Prenatal and Perinatal Psychology and Medicine
Encounter with the Unborn

A Comprehensive Survey of Research and Practice

Prenatal and Perinatal Psychology and Medicine

Encounter with the Unborn

A Comprehensive Survey of Research and Practice

edited by
**Peter Fedor-Freybergh, M.D., PH.D.
and M. L. Vanessa Vogel**

The Parthenon Publishing Group
International Publishers in Science & Technology

Casterton Hall, Carnforth,
Lancs, LA6 2LA, U.K.

120 Mill Road, Park Ridge
New Jersey, U.S.A.

Published in the UK by
The Parthenon Publishing Group Limited
Casterton Hall, Carnforth,
Lancs, LA6 2LA

ISBN 1–85070–181–4

Published in the USA by
The Parthenon Publishing Group Inc.
120 Mill Road,
Park Ridge,
New Jersey 07656

ISBN 0–940813–24–6

Copyright © 1988 The Parthenon Publishing Group

First published 1988

*No part of this book may be reproduced
in any form without permission from the
publishers except for the quotation of
brief passages for the purposes of review*

Typeset, printed & bound in Great Britain by
Butler & Tanner Ltd, Frome and London

Contents

Preface and Acknowledgements   xiii

Introduction

    An overview of prenatal and perinatal psychology and medicine
    P. Fedor-Freybergh and M. L. Vanessa Vogel   xviii

SECTION 1   Developmental psychology

    Part 1
    DEVELOPMENTAL PSYCHOLOGY RELATED TO THE PRENATAL EXPERIENCE

1. The mind of the newborn: increasing evidence of competence
    D. B. Chamberlain   5

2. A new view of the unborn: toward a developmental psychology of the prenatal period
    S. Schindler   23

3. The connection between the course of pregnancy and postnatal mother–child interaction
    G. Schusser   35

4. Perinatal hazards and later schooling
    B. Zachau-Christiansen   53

    Part 2
    STUDIES IN MATERNAL ATTITUDES TO THE PRENATAL

5. Early maternal–neonatal interactions and their impact on the development of maternal attitudes
    Z. Golánska and W. Borkowski   75

6. Prenatal maternal fantasies and postnatal mother–child relationship
    H. von Lüpke   79

7. Maternal attitudes and preterm labor
    X. De Muylder and S. Wesel   87

8. The psychological effects of maternal attitudes in cases of repeated unfavorable pregnancy outcome
    Z. Golańska and A. Bacz   93

Part 3
STUDIES IN PATERNAL ATTITUDES IN RELATION TO THE PRENATAL AND PERINATAL EXPERIENCE

9. The role of the father in care-giving and in the development of the infant: an empirical study on the impact of prenatal courses on expectant fathers
    H. Nickel   101

10. Prenatal problems of future fathers
    I. Krymko-Bleton   123

Part 4
RESEARCH ON BEHAVIORAL DEVELOPMENT

11. The relationship between maternal emotionality during pregnancy and the behavioral development of the fetus and neonatus
    B. R. H. Van den Bergh   131

12. Rhythmicity in parental stimulation of infants
    L. Sanford Koester   143

13. Sexual cross-identity as a fetal response to subliminal parent messages
    M. W. Colter   153

SECTION 2: Psychoanalysis and psychotherapy
Part 1
THE PRENATAL AND PERINATAL EXPERIENCE

14. The concept of cathexis and its usefulness for prenatal psychology
    W. E. Freud   165

15.	The trauma of birth as reflected in the psychoanalytic process L. Janus	177
16.	The role of hypnotherapy in facilitating normal birth L. Mehl, S. Donovan and G. Peterson	189
17.	The conscious and unconscious elements of the experience of pregnancy M. Pál	209

Part 2
STUDIES ON ATTACHMENT AND BONDING DEVELOPMENT

18.	Prenatal attachment, the perinatal continuum and the psychological side of neonatal intensive care W. E. Freud	217
19.	Psychological aspects of prematurity and of neonatal intensive care: a working report H. Bender	235
20.	The importance of early skin contact in emotional development H. Musaph	249
21.	Promoting prenatal and perinatal mother–child bonding: a psychotherapeutic assessment of parental attitudes M. Jernberg	253
22.	A program to facilitate prebirth bonding E. Bowen	267
23.	Parental singing during pregnancy and infancy can assist in cultivating positive bonding and later development L. Thurman	273
24.	Implications of bonding research for adoptive families E. Hormann	283

Part 3
REPORTS ON PSYCHOTHERAPEUTIC METHODS: BIRTH MEMORY THERAPY AND BODY-CENTERED THERAPY

25.	Psychotherapeutic methods for working with birth memories: an introduction to the topic B. R. Findeisen	291

26. Prenatal and perinatal experience and developmental impairment
    R. E. Laibow ... 295

27. Birth, life and more life: reactive patterning based on prebirth events
    J.-R. Turner ... 309

28. Awareness-movement therapy
    U. Kost ... 317

29. A proposed model for prenatal prevention of postnatal disorders
    S. M. Thom ... 321

SECTION 3   Obstetrical and gynecological research
Part 1
PRENATAL DIAGNOSTIC RESEARCH

30. Diagnostic ultrasound in prevention of physical and mental defects
    A. Kurjak, B. Funduk-Kurjak, M. Biljan, D. Jurkovic and Z. Alfirevic ... 333

31. Early ultrasound monitoring and the status of the newborn
    A. Bacz and W. Borkowski ... 343

32. A further contribution to a functional interpretation of fetal movements
    E. Gidoni, M. Casonato and N. Landi ... 347

33. The psychological effects of antenatal diagnosis on pregnancy
    M. Endres ... 355

34. Who's next? – notes on the genetic counseling of pregnant women from studies in conversation analysis
    C. Scholz and M. Endres ... 365

Part 2
LABOR AND PRETERM LABOR: RISK PREGNANCY

35. Prenatal and perinatal psychology: implications for birth attendants
    M. L. Davenport ... 381

36. The midwife as attendant for women with high-risk pregnancies
    E. Pichler ... 391

37. Relationship of psychiatric diagnosis, defenses, anxiety and stress with birth complications
G. Peterson, L. Mehl and J. McRae   399

Part 3
PSYCHONEUROENDOCRINOLOGY

38. Significance of hormone-dependent brain development and pre- and early postnatal psychophysiology for preventive medicine
G. Dörner   419

39. Neurobiochemistry of immersion in warm water during labor: the secretion of endorphins, cortisol and prolactin
M. Boulvain and S. Wesel   431

40. From psychoneuroendocrinology to primal health: new concepts as strategic tools
M. Odent   439

Part 4
IMPACT OF SOCIAL IMPLICATIONS UPON OBSTETRICS AND GYNECOLOGY

41. Maternal psychosociobiological barriers in human reproduction
R. Klimek   447

42. The impact of reproductive technology on society: the donated egg and its mother, and induced abortion as seen via the ultrasound screen
D. Serr, S. Tyano, R. Mane, L. Zabner, S. Mashiach and J. Shalev   461

43. The effects of continual social support during birth on maternal and infant morbidity
M. Klaus and J. H. Kennell   469

SECTION FOUR   Prenatal and perinatal birth transitions
Part 1
BIRTH PREPARATION AND BIRTHING STRATEGIES

44. Childbirth preparation and unfilled transitions
E. Noble   481

45. Effects of a prenatal intervention program
K. Van de Carr, R. Van de Carr and M. Lehrer   489

46. The role of emotional and social support to pregnant teenagers
    E. Scarzella Mazzocchi   497

SECTION 5 Cultural and ethical dimensions of prenatal and perinatal psychology and medicine

Part 1
CULTURAL ASPECTS OF RESEARCH INTO PRENATAL AND PERINATAL DEVELOPMENT AND EXPERIENCE

47. The cultural and historical evolution of medical and psychological ideas concerning conception and embryo development
    D. Gupta and B. Datta   507

48. The use of placental symbols in accessing pre- and perinatal experience
    T. W. Dowling   535

49. Cross-cultural descriptions of prenatal experience
    T. Håkansson   541

50. Sociocultural expectations and responses to the sexual identity of the unborn and newborn in San Jose, Costa Rica
    M. T. Zeledon, R. Flores and M. Villalobos   549

Part 2
ETHICAL CONSIDERATIONS IN PRENATAL AND PERINATAL PSYCHOLOGY AND MEDICINE

51. The ultimate preventive: prenatal stimulation
    B. Logan   559

52. The psycho-technology of pregnancy and labor
    T. R. Verny   563

53. The mother mystique: psychosocio–logical factors which promote an unrealistic view of mothers
    J. Raphael-Leff   581

54. It's better to build children than repair men: preventive aspects of parenting and birthing education
    R. Phillips   599

CONCLUDING REMARKS

55. Future tasks ahead for the ISPP
    M. L. V. Vogel and P. Fedor-Freybergh   607

APPENDICES

Appendix 1 List of contributors. Their research and institutional affiliations, addresses   619

Appendix 2 List of papers of related interest, publication pending in German   625

Bibliography comprehensive, compiled from all papers   639

Index   693

Preface and Acknowledgements

Actually this book is dealing with at least three levels of encounter with the unborn. First and foremost, of course, is the encounter between the mother and the unborn. Here research is focused on acknowledging the competency of the unborn and with improving the dialogue between the mother and her unborn child. Secondly, there is the encounter between the researchers and practitioners of prenatal and perinatal care giving. We especially hope this book helps to break down the barriers existing between them. There is no hierarchy or supremacy of one aspect of qualitative research over another. A great need now exists to promote and expand their cooperation as there is much to be gained in such a collaborative encounter.

Finally to complete the circle is the encounter between the mothers' experiences and that of the researchers and practitioners in prenatal and perinatal psychology and medicine. Here again, there exists the need to bring down barriers, in this case breaking down the typical doctor–patient dichotomy of the competent and incompetent. It is not the case of competent and incompetent, but of different kinds of competencies and their respective limitations. The doctor and other professional birthing practitioners need to recognize the mother's awareness and experience of the unborn as a certain kind of competency; and the mother needs to acknowledge her own competence and not be a passive recipient in this creative process. Her's is an active partnership, mediating her encounter with the unborn child and her doctor and/or midwife.

Born out of the tremendous need at this time to provide a comprehensive survey, this book serves a multiple readership on many different levels. First it is a comprehensive and interdisciplinary presentation of the latest research in prenatal and perinatal psychology and medicine. From the very beginning it must be pointed out that research in this field is not strictly reserved to these two disciplines. For this reason we strove to include research from ethics, sociology, cultural anthropology/ethnology, historical analysis, pedagogy, birth practitioners, and varied approaches to psychotherapeutic practice. Secondly, we wished to present the international profile of this very important research in order to accentuate that the future care of the unborn knows no boundaries. In this regard, the state and nature of the research in prenatal and perinatal studies around the world are represented by researchers from 16 different countries, and reflects only a small sampling of the international flavor of this work. Finally, we saw the need to present a broad spectrum of philosophical and ethical considerations behind the research and practice in prenatal and perinatal psychology and medicine, one which includes the diversity inherent in the myriad of approaches to the study. Many of these differences, it should be added, arise from contrasting ethical, cultural, religious and gender points of view. The consequences of this research necessarily require that the ethical and philosophical questions should not go begging; these issues cannot be avoided and must be faced.

We have tried to produce a work which gives an adequate survey of the field and yet maintains sufficient depth in certain basic areas. However, the anthropological and cultural work is the most weakly represented as there is already a massive amount of research existing here. Unfortunately we had to settle – with too little time and space – to give just a hint of the rich possibilities of what these two disciplines have to offer to prenatal and perinatal studies.

Providing an adequate, up-to-date and comprehensive cross-disciplinary bibliography will be useful not only to the medical and psychological researcher checking up on what is going on in related disciplines, but also for students of the subject and the interested lay person – especially parents and future parents. Indeed the only way to bolster the efficacy of preventive medicine is to enlist the cooperation of conscientious parents so that they will become informed, more competent and responsible for the kind of health care their unborn and newborn child receives. This kind of responsiveness is best effected by sharing with parents the latest research and practice in order that they can make informed choices. It is no longer for an elite to make the choices and decisions concerning the unborn; it is more and more of necessity becoming a choice many of us in our everyday lives are having forced upon us. It is therefore crucial that information, such as that which is contained in these pages, should reach all levels of our respective cultures and societies (with due consideration given to cultural differences).

Unfortunately, we have not adequately been able to account for the cultural and religious sensitivities of our readership. This would have been an impossible task, well beyond our abilities and imagination. Each reader is advised to take what they can profitably use, and to leave the rest. We only ask that our readers approach this material with an open mind. There is much here which goes across cultural and religious boundaries, and will be beneficial and relevant cross-culturally. In this regard WHO has recently acknowledged the need to address these crucial health issues and will be supporting the next International Society for Prenatal and Perinatal Psychology and Medicine (ISPP) congress in Jerusalem in March of 1989.

Perhaps this is a good point to note why a medical doctor and professor, and an ethnologist specializing in the History of Religions are working together in the editing (and some of the writing) of this book. Working from the assumption that all the disciplines have important contributions to offer to prenatal and perinatal studies, and that compiling such a survey would have to cover a broad spectrum of the scientific and the sociocultural dimensions, we saw the opportunity to collaborate and promote this central hermeneutical principle of cross-fertilization. We are – with Peter and his extensive background in both medical and psychological research and practise, and Vanessa with her grounding in the sociocultural, ethnological, ethical, philosophical and religious disciplines – combining the wealth of our knowledge in order to give the most sensitive and fullest interdisciplinary treatment possible in an ever expanding area of concern.

But this book is in no way complete. It is a first attempt at providing a comprehensive survey of prenatal and perinatal psychology and medicine and related fields. As the first such attempt it is certain to have its weak spots (as already referred to above), but it also treads where no one has tread before. So this work fulfils a timely need in providing a survey of a relatively new area of research and showing the state of the art to date. The omissions we regret; even as we were in the final stages of putting the book together more papers and news of developing research were reaching us. Our apologies to those we left out.

We are certain that the last ISPP congress (in Badgastein, Austria) has had much to do with spreading the word of who is doing what and where and how. We hope this book will continue to further that networking of information and people. Indeed we very much welcome such news and feedback; it is the backbone of future efforts to better our understanding of the encounter with the unborn. There are so many different dimensions of prenatal and perinatal research and practice that we can neither work in isolation from one another nor without the participation of informed parents.

Some may find our final selection rather questionable – so many very unhomogenized and so many unscientific papers. But to this we answer that the whole spectrum of ideas about what constitutes knowledge is encompassed by the researchers in prenatal and perinatal studies. Instead of excluding those with widely differing views, we envision this as a challenge to include both parties (the so-called objective and the so-called subjective researchers). Hopefully, this book will serve as a forum for bridging these two divergent orientations in our society and our knowledge. Much could be gained through their cooperation and communication; nothing will be gained through their continued denigration of each other's work. Consequently, our choices here were intentional and motivated by the need to get these two groups talking to each other and recognizing each other's special competency. One group is more clearly competent in scientific insight and research; the others, in their very own individualistic ways, are talented in working with people and eliciting emotions and responses concerning prenatal (during and after the fact) and perinatal experiences.

Some of the research contradicts some of the practice. So be it. We are not here to judge the conclusions but to provide the interested researcher, student and lay person access to the depth and breadth of studies and practices within prenatal and perinatal psychology and medicine. We would have been errant in our task if at this very early stage of the game we chose to exclude work bearing impressive results based upon our own scientific bias — remembering that scientific bias is no less ethnocentric than any other way of knowing. However, this is not to say we either condone or condemn any of these reports. We have tried to present the broad spectrum of responsible work (and there is much which has been left out at both extreme ends of the spectrum).

Necessarily, the contributions in this book have been edited to account for limitations of space. Most of the papers come from the Badgastein congress and, hence, cover some of the same introductory material. Others had to be cut and altered to make the book of a manageable size while still covering a lot of territory — all such decisions were painful and made with great reticence. Our apologies to the contributors and our deep appreciation for their understanding of the necessity for these alterations in their work. We hope that the essence and original intentions of their ideas have been retained in the final product.

Obviously, the final responsibility for the contents and emphasis of this book lies with the editors. For whatever shortcomings and faults due to emphasis or exclusion, these are solely attributable to us. For what is worthwhile — and we think there is much in these pages which is — the credit is shared equally with those who helped to make this book possible. Foremost then, to all the contributors we would like to express our sincere gratitude and appreciation; in so many ways they have helped to pioneer the renewed interest in the encounter with the unborn and neonatal. Their names and addresses are listed in Appendix 1 so that contact can be further encouraged between researchers, practitioners and parents in need of acquiring and exchanging crucial information.

It almost goes without saying that this book would not have been written at all, if it was not for the 1986 Badgastein congress of the International Society of Prenatal and Perinatal Psychology and Medicine (Congress President Peter Fedor-Freybergh). There, over 700 participants (many of whom are contributors in this volume) helped shape and focus much of what is included in this book. Their inspiration is gratefully acknowledged as well.

For their help with typing parts of the manuscript and compiling the bibliography, we should very much like to thank Nicola Brooks, Kay Tabakov and Katarina Blom.

Finally, to our publisher David Bloomer, we are most thankful for his support, encouragement and unlimited patience.

Hopefully, this book is only the beginning in helping to bridge the gaps between the varied disciplines and approaches, ideas and philosophies, researches and practices, care practitioners and parents, but most of all between us and them – between the unborn and the already born.

Peter G. Fedor-Freybergh and M. L. Vanessa Vogel
Stockholm, March 1988

Introduction

Encounter with the unborn: philosophical impetus behind prenatal and perinatal psychology and medicine

P. G. Fedor-Freybergh and M. L. Vanessa Vogel

Prenatal and perinatal psychology and medicine is a relatively recent development within medical and psychological research, and among the many disciplines now engaged in interconnected studies. Behind such work lies a philosophy, concrete and practical both in its aims and methods, which stresses focusing on our future: our children. We recognize that this process begins with the choices we make in giving birth to new life, and with the kind of care we give the unborn. It is the quality of life we need to enhance, not the quantity.

The future of our children can be improved through the quality of care and consideration they receive *in utero*, and also via the care and consideration given to their mothers. No matter the mother's circumstances and/or beliefs, she should be treated with respect, for the quality and value of the mother's life is just as important as that of the unborn.

Those who work within this new interdisciplinary field hope that the pioneering research in which they are now engaged will facilitate further in-depth work and greater understanding of the psychosociological dimensions of prenatal and perinatal development. Underlying this philosophy we need to emphasize that there is no possible separation between the physical and psychological development of the unborn. The continuum of life (see below) begins *in utero*. Even before birth the quality of life can be enhanced or diminished, and these experiences are carried with us throughout life. Through this work we hope to ensure that the future and our children are truly better, not just more plentiful.

PSYCHONEUROENDOCRINOLOGICAL CONTINUUM FOR PRENATAL COMPETENCY: THE PSYCHOBIOLOGICAL BASIS FOR PRENATAL PSYCHOLOGY AND MEDICINE

The new philosophy of prenatal care and birth preparation is carried forward through the mutual co-operation of the medical, psychological and social practitioners. All work upon equally important and mutually interdependent dimensions of prenatal and perinatal psychology and medicine, therefore it is vital that they meet together and share their research and their practice. For this reason an international and inter-disciplinary society was founded in Vienna in 1971, the International Society for Prenatal and Perinatal Psychology and Medicine (hereafter ISPP)[1]. Necessarily, the research of the members of the ISPP and other researchers working in this field has a multidimensional profile: using a psychosocial emphasis to improve the quality of prenatal life through the prevention of disturbances of a physical and psychological nature; and developing preventive procedures to decrease unnecessary premature births and infant mortality through the use of medical and psychotherapeutical methods.

A great deal of such research is the direct consequence of the latest findings of two relatively new and innovative lines of medical research, namely psychoneuroendocrinology and psychoneuroimmunology. Research in these two areas is particularly important in serving as the medical basis for the philosophy behind prenatal and perinatal psychology which we advocate here. Examples of this kind of research can be found in the work of Dörner and Boulvain *et al.* presented in this volume.

Although still operating within a very young discipline, psychoneuroendocrinologists have already elicited useful data from preliminary theoretical research in recording fetal response to and retention of outside environmental stimuli (touch, sound and light stimuli for the most part). Various highly specific biochemical structures (hormones, neurotransmitters and other polypeptide structures) are needed, in direct connection with input phenomena, for the transformation and storage of both sensorial and sensible types of information. Crucial to the formation of the primary central nervous system on the hypothalamic-pituitary-adrenal level, some of these functions are detectable already in the very beginning of the development of the human being. Thus the embryo successively develops a high sensibility and competency for the potential ability for perception.

The implications of these preliminary findings are far reaching. It will require nothing less than radically rethinking of the standard human–embryo development paradigm wherein structure is presumed to precede function. Quite the contrary, recent research in psychoneuroendocrinology (Fedor-Freybergh, 1983) indicates the primacy of function over structure, the morphological apparatus. It is the morphological structure which develops as a result of the inborn primal functional *urge*. An organ would not develop if there were no functional urge compelling it to do so. In the same way, the psychological capacity of the human is not posterior to the completed morphological structure of the human body, nor to its subsequent introduction into and experiencing of a particular sociocultural environment after birth. The unborn already has its psychological processes functioning long before birth; no child is born a *tabula rasa*.

THE PRENATAL LEARNING PROCESS: PREBIRTH MEMORY IMPRINTING AND THE IMPLICATIONS FOR PRENATAL PSYCHOLOGICAL DEVELOPMENT AND COMPETENCY

The initial theoretical conclusions which logically follow such dramatic preliminary results are of great significance. If from the very beginning the building blocks of perception are present and functioning, then firstly, there can be no divisible separation between biochemical processes and psychological processes, between the body and mind (i.e. the substantive and qualitative, respectively). Hence, no *a priori* posturing of one or the other is possible. We cannot reliably prove (pro or con) that subsequent physical and emotional responses are not the delayed, retroactive result of stored sensorial prebirth imprints, although a strong case could be constructed out of and in conjunction with some of the remarkable early successes of various psychotherapeutic methods based upon prebirth imprint theory (see Jernberg's paper).

These two developmental processes are interdependent and make clear, secondly, that the intrauterine experience serves as a learning process for the fetus. This learning process is a vital prerequisite for survival since it makes it possible for the organism to adapt itself to new circumstances. Without adaptation there would be no survival, and one cannot adapt without making and having had experiences upon which to base the adaptation. And such a process requires memory – whether consciously retained or unconsciously imprinted. The information processing which reaches the child from the very beginning of his/her development will be received via the different biochemical pathways and then transformed and stored as memory traces. (This could eventually be useful to a theoretical understanding of certain psychotherapeutical procedures – hypnosis, dream-analysis, etc.) Already the embryo shows evidence of responding to and retaining the impact or imprint of sensory experiences in a biochemical language, which remain as a potential learning source. These prebirth memory imprints may in turn be re-evoked as informational sources (whether negative, positive or ambivalent in character) during later life, especially in regard to emotional response. In this connection, we refer the reader to examine some examples of the varied therapeutical efforts based upon prebirth memories in this volume by Laibow, Findeisen and Turner.

No child is born a *tabula rasa*. The unborn carries psychological experiences from the womb into the outside world. The question is how to understand and foster a psychological development which is not yet conscious, but nevertheless leaves an ineluctable imprint affecting our future experiences – and hence the quality of our lives. How to minimize the negative possibilities and enhance the positive psychological development that begins in this first ecological environment is the practical work before us.

THE EXPERIENCE OF PREGNANCY AND THE PRENATAL EXPERIENCE

Historically both in the West and in many other non-Western cultures, the pregnant woman and the intrauterine experience has been and, very often in an unconscious way, continues to be envisioned negatively. 'A disaster waiting to happen.'

Prenatally and during birth we develop exponentially more than at any other time of our life[2]. To presume, as has been our intellectual and cultural inheritance in the West, that this experience is overwhelmingly and necessarily a negative, painful experience somehow separate from the rest of our life is unwarranted. Equally indefensible is the standard medical assumption that prenatal development *excludes* psychological development.

How can the primary research of prenatal and perinatal psychology and medicine most effectively be transferred over to birth preparation practitioners? And how can we best communicate the latest results of this new wave of research into birth education centers where mothers and fathers will have direct access to it? The following summarizes some of these innovative ideas and approaches concerning the encounter with the unborn and birth preparation, and how these influence and are in turn cross-fertilized by developments in the ethical, cultural, sociohistorical, technological and environmental sciences.

Competency of the mother

We must reaffirm that the mother is not just a 'receptacle' for the child's growth, but an active initiator and participator. Today it is imperative to re-establish the woman as the primary choice maker in this powerfully creative process. Indeed, she is involved in a procreative process with great creative powers of her own. The future mother needs to be aware of these powers and how to be in touch with them in order to be better equipped to guide and augment this creative undertaking.

Pregnancy can also enable the mother to withdraw into a kind of 'creative regression' in order to enter into an intimate dialog with her unborn child. Here it is interesting to note the different research approaches to this fascinating mother–child dynamic as reflected in the work of Schindler, Janus and Freud.

Conscious parenting

New perspectives about the responsibility of parenting involve looking anew at parenting and what is entailed. Finally though, we advocate that it is for the mothers and fathers to choose how they 'will parent', they are the choice makers. Still we need to provide access to an up-to-date family education which strives to show that there are alternative ways to approach family planning; and to outline the important creative role parents play in enhancing their child's development during pregnancy.

But in order to make an informed and stress-free choice, family planning education must begin well before conception. Responsible parenting is not necessarily an automatically bestowed gift from Mother Nature or even an easily acquired talent; very often it needs to be taught. That requires research concerning appropriate socio-pedagogical implementation into our secondary educational systems (high school, college and gymnasium levels), and integration of prenatal and perinatal studies into medical and psychological curricula. Here we point particularly to Schusser's work in outlining a new paradigmatic program for restructuring family education programs.

Birth preparation and birth education

Birth preparation and birth education must go hand in hand. Royal Phillip's paper takes up the ethical and practical concerns supporting the pedagogic work of birth preparation programs. The time during pregnancy also provides a good opportunity for the family to grow together – hence the increased importance of birth education. Indeed there is much which can be done during the prenatal period to enhance and promote bonding and attachment (see Thurman and Bowen's contributions). Most especially pregnancy is the time for actively preparing oneself for what can only be described as a momentous self-transformational event – giving birth not only to another life, but having one's own identity changed, however subtly, in the process. Birth preparation, then, is one of the best and most practical, on-hands preventitive health care measures we have to ensure safe and fulfilling birth experiences (see also Elizabeth Noble's paper). And midwifery has been and continues to be the practice *par excellence* for helping to guide and nurture future mothers through their pregnancy.

Pregnancy as a challenge

Pregnancy can sometimes be experienced by both the mother and the father as a life crisis, which does not axiomatically imply a negatively charged situation. Any crisis may be envisioned as a challenge which can bring about creative and positive solutions or alternatives. We can quite often see that during pregnancy old, latent and unsolved conflicts become manifest (see Elda Scarzella's paper for some further insights on this subject), but frequently these can be worked through during the course of the pregnancy in a very constructive way. Indeed, it should be pointed out that many of the conflicts and problems that a pregnant woman may experience are not the direct result of her pregnancy or her baby. Unresolved issues may re-evoke psychological conflicts within her own personal psyche. In this way the pregnancy often gives the mother (or the parents) a unique opportunity to further her (their) own inner psychological development, sometimes within a psychotherapeutic setting (see von Lupke and Raphael-Leff's papers for further discussion of this subject).

Risk pregnancy

Pregnancy is not just a physical undertaking, the mother has the power to create a psychologically nurturing environment for her unborn child. Physical events may cause psychological stress (i.e. single mothers, unwanted pregnancies, financial and social problems to name a few of the more obvious); and, just as readily, psychological stress can be induced through external sources (e.g. environmental pollution: Chernobyl, the chemical dumping in the Rhine, Three Mile Island – mentioning only a few notable, recent events). For more extended treatments on risk pregnancy, and even its psychosocial implications, see the work of Klimek, Golanska and Bacz, Peterson et al. and Pichler.

The term 'risk pregnancy' is still used almost exclusively in its biological sense, which means it is reserved for those so-called 'somatic' disturbances, physical diseases or handicaps experienced by the mother during pregnancy which could have a bearing on the health of the baby. Here we can see again how firmly institutionalized medicine and medical philosophy, with its static terminology and categorizations, is still embodied within the dualistic outlook of a Cartesian philosophical bent. The net result of such a stand is the continued promulgation of a psychophysical parallelism[3]. In a holistic and comprehensive view of human life we cannot make divisions between so-called 'somatic' and 'psychological' phenomena[4]. Psychologically, medically and anthropologically considered, all life events are experienced as indivisible phenomenological situations wherein body and mind (soma and psyche) represent an entity of mutual influence and interdependence within a particular sociocultural environment. In this way, all events of either a so-called 'somatic' or 'psychological' character, which could adversely affect the well-being and health of the mother or her unborn child, are seen as potential or real risks. It is therefore necessary to create a new kind of prenatal care whereby *all* potential risks can be screened in good time, and where parents would be given the opportunity for comprehensive care, including access to psychotherapeutic counselling (see Endres and Bacz et al. for more on prenatal diagnostics). In this way, risk pregnancy is seen in a fuller, more encompassing light, not only as the physical risk endangering the child's or the mother's life, but also the potential psychological harm that could result. Adequately considering the psychological risks along with and indivisible from the physical risks gives a much more complete and helpful profile of a risk pregnancy.

From the social and psychological perspectives we need to also consider if there is really a possibility for enhancing the quality of life of the child and the mother. Or will the child be forced to bear both extreme physical and psychological handicaps? Will a mother be forced to physically bear a child she will not later be able to psychologically bear? And if so, how will this affect the future child's chances for the right to a quality life experience? There are no answers here. Here, though, there exists a moral challenge to those who advocate only the 'Right to Life'. This challenge extends the parameters of this very crucial question, it includes a consideration of the unborn's 'Right to Quality of Life'. Has the as yet unborn also an adequate opportunity for both physical and psychological self-realization? This is a question for those whose values quantify life at whatever the cost: that includes the possibility for spiritual and mental evolution. By reducing a definition of life to the mere presence of physical energy — tragically divorced from its other psychological self — could be a kind of inhumane torture. Where are the limits, and who is to set those limits? Now that technology can artificially sustain 'life energies' where Mother Nature would mercifully have returned that 'life' to its Creator (or to be reborn, some would say), are we ready to judge for others where those outer limits are?

We do not promote or mean to imply that there is any one right position concerning this moral question. Quite the contrary, our own medical and ethnographic research shows that there is no one morally correct answer to this question which would suffice for all the religio-cultural diversity and spiritual belief worldwide. It is for this reason that we advocate for an *informed* choice. Some will see in such a position a philosophical (and moral) relativism, others will recognize a philosophical realism.

Without guilt

No guilt or inferiority feelings, either consciously or unconsciously, should be imposed upon underprivileged women or moral judgements placed upon the mother's decisions about her pregnancy by medical or birth practitioners. We need be aware that not all pregnant women have the opportunity or possibility to provide their unborn child with optimal nurturing conditions, either economically or emotionally. There should be no psychological anxiety created for those who don't have or don't want the option of abortion, amniocentesis, etc. or whose children after birth show any kind of disturbance or disease (see Serr *et al.*'s work concerning a further discussion of this sensitive topic).

If a pregnancy is carried forward, there is always still present a very creative power within the woman to psychologically improve and enhance the intrauterine experience — and to compensate, no matter what the circumstances are. Actually, there is no such thing as an exclusively 'positive' or 'negative' (attitude toward) pregnancy from the mother's side. We have never witnessed a pregnant woman who, through her whole pregnancy, showed only a positive or negative response toward her child. Pregnancy is always a dynamic process of constantly fluctuating emotions, attitudes and even intellectual discourse. The mother–child dialog is almost always characterized by a mixture of positive, negative and ambivalent emotions, though one of these may very well predominate. Here we strive to help the mother adjust and improve whatever option she has chosen, and to see in that choice a positive, affirming decision.

Moreover, it must be added that a living organism has a strong propensity to adapt and even to repair damage, or to compensate for some failure, something physically and/or psychologically lacking from a previous developmental stage of the life continuum. What is unfulfilled in one stage of experience can be applied to the next and, eventually, worked out to the inner satisfaction of the human being. The point being, no superimposed guilt ever helps to harness healing energy.

Re-education of medical practitioners

The ISPP promotes a holistic medical and psychological approach which is sensitive to the creative process of childbirth and sees the mother as a central actor in that process. Re-educating the medical and psychological professions to readjust their perspectives and techniques, so that they will enhance the quality experience of this most important event, is crucial to improving the working relationship between mothers and doctors. The central question here is one of competency, i.e. recognizing the mother's ability to choose competently.

Methods, which improve the mother's dignity without pain, and thereby enabling a quality enhancing birth event for the mother–father–baby continuum, are just as important from the technological side of the equation. It is the family's indivisible common experience and it should not be hampered or interferred with any more than is absolutely necessary. Freud, Bender and Verny contribute much to this discussion in their papers here.

Preventive prenatal and perinatal care

It has been shown that the highest cause in industrialized nations for infant mortality is premature birth, which is significantly attributable to psychological stress (among other phenomena, see especially Kurjak *et al.* in this regard). Already early results indicate that the treatments developed via prenatal and perinatal psychological research are the most effective way to decrease premature birth and thus infant morbidity and mortality. Today research is being conducted which points to some linking between postnatal immunity (like the SIDS syndrome and other disturbances in the psychoneuroimmunological system, e.g. viral diseases and AIDS) and emotional disturbances in prenatal development.

Practically speaking, the better the total prenatal care, the better the health of the baby will be. If we want healthy adults then we have to go back to the very beginning – our first ecological environment. We all have many good reasons to be concerned about the environment. Few people, however, and this includes professionals, realize that the first environment of the human being (and all differentiated organisms) is the womb. The womb represents the first ecological position of life. It is surprising to see how few psychologists realize this basic fact, and that there are still a large number of obstetricians and gynecologists who merely consider the womb as a 'baby-carrying' anatomical organ. We must begin to be aware of the womb and the development of the human being within – both the possibilities and the risks. Here is where we first begin to nurture and enhance the quality of life – and improve the possibilities for a better, more fulfilling life later on.

ENCOUNTER WITH THE UNBORN

The dialog with the unborn child needs be envisioned as a psychosocial partnership with the child acting as an active participant. In some way, pregnancy can be conceived as an active dialog between mother and child; actually, the dialog does not end here but is further enlarged via the dialog between the mother and father and back again. This discourse is part of a very active and mutually interdependent process taking place on several levels. Minimally these include the psychological-emotional, biochemical and psychoneuroendocrinological.

There may be an exception to this blunt assertion, but we have never heard a mother (or heard of a mother) who would refer to the child in her womb as 'my embryo' or 'my fetus' (see Fedor-Freybergh, 1983). More often the mother says, 'my baby' or even calls the child by a personal name. Generally, pregnant mothers show a high degree of sensitivity and sensibility toward their unborn child which, by contrast, many professionals lack. The child is a very active partner in the pregnancy and an 'active passenger *in utero*' (see Chamberlain's work here). The mother–child interconnection, consequently, has not only a biological but also very much a psychosocial character.

The psychological move from 'it' to 'you'

This mother–child dialog begins on an unconscious level – probably from the very beginning of the unborn child's development. From the mother's side, the dialog will become a reality when she, consciously or unconsciously, makes the move to experience the unborn 'it' as the unborn 'you'. This event initiates her into beginning a conscious encounter with the child, the little person within her. The transition from 'it' to 'you' is just one consequence of the already mentioned sensitivity and sensibility of the unborn – and the enormous creative potential in the psyche of the mother. The dialogical experience is independent of the degree of morphological development of the child (Fedor-Freybergh, 1987 ii).

Primal togetherness

Primal togetherness encompasses the initial quality experiences of intimate unity (or disunity) which can affect or imprint upon all later life experiences and psychological orientation toward relationships. The dialog between the unborn child, mother and father creates a 'primal togetherness', which in turn helps to foster strongly compelling psychophysical predispositions. Potentially any such inborn predilection has the ability to orient and shape forthcoming emotional and social responses, especially in regard to interpersonal relationships. Consequences of these initiatory quality experiences of primal togetherness run along a wide range, from love to ethical behavior. If the first quality experience is a negative one the results are carried forward by predisposing a negative emotional orientation or reaction somewhere along this love-ethic range. Although memory imprinting is still considered a controversial medical or psychological concept, the recent work of psychotherapists open to exploring this possibility show that the prenatal imprinting is there and has the power to affect later life. In this regard see examples of this kind of work in Laibow and Jernberg's papers.

The unborn as a part of the continuum of life

The continuum of life is circumscribed (at the latest) from the time of conception to (at the earliest) the completion of this cycle at the moment of transition into death. Of course, such a definition is a bit ethnocentric and locicentric in that it is fairly well limited to a Western scientific mindset, but it does seek through parenthetical bracketing to accommodate philosophical and spiritual orientations which have a much more encompassing belief about and understanding of the 'beginnings' and 'endings' of life (see Gupta and Datta, and Håkansson here for more on some of these ideas). What follows from the above and needs to be stressed is that the unborn child needs to be considered from the very beginning as a unique individual, indivisible psychosomatically and in terms of the child's mind–body development. The unborn's mind–body entity is involved in a continuing dialog with his/her biological and social environment via his/her dynamic relationship with the dialogical partner (i.e. the mother), and its already developed sensible and sensorial competency. This continuum of life is not separable from the rest of life or the stages of life to be lived outside the mother's womb. It is not possible to separate any stage of human development from the rest of an individual life's continuum. Any discontinuity from the outside, as often we can later witness in the child's life experiences, will violate the basic biological and psychological needs of the unborn individual.

Discontinuity

After birth, the premature taking away of the newborn (thereby separating the newborn from the mother for the first time) creates an unhealthy discontinuity at a crucial psychological moment of bonding and attachment. See Freud and Bender's papers here for more developed ideas on this subject. Such a traumatic separation after nine intimate months of togetherness, through the ups and the downs of pregnancy, promotes a potentially dangerous discontinuity – physically and psychologically. As previously mentioned, the life continuum is one of the basic needs in human life in order to maintain equilibrium and balance. Any disturbance of the individual life continuum on a momentous scale could lead to illness or in extreme cases, where equilibrium cannot be regained, death is the result.

Discontinuity has increasingly become a more serious problem today given the spread of ecological, social and political disturbances throughout much of the world. No one group of people or any nation is wholly immune from the upheaval of disorienting developments on the ecological or social levels. Many in the scientific community are very much aware of the effects of such events, and see in the discontinuity and disequilibrium these beget a source of many of today's mental and social diseases[5]. In the field of prenatal and perinatal psychology and medicine, we are very much aware of the dangers discontinuity can generate in the unborn and the newborn.

Prevention and health reconsidered

In its research and practice, prenatal and perinatal psychology and medicine are becoming more and more *the* preventive interdisciplinary science. It requires the co-operation of many other disciplines – midwives, sociologists, historians, ethicists and anthropologists. The secret to primary prevention and primary health (see Odent for a discussion of primal health) lies buried in the prenatal period of life. This includes the medical, psychological and sociological points of view. It is no coincidence that the theme of the 8th International Congress of the ISPP was concerned with 'The Contribution of Prenatal Psychology to Preventive Medicine, Preventive Psychology and Preventive Aspects of the Socially-Oriented

Professions' (1986). Again we cannot talk about separating the 'somatic', the 'psychological' or, indeed, the 'social' aspects of preventive medicine in considering the health of the human being (compare here similar conclusions by Klaus and Kennell).

Health is not merely defined as either physical or mental health, but is truly a much more encompassing concept taking into consideration the quality of an individual's life. As stated elsewhere, 'health is the dynamic movement along the creative path towards self-realization' (Fedor-Freybergh, 1974). Further, health has to be understood to contain biological, psychological and sociological dimensions. Self-realization evolves from: '(1) the constructive integration of the dialectically changing, individually depending conditions with a simultaneous maintenance of the homeostasis of the "milieu interieur"; and (2) the [inner] balance [created while] striving toward satisfaction of the central intimate vision of the individual during continuous confrontation and adaptation of the psychoendocrine system with and to the "milieu exterieur" of ordinary day-to-day life situations' (Fedor-Freybergh, 1974, p. 6). By adaptation we do not only mean the adaptation of oneself to the environment, but also the possibility to transform the environment to suit oneself.

In any definition, which should necessarily be an open definition, the word dynamic needs to be included and accentuated. Fritjof Capra, in *The Turning Point: Science, Society and the Rising Culture*, uses the term 'dynamic balance' as a useful concept for describing health and as crucial to maintaining the kind of balance which is not merely a 'static equilibrium'. Health is above all a process, an experience which needs to be personally defined (whether consciously or unconsciously). From the side of physics, Capra's thinking corroborates our own ideas from the medical, psychological and sociocultural fields. His definition states, 'Health, then, is an experience of well-being resulting from a dynamic balance that involves the physical and psychological aspects of the organism: as well as its interactions with its natural and social environment' (Capra, 1982, p. 354). Capra's sophisticated psychophysics underscores, as we have previously stated, the ability of the healthy organism to adapt and change itself to its environment, its environment to itself or a combination of both survival techniques. But if there is no dynamism functioning then the flexibility necessary for adaptation is lost and, as Capra puts it, the 'loss of flexibility means loss of health'.

Today, some of the most important work ahead of us is in advocating and implementing a renewed definition of health which reflects the ability of the individual to grow and function throughout the whole of his life's continuum and in such a way as satisfies his/her needs for personal self-fulfillment[6]. Health is not a commercial commodity which can be withheld or denied unless payment is forthcoming; health is an experience, a very personal process which should not be disturbed or the pursuit of which denied anyone because they lack sufficient financial means. When health is defined more and more in terms of a luxury which one can or cannot afford, it will be understood more and more as a 'life option'. The question is, can we afford that option?

The encounter with the unborn is the beginning of the continuum of human life towards its self-realization. We need to extend the standard definition of life's continuum to include the prenatal experience. This experience is part of a holistic life continuum, helping to shape us and determining who we are and will become. For the unborn it is primarily through this imprinting process that this experience is initiated and realized much later along the course of this continuum, often unconsciously. For the mother pregnancy, this encounter with the unborn, is a chance for self-realization. For the rest of us this encounter with the unborn is the chance to extend and deepen our own understanding of this life continuum wherein there can be found no possible separation between physical and psychological dimensions of our existence.

1 Originally the society was known as the International Study Group for Prenatal Psychology, but as the multidisciplinary nature of its members' work developed the name was changed in order to reflect the broader concerns before them. The conclusion of this book deals in more detail with the history, development and work of the ISPP.

2 Here it is interesting to note Leonardo Da Vinci's keen insight and observation of this crucial stage of human development – almost four centuries ago. For his and other remarkable insights into the prenatal and perinatal period the reader is referred to Gupta and Datta's fine interdisciplinary collaboration dealing with a cross-cultural and historical review of our ancestors' medical and psychological knowledge, which was not so 'primitive' as we would perhaps like to believe or have been led to believe.

3 Basically, psychophysical parallelism is the theoretical position which maintains that parallel physical and psychological events do not interact.

4 The word holistic has become something of a trend word today and there is the tendency to misuse it, abuse it and overuse it. For these reasons we tried to avoid using the word holistic, but found there was really no substitute expression for the idea we were trying to convey. Our apologies to those who have heard the word holistic more times than they care to count. Although it may have been abused or overused elsewhere it is employed here in order to convey the idea of an all encompassing and interacting organic (i.e. living) system.

5 Much of the maturation and development of these ideas concerning social and mental

ills today is the outcome of a very fruitful conversation between Sam Tyano, Professor of Child Psychiatry at Tel Aviv University and Peter Fedor-Freybergh in February, 1987.

6   In this regard, see also our conclusion for a discussion of cross-cultural considerations of health and prenatal and perinatal health issues.

Section 1
DEVELOPMENTAL PSYCHOLOGY

Part 1: Developmental psychology related to the prenatal experience

1

The mind of the newborn: increasing evidence of competence

D.B. Chamberlain

ABSTRACT

A brief update on the status of the brain, nervous system, and special senses of taste, hearing, smell and vision provides a reminder of the physical resources supporting mental activity at birth.

Empirical research is cited indicating the range of communication and relationship skills demonstrated by newborns. These include signs of intrauterine communication, crying, dreaming, smiling and other affective signals, entrainment and synchrony, intermodal fluency, listening, hand signals, and quick perception of changes and nuances in relationships.

The significance of newborn learning is demonstrated by classical conditioning, reinforcement learning, habituation, imitation, imprinting, the joy associated with cognition, and by results of infant stumulation programs.

A survey of memory abilities of newborn included documentation of procedural, semantic, episodic, motor, perceptual and affect memory. Finally, evidence is presented suggested that birth memory is the most elaborate expression of the infant mind and its competence.

A human mind is a wonderful thing; you should not leave home without it. With it you respond to others, think, communicate, learn, remember and generally organize your life. You do not really doubt that you have a mind though some days you may wonder. You may wonder even more if a baby has one. The consensus is that they do not because they are too small, too immature, and too dependent to have a mind of their own. Scientific descriptions have not been flattering; infants are 'solipsistic', their pains only 'reflexes', their learning credited to 'conditioning'. Even great talents are obscured; fetal aptitudes are termed 'innate' or 'pre-wired', brilliant perceptual feats are 'amodal'. It does not sound like anything to celebrate.

Infants deserve better. I believe the great weight of evidence now permits us to speak meaningfully of the *mind* of the newborn in a way that Sigmund Freud and Otto Rank would envy. When they developed their theories they had limited clinical contact with infants and almost no research to guide them. Things are different now; we have a century of clinical experience behind us and decades of useful research from which a new synthesis of understanding can be built. I believe that this century will be known as the century in which the world finally arrived at a full and factual appreciation of newborns.

In this paper I will briefly cite the facts I consider most relevant to a new appreciation of the infant mind: the documented competencies of feeling, skilful communication, precocious learning, and astounding memory. More thorough documentation can be found in my monograph, *Consciousness at Birth* (Chamberlain, 1983) and *Babies Remember Birth* (in press, 1988).

PHYSICAL RESOURCES SUPPORTING MENTAL ACTIVITY

Nervous system

The first sign that the nervous system is working comes from contralateral head-turning in response to stroking with a fine hair at 7.5 weeks menstrual age (m.a.)/crown rump (CR) (Hooker, 1952; Humphrey, 1978). Decades of research from stroking embryos and fetuses have charted the development of external sensitivity in all parts of the body. Motion pictures show mouth opening and closing beginning at 8.5 weeks, squint-like and sneer-like expressions at 14 weeks. Swallowing, lip and tongue movements are shown between 10.5 and 12.5 weeks, with strong gagging by 18.5 weeks. Audible crying accompanied by puckering up of the lips, scowling, and muscle tension around the eyes was photographed at 23.5 weeks m.a.

Embryology has charted in great detail the development of physical structures from the first cells to the completed organs. Neuroscience provides the basic time table for development of brain structures in strict temporal order, although there are still many mysteries about their connections and interactions. Subsections of the total brain appear to begin functioning as they are constructed long before birth. Perfection of the nervous system includes development and differentiation of dendrites and dendrite spines of the cortex first noted between 20 and 28 weeks of gestation (Purpura, 1975a). EEG measurements confirm that cortical regions respond to peripheral stimulation via touch, vision, and hearing no later than 32 weeks gestational age (g.a.) (Vaughn, 1975).

Neurophysiology feedback circuits, rather than reflex arcs, are now seen as the elementary circuits in the nervous system, underscoring the importance of self-control, self-regulation and influence *on* the environment as well as *from* the environment. Some see the brain operating as a spectral analyzer recording images by holography so that information on the whole is stored in all the parts (Pribram, 1986).

Current research in neuroendocrinology reveals a profound role for 50–60 known neuropeptides as 'signal molecules' or 'communication molecules'. These busy travelers link the nervous system, endocrine system, and immune system into a bi-directional information network (Pert, 1986). Much of this intelligence system is located *outside* the brain. This confirms the holistic nature of mental, emotional, and physical processes and supports the psychosomatic approach to pregnancy and childbirth.

Orientation and taste

Sensitivity to orientation and disorientation in space can be seen as early as 9.5 weeks g.a. Sensitivity to taste also begins early in gestation. Microscopic analysis reveals taste buds at 8 weeks, surrounded by pores and hair cells by 14 weeks with no essential additions later. Experts conclude that taste buds are working by 15 weeks g.a. (Bradley and Stern, 1967) and that the fetus will experience the taste of citric acid, fatty acids, proteins, salts and a host of other chemicals in the amniotic fluid for 28 weeks before term birth (Mistretta and Bradley, 1977). At birth, many studies document responses to sweet, sour and bitter tastes which are similar to those of adults (Lipsitt, 1977, 1979; Steiner, 1979). Newborns detect minimal alterations in the chemical composition of fluids on the tongue and show typical preferences for degrees of sweetness and for popular flavors like vanilla and strawberry.

Sense of smell

Studies of the newborn sense of smell provide similar evidence: acceptance and satisfaction associated with odors of vanilla, strawberry and banana, and rejection associated with ammonia, rotten eggs and rotten fish. Babies are like the rest of us in this respect. Newborns can expertly detect the specific components in mixtures of anise, garlic, vinegar and alcohol. Within a few days of birth, babies recognize their mother's breast pads by odor, distinguishing them from plain or used pads of other mothers.

Hearing

The structures for hearing are essentially complete by 20 weeks *in utero*. 4 and 5 month-old fetuses react differently to the music of Mozart, Beethoven and rock. (Mozart wins). A group of American and Scandinavian colleagues studying the earliest fetal cries uncovered the fact that the cries of extremely premature infants (900 g) could be matched with intonation, rhythm, and other speech features of the mother – strong evidence for hearing (Truby and Lind, 1965). Studies of fetuses from 16–32 weeks g.a. using a vibroacoustic noise applied to the mother's abdomen over the fetal ear showed (via ultrasound) spontaneous eye, head, arm and leg movements indicative of hearing. Responses were first elicited between 24 and 25 weeks and were consistent after 28 weeks g.a. (Birnholz and Benacerraf, 1983).

Precise electrical measurement of hearing made by brainstem electric response audiometry (BERA) shows that normal newborns hear about as well as adults (Schulman-Galambos and Galambos, 1979). Babies are born with the ability to track subtle auditory speech variations about as well as adults do (Condon, 1977). Newborns note the location of sounds and turn their heads with an expectation of seeing something. They react differentially to recorded sounds of their own crying, the crying of other newborns, the crying of older children, computer-simulated cries and white noise (Simner, 1971). The greatest reaction was to their own cry recordings, including a significant rise in heart beats. Infants become upset when they hear other cries like theirs. Some researchers think this may constitute an innate 'empathic distress reaction' (Sagi and Hoffman, 1976).

Newborns discriminate their father's voice from other male voices but show a preference for high-pitched voices in general and their own mother's voice in particular. Heartbeat sounds hold special interest, have reinforcement value, and disturb them when too slow or too fast (Salk, 1973).

Vision

Vision, an extremely complex phenomenon, has been heavily researched. Although vision matures rapidly in the first 2 months after birth, babies begin life with the ability to extract information from the external environment. Vision, movement, and object perception are coordinated, cross-modal and meaningful from the start (Hofsten, 1983).

Attempts to measure visual acuity at birth indicate competence at close ranges (at least) improving in 3 or 4 months to acuity and accommodation more or less adultlike. One expert says newborn acuity is like that of a domestic cat. Newborns follow attractive moving targets with eyes and hands showing jerky pursuit motions which become smooth by 2 months (Aslin, 1981). Even in the dark newborns are 'all eyes', broadly scanning the field and finely scanning specific targets.

Enough rods and cones are in place to permit response to colors and hues, provided brightness factors are controlled. EEG measurements confirm response of infants to different wavelengths of the color spectrum. Discriminative visual functions have been demonstrated in preterm infants by 31–32 weeks g.a. with horizontal tracking and some vertical tracking. The fully mature pattern is reached by 33–34 weeks g.a. (Dubowitz et al., 1980). Other experiments demonstrate that newborn babies are capable of remembering visual information presented earlier (Slater, Morison and Rose, 1982).

COMPETENCE IN COMMUNICATING AND RELATING

A host of studies, including ethological studies of infants in their natural environment, documents how well newborns utilize their elaborate physical resources to support intelligent communication and development of personal relationships.

The fetus is an active passenger *in utero*, kicking and squirming, engaging in exercise, and responding to changes in the mother's position even before *she* can feel them. Fetal reactions to music, voices, and emotional upset seem appropriate and probably constitute legitimate communications.

Crying

Crying is an obvious communication signal which actually begins before birth (not so obvious). Crying *in utero* (vagitus uterinus) is made possible whenever air is brought into contact with the fetal larynx. This happened in the days of air amniograms. Mothers had to be warned to remain in an upright position after examination lest they have the unsettling experience of hearing the fetus cry in the womb (Goodlin, 1979). Various researchers around the world have recorded cries of abortuses from 21–24 weeks m.a., weighing 650–930 g.

Spectrographic studies of the cry *after* birth have shown them to be meaningful expressions of hunger, pain, loneliness or discomfort, clearly distinguishable from each other. Squeals of pleasure, whimpers, screams and coos, fist clenching and shaking, and other gestures are not random, as once believed, but appropriate to state. The greater frequency of crying associated with early, compared with late, cord cutting probably indicates a preference for late cutting. Intense vocalizing at birth may be a vociferous complaint.

Other affects

Videotapes of babies in the first week after birth reveal clear-cut expressions of affect ranging from pleasure to rage (Eisenberg and Marmarou, 1981). Rage can develop to a full scream in only 30 seconds. After studying many such records, Eisenberg reached the conclusion that if babies were not swaddled and could free their hands they would reach out to hit at whatever or whoever was nearest.

Mothers of newborns, asked to keep a record of emotions seen in the first week reported interest and joy (95%), anger (78%), distress (65%), surprise (68%), sadness and disgust (40%), and fear (35%). Interestingly, none saw any signs of shyness or guilt (Johnson, Emde *et al.*, 1982).

Smiles

Newborn smiles are a delightful communication but experts have generally reduced them to physiological artifacts. Notwithstanding, parents find them unforgettable. Cross-cultural studies show that the first smile is often a signal of special significance, an assurance of safety and well-being prompting feasts, ceremonies, gifts, and renewal of marital sex (Håkansson, 1986). The Japanese call it the 'innocent' smile. After the first Leboyer deliveries, reports of newborn smiles began to increase. After a complete water birth recently, the parents reported the baby smiling blissfully at them for 5 minutes (Star, 1986, pp. 65–6).

Psychologists have usually considered smiles insignificant until the 'social smile' occurs at about 6 weeks. Isn't it time we accepted *all* smiles as authentic and meaningful?

Dreaming

The very first smiles occur in the REM/dream stage of sleep. Premature babies smile most and spend the most time in REM, full-term babies less, and children and adults less and less through the life span. Because of this some experts view dreaming as a mental exercise needed to facilitate completion of the central nervous system in babies and to assist in its maintenance in later years (Roffwarg, Muzio and Dement, 1966).

Observing newborns in dream sleep, researchers noted many signs of consciousness: grimaces, whimpers, smiles, twitches of the face and extremities, and shifting of body and limbs. Dreams were serious. There were frequent 10–15 second episodes of writhing of torso, limbs and digits, and periods of apnea as long as 10 seconds. On the faces of newborns they found adultlike expressions of emotion and thought such as perplexity, disdain, skepticism, mild amusement and the like. In every measurable way, infant dreaming was like adult dreaming. They see no reason why infants cannot be dreaming about their experiences to date, as the rest of us do. Dreaming is a form of communication within the mind itself.

Instant dialog

Recent discoveries that newborns can mimic adult expressions of sadness, joy, and surprise show that they are precisely reading adult faces and moods (Field, Woodson, Greenberg and Cohen, 1982). This form of instant dialog with adults is quite surprising but fits with the earlier surprising discovery that infants synchronize their movements with the structure of adult speech. Elaborate technology and microanalysis was used to show how newborns become 'entrained' syllable by syllable with adult speech, but not to other sounds (Condon and Sander, 1974). A form of *anticipatory* synchrony was captured on film by Daniel Stern (1980). In slow motion his film shows a newborn, just home from the hospital, anticipating his father's moves by making appropriate *opposite* movements of head and arms so that they meet symmetrically in space (Stern, 1980).

Intermodal fluency

This refers to the ability of newborns to store and instantly transfer information from one sense modality to another. For example, in an experiment giving smooth and nubbly pacifiers to blindfolded infants, infants (2–3 weeks) quickly identified by *sight* which ones they had previously *felt* (Meltzoff and Borton, 1979). Similarly, infants shown movies where faces and sound tracks are scrambled often manage to locate the faces which are truly synchronized with the *sounds* they hear. Matching of facial movements with sound is a demonstration of lip-reading (Dodd, 1979). Feats of this kind contradict both the behaviorist assumption that infant awareness starts from scratch and has to be learned, and the developmental assumption that babies begin life with single sense modalities which have to be gradually integrated with other modalities. Intermodal fluency is not developed; newborns have it already.

Listening

When newborns are fully awake they are wide-eyed, curious and attentive – excellent listeners. Videotapes show them lifting their heads and stretching toward sounds being played to them from overhead speakers. Listening is shown by eye-fixation, pupillary dilation, directed head movements, breath-holding, tongue-thrusting and active mouth movements (Eisenberg and Marmarou, 1981).

In the hours right after birth recordings show orderly eye movements, conjugate saccades of varying length and direction in a regular scanning rhythm. The pattern they make is almost indistinguishable, in the speed and precision of the saccades and their binocular synchrony, from that of an adult. This involves delicate neural and muscular mechanisms already coordinated and therefore innate (Trevarthen, 1974). Newborns are equipped for communication.

Relating

Trevarthen and others collaborated in an ambitious program of filming early mother–infant interactions at Harvard University (Trevarthen, 1974, 1980). They found intense *mutual* communication. Films showed the infants *aiming* their eyes, fingers and toes, tracking with their eyes, head, torso, hands and feet. Aiming at mothers was accurate and synchronized. *Looking* movements occurred in advance of efficiency in seeing, delicate *handling* movements appeared long before efficiency in use of hands, and *speaking* movements long before the babies could say anything. To Trevarthen these were acts of intention and purpose (mental events preceding physical events).

In the same study, differences were quickly apparent in how 3-week-old babies related to a furry toy monkey and to their mothers. Gaze could be fixed on the monkey for long periods of study, accompanied by arm extension and grasping movements. With mothers it was different: tentative, rhythmic looking at and looking away, terribly interested but careful not to stare. Researchers could watch film segments of any part of the body and tell whether infants were relating to the monkey or to the mother.

Infants are exquisitely sensitive to *changes* in relationships. In a single feeding on the 7th day of life, experimenters had mothers wear a mask and remain silent. Infants took significantly less milk, later scanned the room anxiously, and had disturbed REM and NREM sleep (Cassell and Sander, 1975). Researchers have obtained similar reactions when they asked mothers to suddenly become silent and 'still-faced' for just 3 minutes (Tronick et al., 1978). Babies only 2–3 weeks old recognize this strange event within 15 seconds, become intensely wary and try different strategies to cope with it. The effect was even worse when mothers were asked to assume a depressed state for 3 minutes. Behavior of these infants (3 months old) was radically altered and one quarter of them cried steadily for 30 seconds.

Such results show that mother–infant communication is goal-oriented and reciprocal; the infant plays a major role, constantly modifying expressive displays in response to feedback from the partner. This is pre-linguistic communication in which the underlying mechanisms appear to be innate, not learned.

Newborns have a special link with their mother's voice. In a cleverly arranged experiment, newborns could suck fast or slow to get different female voices reading the same story (DeCasper and Fifer, 1980). They quickly learned how to obtain their own mother's voice and spent more time listening to her. In doing so they showed they could distinguish between speakers, preferred their own mother's voice, and had technical competence handling various formal aspects of speech: rhythmicity, intonation, frequency variations and phonetics. Infants may be better at listening to us than we are at listening to them.

Hand signals

Hand signals at birth, like the clenched fist, are meaningful communications. Patterns of waving and pointing associated with sound which occur over and over again in infants at 2 months are present in outline at birth. Five communicative hand positions are sketched by the Papouseks (1977).

T.G.R. Bower (1974) has shown that newborns reach out with intention. Polaroid goggles were used to make objects seem reachable when they were not. Infants reaching out for foam rubber spheres were surprised and upset when their hands reached the location of the intangible object and failed to make contact. They could not comprehend their error. Obviously things were not working out as intended. Although most motor activity is awkward at birth and requires practice to become smooth and efficient, studies of hand and arm movements show that these awkward movements are nevertheless directive and purposive.

COMPETENCE IN LEARNING

Learning is usually defined as the change in behavior that accrues over time as a result of experience. Infants have demonstrated their ability to learn in all the ways that learning is usually tested: classical conditioning, reinforcement learning, and habituation. Newborns also show forms of learning – imitation and imprinting – that are best described as innate or instant. Considering all these abilities, I think we can conclude with Lipsitt that the newborn is 'about as competent a learning organism as he can become' (Lipsitt, 1969).

Classical conditioning

The first scientific proof that infants were capable of learning came from Russian psychologists experimenting with the process of classical conditioning pioneered by Pavlov. With repeated trials pairing a neutral (unconditioned) stimulus with a natural (conditioned one), infants were taught to respond to the neutral one by itself. Decades of experiments beginning in the 1920s have succeeded in demonstrating this type of learning in the fetus as well as the newborn (Brackbill and Koltsova, 1967).

Reinforcement learning

Infants learn more quickly when some form of reward follows the behavior being sought. Newborns have been precocious in figuring out which turns of the head (left or right) to a stimulus (bell or buzzer) leads to the reward (sweet solution, milk, sound or light display). They figure out what to do in minutes, even when all the contingencies are reversed (Lipsitt and Werner, 1981).

Habituation

Habituation behavior (the tendency to react less and less to the same stimulus) has also been used to demonstrate infant learning. Reaction to novel versus familiar words, visual displays, sounds, odors or tastes in a series of presentations is a confirmation of discrimination, memory and learning (Kessen, Haith and Salapatek, 1970).

Imitation

More recently, in a series of experiments in several independent laboratories, newborns have shown an unexpected competence in imitating adult gestures and facial expressions. This demonstration of learning without the necessity of tedious repetition, reward or experience takes us to a new level of appreciation of the newborn mind (Meltzoff and Moore, 1983). Newborns as young as 60 minutes old were found to imitate adults sticking out their tongues, opening the mouth wide or moving the fingers in sequence. Newborns 36 hours old discriminate and imitate expressions of happiness, sadness and surprise on adult faces (as previously mentioned). This indicates competent blending of social, perceptive, cognitive and sensorimotor resources in swift and effective communication (Field et al., 1982).

Imprinting

Rapidity of learning by imitation is similar in speed to 'imprinting'. Originally used to explain bonding between animal chicks and their mothers during a critical period after birth, imprinting describes rapid learning in situations of extreme urgency and trauma. This powerful one-episode learning is found in people who have jumped off bridges, survived, and been transformed – in seconds. Sudden, significant changes, both positive and negative, have been seen following near-death experiences in surgery, heart attacks, and grave physical and emotional crises at birth. Using hypnotherapeutic techniques, obstetrician David Cheek (1975) has found specific connections between physical and psychological problems presented by his patients and traumas at their birth. Similar connections have been uncovered in primal therapy (Janov, 1983).

Joy in learning

A happier aspect of infant learning is emphasized by T.G.R. Bower of Edinburgh (1977). He finds that several researchers have reported a connection between learning and smiling and concludes that babies get pleasure out of pulling a string to make a mobile turn, kicking to turn on a projector or turning their heads to get an adult to play 'peek-a-boo'. The joy of learning or having control over something in the external environment is expressed by smiling, cooing or bubbling at the moment they figure out how to do it. He believes that a *love* of learning motivates babies to participate in research. If tasks are too repetitive and no *new* challenges are introduced, babies become bored and stop working. This can complicate interpretation of research findings (Papousek, 1967).

The pleasure of learning to control things is so powerful that handicapped babies have been known to burst into smiles for the first time. Bower (1977) tells of a blind baby who never smiled until he discovered that by kicking his legs he could set off an auditory mobile. This discovery provoked vigorous and forceful smiling. Similarly, Watson (1973) tells of a developmentally arrested infant who had scarcely moved for 8 months and had never been seen to smile. Given a mobile which could be controlled with head, arm and foot movements, the child was moving and cooing within 2 hours!

Earlier researchers gave identical mobiles to two groups of infants in their cribs. One group could set them in motion by moving the crib and the others could only watch. Infants given the opportunity to control the mobiles ended up smiling and cooing while the others did not (Hunt and Uzgiris, 1964). Mental activity is obviously important and gratifying to infants.

Infant stimulation

Infants seem to welcome and thrive on stimulation. Evidence of readiness to learn comes from the relatively new field of infant stimulation. Originally, stimulation was given to assist premature babies to 'catch up' in their development (Rice, 1977); now it is being offered to other babies. Natural stroking, conversation and deliberately arranged sensory experiences seem to enhance development. In this new approach, *contact* replaces isolation and sensory deprivation.

Infants receiving even modest amounts of extra attention and handling by their mothers in the days immediately following birth show signs of improved disposition, language ability and intelligence months later, compared to those who were isolated in nurseries (Kennell and Klaus, 1983). Babies handled more tend to gain weight faster, grow taller, develop motor coordination and muscle control sooner. Even simple programs of prenatal bonding and communication with the fetus seem to pay off in greater alertness and control at birth, earlier talking, independence and better concentration (Ludington, 1985). These are all signs of a mind eager for learning and responsive to loving attention.

COMPETENCE IN MEMORY

Evidence for competent learning in newborns is also evidence for competent memory since memory is required for learning. Memory itself is so complex that it is best described in terms of multiple systems, each system serving somewhat different purposes and operating according to somewhat different principles (Tulving, 1985).

Searching for adequate ways to test for memory has led to appreciation of its many dimensions: 'procedural' memory, semantic memory and episodic memory (including perceptual and affect memory). To this list 'cellular' and 'clinical' memory could be added. As in other aspects of infant study, the actual feats of memory displayed by infants go beyond the theories formulated to explain them.

Procedural memory is a way of describing what enables retention and recall of learned connections between stimuli and responses (Tulving, 1985). This is a recall system involving muscle patterns and coordination as in turning over, sitting up or operating equipment. Such memories are unconscious and automatic. 'Motor memory' is an example. Infants can learn to operate crib mobiles by making certain moves with feet, hands or head and will show memory of it weeks later, provided the same set of features are kept intact (Rovee-Collier, 1985). The same mobile with a different bumper, however, may fail to reinstate the behavior and lead researchers to believe the infant has forgotten. After working with 1500 infants, Rovee-Collier points out that infants may not recognize a mobile out of context any more than we recognize our dental assistant in a line at the movies.

Semantic memory deals with the world of words, a world of internal states of meaning not perceptually present. This type of memory is more conscious than automatic. Checking the memory of newborns (14 days old) for word recognition, workers had mothers repeat unfamiliar words ten times in a row six times a day for 2 weeks (Ungerer, Brody and Zelazo, 1978). After a 42-hour delay at the end of training the infants showed clear signs of recognition as measured by eye activity, head-turning and raised eyebrows. Since they recognized and responded to these words (and not to their own names during this early period) it was thought that frequent and regular exposure helped with storing and recall. A later study (Brody, Zelazo and Chaika, 1984) with newborns only 72 hours old showed that the infants were able to retain certain English words and compare them to novel English words presented in a habituation experiment. The authors believe that the neonates were actually processing speech.

Episodic memory is what we expect memory to be, autobiographical and involving a very personal kind of consciousness. These memories are like time capsules carrying a full spectrum of feelings, thoughts and actions. Infant researchers have confirmed both perceptual and affective memory. Evidence of 'perceptual memory' in newborns comes from experiments with visual forms like faces, double arrows, bellbars, stars and color graphics. Prematures (35 weeks g.a.) showed they could discriminate and remember novel color patterns (Werner and Siqueland, 1978). Other researchers using graphic images in a habituation paradigm found that newborns showed definite recognition of the novel forms and were remembering visual information (Slater, Morison and Rose, 1982). A strange person's face shown for only 1 minute was recognized a week later.

Before birth, pregnant mothers were asked to read the same story twice a day for 6.5 weeks. After birth when the newborns were given a chance to suck for this or a different story, they recognized and preferred the familiar story (DeCasper and Spence, 1982). Tones and music presented before birth have been treated as familiar after birth. As mentioned previously, newborns quickly perceive/remember the odor of their mother's breast pads.

Emotional cues ('affect memory') have also been found crucial to memory. Affects are a language system in themselves, changing little over the life span. We are likely to remember things because of the emotional markers contained in them, and tend to recall them when experiencing these same emotions again. In this way mood and memory are often linked (G.H. Bower, 1981).

Daniel Stern points to an expanded realm of affect experienced by babies which goes beyond the discrete boundaries of fear, anger, etc. These 'vitality affects' or 'feeling qualities', as he calls them, arise directly from encounters with people and involve subtle aspects of intensity, motion and rhythm. Such feelings are often associated with vital processes such as breathing, falling asleep, being awakened, diapered and dressed. Waves of feeling may come from hearing music, jolts from loud noises or seeing someone jump up suddenly (Stern, 1985, pp. 47–57).

Stern reminds us that these vitality affects are expressed by puppets who make emotional impressions by dynamic movement and accompanying voice sounds (but with no change in facial expression), dancers, who make emotional impressions by motion alone, and by animated cartoon characters. These art forms all involve multi-modal crossing and stimulation. Infants have cross-modal fluency and accurately read faces, bodies and intensities. They share with us this wider world of affect.

The durability of memory has been studied in older infants. Memories are found to be surprisingly robust in spite of attempts to deliberately interfere by inserting confusing or irrelevant material. Infants do best when remembering characteristics of objects most salient and important to them (McCall, Kennedy and Dodds, 1977; Cohen, DeLoache and Pearl, 1977). Autobiographical memory is known to decrease markedly and regularly as a function of age but some memories are long lasting and others can be retrieved by stimulus word lists, visualization exercises and other cues (Crovitz and Harvey, 1979).

BIRTH MEMORY: A STUNNING EXHIBITION OF COMPETENCE

People, many years after birth, sometimes recall aspects of their birth experience in psychoanalysis or hypnotherapy. Birth memories arise because the problems presented by these clients are birth-related. The problems are actually *clinical memories* walking around waiting to be recognized and treated. The very existence of the birth-related migraine, depression, fear or breathing problem is living proof that the underlying birth memory is still intact.

During deep experiential psychotherapy, primal therapy, or rebirthing a startling array of contortions and expressions related to trauma at birth may erupt from the physical body. Some describe this as *'cellular memory'* because it is so different from ordinary episodic memory and because specific parts of the body seem to hold and express these memory patterns in perpetuity. Cellular memory is not always traumatic. Intuitive and behavioral assets may be part of the pattern that is stored and released from this deep unconscious level.

Some birth memories arise spontaneously. Reports, still quite rare, come from adults who say they have always had birth memories but were not sure they should believe them or tell anybody about them. More common than the adult memories are the memories coming from very young children (2–4 years old), who blurt them out without warning, or who innocently answer questions about birth when asked. Collections of these stories are beginning to appear (Matthison, 1981; Chamberlain, 1988). I think they constitute an important new category of evidence for the reality of birth memory.

The memories of very young children are disarming and persuasive. Children are resourceful with limited vocabulary, acting out, pointing to parts of the body, repeating conversation and correctly describing the action of those present. One short vignette will illustrate the competence of these young minds. Cathy, helping at a home birth, was left holding the baby when the mother and midwife had left the room. When the baby began to whimper she impulsively put the baby to her own breast. Feeling she should not have been the first to do this, she kept the incident a secret.

Three years 9 months later while babysitting with this child in a group of other children, she asked her if she remembered being born. The child answered yes and proceeded to give an accurate account of who was present and their roles during labor and delivery. Finally she leaned up close and whispered in a confidential tone, 'You held me and gave me titty when I cried and mommy wasn't there.' Cathy said later, 'Nobody can tell me babies don't remember their birth.'

Hypnosis has been a prime means of retrieving birth memories (Kelsey, 1953; LeCron, 1963; Cheek, 1975; Chamberlain, 1981). Cheek (1974) found that ten out of ten adult subjects could demonstrate the correct sequential head and shoulder movements connected with their own deliveries. Raikov (1980) found that adults in deep hypnosis could faithfully reproduce a range of seven newborn reflexes and movements.

Evidence for the *reliability* of birth memories comes from my own research with ten mother and child pairs in hypnosis. This study involved children (average age 16) who had no conscious memories of birth and mothers who said they had never shared details of this birth with them. All of the final subjects were capable of detailed memory in hypnosis. The research yielded narrative reports of the same birth separately obtained from mother and child.

Reports were coherent with each other, overlapped at many points, and contained a rich store of information indicative of alert perception and astute consciousness. Instead of uncovering a pattern of fantasy in the dual reports, analysis of the mother's reports confirmed the general reliability of the children's birth memories.

From the standpoint of understanding the newborn mind, perhaps the most striking feature of these narratives is the *maturity of feeling and thought* one finds enfolded in them. I do not refer to the obvious maturity of adult subjects using mature language; I refer to the maturity of the perceptions and thoughts moving through the *infant* mind at the time. This unexpected maturity is seen in expressions of compassion and love, moral anguish, clear insights about people and their relationships, problem solving and decision making, critical commentary on how birth is handled, and comprehension of what things mean.

Table 1 contains three examples of the characteristic dovetailing and quality of thought found in these reports. A further example comes from a child Linda remembering the situation after delivery. Linda says, 'I was trying to grab for her and she was looking at me. I wanted to turn over and I couldn't. I looked up at her. I wanted her not to let them take me away. But when I saw her face I knew she wasn't going to do that. And then I just give up. Someone wraps me up and hands me over to the nurse and she takes me out.'

After listening to hundreds of these reports, I am left with the strong impression that age is no guide at all to what is on a baby's mind. Babies appear to feel, react, care, think and remember as the rest of us do. This obviously requires a mind.

Summary

Newborns are superbly equipped with a sensory system essentially functional and supportive of mental activity from the start. They are especially prepared for communication, demonstrating innate qualities of attention and perception. Newborn learning is discriminating and precocious; newborn memory is quite beyond what has been predicted by developmental psychology. The facts lead me to believe that newborns feel, react, learn, remember and use their minds essentially as other persons do. They do not become real persons when we think they are ready; they seem to start before we are ready.

CONCLUSIONS

(1) *Psychology* has been wrong about newborns as undifferentiated, egoless, basically incompetent subpersons for most of the first year of life. This view has unfortunately provided an excuse for various forms of neglect and abuse of infants.

(2) *Obstetrics* has been wrong about newborns as insensitive creatures incapable of true experiences, emotion and memory. This false

Table 1 Illustrations of dovetailing in mother and child birth memories

Mother Madeline
They sort of put her on my stomach but they're still holding onto her ... lots of blood and white stuff. She's crying. I can see the umbilical cord. My hands are fastened down because I can't reach out and touch her. I would like them to move her, wrap her up. I'm talking to the doctors ... I think they had a white cap over my hair. They finally undo my hands and the nurse brings her over on my left side. But she doesn't hold her close enough so I can touch her. I really feel frustrated. I do say 'Hi!' to her ... I talk to the doctor about her weight ...

Child Katy
They put me on her stomach, sort of dumped me on her. He's talking to my mom. Everything seems to be okay and she's all right ... I feel bigger and heavier. I can see her but I'm not by her. Her hair is wrapped up, like in curlers or something. She looks tired, sweaty. Nobody's talking to me. They're talking about me, I think, but not *to* me. They act like they know I'm there but like *I* don't know I'm there ... The nurse kind of wiped me. Then they brought me over next to my mother. She wasn't crying but something like that. She's the first one that talked to me. She said 'Hi!'. Nobody else seemed to think that I was really there. Then she talked to the doctor a little bit and they took me away again.

Mother Kathryn
I want to name the baby Mary Kathryn, and Bobby wants to name her Ginger ... You have to have a saint's name (in the Catholic church) so she can be baptized and Ginger is not a saint's name. But he definitely won't go for Mary Kathryn.

Child Ginger
There was a hassle (about the name). My mom didn't like Ginger ... but my dad did.

Mother Irene
I pick her up and smell her. I smell her head. I look at her toes and say, 'Oh God! She has deformed toes!' (She then called the nurse, asked about the toes, and received assurance that they were all right.)

Child Dana
She's holding me up, looking at me ... She's smelling me! And she asked the nurse why my toes were so funny ... The nurse said that's just the way my toes are and that they weren't deformed.

psychology makes many aspects of traditional obstetrics violent and obsolete.

(3) *Medicine and psychology* have confused brain with mind. Preoccupation with the immaturity of the physical brain at birth has

delayed discovery of the true mental competence of newborns and public recognition of the newborn as a real person.

(4) *Developmental psychology* is making the discovery that key elements of the newborn endowment are *not* developmental after all. Dreaming, perception, communication, learning, and memory seem to be functional at birth. This new knowledge could have a positive influence on pediatrics, parenthood and education.

(5) *Newborns* will always be mysterious because they are small and don't talk as we do. They cannot prove their value, wisdom and character to us until they have had some time to grow up. Nevertheless, on the basis of our present knowledge of their competence in communication, learning and memory, I believe we are justified in accepting newborns as full persons, just as human as we are, from the day they are born.

2

A new view of the unborn: toward a developmental psychology of the prenatal period

S. Schindler

ABSTRACT

In textbooks on developmental psychology, human life starts as a development of the organism 'human being'. This organism becomes increasingly interpretable as a psychological being.

This fact would not even be worth mentioning, except that it shows how children are represented at the beginning of their lives: by ignoring their existence as persons.

We know that the pathogeny of a situation also depends on the mental representation of this situation by the 'relevant others'. Preventive concepts in psychosomatic medicine therefore have to take into consideration the view of the unborn as well as the view of other people.

Based on the thesis of Lloyd de Mause, that parents' relationship to their children began to change about the middle of this century, the far-reaching consequences of an inappropriate handling of children will be described.

The child's physiological and behavioral development can be described in connection with information apart from psychoanalytic treatments. Considering the cognitive development and the developmental tasks on the one hand, as well as the child's needs on the other, a concept of developmental psychology of the prenatal period will be outlined.

The development of psychological structures will be presented in terms of their relation to ecological and social-psychological perspectives. It is necessary to re-print the way in which adults view children, especially the parents' understanding of their own children; and we must always keep in mind that these two aspects cannot be separated.

If we ask how the child before birth is typically described in developmental psychology, the answer is revealing: in the earlier scientific literature, little or no attention was paid to the prenatal state, as it was assumed that development began, at best, after birth. Until the 1970s, few textbooks even described the prenatal period of life, and in those few cases that did, the focus of attention was clearly on the physical development of the organism itself. Morphological changes, dependent on growth and maturation, were primarily described in terms of the potentially damaging influences of teratogenes, whereas data on functional development did not appear until much later. The new, revised editions of *Child Development and Personality* by Mussen, Conger and Kagan (1974), provide a good example of this change.

A similar phenomenon appeared one or two decades earlier in relation to another phase of life, that of neonatal development. As Rau (1982, p. 131) states, the newborn was for a long time regarded as a purely physiological being, with all research being concentrated upon the degree of physiological maturity and physical safety. This standard did not begin to change until the mid-1960s. Shortly thereafter, Brazelton (1970) developed the 'Neonatal Behavioral Assessment Scale' for the purpose of better understanding the child's 'interactive behavior'. Subsequent observations made with this instrument have substantially changed the scientific view of newborn capabilities and development. After extensive research, the concept of the 'competent infant' (Stone, Smith and Murphy, 1973) has replaced that of the 'blooming, buzzing confusion' which described the world of the newborn according to William James' view.

This concept of the active, competent newborn is now fully accepted, as elaborated by Rau (1983, p. 83):

'And so arose the picture of a baby that incorporates the essential and psychologically important characteristics – even if they are still only rudimentary – which also form the older child and the adult, respectively. It is the picture of an active organism, one which contributes to its own development in interaction with the world around it. As a result, it can now even be described in terms of subject, not only in objective terms which are already well-known.' (Author's translation.)

When it comes to the child before birth, however, there are still only a few experts who consider the possibility of a similar shift in perspective. Both science and popular opinion adhere to a model which refers to the unborn child in distancing and objectifying terms, rather than viewing such a child as a person with the capacity for autonomous development.

Although the 'intrauterine patient' was discovered more than a decade ago, even now medical mistakes do not generally count in legal terms as regards the prenatal child. The physical integrity of this child is consequently not fully protected, even though under current law he or she can acquire property. That is, the unborn can inherit, in the case where it is born.

Of course, this does not constitute the final legal word. Now lawyers are prepared to take into account new considerations, as a much cited sentence of the Supreme Court in the Federal Republic of Germany indicates. A child who was born with brain damage was granted a compensation claim, since an expert could detect a connection between brain damage and oxygen supply in the fifth month of pregnancy. The mother had considerable circulation problems, and her labor lasted for 2 days. All of this was the result of a traffic accident in which the child's father was also badly hurt (Supreme Court VI ZR 198/3 v. 5.2.1985). Surely this legal decision, which many regarded as sensational, is only a small step on a long road – one which leads from the naive ideas of causal connections in development, to more complex and comprehensive models.

In its effort to recognize plain facts, the study of the unborn first focused upon anatomy, then upon physiology and eventually upon pathology. A scientific approach which attempts to grasp the 'objective' facts is characteristic of research in these fields; a static, realistic manner of presentation is the method of choice. The German language puts this very appropriately: science should be something 'settled' (fest-gestellt) – and if possible, forever. Anatomic models offer perhaps the most suitable examples of such knowledge, with one clear disadvantage: they fail to precisely capture the whole reality of the organism. For example, the child before birth lives in the body of a specific woman, with her own individual and multifarious conditions of living. In her culturally, historically and socially defined situation, she is quite different from other people, and she brings her child into a reality already shaped by a unique world view.

As Peter Fedor-Freybergh (1983, p. 24) has pointed out, no mother talks about her child as 'my embryo' or 'my fetus'. When it comes to her relationship to the child, she is quite void of the scientists' objectifying distance. General statements mean little to her unless they concern her child specifically, or unless they can at least elucidate her view of the child.

The same holds true for the relevant educational institutions. Many students are interested in the contents of lectures only if they are being addressed as expectant or future parents, or if they can relate the material to experiences which they have already had. Otherwise, these students learn objectively-oriented material with little personal involvement, especially if (as is often the case in our field) the material represents only a certain degree of probability. On the other hand, some students of medicine and psychology are concerned about highly objective data, as they are in search of the general and avoid reference to the subjectified specifics of their own lives.

The differences described here will be most apparent in a field, which is more predestined than others to put the knowledge of prenatal psychology into action – that is, to prepare for and to inform the birth process. Elsewhere, one scarcely finds such multifold statements presented with such personal involvement and strong feelings. This is not difficult to understand when one considers that preparation for the child, and for the first encounter with it, can succeed only if one includes one's own relationship to this child, not from a scientific distance but from a more personal perspective.

Ready formulations, as I now use them, are, however, a mere fraction of the new view of the unborn child; more importantly, complementary elements can be seen in practice such as in the 'birthing schools' in Poland, where expectant parents are convinced of the value of close contact with the child. Fetal psychotherapy is introduced, especially through the use of music, and the process of birth even from the viewpoint of the child is the primary focus; at birth, doctors and midwives restrict their incisions to a minimum (Fijalkowski, 1983, p. 140).

But here, as in other fields, there are also scientists who will not allow themselves to be determined *a priori* by the prevalent paradigms. Peterson (1986), for example, has described the phenomenon of 'child arrival' from the mothers' accounts in a way that is not at all conventional.

A few other philosophers have of course tried hard not to disappear into objectifying particulars, but instead to keep the whole context in focus. As early as the first meeting of ISPP Wucherer-Huldenfeld (1973, p. 53) stated:

> 'In indisputable favour of prenatal psychology speaks also its ability to follow the specific human far back. The unity of the prenatal development as well as the total development that comes after birth, becomes more distinct in this way. And so appears a personage that exists and must not be separated in the stages that succeed each other, since they form a unity.'

The concepts of Life-Span Developmental Psychology were already anticipated by him.

From such concepts an important maxim is derived: it is not the one who assumes continuity of development who is obligated to prove it. On the contrary, it is the one who always vindicates fundamental changes between life periods, who is bound to answer. Thus, the competence of the infant, once lacking in the scientific literature, had to first be proven. The fact that it was thought difficult to demonstrate this competence prior to the child's development of language, was nevertheless not sufficient reason to deny the existence of this competence.

Today, developmental psychology calls for the inclusion of the manifold continuity of the entire life course, including the prenatal period. However, the spectrum still extends from the previously mentioned psychologically oriented text books to those of humanistic psychology. It remains to be understood why such inconsistencies ever existed, and why – particularly in the case of prenatal psychology – they continue to persist.

Attempts to answer this question lead us back to early discussions in the beginning of the psychoanalytic tradition, concerning the possible psychological importance of the first stage of life. Here it is important to remember that, in the beginning of psychoanalysis, there was no special treatment of either the prenatal period or of birth traumas. Work with the unconscious and later with the experiences of childhood, led logically to a certain conclusion, as Sigmund Freud and other psychoanalysts began to see the connections between pre- and perinatal experiences. Initially, however, this occurred by chance, as a consequence of the narrative about dream contents (fn. in 3rd edition of *Interpretation of Dreams*, 1908). 'The bridge will be the transition from the other side (not yet born) to this side (life), and when the Human being also imagines death as a return to the womb (to the water), will the bridge also mean a forwarding to death.' Note here the distinction which is clearly made in the choice of words between 'the other side' for the womb, and 'this side' for life after birth. A similar distinction has already been seen in the concepts of contemporary lawyers.

Elsewhere, Freud formulates his ideas a little more carefully, but the fundamental idea remains the same. He recapitulates his thoughts as follows:

> 'The importance of the fantasies and unconscious thoughts concerning life in the womb I didn't condescend to learn until late. They contain ... the most deeply unconscious justification of believing in life after death, which only a projection in the origin of this awesome life before birth describes. The act of birth is, besides, the first experience of fear and consequently the source and the prototype of the affect of fear.'

Again, note especially the choice of words, 'the awesome life before birth'; Freud probably felt this way during his entire life.

Ferenczi's (1913) work on the 'Developmental stages of the sense of reality' represents the first systematic effort to describe prenatal development. In this, he tried to show how the child acquires a concept of reality through a specific line of differentially structured experiences. This process depends on the impelling respectivity which necessarily structures each stage. Furthermore, the conditions of a given stage may be reproduced or re-experienced during regressions. This fundamental idea is invariably of interest to the current topic. It should be emphasized that any communication regarding this early developmental stage is not possible without a revision of the later experiences which inevitably influence our perceptions of the earlier ones (by structure of transference). In other words, neglecting this basic knowledge leads to the mistake that early experiences are interpreted – in this case, misunderstood – on the basis of structures formed out of later experiences. It seems, for example, that considerations of the phenomenon interpreted as the 'castration complex' often overlook the possibility that even a preceding disruption such as the cutting of the umbilical cord can be 'experienced' – in more than just a physical sense – by the newborn child.

A similar theme appears in a discussion of Rank's concept of the 'birth trauma' (published under this title in 1924). In search of a disturbance which could be considered the prototype, or basis for all later disturbances, Rank resorted to the universal event of birth. This event was interpreted as 'trauma', as an injury to a system which was previously intact and able to function within itself. Subsequently this experience became the model for other traumatic experiences which would be encountered in later life. If such a central disturbance does exist, it follows in consequence that the treatment of it will greatly reduce disposition towards later neuroticism. Rank emphasized that every subsequent fear derives from the birth trauma, and that there exists a desire to return to the original intrauterine condition (1924, p. 20).

This concept fails to recognize, however, that many relevant structures and regulation systems are formed postnatally in response to experiences within the world around us, as Ferenczi has already described. Even a detail which became central for Ferenczi and especially for Balint has been overlooked: the beginning of a developmental deficiency (the 'basic fault', as Balint calls it) can be seen in a mismatch or 'lack of fit' between the child and the environment.

Ernst Falzeder's (1984, p. 154) interesting recapitulations follow these thoughts quite logically:

> 'The tragedy begins with a discordance in the needs of mother and child. That is possible already in the prenatal phase. This *unspecified ecological unbalance* has weighty negative effects on the child, whose

entire later development is thereby impaired. Two decisive points in this development are the biological and social birth which, based on these pre-conditions, can only be experienced as traumatic. So, the basic fault becomes 'organized' ... The manifestations of the basic fault are characterized by a fixation on specific ways of coping with these traumata.' (Translation Ernst Falzeder.)

This theme is also rather close to the position taken by Gustav Hans Graber, who already concerned himself with similar questions as early as 1924. For Graber (1967), birth represented above all 'a varied way of existence'. Expressed in more contemporary language, we can say that as the child's environment changes, a new orientation toward the external world must necessarily follow and that this, to a large degree, demands self-activity on the part of the child. This process also leads inevitably to a certain amount of ambivalence.

An observation which has been made by psychoanalysts over and over again is that the child's prenatal, intrauterine existence bears a great deal of continuity with life after birth ('more than the radical caesura of the birth act would lead us to assume', as written by Sigmund Freud in 1926). Furthermore, as Erich Neumann (1955) formulated, 'the psychic reality of this phase can only be realized if it is paradoxically formulated ... it is not possible to be described through subjective or objective relations alone'. He also characterized this situation as 'being in the reality of unity'. Neumann (1955) described this as the phase which connects us to:

'that "oceanic feeling" which appears over and over again even in adults. It appears where the reality of unity completes, breaks through, or replaces the commonplace conscious reality, that which is polarized in object and subject.'

If this is the case, then the question about how the newborn or even the fetus 'experiences' the world takes on a new meaning. Thus, the issue of 'reality of unity' is also expressed in the child's somatic experience: 'In the prenatal state, surely, eros is at work; the object of it must be its own fetal body, whereas the fetal "mind" is "oceanic", or, let us say in very modern words, "high"' (Peerbolte, 1976, personal communication).

Once again, Neumann emphasizes the fact that the experience of the world and the development of Ego takes place originally in relation to the mother: 'It is the first intertwining with the mother that gives nourishment, warmth, and protection, not only through her body but also in the most intimate relation to the mother's whole unconscious proof of love to the child and its body.' Therefore, physiological data and behavioral observation can inform us about the fetus' psychic situation more than in any other period of life.

We would also maintain that Graber's purpose is to avoid making one single stage more essential and determinative than any other. He claims that our thinking must represent a continuous process, as we are accustomed to in psychology, regardless of whether we are referring to life before or after birth. The continuity between prenatal and postnatal existence is once more understandable and accessible even during the analytic process. As Graber (1973) wrote, re-interpreting the previously mentioned metaphor of Freud:

'The bridge to the mother stays for life. No one can lose the infinitely deep psychic solidarity, his prenatal psyche, his unconscious self, that before birth attached him to his mother in a duality – even in postnatal existence. If this spring dries out, then so does life itself. This axiomatic fact may be found in connection with a neurotic attachment to the mother only insofar as the emotional solidarity with our intellectual life and with the external environment can be disrupted in the wake of total regression. But no kind of disturbance and no degree of intensity of it matches that of the drying up. It can be rectified through psychotherapy or deep love; thereby will the live communication be so intense inside and out, that the source of the deep sensibility of the prenatal experience of dual unity rushes into the conscious presence. This makes us feel blissful and as newborns.'

In her discussion of this central problem, Anna Freud (1970) reminds us of the difference between the beginning of personality development on the one hand, and psychic disturbance on the other: 'In my opinion, these oldest influences from the world around us create states that are comparable to the deficiency diseases on the part of the body.' Ernst Falzeder (1984) adds that 'the existence of a deficiency implies that the child has a ... need for something and cannot follow his developmental matrix if this need is not satisfied.' Falzeder refers to Sutherland (1980, p. 839) who connects these concepts to the acceptance of the child's psychic needs: 'A fundamental organizer has been fashioned, not from instinctual satisfactions by themselves, but from these along with the experience of a general fit between the infant's overall psychological needs and the mother's spontaneous acceptance of these.'

And this expresses precisely what the previously mentioned efforts towards preparation for the child and for an optimal experience at birth are striving to achieve. Why then, have the relationships between these efforts and those of psychoanalysis been so little developed?

We know from analogies to physical health that the source of a deficiency may no longer be evident in the overt manifestation: hunger itself wanes, for example, as weakness and apathy set in. Is there a similar phenomenon in the area of psychic-emotional health? There is a great deal of evidence that would lead to this conclusion. The increasing frequency of depressive syndromes may be related to the fact that several generations may also have similarly disruptive birth experiences.

Psychoanalytic concerns about overcoming the fundamental disturbance are also pertinent. When Anna Freud, like her father, says 'this cannot really be a subject for analytic efforts', then she excludes the 'awesome life before birth'.

Hans Graber referred (1967), appropriately, to a 'fundamental resistance'; not only did he struggle against this during his lifetime, but he also provided very concrete references for his vindication. As he asked, 'Isn't the psychoanalytic situation itself such a regression into the prenatal existence, executed both symbolically and in reality by psychoanalyst and patient together?' He was referring to the closed room, the dimmed lights, the generally monotone speech, and the security provided during analytic sessions. The potential counter-transference inherent in this aspect of the relationship often is not analyzed, which does not help to improve the extensive problems.

In a recently published work, Janus explains that such discussions do not call for a break with the psychoanalytic tradition, but for a new interpretation of it. In a similar way, it is possible to refer to Freud's idea of the 'original constriction', thus making the concept of 'original resistance' comprehensible, or to juxtapose this primary process onto the fetal psyche (Janus, 1986b, p. 73). Graber had already referred to the 'almost uninhibited removal of tensions'. Effects of the secondary process and all the 'protective mechanisms' are considered only in terms of later developmental stages. By recognizing and taking into account the prenatal stage, we are compelled to change, not only our view of the unborn, but also the view of all stages in the life circle continuum.

And so, we have returned to the point where this essay began. We could just as easily end here as well, were it not for the fact that a more decisive aspect also needs to be dealt with urgently. Not even in science can we establish a view and allow contradictory evidence to outflank us as if it is of no concern whatever. It is always the case that our view of reality also influences our behavior. The 'secret life of the unborn child' (Verny and Kelly, 1981) must be accepted by us as real, before it can become a subject of scientific investigation. 'If men define situations as real, they are real in their consequences' (W.I. Thomas, *Child in America*, 1928, p. 584).

When we engage in psychology, we have sold our souls to a business which puts the human being itself in the very center of our efforts. That is to say, psychology has already changed our lives more deeply than we ourselves will admit.

Lloyd de Mause (1974) presented the thesis that a new method of handling children, which he called the 'helping mode', began in the middle of this century (Figure 1). As he said, around the 19th century:

'the raising of a child became less a process of conquering its will than of training it, guiding it into proper paths, teaching it to conform, socializing it. The socializing mode ... has been the source of all twentieth-century psychological models, from Freud's 'channeling of impulses' to Skinner's behaviorism. It is most particularly the model of sociological functionalism.'

On the other hand, during the last decade a new development began (de Mause, 1974, p. 52):

'The helping mode involves the preposition that the child knows better than the parent what it needs at each stage of life, and fully involves both parents in the child's life as they work to empathize with and fulfill its expanding and particular needs. There is no attempt at all to discipline or form 'habits'. Children are neither struck nor scolded, and are apologized to if yelled at under stress. The helping mode involves an enormous amount of time, energy, and discussion on the part of both parents, especially in the first 6 years, for helping a young child reach its daily goals means continually responding to it, playing with it, tolerating its regressions, being its servant rather than the other way

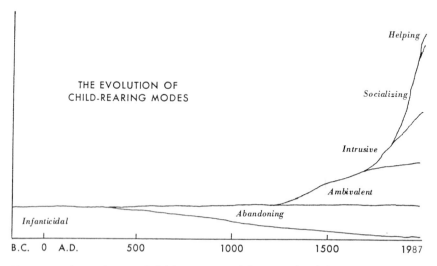

Figure 1 The evolution of child-rearing models. From Lloyd de Mause (ed.) (1974). *The History of Childhood*, p. 53. (New York: Psychohistory Press)

around, interpreting its emotional conflicts, and providing the objects specific to its evolving interests.'

Prenatal psychology has, from its inception, strived for the same goal — that is, to make the child *before* birth the focal point of psychological interests. And although this area of psychological interest arose somewhat accidentally at first (due to parental questions concerning the pre- and perinatal periods as a result of fetal injuries), new directions and publications since that time have increasingly presented the development of the unborn from the perspective of the child's own experience of this crucial period of life.

Setting aside the difficulties associated with the lack of language, Elisabeth Wiebauer (doctoral thesis, University of Salzburg, 1982) aptly described the means of communication available to the young child as follows: 'Children are not in a position to defend their roles with the rationality or morality of adults. Rather, their language is one of the body, of illness, and of death.'

The scientific traditions have struggled for many years to overcome the obstacles confronted when dealing with pre- or non-linguistic subjects, and this is particularly true, of course, for the human sciences. For those of us concerned with the developmental psychology of the prenatal period, we now see this as an especially urgent task, with research implications extending easily into the next century.

3

The connection between the course of pregnancy and postnatal mother–child interaction

G. Schusser

ABSTRACT

After an introductory statement about the relevance of previous research for prenatal psychology in view of acute environmental problems, the theoretical position of the author is outlined.

We start with a critical appraisal of the current research methods and the shortcomings of basic development concepts, and finally request a revised opinion on development which takes into account aspects like wholeness, individual target-seeking, system dependency, self-referentiality and self-reflexiveness of the developing child more than hitherto existing theories have done.

The resulting research conception is described in the second part and the present state of our project is outlined (= nine adapted cases, from the 3rd trimenon until the completion of the first year of birth with various questionnaires, birth protocol, clinical case judgement and various video recordings of mother–child interactions), as well as outlining further project planning.

After a brief characterizing of a few cases, a summarizing sketch of the results is given. It seems to confirm that each case of developing mother–child relationship should be considered as a holistic structure from the beginning and the reconstruction of this structure (= metastructure) allows anticipation about further developments.

INTRODUCTION

The period between the notification and writing of this paper saw the occurrence of the events surrounding Chernobyl. Less than 6 months lie between these events and the ISPP meeting in September 1986 to exchange and discuss the results of our research into and relating to prenatal psychology.

I do not think that I am guilty of misinterpretation in describing these events and their consequences, both acute and chronic, physiological and psychological, as being so grave that faced by them the International Society for Prenatal Psychology and Medicine should devote its research efforts in this direction.

A working party should be appointed which will apply itself intensively to the subject of the endangering of the unborn by environmental pollution – especially through radiation – even if this is initially only a systematic collection, evaluation and interpretation of isolated relevant findings already available in a variety of areas. This could then form the basis of separate studies to be planned by members of the study group.

We cannot, namely, be content to demonstrate the negative effects solely of nicotine, alcohol, coffee and other drugs on fetuses and neonates (DFG-Bericht, 1977, p. 59f.), simply because it is the parents who decide, so to speak, to administer these noxious substances.

At a time when there is no end to reports on ground-water pollution (e.g. through over-fertilization), on the dioxin contamination of mother's milk (Neue Osnabrücker Zeitung, 1986), on pseudo-croup caused by air pollution and now also radioactive contamination, we have rather the scientific and ethical duty to expose as quickly as we can the possible extent of these damaging influences.

After all, the founder of the German section of 'International Doctors for the Prevention of Nuclear War', the professor of nuclear medicine, Dr H. Begemann, describes, with reference to Chernobyl, the unborn as the group at greatest risk (H. Begemann, 1986).

Only such an extension of our work programmes for the coming years could preserve for me the sense that our future scientific activity is truly sufficiently relevant and could dispel the fear that rather we are continuing to concern ourselves with marginal problems while closing our eyes to the real and determining influences on us.

APPRAISAL OF THE PRESENT STATE OF RESEARCH AND ITS UNDERLYING THEORETICAL STARTING-POINT

The initial empirical trends in the results of my own studies, which I present in the second part of my paper, can be judged adequately only in conjunction with the theoretical position adopted here. May I therefore, in four steps, set this out as the first part of my paper.

The predominance of selective project designs

If one attempts to survey the now very substantial number of scientific studies of that part of life delimited by the terms 'course of pregnancy' and 'postnatal mother–child interaction' it becomes obvious that the vast majority of project designs that have become reality have a more or less selective character.

What is meant by selective character?

The central questions posed here relate mostly to temporally very limited stages of the developmental process. The factors discussed and the effects probed into – in other words, what are understood to be independent variables and those believed to be dependent on them – lie very close together in time, so that it might be better to speak of symptomatologies of *situative syndromes* than of sequential causal relationships or series of events. To this category belong all investigations directed to only one of the three wider stages: pregnancy, the perinatal and the postnatal phase. In part these studies do not even cover the whole of their respective individual stages.

Examples of selective project designs

The experience of pregnancy: A considerable number of studies are concerned with the role and/or significance of morning sickness, the various investigations producing widely differing results. Thus, as Schwerdtfeger (1981) reports in her well-informed dissertation on the early experience of pregnancy, Deutsch (1954) interpreted hyperemesis in pregnancy as the expression of a negative, hostile attitude to the child – as large sections of the general public, influenced by the popularizations of psychoanalysis, still do. For Molinski (1972), on the other hand, the cause of vomiting is not so much a direct expression of attitude towards the child (which may quite possibly be an openly expressed, strong desire for one), as rather a particular constellation of personality traits. Yet others, e.g. Uddenberg *et al.* (cited after Schwerdtfeger, 1981), claim to have recognized that moderate vomiting must be considered a virtually normal physiological reaction towards conception, and that in fact such women as experience no nausea or vomiting must even be regarded as having a psychological problem which often only becomes apparent postpartum (e.g. in the form of postnatal depression). Finally, in perhaps the newest of their methodologically significant studies, Ringler and Krizmantis (1983 and 1984) of the Institute for Depth Psychology and Psychotherapy at the University of Vienna have discovered that women who vomit differ from others above all in their more unrealistic perception and anticipation of the events and tasks associated with pregnancy, birth and the raising of children.

Another recently and more frequently studied question is that of the appearance and role of fetal movements during the experience of pregnancy – an area of study presently linked above all with the name of Gabriele Gloger-Tippelt (1985a). In her own study Gloger-Tippelt asked 10 women during the period between the 15th and 27th week of pregnancy to fill in a questionnaire daily on the nature and circumstances of the perceived fetal movements. Thereby she succeeded in distinguishing various phases in the course of the experience of pregnancy in which the first realization of fetal movements takes on an important new orientative function. (I shall here not go into the methodological problem of the daily completion of questionnaires and its effect on the self-perception of the subjects (G. Gloger-Tippelt, 1985b).)

The prenatal vulnerability of the child: Since the scandal of the thalidomide catastrophe, as a result of which funds were greatly increased in the Federal Republic of Germany for research into the course of pregnancy, studies devoted to the vulnerability of the unborn child have become more numerous. To this category belong above all the studies mentioned above on the influence of stimulants and drugs on prenatal development but also on the question, at present much more difficult to answer, of the effect of great maternal stress during pregnancy. At any rate, Charles Spezzano (1981) refers to extensive studies by the Scottish psychologist, Dennis H. Stott, in which impressive evidence has allegedly been found for the effect of strong emotional strain on the fetal development of the child. The very fact that 7% of live births are premature (in West Germany alone at present ca. 40 000 newborn children annually) suggests the urgent need for further clarification of the influence of non-specific extreme stress. Besides maternal and fetal factors for intrauterine disorders a third, placental, is recognized in practical midwifery. From the point of view of modern psychosomatic medicine and its general theory of stress (Th. von Uexküll, 1981, p. 10f. with pp. 107f., 160, 170) both the maternal and the placental factors appear to be easily influenced by psychological stress, conveyed through links such as blood pressure, oxygen transport, hormonal secretion, etc. (especially expert but also short surveys of modern diagnostic aids in early and late pregnancy are given in the three contributions by Halberstadt, Jonatha-Tetternborn and Rüttgers in Hövels et al., 1981).

Other examples that belong here would be studies of the question of the effects of medicines prescribed by doctors, both prenatally and perinatally. Clearly very many more preparations can pass through the placenta than the broad mass of gynecologists previously thought – as Lauritzen has listed (1985).

Studies on rooming-in, behavior in breast-feeding, quality of mother's milk:
A great number of further studies of this selective type are to be found in the area associated with rooming-in, breast-feeding and the advantages of mother's milk. Steingrüber and Pflugmacher (1982) provide a well-informed survey of the state of knowledge regarding the first two aspects. With relation to factors inhibiting or promoting breast-feeding they reach the conclusion, for instance, that it is difficult to evaluate the relative importance of the influential factors so far assembled 'since only few controlled studies are available on this point' (op. cit., p. 467). They are similarly reticent in their estimation of the meaningfulness of the effects of rooming-in (op. cit., p. 470). Wimmer-Puchinger (1985) reports on a more recent and probably methodologically reliable study from the Ludwig-Boltzmann Institute in Vienna on the effect of early (skin) contact between mother and child on the duration of breast-feeding. According to this study the nature of the contact postpartum has a significant effect on the duration of breastfeeding – a result said to have been confirmed in a contemporaneous study by Grossman et al. (1978).

Another example of this topic and type of investigation is represented by studies on the quality and nutritional effect of mother's milk. In this connection I shall mention only two contributions: E. Schmidt (1979), Director of University Clinic B in Düsseldorf, and J. Svejcar (1983), Professor of Pediatrics in Prague. The latter stresses, for instance, that the most recent findings suggest 'that in mother's milk there are more than 100 different substances, about whose significance for the meeting of the nutritional needs of the child we know little or absolutely nothing' (op. cit., p. 236). And Schmidt refers to a sort of large-scale experiment in the western world to force one species, namely humankind itself, to get along without the specific nutrition of its offspring (op. cit., p. 525).

Studies on pre-, peri- and postnatal behavioral competence of children:
Reports of individual observations of the many things that a child at various

stages of its very early development is already capable of have in recent years become very much more frequent, and this knowledge has already sunk fairly far into the public consciousness through a sometimes almost sensational presentation in popular scientific reports: the form and position of the child in the womb, its movements made visible through ultrasonography, thumb-sucking, the swallowing of minute amounts of amniotic fluid, prenatal 'bonding', even fetal conditioned learning have been noted (cf. the very readable, lucid survey of Verny and Kelly, *Secret Life of the Unborn* (1983), and also Nissen, 1982). The same is true of other phases of life: we know a great deal about this too from many individual studies. Those by Bisping and Steingrüber (1984) and also Perrez (1984) on vocalization and the social contingency of the newly born respectively can be described as examples of selective designs.

Studies on early mother–child interaction: Here, too, selective studies vastly predominate, however informative each of the individual sets of findings may be in themselves in their own areas. After the pioneering studies of Colwyn Trevarthen (1979) dominated by the question of the development of 'primary intersubjectivity', or by William Condon (1975) on interactional synchronicity, or Escalona's (1973) and Halliday's (1979) (see Neumann, 1983) studies of the interaction between the child and the person to whom it relates, and the work of the Papouseks (1977) and Grossman (1978) – to name only a few authors – our eyes have literally been opened to that which the senses of a child are already able to perceive. But, as I have said, even these studies require amplification, as H. Keller and H.J. Meyer (1982, p. 124), well acquainted with this very material, opine when in connection with these interactional studies, they observe:

> 'The available preliminary studies do not permit a comprehensively theoretical integration. The majority of researchers have settled for what Osofsky and Connors described as an eclectic standpoint, i.e. an assemblage, relatively devoid of theory, of individual aspects of behavior.'

The predominance of disparate designs in diachronic studies

What is meant by 'disparate'?

Besides the many selective studies a considerable number of diachronic studies on this early period of life have also already been produced. In these the associated variables are separated by a longer period of time, so that genuinely different stages of life are discussed. This longitudinal gain over the types of study outlined above is, however, all too often accompanied by a restriction in the contents, not to say a narrowing of the range of variables included. The variables studied are usually only a very limited extract from the whole gamut of features that constitute and determine human life at the stages in question. In short, the variables discussed are more frequently isolated, disparate aspects and hardly representative of the situative world in which those studied live.

Examples of disparate design

Perinatal deprivation and child cruelty: Vitus Dröscher (1984, p. 51) reports on American studies which claim to have demonstrated a relationship between the placing of children in incubators immediately on birth and their subsequent, statistically more frequent ill-treatment as juveniles. On the other hand, Mingers (In Nissen (ed.), 1982) discovered in his, admittedly relatively small, sample survey ($n = 28$) of grossly ill-treated children not one that had been in a premature baby unit (cf. on this also Kempe and Kempe, 1980, especially p. 85f.).

Early loss of father and adult personality: There is a similar contradiction in the results of investigations of the influence of the early loss of a father (usually as a result of the Second World War) on the subsequent personality development of the child. Whereas, as Ch. Spezzano (1981, p. 27f.) reports, two Finnish researchers claimed to have discovered that the father's loss *before* the birth of the child is more often associated with disorders in subsequent personality development than if the father died during the child's first year of life, Sameroff (1981) could in all find only a very small percentage of disturbed children who had lost their fathers before birth (= no more than the average rate of disturbance in the population at large).

Results of more recent adoption studies: In his book *Kindheit als Schicksal? Die Frage nach den Langzeitfolgen frükindlicher seelischer Verletzungen* (p. 101f.) Hansjörg Hemminger (1982) cites the probably most reliable of adoption studies so far, that of the Swede, Michael Bohman (German version, 1980), as proof that there are virtually no convincingly demonstrable influences from early childhood on behavior and subsequent personality:

> 'There is no correlation in any way between the social adaptation and educational success of adopted children and either complications in pregnancy or on delivery, or the duration of their stay in an institution' (op. cit., p. 101).

The relationship between duration of breast-feeding, sex and personality of the child: In a very new study from the Department of Psychology of the University of Marburg on the relationship between, on the one hand, the intellectual and motor performance and anxiety of 10-year-olds and, on the other, their sex and nursing duration, no connection could be established either between the sex and nursing duration of the child, or between nursing duration and personality at the age of 10.

In contrast, having reviewed the studies by Lukesch and Rottman (1976) and Ferreira (1960) on the relationship between certain maternal behavioral types and neonatal behavior, Kruse emphasized:

> 'Prenatal psychology is still too young a discipline to be able to make definite statements on how the behavioral anomalies of neonates after unwanted pregnancies affect later, adult life. But even for the delayed consequences there are some, admittedly only heuristic and case-orientated means of approach' (Kruse, 1978, p. 9544).

Pre-, peri- and postnatal risk factors and neurofunctional developmental disorders: Jungmann (1983) had available detailed, up-to-date records on altogether 238 children aged between 8 and 16 who, 'during a period of 2.5 years, had been examined in the Department of the Psychiatry and Neurology of Children and Juveniles of the Free University of Berlin on account of behavioral and educational disorders and in whom the involvement of cerebro-organic factors in their problem behavior had to be established' (op. cit., p. 17). On the basis of the medical histories and the anamneses customary at this institute a numerical score was calculated measuring the extent of the burden of anamnestic risk and/or illness in early childhood, for which, incidentally, a system of weightings was used: e.g. gravidic gestosis was weighted 1.5 times, birth weight below 2500 g counted double. This score was then compared with the standard of linguistic development, of statomotoric development and the neuromotoscopic as well as the electroencephalographic findings.

The results showed that none of the four comparisons reached the 1% level of significance; only one, viz. that of the neuromotoscopic findings, just about reached the 5% level.

Jungmann interpreted these findings thus:

> 'In evaluating these results one must bear in mind that the anamnestic details derive from the recollections of the interrogated patients ... An assessment of the relevant elements of this burden, which is as complete as possible, is possible, in the last analysis, only in a prospective examinatory approach ... In the same way, however, the results of the studies available so far show, if anything, fewer connections with subsequent

development ... Deprivatory and compensatory environmental factors become important intervening influences which have a substantial role in determining the prognostic significance of perinatal disorders for further cerebro-organic development' (op. cit., p. 23).

And he concludes:

'Even if there is no doubt that cerebro-organic damage hinders a proper neurofunctional development and therefore can determine psychiatrically relevant disorders as well as neurological abnormalities, the results of our study confirm the problematic aspects of applying above all the discrete findings of neuromotoric examinations aetiopathologically to anamnestic risk-factors' (op. cit., p. 24).

This statement coincides exactly with the views expressed here on selective and disparate project designs.

Critique of the view of development implicit in studies conceived in this way

The implicit additivity

Both types of study outlined here, both the selective and the admittedly diachronic, but disparate, derive from the conviction that it is possible, given a sufficiently large volume of findings added together, gradually to achieve a total reconstruction of the complete mosaic of human development. Such a conviction rests on at least two premises, which are in my opinion not very plausible and certainly not demonstrable.

Firstly, is the premise that the biological development of the complex human organism can, in principle, be divided into discrete stages, relatively clearly distinguishable from each other, and that their specific analysis does not entail a loss of information in the transitions between stages or in the conjunction of series of changes that had originally been studied in a disparate manner.

Secondly, is the premise that, assuming the first assumption to be justified, it is possible to build up a network of such discrete findings, without the underlying discrete analyses having been sufficiently coordinated with each other. No tower can be built from gravel without a binding agent — unless one were to ensure that during the formation of the stones certain shapes had been adhered to. It is this binding agent, i.e. the unifying link on the level of content and methodology between the thousands of individual studies, which I cannot see. In short: how do psychological, physiological and somatic studies etc. acquire a pertinence for developmental psychology? This question was also addressed by Baltes (1979, especially in his Chapter 2).

The implicit reactivity/passivity

The manner in which many studies are conceived and also interpreted often betrays a sort of reactive or passive conception of the developmental process of the subject, as if each identified independent (cause) variable has to result, more or less inevitably and mechanistically, in quite specific and observable or measurable effects. Practically no consideration has hitherto been given in the acquisition of data to the *active* but inner processes of assimilation, which neutralize or reverse these influences, or over-react to them in a sort of allergic response, or, as if creating a depository, 'postpone', 'store' and consign them to accumulate with similar, subsequently occurring influences. One does not even have to be a supporter of psychoanalysis to hold that the processes of assimilation referred to above exist in reality; immunology, allergology, somatic medicine etc. vouch for them just as effectively.

The view of development adopted here

Without presenting their respective supporting arguments or the observations drawn from experience that speak for them, I should here at least like to name the four most important precepts which are essential for a more realistic concept of development in project design.

(1) Development is a holistic/gestaltist process in which the same organism constantly changes, in which the processes of change always affect the whole organism, never therefore concentrating only on component areas, structures or functions. This in itself old insight of developmental psychology should be incorporated more frequently into project designs (cf. on this the distinction made by Reese and Overton, in Baltes, 1979, p. 66f., between behaviorist and organismal developmental positions).

(2) Development is a finalistic process directed towards a goal, conceived of with a view to the future, which in every status quo, that is to say, every momentary situation already anticipates coming situations (cf. the profound discussions of the concept of situation, for instance by Th. von Uexküll, 1981, and K.H. Arnold, 1981). What earlier writers referred to as 'lifeline', 'hope principle', 'anticipatory tendency', 'being ahead of oneself', George A. Kelly calls 'development as a continuing experiment' (cf. Bannister and Fransella, 1981, p. 96f.).

(3) Development is an advancing competence in the interpretation of the objective and subjective worlds and of their relationship to one another. Under this heading it can even be said that the developing

subject gains an ever greater reflexivity in handling both external and internal influencive factors and thereby interprets these factors differently, according to their context, intention and gravity, even if from a purely physical or physiological point of view they are apparently the same. This basic assumption leads to what is described as the 'aptitude for meta-communication' by Watzlawick et al. (1969, p. 41f.), as the 'transactional model' by Schaffer (1978, p. 34) and as the 'reflexive subject model' by Groeben and Scheele (1977, p. 22f.). This quality raises doubts as to whether the strictly operationalized data of traditional research in developmental psychology – even in the case of 'self-report-data' – are really interpreted and understood as the researchers should wish by the objects of research (who are after all in reality subjects and certainly do not lose this quality on entering a laboratory or on facing a researcher elsewhere).

(4) Development is a continuing expansion into adjoining, neighboring and more comprehensive systems and an increasing exchange between these systems. Here I mean what has already been discussed by Lewis and then Bronfenbrenner (1981) in their own respective ways, as well as in the working group on 'Ecology of Development' by Horst Nickel et al. in the Developmental Psychology Section of the German Society for Psychology (cf. for instance B. Wolf, 1983).

THE PRINCIPLES UNDERLYING MY RESEARCH METHODS AND AN OUTLINE DESCRIPTION OF THE PROJECT

The principles underlying my research methods

If one wishes to fill in the most important gaps and blank spaces on the map of human development one must have the courage to embark on long-term studies, even if they do not provide quick results for the academic rat-race. One must, furthermore, attempt to give these diachronic studies as broad a base as possible, adopting, where possible, an interdisciplinary approach to the tools of investigation, even if one occasionally astonishes one's purist colleagues. It should, at the outset, be stressed again, that the assertion is not being made that undertakings of the abovementioned selective or disparate type are superfluous and ought to be replaced, but it should indeed be stressed that they need to be supplemented by approaches derived from the diachronic, broadly based type of study.

The principles underlying this last type, espoused here, have to be of a

(1) diachronic character,
(2) interdisciplinary character,
(3) environmental suitability,
(4) communicative character,
(5) case-orientated character.

The diachronic character must be sufficiently stressed for at least two different phases of development to be studied (e.g. on the one hand the fetal and on the other the postnatal phase). The more different phases are included, the closer the design structure will coincide with the actual biographical structure of the individual life.

In view of the multi-aspect, complex nature of the biography to be produced it is a completely Utopian notion to assume that it might be possible to achieve an even approximately complete reconstruction of a course of events, especially if the representatives of only one discipline are involved. Anyone who has ever struggled to throw as much light as possible on sequences of 'life events' is conscious that it is almost arrogant to believe that as a physiologist, as a psychologist, as an educational psychologist alone, one might even satisfactorily describe, let alone causally account for, the sequences of stages in the life of a human being. For this the collaboration of colleagues from several relevant disciplines is necessary. This research must be on an interdisciplinary character.

It is also essential to ensure that, as far as possible, those studied can remain in their natural, everyday environment during the execution of the enquiry itself. One should manipulate this as little as possible, for instance, by causing some of those studied to behave differently than usual so that the experimental groups of the researcher are sufficiently similar in size. One should also demand as few changes of surroundings and daily routine as possible. The researcher should accommodate himself to the life of the person studied and not vice versa (cf. the modern guidelines and their explanations such as changes in daily routine, ethnomethodology, etc.).

Closely linked with the above is the principle of acknowledging the importance of the original point of view of the person studied and of including this in the data collected. In a society of communications, permeated by the media, in which information technology, code-systems, forms of meta-communication, and the questionable nature of referees is common knowledge, it is simply naive, not to say almost unworldly, to believe that, by correlating some items or other on a questionnaire, one could establish something worthwhile and attract public attention with it! One should not always take as one's model the success of the electoral prognoses of the public opinion pollsters, for the diversity of life cannot be reduced to putting a cross to a text of, at the most ten lines, once every 4 years.

Finally, the term 'case-orientated character' is intended to underline that if the reconstruction of a case (i.e. of a developing individual as well as of a developing relationship) is to be as complete and faithful to its structure as possible, then the interdisciplinary data and points of view must be compared, weighted and *marshalled* into a complete picture. Only then is it at all possible to estimate how significant a particular feature (an expectant mother's lack of partner, Caesarean section, rejection of breast-feeding, or asphyxia, for instance) is in a particular case, that is to say, whether it is of determining influence or not.

Outline description of the project

Investigative plan, tools and timetable

The following plan was conceived in order to fit the research plan as far as possible to the above-mentioned principles.

(1) The family situation (including economic and educational status), attitudes to pregnancy, medical complaints relating to pregnancy, nature of preparation for birth, desire for children, etc. will be enquired into with *three* questionnaires at the beginning of the third trimester (privately drafted questionnaires, SSG, GT-S, which are formal questionnaires for pregnancy, birth, sex, personality, etc.).

(2) In addition, the results of clinical examinations during pregnancy (in the sense of estimations of pregnancy risk) will be recorded.

(3) A record of the birth will be made consisting of condition of the newborn child, course of birth, complications at birth, additional questionnaire for the midwife responsible, report of the supervisory doctor on particular medical indications (and their side-effects, e.g. with regard to the deactivation of the mother and/or the child), risk-factors.

(4) Before release from hospital a video recording roughly 45 minutes long of the mother–child interaction will be made, including, as far as possible, breast- or bottle-feeding, nappy changing and 'free intercourse'.

(5) This will be repeated at home when the child is 6 weeks old.

(6) Similarly a video recording will be made at 6 and 12 months.

(7) A developmental test will take place at 12 months.

(8) A detailed interview will occur with the parents, concentrating on the family, at about 18 months.

(9) Another developmental test will be carried out at 24 months.

(10) Case discussions – for each mother–child relationship – will take place at regular intervals, so that each couple will be discussed in detail at roughly the end of the first and second years by the ten members of the project group (the group consists of three qualified psychologists, two doctors, three qualified educational psychologists, a committee member of the German family association (himself a teacher), and several undergraduate trainees). In these case discussions all important points will be minuted, as intensively as is the practice in educational counselling.

The present status of the project and further perspectives

So far a pilot study covering ten cases is in operation. Its main function is to test the equipment and techniques (video techniques, questionnaires, interviews, tests) as well as to further the cohesion and cooperation between the project group, the hospitals and the families. At the time of the congress the child in the last case was just 5 years old, in the first of the ten cases 14 months old.

The first case of the main study will have been 'taken on' in July 1986; then approximately four cases a month will be added, so that during the course of 4 years approximately 100 cases will have been completely processed.

It is considered important that, apart from the storage of data for subsequent diverse evaluative procedures (which may perfectly well be of selective or disparate character), every collaborator in the project will, in addition, know or, as it were, be able to identify from memory every case, just as, for instance, a teacher can easily know roughly 100 pupils in his classes when he has taught them for 2 years.

Ideally we are aiming to complete a detailed follow-up study when the children are 6 years old (study of the development of the family situation, of the child, video recording of significant parent–child interactions).

Preliminary results – examples

In order to flesh out the concisely formulated outline of the trends in our preliminary results I should like briefly to present examples of three cases chosen completely at random from the ten cases documented so far.

Case A (P): This woman is marked before and during pregnancy by an intense desire for children; after two miscarriages (4 and 2 years previously) this woman, already regarded medically as an 'elderly' mother, hopes, together with her markedly younger student-husband, that this time all will go well at last. She is a 'career-woman', determined to continue working and at present obliged to, as the only bread-winner. She shows a very close relationship with her own mother; her father died 10 years ago. She once had an inflammation of the ovaries and suspected Crohn's disease. Little morning sickness during pregnancy. She tends to keep close control of herself and seeks social recognition, 'wants to get everything just right'.

The birth was very hazardous: the child arithmetically 10 days overdue, the amniotic fluid green, cardio-tokography pathologically = Caesarean section.

The mother–child relationship after birth is at first marked by a physically rather weak and unemotional relationship with a really very lively boy. During the following weeks and months the development of behavioral synchronization was altogether average. Breast-feeding ended fairly early; subsequent style of intercourse is marked by strong sensory stimulation and excessive verbal reinforcement. Very soon — after the mother returns to work — the mother's mother is replaced as a morning caretaker by a friend of the mother (since she can handle the child better).

Case B (S): This woman, of ideal child-bearing age, had from the physiological point of view a problem-free pregnancy, but from the middle of the pregnancy onwards suffered massive stress/quarrels with the child's father, who 'suddenly' rejected all thought of cohabitation or marriage. She did not grow up with her natural mother. Her statements on the use of stimulants during and after pregnancy are contradictory. She tends to act out her emotions and is insufficiently self-critical.

The birth was made difficult by very weak contractions and little 'cooperation' on the mother's part. According to the midwife she was very anxious and sensitive to pain. Epidural anesthetic, Caesarean section.

After the Caesarean her first contact with the child was only possible relatively late. At the first filming session at home it was noticeable that the child was frequently apostrophized as mummy's future protector. At successive sessions the mother–child interaction became more insensitive and formal. The latest reports from colleagues refer to the child often being alone when the mother goes shopping or even visits friends. She is said now to have a new lover.

Case C (C): This university graduate has herself several brothers and sisters and lost her mother at pre-school age. The pregnancy was at the moment of its recognition only partly wanted (she already has a 1-year-old daughter), but then during the course of pregnancy very much wanted. The mother is a strongly-motivated career-woman. Her husband is also a graduate. Complaints during pregnancy: edema (treated by drugs). The husband was not keen on being present at the birth (and wasn't).

The birth was rather problematic: despite the mother's cooperation and being considerably overdue there were virtually no contractions. The child was very jaundiced and received phototherapy for 3.5 days, hence there was only little contact between mother and child.

The mother–child interaction was marked by routine in the tending of the child, by a tendency of the mother to misinterpret the child's interactional tendencies and by breast-feeding by the clock (so too the duration of nursing).

Outline of trends in results

If the cases so far are described according to three situational phases – course of pregnancy, circumstances of birth, quality of postnatal interaction – and these phases are characterized as completely as possible and structured according to the relative importance of various aspects,* there is a clear trend towards a case-specific congruency in these phases. Even if the external influences arising in the later phases (e.g. problems with personal relationships, infectious illnesses) cannot be foretold (how can they be?), the tendency for these possible influences to be 'parried', overcome or endured can be estimated. In other words, both each individual state specific to a phase or stage, as well as their diachronic congruency represent structured holisms (=gestalts) which can be projected. Only knowledge of these variables allows the risk-potential of any external influence to be gauged. Depending on the character of the structure, the effect of one and the same external influence, e.g. the absence of a father through job transfer, a slight infectious illness in the child, etc., could in one case be very dangerous. In a second case, on the other hand, it could be neutral/imperceptible, in a third case perhaps even beneficial (e.g. in the sense of intensifying the relationship between mother and child with its corresponding improving effect on development). From this point of view no amount of studies is of any use, if they concentrate on one particular case structure, since they cannot say anything, for instance, about the cumulative effect of the variants of this structure in conjunction with other influential factors.

The subsequent work in this project will be concerned with identifying the particular constellations in each case that cause particular risk factors described in the literature, in some cases as having an effect and sometimes as not. In this way one might eventually be able to give all known or presumed risk factors a weighting, wherein is encoded in what combinations with what other factors they are particularly dangerous to development or on the other hand neutralized or converted to positive effect.

---

* The criteria for the evaluation of importance being derived from the context, subjective accentuation and professional experience.

FUTURE PROSPECTS

The thesis maintained here of the comprehensive gestalt-like nature of the mother–child relationship between pregnancy and postnatal interaction, and its support in the trends revealed in the analysis and reconstruction of ten cases has nothing to do with a mythologizing of the uniqueness of the relationship between two people when one of them has developed out of the other. It is rather a recognition of the fact that with the implantation of a fertilized ovum two systems begin to interact with each other, each having to adjust to and come to terms with the other. During their life together both systems set up structural as well as functional pathways indicating how the systems will have coped with each other in the past, and will probably most effectively do so in the future. This fixing of pathways – respecting the need to preserve the existence of each separate system in the face of their mutual dependence – can be described at every period of development in terms of the degree of maturity. In turn, one might characterize this in relation to its goal of the best possible development of the systemic quality of both systems. The more predictable, reliable and at the same time more flexible these pathways between the two systems are, the less problematic is the effect of external disruptive factors (noxious substances, influences from third parties, etc.) on each of the coexistent systems. This results because the one can exercise a buffer or compensatory function for the other through these paths.

The decisive point is that the fixing of these pathways between the two systems does not suddenly begin at a particular point in time, but at the very beginning, with the creation of the younger system. Moreover, this process is continuous and without interruption. It merely goes through different phases, the metamorphoric phenotypes. The degree of maturity of these inter-systemic pathways determines, in the last analysis, the extent of the pathogenic valence of external disruptive factors. In order to foretell their effect one requires a knowledge of these pathways, which in its turn is only possible in a holistic examination of the totality of the individual nature of both systems and the relationship between them – and *not* by collecting isolated facts about many diverse cases.*

---

* That many such pathways are already fixed relatively early on is indicated by Schindler's comments on fetal dreaming (in Hau and Schindler (eds.), 1982, pp. 111–18), by Nissen's (op. cit., pp. 29–44) on the intensive intrauterine exchange of experience, by Schmidt-Kolmer (1984, p. 166f) on the concept of 'systemogenesis' and by Kruse (op. cit., p. 9648) on erroneous fetal programming.

4
Perinatal hazards and later schooling
B. Zachau-Christiansen

ABSTRACT

Since 1959 a prospective child development study has been made at the State University Hospital in Copenhagen including 9006 pregnancies referred to the hospital from 1959 to 1961.

More than 200 papers and books have been published during the years from this study and many international presentations can be mentioned.

At the 1-year follow-up 1.7% of full birth weight infants had abnormal CNS findings comparing to 6.7% among low birth weight infants. Most prenatal and perinatal registered complications had some influence upon the development, but the social classification of the breadwinner was of significant importance, the frequencies for CNS findings in social classes IV and V being 3.0 and 12.1%.

This social influence was very important among the low birth weight children of school-age. Among these children with at least one perinatal abnormal sign, besides the low birth weight, no child from social class I became a slow learner or had emotional problems, although 18.2% had reading difficulties. The figures for children from social class V are 18.9, 12.5 and 46.2%.

During school the low birth weight children underwent some school psychological tests together with a random sample of the same age. In this way some tests were restandardized. An important finding seems to be, that using Leiter and WISC we do not find the expected rise in IK between age 8 and 11, so a plateau in IK in these ages in spite of earlier standardization is postulated. This finding must be taken into consideration when children are retested during the first school years, so progressive neurological or mental disease is not presumed.

INTRODUCTION

Everybody can accept that the most dangerous day of a person's life is the day of his death. But it must also be realized that the next most important day of much danger is the day of birth. Every intervention before, through and after delivery, including psychological support, has to be compared with many other factors, especially if an evaluation, including a cost–benefit analysis, has to be done. Often differences can first be measured only later in life.

One method for such an evaluation is a multifactorial longitudinal study.

HISTORY OF LONGITUDINAL STUDIES

Prospective pediatrics, or longitudinal studies of child development, is more than 200 years old, starting in 1777 with Montbeillard's (Scammon, 1927) and in 1787 with Tiedemann's (Murchison and Langer, 1927) descriptions of the development of their sons, continued in 1858 in Austria by Liharzik (1858) describing the growth of a little cohort in his book *Das Gesetz des menschlichen Wachstumes*. In America growth studies were initiated by Harvard University (Stuart et al., 1959) in 1872. Berkeley University (Kagan, 1964) was the first to include psychological development in a longitudinal study, although Gesell and co-workers' studies, with the first publication from 1938 (Gesell, 1965) are better known than the Study of gifted children from Stanford University (Terman and Oden, 1947).

In Britain growth studies started in the 1920s. Best known is the Harpenden Growth Study, including later publications by Tanner (1962). British prospective pediatrics has been especially interested in epidemiological studies: Douglas' (1975) follow-up of 5386 children born in the first week of March, 1946; Court et al.'s (Neligan et al., 1975) study of 1142 children born in Newcastle-on-Tyne in May–June 1947, and Grundy and Fanning's (1957) study of the first year of life for 20 718 infants born in 1952 in southern England. Such studies were only practical when computer techniques had been developed.

In the United States such multifactorial studies, first of all, were related to malformations, as in the Fetal Life Study (Mellin, 1964) from Columbia Presbyterian Medical Center in New York. This study comprises about 12 000 pregnancies from 1946 to 1961 and their outcome, and has been the model for the Copenhagen Longitudinal Study (Zachau-Christiansen and Ross, 1975; Zachau-Christiansen, 1981). The outset for this study was the fear of material irradiation after pregnancy wastages from the nuclear attacks of Hiroshima and Nagasaki had been demonstrated (Neel and Schull, 1956). The University Hospital in Copenhagen has registered information concerned with family history, working conditions, diseases, complications and medication of the mother during pregnancy, delivery and the neonatal period (including two pediatric examinations with neurological implication). At 1 year of age information from 98% of the infants was collected, most of the infants were examined in our outpatient clinic. The children have been invited to health examinations at 3 and 6 years. Two thirds of the families accepted these offers, and we have the school health records for half the probands. For financial reasons, when the children were of school age we had concentrated the investigations on children with low birth weight living in the Copenhagen area.

These financial problems have been related to the biggest and most expensive prospective pediatric investigation in the world, the Collaborative Project of the US National Institutes of Health (Freeman, 1985), commenced in 1959 and comprising 60 000 pregnancies from 14 American centers all over the US. As my group had participated in an international study of infant and perinatal mortality sponsored by the US Department of Health, Education and Welfare (Matthiessen et al., 1967), we had a possibility of American support also for our fetal life study, but the Collaborative Study in the US was so expensive that support for foreign studies was impossible. Although, American support has been received by some of the studies concerning children in our cohort with predisposition for mental disease, including alcohol abuse and children with mothers given hormonal treatment during pregnancy. These are carried out at the Psychological Institute of the Copenhagen Municipal Hospital by Schulsinger and Mednick (Mednick and Baert, 1981) who also described for WHO other ongoing longitudinal studies internationally.

THE COPENHAGEN STUDY

One year follow-up

Our study included 9006 pregnant women from the 20th week of pregnancy. Because of late abortions, still-births, infant deaths and the mentioned minor loss of surviving probands not available for examination, only 7237 full birth weight infants were included in the 1-year analysis (Zachau-Christiansen and Ross, 1975). Of the many parameters for disorders we shall only describe the so-called CNS symptoms, defined as children with convulsive diseases (cerebral palsy, mental retardation or motor retardation, i.e. not able to stand with support at 12 months of age), which could not be explained by congenital malformations (see Table 1).

Such CNS symptoms were found in 1.7% of full birth weight children compared to 6.7% among children with low birth weight. The children of diabetic mothers have developed rather well, although they were delivered 3 weeks before term and have many problems, as only 2.6% had CNS

Table 1 CNS symptoms as defined in the text in different groups of 1-year-old children. Low birth weight (LBW) means children weighing 2500 g or less at birth. Young mothers are 20 years old or less, old mothers over 40. Heavily smoking means at least 20 cigarettes a day

n		%
7237	Full birth weight children (FBW)	1.7
1076	Low birth weight children (LBW)	6.7
88	Children of diabetic mothers	2.6
95	Full birth weight twins	2.1
167	Low birth weight twins	6.5
465	FBW of young unmarried mothers	1.2
49	LBW of young unmarried mothers	4.0
201	FBW of old mothers	3.4
33	LBW of old mothers	12.1
100	FBW of heavily smoking mothers	3.0
27	LBW of heavily smoking mothers	14.8

symptoms. Also twins seem to have been handled well, 2.1% of full birth weight twins and 6.5% of low birth weight twins showed CNS symptoms which are very alike the norms of 1.7% and 6.7% respectively. In Denmark at that time, when marriage was still arranged if a girl became pregnant, we could not show the often described risk to children of unmarried mothers, but to have a mother over 40 years of age at delivery is dangerous, the CNS symptoms appearing twice as often as the norms. The same results were found concerning children of mothers smoking more than 20 cigarettes a day.

The influence of medical complications is only presented concerning low birth weight children (Table 2). For the whole group of such children CNS symptoms as mentioned appeared in 6.7%. The heaviest of these children, with birth weight between 2001 and 2500 g, did better than the norm, only 5.8% showing CNS symptoms. In all the other mentioned groups a significantly higher frequency of CNS symptoms compared to the norm is found.

Low birth weight boys and girls without asphyxia seem to develop equally, although the girls develop somewhat better. The important influence of the social background of the parents is also demonstrated (Table 3). Only 3.7% of children with one or both professional parents (social class I and II in the official British classification, General Register Office, 1951) had CNS symptoms, 6.2% was found when parents are skilled (social class III) against 12.1% when parents are semi-skilled. Children with such parents (social class IV and V) do rather well; when the mother is unmarried,

Table 2 Percentage of low birth weight children at 1 year examination showing CNS symptoms according to medical complications at birth. Comparing frequencies at 10% level between groups of 50 probands each needs a difference of 12% to be significant ($p = 0.05$). Groups of 100 need a difference of 8%, 500 3.5%, 1000 2.5%. At 5% level the significant differences are 8.5, 6, 2.5 and 2

n	Complication	%
624	Born after difficult labor	8.8
91	Born in breech presentation	13.1
127	Born with intrauterine asphyxia	11.8
136	Born with neonatal asphyxia	14.7
14	Rh-sensitized with severe jaundice	7.1
94	Severely jaundiced without sensitization	9.5
13	With neonatal convulsions	23.0
257	With other neonatal signs	10.5
65	Dysmature children	9.2
34	With gestational age >41 weeks	8.8
585	With BW 2001–2500 g	5.8
103	With BW 1501–2000 g	10.4
74	With BW 1001–1500 g	18.9
4	With BW ≤ 1000 g	25.0

Table 3 Percentage of low birth weight children at 1 year examination showing CNS symptoms according to social class

n			%
321	Boys		6.5
358	Girls		6.4
54	Social class I + II,	married	3.7
2		unmarried	50.0
287	Social class III,	married	6.2
34		unmarried	8.8
189	Social class IV + V,	married	12.1
133		unmarried	8.2

only 8.2% having CNS symptoms, which can be explained by young mothers and mothers in education.

Table 4 demonstrates the relation between social class and anemia in 1-year-old Danish children. The most privileged group has only 5% with anemia compared to 29% in children having an unskilled bread-winner with only 7 years schooling, without work and with the family living under bad conditions, or in an overpopulated residence without bathroom and central heating (i.e. Graffar's (1960) group 1).

Table 5 shows the influence the type of domicile has upon respiratory infection and gastrointestinal disorder. When the child is living in a good family domicile, only 7% have respiratory infection at the follow-up; twice as many, 13%, are found in bad domiciles. The best situation was to live with the parents and with the grandparents. Their wisdom or better domicile decreases the frequency to 6%. If the child is living with the

Table 4 Anemia (HB% $\leq$ 80%) at follow-up, distributed according to social class (incidences in %)

General Reg. Office (1951) UK classification		Graffar (1960)	
	Hb $\leq$ 80%	Social grouping	Hb $\leq$ 80%
		9	5
I–II	10	8	10
		7	9
		6	10
III	12	5	13
		4	12
		3	15
IV–V	17	2	19
		1	29

Table 5 Incidence of respiratory tract infections (RI) and disease of the alimentary tract (D) and healthy infants at follow-up, distributed according to housing (incidences in %)

	RI	D	Healthy
Good housing			
with parents	7	2	78
with mother alone	18	2	64
Poor housing			
with parents	13	3	72
with mother alone	19	2	70
Lives with parents, in family	6	2	78
Lives with mother, in family	10	1	77

mother alone, i.e. the child is forced to go to day-institutions, there is no influence of the domicile. The risk of infection, however, of the day-institutions is a leading influence here: 18% had bronchitis living in a good domicile, 19% living in a bad domicile. The development of children with birth weight over 2500 g is also related to social class as seen from Table 6.

Health in school-age

Our investigations concerning school problems of the cohort have been made in two directions. With the permissions of the parents we tried to collect the school health records of the involved children, and an intensive study of the needs for special education among the low birth weight children of the cohort was done.

Only half the school health records were collected (Merrick et al., 1983), see Table 7. The social status of the children with available school health records was similar to the whole population, although the group has less unmarried mothers. This can be explained by the fact that we, by obtaining the school health records at the time for school-leaving, had more recent information about these children and their families. The Metropolitan area, where we made the other part of our school study, was most cooperative in sending us the records.

The prevalence of different diseases, including learning disabilities and psychosomatic or behavioral problems, can be calculated from Table 8, which includes approximately 2000 boys and 2000 girls. 15% of the boys and 10% of the girls had reading difficulties. 1% of the boys had balbuties, or stuttering, sometimes during school age. A very few girls were registered with this problem. 7% of the boys in school-age had had enuresis, only 5% of the girls. The classification of more psychiatric problems is always difficult. We have tried to use the WHO coding. If lines 8, 9 and 10 in Table 6 are summarized it can be seen that behavior problems were seen in 132 boys, i.e. 6.5%, and 42 girls or 2%.

IQ testing in school-age

The children with low birth weight starting school with the Copenhagen municipalities have undergone testing by school psychologists (specially trained for this investigation) and their later school-careers have been followed. They have been compared with a random sample of children in the same schools, and of the same age.

Table 9 shows the results obtained by testing with Binet and WISC. The low birth weight children obtain significant lower scores than the random

Table 6 CNS symptoms at 1-year follow-up related to social class of breadwinner and marital status of mother

Social class*	Status of mother	Birth weight >2500 g (%)	Numerical total	Birth weight <2500 g (%)	Numerical total
I + II	Married	1.5	785	3.7	54
	Unmarried	5.3	19	50.0	2
III	Married	1.6	1995	6.2	287
	Unmarried	1.0	496	8.8	34
IV + V	Married	3.0	1266	12.1	189
	Unmarried	2.6	976	8.2	133
Total			5537		699

* General Register Office, 1951.

Table 7 The Copenhagen perinatal cohort. Representative of health records sample

Proportion (%)	Health record available	Health record not available*
Male/female	50.0/50.0	51.8/48.2
High/low social status of father at birth of child[†]	23.6/76.4	22.0/78.0
Unmarried/married mother at birth of child	29.2/71.8	34.6/65.4
Resident/not resident in Greater Copenhagen, 1976 ratio	80.0/20.0	58.2/41.8

* Excluding cases dead prior to 28 days.
† For details of scale used, see Teesdale (1979).

sample in both tests, and in the two parts of WISC. The Binet test, although in different editions, is still used without modern standardization. The mean for the random sample in our hands is 117, which happens to be the modern norm. Today Danish children handle the WISC performance better than the verbal part (after the standardization made 20 years earlier), but the differences between low birth weight children and the random sample are larger in WISC performance than in WISC verbal.

Table 8 The Copenhagen perinatal cohort. Distribution of major specific diagnoses within ICD group V (mental disorders)

ICD	Males	Females	p
301.50 Observation school or clinic	68	17	<0.01
306.09 Balbutio	23	7	0.005
306.10 Speech retardation or defects	88	63	<0.05
306.11 Reading retardation	299	193	<0.01
306.18 Learning disorders	40	26	NS
306.69 Enuresis	147	98	<0.01
306.79 Encopresis	15	3	0.007
307.99 Transient maladjustment	55	18	<0.01
308.00 Neurosis infantilis	31	9	0.001
308.03 Maladjustment	46	15	0.000
310.99 Inferioritas intellectualis	44	44	NS

Table 9 Intelligence quotients found by Binet-Simon and WISC testing of 159 low birth weight children (LBW) and 171 controls (random sample (RS)) living in Copenhagen county

		Boys	Girls	Mean
Binet-Simon	LBW	110.3	114.2	112.1
	RS	116.3	117.6	117.0
WISC (verbal)	LBW	94.1	92.7	93.3
	RS	96.1	95.0	95.7
WISC (performance)	LBW	101.5	99.9	100.6
	RS	105.7	105.7	105.7
WISC (total)	LBW	97.8	96.0	96.7
	RS	101.1	100.6	100.8

School results, special education

Figure 1 shows that more low birth weight children leave school after 7th grade, than in the random sample. On the other hand more random sample children took their high school examination, including some university level work, i.e. they had at least 12 years' schooling.

In the low weight group girls do better than boys (Figure 2). Children with low birth weight (Figure 3) had poorer school results than children in higher weight classes. These results can partly be explained by the lower social stratification of the low birth weight children than of the random sample, as seen from Figure 4.

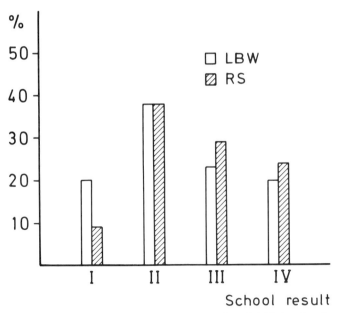

Figure 1 School result measured by which level the child left school. Low birth weight children (LBW) compared with random sample (RS). I: 7th level. II: 8th–9th level without any examination. III: 9th–10th level with examination. IV: 12th grade (undergraduated)

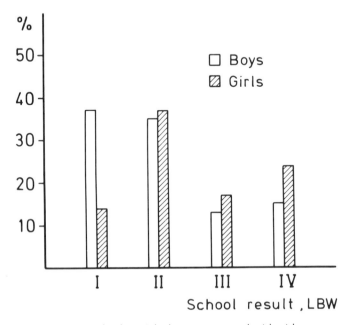

Figure 2 As Figure 1. Low birth weight boys compared with girls

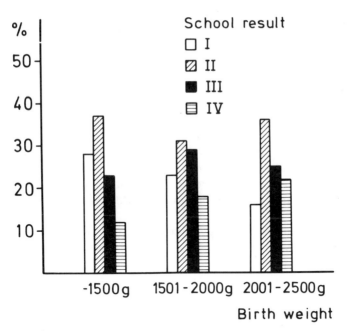

Figure 3 School results of low birth weight children in different weight groups. I–IV defined as in Figures 1 and 2

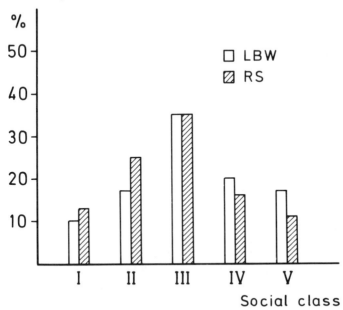

Figure 4 Social classification of investigated low birth weight and random sample children. Social class I professionals, II managing, III skilled, IV semi-skilled, V unskilled

The need for special education is strongly related also to social classification, as seen in Table 10. The probability for a low birth weight child from the lower social classes of having special education in the Danish school system is nearly 50%, a figure which has raised an important debate in Denmark concerning the handling of special education. The low figure for special education for random sample children from social class V, 12.5%, has been investigated more closely. Although the sample used comprises 294 children, the children in social group V included a significant number of children with divorced mothers who had moved out to the county, but became occupied as unskilled workers or did not have any job.

The social influence is stronger, when the figures for the slow learner in Table 11 are considered. No teacher dares to put a child from social class I in a form for slow learners.

Low birth weight children of appropriate or normal gestational age do better than children who have been small for term, i.e. had intrauterine growth retardation (Table 12).

Reading difficulties (Table 13) are also socially related – and very common. Danish is a difficult language, and perhaps reading training is started too late at the age of 7 years.

Special education caused by emotional maladjustment (we called it observation teaching) is only related to social classification for low birth weight children, as seen from Table 14.

Many of the perinatal and delivery complications, which were registered with the low birth weight children in our study, gave rise to a higher rate of slow learners (13%). At age 1 year every child in our prospective study was given a scaling score for general health, motor development and brain damage, all related to the mentioned complications. The figures in Table 15 are obtained by dividing the numbers of low birth weight children in a high risk score group and in a low one. It is possible by such medical scoring to estimate the coming need for special education, as the high risk groups needed education related to slow learning 2–3 times more often.

Plateaux in IQ tests

We have analyzed some of our test results further and made an observation which could be important for psychologists, who do re-testing in the first years of school. In the Copenhagen county investigation with low birth weight children and an equal random sample of the control group, the Leiter, Binet and WISC testing was spread over 2 years. The children were not admitted to school exactly at the same age, as schools only receive children once a year, and it was also necessary to make all tests in the

Table 10 Frequency of special education in 5 years schooling

Social class	LBW (%)	RS (%)
I	14.3	10.0
II	36.7	27.8
III	42.9	27.5
IV	47.1	36.2
V	44.1	12.5

Table 11 Frequency of special education in 5 years schooling for slow learners

Social class	LBW (%)		RS (%)
I	0		
II	6.7		
III	14.3	12.9	1.4
IV	14.3		
V	23.7		

Table 12 Frequency (%) of slow learners in LBW children divided into small for date groups and appropriate weight for gestational age (normal) groups

Social class	Small for date	Normal
I	0.0	0.0
II	9.5	2.6
III	12.2	18.0
IV	26.3	10.0
V	38.9	15.6

same school during a few days. For these reasons the age of children at the test situation was spread over 3 years, so we actually had standardized data covering the age span from 8 to 11 years of age.

As the former Leiter standardizations by Leiter (1966), Arthur (1949) and Smith (1975) had fewer children in the mentioned age groups than we had, our finding (Kruuse and Zachau-Christiansen, 1986) of a plateau in the mentioned age groups may be correctly demonstrated by the declining Leiter IQ (Figure 5).

We have investigated the different WISC tests in the same way, here

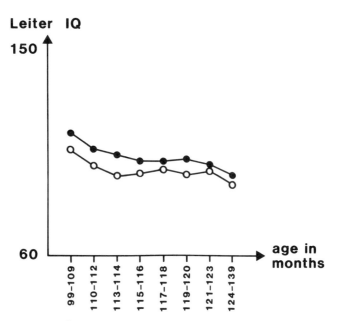

Figure 5 Leiter intelligence quotients found in different age groups of low birth weight children (open circles) and a random sample (dark circles)

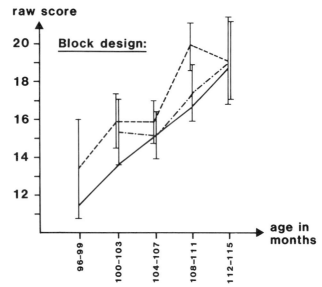

Figure 6 WISC-raw scores in block design found in different age groups of low birth weight children (upper dotted line) and a random sample (dot-and-dash line) compared with a standardization (full line)

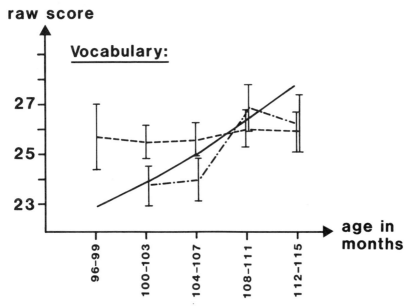

Figure 7 As Figure 6 but showing the results from the vocabulary part of WISC

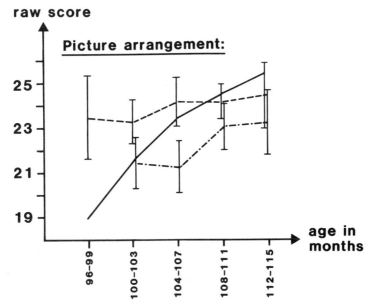

Figure 8 As Figures 6 and 7, showing the results from the picture arrangement part of WISC

Table 13 Frequency (%) of reading disability in children with low birth weight (LBW) and a random sample of children of the same age (RS)

Social class	LBW	RS
I	8.6	5.0
II	21.4	18.1
III	19.6	21.0
IV	25.0	28.9
V	31.8	12.5

Table 14 The frequency (%) of emotional maladjustment in different social classes of low birth weight and random sample children

Social class	LBW	RS
I	2.9	2.5
II	5.0	6.9
III	10.0	4.9
IV	11.4	0
V	15.3	0

Table 15 The frequency (%) of slow learners in LBW children with high risk scores on upper line, and low risk score on lower line at age 1 year

Health at age 1	18.9
	7.6
Motor development at age 1	22.4
	6.8
Brain damage at age 1	30.4
	13.6

using raw scores, and compared the results with the Danish standardization. Figure 6 demonstrates that the block design test shows good accordance, although the children in both groups did better than the standard.

In digit span and picture completion the standardization had plateaux in the mentioned age groups, which we confirmed. But we also showed plateaux in the other eight partial tests: similarities, vocabulary, picture arrangement, object assembly, coding together with information, comprehension and arithmetic. Only our results related to vocabulary and picture arrangements are demonstrated here, Figures 7 and 8.

Children at risk of alcohol abuse

Knop (Knop et al., 1985) has, together with Schulsinger and Mednick, followed a group of children in the cohort with high risk for alcohol abuse, determined by one or both parents having been registered for alcohol abuse. A control group with other parameters equal has been established as a low-risk group. The children in the high-risk group have changed schools more often, they have higher frequencies for repeating a grade, receiving special education and seeing school-psychologists, as seen from Table 16.

Motor dysfunction

Our study has also been used for introducing the concept of minimal brain damage, or as I prefer motor dysfunction, in Denmark. Early in our research, when our children were 11 years of age we drew out seven groups from the cohort, as equal as possible in a number of other parameters (Figure 9). These children underwent a traditional neurological examination, but were also given an examination more related to motor functions, using the test described by Stott and Stott (1966).

Table 16 Some school results of children with high risk for alcohol abuse (HR) and low risk (LR) related to registration of parents for alcoholism or not

	HR (n=134) mean	SD	LR (n=70) mean	SD	Mann-Whitney U p
Highest school grade attended	9.6	1.3	9.8	1.1	NS
No. of schools attended	3.0	1.6	2.5	1.3	0.03
					Fisher's exact
Repeated a grade	20.3%		5.7%		0.007
Supplementary tuition	31.3%		24.3%		NS
Special class	19.7%		11.4%		NS
Referred to school psychologist	51.1%		34.3%		0.026

In the control group, by using Stott's method, we found 20% were motor retarded, but only 4% had a traditional pathological neurological examination.

In group 2.3, consisting of mature children with neonatal brain damage symptoms, the traditional examination did not unmask any abnormality, but the Stott test found 30% diverging. The traditional neurological examination differentiates well for later abnormalities in asphyxiated low birth weight children born small for date, but the Stott test is necessary in group 1.1, where the gestational age corresponds with the birth weight.

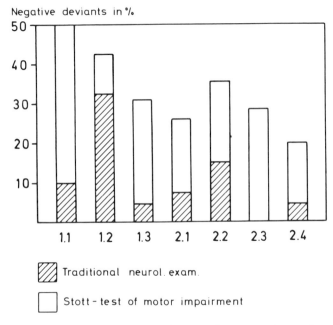

Figure 9 Results from a traditional and functional (a.m. Stott) neurological examination of 11-year-old children with known perinatal history. The children have been divided in seven groups defined as follows:

  1.1: asphyxiated children, born prematurely
  1.2: asphyxiated children, born small for date
  1.3: asphyxiated children, born maturely
  2.1: non-asphyxiated children, born prematurely
  2.2: non-asphyxiated children, born small for date
  2.3: non-asphyxiated children, born maturely with neonatal signs of cerebral damage
  2.4: non-asphyxiated children, born maturely, without such signs

CONCLUSION

A tremendous amount of biomedical and social factors determine the development of infants and children. Also the measurement of this development was problematic, some methods had to be re-standardized, new methods had to be developed – although prospective studies give a possibility of measuring interventions. Today I would have included prenatal stimulation and postnatal psychological intervention, if I were to start a new cohort. Studies until now have shown that large cohorts are often necessary for obtaining results of statistical significance.

Part 2: Studies in maternal attitudes to the prenatal

5

Early maternal–neonatal interactions and their impact on the development of maternal attitudes

Z. Golańska and W. Borkowski

ABSTRACT

The development of maternal attitudes was studied after delivery in 50 mothers of preterm babies and compared with attitudes of mothers who had given birth to term infants. There were statistically significant differences between the two groups in respect of development of pathologic attitudes in mothers of premature babies.

The birth of a child is the most important stage in the formation of maternal attitudes. Just after delivery the mother learns to love the child and learns the basic ways of acting towards it. At this moment, declared attitudes come into contact with reality for there exists a real object, the child, towards which these attitudes are directed. The type of maternal attitudes are dependent on individual experience and on the particular situation in which the mother finds herself.

Taking into account the fact that a woman who gives birth to a premature baby is in a very difficult situation from the psychological point of view, it is to be expected that attitudes to the child will be disturbed.

The aim of our work was to examine attitudes to maternity in women who had borne premature infants and to compare them with those of women whose children were born at term.

PATIENTS AND METHODS

We have studied a randomized group (A) of 50 women who had given birth to premature children. The control group comprised 30 women who had borne term babies, group (B).

The age of the subjects was 22–29 years. In terms of education they were divided as follows: group A, 52% secondary school education and 42% university level education and group B, 48% and 42% respectively.

In order to determine maternal attitudes, a clinical interview was conducted on day 2–4 after delivery along with a test involving the completion of sentences, based on Sacks test and compiled especially for research purposes (Bell, 1948). The results were analyzed by the χ^2 test.

RESULTS

Table 1 presents the results of the study. An analysis of the data indicates significant differences between the two groups of women in maternal attitudes represented.

A negative attitude in group A occurred in the case of a woman in a difficult personal situation (a single mother). There were also some negative attitudes in group B, when the child constituted an obstacle in the attainment of some personal goal.

An attitude of anxiety amongst the mothers of prematures mainly concerns a situation connected with separation from the child, the lack of contact and impossibility of nursing it. Another frequent cause was the lack of full information concerning the chances of the child's survival. Such a situation causes a state of frustration which may be the principal etiological factor in the appearance of anxiety towards maternity.

In the case of a mother giving birth to a premature infant who is usually taken to the neonatal intensive care unit and for a long period of time is separated from the mother, the development of a positive attitude to maternity, an attitude connected with the moment of birth, is rendered more difficult in the clinical conditions. The need for a natural link between

Table 1 Comparison of maternal attitudes

Group	Positive	Anxiety	Negative	Total
A	14	35	1	50
B	20	6	4	30

$\chi^2 = 19.5957$; $p = 0.05$

mother and child is too often insufficiently stressed, with more emphasis laid on rational conditions and technical perfection.

DISCUSSION

After the birth of a healthy term infant the mother always experiences feelings of pride and joy. If the child is born prematurely or with defects, the parents regard this fact as a failure. This situation is made worse by the fact that the premature baby is separated from the mother, which causes a break in the natural links which arise between mother and child during pregnancy and after delivery, and disturbs the formation of a normal attitude to maternity. Disturbances in maternal attitudes are particularly dangerous for women who do not have normal parental motivation previously formed. In mothers of preterm infants, there exists a danger of the appearance of an attitude of excessive concern for the infant just after delivery and in the future.

Hitherto research on the mother's postnatal contact with the child indicates the necessity of maintaining direct links between mother and child (Bowlby, 1969; Golanska and Borkowski, 1985; Klaus and Kennell, 1976; Odent, 1984).

Our work was intended to reveal that in the birth of a premature child, who is separated from the mother, the situation may lead to disturbances in maternal attitudes, particularly in the emotional components, and as a result may give rise to many malfunctions in the development of the child.

6

Prenatal maternal fantasies and postnatal mother–child relationship

H. von Lüpke

ABSTRACT

The prognostic significance of fantasies about the future child during pregnancy can be found less in their contents than in their relational context. Based on the fundamental relationship of mutual incorporation with fantasies of omnipotence, on the one hand, and anxiety of annihilation on the other, the need for the other's survival and the waiting for his proposal becomes the essential element of the dialog.

An example shows the development from the mother's fantasies about the future child to the mother–infant relationship in a case of defective dialog. The analysis focuses on the psychotic and the psychosomatic defences as elements of a fused relationship based on a fantasy of mutual incorporation. The evaluation of these elements is not viewed as pathology, but is understood as part of a balance between identification and integration. In the context of dialog even these elements seem to be essential for normal development.

Fantasies about an expected child accompanied by the selection of name, baby clothing and furniture are normally considered to be favorable signs for the future relationship of mother to child (Caplan, 1960). Cohen (1966) believes, in fact, that 'the absence of any preparatory behavior especially during the last trimester (including fantasies about what the baby will be like to take care of)' is one of the 'danger signs' for the improper adjustment to pregnancy and for the lack of the development of a strong relationship to the child.

With this as a background it was surprising to me to discover that women who expressed the most vivid fantasies about their child during pregnancy sometimes were not capable later of developing a stable mother–child relationship (von Lüpke, 1984). On the other hand, I have spoken with pregnant women who could express no fantasies about the child and in some cases clearly rejected the child during pregnancy, but who from the moment of birth appeared to have developed a good relationship with their child. It would appear that due to complex factors it is not possible to correlate fantasizing during pregnancy with the later mother–child relationship.

On the other hand, in later work with mother and child, themes continually appeared that were already evident from the time of the pregnancy. From this followed an attempt to proceed less from the content of the fantasies as from the relational context. Not only the relationship of mother to child had to be considered but also her relationship to the family, to her partner, and to the therapist. Finally the active role of the child would have to be considered. In order to clarify this process at least to some extent, I have chosen an example that varies greatly from the norm. There are two reasons for my choice. First, because of my work in a mother–child home, it is within the realm of my experience. The second reason is the notion that normality and pathology distinguish themselves not in substance but rather through the available regulatory mechanisms. Furthermore, pathology makes underlying structures more visible while in normal situations it is difficult to analyze the underlying entanglement of constructive and destructive forces.

CASE STUDY

Andrea was 20 years old and in the sixth month of pregnancy as our discussions began. She limped – I was aware that she had a congenital hip joint luxation. During our first conversation she sat on the edge of her chair. She appeared to be someone who was always on the alert. She spoke loudly – almost shouting – as if she felt she had to defend herself. Although she asked questions she did not wait for an answer. What she had to say seemed to be a long monolog.

Andrea began by telling about her very intense perception of fetal movement. She felt not just the kicking of the liver, stomach and bladder but also such a strong tickling of the liver that she had to laugh. This part of the story was accompanied by the tickling motion of her fingers. Already in the first weeks of pregnancy she dreamed of holding the child, feeding it, and taking it for a walk. She thought it would be a boy because of hair growth during her pregnancy and she had always considered herself to be more masculine. The whole family, including her mother, was 'masculine'. 'Boys are more assertive.' But, 'It is only important that the child is healthy.' She had names for both a boy and a girl, but did not tell me what they were.

Andrea had spent most of her first 3 years of life in the hospital due to her hip condition. She remembered how she rocked her head while she repeated the name of her favorite nurse. She was in a childrens' home from the ages of 10–16. Her parents have still not given her an explanation for why she was put in the home. Perhaps it was because she had stolen something or because she wet the bed. She stopped wetting the bed at 14 years of age – 4 years after being sent to the home. Since then Andrea has suffered from stomach pains. In the home, anyone who showed signs of weakness was 'taken care of' by the others. Even today Andrea hates nothing more than self pity. When her pain is particularly bad, she shuts herself in the toilet. Soft stroking of her body she perceived as 'ants crawling on her entire body'. She prefers that her present boy friend treat her roughly, pulling her hair, and that he use rough, abusive language with her. She called her child a 'parasite'.

A year before Andrea had had an abortion in the third month of pregnancy. She had been told her pelvis could crack. Just before the abortion she saw her child's movements on the ultrasound screen. From then on she considered herself to have killed her child. For several months thereafter, she tried to kill herself by drinking large quantities of alcohol. At the end of this phase she experienced a nightmare: her entire body was covered by insects that were slowly devouring her. As she related this she imitated the sound of the insects' jaws. She awoke with a scream that could be heard throughout her apartment building. From then on she stopped drinking. She continues to hear screaming in the night and because of this is thinking about moving.

As quickly as possible Andrea tried to get pregnant again. She used two partners and was successful. She learned of this new pregnancy in the same hospital in which she had had the abortion. She was so overcome that she was not sure if she was experiencing emotions of joy. She was forced to move into the mother–child home due to financial problems including eviction from her apartment.

Andrea's fantasies about the child centered around the themes of protection and mutual help. She held her uterus with both hands in the elevator in order to protect her child. The baby 'stroked' her from within and alleviated her pain. If necessary, she planned to prostitute herself in order to support her child. One nightmare repeated itself. Andrea was holding her child and feeding him. The child was a black-haired boy. As she was leaving her house a masked man approached her and grabbed the child. She thinks the man in the dream could have been one of the possible fathers.

Another theme appears in ever new variations: namely food. Andrea was never able to cook for herself. Even though she ate enough she lost weight. She could not stand the thought of milk even though she always had been able to drink milk 'by the liter'. When she was excited she vomited. The fetus moved the most when she was eating. Andrea considered this to be a sign of her baby accusing her: 'You care for yourself more than for me.' Andrea experienced the desire to be cared for herself. 'Here, I am the biggest child.'

In the 33rd week of pregnancy she was admitted to the hospital due to premature labor contractions. A daughter, Danielle, was born without complications in the 37th week of pregnancy. Andrea was greatly relieved that the baby's hips were normal. Andrea breast-fed the baby briefly but gave up, doubting her ability to nurse. She was not able to link the words 'I' and 'mother' in her imagination. Danielle did not burp well, spit up her milk, screamed and then was too tired to drink her milk. Even though the baby was hardly $3\frac{1}{2}$ months old Andrea thought she screamed because: 'The mouse is furious because her toys were hung too high; she expects the pictures on the wall to talk to her; she wants to hold her bottle herself.'

Andrea feared that Danielle would suffocate under her covers, and that water would get into her ears during bathing and be dangerous. Danielle was frequently cramped and retroflexed. She cried until she was blue. She would then play by herself and Andrea thought that the baby wanted to be left alone.

Andrea attempted to cut her wrists after a conflict in which a new partner and the baby's probable father were involved. She remembered the incident as chaotic. A week later she remembered, 'There was blood everywhere. At first I did not know whose blood; then I saw that it was mine and it was about to run over my daughter.' Andrea considered herself to be more mature: 'I am no longer the biggest child.' But it was at the same time that another change occurred. Danielle became a stranger to her mother. Andrea was no longer capable of caring for the baby. Danielle needed to be placed in the ward of the home while Andrea herself saw more and more of her boy friend. The baby was frequently with her potential father who was attempting to obtain legal guardianship of the child. At first this was unacceptable to Andrea even though she admitted that there was 'fresh air' where the father lived. Andrea herself was suffering from stomach pains, could eat nothing even though she was hungry and had migraine headaches. At night she dreamed she had denounced the other potential father of her child. In the dream she held him while he was decapitated. Andrea was afraid of black objects, imagined a man to be climbing up her balcony and was frightened by the sight of a bicycle in spite of the fact that she had heard it in advance.

Danielle developed a particularly stubborn obstructive (asthmatic) bronchitis and was losing weight. At $9\frac{1}{2}$ months she began to rhythmically beat her head against objects. Her mother's comment was: 'Perhaps she wants to get herself in shape.' At 11 months Danielle was placed in a foster home during the week and at the weekend she was with her potential father, and was cared for there by his wife. Andrea herself was working in a bordell that passed as a 'Sauna'. The bordello belonged to the other potential father. Thereafter the foster care was changed into adoption.

How was it that the lively fantasies during pregnancy did not lead to a sound mother–child relationship? According to Caplan (1960), aren't dreams about caring for a baby while holding it in your arms a particularly favorable precondition for caring in reality? Caplan's assumption is that we can expect a shorter 'maternal time-lag', that means a shorter time span between the birth and the development of 'full maternal feeling', when in the dreams during pregnancy the child appears as a young baby, rather than as an older child or even a grown-up.

As a first response one could say: the deficiencies of the mother were so great on account of her own socialization, that she was fantasizing about the child not as dependent and in need of care, but rather as a care-giving partner, as a mother: 'Orphans or women having experienced maternal deprivation, who express the fantasy of giving birth to their own mother, provide themselves with a mother by giving birth to a child' (Bydlowski, 1984). The imagined boy was strong and aggressive, he was supposed to take care of himself and the mother as well. These wishes are again apparent in her fantasies about the baby in her first few months, already enraged because her toy is hanging too high or looking for answers from pictures, and the girl at $3\frac{1}{2}$ months, trying to hold her bottle.

This interpretation is no doubt correct, but it does not yield a conclusion: it only deduces a pathological result from a pathological assumption. My concern here is to use extreme situations to enlarge our knowledge and understanding of possibilities for regulation, meaning health, not to delineate them as pathological manifestations.

Bibring (1959) says:

'A great number of these cases presented in our conferences by the screening team and by the psychotherapists working with the prenatal clinic patients were at first diagnosed by a majority of staff members as 'borderline' cases, i.e. as ambulatory, beginning or arrested psychoses. The content of these interviews was remarkably similar to that which we usually find in severely disturbed patients. Magical thinking, premonitions, depressive reactions, primitive anxieties, introjective and paranoid mechanisms, frequently associated with the patient's relation to her own mother, seemed to prevail.'

It turned out that such anomolies were not in all cases accompanied by disorders during pregnancy, birth and childcare. Bibring comes to the conclusion 'that this picture may pertain more to the condition of pregnancy in general than to the specific problems of the individual.'

What Bibring labels as psychosis could also be seen as the flip side of a coin called Object Relationship with fusion (the extension of the self through the lifting of the barriers and incorporation of the other): as the destruction of the self. Here, feelings of dismemberment or alienation of a part of one's self would already constitute defense mechanisms against the total destruction in the sense of a loss of identity. 'On the oral level of the organization of libido, to be overcome with love still coincides with the destruction of the object' (S. Freud, 1920).

Concerning the state of the fusion, it is not known who is doing the swallowing and who is being swallowed, who's being completed and who is being destroyed. Thus, in this manner, gratification and fear of destruction remain inseparably intertwined.

Beside the mentioned psychotic defense mechanism which defends the identity (if only in a rudimentary form) at the cost of great fear, a psychosomatic defense can be developed in the form of an 'allergic object relationship' (Marty, 1958). 'In fact, this is a progressive mutual permeation of subject and object whereby the difficulties and distances between the partners are eliminated' (Marty, 1958). Here, the fear of destruction which comes with fusion is being neutralized via transferal onto a physical level, for example, into the vital somatic threat of the asthma fit. Somatization into an itch and scratch fit would be another example of how the combination of fusion and dismemberment can be experienced without fear. Marty himself stresses the significance of allergies as a protection against disintegration and points out that psychoses are rarely found in patients suffering from allergies. Perhaps one can say: the psychosis defends the identity at the cost of integration while the allergic object relationship gives up identity in order to avoid disintegration.

In another vein, the development of an object relationship which not only knows the merciless incorporation of an object, but also entails concern for the survival of the object, follows a completely different path: 'In adult and mature sexual intercourse, it is perhaps true that it is not the purely erotic satisfactions that need a specific object. It is the aggressive or destructive element in the fused impulse that fixes the object and determines the need that is felt for the partner's actual presence, satisfaction, and survival' (Winnicott, 1978).

This concept of Winnicott is expanded in the 'dialog' of Milani Comparetti (1985). Here, instead of calculable reactions we have 'propositions' and 'counterpropositions', giving the partners the freedom to decide what they want to share and what they want to keep to themselves. Perhaps it is this unshareable, this 'secret' as an integral part of the dialog which constitutes the most decisive rebuttal of any form of fusion. It is no coincidence that silence as an expression of a 'niche of subjectivity' (Milani Comparetti, 1985) is obviously viewed as a threat by totalitarian systems, a threat which prompts them to realize psychotic fears by way of torture.

Let us return to our example. Already at an early stage in Andrea's life we can see manifestations of fusion (as bed wetting) and incorporation (as stealing). The combination of fusion and destruction is evident during the alcoholism episode. In her nightmare, Andrea is being eaten alive by insects with crackling jaws: destruction without fusion, the pure psychotic part, reverberating later during stroking which to her feels like 'ants on my body'. Incorporation and rejection: she has eating problems, she is repulsed by milk, she vomits when excited: fusion and destruction are pushed to a somatic level here. The child, also, reacts at this level initially: a weak drinker, failure to burp, vomiting. Then, Danielle moves on to the next level of somatic reactions, to an allergic object relationship in the form of an obstructive ('asthmatic') bronchitis.

In between lies that break in the relationship of the mother and child which coincides with the suicide attempt. What had happened? It is possible that up until this point, Andrea had still seen in Danielle the aggressive boy whom she had fantasized about during her pregnancy: the boy who was able to protect his mother with his strength and revenge her for all the humiliation she had suffered. In another humiliating situation, Andrea, perhaps, becomes aware of the reality: her small, helpless daughter has nothing in common with the hero-son she'd fantasized about. 'I have become more mature', says Andrea. As with alcohol before, she is now seeking refuge in another destructive fusion. But the bloody fusion does not succeed: it was only her own, the mother's, blood that ran over her daughter's face. She has become a stranger to her. After the loss of the fantasized baby, it is apparent that she has until now barely been aware of the real child. The stage of the 'concern' or 'dialog' had not been reached; there was no image of the partner that could have survived the disappointment. Andrea attempts to keep the approaching psychosis in check by anticipating her pursuers and bringing about her own destruction: of her own accord she now hands the child over to the man who was repeatedly trying to take it away from her in her nightmares during pregnancy. She becomes a prostitute, not in order to support her child, but rather to surrender to the clutches of brutality.

I believe that it is clear that almost all the themes important to the mother–child relationship show themselves already in pregnancy. That does not mean that they could not have developed differently. It has often been observed that after birth the child takes the initiative and as a result dialog between mother and child is possible even in difficult relationships. The first $4\frac{1}{2}$ months of Andrea's and Danielle's relationship were evidence of the possibility of the relationship developing favorably. At 5 weeks Danielle sought contact by smiling. At 4 months she actively sought contact through cooing noises. Then came her mother's suicide attempt. The role played by the intensive relations with a then 16-year-old boyfriend in the further development of Andrea's relationship with Danielle must remain open. Here, the limits of prenatal prognosis make themselves clear. A prognosis can only state the themes but never their final meaning.

But that also means that elements that appear highly pathological at first do not by themselves point to a poor prognosis. This corresponds to Bibring's experience as quoted at the beginning of my remarks.

Perhaps it can be said that it is the cannibalistic basis of human relationships that gives color, depth and vitality to the dialog of a mother with her unborn child, infant and partner. 'I could eat you up', is not by accident one of the most frequent expressions of love to an infant.

Perhaps it is also the discrepancy between the fantasized child and the real child that gives the relationship a chance. This discrepancy allows the child to more easily go its own way and avoid the danger of Peter Pan, who fulfilled his mother's wishes at the expense of his own growth (Gidoni et al., 1983).

In lullabies and myths, caring for and destroying are closely related. A Hebrew myth tells of a woman before Eve – the demon, Lilith. The children of Lilith and Adam were demons 'that still plague humanity'. Lilith was commissioned by God to take all newborns into her protection but rather she destroyed all human children who did not wear the amulet of the three angels. Von Ranke-Graves and Patai (1963) describe an apotropaic rite used for the protection of male infants considered to be in particular danger. 'When Lilith succeeded in getting close to and kissing a male infant, the child would laugh in his sleep. To ward off the danger of Lilith it was thought necessary to stroke the lips of the sleeping child with a finger. Then Lilith would disappear.'

7
Maternal attitudes and preterm labor

X. De Muylder and S. Wesel

ABSTRACT

A prospective study of psychological factors during pregnancy investigated 47 pregnant women around the 24th week of gestation by means of a self-reporting multiple choice questionnaire. After delivery, the patients were classified in two groups: A, those who presented with preterm labor and were admitted for treatment in the hospital and B, those who did not develop preterm labor and delivered at term. Analysis of the answers to the questionnaire reveals that preterm labor mothers found more difficulty in accepting the pregnancy, had poorer communication with their baby, had less support from their husband and reacted more negatively when they first menstruated. The implications of these findings in the process of motherhood are discussed.

In 1986, preterm labor (PTL) remains the most important cause of perinatal morbidity and mortality. Management of this common obstetrical problem should include prevention, early diagnosis, arrest of premature contractions and intensive care of the neonate. However, though some conditions like cervical incompetency, uterine anomalies and overdistension are well known to predispose to PTL, the precise cause remains, in the majority of instances, unidentified.

Amongst theses on idiopathic PTL, Papiernik (1969) has identified constitutional, gynecological and socioeconomical problems that could increase the risk of preterm delivery. In the same way, some psychological features have been suspected to be more prevalent in groups of mothers of premature neonates than in controls (Gunter, 1963; Blau et al., 1963). In a previous study (De Muylder, 1986) we also observed that negative attitudes toward pregnancy, emotional immaturity, unresolved conflicts with the mother, history of a traumatic experience during a previous pregnancy, high level of anxiety and feeling of inadequacy in female roles were more frequent amongst mothers admitted for PTL than amongst controls.

All these studies, however, are retrospective and it cannot be excluded that the experience of hospitalization for PTL or the delivery of a premature neonate did not modify the answers given to the investigators. This is the reason why we decided to start a prospective study investigating around the 24th week of pregnancy, these psychological factors in a large group of pregnant mothers. We wanted to know if there was any significant difference between the mothers who afterwards developed PTL and those who delivered at term. This paper presents preliminary results of this study.

PATIENTS AND METHOD

A self-reporting multiple choice questionnaire of 67 items was devised in order to assess eight aspects:

(1) Attitude toward pregnancy: planned?, wished?, invested?; preparation of the nest; general feelings and modification of activities and attitudes.

(2) Feto-maternal relationship and communication with the fetus *in utero*.

(3) Anxiety, fears and dreams.

(4) Maturity, self-confidence, independency.

(5) Adequacy as a female, feelings about feminine identification and development.

(6) Support from the husband, the family and friends.

(7) Relationship with the mother during childhood.

(8) History of previous traumatic obstetrical experience.

This questionnaire was distributed to the pregnant mothers during an antenatal visit 20–24th week. It was requested that it should be filled in at home and brought back at the next visit. These questionnaires were stocked for analysis and, after delivery, the data about pregnancy, labor, delivery and postpartum were extracted from the medical charts. The age, gravity, parity, marital status, socioeconomical level and previous medico-obstetrical complications were also recorded. The socioeconomical level was evaluated by means of the number of schooling years and the husband's profession.

The mothers were divided into two groups: group A consisted of the patients who had been admitted for PTL whatever the evolution has been (successful arrest of the contractions or tocolysis failure and preterm delivery). Preterm labor was defined by regular uterine contractions producing a modification of the cervical score and occurring before 37 weeks of pregnancy; group B consisted of all the other patients who had not been admitted for PTL and who delivered at term.

The questionnaires were analyzed by two methods. First, the distribution of the answers to each question were compared in the two groups. Secondly, for every patient, a score of Unconscious Rejection of Pregnancy (URP) was established by using the responses to 14 questions thought to be adequate to evaluate the maternal attitude toward the pregnancy and the fetus (mainly directed to points 1 and 2 of the eight aspects).

The first 50 patients who delivered after completing the questionnaire were analyzed in this study. Unfortunately, three mothers whose clinical data were incomplete had to be excluded. So, 47 charts were available for analysis: 11 preterm labor cases and 36 controls.

RESULTS

The distribution of age, parity, marital situation and socioeconomical levels in the two groups are presented in Table 1. There is no difference between patients admitted for PTL and controls.

The analysis of the answers to each question of the self-reporting questionnaire shows that four items present a very different distribution in the two groups. As indicated in Table 2, mothers who have later been admitted for PTL declare more frequently that

- the pregnancy has been difficult to accept;
- they have a poor communication with their baby (or even no communication at all);
- their husband offers little help or support;
- they reacted negatively when the first menses started.

The comparison of the URP score in the two groups also reveals a very significant difference between PTL mothers and controls. Whereas the mean score is 4.82 ± 2.21 for the PTL mothers it is only 2.69 ± 1.31 for the controls. Figure 1 shows the difference in the distribution of these scores. Moreover, a URP score greater than or equal to 5 carries a relative risk of preterm labor equal to 5.7!

Table 1 Sociodemographic data of 11 PTL and 36 control mothers

	Preterm labor	Controls	
Age			
<20	0	1	NS
20–24	5	14	
25–29	4	14	
30–34	1	5	
⩾35	1	2	
Parity			
0	3	16	NS
1	7	17	
2	1	2	
⩾3	0	1	
Marital situation			
Married	11	32	NS
Single	0	4	
Socioeconomic level			
1–2	0	2	NS
3–4	3	13	
5–6	5	12	
7–8	3	8	
9–10	0	1	

Table 2 Psychological features in 11 PTL and 36 controls

	Preterm labor	Controls	χ^2
Number	11	36	
Poor or no communication between mother and fetus	4	3	5.22*
Negative reactions at menarche	4	4	3.80*
Difficulty in accepting the pregnancy	3	2	4.18*
Little or no support by the husband	6	9	3.40†

*$p<0.05$; †$p=0.06$

MATERNAL ATTITUDES AND PRETERM LABOR

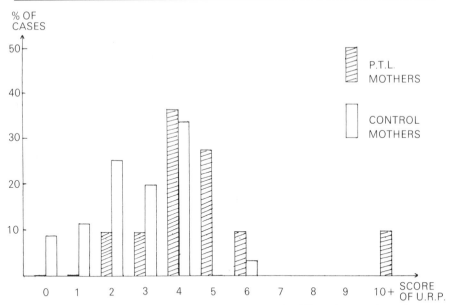

Figure 1 Distribution of the URP scores amongst the PTL and control mothers

DISCUSSION

Although only preliminary, these results suggest there could be some important differences in the mental attitude of mothers who develop preterm labor compared to a group of controls.

An important methodological difference between our study and most of the preceding published papers is that this work was prospectively conducted, the patients being investigated well before the occurrence of the premature labor. By so doing, we planned to avoid the tainting of the responses by the pregnancy evolution and its outcome.

For this study, we mainly used a URP score based on the answers to 14 predetermined questions and aimed at evaluating the pregnancy investment realized by the mother as well as the quality of her relationship to the fetus. The mothers who will later present with preterm labor tend to have much higher scores than the controls, meaning that, among these mothers, pregnancy was less desired, less invested and the relationship with the fetus was poorer.

According to Bibring (1959), pregnancy can be regarded as a period of crisis involving profound psychological and somatic changes, like puberty and menopause. This crisis represents important developmental steps and significant adjustments are needed. Bibring described three tasks for the pregnant mother: first, to accept the pregnancy and the fetus as part of herself; then, to accept the fetus as an independent individual; and finally, to wish the delivery will occur. Through the successful implementation of these three tasks, the woman realizes an important maturational evolution called motherhood.

The fact that a greater number of PTL mothers admit that pregnancy was difficult to accept points out to difficulty in the realization of the first task. Other authors like Berkowitz and Kasl (1983) and Blau et al. (1963), Nuckolls et al. (1972) and Laukaran and Van den Berg (1980) also found a link between pregnancy desirability and either PTL or other obstetrical complications.

The poorer communication between mother and fetus as well as some negative attitudes to quickening, also suggest some defects in the acceptance of the fetus as an autonomous individual, i.e. the second task of Bibring. This failure to develop emotional affiliation could be of serious significance and could predispose to ulterior bonding defect. It can be hypothesized that, in some cases, preterm labor could be a precursory sign of a disturbed relationship between mother and baby.

Our study also indicates that support provided by the husband during pregnancy seems to be less adequate in cases of PTL. Although Berkowitz and Kasl (1983) did not find any difference between partner support to mothers of premature neonates and to control mothers, Nuckolls et al. (1972) showed that obstetrical complications could be related to a balance between stressful situations and the nature and strength of the supportive elements.

Finally, the patients at risk of PTL also demonstrate more negative attitudes at menarche. This is in line with the observations already made by Gunter (1963) and by Blau et al. (1963) that some mothers of preterm babies more frequently feel inadequate as females and express uncertainty about their feminine identification or development, rejecting heterosexual relationships and associating sex with guilt.

In conclusion, these preliminary results of our study tend to suggest that preterm labor could be more frequently observed in pregnant women with a difficult motherhood process, feminine inadequacy and defective partner support. However, further studies are needed before definite conclusions can be reached.

8

The psychological effects of maternal attitudes in cases of repeated unfavorable pregnancy outcome

Z. Golańska and A. Bacz

ABSTRACT

Attitudes towards maternity as well as emotional problems of 50 childless women who aborted at least one pregnancy, and of 30 healthy primigravidas are presented in this study. The psychological examination consisted of a clinical interview, a test involving the completion of sentences which was a modified version of a Sacks test, and a projection experiment constructed along the lines of a thematic apperception test (TAT). An ambivalent maternal attitude was stated significantly more often in women with pregnancy losses than in primigravidas. On the contrary, a positive attitude appeared significantly less frequently in women who aborted as compared to the primigravidas. Both groups differed in the degree of intensity with which emotional problems were experienced. Above all feelings of guilt, fear, anxiety, attitudes to abortion, and ambitions as regards the future were the concerns most often expressed. In every one of the 50 women with unsuccessful pregnancies there appeared at least one conflict of notable intensity, and in the primigravidas this occurred only in one third of the women. It is stated that abortion is a traumatic experience and disturbs the formation of attitudes towards maternity and is a cause of emotional disturbance. A psychotherapeutic program for this group of women, as well as a psychotherapeutic approach for the nurses, was introduced.

INTRODUCTION

Maternity is regarded as a primary value, being the essence of the life of every women irrespective of the age in which she lives. The child, the object of love, allows the mother to satisfy a fundamental psychological need, which expresses itself amongst other maternal attitudes.

Limited fertility today concerns one in four marriages. Infertility, the inability to carry a pregnancy to term, or serious somatic illness preventing the normal development of pregnancy are examples of situations in which the achievement of the model of woman as mother is made more difficult. All obstacles on the way to the attainment of maternity are the cause of increasing psychological disorders. The psychological factor is increasingly taken into consideration in the analysis of cases of infertility and pregnancy losses (Motyka and Golańska, 1981; Coghi et al., 1979). This problem is creating more and more interest amongst both psychologists and physicians; however, the problem of unfulfilled maternity (including attitudes to maternity) is too rarely the subject of research.

The aim of the present work is to evaluate attitudes towards maternity and emotional problems in childless women who in the past have had at least one unsuccessful pregnancy.

MATERIAL AND METHODS

For the research a group of 50 women was selected, all in the first trimester of pregnancy and hospitalized because of repeated early losses of pregnancy*. A control group was comprised of 30 primigravidas in the first trimester of pregnancy who were attending the Cracow School of Childbirth.

The psychological examination consisted of a clinical interview, a test involving the completion of sentences which was a modified version of a Sacks test (compiled especially for the purposes of the examination), and a projection experiment constructed along the lines of the thematic apperception test (TAT) of Murray. Apart from the psychological examination, the age, level of education, place of residence and the duration of the marriage of the women under examination were analyzed.

---

* At the Department of Endocrinology, Institute of Gynecology and Obstetrics, Copernicus University School of Medicine, Cracow, Poland.

Table 1 Distribution of age in years

Age	Pregnancy loss n	%	Primigravidas n	%
22–25	15	30.0	8	26.8
26–30	30	60.0	19	63.2
31–35	5	10.0	3	10.0

$\chi^2 = 0.21; p > 0.05$

Table 2 Level of education

	Pregnancy loss n	%	Primigravidas n	%
Elementary	1	2.0	2	6.7
Technical	2	4.0	3	10.0
Secondary	26	52.0	12	40.0
University	21	42.0	13	43.3

$\chi^2 = 2.74; p > 0.05$

Table 3 Area of residence

	Pregnancy loss n	%	Primigravidas n	%
City/town	37	74.0	24	80.0
Rural	13	26.0	6	20.0

$\chi^2 = 0.33; p > 0.05$

Table 4 Duration of marriage in years

Year	Pregnancy loss n	%	Primigravidas n	%
1–2	11	22.0	12	30.0
3–4	18	36.0	11	36.7
5–6	7	10.0	3	10.0
>6	14	28.0	4	12.0

$\chi^2 = 4.1; p > 0.05$

RESULTS AND DISCUSSION

The women under examination did not vary in age (Table 1), level of education (Table 2), place of residence (Table 3) or duration of marriage (Table 4) – in other words in those factors which could have an influence on maternal attitudes.

From an analysis of the psychological tests, it appears that maternal attitudes can be qualified into three categories: a positive attitude, an ambivalent attitude and a negative one. The groups of women examined varied in the frequency of the appearance of particular maternal attitudes (Table 5); with the group of women with failed pregnancies an ambivalent attitude appeared significantly more often, and a positive one less frequently. Both groups also differed in the degree of intensity with which emotional problems were experienced – above all feelings of guilt, fear, anxiety, attitudes to miscarriage, and to future ambitions. In every one of the 50 women with unsuccessful pregnancies there appeared at least one conflict of notable intensity, and in the control group this occurred only in one third of the women (see Table 6).

The results of the psychological tests and the data from the clinical interviews bear witness to the fact that abortion, as it is a traumatic experience, disturbs the formation of attitudes towards maternity and is the cause of emotional disturbances. Women with a problematic obstetric history are decidedly more depressive, and more inclined to fear. They manifest various forms of changes of mood, mostly of a depressive nature, and increased sensitivity along with outbursts of anger. All the women in this group were characterized by a lack of emotional stability. Furthermore, they had a decreased sense of their own worth and revealed increased activity of psychological defense mechanisms.

The information supplied by other authors (Edwards and Jones, 1970; Spielberger and Jacobs, 1979) shows that potentially any emotional stress in a mother can lead to complications in birth, a lower birth weight of the fetus, and clear psychomotor overexcitability in the infant. Similarly,

Table 5 Attitudes towards maternity

Attitude	Pregnancy loss n	%	Primigravidas n	%
Positive	18	36.0	21	70.0
Ambivalent	30	60.0	8	26.7
Negative	2	4.0	1	3.3

$\chi^2 = 8.85; p < 0.025$

Table 6 The occurrence of high degree conflicts (%)

Conflict	Pregnancy loss	Primigravidas	p
Fear and anxiety	98.0	23.3	<0.001
Feeling of guilt	96.0	10.0	<0.001
Mother	10.0	16.7	NS
Father	22.0	20.0	NS
Husband	4.0	6.7	NS
Doctor	8.0	10.0	NS
Pregnancy	16.0	6.7	NS
Abortion	96.0	0.0	<0.001
Sexual life	6.0	10.0	NS
Goals	66.0	3.3	<0.001
Future	28.0	6.7	<0.025
At least one conflict	100.0	33.0	<0.001

Laukaron and Van den Berg (1980) and Goshen-Gottstein's (1969) research seems to indicate that disturbance in attitudes to the child can become the cause of complications in birth or even lead to intrauterine death.

Our study was of an exploratory nature. In Poland no research has thus far been conducted on the maternal attitudes of women with unsuccessful pregnancies. The research hitherto of the aforementioned authors was of a prospective nature and was conducted collectively on large populations. Our study was conducted individually and included both conscious and subconscious emotional spheres, and attitudes to the child. Furthermore, individual contact with each of the patients allowed simultaneous psychological examination to be conducted and the case studies to be examined, which provided a basis for the compilation of a psychotherapeutic program for that group of women. A program of psychotherapeutic approach for the nurses taking care of the women was also produced. The effectiveness of these programs is the subject of prospective clinical works and will be the subject of future reports.

Part 3: Studies in paternal attitudes in relation to the prenatal and perinatal experience

9

The role of the father in care-giving and in the development of the infant: an empirical study on the impact of prenatal courses on expectant fathers

H. Nickel

ABSTRACT

The role of the father as care-giver has been discussed more and more in recent years. Together with the expectant mothers a growing number of expectant fathers participate in prenatal courses. The impact on their later care-giving behavior has, however, hardly been investigated empirically, and the influence of fathers' participation in care-giving on the development of infants has also not been studied. For this reason a longitudinal pilot study on prenatal courses and parent–child interaction in the first year of life focussed on these questions.

Two groups of fathers ($n = 69$) have been compared: one with fathers who attended preparatory courses for infant care-giving together with the expectant mothers ('prepared'), and one control group without such a preparation ('unprepared'). The method of this study consisted of a quasi-experimental group comparison based on an accidental sampling with the help of gynecologists, midwives, and teachers of prenatal classes. The data were collected by use of questionnaires (in the 1st and 6th week and the 9th month of life) and through observations in a quasi-experimental laboratory situation (in the 3rd and 9th month).

The questionnaire data yielded some important differences between the two groups of fathers which appeared already at birth and later in daily routine of care-giving as well as in exceptional situations, e.g. prepared fathers already felt a stronger attraction to the child after delivery, and later they changed nappies and carried the baby on their body significantly more often than unprepared fathers. The quasi-experimental observations consisted of two settings each: in the 3rd month of life free play and face-to-face interaction, in the 9th month of life free play and a test of attachment behavior. The data were analyzed by trained raters according to quantitative and qualitative characteristics. This analysis yielded some significant differences for fathers' behavior in the 3rd month of the babies' life, e.g. prepared fathers showed stronger proximal body contact, more emotional warmth and empathy, which, however, existed only as a tendency in the 9th month. However, the two groups of the 9-month-old infants differed significantly; babies with prepared fathers showed a higher degree of responsiveness and uttered more positive vocalizations. Further, a developmental screening revealed an advantage in some aspects of social behavior.

In sum, these findings may point to the interpretation that participation of fathers in prenatal classes influences their later care-giving behavior and also promotes the psychic development of the children. Consequences for planning preparatory courses with a stronger psychological orientation are also discussed.

THEORETICAL FRAMEWORK, OBJECTIVES AND HYPOTHESES

The investigation was conducted within a longitudinal pilot study on the preparation of parents for their first child, experiences in birthgiving, and the parent–child interaction in the first 9 months of the infant's life. The aim of the study was the construction and preliminary evaluation of hypotheses regarding which kind of the various factors of birthgiving preparation, and of the infant's early life influence the parent–child interaction. Furthermore, the question was taken up how different forms of participation of fathers influence the behavior and development of their infants. From that, this pilot study is concerned with basic developmental psychological objectives as well as with applied intervention-oriented objectives. We also refer to a broader theoretical framework by taking into account social psychological and sociopolitical factors as well.

In terms of developmental psychology this study started on the assumption that the mother should not be considered as the only or dominant person with a close emotional relationship to the newborn baby and infant, but that for the optimal development of the children the father's role is already of substantial importance at birth. Within this, the father's functions are not the same as those of the mother, and they are not exchangeable but have a kind of subsidiary role. The results of investigations in the United States (see Parke et al., 1975, 1976, 1980, 1981; Kotelchuk, 1976; Lamb, 1976a,b, 1977, 1979a,b, 1982) have since then been recognized internationally, and they have been confirmed in a number of following studies in other countries (see Fthenakis, 1984, 1985; Köcher and Nickel,

1985; Nickel and Köcher 1986a,b). Whereas Lamb et al. (1985) point to positive effects of a growing participation of fathers on the development of the children, respective empirical results had not been presented in the German-speaking countries at the time of the beginning of our study.

The reference to an applied intervention-orientation has been taken up because of the fact that a growing number of fathers have participated in preparatory classes together with expectant mothers in recent years. Whereas since the 1970s preparatory training courses for parents, and some especially for fathers, have been developed (see Lally, 1974; Barnhill et al., 1979; Parke et al., 1980) no respective scientifically evaluated programs have been established in the German-speaking countries. However, in practice fathers participate in these classes which originally had been developed for expectant mothers. Most of them are a kind of babycare course. The relevance of such preparatory training programs for fathers and possible effects on later child behavior have not yet been evaluated empirically; our study is conceived of as a respective preliminary contribution.

Therefore, this study focusses on the following main questions. Do prepared and unprepared fathers differ in their behavior towards newborn babies and infants? Do such differences also exist in the behavior of the children?

These two questions are drawn from two-sided hypotheses because specific and reliable results are still lacking and a formulation of specified one-sided hypotheses is not possible. These hypotheses can be summarized as follows:

(1) Unprepared and prepared fathers differ in their personal experience and their behavior towards newborn babies.

(2) Unprepared and prepared fathers differ in their personally experienced adaptation to the child during the first 6 weeks.

(3) Unprepared and prepared fathers differ in babycare and care-giving behavior with 3-month-old infants.

(4) Unprepared and prepared fathers differ in play and interaction when dealing with infants in the 3rd and 9th month of life.

(5) Children of prepared and unprepared fathers differ in interactive behavior in the 3rd and 9th month.

(6) Children of prepared and unprepared fathers also differ in some characteristics of their psychic development.

METHOD

Research design

In a quasi-experimental research design with an accidental sampling three groups of parents, expecting their first child, were investigated. These groups differed in regard to the kind of preparation:

Unprepared (U): fathers do not attend prenatal classes and do not have practical experience with infants,

Prepared (P): fathers attend prenatal classes in babycare and have practical experience with infants,

Well-prepared (WP): fathers with the qualifications of group P who also participated in a developmental psychological parent training course.

These three independent groups have been compared in regard to the following variables:

Kind and frequency of the father–child interaction in the first months of the infant's life (questionnaire),

The parents' personally experienced adaptation to the child (questionnaire),

Developmental progress of the child as described by the parents (baby diary),

Quality of the father–child interaction in the 3rd and 9th month (video-taped quasi-experimental laboratory study),

Attachment of the child to the parents in the 9th month (video-taped quasi-experimental study).

Subjects

69 parents and their respective 69 infants were investigated. The parents entering the study had to fulfil the following conditions: German mother tongue and German cultural background, married or living in similar arrangement (2-person household), expecting first child, mother's first pregnancy, medically unproblematic pregnancy, father's profession not within medicine, psychology, social science, child care or child education.

The following criteria caused a drop-out: birth complications, illness of the child, critical living conditions influencing the normal parent–child interaction within the first year, withdrawal of the parents.

The sampling was done through a 'first-contact questionnaire' which was distributed by project cooperators or gynecologists, midwives, and

Table 1 Sampling in the two stages of the study

Age of infant	n	Unprepared (U)	Prepared (P)	Well-prepared (WP)
Questionnaire study				
3 months	69	27	36	6
9 months	60	26	28	6
Laboratory study				
3 months	27	10	14	3
9 months	26	8	16	2

teachers of prenatal classes in the cities of Düsseldorf and Duisburg (Northrhine-Westfalia, FRG). The subjects did not receive any financial rewards but they did not have to pay for reposting the questionnaire. The sampling was completed during May 1981 to June 1982. 450 first-contact questionnaires were distributed with 140 returning. From among them, 31 parents could not be included because of the mentioned preliminary exclusion criteria and another 49 parents dropped out during the investigation.

In the first part of the investigation (from pregnancy up to the third month of life) 69 parents participated in the longitudinal questionnaire study. They predominantly belonged to the middle or lower middle class (cf. Kleining and Moore, 1968). The 69 parents were assigned to the three groups 'unprepared' (U), 'prepared' (P) and 'well-prepared' (WP) fathers (see Table 1).

The first two groups U and P, differed in respect to the father's participation in prenatal classes for babycare. The subjects were classified according to the first-contact questionnaire which listed the different kinds of preparatory courses. The trained group WP constitutes the third stage of the independent variables. Fathers of this group not only fulfilled the conditions of group P but attended a developmental psychological training course for expectant parents as well, which was especially developed for this study by the two cooperators. Fathers and their wives who had already attended babycare prenatal classes were invited to this course which was run before the birth of the child.

Between these groups no significant social class differences were found. The small number of parents in the WP group is due to the difficulties in the organization of the psychological training course and because of many drop-outs in this group. Although strong efforts were made to find convenient dates to allow all parents to participate, it was not possible to gain the aimed number of parents (who already had attended prenatal babycare classes) for an additional participation in this course. Furthermore, because of events which led to a drop-out of some parents, this group of well-prepared fathers was outnumbered. Therefore, it was not possible to include this group in the comparative data analysis.

From among the 69 parents 27 young families participated in the quasi-experimental laboratory study in the 3rd month of the babies' life (see Table 1).

In the second part of the investigation (3rd–9th month) the sample consisted of 60 parents, and in the second quasi-experimental laboratory situation in the infant's 9th month 26 parents participated (see Table 1).

Research procedure

A summarized overview of the course of the longitudinal study starting with the first contact is given in Table 2. Due to the different dates of the first contact in the 3rd to 8th week of pregnancy the length of the investigation varied within the families between 10 and 15 months. The data collection referred to the following areas: pregnancy, birthgiving, care in hospital, the first weeks, care for the baby in the first 9 months, father–child interaction in the 3rd and 9th month, development of the child in the first 9 months, attachment behavior.

Table 2 Procedure of the longitudinal study

Date	Method
3rd–8th week of pregnancy	First-contact questionnaire
1st week	Questionnaire (Q) on birth and hospital: general Q on delivery for the mother Q on delivery for the father Q on hospital for the mother Q on hospital for the father
6th week	Questionnaires for the first weeks Q for the mother Q for the father Q on the social context
11th week	1st laboratory study
9th month	2nd laboratory study
4th week–9th month	Baby diary
9th month	Final Q for the father Final Q for the mother Q on the social context

The psychological training program

As basic intentions of this course three aims were set:

(1) *Impart of knowledge:* the parents' knowledge of the development of the child during the first year of life was enhanced by introducing developmental psychological facts. The parents, and especially the fathers, were instructed by use of examples how they could promote the development of their children through play etc.

(2) *Sensitization:* the parents were sensitized for recognizing abilities and needs of newborn babies and infants so that they could interpret the infant's signals competently and react in an empathetic way.

(3) *Motivation:* fathers were motivated to practice the learned skills in babycare and to engage in bodily contact with the infant. Mothers were stimulated to give support to their husbands' self-confidence in baby care-giving.

The practical realization consisted of lectures with situation-centered and vivid information on the development of children in the first year, examples given through video- or film-clips, and open discussion.

Data collection instruments

The data collection was based on several questionnaires and video-taped observations in quasi-experimental laboratory situations. Each of the instruments had been tested and modified before being used in the main investigation.

Questionnaires

The questionnaires for assessing the relevant variables for the period of pregnancy, birthgiving, and the first weeks of the child's life had been developed and tested especially for this study because no adequate standardized questionnaires for these special objectives had been available.

The following instruments were used:

(1) *First-contact questionnaire* It included, apart from particulars and a declaration for further participation, mainly questions on the course of the pregnancy, and the perinatal situation, e.g. expected date of delivery, hospital, aims of the parents as to rooming-in and attendance of the father at delivery.

(2) *General questionnaire on birth and hospital* It assessed the date of

birth, gender and health of the infant, the place of delivery, name of the hospital.

(3) *Questionnaire for the mother on delivery*   This questionnaire was used for a description of the delivery, the situation in the delivery room, and the personal experiences at the first contact with the child.

(4) *Questionnaire for the father on delivery*   It assessed whether the father was present at the delivery, his personal experiences of the birth, the kind and length of the first contact with the child and the experienced feelings, wishes, and suggestions for the first parent–child contact.

(5) *Questionnaire for the mother on the hospital*   This questionnaire drew on the conditions in the hospital for mother and child (length of stay in hospital, rooming-in, participation in care, help for care and breast-feeding, wishes and suggestions for improving the situation in the hospital).

(6) *Questionnaire for the father on the hospital*   It assessed the following information: frequency of visits to the hospital, personal feelings of the father during his wife's stay at hospital, kind of contact with the child, earlier experiences with newborn babies.

(7) *Questionnaire for the first weeks*   This was used for characteristics of the first 4–6 weeks with the baby at home and is identical both for mothers and fathers, apart from an introductory part for the mother for general data on the health, feeding and development of the child. Main issues are the actual job situation, shifts in leisure time activities, the first weeks with the baby (personal experiences in adaptation to the child, participation in care-giving, problematic issues in the relation of the three, frequency of contact with the child on weekdays and weekends).

(8) *Questionnaire for the social context of infants and preschool children* (similar to Schmidt-Denter, 1984)   The questions were answered in cooperation with both of the parents. With reference to the daily routine, information is given on the main persons in close relation to the child and their social functions, kind and frequency of contact with the child, care-giving behavior, and activities in play.

(9) *Final questionnaire*   At the end of the investigation (in the 9th month of the child's life), mothers and fathers had to give retrospective answers on topics such as job situation, leisure time activities and the first 9 months with the child. Additional questions for the mother concerned breast-feeding and food for the child, and the corresponding care-giving activities.

The baby diary

The parents had to write a kind of diary on the development of their infant according to the given criteria: psychomotoric development, perception, vocal utterings/language and social behavior. The diary is preceded by a part with questions on dealing with the infant.

Quasi-experimental observations on parent–child interaction

In the 3rd and 9th month of the infant's life the parent–child interaction was observed and video-taped under quasi-experimental conditions in a laboratory (see Figure 1). The observation situations consisted of three different kinds of situations:

(1) In the *free-play setting,* mother/father were stimulated freely to play with the child on the blanket using a provided toy (see Figure 1a).

(2) In the *face-to-face interaction,* they were asked to attract the baby's attention while sitting together with the baby in the armchair but subjects were not allowed to use toys (see Figure 1a).

(3) The *decision-situation* consisted of a test of the attachment behavior, similar to Ainsworth's test (see Ainsworth and Wittig, 1969). The baby had to decide whether to crawl to the mother or to the father (see Figure 1b).

Whereas the first setting was used in both parts of the laboratory study, the second setting was only used in the first part while in the second part of the study the first and the third setting were used:

(1) 3rd month:
 first setting: free play (5 min each with father/mother)
 second setting: face-to-face interaction (3 min each with father/mother).

(2) 9th month:
 first setting: free play (4 min each with father/mother)
 third setting: decision situation (2–4 min with both of the parents).

The parent–child interactions were video-taped with fathers or mothers alternating. Because of research technique reasons (e.g. possible overstraining the child) a permutation of the sequences was not possible, but not necessary because the fathers' behavior was of greater interest.

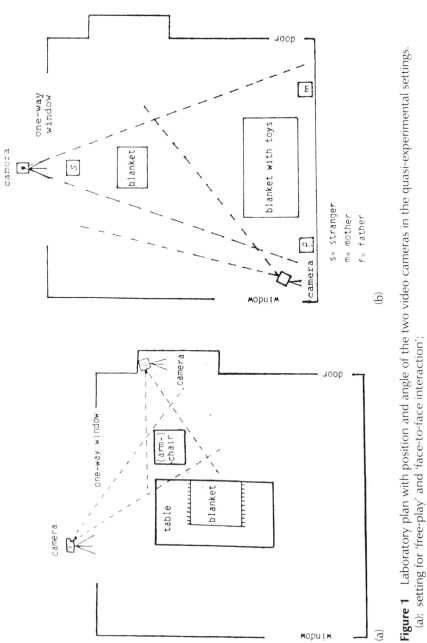

Figure 1 Laboratory plan with position and angle of the two video cameras in the quasi-experimental settings.
(a): setting for 'free-play' and 'face-to-face interaction';
(b): setting for 'decision situation'

Data analysis

Within each thematic area a description of the whole sample and an inferential statistical analysis of the behavior is given comparing the group of prepared (P) and unprepared (U) fathers. Because of the low frequency in the well-prepared (WP) group ($n = 6$) this group could not be included in this comparison.

The data from the questionnaires were analyzed by calculating the frequency distributions of the given answers. The questionnaire data were either at the nominal or the ordinal level so that for determining group differences either the Chi^2-Test or the Rank-sum-test by Raatz (a variant of Wilcoxon's Rank-sum-test) was used.

The analysis of the video-taped situations was carried out by trained raters with regard to quantitative and qualitative characteristics of the fathers' and children's behavior. In the quantitative analysis the occurrence of given variables of father and child behavior was registered in intervals of 10 seconds. For evaluating the qualitative characteristics eight scales were used, four each for father and child behavior:

Father behavior	Child behavior
Emotional warmth	Cheerfulness
Empathy	Quality of vocalization
Quality of stimulation	Responsivity
Assuredness and confidence	Decision behavior

The scales 1–3 for father behavior and the scales 1–3 for child behavior were taken from an earlier study on maternal behavior and behavior characteristics of infants (see Nickel et al., 1981) and have been adapted for this study. The other scales were constructed on the basis of an analysis respective to other research and specific observations.

For determining group differences in the analysis of the data from the systematic observation in the laboratory the Mann-Whitney-U-Test was used.

RESULTS

From among the many results within the different areas, mainly those relevant for the comparison of the two father groups will be presented. The other findings are documented in Bartoszyk and Nickel (1986a,b) and Nickel et al. (1986).

Results from the questionnaires

First contact

In regard to the variables – course of the pregnancy, pregnancy check-up, contact with other parents, household matters and the desired developmental promotion in the analysis of the first-contact questionnaires – no significant differences were found for the groups of unprepared and prepared fathers. However, as to the different preparatory measures several significant group differences appeared. As already fixed by the definition, unprepared and prepared fathers differed in the variable 'participation in babycare prenatal classes'. Furthermore, significantly more prepared than unprepared fathers also participated – together with their wives – in prenatal training programs as developed by Read, Lamaze and others. In addition, more prepared fathers attended lectures on the physical development of infants, they had read more related books and used other kinds of information sources.

Delivery and stay in hospital

From among the 69 fathers of the whole sample 78% ($n = 54$) were present all the time during delivery, 13% ($n = 9$) took part only in the beginning or in the end, and only 9% did not attend delivery. During the course of delivery 55% ($n = 38$) felt very confident, 33% ($n = 23$) confident and 10% ($n = 4$) felt sort of unassured; only one father reported to have been very unassured. 61 of the mothers answered the question on their evaluation of the participation of their husbands: all of them gave positive answers, 97% ($n = 59$) thought their husband's participation as being 'very supportive'; in no case was this characterized as unpleasant or bothering.

In most of the cases (80%) fathers had a first contact with the child straight after birth. Some fathers had the opportunity to cut the umbilical cord and described this as a great experience. The duration of this first father–child contact varied between 1 and 150 min according to the form of contact and medical particularities of delivery.

Fathers described their first encounter with the child differently, given emotional categories. As to the two categories, significant differences between the two groups were found. Prepared fathers felt more strongly 'attracted to the child' and more 'moved'. Further, significantly, more prepared than unprepared fathers engaged themselves in nappy changing or bottle feeding while in the hospital.

The first weeks at home

The main results from the questionnaire on the first weeks were as follows. Although within the whole sample the greater part of total babycare was done by the mothers, 91% of the fathers ($n=63$) took part in babycare in varying degrees; only 9% ($n=6$) did not engage themselves in babycare at all.

In the prepared group the majority of fathers frequently or always took part in babycare and care-giving, 39% ($n=14$) seldom, and 8% ($n=3$) not at all. In the unprepared group no father took over babycare totally, 33% ($n=9$) took part frequently, 56% ($n=15$) sometimes and 11% ($n=3$) never. Although a general difference for the two groups could not be proved in terms of inferential statistics, one significant difference was found for the answer on the question 'What do you enjoy most while being with your baby?' Prepared fathers pointed to proximal contacts such as bathing, playing, cuddling, etc. significantly more often.

With regard to the actual burden as experienced by the fathers within the first weeks after birth no significant group difference was found. The majority of prepared as well as unprepared fathers experienced a stronger burden. The question on the possible cause for this additional burden was answered by 26 prepared and 21 unprepared fathers. The prepared fathers referred to babycare and care-giving significantly more often whereas unprepared fathers regarded non-familial responsibilities as burdensome.

Care-giving and babycare

The comparison of the two groups of fathers as to the daily routine in babycare and care-giving was based on the questionnaire for the social context. The results showed that prepared fathers changed nappies and took over the 'going-to-bed ceremony' in the evening significantly more often than unprepared fathers. Furthermore, there was more of a tendency, among the prepared fathers, in the area of bodily contact such as carrying, helping to burp, etc.

With regard to special care giving functions we found two statistically significant group differences: prepared fathers carried their child in a baby sling on their body more often than unprepared fathers. Whereas in the prepared group 11 fathers (38%) reported to carry the baby on their body, this was the case only sometimes with one unprepared father. Furthermore, prepared fathers took their babies in the pram for a walk significantly more often than unprepared fathers.

Results from the laboratory situation under quasi-experimental conditions

Analysis of father's behavior

In the *quantitative analysis* of the video tapes the behaviors of the fathers were registered in intervals of 10 seconds each, and were assigned to 11 fixed behavior categories. Four of these categories (eye contact, restriction, modeling, no stimulation) have only been registered seldom or not at all; they are therefore not described in the following. The remaining six categories can be distinguished as proximal and distal behavior. In both the settings distal behavior of father occurred more often. By far the most frequent form of interaction was vocalization, i.e. speaking to the child, singing or imitation of the baby's vocalization.

The group comparison between prepared and unprepared fathers with children in the 3rd month did not lead to significant differences in regard to the first setting (free play). However, in two behavior categories the analysis of the second setting (face-to-face interaction) yielded significant differences: prepared fathers showed more 'whole body movements' in dealing with the child, unprepared fathers more often only touched the child's body (see Tables 3 and 4).

In the second part of the study with children 9 months old, distal

Table 3 Comparison of fathers' behavior in 'free play' with the infant aged 3 months (quantitative evaluation)

	Group medians		
	Unprepared	Prepared	U
Distal			
mimic	39.0	29.0	56.0
vocalization	85.0	88.5	68.5
showing	44.0	40.0	64.5
Proximal			
touch	46.5	35.0	53.5
cuddling	0.0	1.5	67.5
whole body movement	18.5	31.5	57.0
Care	0	3	49
Eye contact	—	—	—
Modeling	—	—	—
Restriction	—	—	—
No stimulation	—	—	—

Table 4 Comparison of fathers' behavior in the 'face-to-face interaction' with the infant aged 3 months (quantitative evaluation)

	Group medians		
	Unprepared	Prepared	U
Distal			
mimic	62	66	69.5
vocalization	100	94	55.0
showing	0	0	60.0
Proximal			
touch	68.5	12	24.0*
cuddling	0	0	57.5
whole body movement	20.5	44	26.5*
Care	0	0	64
Eye contact	—	—	—
Modeling	—	—	—
Restriction	—	—	—
No stimulation	—	—	—

* significant difference ($\alpha = 0.05$)

behavior of fathers also occurred more frequently. The behavioral categories 'showing', 'eye contact' and 'vocalization' are by far the preferred forms of interaction. The proximal behavior 'touch' (= touching single parts of the body) and 'whole body movements' appeared more often than 'cuddling'.

The comparison of the two groups of prepared and unprepared fathers did not, however, yield significant differences.

The *qualitative analysis* of both of the settings yielded that fathers showed, in general, a positive behavior as characterized through middle or even high scores on all rating scales. The results of the group comparison are given in Table 5.

In the infants' 3rd month of life in the first setting (free play) a tendency appeared that prepared fathers had higher means than unprepared fathers. However, only in the scale 'empathy' a significant difference could be gained on the 10% level only.

Similarly, in the second setting (face-to-face interaction) the group of prepared fathers reached higher means than the unprepared group. This difference was significant on the scale 'emotional warmth'.

By and large, the analysis of the first laboratory study with children in their 3rd month resulted in the following significant differences for the two

Table 5 Comparison of the distribution of the groups of prepared and unprepared fathers with children in their 3rd month

Rating scale	Group U median	Group P median	U
First setting (free play)			
Emotional warmth	3.8	4.4	47.0
Empathy	3.8	4.5	48.5*
Quality of stimulation	3.0	4.0	50.0
Assuredness and confidence	3.9	4.9	60.0
Second setting (face-to-face interaction)			
Emotional warmth	3.0	4.3	26.0†
Assuredness and confidence	4.1	4.5	44.0

* significant on the 10% level; † significant on the 5% level

groups of fathers: prepared fathers showed whole body movements more frequently, whereas unprepared fathers only touched the child. Prepared fathers also produced more emotional warmth and a stronger empathy.

In analyzing the data from the second laboratory study with children 9 months old the behavior of prepared fathers in comparison with unprepared fathers was rated higher on all scales (see Table 6). However, the group differences were lower than in the first laboratory study. The statistical analysis only yielded a significant difference on the 10% level in regard to the stronger empathy of prepared fathers.

Table 6 Comparison of the distributions of unprepared and prepared fathers with their children 9 months old in the first setting (free play)

Rating scale	Group U median	Group P median	U
Emotional warmth	3.1	4.0	38.5
Empathy	3.4	4.2	35.0*
Quality of stimulation	3.3	3.4	56.5

* significant on the 10% level

Analysis of the children's behavior

As to child behavior in the first laboratory study with 3-month-old infants statistically significant differences were not found (see Table 7).

Table 7 Comparison of child behavior at the age of 3 months with unprepared and prepared fathers

Rating scale	Group U median	Group P median	U
First setting (free play)			
Cheerfulness	3.9	3.6	61.0
Quality of vocalization	3.2	3.1	52.0
Responsivity	4.1	3.3	58.0
Second setting (face-to-face interaction)			
Cheerfulness	2.0	2.5	56.0
Quality of vocalization	3.0	3.0	59.5
Responsivity	1.3	1.3	67.0

However, the qualitative as well as quantitative analysis of the data from the second study revealed significant differences (see Table 8). In the quantitative analysis we registered twice as many negative vocalizations of children with unprepared fathers compared with prepared fathers. The qualitative evaluation of the child behavior in the first setting (free play) led to the result that children with prepared fathers were rated higher on the scales 'quality of vocalization' and 'responsivity'. The raters also reported these children to be more cheerful, but this difference was significant just above the 10% level. In the third setting (decision situation), children of prepared fathers had higher scores too, a significant difference was only proven on the 10% level for the scale 'cheerfulness'.

Table 8 Comparison of child behavior at the age of 9 months with unprepared and prepared fathers

Rating scale	Group U median	Group P median	U
Setting 1 (free play)			
Cheerfulness	3.3	4.1	38.0*
Quality of vocalization	3.1	4.0	24.0†
Responsivity	2.9	4.2	23.5†
Setting 3 (decision situation)			
Cheerfulness	2.2	3.9	33.0*
Quality of vocalization	1.85	4.2	36.5

* significant on the 10% level; † significant on the 5% level

The analysis of the decision situation led to the following picture. Within the group of prepared fathers eight out of 16 children, exactly half, directly approached the mother, another child showed such behavior as a tendency; five children could not decide, one tended to the father, and one unambiguously crawled to the father. In the unprepared group three out of eight children approached the mother, one tended to do so, three could not decide, and one child showed a slight tendency towards the father; however, none decided unambiguously for the father.

All in all, approximately half of the children in both groups decided to approach the mother while the others did not show a clear decision or had a tendency for the father. It was not possible to differentiate clearly the two groups of prepared and unprepared fathers on the basis of the given sample.

The analysis of the baby diary — which cannot be discussed here in detail — showed some important differences, especially in regard to the social behavior. For instance, children with prepared fathers smiled at their father and/or mother significantly more often.

DISCUSSION

Experience of birth and first contact with the newborn baby

In this study, 91% of the fathers have been present at birth. The growing number of fathers participating in delivery reflects a social trend which has been observed not only in the United States, but also in European countries in recent years (see Nickel and Köcher, 1986a,b). Parents regard this shared experience as of positive emotional value. This participation in no case had the effect of a 'birth shock' on the part of the father, the overwhelming majority of fathers having been confident. With no exceptions, mothers reported the participation of their husbands to have been supportive.

Comparing prepared and unprepared fathers, we found an important difference in their description of experience at their first sight of the child. Prepared fathers reported to be 'emotionally moved' and 'attracted to the child' significantly more often. Greenberg and Morris (1974) also point to such an emotional effect of the birth experience for fathers, which they describe as 'engrossment'. It is evident that prepared fathers are more eager to get emotionally involved and to accept feelings which by custom are labeled as non-masculine. In this respect, such variables as outlined by Parke (1978, 1979, 1980) in the cognitive model for preparation for parenthood seem to be relevant.

The socialization function of the father

Although in almost all families in this study the mother mainly cares for the baby, as many as 91% of the fathers participated in care-giving and babycare. This markedly contrasts with results of an earlier American study by Kotelchuk (1976), with 43% of fathers reporting never having changed a nappy. These divergent results not only reflect specific cultural but also generational differences (cf. Josselyn, 1965; Field et al., 1981).

In comparing the two groups of fathers, a strong tendency towards more engagement in babycare was found for the prepared fathers. Furthermore, the results showed that prepared fathers take over such activities, which previously have been looked upon as feminine activities (e.g. carrying the baby on the body, cuddling, singing a lullaby, etc.). Prepared fathers, more often than the unprepared, reported that they enjoyed these forms of 'proximal contact' in dealing with the child. Assuming that, for the most part, the interaction with the infant develops within a daily routine, in babycare this result can be interpreted in the way that an early participation of the father in this area of babycare positively influences bodily relations in general.

The interactive behavior of fathers

The results from the video-taped observations in standardized laboratory conditions showed that prepared and unprepared fathers differ especially in face-to-face interaction with the child. Prepared fathers prefer proximal behavior such as whole body movements, and this seems to be a sign for a more assured and intimate contact in dealing with the infant. Besides this, already in the first study with the 3-month-old infants prepared fathers interacted more empathetic and cheerfully, and this is still a tendency with the 9-month-old children. Furthermore, significant differences in child behavior were found at this second stage of the study. Children with prepared fathers react more responsively than children with unprepared fathers, they utter only half as many negative vocalizations and their general quality in vocalization is better. These results seem to be important because they confirm that already within the first year of life the behavior of fathers begins to mould child behavior. Within this we could point to a tendency of important differences in the area of social behavior with an advantage for children with prepared fathers.

CONCLUSIONS

Altogether the conclusion seems to be justified that the participation of an expectant father in babycare prenatal classes positively influences his later dealing with the infant and promotes child development. However, the question remains to what extent such results are influenced by other factors apart from attending prenatal classes. For instance, the preliminary motivation of fathers within the two groups might have been different. An evaluation of such factors was considered at the beginning of our study but it was not possible to include them because of the many practical difficulties. However, there are some clues for a higher preliminary motivation of prepared fathers such as their stronger interest in more related information and more participation in various forms of preparatory classes and lectures. If one takes into account that in their interactive behavior, the unprepared fathers came closer to the prepared fathers' responses this could be regarded as supporting the assumption that the different behaviors of the two groups might be caused by different learned experiences. Whereas prepared fathers had already learned such experiences before the birth of their child, the unprepared fathers had to gradually acquire the respective skills in dealing with the infant.

Although positive influences have been confirmed in this study, these considerations lead to the question whether prenatal classes for babycare are really the optimal form for preparation of fathers, or whether an additional training program for expectant parents should be considered. Such a program should go beyond ordinary babycare classes and should incorporate consequences of recent psychological research on the development of children in the first year of life so as to present a better preparation for expectant parents. A first concept for such a psychologically oriented training program has already been developed within this study. It was, however, only possible to conduct it within a small group — the experiences and the feedback from the parents are nevertheless very stimulating. In the meantime, Auerbach et al. (1985) have developed a similar training program with mothers in Israel for how to deal with a newborn baby, although only with a cognitive orientation. Perhaps one should pay special attention to attitude components. Recent observations in parent–child playgroups (see Köcher and Nickel, 1985) refer to the fact that fathers have to overcome high emotional barriers in their attitudes towards care-giving functions. Because of this, they need early help, which should be considered as a part of prenatal classes. Developing and evaluating such adequate preparatory training programs for mastering the critical event of the birth of the first child open up a new area for an intervention-oriented prenatal developmental psychology, an area of research still not worked on to a great extent but with high practical relevance.

ACKNOWLEDGEMENTS

This research project was subsidized by the Minsterium für Wissenschaft und Forschung des Landes Nordrhein-Westfalen and was conducted at the Institut für Entwicklungs- und Sozialpsychologie der Universität Düsseldorf with the author as head and Dr Jutta Bartoszyk and Dipl.-Päd. Hiltrud Wenzel as cooperators.

10

Prenatal problems of future fathers

I. Krymko-Bleton

The birth of a child transforms the pair of lovers who conceived him into parents. Confronted by this change in roles, the new mother and father are obliged to assume their altered identities. Whereas the mother has been prepared physically for the change by 9 months of pregnancy, during which she has experienced the gradual transformation of her body, the father's preparation has been purely psychological. He has witnessed the change from the outside, and has spent the pregnancy in a state of expectation. In one study according to one future father, who often came back to the subject, 'She's been carrying the baby for 9 months now – and I've spent the last 9 months waiting.' Another father told us that 'It took 9 months for the baby to be born. And I had 9 months to "think" him into existence.'

While the above-quoted fathers spent their partner's pregnancy preparing themselves for the birth, one should not conclude that future fathers are able to form an accurate mental image of the baby carried by their spouse. Such representations remain as inaccessible to them as the physical sensations linked to the presence of the fetus in the mother's womb. Research conducted among expectant fathers has shown that, as a rule, they begin to form a mental image of the child only once the pregnancy has become highly visible, for example, at the moment when they can feel the fetus move in their partner's womb or following an ultrasound examination which has enabled them to perceive the baby 'directly'. If one excludes the latter situation, one finds that the greatest number of fathers imagine the future being as a child old enough to take part in activities, rather than as a newborn. As one father told us, 'My wife was very active, very thoughtful (of the future child) – she spent a good deal of time arranging the apartment, decorating. She bought a lot of plants, and prepared for E's birth. She got everything ready. I remember her showing me some toys, and I hadn't really grasped that we were going to have a baby. She bought baby clothes. I still didn't realize the full significance.'

Nevertheless, the frequency of psychosomatic symptoms among expectant fathers (increasingly referred to as the 'couvade' syndrome[1]) is proof of the subconscious participation of men in their wives' pregnancies. Among the signs of the couvade syndrome, which disappear as soon as or soon after the subject's wife gives birth, one finds minor problems such as digestive difficulties, weight gains, dental problems and swellings of various sorts – inflamed tonsils, aerophagia and even sties on the eyelids.

Men have always been fascinated by maternity, the capacity at once marvelous and terrifying of the female body to give birth. The awakening of the timless 'mother' image, and the ambivalent feelings engendered by it, are the source of various prenatal problems among expectant fathers. I will be dealing with certain aspects of this phenomenon in the course of this paper.

To illustrate my findings, I will be quoting answers given by recent fathers to students carrying out a study organized by the Laboratoire de recherches sur la paternité, at the Université du Québec à Montrèal, directed by myself. The subjects of the study were normal, socially well-adapted young men who had accompanied their spouses to prenatal classes, and had subsequently been present at the birth.

When a couple is transformed into a family by the appearance of a child, the mother and baby are seen as the principal protagonists. The role of the third person in question is, in our culture, given little attention despite the fact that the progenitive function constitutes the central conflict of the male adult.

The birth of a child situates men within the history of their families just as it does women. From sons of their fathers, they are transformed into fathers of their own children. Hence, paternity definitively alters a man's relationship with his father. This fact is well-known. It is very common for young men, upon the birth of a child, to think of themselves in relation to their fathers, indicating that they wish to be as good to their children as their fathers were to them, or, to the contrary, vowing to provide their children with everything their fathers never gave them. Thus, a man's reaction to paternity is intimately linked to how he identifies with his father.

A rather more controversial subject is the importance, for the expectant father, of precocious memories, archaic images related to his relationship with his mother. The sight of his partner's distended stomach awakens fantasies as to the contents of the womb.

In reply to questions about their reactions to the transformation of their wives' bodies during pregnancy, the subjects of our research answered first of all in terms of beauty, stating that, despite their partners' worries about their figures, they found them attractive. However, beneath a certain air of neutrality lay other incipient emotions. One future father revealed the ambiguity of his feelings to us in rather striking terms: 'It's beautiful, but awfully big.' Another father stated, 'A bit of a paunch is attractive — but by 9 months it's best to keep it covered. When a pregnant woman passes by in the street, there's nothing more beautiful, it's beautiful to see her move — but I still didn't particularly like seeing my wife naked at 9 months ...' Other fathers informed us that their wife's pregnancy had enabled them to master their emotions, to get over their embarrassment when confronted by pregnant women — or even to talk to them! 'Now, from an aesthetic point of view, I find them attractive. It's not that I didn't find them beautiful before, they just didn't attract me. I was even more inclined to talk to a woman who wasn't pregnant than to one who was.'

Certain fathers spoke to us of the decrease in their sexual desire during their partner's pregnancy: 'Towards the end, she had the body of a pregnant woman. Quite honestly, I found that less ... I was more loving than ever, but less attracted sexually (...) The more she took on her pregnant-woman personality, the more tender I became. But I was less physically attracted.' We thus found that the mother image, with its related taboo, overshadows the image of the woman as lover.

Men also indicated that they felt threatened by the content of their partner's womb. One father described the evolution of his sexual desire as follows: 'There were several phases. The first 3 months, I saw strictly nothing; her pregnancy didn't change much. After 4 or 5 months, when I touched her stomach ... I didn't really want to touch it too much ... I was afraid my weight would hurt the baby. I didn't consider it immoral but ... I was ill at ease. At 7 or 8 months it was really too big! ... It was as if I had become somewhat "platonic" towards her — there was always a witness present.'

Thus, once the pregnancy becomes visible, men often have the impression that they will harm the fetus if they make love to their partner, or find themselves under the sway of the fantasy whereby the fetus is seen as a third party watching the couple from within the mother's womb and capable even of causing them harm.

The pregnant woman's protuberant shape reawakens her spouse's infantile impression of maternal power: the mother's ability not only to create life, but to keep it enclosed within her body. The promise of life is thus coupled with a sense of danger and death.

Feelings of helplessness in the face of this maternal power may generate aggression and hatred. The example of a 4-year-old boy whose mother was expecting a baby serves to illustrate this phenomenon. The little boy knew that his mother was pregnant, that there was 'a baby in her stomach'. When the pregnancy became clearly visible, the child, who was normally very affectionate, became highly aggressive towards her, attacking her both verbally and physically. Finally, worried by this change in their son's character, the parents realized that the little boy thought that his mother, like a wicked witch, was holding the baby prisoner in her stomach. He had identified closely with the fetus. Following a suitable explanation, the situation returned to normal. The little boy once again became affectionate towards his mother while awaiting the birth of his sibling. One can only speculate as to how many adults experience subconscious fantasies similar to the confused little boy's conscious belief.

Worries as to the state of the fetus may be seen as indicative of the destructive powers attributed to the mother's womb, or, at least, as an indication of uncertainty with regard to the environment enclosing the developing baby. 'You're worried before (the birth). You're always scared of having a crippled or deformed baby ...' explained one father. Others indicated that, following their child's birth, they had immediately verified whether or not the newborn had all four limbs, or was deformed. One father was struck by the fact that, following the birth, '(the baby) was so alive!'

For fathers, childbirth is a critical period. The culminating moment, for those who witness it, is the actual delivery of the baby. During the delivery, the notions of danger and death (of the child, of the mother – and also of the father) are ever present.

The father's identification with the baby is a particular cause of anxiety and of fear for corporal well-being. The child passes from the fetal state to that of a newborn baby 'at its own risk'. During this perilous transition period, the father witnessing the delivery remains powerless, unable to assist the newborn through the adventure. Identifying with the baby, he relives his own birth. 'It was as if', recounted one father, 'he (the baby) had just gone through an experience requiring a tremendous physical effort, account taken of his size and weight.'

Accordingly, one should not be surprised that men often insist that their wives endure their labor pains as long as possible, or become angry with the delivery team. As one father stated, 'I wasn't at all disturbed by my wife's suffering. I was only afraid she wouldn't tough it through.' Another father, who had counted on an 'all-natural' birth for his child, told us,

PRENATAL PROBLEMS OF FUTURE FATHERS

'When they decided to give her an epidural, I found it a bit too soon; I would have waited, even if it was a bit hard for her ... I would have waited until she found it harder to take – I know my wife.' Yet another continued: 'If the doctors arrive and find your wife can't take it any more ... the husband can tell them he thinks she's capable. I encouraged my wife to continue without anesthetics. I said to her, "It's coming, don't give up, it's on the way!"'

With the popularization of psychoanalytical theories, much discussion has been devoted to the envy women supposedly feel with regard to men's bodies and functions. However, uptil now, very little has been said about male envy of the female body and functions. Accordingly, we are still far from recognizing the full extent of the man's deep-seated identification with the mother during the process of becoming a father.

Already manifest during the pregnancy, the future father's identification with his spouse – highly encouraged during prenatal classes – is also a source of anxiety. According to one father, who quickly corrected himself, 'They called me at six o'clock and then I gave birth ... I mean, I went to the delivery room ...' Another father told us, 'We were at 6–8 centimeters in one hour.' A third subject stated, 'I'd say we had a good delivery.' A father who described the postnatal bath he gave his newborn daughter described the experience as follows: 'Then the doctor cut the cord and gave her to me. I dipped her in a bath heated to maternal temperature.' The latter father, who subsequently spent a good deal of time caring for his daughter, regretted the fact that his wife had not breast-fed her longer. He spoke in the following terms of his own birth: 'I know that, personally, I had an atrocious birth. And, what's more, I wasn't breast-fed.' Was the subconscious memory of his birth so traumatic, and that of his mother so terrible, that he fantasized that he himself had given birth? One wonders whether this father was subconsciously hoping to recuperate something of his own birth when he spoke of the nutritive virtues of the placenta. First of all, he hesitated to speak openly about the fantasy of eating the after-birth, telling us that he had heard that 'there are women who eat it'. He went on to say, 'I'm rather disdainful of blood and cuts. We aren't used to it, we live in such an antiseptic society (...) Then I saw that it was in a disinfected basin. My first reaction was that it seemed ... that it wasn't so ...' Then his defensive reflexes gave way: 'You know, fried or dipped in butter it must be better, but, as it is, I found the idea of eating it a bit disgusting ... But I was tempted. I saw it and said to myself, "Why not eat it if it's recommended, seeing there are supposedly lots of good, nutritive things in it?"'

The birth of a child causes the father to regress towards his earliest relations with his mother. At the same time, by situating him in the order of generations, it directs his attention to the other end of the temporal axis, causing him to realize that he is mortal, and that he has just taken a large step in the fatal direction. Men affirm that paternity renders them more responsible, less carefree.

The childbirth process, seen from the man's point of view, reactivates the father's repressed conflicts. He finds himself caught up in a psychological situation involving regression, and infantile maternal identification. His very identity is menaced. The resolution of this crisis, which determines the man's relationship with his wife and child, depends not only on his level of maturity and the manner in which he has assimilated the earlier stages of his psychological development involving identification with male and female figures, but also the reference base and support provided to him by society.

At present, men are encouraged to give free expression to the feminine side of their personality. They are encouraged to look after their newborn children, invited into the delivery room, asked to accompany their wives to prenatal classes. It seems to me that little – if any – thought is given upon such occasions to the potentially conflictual aspect of this relatively new role for fathers. Recognition of possible psychological conflicts, and, to an even greater degree, points of reference for expressing such problems, are sorely lacking.

The customs and rituals of certain so-called primitive societies appear strange to us – for example, the 'couvade', which, although considered by such cultures as socially acceptable, is now seen as psychopathic behavior in the west. Nevertheless, we have not yet found any suitable mechanism to replace such customs.

This phenomenon seems to me to have a bearing on the present-day crisis of the family unit, which has become one of the major preoccupations of the various agencies dealing with child-care problems. In the province of Québec, for example, the massive growth in the number of one-parent families consisting of mothers and their children may be seen as a sign of the family crisis, which may be attributed, in part, to the problems encountered by men in assuming their role vis-à-vis their children.

The prenatal problems of future fathers, linked closely to their identification with the fetus carried by their partners and to their earliest relations with their own mothers, may thus be seen to have certain large-scale social repercussions. Further research is essential if we are to fully understand the psychological process of becoming a father.

---

[1] *Editor's note:* couvade, French from *couver*, 'to brood, to hatch'. The custom among many so-called primitive societies wherein the father takes to bed as if for (preparing himself for) childbearing while the mother is in labor.

Part 4: Research on behavioral development

11

The relationship between maternal emotionality during pregnancy and the behavioral development of the fetus and neonatus

B.R.H. Van den Bergh*

INTRODUCTION

Scientific advances in the area of embryology, teratology, genetics and the developing sciences clearly show us the vulnerability of the human embryo and fetus; the human being is subject to environmental influences which may either contribute or interfere with its development from the moment of conception.

During the last decades psychologists have taken part in the search for prenatal developmental factors which threaten the developmental integrity of the offspring. The belief that the emotional state of the pregnant woman may affect the child she carries has become the proper subject of scientific inquiry. Specifically, it has been hypothesized that increased levels of negative emotionality in the pregnant woman may produce pregnancy and birth complications as well as developmental irregularities in the newborn (Carlson and LaBarba, 1979, pp 343–4).

The literature concerning the relationship between maternal emotion-

*Research Assistant at the National Fund for Scientific Research (Belgium).

ality and reproductive outcome is extensive, diverse and fragmented. (For a review see for example Barrett, 1982; Brown, 1964; Carlson and LaBarba, 1978; Chalmers, 1984; Farber et al., 1981; Ferreira, 1965; McDonald, 1968; Newton, 1985; Rizzardo et al., 1985; Van den Bergh, 1983.) Anxiety seems to be the emotional factor most often studied and implicated in reproductive complications. In Figure 1 we have tried to integrate the literature concerning the implications of maternal anxiety during pregnancy upon the process and product of reproduction, using a self-constructed heuristic model. Built on a time variable and a subject variable, this model includes six conditions which represent the successive conditions of mother and child during the pre-, peri- and postnatal period. There seems to be no single or critical etiological factor of anxiety during pregnancy. Maternal anxiety can exert an influence in several ways; it can either directly influence one of the conditions (for example anxious women tend to have more pregnancy complications) or modify the relationship(s) between two or more conditions (for example: the occurrence of hyperemesis gravidarum may cause alimentary derangements in the fetus which can interfere with the food supply and development of the fetus). The full lines in Figure 1 represent relationships between one or more conditions that were established in one or more studies; the dotted lines represent possible relationships that are not yet scientifically explored.

The results of the studies have to be interpreted very cautiously because many of them show methodological shortcomings. Among these shortcomings are failure to specify sample characteristics, insufficient controls, conclusions based on retrospectively obtained data, inadequate assessment of independent and dependent variables, inadequate use of statistical methods and the problem of causation versus correlation.

While the results of the methodologically most acceptable studies do support the notion of an overall relationship between maternal emotionality and reproductive outcome, little can be said about the specific nature of this relationship. In our opinion, this lack of more specific findings can be explained, at least partially, by the fact that some fundamental questions regarding the relationship between maternal emotionality during pregnancy and reproductive outcome have not been scientifically explored, namely:

(1) Can the influence of maternal emotionality upon the fetus be established in the prenatal period? (Or can we detect some parameters, e.g. fetal behavior states, fetal activity, which are sensitive to the influence of maternal emotionality during pregnancy?)

(2) Is the prenatal influence reflected in the postnatal behavior of the child? (Or can we find significant correlations between prenatal

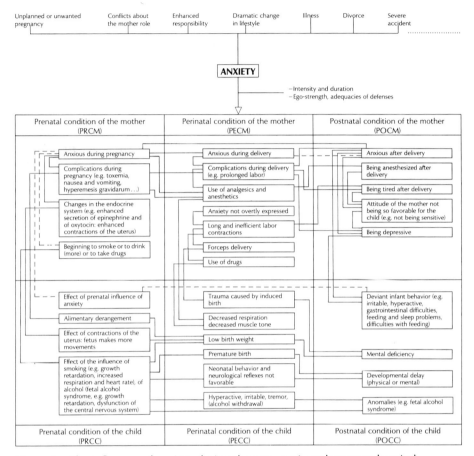

Figure 1 The influence of anxiety during the pre-, peri- and postnatal period.
Code: ──── established relationship; ---- possible relationship (not yet established)

parameters on the one hand and neo- and postnatal parameters, e.g. neonatal neurological examination, behavioral states, feeding behavior, mother–child interaction, on the other hand?)

Recently we have been able to explore these problems because the introduction of the ultrasound techniques (particularly of the real-time ultrasound) have made it possible to study the behavior of the fetus in its intrauterine surroundings. Now valid measures of maternal emotionality and adequate neonatal and postnatal behavioral assessment scales are available. The two problems we just mentioned are the leading questions of the research project we are now engaged in at the Department of Obstetrics and Gynecology and the Department of Pediatrics and Neonatology at the University Hospital of Leuven. Concerning the first question we have already conducted a study at the University Hospital of Groningen. It was a controlled study on the effect of acute (induced) maternal emotions on fetal behavior. I will present this study in the first part of my paper, while in the second part I will present my current follow-up study, in which we want to study the relationship between more chronic maternal emotional conditions and the behavioral development of fetus and neonatus.

STUDY 1: THE EFFECT OF (INDUCED) MATERNAL EMOTIONS ON FETAL BEHAVIOR (A CONTROLLED STUDY)

Regarding the relationship between prenatal emotional stress and fetal behavior we have only found some case reports in the literature, indicating that mothers under severe emotional stress tend to have a hyperactive fetus (Ianniruberto and Tajani, 1981; Sontag, 1941; Whitehead (1867) as mentioned by Ferreira, 1965 and by Montagu, 1962). It has also been suggested that less severe maternal emotional conditions can affect fetal behavior (e.g. Sontag, 1969; Zimmer, 1982).

As we found no controlled study on this subject we ran this study to investigate (a) whether induced maternal emotions have an effect on fetal behavior and (b) whether there exists a relationship between maternal base level anxiety and fetal behavior. Fetal behavior was recorded by real-time ultrasound and external cardiography. Emotions were induced by showing a film of normal delivery. Anxiety was measured with the State-Trait Anxiety Inventory (STAI, Spielberger et al., 1970), other emotions with an ad hoc questionnaire. A preliminary study was undertaken to examine whether or not the film induced emotions in pregnant women. The results of this study, conducted on a sample of 66 pregnant women indicated that the film proved effective as an emotion-inducing stimulus.

Method

Subjects

Ten healthy women with durations of pregnancy between 36 and 40 weeks volunteered to participate in this study. None of the women had seen the film before. Mothers' ages ranged from 19 years to 31 years 5 months (mean 26 years 6 months). Most of the women (seven out of ten) were primiparous. From the medical records it was concluded that a fairly normal group of mothers has been recruited and that the children on whom the recordings were made turned out to be healthy babies.

Design

All recordings were made between 2.00 and 5.00 p.m. and had a duration of 120 minutes. The film (26′) was shown during the second half hour on the experimental day. In all women a standardized 2-hour control period was made. Control and experimental day fell on two successive days in a counterbalanced order. This means that two sequences were run: experimental session followed by control session (sequence 1) and control session followed by experimental session (sequence 2). The women were randomly allocated to either sequence. Each session was divided in four half hour periods. Figure 2 summarizes the experimental design used in this study.

Maternal emotionality measures

In order to examine the emotional state of the mother the State-Trait Anxiety Inventory (STAI; Spielberger et al., 1970) was administered before and after the film. This standardized questionnaire differentiates between an anxiety state (that reflects current tension or apprehension and is fluctuating) and an anxiety trait (of a characterological nature, a disposition, anxiety proneness). On the experimental day a 10-item ad hoc questionnaire and a semistructured interview regarding feelings during the film were administered.

Fetal behavioral measures

Since the introduction of real-time ultrasound it has been possible to visualize the fetus and to study fetal motor patterns in a standardized way. In our study fetal general movements were used to obtain one measure of fetal behavior. These general movements were defined by de Vries *et al.* (1982) as 'movements of the whole body in which no distinctive

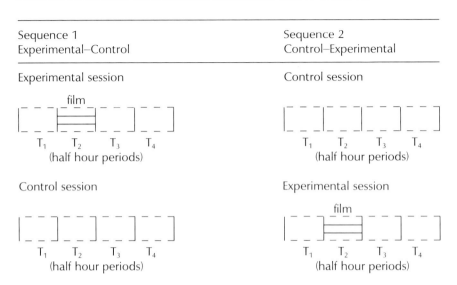

Figure 2 Experimental design of the study. $n = 5$ for each sequence

patterning or sequencing of the body parts can be recognized'. The percentage of time that general movements are present during observation time is named fetal activity A.

Fetal behavioral states were used as a second measure of fetal behavior. Put bluntly, these states refer to different patterns of rest and activity in the human fetus. Although behavioral states have an important meaning for the assessment of the maturation and integrity of the fetal nervous system, they were used just as a measure of fetal behavior in this study. Fetal behavioral states were identified according to the criteria as defined by Nijhuis et al. (1982). They defined four behavioral states in the fetus, in terms of three variables: heart rate, eye movements and body movements. In order to accept the presence of states, certain criteria with regard to these variables have to be fulfilled (see Study 2). Put in a somewhat oversimplified way, a state of 'deep sleep' (Nijhuis et al., 1F), and a state of 'REM sleep' (Nijhuis et al., 1F–2F) were distinguished in our study. In order to study the effect of induced maternal emotions on fetal behavioral states we tried to find out if, during the observation time, the percentage of time that each of the two states occurred was different on the experimental day and on the control day.

It has been experimentally verified that the responses to different stimuli in various behavioral states may be different (Visser, 1983). Till now the data seem to indicate that natural stimuli are incapable of eliciting a response in the 'deep sleep' state but applied during 'REM sleep' state they produce responses of various magnitude (Timor-Tritsch, 1986). As the kind of emotions the film induced can be regarded as natural stimuli their effect should be the strongest in the state of 'REM sleep'. To measure this state-related effect we tried to find out if the percentage of time that general movements occurred during the state of 'REM sleep' were different on experimental and control days. This percentage of time was called fetal activity B.

To sum up then, three measures of fetal behavior were used:

(1) Fetal activity A, i.e. the percentage of time that general movements occurred during observation time.

(2) Fetal activity B, i.e. the percentage of time that general movements occurred during the state of 'REM sleep'.

(3) Fetal behavioral states, i.e. the percentage of time that the state of 'deep sleep' and the state of 'REM sleep' occurred during observation time.

Results (on fetal behavior) were analyzed in half hour periods. In order to have comparable time periods before (T_1), during (T_2) and after (T_3 and T_4) the film period, the results of the third and fourth half hour were summed and divided by 2.

Results

Induced maternal emotionality and base level anxiety

The difference between the state anxiety scores before and after the film was not significant ($t_{(9)} = 0.88$, $p > 0.05$, two tailed paired t-test). Only for a few women was anxiety the dominant feeling during the film. Direct observations of the women, as well as results from the questionnaire and the semistructured interview revealed that, on the whole, feelings other than anxiety (e.g. being emotionally touched) were dominant.

Fetal behavior

To answer our first question whether induced maternal emotions have an effect on fetal behavior, a 3 × 2 × 2 (Time × Condition × Sequence) analysis of variance (ANOVA) was performed on the data on fetal behavioral states and fetal activities A and B. If the film has an effect then the flow of fetal behavior over the three time periods considered, should be different in the experimental and the control conditions. Or somewhat technically, the ANOVA will reveal a significant Condition × Time Interaction.

For all three measures of fetal behavior the expected interaction between Time and Condition failed to emerge.

Results with regard to the second question (does there exist a relationship between maternal base level anxiety and fetal behavior?) were somewhat more encouraging. The state anxiety averaged across both measurement points (before and after the film) was used as a measure of base level anxiety on each day. These measures (two for each mother: one a day) were correlated with the three measures of fetal behavior for the corresponding day. A significant correlation was found between mean state anxiety and fetal activity A ($r_{(16)} = 0.49$, $p < 0.05$) and mean state anxiety and fetal activity B ($r_{(16)} = 0.57$, $p < 0.01$).

Discussion

The most striking result in this study is that the analysis of variance did not reveal a significant Condition × Time interaction for any of the three measures employed. From these results it is concluded that emotions, induced by a film of normal delivery, do not affect fetal behavior in the near-term fetus. Moreover, the fact that this interaction failed to emerge for fetal activity B indicates that there was no state-dependent effect of induced emotions.

With regard to our second question, however, a significant correlation was found between mean state anxiety and both measures of fetal activity. These results indicate that, irrespective of the emotions the film induced, the state anxiety level of the mother correlates with fetal activity.

Some cautious remarks are in order. From the correlational results we obtained we cannot make any statements in terms of causality, e.g. that maternal emotions have an effect on fetal activity. It is also possible that either fetal activity influences maternal emotions or that a third factor influences both. Clearly our knowledge about the underlying mechanism is insufficient.

Conclusion

From the results of our study we can conclude that maternal emotions induced by a film of normal delivery do not affect behavioral states or activity in the near-term fetus. However, there exists a significant relationship between maternal anxiety level and fetal activity. Both results seem to be important. The first question has important practical implications since films of delivery are increasingly used in pregnancy courses. The second result warrants researchers to take into account maternal anxiety levels when studying fetal motor behavior. In addition, it has important implications for the counselling of pregnant women who worry over complex medical registrations.

As this study was conducted on only ten women we need supporting evidence from other studies in order to make firm conclusions regarding the relationship between maternal emotions and fetal activity.

STUDY 2: THE RELATIONSHIP BETWEEN MATERNAL EMOTIONALITY DURING PREGNANCY AND THE BEHAVIORAL DEVELOPMENT OF FETUS AND NEONATUS – PROPOSAL OF A FOLLOW-UP STUDY

With regard to the fundamental questions stated in the introduction, some promising results have been obtained in our first study. While some caution is in order in view of the correlational nature of the findings, the data seem to indicate that fetal activity is a parameter that is sensitive to the influence of acute maternal emotions during pregnancy. In our second study, which is currently underway, we want to explore (1) whether there exist fetal behavioral parameters that are sensitive to the influence of more chronic maternal emotions during pregnancy, and (2) whether these fetal parameters correlate with neonatal behavioral parameters. To explore these questions a prospective longitudinal study has been started.

Subjects

The final sample will comprise 70 primiparous women, 18–30 years old and without obstetrical complications at the beginning of the study. The selection of the women for the experimental group (high levels of negative emotionality; $n = 35$) and the control group (low level of negative emotionality; $n = 35$) is normally conducted at 16–20 weeks of pregnancy and is based on combined state-trait anxiety scores.

Measures

Three types of data will be collected: maternal emotions, fetal behavior and neonatal evaluation of both mother and child.

Assessment of maternal emotionality

The maternal condition is measured at several times during pregnancy (16–20, 26–30, 36–40 weeks of pregnancy), with the use of psychological tests.

Anxiety scales: In addition to the State-Trait Anxiety Inventory (STAI), which just provides the overall level of anxiety, a Pregnancy Anxiety Scale (PAS) was constructed, which probes for specific worries in the third trimester of pregnancy. Building on earlier efforts (Blau et al., 1964; Kumar et al., 1984; Pleshette et al., 1956; Schaefer and Manheimer, 1960) and clinical experience, a 58 item scale was constructed. Results of a preliminary study on 38 pregnant women indicate that the scale has content validity, as judged by medical experts, as well as concurrent validity. A significant correlation was found between the PAS on the one hand and the state anxiety ($r_{(38)} = 0.68$, $p < 0.0001$) and trait anxiety ($r_{(38)} = 0.70$, $p < 0.0001$) on the other hand. Psychometric qualities of the scale will be tested on a larger sample.

Symptom Checklist: Furthermore a Symptom Checklist was used which provides a combined measure of general adaptational distress (GAD, Fagley, 1982) and psychosomatic complaints (pregnancy symptoms) (Luteyn, 1984; Kumar et al. 1984; Wolkind, 1974; Schaefer and Manheimer, 1960). This instrument showed a significant correlation with the state anxiety ($r_{(32)} = 0.64$, $p < 0.0001$), trait anxiety ($r_{(32)} = 0.49$, $p < 0.005$) and the PAS ($r_{(29)} = 0.619$, $p < 0.0005$).

Maternal–Fetal Attachment Scale: This 24 item checklist represents a Dutch version of a scale originally developed by Cranley (1981a). The instrument measures the construct of maternal–fetal attachment, which was defined by the author as the extent to which women engage in behaviors that represent an affiliation and interaction with the unborn baby. Preliminary analyses indicate that there was a significant negative correlation between the Maternal–Fetal Attachment scale and trait anxiety ($r_{(50)} = 0.29$, $p < 0.05$).

In short, the encouraging results of a preliminary study revealed that the set of measures employed yield converging results on mothers' emotional state, experience of pregnancy and related variables.

Assessment of fetal behavior

At 36–38 weeks of pregnancy fetal behavior is recorded with the use of ultrasound and external cardiography.

Fetal behavioral states: Behavioral states in the fetus have been defined in terms of three variables: heart rate, eye movements and body movements. In order to accept the presence of states, certain criteria with regard to these variables must be fulfilled:

(1) Particular conditions of these variables must recur in a specific, fixed combination.

(2) These associations must be temporally stable.
(3) The variables must change their properties simultaneously at the onset and end of a particular state epoch (Nijhuis et al., 1982).

The emergence of behavioral states in the fetus, normally occurring at 36–38 weeks of pregnancy, can be seen as a confirmation of the integrity of the fetal central nervous system.

With regard to our first question we want to investigate if maternal emotions alter the emergence and occurrence of fetal behavioral states.

Fetal motor and breathing patterns: These patterns also will be used as measures of fetal behavior.

Assessment in the neonatal period

Assessment of the child: To examine the relationship between fetal and neonatal behavioral parameters, the following neonatal assessments are planned:

A standardized neurological examination (Prechtl, 1977),

An observation of neonatal behavioral states (Prechtl and O'Brien, 1982),

An observation of feeding behavior to obtain a feeding score (Daniëls, 1985),

Parts of the Brazelton Neonatal Behavioral Assessment Scale (Brazelton, 1984).

Data on labor and delivery: Since different aspects of the labor and delivery can mediate the relationship between fetal and neonatal behavior, several data of labor and delivery will be gathered from the medical records (length of labor phases; use of anesthetics and analgesics; birth complications; Apgar scores; umbilical pH; sex, weight, length and head circumference of the baby).

Assessment of the mother: In an interview (Keller, 1985) the mother's experiences of labor and delivery will be explored. The STAI will be used again as a measure of anxiety. Several neonatal perception inventories (Daniëls, 1985) will be used to give an idea of how a mother feels about the different aspects of the baby's behavior (e.g. sleeping, feeding, crying and motor behavior).

Assessment of the mother–child interaction: The AMIS scale (Assessment of Mother and Infant Sensitivity Scale, AMIS, Price, 1983) which was developed in order to measure the quality of early mother–infant interaction in a feeding context within the first quarter-year postpartum, will be used to observe the mother–child interaction.

Conclusion

With this study we hope to answer the two fundamental questions outlined above and to clarify the specific nature of the relationship between maternal emotionality during pregnancy and reproductive outcome.

ACKNOWLEDGEMENTS

This paper presents parts of the author's doctoral dissertation under the supervision of Prof. A. Marcoen, to whom she is highly indebted. The assistance of P. De Boeck and R. Stroobant in data processing and L. Goossen's helpful comments on previous drafts are gratefully acknowledged. Special thanks go to E. Mulder, G. Poelman-Weesjes and D. Bekedam for their help in data collection and recording, and to G. Visser for his insightful suggestions.

12

Rhythmicity in parental stimulation of infants

L. Sanford Koester

ABSTRACT

Face-to-face interactions between care givers and infants represent an important context for infant development as well as opportunities for scientific observation of the early relationship. One of the many interesting features of these dyadic interactions is that of timing, particularly as it contributes to the reciprocity between partners. Other researchers have demonstrated the significance of the temporal patterns of the overall parent–infant dyad. In this study, the specific temporal patterns of the repetitive stimulating behaviors used frequently by parents have also been examined microanalytically. In 17 pairs, all examples of repeated stimulation by mothers to their 3-month-old babies were analyzed from brief, video-taped observations. The following questions were addressed in the present study:

(1) In what ways are the temporally-patterned stimuli used by mothers with their infants coordinated across multiple sensory modalities?

(2) What modifications or preferences are evident in maternal stimulation according to the behavioral signals of the infant?

(3) Is there evidence of prenatal/postnatal continuity in the rhythmic stimulation used spontaneously by mothers in interactions with their infants?

Results support the notion proposed by Papoušek and Papoušek (1982; 1987) that parental behaviors are well suited to support the behavioral organization and adaptation needs of the young infant. Parents alter their behaviors rapidly in conjunction with infant behaviors, and supplement their own vocalizations to the preverbal child with a rich repertoire of tactile, kinesthetic, vestibular and visual stimulation. However, the tempos of maternal stimulation documented in this study show little evidence of being related to or determined by rhythms which might be experienced prenatally, such as the maternal heart beat.

THE PARENT–INFANT INTERACTION SYSTEM

Much attention has been paid in recent years to issues of reciprocity and even synchrony between interacting partners such as those typically observed in infancy research (e.g. Brazelton *et al.*, 1974; Bullowa, 1973; Condon and Sander, 1974). Von Bertalanffy's (1968) general systems theory has helped to focus this attention on the impact which each member of the dyadic system has on the other. That is, an interaction proceeds in a continuously fluid manner, during which the 'changer' is also 'changed', as elaborated upon by Koester, Papoušek and Papoušek (1987). Application of microanalytic techniques to filmed observations of parent–infant interactions has yielded an impressive but cumbersome array of data bearing upon these issues; in an effort to simplify such data for interpretation, Bakeman and Brown (1977) proposed the notion of 'dialog' as a guiding metaphor for revealing the underlying structure of an interaction. One of the obvious advantages of such a metaphor is that it encompasses both vocal and non-vocal parameters, and yet allows one to examine the flow of behaviors over time, and the interconnections among various modalities.

TEMPORAL PATTERNS OF THE INTERACTION DIALOG

In any form of dialog, timing is of utmost importance; while not all behaviors emitted by each partner call for silence or a behavioral pause on the part of the other, a satisfactory exchange must include some turn-taking and some signalling of readiness for one's partner to 'take the floor' (Jaffe and Feldstein, 1970; Mayer and Tronick, 1985). Yet another aspect of timing, on a more micro level, is that of the temporal patterns inherent within each vocal or behavioral episode (e.g. the rhythms of speech, of a mother stroking her infant, of an infant kicking its feet, etc.). Just as melodic contours and vocal patterns may convey certain specific messages, so may these rhythmic features of an interaction signal the onset of a new behavior, efforts to soothe, playful opportunities, or reinforcement for a specific accomplishment. Therefore, in the present study we have analyzed all temporally patterned, repeated stimulation provided by mothers to their infants during a brief, video-taped, face-to-face interaction. The purpose was first, to document temporally patterned interventions spontaneously displayed by parents in all modalities (tactile, visual, kinesthetic, vestibular), and secondly, to compare these strategies with those suggested in the research literature as being most effective in situations such as soothing or eliciting infant attention.

PRENATAL/POSTNATAL RHYTHMIC CONTINUITIES?

Salk's (1962, 1973) assertion – that rhythms experienced prenatally (such as maternal heartbeat) are most appropriate for soothing the infant postnatally – has been referred to frequently but not yet adequately substantiated by further research. Ter Vrugt and Pederson (1973), for example, have noted that rhythms to which the fetus is exposed vary considerably in frequency, from a low of around 0.25 Hz (maternal breathing) to a high of more than 2 Hz (maternal walking and fetal heartbeat). Nevertheless, the notion of the maternal heartbeat as a pacesetter for later maternal behaviors continues to find popular appeal, perhaps because of the romantic association of the heart with expressions of affect such as love and attachment.

Investigating postnatal stimulation only, Ashton (1976) found certain commonalities between induced (simulated) and self-generated stimuli (infant sucking rate) in terms of their efficacy for calming the infant: one criterion was that of repetitiveness of the stimuli; the second criterion was a frequency of approximately 1 Hz (60 bpm, or slower than the 72 bpm average maternal heartbeat typically cited by Salk and others). It is of interest then, to examine spontaneously generated temporal patterns used by parents with their infants, and to compare them with those mentioned in the experimental literature as having some potential relationship to prenatal rhythms.

PARENTAL SUPPORT OF INFANT INTEGRATIVE COMPETENCE

The model of intuitive parenting developed by Papoušek and Papoušek (1978; 1982; 1987) provides a useful heuristic for approaching these questions. According to this view, parents incorporate many non-conscious behaviors into their daily interactions with their infants – behaviors which are strikingly similar to those espoused in the scientific literature as most effective in facilitating the growth and development of the young organism. That is, without conscious awareness or ability to articulate their own strategies and intentions, adults modify their vocal and non-vocal behaviors dramatically when interacting with an infant as compared to an older child or another adult. For example, parents regulate their visual distance with an infant, provide ample reinforcement for social reciprocity, modify their speech patterns and melodic contours, use an extraordinary amount of repetition, and structure their stimulation in ways which accentuate and enhance the learning capabilities of the infant partner. These adjustments occur so rapidly and frequently during face-to-face interactions that it is reasonable to assume that they cannot be the result of conscious, cognitive processes or of planned strategies; thus the term 'intuitive' is used to refer to the subtle parental behavior patterns which are observable uniquely in interactions with young infants.

With this conceptual framework in mind, the following questions were addressed in the present study:

(1) In what ways are the temporally-patterned stimuli used by mothers with their infants coordinated across sensory modalities?

(2) What modifications or preferences are evident in maternal stimulation according to the behavioral signals of the infant?

(3) Is there evidence of prenatal/postnatal continuity in the rhythmic stimulation used spontaneously by mothers in interactions with their infants?

METHODS

17 mothers and their 3-month-old infants were observed and video-taped during a face-to-face interaction in a laboratory setting. Mothers were given no special instructions other than to play with their infants, who were placed in an infant seat on a table in front of the mother's chair.

Stimulation by the mother was considered rhythmic if the same behavior occurred at least three times consecutively within one coherent behavior episode. The onset and offset times, number of 'beats' or occurrences of a given behavior within each episode, and the tempo (beats per second) were coded for each of the following maternal behaviors:

Tactile stimulation of baby: stroking; tapping/patting; tickling or finger games.

Kinesthetic stimulation of baby: shaking foot or hand; moving two limbs alternately or simultaneously.

Vestibular stimulation of baby: rocking infant seat in vertical plane.

Visual stimulation of baby: nodding or shaking head; repeated tongue protrusions by mother.

The general behavior and focus of visual attention of the infant were also coded in relation to each maternal behavior sequence, as follows:

Focus of infant attention when awake and calm:
  attends to mother,

attends to mirror (next to infant),
attends to other (self, environment or undeterminable).

Infant transitions:
fussy vocalizations and/or crying,
drowsy, eyelids drooping/closing, fingers relaxed.

RESULTS

Commonalities of temporally-patterned stimulation across modalities

As can be seen in Table 1, maternal behaviors formed four distinct clusters when categorized according to average tempos. The two slowest categories each included only one behavior each, with maternal head nodding being the slowest and maternal head shaking occurring next in order of tempo. In the German sample upon which these findings are based, these two behaviors in particular are typically used to signal either approval and agreement (head nod), or negation and prohibition (head shake). Therefore, it is of interest that they are also characterized by different temporal qualities which may assist the infant in discriminating between these and other messages. Similarly, the maternal head shaking

Table 1 Classes of tempos of maternal stimulation behaviors

Tempo	Behaviors	x̄ tempos (bps*)	SD	Mann-Whitney U	p
Slow	head nod (mother)	0.51	0.30	3.5	<0.001
Medium-slow	head shake (mother)	1.28	0.74	52.5	<0.05
Medium-fast	stroke shake foot shake hand move 2 limbs rock	1.72	0.13	15.5	<0.001
Fast	tap/pat tickle games tongue play	2.64	0.35		

*bps = beats per second, or Hz

tempo had been shown previously (Koester, Papoušek and Papoušek, 1985) to be closely coordinated with the rate of maternal vocalization to the same 3-month-old infants. In addition, the average tempo of the medium-fast behaviors (see Table 1) was similar to that of the mothers' singing; the faster, more playful behaviors such as tickling games were more related to the tempo of repeated syllables, often used by the mothers during playful interactions.

Maternal stimulation in relation to infant behavior

Mother–infant interactions are characterized by a great deal of variety and rapid changes of maternal behaviors, often in response to subtle fluctuations in infant mood or level of attention. As Figure 1 indicates, even when the infant is calm and alert, mothers employ different strategies depending on the focus of the infant's visual attention. That is, tactile and visual stimulation are offered with almost equal frequency when the infant is looking toward the mother. When the infant looks away, however, the mother often increases her level of both tactile and kinesthetic stimulation, as if to elicit the child's attention to her once more; concurrently, she reduces stimulation which would involve the infant's visual attention since this has already been diverted.

When the infant signals a transition to an inattentive state such as fussiness or drowsiness (see Figure 2), the profile of maternal behaviors again takes on quite different characteristics. In the case of fussiness, maternal head shaking (again, possibly an attempt to prohibit crying) becomes the most prevalent maternal response; rocking the infant also increases, compared to when the infant is alert and attentive. When the infant becomes drowsy, the mother typically reduces the complexity and variety of her stimulation, but dramatically increases her use of rocking which may facilitate the onset of sleep.

Little evidence of prenatal/postnatal continuity of tempos

Figure 3 illustrates the relative scaling of prenatal rhythmic tempos (as indicated in the research literature), and those tempos characterizing maternal stimulation to infants postnatally (as documented in this study). With only one exception (head shaking) out of ten behaviors observed, maternal stimulation to 3-month-old infants had little in common with the maternal heart rate so often cited as the most salient rhythmic stimulation for the fetus. More comparable to the data presented here would be the pace of maternal walking or of the fetal heartbeat (Ter Vrugt and Pederson, 1973) which is close to that of the cluster of medium-fast behaviors found in mothers with 3-month-old infants (see Table 1).

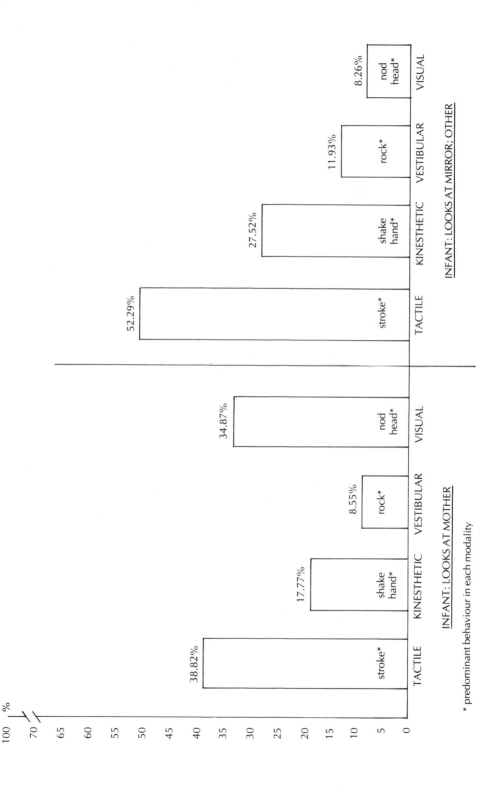

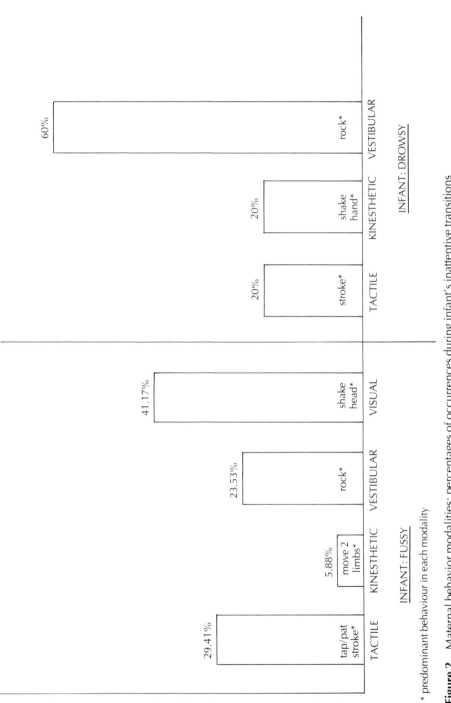

Figure 2 Maternal behavior modalities: percentages of occurrences during infant's inattentive transitions

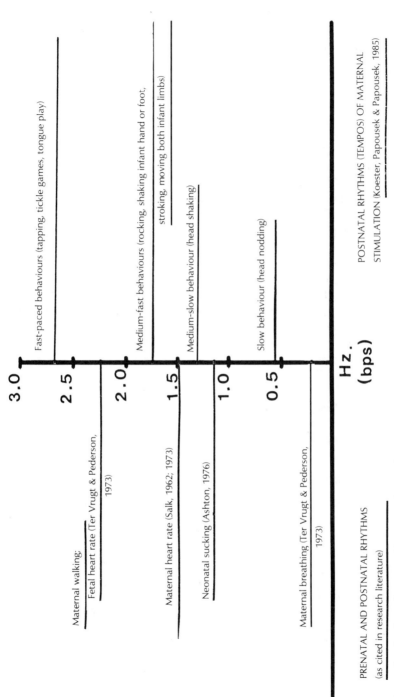

Figure 3 Scaling of prenatal/postnatal stimulation tempos

CONCLUSIONS

In many cultures, face-to-face interactions between parents and infants represent a frequent and important context for early infant development. Not only are such exchanges characterized by a narrowly conscribed visual range, but they also involve subtle intrapersonal and interpersonal patterns of timing which contribute to the sense of reciprocity between parent and infant. In this paper, it is asserted that there is significance not only in the temporal features of the overall parent–infant dialog (Beebe et al., 1985; Schaffer, 1979), but also in the specific temporal patterns found within the repetitive stimulating behaviors used so frequently by parents during such interactions. These microrhythms help to provide some coherence to the multimodel package of stimulation to the infant, and appear to convey, non-vocally, certain messages which are substantiated or elaborated upon by parental vocalizations.

Results of the present study support the notion that parental behaviors are well suited to the behavioral organization and adaptation needs of the young infant. Parents alter their behaviors rapidly in accordance with the infant's signals, and reinforce their own vocalizations to the preverbal child with a rich complement of tactile, kinesthetic, vestibular and visual stimulation. However, the tempos of maternal stimulation observed in this study show little evidence of being determined or 'driven' by prenatally experienced rhythms such as the maternal heart beat. It will be of interest for further research to investigate ways in which these early temporal patterns are gradually transformed, as the infant develops and imposes different requirements on its social environment.

ACKNOWLEDGEMENTS

Appreciation is extended to the following people for their assistance in the development and preparation of this research: to Doris Winter for her support and technical assistance with the manuscript; to Betty Harris for reliability coding; to Drs Hanuš and Mechthild Papoušek for conceptual and methodological collaboration; and to Herr H. Rohde for statistical and computer consultation. This research was completed while the author was a stipendist at the Max-Planck-Institute for Psychiatry (F.R. Germany), and Adjunct Associate Professor at the University of North Carolina at Greesboro (USA).

13

Sexual cross-identity as a fetal response to subliminal parent messages

M.W. Colter

ABSTRACT

There has never been a satisfactory explanation of the etiology of the 'congenital' homosexual, the man who, from the earliest period of his life, often from the age of 3 or 4 years, was aware of his 'differentness'. The theories advanced never cover enough of the cases, suggesting that there may indeed be another factor. This paper suggests that the factor may be the influence of extreme ambivalence in the psychological states of both parents via the sex of the child while it is in utero. This parental indecision is mediated through constant and repetitious overt verbalization and, of greater importance to the fetus, mother's covert subvocalizations.

Three 'scenarios' are suggested that might influence the parents to strongly desire their unborn child to be one sex or the other. Since the sex of the fetus is rarely known (amniocentesis is not in common use for this purpose), confusion, 'future guilt', ambivalence and 'future resentment' may all come to play their part in changing the ambience, the subtle chemistry and the cognitive engrams (extremely early mental imprinting) of self-sexual identity.

Several case histories are used to explicate these suggestions of uterine conditioning and several seminal studies are cited in which fetuses show evidence of verbal conditioning.*

---

* This chapter is part of an unpublished manuscript concerned with the vulnerability and the development of mind and the loss of sensual bonding between parents and their same-sex children. Expected publication date: Spring 1989.

We have gone just about as far as we can, it would seem, to give the human infant the best environment possible. We know that certain ingested substances affect fetal development and so expectant mothers are warned that tobacco, alcohol, psychedelics, some medications and some foods will alter the normal development of the child. We have changed forever, for millions of newborns and their parents, the ambience of the delivery room with physically humane and psychologically sensitive techniques. We have raised the consciousness of prospective parents through organizations like La Leche and the YMCAs and Planned Parenthood groups that teach anxious fathers and mothers the methods that will help keep their babies physically and psychologically healthy. And finally, though not accepted by all, we have invoked an attitude that is unique to the human being. We have publicized and legislated into existence voluntary abortion and anticonception methods, a position that recognizes that the quality of living is far more important than the quantity of lives. What more then, can a relatively enlightened civilization do to ensure the welfare of its future members?

It can begin to pay attention to what may well be the last frontier: *fetal development.* This paper attempts to assess the effect of parent expectations and parent psychological status on the fetus' gender identity which, by extension, will become the individual's basis for his sexual orientation.

Nowhere in the long history of the human race has there ever been suggested a fully adequate explanation for the etiology of the 'congenital' homosexual. For the purposes of this paper it is essential that we identify clearly the types of persons being discussed. We are interested here in the male whose sexual identity was female from his earliest years (some case histories being as early as the third or fourth year) and whose sexual orientation (i.e. a marked interest in and attraction to other males) appears to date also from such a young age. There does not appear to have been time for 'socializing' forces to account for these persons' same-sex predilection. (My use of the male gender is solely for purposes of grammatical simplicity. The subliminal influences noted are true for both females and males.)

Specifically, then, we will explore how the parents' attitudes and expectations about the child's gender affects its sexual identity.

We are looking here at those males whose sexual identification appears 'set' prior to their sixth year. These boys share the following characteristics:

Body shape: Generally ectomorphic with delicate bone structure, height being inconsequential. Rarely muscular with heavy bone structure.

Intelligence: Generally above average with heightened awareness and social sensitivity.

Feminine identification: Frequently interested in the softer clothing, underwear and outerwear, usually associated in western cultures with women. Generally prefers less 'aggressive' toys; often prefers the company of girls and women; usually exhibits social interest in other males, especially older ones such as sisters' male friends, male cousins and uncles, but almost always has trouble bonding closely with his own father or with his own brothers, toward whom the female-identified male feels confusion and unacceptable emotionality.

Male-to-male orientation: These young boys frequently have a history of sexual contacts with adolescents and men far earlier than their peers have sexual contacts, frequently before they themselves are pubertal.

With such an early onset of a syndrome of characteristics that will later be called homosexual, we are compelled to look elsewhere for clues regarding its occurrence. The needs, wishes and attitudes that accompany this complex occur far too early for the usual psychosocial family forces to have had time to act.

Here, then, in the area of sexual identification (and later sexual orientation) we have to look at far more subtle influences than those mentioned above. We must begin to pay attention to how the parents' *attitudes* toward this as yet unborn child bear on these issues.

Let me outline some possible scenarios and then we will look at three case histories.

Scenario 1: Mother's husband dies, is divorced or separated from her while she is pregnant. She thinks a lot about her situation, talks a lot about it with friends, and spends countless hours having 'conversations with herself' (subvocalizing) about her love–hate feelings toward this absent male. She is angry at her loss of this important male, frustrated at the shattering of her dreams because this man is no longer with her, and experiences deep sadness and perhaps depression at what she may see as an 'unjustifiable' loss of the male who impregnated her. This woman knows that the child she bears may be male. Her ambivalence at this important time in her fetus' development leads her to 'talk to her baby', something all women do as a normal prebirth bonding process. In this case, however, almost all the mother's *subvocal, covert messages* will be consistently in the direction of *indecision about her infant's sex*. Taken together, the repetitive, covert subvocalizing and overt messages appear to predispose the infant to adopt that sexual identity that conforms closest to the degree of ambiguity in the mother's 'communications' to her fetus.

Let us develop another probable scenario.

Scenario 2: Both parents are expecting their first child. As is true for most new parents, a male child is preferred as the eldest. In this particular case, the expectant father is so set on a male child that he causes the mother to begin to experience 'future guilt' for having a girl even though she hasn't given birth yet. Once again, mother is made painfully aware that father expects her to deliver 'his' son, and engages in repetitive and constant subvocalizing. These messages of confusion, guilt and reproach toward her husband for being so insistent about the gender of the baby, all become subliminal messages delivered into the developing consciousness of the fetus which is, of course, utterly defenseless against anything at all that is done to it or impinges on its womb-space.

Let us put together yet one more possible chain of events.

Scenario 3: Mother has already two or more children and is preparing for another one. All the previous children are of one sex, either male or female. Both she and her husband dearly want a child of the other sex: if they have boys, they want a girl. If girls, they want a boy. But both know full well that they cannot predict the baby's gender, so once again the mother, with father's wishes well known to her, begins both the subvocalizing and the overt talking about the sex of the baby. And once again the theme is confusion, ambivalence, 'future-guilt', repeated endlessly and consistently by both the mother's own process as the 'child carrier' and father's constant input as a very interested party.

So we see that in the case of the human neonate we are confronted with imprinting on a far broader level than that put forward by Lorenz. Here we see the earliest fetal 'learning', a learning of needs and attitudes that appear to affect the developing fetus on multiple levels of body structure, intellect and sensitivity, levels of aggressiveness, and self-sexual identity. And we see symptoms of the complex far in advance of the possible effect of the postnatal social enforcers that you would suspect might have such an influence.

Recent research, some of it unpublished, presented at a variety of professional conventions and colloquia corroborates, on the sensory level, that 'human fetuses do hear *in utero* and that they can learn through hearing' (De Casper, *Monitor*, November 1984). De Casper also found that 2-day-old infants who had had a story read by their mothers during their final 6 weeks *in utero* preferred the story that had been read to them rather than another story they had not heard as fetuses. The unresearched assumption is that the fetuses and infants are responding to verbal rhythms learned before birth. Some fetal conditioning has been demonstrated as well (Gottlieb and Krasnegor, *Monitor*, Nov. 1984).

Apparently another 'sacred notion' is about to fall. The 'sanctity of the womb' is about to go the way of the 'idyllicism of childhood' known now to be a fantasy far more than a truth. Not only is the chemistry of the womb highly susceptible to, and easily changed by, the hormones secreted into the mother's system at times of acute stress, chronic indecision and doubt, but the primitive matrix of consciousness that is developing in the fetus from the fifth month of gestation is also highly susceptible to the 'ambience', the 'social climate', of the womb.

Folklore tells us that to have a child mature into a musician, mathematician, singer, etc. the mother should immerse herself in the relevant activities. Just what is presumed to be occurring here in these 'best of cases'? It is that mother and infant's shared environment will be affected by thoughts, feelings, subvocalization and subliminal suggestions, and that 'bathing' the fetus in such a barrage of stimulation will aid the infant with being born with an 'implanted' program. Not the 'tabula raza', the *untouched mind* waiting for life, after birth, to write on it, but *the mind* stamped with patterns that may well be nearly totally resistant to any influences later brought to bear on the growing or grown person. We must therefore add the psychological state of *both* parents to the other two categories of fetal influencers, those of ingested substances, and structural abnormalities.

The fetus is a 'captive audience' beyond the dreams of the most fanatic 'brain-washer'. Never again in the long life of the person will his mind and his body be more vulnerable. For it is truly in the womb, where impinging stimuli and cellular growth are inextricably and inescapably mixed, where self-defense is unthinkable, that those life experiences yet to come are indeed fore-ordained, where the personality receives the primary, the basic, the core-level engrams that will shape the content of the person's life, perhaps unalterably.

Let me now become more specific and take you on a 'fetal journey' from preconception to postbirth to give you a more graphic picture of the process.

> We have two men, one married and entering his forties, the other single and in his thirties, both plagued by pain, pain described by them as anxiety, tension, doubt, uncertainty. Pain felt in all their muscles: in the older man localized in his shoulders and chest, in the younger, in his lower back and legs. Both have constant complaints about their breathing and feel tightness in their chest. Both men are hypersensitive to their environment, the older tormented far beyond normal empathy by those world events characterized by violence, death and injury. He is in a constant state of expecting these events to happen to him or, conversely, that he could be the perpetrator of these terrible acts, harming himself and those he loves. The younger is constantly adjusting his environment so it doesn't impinge too hard on his various sense organs causing him discomfort. He is extremely sensitive to sounds, light, temperature, pressure, textures of cloth and his own skin. He is rarely satisfied with anything he does and often thinks he will not live into old age. The older man is intensely heterosexual while also expressing much interest in sensual and sexual contact with men. The younger is bisexual, feeling far more comfortable with males while preferring women for sex.

The intrauterine environment for both people was surprisingly similar. For the older man, his parents' marriage ended when he was 18 months old after years of increasing difficulty, and there is every reason to believe that his conception was one of those designed to 'save the marriage' in some poorly defined way. The younger man has two older sisters and according to family history was conceived as the byproduct of a faulty condom. Other facts that are known: both pregnant women were very religious, both husbands made good livings and were not demonstrative with their wives or children.

Some assumptions that grow out of what we know are these:

(1) All four parents wanted boys, one family as the oldest child, the other family because they had no children.

(2) Both women, probably in conjunction with their husbands, were at best ambivalent about the oncoming event, in the first case because of a deteriorating marriage, and in the second case because of the accidental nature of the event, and finally, of course, because they could not guarantee a male child.

Now let us construct the scene from the *fetus' point of view*. They float, totally dependent, their tissues absorbing uneasiness from the subtle and constant chemical fluctuations that are produced by their mother's (and father's) feelings of anxiety and doubt about the 'correctness' of having another child. The fetus' earliest 'learning experiences' are a mental absorption of the unremitting uncertainty, the endless chain of subvocalized ambivalence, about their sexes. The learning for these fetuses is on a tissue level, their developing organs bombarded by toxic chemical/hormonal levels, so basic, that later on, these men will not be able to remember ever feeling at peace with themselves or their environment. They do not experience themselves as fully realized males; they are in constant pursuit of women who, they say, will 'validate their masculinity'. One is overtly bisexual, the other too fearful of the fantasies of homosexual entanglement to allow this part of his need-system any externalization at all.

While it is tempting to imagine that the fetuses could 'overhear' and 'understand' their mother's intensely confused internal conversations, there is no need to invoke such a fantasy. It is sufficient that on the level of psychological influences, the subtle, consistent and constant effect of months of repetitive subvocal and subliminal messages has been to alter these mens' ability to identify as authentic males.

For the fetuses, what should have been time spent in the idyllic security of the womb was anything but, infused and permeated as they were with the soluble essence of their parents' problems.

SEXUAL CROSS-IDENTITY

Here is another case involving chronic doubt and ambivalence about the sex of the coming child. The only concern in this middle-class family was that the baby should be a boy, there being two older girls already, and one miscarriage, but in those days (before amniocentesis) the sex of the child was hidden until birth. The father in this case was not at all child-oriented, given far more to pursuits that took him out of the home. Moreover, he was not a man comfortable with his own masculinity. His wife, on the other hand, was a woman who loved dressing up her children with fancy clothes, and keeping them clean. While she agreed with her husband that a boy was what was wanted, this did not suppress her own doubts about bringing up a boy when she already had two girls, from being added to the normal uncertainty about the child's gender.

The woman herself was the second daughter of two eldest girls and had always been more gutsy than her older sister, the 'tom-boy' of her family, in fact. Her intelligence was of a broader, more inquisitive kind than her husband's. He was the second son of two eldest boys. European-born, he came with his parents to the US as a long-haired tot of four. He was always too loud in groups and in fact appeared somewhat uncertain about his adequacy as a male. Both wife and husband felt themselves to be 'on the spot' with their extended families, all of whom kept saying 'how wonderful it would be' for them to have a boy now. These are some of the facts of this couple's psychological environment. These facts also indicate, with broad strokes, the degree of ambiguous emphasis brought to bear on the developing sexuality of the fetus, whose gender was decided at the moment of conception but whose identity was not. This would be decided during the long course of 4 or 5 months as he absorbed his parents' confusion which will become part of his and his mother's internal environment. It is suggested that these are the factors that produced a boy who, at the age of four knew that he was 'not like' all the other little boys. Did his mother's behavior in dressing him beautifully, his father's absence, disinterest, and fear of another male presence in the home, tip him in the direction of cross-identity? If you think so, then what of the thousands of boys whose parents were similar to these, yet grew up to be decidedly heterosexual, comfortably self-identified as males?

Perhaps it is here, in the womb, bathed in the fluid distillate of parental anxieties, hopes, ambivalence and fears, that the basic shape of the personality is laid down. A shape that dictates the person's predilections, sensitivities, moods, vague expectations and trust and that is as much a part of his psychological socio/sexual structure as the skin that covers him. Complexes largely inaccessible to the words that a future therapist may use, for while the meanings of words are not a part of our womb-time, the feelings contained in the words, of doubt, confusion and uncertainty are. We develop into being what our parents' (mother's) messages 'communicated' to us: to be ambivalent about our sexual identity or deny our gender-identity entirely. Our developing mind absorbs unconsciously these engrams of self-doubt and self-confusion, in truth the 'tabula rasa' accepting without question everything that comes to it.

The research cited earlier and the clinical findings of some therapists are beginning to point insistently to the early accessibility of the human fetus to learning. This paper has explored fetal learning too, but learning on a level so basic that it would be quite beyond any individual's recall, a process we may call 'fetal communication'. Such a process underscores the need for sensitivity and knowledge on the part of prospective parents. To embark on the conception of a human being is to undertake the most difficult and long-term task imaginable. To approach the development of a child casually or with parent-states at risk, or with ignorance as to the child's needs or how it will grow, is to affirm that there is nothing very special at all about being human. Indeed, we are placed then on the same level as cats and rabbits, cute but of no great importance. None but the most unthinking and therefore the least human among us would knowingly agree with such a position when all the evidence underscores the fact that the unborn child of 5 or 6 months is exquisitely sensitive to anything that impinges on its womb-time mind.

Section 2
PSYCHOANALYSIS AND PSYCHOTHERAPY

Part 1: The prenatal and perinatal experience

14

The concept of cathexis and its usefulness for prenatal psychology

W.E. Freud

ABSTRACT

To facilitate integrating the subject matter of prenatal psychology into the conceptual framework of psychoanalysis the author considers the term, 'cathexis' (emotional investment), to be as useful as the concepts of attachment and bonding (Bowlby 1969; Klaus and Kennell, 1976). The topic will be elucidated from the vantage point of the researcher and from the side of the mother, the father, the family and the fetus himself. It is hoped that the non-analytic healthcare professional may also benefit from viewing the problem area of wanted and unwanted pregnancy from a slightly different perspective than the accustomed one.

If we speak of the usefulness of a term (like 'cathexis') we mean that in order to reach a better understanding we have to work from a broad basis and make use of everything that can make a contribution. In other words, only a multidisciplinary approach is likely to yield a rich harvest. It is felt that the use of the term 'cathexis' can help to bridge the gaps between psychoanalysis and other disciplines. This presentation addresses two interconnected issues: first, the contribution psychoanalysis can make to prenatal psychology, and secondly, the contribution prenatal psychology can make to psychoanalysis.

THE CONTRIBUTION PSYCHOANALYSIS CAN MAKE TO PRENATAL PSYCHOLOGY

For our purposes it may suffice to say that 'cathexis' simply means 'emotional investment'*. In S. Freud's libido theory the libido is sent out from the ego on to objects. He illustrated what he meant by an analogy from zoology:

> 'Think of those simplest of living organisms (the amoebas) which consist of a little-differentiated globule of protoplasmic substance. They put out protrusions, known as pseudopodia, into which they cause the substance of their body to flow over. They are able, however, to withdraw the protrusions once more and form themselves again into a globule. We compare the putting-out of these protrusions, then, to the emission of libido on to the objects while the main mass of libido can remain in the ego; and we suppose that in normal circumstances ego-libido can be transformed unhindered into object-libido and that this can once more be taken back into the ego' (Freud, S., 1917, p. 416).

The concept can be used as a noun, as a verb or as an adjective. Cathecting (emotionally investing) is a flexible, fluctuating, dynamic process, neatly illustrated, for example, in A. Freud's (1967) paper 'About losing and being lost'. By 'putting out feelers' in trying to make contact with other people we risk, of course, the possibility of being rebuffed and rejected, but that seems inevitable. We cathect just about everything, animate and inanimate objects alike. The infant builds up an image of his body by cathecting parts of his body, and in the course of his development different body zones are maximally cathected at different times (e.g. the oral, anal and phallic phase). In the service of need-fulfilment the newborn at first cathects the nipple of the mother's breast.

In the mental sphere we cathect thoughts, ideas, fantasies, beliefs, convictions, ideals, and the cathexis of our wishes for material things not infrequently clashes with our ideals and with what is possible in reality. We speak of over- and under-cathexis. If, for example, our ideal is to be slim and we have over-cathected food we are likely to have a tough time. If we have set our heart on a luxury car or on an expensive dress or a custom-built house but barely earn enough to make ends meet we suffer accordingly. The intensity of cathexis ranges from shallow to deep. Institution children, for example, quickly form relationships with many different people, but these relationships are superficial (see Provence and Lipton, 1962). Others form few but deep and lasting relationships that are

---
* For the intricacies and the history of 'cathexis' I would refer you to Freud, S. (1917) and to Ornston, D. (1985), for definitions to Rycroft (1968) or Laplanche and Pontalis (1973).

firmly rooted, but which correspondingly cause greater upset when they come to an end. We speak of positive and negative cathexis, we cathect and de-cathect. If a child feels hurt by a loved person who has given him a toy he withdraws his positive cathexis from that present, i.e. de-cathects it, and is likely to maltreat or destroy it. In other words, it has lost its value for him. More often than not cathexis is neither wholly positive nor negative but ambivalent, and much of the time cathexis fluctuates. When something very disturbing has to be kept out of consciousness a counter-cathexis is set up to prevent the emergence of the unpleasant. In each case the meaning and purpose of a cathectic maneuver becomes intelligible only from the context in which it happens and from elucidating the underlying motivation and purpose. Often several determinants contribute to the outcome (Waelder, 1936). From this somewhat cursory and superficial review you may already have gathered how useful the term 'cathexis' is for psychoanalytic thinking. If it can be equally profitably applied in the realm of prenatal psychology we will have gained. In the following the usage of the term, 'cathexis', will become self-evident.

THE CONTRIBUTION PRENATAL PSYCHOLOGY CAN MAKE TO PSYCHOANALYSIS

There may be many motivations for a woman to become pregnant, and they are not mutually exclusive (e.g. competition with siblings, friends, relatives, her own mother; prestige values; neighborhood pressures; perpetuation of the family). It is always interesting to see which motivation is cathected most. Each pregnancy is different from any other, and the various stages of pregnancy are differently cathected, some more positively than others. As a colleague and mother once said: 'In the whole course of antenatal classes I was really only optimally interested when problems were discussed that corresponded to my prevailing state of pregnancy. It meant that a·certain topic would already have been dealt with when it was still comparatively meaningless to me; or that I had to wait, sometimes for a long time, until my own particular problem could be aired. But by then it was no longer topical for me. In other words, my anxieties could hardly ever be discussed when they were most acute.'

One can think of a multitude of developmental 'micro-stages' of pregnancy, each cathected by the mother with different nuances. Perhaps she is 'programmed' to cathect each micro-stage of pregnancy optimally only at the time she goes through it.

The prospective mother has many hopes (in German: she is in hope, 'in der Hoffnung') and expectations (she 'expects'). As the pregnancy proceeds, cathexis from academic studies or work is withdrawn, and she has many fantasies about the child to be. Her fantasy relationship with the unborn reflects the meaning this particular child has for her in terms of whom it represents, whether, for example, a loved brother or a hated sister, a firstborn like herself, etc. A clue to it can already be found in the choice of the baby's name. Not infrequently it is a name that could be used for a boy as well as for a girl. If it has a strong male component, as in Alexandra, Gerhardine or Ulrike and the mother claims to have a strong wish for a girl we can surmise that latently the wish for a boy is more strongly cathected. There is now a growing and widespread belief, that prenatal influences, whether from without or within play a decisive role in shaping the personality of the unborn (Graber and Kruse, 1973; Grof, 1975; Verny and Kelly, 1981; Gross, 1982; Hau and Schindler, 1982; Schindler, 1982; Schindler and Zimprich, 1983; Grof, 1985) and some studies explicitly point to the share the emotional attitude of the mother has on postnatal outcome (e.g. Ferreira, 1960; Blau et al., 1963; Stott, 1973; Rottmann, 1974), pointing to the importance of the influences that come from within, i.e. from the way in which the mother is able to cathect the fetus.

Lest it be thought that only the mother's cathexis is of major importance let us remind you that her attitudes are very much influenced by others around her, notably by the members of her family. Her partner also plays a decisive role, as well as the quality of the partnership itself. For example, a divorced mother's rejection of her partner can transfer itself to the intimate relationship with her infant whom she then cannot breastfeed (Lukesch and Rottmann, 1976).

Fathers, too, were once small, and as little boys they had, just like little girls, wishes to have a baby (Brunswick, 1940; Jacobson, 1950). They too spent many hours of their childhood puzzling about where babies come from and how babies are made (Freud, S., 1908). Needless to say, little boys and girls can consider and comprehend such problems only within the realm of thinking that corresponds to their prevailing state of emotional development. It means that, for example, an infant in the oral phase will think of baby-making in oral terms and a child in the anal phase will connect it with some anal activity, and so on. These thoughts and wishes remain cathected and are revived in later life. With such a history of strongly cathected wishes the prospective father feels a bit left out when his partner becomes pregnant. Greenacre (1953) speaks of exclusion anxiety and Bettelheim (1954) of the envious male. The culturally sanctioned custom of couvade (Trethowan and Conlon, 1965) is no longer available to him, and he has to face that he cannot give birth to the baby nor breastfeed the newborn. However, as a male, with a reputation for inventiveness, he found ways of harnessing his cathexis in a roundabout way: all he had to do was to become an obstetrician or a pediatrician and he could have babies unlimited. It is no coincidence that the key positions in these professions are held by men. They have neatly cornered the market: during the mother's pregnancy the babies belong to the obstetrician, and at the moment of delivery the pediatrician stands already waiting to receive the newborn and to look after him.

You will not be surprised to hear that during his partner's pregnancy the father also demonstrates his creativity. Liebenberg (1973) found in her sample of men that 52% of the prospective fathers took up heavy work or engaged in class schedules. At the same time fears of passivity are mobilized, which have to be countered. Liebenberg found a higher incidence of reckless and physical daring, resulting in car accidents, during this time, as well as heavy drinking and resorting to other women. Interestingly, 65% of the men developed 'pregnancy symptoms', like fatigue, nausea, backache, headaches, vomiting and peptic ulcers. Some of them put on 4.5–5.5 kg of weight, which they lost again after the birth of the baby. Several stopped smoking giving the reason that it was 'for the baby'. All this goes to show that the pregnancy was heavily cathected by them too.

When there is an older sibling he too cathects the pregnancy, albeit in his own way. Whatever he is told, he usually expects a playmate of even age who walks and talks and generally reacts like a sensible human being. He also identifies with the pregnant mother and fantasizes that the baby is inside himself and that he will give birth to the baby. However, it is not only the sibling in whom dynamic shifts of cathexis can be observed. The pet in the family will sense the mother's preoccupation with the baby inside herself, and dogs and cats have been known to react by refusing food or withdrawing. Sometimes one feels that the father, the sibling and the pet get the birth trauma rather than the newborn himself.

Ultrasound scanning (USS) affects the parents' cathexis of the fetus, who can now first be seen before his movements are felt (Brenot and Brenot, 1984). A mother comes to mind who had several screenings. On the first occasion she could only discern separate 'pieces' and compared the picture to a jigsaw puzzle. On the second occasion the husband was present, and together they could see the fetus. From then on she cathected the image. She stressed that the support from her husband was crucial. One can understand this, because the strange image may have looked too frightening for her to cathect it fully. Another mother's USS showed three fetuses, which was unexpected and came as a shock. It required considerable readjustment of cathexis, but eventually the mother accepted the idea of having triplets. When a later scan revealed four fetuses we expected an even more anxious reaction. To our surprise, however, the mother felt relieved: she thought that four was a much better number for her than three, and she actually preferred it. Asked why, she said: 'At least two won't always gang up against the third; it will be two against two.'

When we now view 'attachment' from the vantage point of the fetus the meaning of 'cathexis' has to be modified. Instead of thinking in terms of 'emotional investment' we may conceptualize in terms of experiential awareness. The question is perhaps not so much whether or to what extent we should endow the fetus with human characteristics (anthropomorphize) but from what stage of his development onwards this becomes plausible. Albert Liley (1972) wrote a charming and at the same time scientifically unreproachable paper on 'The foetus as a personality', which has remained a classic. He regarded the fetus as an active, co-operative, if not controlling being:

> 'Far from being an inert passenger in a pregnant mother, the foetus is very much in command of the pregnancy. It is the foetus who guarantees the endocrine success of pregnancy and induces all manner of changes in maternal physiology to make her a suitable host ... It is the foetus who determines the duration of pregnancy. It is the foetus who decides which way he will lie in pregnancy and which way he will present in labour.'

Graves (1980) concluded that the fetus is a sentient, active organism who is capable of regulating and monitoring his environment: 'This picture of a "competent fetus" forcibly suggests that our search for the origins and early developmental phases of human mental life must begin with the fetus.'

The fetus is growing up in the environment of his mother's biological rhythms. There is the rhythmic beating of the mother's heart, a 'rhythmical wooshing sound, punctuated by the tummy rumbles of air passing through the mother's stomach' (MacFarlane, 1977), and there are the sounds of her breathing and her voice. Her sleep-wake pattern and her general style of functioning (slow, lethargic; fast, hectic) impinge on his awareness. Rhythm, which Clauser (1971) regards as the organizer of human development, is so reassuring because it holds the promise of repetition and continuity. The fetus lives in a 'cradle' of sound and movement. Milano Comparetti (1981) points to the 'embryo-genetic need to change contact with the surface of the uterine cavity'. The vestibular-proprioceptive system matures at 21 weeks gestational age (wga), myelinization of the vestibular system begins at 4 months, is well under way at 6 months and is quite heavy at term (Korner and Thoman, 1972, quote Langworthy, 1933). John Lind (1981) thought that the fetus experiences cessation of movement as deprivation. Plato's Athenian already spoke of the importance of movement:

CATHEXIS IN PRENATAL PSYCHOLOGY

'So let's take this as our basic principle ...: all young children, and especially very tiny infants, benefit both physically and mentally from being nursed and kept in motion, as far as practicable, throughout the day and night; indeed, if only it could be managed, they ought to live as though they were permanently on board ship. But as that's impossible, we must aim to provide our new-born infants with the closest possible approximation to this ideal.' (The Laws, Book VII)

According to Feher (1980) bodily sensation is the medium of expression most accessible to the infant. Body movements in the womb are also significant in that they may affect later emotional states and mental development. She writes: 'According to Corliss (1976), movements create sensations which have patterns. These patterns are actually imposed on the musculature, and then on the cortex itself, as imprints or memories, which remain like a permanent "motion picture" to influence our consciousness and future reactions'. Greenacre (1953) speaks of unique somatic memory traces, and the question arises to what extent the fetus cathects the mother through body memories.

One wonders whether he cathects movement as such. In general, if the fetus does cathect, how are we to imagine this? Does he cathect tangibles, i.e. that which he can touch (like the amniotic fluid, the placenta, the uterine wall, the umbilical, parts of his own body)? Or does he cathect intangibles like interaction, continuity, rhythm and sound? Does he cathect stimulation?

Liley (1972) points out that the fetus has a much larger number and a much wider distribution of taste buds in his oral cavity than the child or adult, which are already developing between the 11th and the 20th week of gestation. Graves (1980) quotes a suggestion from Bradley and Mistretta (1975) that the shifting ratios of fluid and urine contribute to the stimulation of taste buds *in utero*. One wonders to what extent he scans the amniotic fluid for a number of different parameters and whether through thumb- or finger-sucking the oral cavity and snout area are not already over-cathected and therefore libidinized *in utero*.

Sontag (1941) found that deeply disturbed maternal emotion produces a marked increase in fetal activity. Lieberman (1963) denied habituated women smokers cigarettes for 24 hours and then offered them a cigarette. Even before the cigarette had been lit a significant acceleration in fetal heart rate could be demonstrated. Ianniruberto and Tajani (1981) observed what happened to 28 pregnant women when severe tremors shook the area near their maternity hospital during the earthquake in southern Italy in November, 1980. The women, who were panic stricken but had suffered no physical trauma were examined with ultrasonography: 'All the fetuses (between 18 and 36 wga) showed intense hyperkinesia which lasted from 2 to 8 hours. In 20 cases this was followed by a period of reduced motility lasting from 24 to 72 hours; the remaining eight fetuses recovered immediately.' How this works out in terms of cathexis will give food for thought.

Now let us briefly look at the remedies at our disposal when maternal cathexis of the pregnancy is less than optimal. Lind and Hardgrove (1978) recommend singing lullabys to the baby *in utero*, while Kestenberg (1980) systematically teaches pregnant women to notate tension changes that occur in fetal movement. Prospective mothers learn to accommodate the fetus's body by widening, lengthening or bulging; the idea of co-operation with the fetus is in the center: 'Becoming acquainted with, and attuning to the baby's movement is a preparation for child care in extrauterine environment'. Working with mothers in this way not only promotes prenatal attachment through a primarily physical approach but also serves to focus on reasons for less than optimal cathexis of the fetus.

Carter-Jessop (1981) systematically studied the effect of specific prenatal 'bonding intervention' on the frequency of postnatal maternal attachment behaviors. It serves the two-fold purpose of preparing mothers to optimize the growth and development experience for their children throughout childhood, through being 'tuned in' to identifying and acting on the individual child's needs, and to help them to weather threats to the relationship, e.g. separation in prematurity, illness or handicaps of the child.

One of the most intrigueing studies is that of De Casper and Spence (1982). They wanted to find out how prenatal experience affects postnatal auditory perception of the mother's voice. Five weeks before delivery a story was read twice daily to the fetus until delivery. Within 3 days after delivery two stories were read to the infant, whose reactions were measured by sucking interburst intervals. The infant preferred the known story by maximizing input: the preferences shown suggested that prenatal auditory experience may be important for speech perception. The fetus had cathected the known story more.

Most striking is the work of Veldman (1982). He shows the pregnant woman how, by gently laying her hand on the side of her abdomen and letting her feeling of love for the child flow into her hand, she can induce the fetus to nestle into it. She can thus 'rock' him from side to side. If the parents play with the fetus in this way at the same time every day he will kick if for once the game does not take place. In the course of the last few years prenatal bonding enhancement programs have been offered to pregnant mothers in several centers all over the States.

The relationship between the mother and the baby inside her should be evaluated from both sides, i.e. we should consider the mother's cathexis of the fetus and the fetus's cathexis of the mother. But now let us look at those pregnancies in which the cathexis is mainly negative. Hau (1973) coined the useful term 'intrauterine hospitalism' to describe conditions in which the mother's aversion to pregnancy is of such magnitude that it threatens the survival of the fetus. Could one imagine that he reacts like the babies Tronick and Adamson (1980) studied in so-called 'still-face' situations, in which the mother no longer responds to the infant's attempts at eliciting interaction and feedback until eventually he resigns and withdraws? It would then only be a small step towards quitting altogether. The fetus may 'decide' that it is no longer worth staying inside and try to escape prematurely or whither away.

While we are aware that it takes time to mourn a baby when termination has been indicated on medical grounds, as, for example, when the mother contracts rubella, similar needs of a mother who has negatively cathected her pregnancy are often discounted. Abortion is still taboo, and there is often a tendency to unconscious collusion between mother and healthcare professional to get the whole matter over as quickly as possible and to deny that it ever existed. Even in the negatively cathected pregnancy there are positive cathexes and the mother who decides that she wants an abortion also needs help to come to terms with her conscious and unconscious feelings of guilt and to work through them. So we have to strive for solutions that are, in the first place, compatible with the ego-syntonic needs of the mother and, if possible, with those of the father too. At the same time we have to avoid the unconscious collusion of denial.

In the States, and now increasingly in Western Europe, the group of mothers with the most precarious cathexis is the COMP-group (so called, because it is compounded with multiple handicaps). These disadvantaged mothers are teenagers, unwed, have no partners or several, their IQ is average or below and they come from social class IV or V. They have no support systems, live on poor or the wrong kind of nutrition, are usually addicted to heavy smoking, drinking or drug-taking, come from broken homes and have themselves not had good mothering or fathering experiences. They do not attend antenatal classes and come in as emergency admissions, often with obstetric complications which require a Caesarean section. We know nothing about them but have to make quick decisions without background information. They are at-risk mothers and more likely than not give birth to an at-risk baby, which means drastic separation from the newborn through neonatal intensive care. Pursuit of this topic would lead us too far and has been discussed elsewhere (Freud, W.E., 1980) but a few words on prophylaxis might not be out of place. It could focus on two approaches. One is early intervention with those girls who later drift into the COMP-group. We still have contact with them when they are in school, and it is not difficult to provide a curriculum that harnesses the consuming interest in babies among boys as well as girls during their school career. In former times, when large families were the rule, children were used to holding, handling and carrying their younger siblings, something that nowadays is the exception. In the States there are already school programs that invite mothers to breastfeed, and that give pupils responsibility for bottle-feeding, cleaning and carrying babies.

The second approach would be from the side of the prenatal bonding enhancement schemes. Hitherto the emphasis has been on encouraging the mothers to invest more in their positive cathexis of the pregnancy (Lind and Hardgrove, 1978; Kestenberg, 1980; Carter-Jessop, 1981; Barglow et al., 1984). Only secondarily, it seems, does the fetus get attention. Veldman's (1982) method seems to be the most promising, because his concern is more explicitly with the fetus. A new strategy could be suggested which addresses itself in the first place to the fetus. To find out the best times during pregnancy for such a venture would be one of the tasks.

It has been our impression that prenatal psychology is under-cathected by many psychoanalysts. The reasons for this are none too clear, but may be connected with the historical differences between Rank (1924) and Sigmund Freud, so that birth and the prenatal were not 'sanctioned' as being wholly acceptable as subject matter for further thorough exploration. An excellent review of this has just become available (Janus, 1986b).

From a psychoanalytic perspective the scope of the genetic point of view has been steadily widened (see Freud, W.E., 1975), although not without resistance, and there is a lot to be said for extending the genetic point of view further and to regard the prenatal dimension as earliest infancy, which should be included in the psychoanalytic training syllabus.

Perhaps mother–infant observation, as we know it (Bick, 1964; Freud, W.E., 1975) needs to be extended. By linking ultrasonic impressions with subsequent observation of mother and newborn Piontelli (1986) has made a start. The pregnant mothers still remain our most reliable source of information (Bibring, 1959; Bibring et al., 1961).

SUMMARY

In the first part of this presentation we tried to create more common ground for communication by recommending the usefulness of the term, 'cathexis', for prenatal psychology. In the second part of the presentation we drew attention to some of the things the fetus experiences *in utero*, bearing in mind that there is probably a psychological component to intrauterine manifestations. In conclusion it is suggested that more detailed knowledge and observation of the prenatal would help the analyst in his therapeutic work.

15

The trauma of birth as reflected in the psychoanalytical process

L. Janus

INTRODUCTION

The term 'the trauma of birth' in the title of this chapter is meant to call to mind the trailblazing work of Otto Rank. As to the contents of the chapter, the first part is devoted to the development of the theme of birth in the history of psychoanalytical treatment, while the second part deals with modern perspectives for the significance of the birth theme as far as treatment techniques are concerned. To facilitate this presentation, I will begin with some systematic preliminary remarks on two subjects – the symbolism of birth and the significance of the birth process for theoretical concepts of psychoanalysis.

PRELIMINARY REMARKS ON THE SYMBOLISM OF BIRTH

The interconnection between symbols and real experience should never be overlooked in birth fantasies. These two elements are the reverse sides of one single process. The realities of experience determine the embodiment of the symbol, with birth as renewal or as destiny; at the same time, the symbol, as a primary fantasy or archetypical representation, determines the course of experience. Thus, a traumatic birth signifies that the corresponding symbolic structure has been marked by a certain negative initial influence. Later processes of maturation and change which are analogous to birth – such as the transition to adulthood as celebrated in initiation rites symbolic of birth – may then be determined by symbols of birth marked by a birth trauma. Symptoms of anxiety prior to an examination are a typical example of this.

Therapeutic processes of regression and healing – from the ancient mysteries, Buddhist immersion, and individuation processes focused on mythical heroes to treatment processes in depth psychology – have always been experienced and represented in symbols of regression to the womb and rebirth. Due to the primacy of the Oedipus complex, this symbolism of birth and rebirth has not been systematically worked out in psychoanalysis. Nevertheless, noteworthy initial efforts have been made – by Freud himself, as well as by Ferenczi, Rank, Graber, Fodor, Rascovsky and others.

PRELIMINARY REMARKS ON THE METAPSYCHOLOGICAL SIGNIFICANCE OF THE CONCEPT OF BIRTH ANXIETY

If the prenatal period and the birth process are incorporated into a comparison of the prenatal and postnatal periods, some of the conclusions reached concerning certain theoretical concepts of psychoanalysis may be surprising at first glance. Whereas Freud designated the archaic infantile as the unconscious, this position is qualified by Rank's statement that the nucleus of the unconscious is the fetal, in the same way that repression is qualified by primary repression, which in turn qualifies repression to after-repression. Primary repression, for its part, coincides with the trauma of birth (Janus, 1986b, p. 73 et seq.). The fetal nucleus of the unconscious comprises primary fantasies that are phylogenetically determined and function as hallucinatory wish fulfillment, that is, as a fetal psychism, as early as in the intrauterine stage. For this reason, then, one is ultimately correcting primary repression of the birth trauma in correcting traumatic repressions. Since birth represents the real beginning of our consciousness, making someone conscious of something is actually a kind of birth; it is a reunification of the unconscious with the conscious or of the prenatal self with the postnatal self, the former having been separated from the latter by traumatic repression or, more precisely, by the birth trauma. This concept likewise implies that the primary process corresponds to the fetal psychism, while the secondary process designates the intervening processes of control with reference to reality. Primary resistance corresponds to the regressive tendency to avoid the transition from the prenatal to the postnatal level of functioning, with birth anxiety representing a threat to this transition. These preliminary reflections are intended to render possible a clear portrayal of the development of the concept of birth in analytical treatment techniques.

THE SYMBOLISM OF BIRTH IMPLICIT IN THE STUDIES ON HYSTERIA

Breuer's account of the treatment of the patient Anna O. contains numerous associations with birth. A collective symbol for the birth canal may be seen in the description of the treatment as 'chimney sweeping'. Breuer assumes the role of a midwife who relieves the patient of the fantasms born every day. The introvertive disappearance of the patient into an inner zone of 'hallucinatory self-hypnoses' symbolizes regression into the womb, as Freud later established with respect to dreams (Freud, 1917, p. 413). The symptoms experienced by the patient Anna O., with her peculiar contortions and manifestations of tension, also exhibit characteristics reminiscent of birth positions (Freud and Breuer, 1895, p. 21). The following interpretation seems admissible: having grown disappointed in her father, the patient regressed to her unhappy relationship with her mother; she acted out her having become mired in the negative symbiosis with her mother by imitating agonizing birth positions, symptoms of a conversion neurosis. Rank later called attention to the repetitive nature of birth symbols as exhibited in numerous symptoms of conversion neurosis in *Trauma der Geburt* (The Trauma of Birth). These indications with respect to the level of birth symbolism in the treatment of Anna O. are consistent with the fact that she is said to have experienced the labor pains of a hysterical birth at the end of the treatment (Jones, 1960, p. 268), thereby expressing her unconscious wish for inner renewal and for integration of the primary separation of birth, which was repeated in the separation from the therapist. The reduction of the symptoms to the desire to bear the father-therapist a child was not completely understood at the time.

Judging by his treatment reports in the studies on hysteria, Freud appears to have been more active during therapy than Breuer. Using the technique of pressing on the patient's forehead, in which the therapist apparently holds the head from the front with both hands, a birth-like situation is directly evoked in psychomotoric re-enactment. The hollows of the hands symbolize the pelvic girdle, the bearing down and pushing of the process of labor, and the interplay between pressure and counterpressure in the birth process. The symptom is symbolized in the image of a birth that can proceed no further or an emotion that finds no outlet, the release of which brings relief and a solution. The therapeutic process may be portrayed as 'opening a locked door' (Freud and Breuer, 1895, p. 228) in the face of resistance. The connection between the origin of the concept of resistance and the symbolism of birth is immediately evident here. The pushing and bearing down, as well as the intensification of pressure when the unconscious enters the consciousness, takes on an almost dramatic birth-like atmosphere in Freud's account. The symbolism of birth is also found in the concept of catharsis: 'Through the horror (phobos) in the face of the inescapable power of fate (emotions during the beginning phase of birth) and the misery (eleos) in view of the elementary affliction of man (the expulsion phase of birth), the observer arrives at a cleansed, intensified feeling of existence (feeling of novel animation subsequent to birth) (Brockhaus, 1970, p. 17).

THE CONCEPT OF BIRTH ANXIETY IN FREUD'S WORKS

The theme of birth, implicitly present in the studies on hysteria, becomes explicit in the concepts of birth anxiety (1909) and the intrauterine state as a form of primary narcissism (1917). Freud introduced the concept of birth anxiety in passing in the new edition of *Die Traumdeutung* (The Interpretation of Dreams) in 1909: 'The act of birth is, by the way, the first anxiety experience and therefore the source and model of the emotion of anxiety' (Freud, 1909, p. 390). The identification of the intrauterine state with primary narcissism becomes evident from the following quotations:

> 'Sleep is a somatic reactivation of the period in the womb, fulfilling the conditions of position of rest, warmth, and deflection of stimuli; indeed, many people reassume the fetal position while asleep. The psychic state of a sleeping person is characterized by a virtually absolute withdrawal from the world of his environment and a cessation of all interest in it. When investigating psychoneurotic states, one must emphasize the so-called temporal regression in each of them and consider the retrogression in development peculiar to each. One differentiates between two such types of regression – that of ego development and that of libido development. The latter extents in the state of sleep as far as the development of primary narcissism; the former, as far as the stage of hallucinatory gratification of desires' (Freud, 1917, p. 413).

The following quotation is also pertinent in this context:

> 'Thus, in being born, we have taken the first step from absolutely self-sufficient narcissism to the perception of a changeable outside world and to the beginning of exteriorization. Bound up with this is the fact that we can not continually endure this new state, that we periodically negate it and return in our sleep to the earlier state of lack of stimuli and object avoidance' (Freud, 1921, p. 136).

For therapeutic purposes, the theme of birth was discovered as a reaction to the fact that a deadline was set for terminating the treatment of the wolfman (1918).

THE TREATMENT-ORIENTED TRANSFORMATION BY RANK

Rank likewise viewed the analytical situation essentially as a symbolic re-enactment of the fetal situation as influenced by the reality of birth. He described the spontaneous appearance of this perinatal regression and its manifestations. This regression can express itself in images of being immersed into a body of water, for example, or being placed in a subterranean cave, and so on. The consistent interpretation of these associations, that is, the demonstration of connections between the individual's life history and traumatic moments during birth, paves the way for the eventual separation from the therapist, which regularly ensues in images of being born. Rank's ideas (1923, 1924) were taken up by a small number of analysts. Hollòs (1924) reported on the treatment of a prematurely-born patient who experienced the trauma of his birth over and over during therapy. Alexander (1925) described the deep regressions in the analytical process, and Sadger (1947) stated irrefutably that one could speak only of a 'relative analytical cure' if the trauma of birth was not reached. However, the majority of the analysts, who were under the governing influence of Abraham, Jones and Sachs, did not accept Rank's theories. In this connection it should be taken into consideration that the circle of truly competent analysts was very small at the time and that discussion was burdened by political considerations as to who would succeed Freud.

THE DISAPPEARANCE OF THE BIRTH THEME FROM PSYCHOANALYSIS

Freud's work *Hemmung, Symptom und Angst* (Inhibition, Symptom and Anxiety) (1926) was his last contribution to the discussion of the viewpoints held by Rank. In it, the primary emotions are qualified by the concept of signal anxieties and emphasis is placed on the ego and ways of understanding it, which diverts attention from manifestations of deep regression in the analytical situation. This set a course which was pursued by the proponents of ego-oriented psychoanalysis, including Hartmann and Rappaport, and supplanted the birth theme from the realm of psychoanalysis. According to this school of thought, the innate ego functions survived the trauma of birth more or less intact, such that they appeared to be released from the dynamics of this conflict. These concepts were oriented more towards securing the status quo in psychoanalysis than towards promoting continued creative development in the field.

THE SYMBOLIC EMBODIMENT OF THE BIRTH THEME IN JUNG'S WORKS

Following up on an idea set forth by Silberer (1914), Jung described the aspect of transference in the therapeutic process paradigmatically as symbolic regression into the womb and rebirth, making use of a series of pictures such as were used by the alchemists. Transference as a mutually and unconsciously activated phenomenon is portrayed symbolically in these pictures as the beginning of a stream which originates in the 'Fountain of Mercury', the 'uterine vessel of transformation' (the 'unconscious'). The picture entitled 'Immersion in the Bath' symbolizes 'being returned to the dark initial state, to the amniotic fluid of the gravid uterus' ('regression'). It is here that the transformation process of 'dying and coming into existence' takes place in images of death, decay ('analysis') and reanimation ('sublimation'), with the latter being manifested in rejuvenation through new birth.

THE CONTINUATION OF THE IMPETUS GIVEN TO THE BIRTH THEME IN EARLIER PSYCHOANALYSIS

The innovative power of the dimension of the birth experience set forth in the works of earlier analysts was developed further in a creative fashion, in particular by Graber, Fodor and Kruse. I would like to indicate briefly the different focal points that resulted.

With respect to treatment techniques, Graber concurred with Rank, emphasizing the powerful nature of the prenatal experience and the significance of the original, basic self of the fetal existence as a determining factor. The concepts of total regression (intrauterine regression) and 'primary resistance' (avoiding the repetition of the birth trauma) are new. Graber summarizes the important points in his conception of treatment as follows:

> 'It is the patient's attitude of resistance, which often appears unassailable and inalterable, that jinxes our efforts by means of an inflexible, primary-fixated, regressive posture of making existential embryonic claims to absolute security, being loved as God loves one, absolute goodness, etc. As early as twenty years ago, I stressed – as I have been doing ever since – that the main task of psychotherapy is to nullify the ego-like structure resulting from identification with what is foreign and having an external character (false self), thus enabling the self, the most original and inherent part of the soul, to develop ... and yet, provided that we possess the faculty to do so, we can experience daily in our practices how the smallest success in psychic healing is basically a kind of rebirth out of a bound existence into a freer one' (Graber, 1966, p. 64).

Aside from Graber, it was no doubt Fodor (1949) who described the significance of actualizing the birth experience in the treatment situation most comprehensively. Like Sadger, Fodor stresses the immediacy of the repetition of one's birth as a decisive factor in treatment. He places special emphasis on the meaning of prenatal dreams and their integration.

Kruse's treatment style, as evident from his treatment reports (Kruse, 1969), has an active, dynamic character similar to that of Adler. His approach is to confront conflicts as a means of working out traumatizations suffered in early childhood, with the treatment process being viewed as a symbolic repetition of the individual's development. Kruse attaches special importance to dreams about the womb and birth:

> 'Dreams about the womb and birth which have no engram of their own (i.e. do not originate from a birth trauma) have a favorable meaning for prognosis, almost without exception. They indicate that the climax of treatment has been passed, the conflicts of life uncovered, and that the actual process of recovery is forthcoming or has already begun. The patient, protected by the transference attachment, regressed to the period prior to the emergence of neurotogenic causes in his life. In symbolic terms, he was able "to enter his mother's womb a second time and be born again" (John, 3,4). A comparison with a train suggests itself, a train that was misdirected as a result of the switches having been improperly set and has to back up to a point beyond the decisive switch. Only then does it once again proceed full steam ahead towards its destination' (Kruse, 1969, p. 173).

In cases of fixation on the trauma of birth, Kruse cites very striking examples of the birth process becoming more and more successful in the succession of dreams about birth, thus reflecting the progress being made during treatment. His ideas as to the treatment of agoraphobia and claustrophobia, both of which can apparently be very directly influenced by incorporating the birth theme, are far from exhausted.

Looking back on the extensive research work alluded to here that has been done in the last 60 years, since the publication of Rank's book — whereby Caruso, E. Freud, Hau, Rascovsky, Verney and others should be mentioned — the way has now, in my estimation, been paved for an attempt at formulating some systematic ideas on the significance of the birth experience and the prenatal period for the treatment process. I would like to proceed to do so, taking into consideration the three aspects of the trauma of birth, serial trauma and the symbolism of birth.

THE TRAUMA OF BIRTH AS REFLECTED IN THE PROCESS OF ANALYTICAL TREATMENT

In cases involving a traumatic birth where later conditions in life did not allow this traumatic experience to be integrated and reabsorbed, so to speak, the birth trauma is generally one central focus of treatment which proves effective from the beginning, according to my observations. Thus, the various forms of defensive behavior exhibited by a compulsively neurotic patient, whose birth was both overdue and difficult, were ultimately intended to prevent a genuine relationship from developing at all, that is, to prevent a therapeutic birth from taking place. To this end, the patient spoke eloquently, keeping me at a distance in this way and by other means as well. His central fantasy was that I wanted to crush his head and that he resisted these efforts. This was the repetition of the archaic situation of birth in which the doctor kneeled on the mother's abdomen to force the birth to proceed, crushing the head of the fetus in the process. This traumatic primary experience assumed various symbolical representations, e.g. being beaten, decapitated, dismembered, put through machines that tear one to pieces, finding oneself on board a ship caught between rocky cliffs, and so on. The patient's means of symbolic defense and armament in the face of these imaginary dangers were accordingly diverse. At the same time, all of this was viewed as renewed and repeated attempts on the patient's part to integrate the traumatic birth experience, in much the same way as an accident may be relived again and again in nightmares in order to integrate the overwhelming danger.

In this respect, therapy is an overcoming of the trauma of birth which takes place on various yet interconnected levels: the level of transference, the level of the psychic content of feelings and one's defense against them, the level of symbolic images and gestures, and the level of bodily experience. The actualization of a reference to birth can thus manifest itself in a fantasy concerning a relationship, in a dream, in an anxiety or its warding off, in a bodily experience, or in some combination of these components. Thus, a patient who experienced a difficult breech birth after the expected delivery date perceived the setting of an appointment for therapy, like all other appointments, as something which pinned him down in an unbearable fashion. On the way to analysis, he felt immensely fatigued, burdened down, and he broke out in perspiration. In his dreams, he often saw corridors and staircases in which he got caught, unable to get through them. He said that when he was confronted with a task, he did not envisage it as something ahead of him but saw it rather as something wound around himself through which he had to pass. Accordingly, he reacted to stressful situations by developing diffused rheumatoid pains in his muscles. He said that entering caves was a test of courage for him. However, he explained that he had to avoid imagining them as being too narrow or in danger of collapsing; otherwise, he would dream about such things at night.

As the above-mentioned authors have described, a careful analysis of associations with a traumatic birth leads to a gradual integration of the complexities of the birth trauma. A patient born by Caesarean section felt himself to be a foreign body, in all kinds of situations in life and during analysis as well; he had the impression he offended others and felt battered and worn down. The traumatic process of his delivery by Caesarean section, together with the sudden, overwhelming change of environment, assumed the most varied symbolic forms, such as being flung back and forth, being blown away, or experiencing frequent uneasiness, and so on. The patient's outlook on life was correspondingly gloomy. The integration gradually effected during the treatment process was reflected in a dream in which he drove a motorcycle along a winding road to the coast, maneuvering the vehicle elegantly and ending up in an area of the countryside that he loved. This dream and similar ones signalled a substantial change for the better in his outlook on life.

THE SERIAL TRAUMA

My observations indicate that the theme of traumatic birth plays a particularly important role in treatment if conditions at birth were traumatic and if, at the same time, the conditions in the family during early childhood were unfavorable and if, moreover, the dynamics of conflict in the family exposed the child to similar conflicts during the various phases of his development. This could be a certain depressiveness on the part of the mother, for example, with which the child tries unsuccessfully to come to terms in various ways during the various phases of his development. Scenarios of this kind can result in the traumatic experience of birth being left unresolved, so to speak, as a consequence of a series of similar traumatic situations, with the corresponding roots making themselves felt very quickly in stressful situations. It may also happen that the experience of an insignificant birth trauma is reinforced through serial traumatization, because later anxieties may be experienced as a reflection of the anxiety experienced at birth.

THE SYMBOLISM OF BIRTH IN THE THERAPEUTIC PROCESS

The process of healing has always been characterized by the basic form of 'dying and coming into being', of a journey into the depths, of introversive regression, and the like. While this process was carried out in ancient times by projecting one's experiences onto the fates of mythical heroes or by participating in the collective rites of the mysteries, it is interiorized in the analytical process to the experience of a relationship entered into in mutual agreement. Nevertheless, the dynamics of this experience are determined by the same symbolism as in those earlier processes, as Jung succeeded in showing with reference to alchemy, which is more familiar to us than the techniques employed in ancient times.

The consideration of these dynamics of birth symbols in all processes of transformation and change, as is implicit in psychoanalysis, offers a decisive orientation when assessing the psychoanalytical process and allows several elucidative reflections on the problems of treatment techniques. An approach oriented on the model of unilateral healing or recovery is of necessity incomplete, neglecting as it does the inalterable fact that what has been outlived must die in all processes of rebirth. It was Sabina Spielrein who developed this viewpoint to its full extent in her work *Destruktion als Ursache des Werdens* (Destruction as the Cause of Coming into Being) (1912). In my estimation, the creative strength of the process model set forth by Fürstenau (1978, p. 66 *et seq.*) lies in the fact that this principle of dying and coming into being is explicitly contained, albeit abstractly, in the concepts of 'revising the traditional pattern of relationships' and 'establishing a new pattern of relationships'.

A further viewpoint is that of regression. With respect to the dynamics of the symbolism of birth, it is immediately evident that a process of transformation can take place only via a creative, crisis-like regression. While Freud virtually opened up the regressive space of the unconscious and the infantile, he emphasized the aspect of insight in doing so, which is a sound approach to hysterical disturbances. The aspect of repetition, the experience aspect, receded by comparison, to be accentuated later by Ferenczi and Rank (1924). The development of ego psychology in psychoanalysis was in danger of allowing the aspect of insight to be stressed exclusively, as witnessed, for example, in Greenson's overemphasis of the working alliance (1967). In terms of practical treatment, these considerations compel the therapist to recognize that perinatal transference fantasies are to be accepted in countertransference rather than ignored a priori. This holds particularly true for short-term therapy or analytically-oriented psychotherapy. Failure to heed this connection is, in my opinion, one reason why the concept of short-term focal therapy has stagnated (Janus, 1986b, p. 87).

Likewise, the division into psychoanalysis and analytically-oriented psychotherapy appears to be partially due to a failure to appreciate the dynamics of the birth experience. It is widely held that patients, who have less marked early fixations and who are able to engage in regressive and progressive interaction in the therapeutic process without suffering a crisis-like situation or becoming entangled with the therapist, are good candidates for therapy.

According to this view, analytically-oriented therapy is indicated in cases involving early fixations, whereby the dynamics of the roots of the birth trauma are masked by an 'active' approach to therapy in order to attain the goal of partial adjustment. In my opinion, the distinction between psychoanalysis and analytically-oriented psychotherapy is qualified by including the earliest period of life in the process of treatment and the therapeutic relationship. For example, a patient of approximately 30 years of age comes in while suffering a depressive-narcissistic crisis, which has already been going on for some time and is jeopardizing his ability to work. He feels threatened by insecurities in a difficult relationship. He has the feeling that he is losing the ground under his feet, that he no longer has a grip on things and is falling into a void. It first appeared to be a situation involving the repetition of an Oedipal deprivation that he had suffered when his mother returned to work. This experience, however, weighed even more heavily because of the fact that his birth had been difficult and premature and that he had not received adequate care at first. This deep layer of conflicts became more clear to me through countertransference, as I became aware of strong feelings of not being provided for in myself; in this way, I arrived at a better understanding of the existential impact of the patient's fear of deprivation. By incorporating this early dimension of his experience as I now understood it into my interpretations, I was better able to work out with the patient the effects that his anxieties about not being cared for and his defense against these anxieties had on his life. Thus, in approximately 25 sessions the repetitive nature of the patient's symptoms was clarified to such an extent that he felt unburdened and was able to individuate without fear of separation, even in the therapy situation, and to face the real problems of a difficult situation in life. It is my conviction that analytically-oriented psychotherapy focused on ego building would have led only to an unsatisfactory understanding of the aspect of the relationship conflict in this case and that psychoanalytical treatment in the more restricted sense would have protracted the symptomatic regression. Through his therapeutical acceptance of the deep regression in which he found himself in his conflict, the patient was able to reach the level of the Oedipal conflict that triggered his difficulties more quickly.

The therapist faces a particular challenge when the theme of birth is expressed exclusively in terms of bodily experience, e.g. in the form of headaches, respiratory distress, chills, and so on, or when it is acted out. Thus, one patient was able to perceive and express her desire for regressive fusion only through her real desire to move into an apartment I had formerly occupied. Another patient actualized his desire for regression through agonizing physical feelings of being cornered. Much research remains to be done in this area.

Blarer (1982) was correct in emphasizing that all changes and crises in the therapeutic process can be represented in symbols of birth, especially at the beginning and end of treatment. One patient expressed his hope of experiencing a psychic birth during analysis in the following dream: 'I was in a shaft that narrowed towards the top. There was wooden scaffolding leading to the top, which I wanted to climb up on. It started to wobble in the middle, and the rungs ended there. It was just a very smooth pole. It was still quite a distance to the top. I ventured to try it, thinking, "if only you were nimbler and not such a coward."' The dream illustrated his confinement in the archaic maternal symbol of the shaft and his efforts to free himself. Such are the familiar images of the cave, the swamp, the forest, the subterranean passage and so on, which are ever present in fairy tales and in therapeutic processes like the catathymic experience of images. These images, which represent the regressive movements, desires and anxieties of the patient, can offer the therapist helpful orientation. The end of therapy may be symbolized in images of birth, weaning and learning how to walk.

Perhaps the time has now come to do justice to the extensive influence of the birth experience by adding the concept of the natal phase to the developmental phases already known. While Schwidder once described the theme of the Freudian libido phase as loving and being loved, killing and being killed, devouring and being devoured, the natal phase is concerned with the dying and coming into being of birth, or the dimension of experience relating to death and rebirth. Whatever one may hold of this view, one must today in any case contradict the claim made by Stone (1961) that the analyst represents the mother subsequent to separation; in the therapy situation, the analyst assumes the function of the mother prior to separation as well, and both the prenatal and postnatal functions of the mother are conveyed through the process of real and symbolic birth.

16

The role of hypnotherapy in facilitating normal birth

L. Mehl, S. Donovan and G. Peterson

ABSTRACT

This study used a multivariate approach to isolate psychological factors that are associated with normal and abnormal birth outcome. Secondly, the study aimed to examine the relationship between hypnotherapy and birth outcome. Two psychological factors, fear and support from the woman's partner, most strongly discriminated between the normal and abnormal birth outcome groups. Other psychological factors, anxiety-stress, maternal self-identity, beliefs, support from the woman's mother, and support from friends, distinguished between the groups. High levels of fear, low support from the woman's partner, anxiety-stress, poor maternal self-identity, negative beliefs, and lack of support from the woman's mother and friends, were found to be associated with an abnormal birth outcome. Low levels of fear, support from the woman's partner, low levels of anxiety-stress, a positive maternal self-identity, positive beliefs, and support from the woman's mother and friends, were found to be associated with a normal birth outcome. Hypnotherapy played a significant role: its presence inhibited negative emotional factors from being related to abnormal birth outcome. A prediction model was formed to discriminate pregnant women at risk for an abnormal birth outcome.

INTRODUCTION

There is a growing interest in the role of psychosocial risk in health and disease[1]. Physicians have begun to question the influence of psychosocial risk on health. Obstetricians wonder if psychosocial risk factors contribute to the outcome of childbirth.

Nuckolls et al. (1972) have suggested that urban society, with its breakdown of the extended family system, may expose women to more psychological stress regarding pregnancy than occurs in the extended family structure. Their research indicated that realistic, accurate, social support during pregnancy facilitated a healthy obstetric outcome.

Smilkstein (1984, 1986) has provided a model to conceptualize the effects of psychosocial factors on health and disease called the Cycle of Psychosocial Risk. In Smilkstein's model, multiple stressors impact upon an individual each day. A response is generated reflecting the individual's cognitive appraisal of the stressor. The 'black box' within which cognitive appraisals are made is the individual's belief system (beliefs for short). Beliefs are influenced by many factors, including the person's past experience with similar stressors. Beliefs represent the results of prior learning. Smilkstein notes that the cognitive appraisal process is affected by the person's psychosocial equilibrium at the time the stressor is received and by the number and intensity of other stressors being processed by the person.

Pregnancy is an unresolvable stress. The birth and the coming of parenthood cannot be prevented. We wondered if women who used 'mature' coping strategies and who have social support would be more likely to suffer less physiological impact from anxiety and therefore would experience more normal labors[2].

Nucholls has pointed out how pregnancy and parenthood are becoming much greater stresses related to decreasing support for the family in our state of urban mobility. Peterson (1984) and Mehl and Peterson (1978, 1985) have written about the ambiguity and inherent contradictions in woman's role in our society today. The struggle to integrate career and motherhood is often intense for many women, whose mothers only served as negative role models.

Kobasa (1979) applied the term 'hardiness' to subjects in her studies who demonstrated a low incidence of illness in the face of high stress. Will 'hardy' pregnant women have more physiologically normal labors than other women? Hardy individuals have been characterized as having: (1) a greater sense of control over what occurs in their lives, (2) a feeling of commitment to the various activities in which they are engaged, (3) a view of change as a challenge rather than a threat, and (4) a sense of a meaningfulness to their lives.

Mehl and Peterson (1986) reported a prediction equation for Caesarean birth that included beliefs, attitudes, lifestyle, behavior and environment. These authors suggested that the increasing cultural stress on women's roles and decreasing social support may be important contributors to the rising Caesarean delivery rate.

Our purpose in this research was to consider the question of whether high stress and low social support contribute to birth complications, and to determine if an intervention program of experiential psychotherapy, utilizing primarily hypnosis would protect the high stress–low social support woman from developing birth complications.

METHODS

We chose to study the patients of a certified nurse midwifery practice group in the San Francisco Bay Area. These midwives were appropriately obstetrically supervised and delivered their clients at a local hospital. Obstetrical perinatologists supervised the development of the nurse-midwifery protocols. Only medically low-risk women remained with the midwifery group. The Popras Risk Screening System, developed by Dr Calvin Hobel, was used by these groups.

We reasoned that midwifery service patients subjected to these protocols would be medically low-risk, and therefore, ideal for our purposes. 64 consecutive women receiving midwifery care after initial evaluation and screening were studied. Age varied from 20 years to 38 years with an average of 28 years. Years of education ranged from 9 to 19, with an average of 14 years. Of the women, 38 were nulliparous, 14 were primiparous and 12 were multiparous.

A more complete medical and psychosocial history was obtained, including:

(1) Demographic information,
(2) A complete family medical history,
(3) Ob/gyn health history,
(4) Psychosocial history,
(5) Past medical history, and
(6) Review of current symptoms.

The Homes–Rahe Life Stress Inventory was used, along with the Taylor Manifest Anxiety Scale, and the Dyadic Adjustment Scale. Each couple was interviewed by a member of the research team. The woman was seen 2–4 weeks later for body assessment, particularly the woman's relationship to her body, awareness of body symptoms and tension, and pattern of body tension.

During the couple's interview, information was solicited from which an assessment of the couple's beliefs, experiences, expectations and affective states was made. Assessment was also made of the women's stressors, fears and social support.

Follow-up interviews were offered to all patients. During these interviews, hypnotherapy, relaxation training and other methods of anxiety management were used. The average number of prenatal interviews was 10. The minimum was two, and the maximum, 24. Two of us (LEM and GHP) provided the majority of the interviewing, assisted by two psychology graduate interns.

The approach used for the experiential psychotherapy and hypnotherapy has been described elsewhere. In brief, we are using a problem-oriented approach, guided by biofeedback and somatic observations of patterns of muscular tension. Hypnosis is used widely. Suggestions are consonant with a problem-solving approach. Occasionally other family members would be brought to the interview. We are not doing insight-oriented psychotherapy or any type of psychoanalytically based psychotherapy. Our goals were increased relaxation, decreased anxiety, increased sense of trust of social support, and realistic fear. Hypnosis was used to guide the woman through an imaginary experience of giving birth, thereby decreasing fear and anxiety. Careful notes were made of the interviews.

Interviews aimed to establish a close rapport with each patient, so that feelings, fears and complaints could be freely expressed. Interviews lasted one hour and were timed to coincide with the woman's visit for prenatal care. They were done in the midwives' offices. In addition to questions related to the seven major research categories, information about the patient's past and currect reactions toward herself, her family, her partner, work, social, religious and physical experience was elicited. Her knowledge of the physiology of pregnancy and birth, her menstrual experience, family patterns of pregnancy and birth, changes in sex relationships, attitudes toward body changes, the baby, nursing, and the general experiences of pregnancy and birth were assessed.

Careful note was made of the subtle and revealing shifts in attitudes and reactions indicated by changes in tempo and intensity of verbalizations, slips of the tongue, innuendo, facial expression, vasomotor activity and tone of voice.

Because an unselected group was interviewed, the interest or capacity of each woman for participation varied. Some had but little experience thinking about themselves or that which had happened to them and expressed themselves poorly. However, some subjects who verbalized poorly gave crucial, pertinent material once they were encouraged to talk about themselves. Others were defensive and produced scanty material.

These interviews represented different experiences to different patients. To most, they gave a much needed feeling of being an individual in whom the midwives were interested. To a few, the interviews were simply an opportunity to be a part of a study, and to a couple of women, the interviews provided a serious threat. Most of the patients, however, soon came to regard the interview as a helpful experience – an opportunity to talk about anxieties and problems.

Observations of the behavior and emotional reactions of these patients to their prenatal and subsequent examinations were recorded by the interviewer. Some patients chose to see the researchers for hypnosis, brief psychotherapy, relaxation training, visualization, marital or couples counseling. The researchers interacted with the women's childbirth educators, to give and receive information helpful to all. Obstetric data and all physical examination findings during the course of pregnancy and childbirth were recorded. Every effort was made to learn as much as possible about the patients in terms of their psychological functioning, cultural background and life experiences. When possible, data were gathered on their reactions to pregnancy, from the time of their first clinic visit, as well as before, during and immediately after delivery.

Verbal responses from the women were recorded and the relationship between the verbal expression and the clinical impression of affective states was noted. For example, the statement, 'I am afraid of pain in childbirth', signifies the pregnant woman is herself afraid. This indicates something about the internal state of the woman. By taking the verbal statements, categorizing the expression and weighting the intensity, a measure of the psychological factor was obtained. Thus, 'I am afraid of pain in childbirth', was categorized as a 'Fear' type of statement.

Statements from the women were categorized in the following content areas:

(1) Fear,
(2) Anxiety-stress,
(3) Maternal self-identity,
(4) Beliefs,
(5) Psychosocial support from the partner,
(6) Psychosocial support from the mother's mother,
(7) Psychosocial support from friends.

Since the women were likely to present verbal evidence of their internal psychological state, frequency of occurrence of a specific response and the magnitude or intensity of the responses were noted. Comparative adverbs: 'very', 'mildly', etc., were included as indicators of the magnitude of the psychological state. The verbal responses of the women were differentially weighted in the specific content categories in proportion to the assumed intensity represented by statements classifiable in certain content categories. Values were assigned to all the verbal responses made. Values ranged from negative (-3) to positive $(+3)$, with $+3$ the most theoretically conducive to a normal birth outcome and −3 the least. One type of direct verbal report of the subjective affective experience, such as, 'I am anxious', would be classified in the 'anxiety-stress' category, and have a weighted value of a −2, while the same statement with a greater intensity, 'I am very anxious', would be weighted −3. Each of the women's responses were assessed with the value weighted on each variable to develop a profile of her psychological attitude during pregnancy.

RESULTS

A prediction equation was developed which correctly classified 89.1% of the cases correctly into the normal birth outcome group (group N) or the abnormal birth outcome group (group A). Women having normal deliveries were classified correctly with 88.2% accuracy, compared to 90.0% for women having abnormal births. The complete prediction model is shown in Figure 1. (The codes for the variables are provided in Table 1.) The numbers in the equation are the coefficients for canonical variables provided by the discriminant analysis. A y-value greater than 0.7488 predicts an abnormal birth. Current research is improving the equation of Figure 1 through modifications toward a non-linear structure. For the linear model, the canonical correlation was 0.772, meaning that, about eight times out of ten, the equation correctly classified group membership. The most significant psychosocial factors were *fear* and *support from the baby's father*.

$$Y = 2.07956 - .41895R - .25862T + .21757D + .86444O - .31573I - .89256N \\ + .34529Q - .38230V + .10873C - .28286Y + .17197S + .26531F + .12293B \\ + .01820K - .02270A - .11385J + .14981P + .09632W - .08914G - .02173AA \\ + .10729L + .04648E + .03045V - .01520Z - .07954H + .07954H + .04495A \\ + .00702X$$

Figure 1 Prediction model for a normal or abnormal birth outcome

Contribution of medical and demographic variables to risk

Table 2 shows that no significant differences were found between the normal and abnormal birth outcome groups on age, years of education, religion, place of birth and marital status. Table 3 shows no differences in the two groups for members having previous live births, previous abortions and previous miscarriages. Table 4 shows differences between the two groups in past medical history. Women in the abnormal birth group

Table 1 Key to the names and codes for all variables

Code	Variable represented in analysis
A	Age
B	Years of education
C	Religion
D	Place of birth
E	Marital status
F	Previous live births
G	Previous abortions
H	Previous miscarriages
I	Physical activity
J	Past relationship with mother while growing up
K	Past relationship with father while growing up
L	Past infections
M	Past injuries
N	Past surgeries
O	Past hospitalizations
P	Past illnesses
Q	Drug use
R	Fear
S	Maternal self-identity
T	Support from partner
U	Support from mother's mother
V	Support from friends
W	Support from other sources
X	Anxiety-stress
Y	Beliefs
Z	Interventions
AA	Psychotherapy sessions
BB	Birth outcome
CC	Gestation
DD	Length of 1st stage of labor
EE	Length of 2nd stage of labor
FF	Birthweight
GG	Apgar score at 1 minute
HH	Apgar score at 5 minutes

showed significantly more previous (to the pregnancy) infections, injuries and hospitalizations. These events were not obstetrical or gynecological and did not increase their risk on the Propas Obstetrical Risk Screening Criteria. There were no differences in number of prior surgeries or diagnosed illnesses.

Table 2 Comparison of means and standard deviations for the demographic variables between normal and abnormal birth outcome groups

Demographic variables	Normal Mean	SD	Abnormal Mean	SD	t-value
Age	28.26	4.96	27.85	4.18	−0.34
Years of education	13.97	2.53	14.20	2.22	0.38
Religion	1.97	2.47	2.13	2.36	0.27
Place of birth	3.41	2.08	3.87	2.67	0.76
Marital status	2.44	1.19	2.27	1.11	−0.60

Table 3 Comparison of means and standard deviations for the past obstetrical history variables between normal and abnormal birth outcome groups

Past obstetrical history variables	Normal Mean	SD	Abnormal Mean	SD	t-value
Previous live births	0.76	1.02	0.57	0.82	−0.85
Previous abortions	0.91	1.24	0.87	1.17	−0.15
Previous miscarriages	0.00	0.00	0.13	0.51	1.53

Table 4 Comparison of means and standard deviations for the past medical history variables between normal and abnormal birth outcome groups

Past medical history variables	Normal Mean	SD	Abnormal Mean	SD	t-value
Infections	0.53	0.56	0.97	0.81	2.53*
Injuries	0.26	0.48	0.70	0.75	2.86†
Surgeries	0.68	0.77	0.97	0.72	1.56
Hospitalizations	0.76	0.78	1.27	0.83	2.50*
Illnesses	0.47	0.51	0.67	0.76	1.23

* Significant at the 0.05 level ($p > +1.96$); † significant at the 0.01 level ($p > +2.57$)

Table 5 shows differences in past habit history. Women in the abnormal birth group showed more frequent past drug use. Neither group was using drugs during the pregnancy. Such usage would have prompted rejection from the midwifery service population. Women in the normal birth group tended to be more physically active.

Table 5 Comparison of means and standard deviations for the habit history variables between normal and abnormal birth outcome groups

	Normal		Abnormal		
Habit history variables	Mean	SD	Mean	SD	t-value
Drug use	0.79	1.25	1.50	1.22	2.28*
Physical activity	1.32	1.25	0.80	0.81	−1.96*

* Significant at the 0.05 level ($p > \pm 1.96$)

Emotional state variables

Table 6 shows the differences in the emotional state variables. All four variables were significantly different between groups. Women in the abnormal birth group showed more *anxiety-stress* and *fear*. Their beliefs (cognitive appraisal modes) were more negative toward birth. They showed less maternal identity.

In Table 7, we compare the means on the anxiety-stress variable between the normal and abnormal birth outcome groups when grouped for hypnotherapy. No significant differences were found. Both groups, under the condition of hypnotherapy, showed high levels of anxiety-stress. These results indicate that the presence of hypnotherapy inhibited cases of high anxiety-stress from being related to abnormal birth outcome. Under the absence of hypnotherapy, the abnormal group showed higher levels of anxiety-stress, and the normal group showed very little anxiety-stress. This indicated that, in the absence of hypnotherapy, high anxiety-stress was associated with abnormal birth outcome.

In Table 8, we compare the means on the anxiety-stress variable between the hypnotherapy and no-hypnotherapy conditions for the normal birth

Table 6 Comparison of means and standard deviations for the emotional state factors between normal and abnormal birth outcome groups

	Normal		Abnormal		
Emotional state factors	Mean	SD	Mean	SD	t-value
Anxiety-stress	−0.23	1.99	−1.72	1.46	−3.39*
Fear	1.09	2.09	−0.89	1.74	−4.10*
Identity	0.93	1.83	−0.25	1.81	−2.59*
Beliefs	1.31	1.45	0.17	1.30	−3.29*

* Significant at the 0.01 level ($p > \pm 2.57$)

Table 7 Comparison of means and standard deviations for the emotional state factors between normal and abnormal birth outcome groups when grouped for hypnotherapy

Emotional state factors	Normal Mean	SD	Abnormal Mean	SD	t-value
Anxiety-stress					
Hypnotherapy	−1.59	0.78	−1.91	0.59	−1.29
No hypnotherapy	0.73	2.03	−1.51	2.06	−3.13†
	4.05†		0.75		
Fear					
Hypnotherapy	0.31	2.21	−1.03	1.27	−2.07*
No hypnotherapy	1.65	1.86	−0.74	2.20	−3.41†
	1.91		0.46		
Identity					
Hypnotherapy	−0.19	1.50	−0.48	1.42	−0.56
No hypnotherapy	1.72	1.64	0.02	2.19	−2.58*
	3.44†		0.76		
Beliefs					
Hypnotherapy	1.60	1.29	0.11	1.16	−1.54
No hypnotherapy	0.89	1.60	0.24	1.48	−2.84†
	1.43		0.28		

* Significant at the 0.05 level ($p > \pm 2.048$); † significant at the 0.01 level ($p > \pm 2.763$)

outcome group. No significant differences were found. In the absence of hypnotherapy, the normal birth outcome group had no anxiety-stress. In comparing the mean scores on the anxiety-stress variable between the hypnotherapy and no-hypnotherapy conditions for the abnormal birth outcome group, no significant differences were found. Under both the hypnotherapy and no-hypnotherapy conditions, the results showed similar mean scores for the anxiety-stress variable in the abnormal birth outcome group. This result indicates that under the no-hypnotherapy and hypnotherapy conditions, the abnormal birth outcome group had high stress and anxiety. These results indicate that the presence of hypnotherapy stabilized cases of high anxiety-stress in the normal birth outcome group and may have inhibited women from having an abnormal birth outcome.

Table 8 Comparison of means and standard deviations for the emotional state factors within normal and abnormal birth outcome groups when grouped for hypnotherapy

Emotional state factors	Hypnotherapy Mean	SD	No hypnotherapy Mean	SD	t-value
Anxiety-stress					
Normal	−1.59	0.78	0.73	2.03	4.05*
Abnormal	−1.91	0.59	1.51	2.06	0.75
Fear					
Normal	0.31	2.21	1.65	1.86	1.91
Abnormal	−1.03	1.27	−0.74	2.20	0.46
Identity					
Normal	−0.19	1.50	1.72	1.64	3.44*
Abnormal	−0.48	1.42	0.02	2.19	0.76
Beliefs					
Normal	1.60	1.29	0.89	1.60	1.43
Abnormal	0.11	1.16	0.24	1.48	0.28

*Significant at the 0.01 level ($p > \pm 2.57$)

Fear variable

In comparing the mean scores of the fear variable for the normal and abnormal birth outcome groups, significant differences were found. The abnormal birth outcome group showed higher fear scores than the normal birth outcome group, indicating that high fear is associated with abnormal birth outcome. See Table 6 for a summary of these results.

When grouped for hypnotherapy, in comparing the means on the fear variable between the normal and abnormal birth outcome groups, no significant differences were found. Both groups under the condition of hypnotherapy showed the presence of fear, although the abnormal birth outcome group's mean scores were slightly higher. These results indicate that hypnotherapy has a tendency to inhibit cases of fear from being related to abnormal birth outcome. In comparing the means on the fear variable between the normal and abnormal birth outcome groups under the no-hypnotherapy condition, significant differences were found. The abnormal birth outcome group had high fear, and the normal birth outcome group had no fear, indicating that, in the absence of hypnotherapy, high fear is associated with abnormal birth outcome. See Table 7 for a summary of these results.

When comparing the means on the fear variable between the hypnotherapy and no-hypnotherapy conditions for the normal birth outcome group, no significant differences were found. Under the conditions of hypnotherapy and no hypnotherapy, the results showed similar positive mean scores for the fear variable in the normal birth outcome group. When comparing the mean scores on the fear variable between the hypnotherapy and no-hypnotherapy conditions for the abnormal birth outcome group, no significant differences were found. Under the hypnotherapy and no-hypnotherapy conditions, the results showed similar negative mean scores for the fear variable in the abnormal birth outcome group. These results support those reported in the previous paragraph stating that in the absence of hypnotherapy high fear is associated with abnormal birth outcome. See Table 8 for a summary of these results.

Maternal self-identity variable

When comparing the mean scores of the maternal self-identity variable for the normal and abnormal birth outcome groups, significant differences were found. The abnormal birth outcome group showed greater negative maternal self-identity scores than the normal birth outcome group, indicating that a negative maternal self-identity is associated with abnormal birth outcome. See Table 6 for a summary of these results.

When grouped for hypnotherapy, in comparing the means on the maternal self-identity variable between the normal and abnormal birth outcome groups, no significant differences were found. Both groups under the condition of hypnotherapy showed a similar tendency toward negative maternal self-identity. When comparing the mean scores of the maternal self-identity variable under the conditions of no hypnotherapy, significant differences were found. The abnormal birth outcome group had a greater negative maternal self-identity, and the normal birth outcome group had a greater positive maternal self-identity, indicating that a positive maternal self-identity is associated with normal birth outcome and a negative maternal self-identity is associated with abnormal birth outcome. The presence of hypnotherapy has a tendency to inhibit cases of negative maternal self-identity from being related to abnormal birth outcome. See Table 7 for a summary of these results.

When comparing the means on the maternal self-identity variable between the hypnotherapy and no-hypnotherapy conditions for the normal birth outcome group, significant differences were found. Under the condition of hypnotherapy, the mean score was mildly negative on the maternal self-identity variable, and under the condition of no hypnotherapy, the mean score was positive. These results indicate the presence of negative maternal self-identity for women undergoing hypnotherapy in the normal birth outcome group, and the presence of positive maternal self-identity for women not undergoing hypnotherapy in the normal birth outcome group. When comparing the mean scores on the maternal self-identity variable between the hypnotherapy and no-hypnotherapy conditions for the abnormal birth outcome group, no significant differences were found. Under the conditions of hypnotherapy and no hypnotherapy, the results showed a similar tendency toward negative maternal self-identity in the abnormal birth outcome group. These results indicate that the presence of psychotherapy stabilized women with negative maternal self-identity and inhibited them from being related to abnormal birth outcome. See Table 8 for a summary of these results.

Belief variable

When comparing the mean scores of the beliefs variable for the normal and abnormal birth outcome groups, significant differences were found. The abnormal birth outcome group showed lower belief scores than the normal birth outcome group, indicating that positive beliefs are associated with normal birth outcome. See Table 6 for a summary of these results.

When grouped for hypnotherapy, in comparing the means on the beliefs variable between the normal and abnormal birth outcome groups, no significant differences were found. Both groups under the condition of hypnotherapy showed a similar tendency toward positive beliefs. When comparing the mean scores of the beliefs variable under the condition of no hypnotherapy, significant differences were found. The abnormal birth outcome group had more negative beliefs than the normal birth outcome group, and the normal birth outcome group had more positive beliefs than the abnormal birth outcome group. These results indicate that positive beliefs are associated with normal birth outcome and negative beliefs are associated with abnormal birth outcome, although in the latter case the association is weak. See Table 7 for a summary of these results.

When comparing the mean scores on the beliefs variable under the conditions of hypnotherapy and no hypnotherapy within the normal birth outcome group, no significant differences were found. Under both the hypnotherapy and no-hypnotherapy conditions, the normal birth outcome group showed positive beliefs, although under the hypnotherapy condition, the mean scores were less positive. When comparing the mean scores on the beliefs variable under the conditions of hypnotherapy and no hypnotherapy within the abnormal birth outcome group, no significant differences were found. Under the hypnotherapy and no-hypnotherapy conditions, the abnormal birth group showed similar scores indicating a very slight tendency toward positive beliefs. See Table 8 for a summary of these results.

Support from the baby's father variable

When comparing the mean scores of the support from the mother's partner variable for the normal and abnormal birth outcome groups, significant differences were found. The normal birth outcome group showed higher support scores than the abnormal birth outcome group, indicating that positive support from the woman's partner is associated with normal birth outcome. The mean score of the support variable for the abnormal birth outcome group was negative, indicating that negative support is associated with abnormal birth outcome. See Table 9 for a summary of these results.

When grouped for hypnotherapy, in comparing the means on the support from the baby's father variable between the normal and abnormal birth outcome groups, no significant differences were found. While the differences between the mean scores were not significant, the abnormal birth outcome group showed a tendency toward negative support from the woman's partner and the normal birth outcome group showed a tendency toward positive support. When comparing the mean scores of the support from the baby's father variable under the conditions of no hypnotherapy, significant differences were found. The abnormal birth outcome group showed negative support from the baby's father, and the normal birth outcome group showed positive support from the baby's father. These results indicate that positive support from the baby's father is associated with normal birth outcome, and negative support is associated with abnormal birth outcome. See Table 10 for a summary of these results.

When comparing the means on the support from the baby's father variable between the hypnotherapy and no-hypnotherapy conditions within the normal birth outcome group, significant differences were found. Under the condition of hypnotherapy, the mean scores were only mildly positive on the support variable, and under the condition of no hypnotherapy, the mean scores were more positive than under the hypnotherapy condition. When comparing the mean scores on the support from the baby's father variable between the hypnotherapy and no-hypnotherapy conditions within the abnormal birth outcome group, no significant differences were found. Under both the hypnotherapy and no-hypnotherapy conditions, the results showed similar mean scores for negative support from the baby's father within the abnormal birth outcome group. These results indicate that the presence of hypnotherapy stabilized

Table 9 Comparison of means and standard deviations for the psychosocial support factors between normal and abnormal birth outcome groups

Psychosocial support factors	Normal Mean	SD	Abnormal Mean	SD	t-value
Partner	1.22	1.64	−0.46	2.04	−3.64†
Mother's mother	0.38	1.62	−0.42	1.43	−2.07*
Friends	0.85	1.23	−0.12	1.04	−3.34†

* Significant at the 0.05 level ($p > \pm 1.960$); † significant at the 0.01 level ($p > \pm 2.576$)

Table 10 Comparison of means and standard deviations for the psychosocial support factors between normal and abnormal birth outcome groups when grouped for hypnotherapy

Psychosocial support factors	Normal Mean	SD	Abnormal Mean	SD	t-value
Partner					
Hypnotherapy	0.51	1.77	−0.31	1.96	−1.18
No hypnotherapy	1.72	1.38	−0.63	2.18	−3.85*
Mother's mother					
Hypnotherapy	0.05	1.85	−0.53	1.16	−1.04
No hypnotherapy	0.64	1.45	−0.29	1.73	−1.65
Friends					
Hypnotherapy	0.86	1.23	−0.19	0.54	−3.07*
No hypnotherapy	0.85	1.27	0.01	1.43	−1.86

* Significant at the 0.01 level ($p > \pm 2.576$)

cases of lower support from the partner from being related to abnormal birth outcome. See Table 11 for a summary of these results.

Support from the mother's mother variable

When comparing the mean scores of the support from the mother's mother variable for the normal and abnormal birth outcome groups, significant differences were found. The normal birth outcome group showed positive support scores, and the abnormal birth outcome group showed negative support scores. These results indicate that positive support from the woman's mother is associated with normal birth outcome. See Table 9 for a summary of these results.

When grouped for hypnotherapy, in comparing the means on the support from the mother's mother variable between the normal and abnormal birth outcome groups, no significant differences were found. Under the no-hypnotherapy condition, when comparing the mean scores on the support from the mother's mother variable, no significant differences were found. See Table 10 for a summary of these results.

When comparing the mean scores on the support from the mother's mother variable within the normal birth outcome group, no significant differences were found. When comparing the means on the support from the mother's mother variable within the abnormal birth outcome group, no significant differences were found. See Table 11 for a summary of these results.

Support from friends variable

When comparing the mean scores of the support from friends variable for the normal and abnormal birth outcome group, significant differences were found. The normal birth outcome group showed positive support scores, and the abnormal birth outcome group showed negative support scores. These results indicate that positive support from the woman's friends is associated with normal birth outcome, and negative support is associated with abnormal birth outcome. See Table 9 for a summary of these results.

When grouped for hypnotherapy, in comparing the mean scores on the support from friends variable between the normal and abnormal birth outcome groups, significant differences were found. The abnormal birth outcome group showed negative support scores and the normal birth outcome group showed positive support scores. When comparing the mean scores of the support from friends variable under the no-hypnotherapy condition, no significant differences were found. See Table 10 for a summary of these results.

When comparing the means on the support from friends variable between the hypnotherapy and no-hypnotherapy conditions within the normal birth outcome group, no significant differences were found. Under both the conditions of hypnotherapy and no hypnotherapy, the results showed similar mean scores for positive support from friends. When comparing the mean scores on the support from friends variable between the hypnotherapy and no-hypnotherapy conditions within the abnormal birth outcome group, no significant differences were found. The results showed similar mean scores for the absence of support from friends under both the conditions of hypnotherapy and no hypnotherapy within the abnormal birth outcome group. See Table 11 for a summary of these results.

Birth data

In comparing the mean scores between the normal and abnormal birth outcome groups on birth data variables, first stage labor length, Apgar score at 1 minute, and Apgar score at 5 minutes, significant differences were found. These results indicate first stage labor length was shorter, and the Apgar scores at 1 and 5 minutes were better, for the normal birth outcome group than for the abnormal birth outcome group. However, no significant differences between the mean scores for the normal and abnormal birth outcome groups were found for gestation, second stage labor length and birthweight. These results are summarized in Table 12.

DISCUSSION

A review of the prediction equation developed from discriminant analysis shows that many factors interact to engender susceptibility to birth complications. In this paper, we have focused upon the seven major psychosocial variables, showing their important correlation to birth problems, and that an intervention program can mitigate the contribution of these risk factors. In other research we are working with all the variables to create a systems dynamics computer model for susceptibility to birth complications.

From our results, we suggest that prenatal providers should incorporate a consideration and reduction of these psychosocial risk factors into routine prenatal care. This can be done cost-effectively, through utilization of a mental health professional trained in birth psychophysiology, hypnotherapy and family systems therapy. Knowledge of somatics and biofeedback is also helpful. This practitioner can interact with nurses and childbirth educators to improve co-ordination of patient care and provide attention to psychosocial risk. Specifically, psychosocial risk reduction involves:

(1) Identification, acceptance and resolution of fears.
(2) Identification of states of high anxiety-tension, with helping the client learn more effective coping styles.
(3) Identification of negative beliefs about birth and parenting, with provisions for reframing and emotional relearning.
(4) Identification of low maternal identity with anticipatory guidance for the mothering role and hypnotherapy to improve self-esteem.

Table 11 Comparison of means and standard deviations for the psychosocial support factors within normal and abnormal birth outcome groups when grouped for hypnotherapy

Psychosocial support factors	Hypnotherapy Mean	SD	No hypnotherapy Mean	SD	t-value
Partner					
Normal	0.51	1.77	1.72	1.38	2.24*
Abnormal	−0.31	1.96	−0.63	2.18	−0.43
Mother's mother					
Normal	0.05	1.85	0.62	1.45	1.00
Abnormal	−0.53	1.16	−0.29	1.73	0.46
Friends					
Normal	0.86	1.23	0.85	1.27	−0.02
Abnormal	−0.19	0.54	0.01	1.43	0.45

* Significant at the 0.05 level ($p > \pm 2.048$)

Table 12 Comparison of means and standard deviations for the birth data between normal and abnormal birth outcome groups

Birth data	Normal Mean	SD	Abnormal Mean	SD	t-value
Gestation (weeks)	40.06	1.01	39.07	3.95	−1.42
Labor length (hours)					
First stage	7.03	5.65	10.91	7.61	2.34*
Second stage	1.48	3.06	2.05	1.92	0.89
Birthweight (g)	2 455.06	375.44	3 574.70	840.62	0.75
Apgar scores					
1 min	8.16	1.32	6.70	2.22	−3.25†
5 min	9.09	1.22	8.33	1.56	−2.17*

* Significant at the 0.05 level ($p > \pm 1.96$); † significant at the 0.01 level ($p > \pm 2.57$)

(5) Consideration of strengths and stresses of the woman's support system. Needed interventions include:

    (a) Couple's therapy to decrease stress, increase husband's emotional availability, improve lifestyle, etc.,

(b) Individual counseling for the husband to address his concerns,

(c) Network therapy (environmental intervention with the mother's friends (which can be done in childbirth classes),

(d) Therapy with the mother and her mother to facilitate transition and change of that relationship, and/or,

(e) Helping the woman with no psychosocial support to establish needed relationships and resources.

On a broader level, these findings may presage a time when all medicine is practiced as a team endeavor, with the behavioral medicine specialist or medical psychologist as an important member of that team. When the way medicine is practiced changes to reflect our new understanding of the interactive nature of all aspects of the patient's life on health, we will have come far.

---

[1] *Editors' note:* bibliography and rating questionnaires determining high-risk pregnancies are available through the authors.
[2] These more 'mature' strategies include altruism, anticipation, humor, resource sharing, role adjustment, sublimation and time-out.

17

The conscious and unconscious elements of the experience of pregnancy

M. Pál

ABSTRACT

The paper gives an account of the psychological examination – conducted at the Department for Obstetrics and Gynecology of the Central State Hospital in Budapest – of women going through their first pregnancy exempt of complications or complaints.

The examination implied projective tests and goal-oriented exploration. The total population subjected to the examination consisted of 30 patients.

The results can be summed up as follows:

(1) Women with a higher education degree and having a professional job consider their pregnancy as a task to be fulfilled.

(2) In the case of psychologically normal pregnant women phenomena of regression are manifested in fantasies concerning the parturition as well as the health personnel serving during the process.

.(3) Considering pregnancy as a task to be fulfilled results in an averting mechanism; it slows down and hence facilitates the integration of the embryo. Moreover it constitutes an object which helps to diminish the anxieties hiding near the level of consciousness.

The investigation described here was carried out at the gynecological department of the Central State Hospital of Budapest. There has been co-operation between the Departments of Obstetrics–Gynecology and Psychotherapy of the hospital for a long time. The psychiatric diseases encountered in the Gynecological Department (lactation psychoses, states of depression following major gynecological operations, etc.) are treated at the Department of Psychotherapy. It was during this co-operation that the idea was raised of giving regular psychological care to pregnant women. While trying to understand and treat abnormal forms of behavior, we realized how little we actually know about 'healthy' pregnancy without complaints which we used as a basis for comparison in our procedures. For that reason we came to the common view while designing our work that, in addition to the data found in literature, it was worth taking a closer look at the evident facts and those which are generally considered to be commonplace. Research carried out all over the world is primarily concentrated upon pathological phenomena and there is considerably little reliable material concerning the psychological phenomena of healthy pregnancy. Thus, in the present phase of our investigation we are trying to find an answer to the question as to whether we encounter characteristic psychic forms of behavior of pregnant women who are expecting their children without complaints in both the physical and the psychological sense.

As a starting point, we accepted the research results of Bibring (1961) and her colleagues. They consider pregnancy – together with puberty and menopause – a maturational crisis differing from other crisis situations of life in that it involves a high degree of hormonal and somatic changes and they are always resolved in one direction (the adolescent may no longer be a child, the mother may no longer be alone). The conflicts of the earlier life period appear in the crises of maturity in a more condensed manner and they make the whole personality face new libidinal and adaptational problems to be solved.

During the first pregnancy as a normal crisis of maturity, the expectant mother must accept the embryo as the representation of the beloved companion and herself and then – mostly beginning from the first perceptible movement of the embryo – she is to prepare for giving birth to her offspring as an anatomical separation. The characteristic sequence of libidinal positions is repeated as it were in the connection between the child born and its mother: she must be able to accept the child and in the meantime prepare for letting it go when it grows up.

No matter how natural, 'normally' a crisis like that is taking place while it lasts; it can easily tip over in a pathological direction – just as it frequently does in pregnancy, adolescence and menopause.

It was on the basis of the considerations described very briefly here

CONSCIOUS AND UNCONSCIOUS ELEMENTS OF PREGNANCY

that we elaborated our working method as follows: every patient coming to us with her first pregnancy is sent by her medical attendant for a psychological test. If he finds any kind of disorder, be it in the somatic sense or in relation to her circumstances or behavior, he will report about it to us.

In the investigation I applied projective tests and guided exploration; in this presentation I make use primarily of the results of the exploratory material, and I only wish to make a few references to the data of the projective tests.

So far 30 pregnant women have participated in the investigation. The youngest is 19, the oldest, 31 years old. All of them have white-collar jobs, having gained at least secondary school-leaving certificates, and 50% of them are university graduates. Since the patients were included in our research program without any selection, this high level of schooling must be characteristic of the patients of the hospital. The family background of the married couples is not so homogeneous in relation to schooling: the majority of pregnant women have higher qualifications than their parents and only one third of them come from professional families.

Their financial circumstances are at least average. Two young couples are provided for by their parents since they are still studying.

In the case of six patients the obstetrician indicated somatic problems or supposedly psychological disorders. In these cases, after having analyzed the personality, motivations and the circumstances, I applied psychotherapy that was intended to help rather than explore. Two of them required a more thorough settlement of the conflicts. This will take place after confinement and the separation of the baby. Up to the time of the completion of this paper three of them had been confined; delivery was uncomplicated in the psychological sense in all the three cases. These pregnant women, in contrast to their earlier anxieties, were able to cooperate with the obstetrician and behave in the way they had expected of themselves. I shall return to this aspect later.

The material collected so far is perhaps not sufficient for drawing definite conclusions but it probably allows us to pose questions and perhaps evaluate certain phenomena as tendencies.

Much to our surprise, every woman tested and interviewed displayed some uncertainty or conflict in relation to her own femininity. It seems that, in addition to the conflicts defined by the individual personality development, the relationship to sexual identity is the common conflict, which again comes to the surface during pregnancy and forces the personality to find new solutions. Besides the signs of the projective tests to this effect, it is primarily dreams that point in this direction. Allow me to quote a few of them.

Case 1 Judit, aged 31, has never been pregnant before although she has never used any contraception. For that reason she consulted a doctor several years ago but she did not undergo a thorough fertility test. She considers her pregnancy to be a gift received by accident. As an important change in her way of life, she mentions that since she has been expecting a child she has regularly visited the hairdresser and the beauty parlour which she had never done before and has bought a lot of clothes although she is now unable to wear most of them. She really is conspicuously well-groomed and elegant. Her dream is the following: someone tells her that she is going to give birth to a baby, but nothing happens although in her dream she knows she ought to feel pain and she seems to see her baby too. All of a sudden her husband tells her that she should stop trying, it looks as if she is unable to carry out the task and he takes over. And the baby is born by her husband.

Case 2 Mónika is 19 years old. She did not want a baby yet but when she became pregnant she and her husband did not dare to take the risks of an abortion. She has always been disturbed by her petite and fragile stature which makes her out to be younger than her age. Her body weight has not increased as much during her pregnancy as she expected. In her dream one of her sisters, who is a very beautiful girl, gives birth to a baby all of a sudden. She asks Mónika to give her the clothes purchased for her own baby and says: 'They would be too large for your child anyway'. In another of her dreams she suddenly sees her mother delivering a child at home. Her father is assisting her and praises her for her discipline and efficiency. In her dream Mónika knows that he says so because she will not behave so well.

Several other examples could be cited. Anyway, it seems as if these women were uncertain whether their pregnancy was the fulfilment of their femininity, as is generally supposed, and were unconsciously questioning their role and adequacy.

When summarizing our partial results, another common feature was that the mothers looked at motherhood as a task to perform. Here the word 'task' is used in the following sense: 'What is going to happen is in no way an event to occur naturally and necessarily but is the result of my conscious enterprise; besides that, the pressure of external expectations plays at least as important a role in it as my own internal inclination.'

Let us survey the manifestations referring to this. Every woman considers her pregnancy as something she herself wanted. All of them wished to have children from their present relationships and the majority of them also consider the time to be optimal. Allow me to quote some relevant details of the explorations.

'We have been married for two years. We actually wanted to wait for another half year, planning to have the flat done first, but when we learnt that I was pregnant we were very happy. The parents of both of us asked us almost the day we got married when we were to have a baby, for both my husband and me were born when our parents were not so young any more. Thus we concealed the matter from them till they themselves would have noticed it anyway.'

Another details runs as follows:

'We planned with my husband long ago when I should have a baby and we were punctual almost to the month. We would like to have two children but if both of them turn out to be of the same sex we want a third one as well. The only thing we could not take into account was my job: as far as it is concerned they may only be born at the wrong time.'

We do not believe that these calculations and ponderings about the children to be born should reflect ambivalences of a nature and extent that we would have to think of an unconscious rejection of pregnancy. Instead, the thing is that planning to have a baby has been included among the realistic plans of life requesting pragmatic considerations.

An important place is occupied by the personal things of the baby in the future mother's world of fantasy and thinking. Still alive, but increasingly less effective, is the popular belief that the bed and diapers of the baby may only be prepared when the healthy child has already come into this world; otherwise the detrimental attention of the bad spirits is called too early. In the group examined only one woman referred to this, saying that she had not dared to buy anything yet. The majority of the women arrange the environment of the baby to be born in the second half of pregnancy. Beyond the realistic requirement of proper care, here some kind of role is probably played by substitutive cathexis too. However, the plans of purchasing are accompanied by an unproportionate and therefore inadequate tension. And in the projective tests — also as a tendency — an enhanced degree of introverted behavior appears, simultaneously with an intensive defense against it, mostly in the form of an extroverted uneasiness. This phenomenon, I believe, allows the following question to be raised: perhaps the personal things of the child substitute and represent the child itself for the libido, and they do so not only in the course of pregnancy. Transforming care into a task and an accomplishment somewhat delays, slows down and thus facilitates for the personality the integration of the embryo, the alien body.

The third field in which we experienced a strongly task-like behavior of pregnant women was when they imagined the process of delivery. Those who are still at the beginning of their pregnancy do not yet indulge in such fantasies. As time goes on, approximately in the last third of pregnancy, the question arises which may be summarized as follows: 'How shall I be able to behave properly during confinement?'

The character and wording of the anxieties are very much alike: 'I shall be crying and screaming, which is not the right thing to do', 'I shall not have enough strength'; 'I shall not be able to stand up against the pain'; 'I shall not be able to listen to the obstetrician and if I do something wrong I might hurt my child'; 'if I do not appear strong and patient enough, they will be angry with me'; etc.

In the centre of these regressive fantasies of anxiety stands the picture of the obstetrician and the midwife in a strongly magnified form, very similar to the picture formed by the little child of its parents; the obstetrician appears as an omnipotent, severe father figure, alleviated only by his serene and permissive indifference, and the midwife appears as a mother figure, irritable but catering for bodily requirements. All this is accompanied increasingly more strongly by the desire that in the course of delivery somebody should be with her who is taking care only of her, the woman in labor. It occurs increasingly more frequently that the father is present at delivery, but we do not yet know anything about the extent to which his presence alleviates the elementary loneliness of confinement.

Summarizing the experience gathered so far, the following working hypothesis to be tested in the future may be set up: in the case of professional women living in urban areas, changes in relation to the earlier knowledge and assumptions are presupposed in the psychological process accompanying the physiological and hormonal occurrences of pregnancy and in the sequence of libidinal positions. First of all, women consider their pregnancy as a task. It has not yet been clarified whether it is a general tendency accompanying every case of a pregnancy or rather, which is easier to assume, a new phenomenon of a task-oriented world.

Secondly, in the case of healthy pregnant women, regression, described in the literature too, appears in fantasies related mainly to confinement, and the persons assisting it.

Thirdly, pregnancy and confinement experienced as a task assist the integration of the embryo, the narcissistic cathexis of the self. It seems that this is undergoing transformation in the case of highly differentiated and individualized personalities. We cannot know whether it is an experience of instinctive processes on a level rather close to consciousness, or perhaps there is a change in instinctive processes themselves. From what we have seen so far, however, the tendency is outlined quite markedly that if the patients experience their pregnancy as a task, it operates as a defense mechanism. By slowing down the process, it facilitates adaptation; coming closer to consciousness, the anxieties, objectivized in the tasks, are alleviated.

Part 2: Studies on attachment and bonding development

18

Prenatal attachment, the perinatal continuum and the psychological side of neonatal intensive care

W. E. Freud

INTRODUCTION

After teaching infant observation for many years at the Hampstead Child Therapy Clinic and the Institute of Psycho-Analysis in London the author, a non-medical psychoanalyst, had the unique opportunity of observing for extended periods of time in a great many neonatal intensive care units (NICUs) in England, North America, Canada and in the German-speaking countries of central Europe. His overall impression is one of superb medical technology in these units, of devoted intensive care for the tiny babies by nursing and medical staff and of ample room for improvement of the psychological side of neonatal intensive care (NIC). As in other hospital departments, established routines, schedules and procedures, which have proved themselves in the past, have become firmly rooted in the practice and in the minds of those who have been there for a long time. Therefore, it is not always easy to kindle enthusiasm for hitherto untried approaches, especially when it can be argued that the rapid and impressive advances on the medical-technological side have enabled us to save ever more and ever lighter babies, even when separated from their mothers. It is my contention, however, that premature babies and premature mothers usually need each other more than healthy newborns and their mothers need each other (Anderson, 1977). By separating them we are approaching the limits of human adaptability (Lozoff et al., 1977). The togetherness of mother and newborn will be the leitmotif of this presentation.

The trailblazing observations by James Robertson (Bowlby et al., 1952), who went into the childrens' wards of hospitals with a cine camera, showed that an independent, unattached and psychoanalytically trained observer (with a flair for viewing events from a slightly different perspective) is in a particularly favorable position to spot flaws and drawbacks in the system. These are flaws and drawbacks which can otherwise remain unnoticed in the course of habituation or are scotomized by hospital staff who have to work there day and night.

The kind of mother–infant observation developed for the training of psychoanalytic candidates in London (Bick, 1964; Freud, W. E., 1975) proved, in slightly modified form, suitable for observing in NICUs. All the observer then had to do was to make himself as inconspicuous as possible while identifying and empathizing in turn with everyone he encountered there. This includes everyone from the premature baby, the parent and other visitors, to midwives, nurses, physicians and ancillary staff (cf. Freud, W. E., 1980). Such a method is in keeping with the use of free-floating (evenly distributed) attention employed by the psychoanalyst.

In the following I will convey some of the impressions that led me to suggest changes in order to bring the psychological side of NIC more in line with the achievements of present-day computerized medical technology. The opinions expressed here are mine, though they were not infrequently shared (albeit sometimes secretly) by parents of prematures, nurses, midwives and physicians alike.

NIC makes sense only when seen in the wider context of a developmental perinatal continuum that takes full account of prenatal experience. I am aware that whenever it comes to attempts at describing prenatal psychological events we are up against the problem of having to conceptualize prenatal phenomenology in postnatal language, which may not always be the best way to understand the intricacies of prenatal manifestations. However, it proved too tempting not to extend Klaus and Kennell's (1982) concepts of attachment and bonding to the prenatal. The term 'attachment' is used here in the sense of 'forming a bond', the term 'bonding' to denote a more intense attachment. Sometimes I use the flexible psychoanalytic term, 'cathexis', in the sense of emotional investment (cf. Ornston 1985; and also see pp. 165–75 in this volume).

Prematurity presents us with a unique 'experiment of nature', in which we can observe a bit of prenatality postnatally – a circumstance that also has a bearing on our therapeutic efforts in NIC. We want to make the premie feel as much 'at home' as we can. When we try to simulate

PSYCHOLOGY OF NEONATAL INTENSIVE CARE

intrauterine conditions (e.g. by rocking the incubator at regular intervals) our efforts appear crude and remain non-contingent (i.e. not necessarily fulfilling the premature's needs just when they arise). Such crude approximations also highlight what Als (1984) has called 'the mismatch of organism and the neonatal intensive care-giving environment'.

Against the background of a perinatal continuum one can select certain 'constants' of fetal experience to signpost the route which NIC should take. In this sense one can think of prenatal aspects, like host-togetherness (togetherness with mother), contact (body-contact by touch), continuity, contingency, movement, interaction, feedback and rhythm. One can then ask to what extent currently practised NIC meets such prenatal criteria. So let us first look at prenatal attachment.

PRENATAL ATTACHMENT

The mother

The emotional investment (cathexis) in the idea of having a baby begins in the parents' own childhood with childhood interest in where babies come from and how they are made (Freud, S., 1908). The fact that boys also have wishes for a baby (Brunswick, 1940) should make us give more thought to how we can help the fathers of newborns. A wish for offspring comes up in many guises and can express itself consciously as well as unconsciously. It is always intrigueing to note what is spontaneously mentioned by the parents, and then to compare it with what we think are the really important underlying motivations for a pregnancy[1]. There are usually quite definite expectations and hopes (the mother is 'expecting'). The wish for a child may be predominantly positively or negatively cathected and is in any case ambivalent. Not infrequently we find a conscious positive wish for a child, but underlying it a stronger unconscious rejection. It is widely assumed that a strong emotional cathexis decisively influences prenatal fetal development and has a bearing on outcome. By contrast, there is widespread evidence that if a woman wants to get rid of a child her most ardent wishes remain ineffective, and one cannot help wondering to what extent an even stronger unconscious wish to keep the child is not the stronger one. Though the area of prenatal influences is a fascinating one, I do not want to enter into it here.

Once the mother is pregnant she often has a vivid fantasy-relationship with the fetus (see Lüpke, 1984) that is characterized by projections of her wishes. Just as the later real relationship with her child, the fantasy-relationship will already be influenced by the unconscious meaning this particular pregnancy has for the mother, i.e. whom the fetus represents (e.g. a sibling, parent or other family member, or herself). What gender this person is also plays a role.

The fetus

Albert Liley's (1972) charming paper dispelled the last doubts, if there had been any, that the fetus can be regarded as a lively and active personality. Additionally, Graves (1980) speaks of the fetus as sentient and competent. He is growing up in the environment of his mother's biological rhythms, which is of cardinal relevance for NIC.

Through the early maturation of hearing and of the labyrinth (Clauser, 1971; Korner and Thoman, 1972) he is particularly receptive to sound and movement. There is the constant background rhythm of his mother's heartbeat (perceived by his ears or by conduction via the more solid structures of his body), and he may be aware of 'the rhythmical wooshing sound of her bloodflow' (MacFarlane, 1977) 'punctuated by the tummy rumbles of air passing through his mother's stomach' and the noise and rhythm of her breathing, just as he may be aware of her wake–sleep pattern and her general style of functioning (lethargic, smooth, hectic, abrupt). Rice (1979) quotes Salk (1962) when she wonders about 'imprinting' to intrauterine sound. In any case, rhythm itself provides a most reassuring 'cradle' through its promise of repetition and continuity. Last, not least, there is his mother's voice, which he can distinguish from the voice of others (De Casper and Spence, 1982), and there are suggestions that he may also be aware of the emotional under- and overtones of peoples' voices (Verny and Kelly, 1982).

Clauser (1971) regards the mother's movements and the rhythmic rocking of her gait as the most frequent stimulation which the fetus experiences and speaks of the prenatal experience of the mother as an acoustic-rhythmic happening. John Lind regarded movement as so important that he thought cessation of movement is experienced as severe deprivation (personal communication, 1981). Graves (1980) quotes Dawes (1973) as stating that the fetal need for activity is recognized and connected with the need to practise and to exercise. Such practise is considered a necessary prerequisite to normal functional development and morphological maturation – a view also held by Milani Comparetti (1981). The exercising aspect of fetal movement reminds one of Bühler's 'Funktionslust' (pleasure of functioning). Maybe, the fetus has to be so active during certain periods of his maturation because, with his increasing size, there will later be less space for him in which to frisk about.

Milani Comparetti (1981) pointed to the embryonic need to change contact with the surface of the uterine cavity. Kulka *et al.* (1960) take motion to be the first means of tension discharge and state that contact needs are probably fully gratified in intrauterine life. Blechschmidt regards the amnion (the innermost membrane enveloping the fetus and enclosing the liquor amnii) as a swing (personal communication, 1983). Plato (1970 edition) was of the opinion that

> 'all young children, and especially very tiny infants, benefit both physically and mentally from being nursed and kept in motion, as far as practicable, throughout the day and night; indeed, if only it could be managed they ought to live as though they were permanently on board ship. But as that's impossible, we must aim to provide our newborn infants with the closest possible approximation to this idea.'

One wonders to what extent movement serves communication. Verny and Kelly (1982), who elaborate on behavioral, sympathetic and physiological channels of communication, think that mother–child communication is an important part of bonding, especially during the last 2 months of pregnancy. Mothers often take kicking as a message. Veldman (1982) found that if the fetus is 'rocked' regularly at a certain time through laying hands on the sides of the mother's body he will 'knock' if the practise is discontinued. This presupposes some kind of memory. How are we to imagine this? Feher (1980) thinks that bodily sensation is the medium of expression most accessible to the infant, and that body movements in the womb are also significant in that they may affect later emotional states and mental development. She writes: 'According to Corliss (1976) movements create sensations which have patterns. These patterns are actually imposed on the musculature, and then on the cortex itself, as imprints or memories, which remain like a permanent "motion picture" to influence our consciousness and future reactions.' When we observe a premature pressing hands or feet against the wall of his incubator we wonder whether a 'body memory' is at the back of it. Greenacre (1945) speaks of unique somatic memory traces. To what extent does the fetus 'cathect' his mother in terms of body memories?

Verny and Kelly (1982) hypothesize an 'organismic memory' that would allow even a single cell, like an ovum or a sperm, to carry 'memories' and link it to the Jungian concept of the collective unconscious.

There are other communication systems, like the one by which the mother becomes aware of the moment of conception (Peterson, 1983) or the co-enesthetic organization (Spitz, 1945a)[2]. Before we ask what is important for the fetus to remember, one other aspect should be mentioned: the fetus has a much larger number and a much wider distribution of taste buds in his oral cavity than the child or adult (Liley, 1972). Graves (1980) quotes a suggestion from Bradley and Mistretta (1975) that the shifting ratios of fluid and urine contribute to the stimulation of taste buds *in utero*. Taste buds are already developing between the 11th and 20th week, and one wonders to what extent the fetus may be monitoring his liquid surround and whether some parameters (like chemical composition, pressure, temperature or other fluctuations) are more important to him than others.

Could one hypothesize that the fetus 'bonds' to tangibles (i.e. to that which he can touch), like parts of his own body and parts of his environment (such as the amniotic fluid, the placenta, the uterine wall, etc.). Likewise might this same idea be extended to 'intangibles', like togetherness with his mother, his mother's voice or certain affective intonations of it (cf. Lind and Hardgrove, 1978), continuity, rhythm(s), movement and other forms of intangible stimulation? All aspects of psychological prenatal bonding may serve as stepping stones that facilitate moving along the prenatal sector of the perinatal continuum.

THE PERINATAL CONTINUUM

For our purposes and in order to emphasize the importance of togetherness I will widen the concept of the perinatal continuum, extending it from conception to the end of exterogestation, i.e. until the child can crawl (Portmann, 1944; Bostock, 1958; Kovács, 1960; Montagu, 1961). The sensitive period (Klaus and Kennell, 1982) is at the beginning of exterogestation, when after the brief interruption through delivery mother and newborn are reunited again. A long stretch of this continuum, from the pregnancy test to postnatal care has, in Western industrialized societies, become institutionalized, which is in sharp contrast to the so-called underdeveloped countries and the societies of traditional peoples (cf. Liedloff, 1976; Montagu, 1978; Kitzinger, 1978). Institutionalization tends to crowd out the humane aspects, which means that constant efforts are needed to reinstate them.

There are striking and intrigueing 'parallels' between intra- and extrauterine life. To name but a few, Milaković (1967) thinks that the drinking of amniotic fluid by the fetus represents the consummatory act of a prenatal stage of libidinal development, and stresses the great importance of fetal oral experiences. Hoffer (1949) pointed out that already in intrauterine life the hand becomes closely allied to the mouth for the sake of relieving tension. He saw in this alliance the first achievement of the primitive ego. Kulka *et al.* (1960) postulate a kinesthetic phase, which predates the oral and has its own primacy and specific modality of expression[3].

Greenacre (1953) stresses that intrauterine life and early infancy form a continuum and that 'the fetus reacts to discomfort with an acceleration of the life movements at its disposal', stating that these responses represent an earlier form of anxiety-like response. She further postulates that the fetus derives some pleasure from moving and from contact with the maternal body. Graves (1980) thinks that, given the level of auditory responsiveness and the repertoire of fetal movements, it is not impossible that already *in utero* some synchronization between fetal movements and intrauterine sound variations may occur. Truby (1971) holds that the fetus moves his body in rhythm to his mother's speech, reminiscent of the synchrony between the neonate and his mother (Condon and Sander, 1974).

How can the essential ingredients of maternal–fetal interaction be pinpointed? Does the mother's contribution always have to be contingent? Could it be that in the absence of one or more essential part-interaction components the fetus reacts like Tronick and Adamson's (1980) 'still-face' infants whose mothers had been instructed to withhold feedback? Would the fetus, after being exposed to certain amounts of the mother's ambivalent cathexis become entrapped between contradictory messages, so that eventually his co-operation is impaired when it comes to labor and delivery (cf. Hau's 1973 concept of 'intrauterine hospitalism')? Or, if the mother's unconscious negative cathexis of the pregnancy becomes too strong and unpleasant, might he be thought to refuse nourishment or make an unexpected premature getaway?

The question also arises under what conditions and at what point in time fetal activity contributes to the onset of labor. Milano Comparetti (1981) stated that 'the fetus himself triggers parturition when his humoral message makes the womb responsive to the stimulus of his thrusting. Propulsion then is not only mechanical collaboration in labor, but also a fetal timing mechanism for the saccate rhythm of delivery.' The fetus sometimes confronts us with dilemmas by the way he chooses to lie, especially when he shows no inclination to conform to our attempts at turning him – or perhaps we are not going about it in the right way. There are reports of inducing him to assume a position which we think is best for delivery by talking to him or to his mother (Groddeck, 1926). There is probably something in Veldman's view (personal communication, 1985) that the intentions of the fetus should be respected if, after the second attempt at turning, he reverts to the position from which he does not want to be dislodged.

The principle of 'following' a person's natural inclinations is reflected in the psychoanalytic model of therapy, where observing and listening have pride of place. It has found ample expression in the Hampstead Well-Baby Clinic where this approach is one of the cornerstones of the service (Freud, W. E. and Freud, I., 1976)[4]. Such a model differs from the medical model, which requires that something should be 'done' most of the time[5]. This is not to underrate the merits of the medical model, only to suggest that it be suitably complemented by the analytic one.

On another part of the perinatal continuum Sosa et al. (1980) followed the same principle when they demonstrated the importance of a supportive companion during labor. The mere presence of the 'Doula' favorably influences the mother's interaction with the fetus resulting in shorter labor, fewer obstetric complications and less maternal anxiety. Leboyer (1975) had already prepared the way for a smoother transition, and Odent's (1984) flair for capturing the spirit of being in tune with parent and fetus at a crucial point along the continuum is exemplified in the communal singing and dancing in his unit. Mixed groups of prospective parents, and parents who have already had their babies, are joined by doctors and nurses in the merrymaking. I can personally testify to the warm emotional climate and the feelings of support and friendship this creates. It goes a long way towards creating and strengthening the parents' confidence in themselves and the feeling of belonging. Meeting familiar persons again along the continuum is reassuring. We would be well advised to bear this in mind when selecting teachers for antenatal classes as well as for follow-up visits, and ultimately for home visits in the course of long-term follow-ups.

'Following' also has a bearing on the design of antenatal preparation. The term, antenatal 'class' reveals the emphasis on 'teaching', in which the parental share of anxieties and attendant questions usually get an insufficient hearing. As a colleague mother once put it to me:

> 'In the whole course of antenatal classes I was really only optimally interested when problems were discussed that corresponded to my prevailing state of pregnancy. It meant that a certain topic would already have been dealt with when it was still comparatively meaningless to me; or that I had to wait, sometimes for a long time, until my own particular problem could be aired. By then it was usually no longer topical. In short, my anxieties could hardly ever be discussed when they were most acute.'

It should make us think again whether antenatal preparation is best done, as it is now, in groups of mothers in different stages of pregnancy or whether better ways can be found.

Field (1979), in her studies of imitation vs. stimulation of the premature, also followed the principle of taking cues primarily from the baby, by 'following' his signs and signals in order to be in tune with what he needs and wants at any given time. Only in this way can truly contingent care giving be assured.

The 'amazing newborn' (Klaus and Klaus, 1985) is programmed to interact with his mother from the beginning, and it is important not to deprive him of this opportunity. As De Chateau and Wiberg (1984) said: 'The alertness of the newborn is highly significant and complements parental receptivity, thus preparing for a sensitive synchrony of responsiveness of infant and caretaker. In fact, the early parent–infant interaction is felt to determine the amount and quality of sensory stimulation received by the newborn later on.' Klaus and Kennell (1976) had already laid the foundations, and the kangaroo method more recently brought the whole issue into the limelight again (Sanabria and Gomez).

PRELIMINARY SUMMING UP – RELEVANCE TO NIC

By placing the newborn on his mother's body immediately after delivery, he is 'plugged in again' into the familiar environment of his mother's biological rhythms. This may well be the decisive ingredient in the soothing effect of maternal holding and in the kangaroo method of carrying the premature between the mother's breasts. Other things being equal, optimal conditions for transition from the intrauterine to the extrauterine state are thereby given and least demands made on the newborn's integrative capacities. Skin-to-skin contact between mother and newborn is a vital component. Feher (1980) supports her statement that touch epitomizes continuity by referring to Spitz's 1945b and 1946 studies on hospitalism, and Kitzinger (1978) stresses that it is not only the sight or sound of the baby which provide clear signals in the bonding process between mother and newborn but the physical contact through touch that initiates an onrush of feelings, which is 'perhaps the most significant element in attachment to the neonate'. Touching, holding and stroking play a major role.

Optimal entrainment, reciprocal interaction, dialog, feedback, synchrony, and mutual care giving can only occur in the context of mother–baby togetherness, which confers psychological immunity (cf. Freud, W. E., 1980). The mother is not only the best incubator, but, if given half a chance, also the best monitor of her baby's well-being.

THE PSYCHOLOGICAL SIDE OF NEONATAL INTENSIVE CARE

Psychologically, the premature can, like his 'premature' parents, be regarded as traumatized. After delivery he is 'plugged out' of the biological rhythms of his mother and is, unlike the healthy newborn, not immediately 'plugged back in again' into his familiar environment. On the contrary, he is whisked away to the NICU or to a specialized perinatal center, i.e. to the pediatricians and to the nurses. He is no longer regarded as belonging to his family. The perinatal continuum has thus become a discontinuum. Uterogestation has been shortened by prematurity and exterogestation has been lengthened. By radically separating the at-risk newborn we are making exterogestation longer still. It seems as if we took the wrong turning

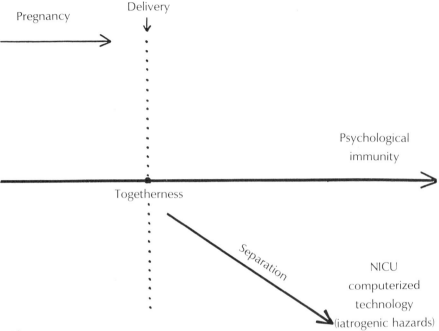

Figure 1

at the fork in the road (see Figure 1) instead of continuing along the road of togetherness.

The premature parents feel they have failed and lose their self-confidence. Within an achievement-oriented society they feel that they have not 'produced' as expected. They have lost face within their wider family and are shunned by their friends, who do not know how to cope with such situations except by embarrassment, pity and avoidance. Hospital and NICU staff subconsciously also do not trust them, because they have not produced a healthy newborn, and they take over the baby.

Traditionally, psychoanalysis has always stressed the importance of keeping mother and infant together (cf. especially Bowlby, 1969, 1973, 1980; Robertson, 1970; Winnicott, 1958, 1965). In the light of what we now know about intrauterine existence and in view of the importance of safeguarding the perinatal continuum, it is my contention that if mother and premie were kept together from the outset many pathological conditions in the at-risk newborn that now seem almost inevitable might simply not arise while other problems which do arise may be more benign.

The separation issue has not only been on the minds of the parents but very much on the minds of the care givers too. Jonxis (1967) thought of using the whole NICU as an incubator so that the mothers could stay together with their sick newborns. This worked well until we became too adept at saving ever lighter babies, who in turn required ever higher temperatures for their wellbeing. The NICU then became too warm for the personnel (Okken, personal communication). Kahn et al. (1954) and Bell (1969) tried to do something similar in Johannesburg. Garrow's NICU in High Wycombe, England, which is built like a wheel, with the NICU at the hub and the mothers' bedrooms, like spokes, right next to it, has become a model for NICU design (personal communication). In Pithiviers incubators are kept alongside the mothers' beds (Odent, 1984), but these are the exceptions.

Separation means additional stress for parents, premies and the caregiving personnel. Not infrequently the premie remains 'plugged out' for weeks. In the absence of close contact with him the mother's fantasies tend to get out of hand: she worries and expects the worst. Uncertainty about their baby's further development and possible permanent handicap is never far from the parents' minds. Trying to strengthen the invisible bond by providing the parents with a polaroid photo helps, but does not go far enough. A hospital in Grand Rapids, Michigan, has a film of the NICU, which is shown to the mother while her baby is stabilized for transport to the perinatal center, and in future there may be closed-circuit television for those who want it, but these are only palliatives. The road along separation has been buttressed and consolidated by medical technology. Now we need a new technology in the service of togetherness. A start has been made in a maternity unit in W. Germany, where the newborn can enjoy receiving phototherapy on his mother's tummy[6]. Consequently there are no longer crying babies nor anxious mothers during phototherapy in this unit.

One way to approach the issue is from the side of basic needs. The first task here is to identify the psychological needs of those concerned. In trying to do this for the mothers and for the prematures (Freud, W. E., 1980) it became evident that the whole issue of visiting needs reappraisal. Is it not surprising that, if mother and newborn belong together so much, parents of prematures don't visit more often, and when they do don't stay for very long? The real question is why don't we let the babies belong more to their parents, especially to their mothers. The 'whose baby?' syndrome goes some way towards explaining it. One reason is that we do not really want visitors in the NICU, where they are subconsciously regarded as being in the way. Another reason has to do with our reticence to consider and accept change (cf. below).

Until Barnett et al. (1970) showed that the bacterial hospital flora constituted a greater threat to the baby's health than that of the visiting mother and that the mother's presence did not appear to increase the risk or the occurrence of infection, visiting parents were held at bay behind the glass walls of the corridors. NICUs were not designed for the comfort of visitors and this message is brought home to them by the lack of basic provisions which would make them welcome. While many NICUs display notices to the effect that no responsibility is taken for valuables, few units provide lockers for the mothers' handbags. There are usually no facilities for making visitors physically more comfortable in the well-heated units. There are neither changing rooms nor shower facilities, let alone lockers for the parents' clothes. There are also still too few high stools in the units to enable the parents to get a comfortable view of their baby in the incubator, and in middle Europe the rocking chair in the NICU is conspicuous by its absence.

The parents still have no 'territory' within the unit and feel themselves as guests who can be asked to leave at any time. The greatest drawback, however, is that they do not have a well-defined role which would enable them to participate more actively in their baby's care. A start has been made since it became clear that premies benefit from being touched, stroked, held and talked to, and the more progressive units also allow the parents a slightly bigger share in the cleaning and tube-feeding of their baby (Baum and Howat, 1978), but to my knowledge no unit has as yet integrated one or both parents into the care-giving team. It should never be forgotten that active participation is still the best form of occupational therapy!

The needs of the premature

The needs of the premature, like the needs of infants, clamor for immediate gratification. Because he is so small and light and lonely the premie needs his mother all the more. In the context of prenatal togetherness I assume his basic needs to be for continuity (e.g. of the mother's biological rhythms), contiguity (body contact), contingency, interaction and feedback, and we have to ask ourselves to what extent they are adequately met. In a NICU togetherness is primarily with inanimate objects, i.e. with machines, like the ventilator and the monitors, and in an abstract sense with routine procedures, schedules (e.g. feeding, cleaning, temperature-taking) and interventions (many of them painful). The rhythm of the ventilator and the background sounds of the monitors do not readily lend themselves to adequate feedback. Attachment then, is in the first place, to the machine, with the tendency to hold on to the familiar problems of weaning from the machine(s) which may subsequently arise. Marton et al. (1979) have pointed to the human interaction deficit, and what human interaction there is, is usually unpleasant. This is in stark contrast to the analytic view that maximal pleasure should be experienced at each developmental stage before the infant moves on to the next one. Additionally, NIC requires intervening steps, which have to be negotiated (e.g. from parenteral feeding to tube-feeding to bottle-feeding before he gets to his mother's breast). Too many intervening steps may overtax the premie's capacity for integration, especially when transition from one step to another is not smooth.

Another stress imposed on the immature organism is that of having too many different care givers. Minde et al. (1975) observed 70 different nurses during a period of approximately 7 weeks and, of course, each nurse has her own individual style of care-giving. On top of it all we may unwittingly delay integrative processes by not providing enough opportunities, as for example for unlimited non-nutritive sucking and for exploring the mother's skin (especially the breast) with lips and tongue (Bonnard, 1960).

In spite of individually tailored stimulation programs (e.g. Brown and Helper, 1976) it is difficult to discern the cues the premie may be giving us, which is partly due to our inexperience in clearly understanding his signs and signals. There are, furthermore, wide individual differences in the premies' abilities to communicate. Communication could be via one, several or all sensory modalities. But in view of the separation from his mother the vital channel of bodily communication is usually not at his disposal; with the kangaroo method of nursing it is.

All the 'vehicles' for facilitating, promoting and consolidating mother–infant interaction presuppose togetherness. Traditionally, breastfeeding and skin-to-skin contact have been the most effective ones. The kangaroo method, whereby the baby is carried between the mother's breasts (Rey and Martinez, 1984; Anderson et al., 1986) combines many of the essentials, notably closeness, continuity, movement and unlimited sucking time, which is the best preparation for breastfeeding. For the mother of a premature avoidance of a second 'failure' assumes special importance and needs extra encouragement (Lowen, 1982).

The psychological needs of the nurses

This somewhat isolated elite group of specially trained nurses, who are attending the at-risk newborns round the clock, has in essence been given an impossible task. The nurses provide substitute mothering of a kind that requires constant over-cathexis of their charges, whose lives they repeatedly save. And yet, they are not usually accepted as 'family'. On the other hand they are doomed to lose 'their' babies in any case, if not to the family when the baby gets well, then to death. Mortality in NICUs is usually higher than in other units of the hospital.

Their medical and technical competence puts them on a level with the physicians, who often rely on their superior skill and experience. Most of their time is taken up by routine ministrations to babies and machines, leaving little scope for creative activity in connection with their work. In addition they often have to give psychological support to the parents, usually without having received formal training in this. Little wonder then that the cumulative emotional stresses expose them to the burnout syndrome (Marshall and Kasman, 1980; Marshall et al., 1982; Duxbury and Thiessen, 1979). Their own need for ongoing emotional support is only just beginning to be recognized, but as yet far too little provision exists for regular support groups (Bender, 1981) or for individual support. Their impressive potential for instruction and supervision, for which their experience amply qualifies them, remains largely untapped.

THE RISKS OF CHANGE

The challenge to save lives in the face of the well-nigh impossible and the attendant need to develop and perfect defenses, which enable one to cope with that task, may explain why suggestions for change seem to meet special opposition in the NICU. Understandably, there is great reticence to exchange the precious footholds that have been gained in the fight against death and disease and replace them with new and unproven ones. It is, therefore, not surprising that suggestions for even minor alterations usually meet with firm resistance. Resistances are usually easily 'rationalized', i.e. supported by convincing-sounding justifications for holding on to the known and predictable. The most frequently met rationalizations are: lack of space, lack of time, lack of staff and lack of resources – with medical safety often thrown in for good measure ('Can it be proved statistically?'). Not infrequently the need for further research is put forward before anything new is accepted. Closer scrutiny, however, often reveals that these rationalizations are neither convincing nor valid. For example, it may be argued that there is really no space, but at the same time a room nearby is cluttered with rarely used apparatus. It should not be beyond the ingenuity of those concerned to find a quiet area for mothers who want to breastfeed and to relegate the rarely used appliances to other quarters. Once the underlying anxieties, which are at the bottom of many resistances to change, have become more accessible to conscious consideration by discussion, the way is open to consider even seemingly unacceptable proposals for improvement with greater equanimity. A patient, analytically-trained outside observer can often act as a catalyst, if not as a midwife to new ideas.

THE IDEAL NICU – A REALITY

I submit that the future of NIC lies in the direction of keeping mother and premie together from the outset, however unconventional that may sound in view of the specialized care the sick at-risk baby should receive. Though we are only at the beginning of evaluating the advantages of the kangaroo method (Whitelaw and Sleath, 1985), preliminary studies sound most encouraging. A start has been made with developing appliances that allow mother and sick newborns to remain together, as with phototherapy and cots that hinge on to the mother's bed. Another area awaiting development is the more active participation by the premie himself. Mary Neal (1968) made a promising start by putting little hammocks inside the incubator in which the premie could push himself off from the incubator wall whenever he needed more motion. Surprisingly, this method has not been developed further. The sick premature is isolated in an incubator ('Incubator Prem', for short), but, as Kulka et al. noted in 1960:

> 'Premature infants are particularly vulnerable to increased muscular tension. It may be postulated that for their particular state of neuro-muscular development, close cuddling and rocking should be as constant as in the mother's womb. If this is so, the modern incubator falls far short of a good environment for a premature infant.'

Prematures, whose condition is sufficiently stabilized to allow for graduation to an open cot, where they can breathe room air unassisted ('Cot Prems', for short) pose a similar challenge. They spend most of their time sleeping, and with some of them one wonders whether so much sleep is really necessary. It is an intriguing question to what extent their long periods of sleep are due to physiological needs and to what extent they are an expression of conservation-withdrawal (Engel and Schmale, 1972). After all, neglected children and adults, who are deprived of human contact and attention, also spend long periods of the day sleeping, if only because there is not much else that life can offer them (cf. also Spitz, op. cit., 1945b, 1946). The cot prems' relative isolation from human contact (apart from being taken up for schedule feeds and ministrations or when their parents come visiting for short periods of time) should give cause for concern.

Be that as it may, if the cot prem must sleep he should sleep on his mother's body in order to be 'plugged in again' to her biological rhythms.

The perinatal continuum would thereby be safeguarded again. In view of care-giving, as well as of holding, being a mutuality (Anderson, 1977; Kestenberg, 1977) there should really not be any valid objections to creating conditions that allow the mother to be together with her newborn as long as she wishes. I envisage a nursery where mothers sit in rocking chairs (preferably in skin-to-skin contact for those who want it) with their premature babies or carry them kangaroo method between their breasts. Then mother and premie would have unlimited opportunities for getting to know each other, and the premie would have ample leisure for exploring his mother's skin with tongue and lips by touch, smell and taste besides enjoying endless sucking time. Instead of being fed at regular intervals, topped up to imbibe the 'required' amount of fluid and then put back into the loneliness of his cot to sleep some more, the premie would doze off satiated in his mother's arms or in her lap. It would have the added advantage of experiencing his maturational spurts during sleep within an environment he has been used to during his prenatal existence. When he is sufficiently rested he will wake up again and if hungry again will communicate his need for more. Even if he takes less than the prescribed amount at any one feed there are suggestions that over a cycle of 24 hours he will take as much food as he needs without being forced to do so (Ounsted, personal communication). An interesting research area beckons: would prematures who have unlimited non-nutritive sucking and exploring time on their mothers' bodies achieve an earlier integration of breathing-sucking-swallowing, enabling them to breastfeed sooner?

A mother is probably the best observer of her infant, being intuitively in touch with him. Bender (1981) describes how the mother of a 30-week-old premie noticed her daughter in the incubator sucking the corner of the sheet. She showed the nurse, who simply suggested putting the baby to the breast, and it turned out that the baby could fully breastfeed. We could encourage observation of prematures as part of NIC, perhaps with an interdisciplinary team composed of a pediatrician, a nurse, a psychologist, child psychiatrist or psychoanalyst, and at least one parent. If this team sat around the incubator for a period of half an hour or an hour at a stretch and then discussed their observations, we would soon know with which parents we could work together as a team apart from learning a lot from the pooled observations. It would not only cement the relationship between family, nurses and physicians but would also make it easier for the nurses to let the mothers do a good part of the routine ministrations themselves. Initial bonding would be enhanced and the mother's confidence in handling her baby after discharge from the NICU would be strengthened. At the same time the nurses would be freed for more creative activities. The role of the NICU nurse would change to being advisor to the parents. Nurses would thus have more time to supervise the parents' acquisition of necessary skills and to give them more emotional support. As nurse-consultants they would have a different status and could more easily be drawn into independent research.

One of the maternity hospitals to which I was attached in London had a nurse who specialized in advising mothers about breastfeeding. Fittingly, she was known as the 'milk-lady'. Even so, there were always more questions than she could answer in the available time, especially from primaparas without previous experience of how to breastfeed. There is no reason why different nurses should not, acording to their special interests and skills, become 'experts' for certain aspects of NIC over and above their general competence of NIC-nursing. I can think of several such specialized aspects, like visiting, communication of mother and premie, non-nutritive sucking, baby-massage (Rice, 1977, 1979), father-bonding, parent participation in NIC, discharge problems, follow-up, etc. Such drastic changes would require a reassessment of the training syllabus for midwives and nurses.

Lest it be thought that these changes could be brought about without extra effort, let me hasten to add that such transformations require well thought-out preparation and probably ongoing nurse and physician support apart from the feedback needed from parents' self-help groups. Obviously, what matters most in all this is that we can create the right 'climate' for such an undertaking.

Spitz (1950) regarded affective perception, emotional development, as the trail breaker for all other development of the personality in the first year of life. This has been amply borne out in the psychoanalytic treatment of children, where we can observe how, for example, learning disturbances disappear once emotional conflicts have been resolved. The emotional aspect is the main carrier. In the Hampstead War Nurseries, Dorothy Burlingham and Anna Freud (1942, p. 76) observed that regression occurred while children who were separated from their mothers passed through the 'no-man's land' of affection, i.e. during the time after the old love object had been given up and before a new one had been found. One of the children, John, aged five, expressed his own state of mind in words which have since become famous: 'I am nobody's nothing'.

We do not know how many of the infants who went through NICU and especially through an incubator experience for any length of time, encounter serious difficulties in their further emotional development and what the quality of their adult relationships will be like. We can only hope that they will feel better about themselves than little John. Unfortunately, a certain number of them end up needing therapy, either as children or as adults. It would be interesting to know whether they develop characteristics that are specific for their NICU experience and especially their incubator experience[7].

---

[1] The wish to have a child before one gets too old; perpetuating the family; competition with siblings, friends, relatives or with one's own mother; to keep a marriage together; to have a 'live doll' on whom one can lavish affection; to recreate a childhood that is better than the childhood one experienced oneself; to get away from the parental home; to have someone 'who really cares for me and will look after me', etc.

[2] Perhaps the key to the kind of affective prenatal attachment, in which we are most interested lies in these regions, but to the best of my knowledge this has not been systematically researched further.

[3] By kinesthetic they mean 'all incoming sensory modalities: light, touch, pressure, temperature, visceral afferent, and also their central representations'.

[4] The Hampstead Well-Baby Clinic is attached to the Hampstead Child Therapy Clinic, now called The Anna Freud Centre.

[5] For a striking illustration in connection with sewing up episiotomies, cf. Jordan, 1980, p. 44.

[6] This is a device jointly developed by Dr G. Eldering, his engineer, and the author.

[7] I will close with a request that those of you who have treated or are treating such cases acquaint me with what you have found.

19

Psychological aspects of prematurity and of neonatal intensive care: a working report

H. Bender

HOW THE WORK CAME ABOUT

The work described in this paper arose out of a tradition of good liaison between the Department of Pediatrics and that of Child Psychiatry. Some 12 years ago requests were received to see parents of babies on the Neonatal Intensive Care Unit. There was a growing awareness that although the provision of emotional support for families was important and ideally should be part of the routine pediatric care of the newborn, it was becoming increasingly difficult for the nursing and medical staff to provide this. This was particularly so in cases where staff believed parents to be exhibiting 'pathological' behavior. They began to feel that more specialized care would be appropriate.

The request also revealed some awareness of stress and anxiety on the part of the staff and led me to consider what might be the aim of liaison work and how this might be achieved.

Focusing on the psychological aspects of prematurity and neonatal intensive care (NIC), one is immediately struck by the realization that there are many diverse needs to be met and fulfilled in order to create optimum conditions within the neonatal intensive care unit. Although medical care of the unhealthy newborn has become increasingly sophisticated and innovative, a greater awareness of the psychosocial aspects of prematurity is necessary if we are serious about ensuring the overall well-being of preterm babies. This involves recognition of the fact that in looking at this field we are presented, simultaneously, with three 'at risk' populations: the babies, the parents and the staff.

NEONATAL BABIES

The babies are at risk, not only because of their precarious physical conditions but because of the onslaught of stimuli, noise, light, pain and multiplicity of handling, occurring at a time of incomplete psychological and physiological development.

The preterm infant is a medical artefact who has a special psychology which we are still struggling to understand. The intrauterine baby has everything provided by his mother in a natural idling space. In contrast, the extrauterine baby has to look to a life-support system, requiring a change in respiratory effort. He is now exposed and uncontained with fewer benign cutaneous experiences. Routines and life-saving procedures often impinge on the infant and constitute a violent assault, both from a physiological and a psychological point of view.

Some of the most disturbing procedures such as suction, chest physiotherapy, X-rays, positioning, rectal temperatures and nappy changes, disrupt the infant's sleep state and may therefore predispose him to greater risk of apnoeic attacks, particularly since prematures under 32 weeks gestation cannot yet achieve a state of deep sleep.

The current shift system amongst staff virtually ensures that during his stay on the unit, the baby will be handled by innumerable care-takers, each with her own style. In contrast, parental handling tends to be more benign and consistent, allowing babies to begin to differentiate the parents' touch. Babies have been found to open their eyes and move more frequently in response to this parental handling.

Noise

Noise levels both on the unit and within the incubator itself often reach decibel levels which would be intolerable to the adult ear. The premature infant is assaulted by numerous sounds: the monitoring equipment with its alarms and beeps, the metallic sounds of instruments often thoughtlessly placed on top of the incubator, blaring pop music on radios turned up to alleviate the atmosphere for staff and a mêlée of human voices.

Some of these findings have serious implications on our neonatal units, and seem to indicate that babies could benefit from a more individualized developmental care plan, involving primary nursing care.

More detailed observation by staff before, during and after care-giving sessions, would highlight the babies' distress as well as fluctuations in their states, and serve to bring to our attention which babies are most vulnerable (in a more global sense).

Staff would need to evaluate the timing and sequencing of procedures and attempt to facilitate the babies both during and after painful procedures, respecting deep sleep states in older prematures.

As the baby progresses, a behavioral assessment could aim to increase the limited visual opportunities of incubated babies, which often result in a delayed visual experience (compared with the term baby). Benign tactile experiences, such as lambskins and parental massage could be implemented to increase opportunities for early learning through sensory and motor experiences.

The premature baby is unable to influence his environment and this sense of impotence, which is often a feature of neonatal intensive care, is reflected also in the feelings of both parents and staff.

CARE-TAKERS

There is reason to believe that, apart from their precarious physical conditions, the infants are additionally 'at risk' because their care-takers are at risk.

Both parents and professionals are subject to similar forces which work for both detachment and attachment. Medical staff are susceptible to the same factors associated with an infant's immaturity which cause parents either to approach or to avoid their infant.

Before moving on to examine the factors which constitute stress for parents and staff and the coping strategies each group seeks to employ in order to survive, it should be stressed that any discussion about prematurity requires a fuller understanding of the early factors influencing parent/infant relationships. This also requires an appreciation of the impact of prematurity on this process.

The work of, amongst others, Bowlby in the UK, and Klaus and Kennell in the USA, has indicated how vital the earliest period is to the sense of well-being of the parents, and the subsequent emotional development of the child. Bonding is not necessarily automatic and is an extremely complex psychological process, even under normal circumstances. It seems to develop through a subtle interaction between parents and infant, and depends on many factors such as the temperamental characteristics of the parent/baby couple, opportunities for extended contact, the sensitivity and intensity of parental interactions.

Attachment depends on this reciprocal feedback and on what Winnicott has called 'a facilitating environment' (in both a physical and an emotional sense).

Those familiar with Neonatal Intensive Care Units (NICU) will agree that most of the factors acknowledged as important in bonding are absent in the typical NICU. With the rare exceptions of certain units designed to take cognizance of these difficulties, separation still tends to be the predominant feature of NIC. Mothers are often separated from both their babies and their partners. Units often have elaborate entry systems. Parents are frequently asked to 'gown-up', depriving the babies of skin-to-skin contact. When the parents finally see their infants, a plastic box and a mass of equipment may further complicate contact.

PARENTS

Prematurity has been described as an 'accidental psychosocial crisis' and parents' responses to this situation are conditioned by several factors.

Factors which pre-date admission

Parents of prematures may often already form an 'at risk' category before their encounter with the NICU for the following reasons.

Many come from socially deprived backgrounds and have had poor antenatal care. They often live far away from their family support systems. It is not unusual to find a complicated obstetric history of infertility, miscarriage, abortion, stillbirth and neonatal death. Therefore they may bring many pre-existing psychological conflicts to the intensely and peculiarly stressful situation of having a baby on such a unit.

Mothers express conflicts such as feeling themselves to be inadequate containers. They speak of feelings of failure that their bodies were not able to grow a baby to term. Fathers experience feelings of disappointment and shame at having produced such a puny, sick infant which constitutes a blow to their virility, particularly in an area where weight is erroneously equated with quality.

Factors associated with the birth

In general, there will have been emergency aspects of the labor and delivery, involving a transfer of hospitals, perhaps with little or no time for communication and explanations at the time of the delivery. Also the mother may have experienced full or partial analgesia leading to a period of separation, which may have increased the parents' anxiety about what they will discover upon seeing the baby.

Factors associated with the setting

Often, first exposure to the baby's unexpected fetal-like appearance is shocking. The preterm infant is often naked, hairy and bony, with transparent skin revealing the body contents. Occasionally the baby is badly bruised after a difficult birth or severely jaundiced. This precious encounter takes place in an unwelcoming, unfamiliar, hot environment dominated by complex equipment which appears to be assaulting the baby's every visible orifice and body surface.

In response to the ever present fear that their baby might die, parents exhibit all the features of grief — depression, sadness and crying, loss of appetite, sleep disturbances and even phobic symptoms. Their distress may take the form of somatic symptoms such as shortness of breath, palpitations and tightening in the throat. At an unconscious level, this may be understood in terms of the parents' identification with their sick baby (for whom respiratory problems are usually a major concern).

These symptoms are neither uncommon nor pathological, but may be considered as healthy responses to what one could describe as *pathology of circumstance*.

The need to respect parental defenses is underlined, particularly in the context of how to assess and identify those parents who are having special difficulty in adapting to the situation. Some workshop members felt a re-evaluation of bonding was necessary because both medical and nursing staff had sometimes overdramatized the effects of 'bonding failure' and they were in danger of becoming persecutory, particularly when parents distanced themselves from a very sick baby whom they anticipated might die. It is clearly important to understand the reason for this apparent failure to attach *before* reacting.

Naming the baby

Linked to the above, the significance of naming or *not* naming the baby was sometimes misinterpreted by staff. The meaning of the name itself varies in different cultures. In Judaism, for example, it is customary to name the child after a loved, deceased close relative, such as a parent or grandparent. However, it is also customary not to name the baby, in the case of a son, until his circumcision which, obviously in the case of a preterm, would be considerably delayed until the baby was fully fit.

In other cases names are sometimes withheld until such time as the baby's survival seems more certain, for fear that the 'special' name the baby carries might be lost. A baby's death means both a loss of future and a severance with the past.

Example 1

Mr and Mrs A were a couple who had not known they were expecting twins until the moment of delivery. In a prior discussion they had only chosen one girl's name which they had always loved – Laura. Following the birth, both babies' conditions deteriorated and the priest was called to baptize them. The parents decided to name the apparently stronger twin Laura and the weaker twin, Lucy. As it turned out, Laura died after a few hours. The father said, 'It felt as if the wrong baby died. The baby we were waiting for died and the newcomer survived. Now the name has been lost to us forever.'

Sometimes a name may signify a replacement baby or somehow a wish to resurrect the dead baby and merge its identity with the new baby, as in the case of Lisa.

Example 2

Lisa (a derivative of Elizabeth) was born on the second anniversary of her sister Elizabeth's death. In this case the parents believed that their daughters' souls were somehow inextricably linked and this belief was reflected in the choice of name.

Anniversaries

Many workers have observed the frequency with which anniversaries featured among the population of parents of premature infants, e.g. the birth of a premature on the anniversary of a sibling's death (as above). The forthcoming anniversary and the attendant emotions it aroused were sometimes cited by parents as a possible reason for the premature onset of labor. Parents reported feeling depressed on the anniversary of a miscarriage, a baby's death or around the time of a dead child's birthday, had he/she survived.

Some units have explored ways in which they might commemorate the baby's death and display solidarity with the parents, perhaps by sending a card from the staff on the first anniversary.

The author describes her own involvement with parents and staff and the contribution of psychoanalytic understanding to this area of work, enhanced by Ernest Freud.

It was felt that a psychotherapist, by focusing on the *internal* subjective world of parents, babies and staff, could help alleviate the anxiety which often permeates a NICU. It was also hoped that she could partly unravel the complex psychological processes which inhibit:

PSYCHOLOGICAL ASPECTS OF PREMATURITY AND NIC

(1) unit policies intended to alleviate stress,
(2) optimal functioning by the staff, and
(3) attachment between parents and babies.

This understanding can enable staff to help reinstate parents in their parental role, and hopefully free the care-takers from the distortions of their perceptions, enhancing their ability to confront the infant's illness as realistically as possible.

It is perhaps helpful to both parents and staff to be able to discuss important emotional issues with someone who is not directly responsible for the baby's care.

Working with parents

There are different forms of psychotherapeutic interventions which may be of benefit to parents.

Observation

Psychoanalysts have emphasized the value of attentive observation and reflection as a healing process in itself. Others maintain also, that sharing the baby's observable behavior and reactions with the parents can become a powerful technique for establishing a good working relationship with the family.

Assimilation

The whole experience of childbirth which culminates in a baby's admission to the NICU, may remain confused, unresolved and unassimilated in the parents' minds.

The opportunity of going over the sequence and unique details of the birth allows the parents to integrate the experience, enabling them to move on and attend to the entirely new set of physical and psychological demands of being parents. Through discussion, these 'undigested' experiences may be assimilated and become more bearable. Thus in caring for the parents one can, in turn, help them to mobilize their own capacities as care-takers.

Airing of irrational fears

Many parents have irrational fears and fantasies which need to be listened to before they are able to take in the reality. These range from questions relating to the reasons for premature labor and, for example, 'should I have had sexual intercourse during pregnancy?' to irrational fears about the dangers of touching the baby. Worries about hurting or infecting the baby may stem from a mother's feeling that she is bad or inadequate and are often based on guilt. For example, Mrs A was observed to be expressing reluctance over handling her daughter (aged 30 weeks gestation). During a talk with the unit psychotherapist it emerged that Mrs A yearned to hold her baby but had been warned by her own mother of the dangers of infecting such a tiny baby and therefore stifled her longings. She also revealed that she had suffered a neonatal death a year earlier during a time when the dustmen were on strike and somehow she retained the fantasy that the dirty environment outside the hospital had given rise to a fatal infection.

WORKING WITH MEDICAL AND NURSING STAFF

It was agreed that just as mothers are mirrors for their infants, so do staff often mirror parental feelings, doubts and anxieties. In order to effect any changes in the routine and procedures, the emotional needs of the medical and nursing staff must be considered, since they are essential primary care-takers.

Although policies can be introduced which have been formulated to keep abreast of any developments reported in the literature, their success or failure will in turn be related to how these affect the staff at an unconscious level. Unit policies of parental involvement in the care-taking team, for instance, although theoretically acknowledged to be beneficial, may arouse very ambivalent feelings amongst the staff.

Example

Some nurses reported experiencing involved parents as offering an additional pair of hands; whilst other (less confident) staff experienced the same parents as an extra pair of scrutinizing eyes, watching them make mistakes.

Factors constituting stress for staff

It is clearly a multiplicity of factors which leads to the high rates of stress-related illness, low morale and absenteeism. Termed 'burnout', this is defined as 'loss of motivation for creative involvement' – a way of feeling and behaving.

Amongst these stress factors are: responsibility for the lives of very fragile babies; constant exposure due to the nursery layout necessary for the intensive care of neonates; the need to have understood considerable technological complexities; the need to make quick, unsupported decisions during crises; the expectations of expertise sometimes put on very inexperienced staff; disruptive shifts and rotations; staff shortages; the low status and pay of nursing staff; frequent death and loss of babies; rage, frustration, envy and other very strong feelings as well as the moral and ethical dilemmas of working on such a unit.

Suggestions and attempts to alleviate stress have been diverse, but certain features recur as important:

(1) That there is a need for quiet, reflective moments within a setting where action sometimes takes the place of thought;

(2) That there should be a forum for expression – neutral territory in which everyone can contribute equally irrespective of hierarchical structures; and

(3) That time be given to the interpretation of observations and opportunities be opened to explore and encourage intuitive feelings.

Issues common to both staff and parents

Some common themes have arisen for both staff and parents and are characterized here as rivalry, identification, guilt, separation and mourning.

Rivalry

Parents often felt rivalry with staff because they felt that their baby had been 'taken over'. They felt that the staff spent more time with babies, fed them, understood the technology and seemed to be more confident with them. We know how easy it is to undermine any new parent's confidence, and parents of babies on a NICU are especially vulnerable. Most parents reported that they did not feel that the baby was really theirs until he or she was at home.

Staff quite readily acknowledged feelings of rivalry, anger and hostility, and sometimes said that in a similar situation they would be better mothers and visit unfailingly. They frequently felt irritated by mothers who, for example, had not understood the conversion of imperial into metric units. This was understood in terms of the staff projecting their own feelings of inadequacy onto the parents. The difficulty centred around the fact that the staff were constantly feeling the helplessness and pain of not being able to save babies, yet at the same time were needing to contain parental projections of hope, potency and idealization. It was extremely difficult to be in touch with the parents' envy of them as coping, capable surrogate mothers when, at times, they felt so helpless themselves.

Identification

Parents often identify their own confused, hurt feelings with that of their baby, and in consequence need parenting themselves in order to parent their baby.

Mrs W, whose baby was very ill with respiratory distress syndrome and heart failure, sat crying with her baby, talking about his pain and wondering aloud how she could have been so selfish that she could want a baby so much that she could put him through this.

Student nurses seemed particularly aware of the impact of the NICU on parents, and could identify with their feelings of inadequacy. One nurse recalled how her rosy fantasies about intensive care nursing – 'plumping up and nurturing somewhat undersized infants' – were shattered by the reality of accepting that 'caring' frequently involved inflicting painful procedures on infants whose future life and development were uncertain. Staff, like parents, were reminded of some of their own distressed babyish feelings by these distressed babies.

The theme of *separation and attachment* is a central preoccupation for both parents and staff.

Fatigue, fear and helplessness can make parents long to be away from the unit. Once away, however, there is often a strong anxiety that something might have happened to the baby; this is realistic, but fuelled by unconscious guilt and conflicts about anger and dependency. Some parents described feelings akin to agoraphobia, and others reported a feeling of numbness and being suspended in time, always with a nagging sense of wanting to be somewhere else.

That there is meaning to relationships from the very beginning of life and an interest in people above objects is no longer the unproven conjecture of psychoanalysts. It is particularly important that staff acknowledge the value of the nurturing aspects of their care rather than somehow believe these to be 'unprofessional'.

Occasionally, it was necessary for staff to consider the *baby's* primary need to have one care-taker and to discuss with them the possibility of consciously allowing themselves to become attached in order to provide an intermediate attachment figure when the real parents were unavailable. This was the case with a 28-week-old baby, whose mother had a fit during the labor, choked on her vomit and was admitted to intensive care, with little chance of recovery.

However, rotational policies, day and night duties and the shift system often militated against the formation of very close attachments to babies and parents. Some nurses saw this policy as a disadvantage and felt the need to augment and cement their attachments by discreetly popping in on off duty days. Others felt grateful 'no-one gets stuck with the really sick babies'. The system allowed them to maintain a distance. It protected them from the overwhelming pain and acute distress when 'their' baby died.

Mourning/attachment/guilt

Parents of a preterm baby always experience some mourning and grief. The loss of the experience of the last trimester of pregnancy contributes towards making attachment to the baby difficult, as does the loss of the wished-for normal baby and the threat of losing this baby. These losses can evoke former unresolved grief and mourning which then becomes overwhelming. This is especially true of parents who have experienced a previous miscarriage or stillbirth.

Mrs M was causing concern to the staff because of her rejecting statements about her baby after his birth, and then her apparent lack of feeling when he died after 24 hours. A long talk with her revealed that her beloved mother had died of cancer 2 years previously, and she had been very stoic about this. During several sessions she cried for her mother, and on leaving the hospital said that she felt much better and might really want another baby in the future.

The constant reality of babies dying on the unit made death, and the feelings of tremendous guilt and depression that are aroused, the most difficult thing of all for the staff to deal with. The effects of the sudden death of a long-stay baby would resonate throughout the unit. A superhuman effort was made for a particular baby who had spent 8 weeks on the unit. Having survived major setbacks he just 'went off' one night. After unsuccessful attempts at intubation he sustained massive brain damage and died despite weeks of care and effort. The entire staff's grief was most acute, and the unit went into a state of mourning. I had seen the parents both prior to and immediately following the baby's death. I had also accompanied the parents to the mortuary, where the mother finally felt free to hold the baby, unencumbered by the machinery which had hampered their contact during his lifetime. Afterwards, Mrs S, feeling unable to return to the unit, asked me to please convey her gratitude to the staff for all the loving care she, her husband and her baby had received – they had all become 'family' to her. In the group, when I described the details of Mrs S's leave-taking of her baby, almost every member broke down and cried freely. It had been the staff's own pain at losing the baby which had led to the hasty dispatch of the body from the ward, and accounts for their attempts to dissuade me from supporting the mother's wish to hold and say goodbye to her dead baby.

Defense mechanisms common to both staff and parents

Workers have observed that parents and staff employ various defense mechanisms to help them deal with the psychological stress, pain and conflict thrown up by the birth of a severely ill baby. The most common of these seem to be avoidance and denial, displacement, splitting and projection, manic reparation and magical thinking.

Denial and avoidance

This takes several forms. For example, Mrs P reported that, on looking at her critically ill baby for the first time, she said to herself that there was nothing wrong with him and he would be out of the unit in a few days. Some parents begin to say that they are too busy to visit their baby, and one 15-year-old mother said that she could not visit because she had to go shopping for clothes so that she could be presentable to the doctors. A common phenomenon is that parents ask questions about their babies and are then unable to hear the answers so that the staff have to be infinitely patient in repeating simple information. If the underlying fantasies are first elicited from parents, staff find it easier to convey the real facts.

An example of avoidance of the group sessions by medical and nursing staff paralleled this avoidance in the parents. The therapist would arrive for the group meeting, and suddenly doors would close and staff seemed to disappear. Some staff admitted that this was often the only way they could deal with their anxiety when the parents of a dying baby arrived to visit. Again, for example, there was a nurse who was adamant that, unlike in adult intensive care nursing, one could not get involved with babies. Nurses often reported losing interest in a very sick baby who might die, or a feeling of anger towards that baby. Sometimes they requested to be moved into a different nursery within the unit.

Displacement

Some parents deal with their feelings by displacing them onto other things or events. The focus of those feelings almost always has a basis in reality, but may become emphasized to the exclusion of other feelings about the baby. One father, for example, was only able to talk about his baby's life-support equipment, worrying whether the dials were accurate, etc. One mother decided that the baby's room was inadequately decorated and exhausted herself redecorating it.

Projection/splitting

These are complex defense mechanisms involving blaming other things and people for things for which one unconsciously blames oneself, and splitting feelings into those which are all good and those which are all bad. We often see how obstetricians are blamed for everything which has gone wrong, and how staff on the NICU are idealized. At other times it is the NICU that receives all the blame, or one particular doctor. Parents can often blame each other. Mr H, the father of a child irreversibly brain damaged at birth, pointed out that his wife's uncle was mentally handicapped, and blamed his wife's blood for his son's condition.

Not surprisingly, marital tensions are particularly common among parents whose emotional needs are individually so great, and only very well adjusted relationships survive the stress without difficulties.

Manic reparation

Parents sometimes deal with the guilt about their own damaging infantile feelings by compensating for them. This is normally quite an adaptive defense as it involves care-taking and such activities as fund raising for the unit. Clearly not all care-taking is defensive, but staff need to be aware that when it has a manic quality other, more painful, feelings may be behind it. Following a baby's death, it was not uncommon for staff to console themselves with the thought that the mother would soon be pregnant again.

Following discussion about staff groups a further area has emerged about which little has been written, i.e. the feelings and experiences of the worker attached to a neonatal unit, who has a therapeutic function.

Therapist's area of difficulties

In the early days of liaison with the NICU the author experienced some reluctance and difficulty over feeding back information about parents to staff – even when this was agreed by the parents. This was understood as a reflection of a difficulty the staff themselves were experiencing in relation to the parents. The conflict began to clarify and indeed contained a core issue. To what extent are parents and staff able to regard one another as co-workers working together for the infant's health? The therapeutic task was to understand the issue of trust and the use or misuse of information.

A feeling that I, as a lay person, often experienced whilst observing babies on the unit, was an acute feeling of impotence – a wish to be able to demonstrate in some concrete way that what was being offered, i.e. an attempt to examine the baby's and parents' psychological needs, was equally good and valuable and would promote the baby's health. It made me aware of not only how peripheral and useless parents feel when faced with the powerful life-saving equipment and potent doctors and nurses, but also *why* the staff so often needed to be involved in active management of the infants. 'If only they'd had such and such a machine, then baby X would have survived.' The ever-expanding technology also served another function, it allowed the staff to collude with the parents' magical fantasies and expectations concerning their impressive god-like powers and often made it incredibly difficult for them to acknowledge the limits of what was possible. Helplessness was dealt with by delusional impotence – a feeling that we can and must save life at all cost – a sort of denial of mortality. The use of machines has allowed us to desensitize ourselves to the actual act of death and the taking of life – we 'turn off the respirator' or a baby just 'goes off' one night. It was this painful sensitivity that one was trying to re-introduce into the work and to recognize that the staff's reflex responses (of activity and intervention) could often be instead of thought and inhibiting to thinking. In a parallel way, I had on many occasions to contain and tolerate my own feelings of inadequacy, and not jump in to offer interpretations or explanations.

The feelings of hopelessness, impotence, isolation and rejection experienced by the therapist become the key to understanding at an experiential, rather than intellectual, level the essential problems facing staff and parents in neonatal intensive care.

CONCLUSIONS

Although, in general, there is now a greater recognition of the emotional stresses and psychological conflicts that parents experience during their premature baby's precarious course from traumatic and unexpected birth through to the homecoming and integration into the family, steps taken to implement the facilitation of relationships within this setting are often fraught with difficulty.

It is my contention that work which does not take cognizance of new developments in prenatal and perinatal psychology and medicine will ultimately lead to diminished experience of childbirth and childcare for both the parents and the professionals in this field.

20

The importance of early skin contact in emotional development

H. Musaph

Every scientist engaged in perinatal psychology has to overcome immense difficulties. The critical spectator will put methodological questions, which cannot be answered. The scientist will claim that impregnation, pregnancy and the time afterwards are such unique happenings in the life of mother, child and father, that figures can only reveal the exterior of the problems. The parents have already passed through an emotional development, which differs from person to person. If one tries to compare a pregnant woman with another pregnant woman, one does not take into account the immense diversity in human beings. Talking about perinatal psychology it is necessary to give details about subculture patterns, personal circumstances and personality structures of the women concerned. These variables determine diagnosis, prognosis and therapy in a given situation. We have to include the psychology of the researcher in our considerations as well.

The psychologist who is specialized in methodology will speak in these cases of an anecdotal approach and perhaps he will condemn it. Our answer is that in perinatal psychology relations and emotions take a central place and are of paramount significance. We need the methodologist in order to quantity the accompanying symptoms of emotion, but we are unable to measure emotion itself. Who can measure love or bereavement?

So we know a lot about the autonomous response patterns of mother and child, for instance the relation between their heart rate in the first days after delivery. But these parameters, important as they are, always give partial information. We have to combine this information with all the little things we experience in investigating mother, father and infant in a given case.

THE SHADOW OF DECEASED MEMBERS OF THE FAMILY

A Jewish boy, born shortly after World War II, told me the following story:

> His parents were Polish refugees, who came to Holland together with his grandparents from the father's side. This grandfather was a famous scholar in Judaism. He died shortly after his son's marriage. A few weeks later his daughter-in-law was impregnated and when the young woman told the good news to her mother-in-law, this widow answered: 'You will see, it will be a son, his name will be the name of his grandfather, who just died and he will become a light in Israel.' I think in this prediction there is belief in evidence of reincarnation. The grandmother was right. Her daughter-in-law gave birth to a son, who was named after his grandfather. It is clear that directly after birth the skin contact between mother and son was very close. The child was wanted, his gender was wanted and she had great expectations in holding a very promising baby against her breast. This attitude did not change in the years to come, especially because of the fact that her husband had the same belief in his son, the substitute baby. It turned out that this boy, in his adulthood, had no difficulties at all in making emotional contact with his fellowman.

THE SHADOW OF TRANSGENERATIONAL TRAUMATIZING

> A married woman, mother of a daughter of eight and a son of six years of age, consulted a psychiatrist because of serious contact difficulties with her husband and children. She hardly had sexual contact. Her husband was indignant about the situation. The children were more fond of the father. She could not endure stroking, fondling or caressing. In such situations she was immediately blocked emotionally and this condition had already existed since the early childhood of her children. She loved her husband and children very much, so she suffered from her own incapacity to stroke and fondle and caress. Her parents were both in German concentration camps during the Second World War, because they were Jewish. These heavily traumatized parents reared their three children in a conspiracy of silence concerning their own experiences in the concentration camps. Furthermore, our patient could not remember a situation in which she was sitting on the lap of one of her parents or was stroked, fondled or caressed. When she came to other families and saw that this behavior was normal, she developed feelings of jealousy and grudge.

The difference in both examples is striking. It is not true that our second patient is deficient in her attachment behavior in general. But she was unable to give skin contact from the very beginning of her emotional development, because of deprivation of skin contact in the very early stages of her relationship with her parents.

We know that there exists an identical pattern of skin contact between mother and child, mother and love partner, and mother with her own body. The following deductions can be made from this statement:

(1) Everybody has a fixed behavior pattern in giving skin contact.

(2) In all probability this pattern is an inprint during the first weeks of life.

(3) This archaic pattern is very difficult to change in adulthood.

(4) Deprivation of skin contact in the first weeks of life most probably goes hand in hand with other deprivations, such as eye contact, singing, fondling contact, parameters of emotional contact.

(5) We see skin contact as part and parcel of emotional contact, which is of paramount importance in the mother–child and the father–child relationship.

(6) It is important to diagnose skin contact between the infant and his key figures of influence. In case of deprivation of skin contact, it is then easier to change this pattern as soon as possible.

(7) We have to avoid an impeachment situation, provoked by the doctor or the nurse, who try to change the behavior of deprivation.

(8) Therapy of deprivation behavior of skin contact can be given by members of a child guidance clinic. The counselor could advise the mother by caressing the baby and asking the mother to repeat this behavior. It goes without saying that follow up in this situation is necessary.

(9) If the mother is not able to give skin contact, we have to teach the father or other key figures to do it and to follow our instructions.

(10) If breastfeeding is impossible, the baby should be placed to the naked breast of mother or father while bottle-feeding.

I have already mentioned the impossibility of giving a cast-iron proof that there is a linear connection between deprivation of skin contact in the first months of life, and a disorder in attachment behavior in adulthood. The diversity in human life, in experience and personality structure, in nature and nurture, is too much present in all human beings. Nevertheless, there is enough clinical evidence to state that this connection is most likely.

The same diversity is responsible for the fact that not all babies, suffering from deprivation of skin contact in the first months of life, are condemned to disorders of emotional attachment behavior in adulthood. But this does not relieve us from our obligation and responsibility to do our utmost to prevent empathatic disorders in adulthood.

21

Promoting prenatal and perinatal mother–child bonding: a psychotherapeutic assessment of parental attitudes

A. M. Jernberg

ABSTRACT

The process of forming an attachment between mother and child is a process which begins long before the infant is born. For most mothers it is quite natural to begin to incorporate the baby into their everyday thinking and, during the second trimester, into the way they view themselves. For most mothers the third trimester is a time of coming to see the baby as a separate human being. Yet there are mothers who lack these perceptions or find them difficult. Obstetricians, neonatologists and infant mental health specialists worry that attachment and bonding may be deficient and/or of poor quality in this group of mothers and their babies.

The Prenatal Marschak Interaction Method (MIM) is a method for observing and, when indicated, offering intervention into the attitudes and behaviors of mothers towards their unborn infants.

This paper gives the history of the MIM and describes how to administer, observe, and make evaluations of the mother's attitudes and behaviors toward the fetus. It offers guidelines for conducting the feedback session; and, finally, it describes when and how to intervene if help and guidance are necessary.

References are made, both to the tasks assigned and to the responses to the MIM, which are typical of women who intend to keep their babies as against those who, for example, plan to place them in adoption. A case study of one young woman referred for help is offered as one example of how the method is conducted. This account follows Miss R from initial Prenatal MIM to feedback session, to intervention and, finally, to the Postbirth MIM which she performed with her small daughter.

INTRODUCTION AND RATIONALE

Attitudes of women toward their pregnancies and toward their unborn children may both reflect their own happiness or distress and be reflected in the 'happiness' or distress in the fetus and newborn. 'The belief that events can influence the unborn child – and may be caused by such factors as magic, the gods, and the planets, or by the infant's own actions, or by events affecting the pregnant woman – has been held through all of recorded history in all cultures,' writes Macfarlane (1977, p. 5). We have all known intuitively and certainly folklore has told us (Alexander, 1950) that the happiness of the expectant mother has some relationship to the success of her pregnancy. Indeed, Macfarlane writes about the prenatal clinics run in China 1000 years ago; 'not so much in the interest of physical well-being as to ensure tranquility in the mother and, through her, in the baby'. A prospective mother's own happiness, in turn, may be influenced by society's messages regarding pregnancy, by her history, and by her current relationships – particularly with her mate. Her attitudes toward pregnancy in general, her present pregnancy, in particular, and other factors having to do with her internal and external reality all play important roles.

As ever-more research demonstrates the sensitivity of the fetus to its mother's state of mind, to her attitudes toward pregnancy and to her behaviors, it becomes increasingly evident that it is the job of helping professionals to understand, identify and intervene when necessary.

With respect to the fetus's sensitivity to maternal state of mind it is relevant to note the findings of Grinker and Walsh (1978) that, more than is true for two control populations, the population of schizophrenic young adults had experienced the death of a grandparent-to-be even before they were born. Bottari and McLaughlin (1984) write, 'The moderate relationship between mothers' prenatal psychological adjustment and infant birth weights is remarkable and suggests a link between mother's psychological condition and the physical condition of her offspring,' (p. 6). Lieberman's (1973) findings suggest that a woman even thinking of having a cigarette – to say nothing, of course, of her actually having one – brings about an increased fetal heart beat. With respect to the fetus's sensitivity to its mother's behaviors, De Casper and Spence's work in 1982 is quite consistent with the work done by Sontag (1941, 1944) well over 40 years ago. De Casper and Spence's (1982) cleverly designed experiments demonstrate that neonates prefer to hear a tape recording of their mothers reading the same poem they had heard them read prebirth rather than tapes of their fathers reading that same poem or their mothers reading another poem.

Those findings are as significant in their implications as are the studies of Connolly and Cullen (1983) demonstrating that mothers' negative attitudes toward the pregnancy correlate with abnormalities of the limbs in their newborns at the 5% level of significance, a finding consistent with that of Dorman and Olds (1983) which showed that maternal attitudes prebirth are predictive of perceived infant temperament postbirth. Brazelton (1974) observes that if the communication system is established before birth, there will be meshing immediately after birth. Of greatest relevance to this point is Leifer's (1980, p. 69) work, which was designed to answer the question, '... to what extent do pregnant women develop an emotional attachment to the fetus and is this related to attachment toward the actual baby?' '... a very striking finding of this study', writes Leifer, 'was that the degree of emotional attachment toward the fetus during pregnancy is related to the intensity of maternal feelings shown toward the infant after birth ... all of the women who had developed only minimal emotional ties to the fetus during pregnancy experienced a greater sense of distance toward their babies ... These women were clearly distinguished during pregnancy by their conflicted negative feelings toward the fetus and by their lack of any form of playful communication with it' (pp 86–7).

Winnicott (1957) stresses the importance of the mother getting to know the fetus 'as a person' before birth if there is to be a 'good mother–child relationship' after birth. Addressing new mothers-to-be, he writes, '... I think the most important thing is that you feel that your baby is worth getting to know as a person and worth getting to know from the earliest possible moment ...' and he goes on to say, '... Even in the womb your baby is a human being unlike any other human being, and by the time he is born he will have quite a lot of experience, unpleasant as well as pleasant ... If I were you', Winnicott continues, 'I should not wait until the psychologists have decided how human a baby is at birth – I should just go right ahead and get to know the little fellow and let him get to know you' (p. 5). Verny and Kelly (1981) are more detailed yet in their advice to expectant mothers: 'Soft, soothing talk makes him feel loved and wanted ... He is mature enough intellectually to sense the emotional tone of the maternal voice' (p. 22). 'This communication is an important part of bonding', they continue. 'And since every investigator who has studied bonding after birth agrees that it is immensely beneficial to both mother and child, it stands to reason that bonding before birth would be equally important' (p. 27).

With the advent of the ultrasound technique for early diagnosis, mothers have been able to relate to their fetuses as 'separate people' in a brand new way. Fletcher (1983) describes, as clear evidence that they had formed a bond of loyalty toward them, two women's thoughts about and feelings toward their fetuses following ultrasound examinations in early to midpregnancy. He refers to this awareness as enhancing of early bonding and describes the experience of viewing the fetus as a 'shock of recognition'. Reading (1980) maintains that the increasing use of ultrasound scans during pregnancy may increase women's perceptions of their babies as 'separate' persons. Given how important it clearly seems to be for mothers to attach early to the child inside them and to perceive and relate to that child as a separate human being, it would seem useful to develop methods other than ultrasound for helping this process along. The Prenatal Marschak Interaction Method (PMIM) is one such method.

The Marschak Interaction Method (MIM) (1960a, 1960b, 1967, 1980) was originally developed as a tool for observing the interaction between parents and their preschool children. The MIM provided information about the behavior of each of the two participants within the interaction. It assessed such parental capacities as that for giving the child affection, for guiding the child's purposeful behavior, for reducing the child's stress, and for alerting the child to the environment as well as the parental ability to be playful.

Over the past two decades we have responded to more and more requests first, to assess the quality of attachment between parent and child and secondly, to intervene in the interaction if poor attachment is evident. During this period the staff have utilized ever younger levels of the MIM and thus have observed more and more parents interacting with younger and younger children. With this drop in age level it has become ever more apparent that the foundation for the behaviors we see in the *Infant MIM* (Jernberg et al., 1983) is established and can be improved upon, if necessary, even before the baby is born (Jernberg et al., 1985). The *Post-MIM Intervention* often offered a mother and her 6-month-old child is most certainly useful for enhancing attachment. That same intervention begun even before birth allows mothers first, to develop wholesome attitudes toward their fetuses, their pregnancies and themselves as future mothers and second to 'practice' behaviors which will later benefit the mother–child relationship.

METHOD

The MIM, as originally conceived by Marschak (1960a), consists of a series of tasks covering a number of different parenting dimensions which are administered to parent and child as they sit side by side on chairs facing a table top. If the child is too young to sit, the child lies on a mat on the floor while the parent, leaning against a backrest, sits beside him/her. The instruction cards stacked up in front of the parent direct how to do each task. Numbered envelopes contain materials called for in the instruction cards.

Some MIM tasks appear, virtually unchanged in purpose, right up the developmental ladder from newborn to infant. This universally useful list includes tasks such as:

Talk and play together,
Reduce child's stress,
Talk to the child about his or her future,
Parent leaves the room for a minute,
Tell the child a story beginning, 'When you were brand new . . .'

Of the 15 or so items geared for each level, about seven are selected for each individualized administration. Which tasks are selected depends upon the kinds of hypotheses being tested (e.g. 'Is this a mother who is "exploiting" her child?' 'Will these parents have difficulty allowing their child autonomy?' 'Does this father require his son to identify with his own too-ambitious behavior?' etc.)

While parent and child are performing the tasks of the MIM, or in reviewing the tape if the session has been video-recorded, the observer takes extensive notes as to the verbal and non-verbal behaviors of each of the two participants and also notes the nature of the 'climate' between them. It is recommended that, whenever possible, a video camera rather than a human hand be used to do the recording. In a session subsequent to the MIM session(s) both parents (in a two-parent family, one parent in a one-parent family) are invited to a 'feedback session'. As they review the videotape during the feedback session the parents are encouraged to begin to think about what happened as they participated in the MIM. They are helped to look at their interactions with their child and to try to come to understand the complexities of the relationship.

Parents are never 'blamed' for inappropriate behavior. Indeed, it may well be that they come to see that, as is often true with adopted children, it is the child's behavior, not their's, which sets the stage for parental feelings of rejection and hurt (Koller, 1981). It is in the feedback session that a parent may be told, 'Look at those lovely things you do with him, how playful you are with him and how warm. Any other child would adore interacting with a parent like you. But not Johnny. Notice how he keeps looking away from you and shifting his body away. That must surely hurt you when he does that.' For many a parent, mothers particularly – for, as Koller has observed, it is usually the mother, not the father to whom this treatment is directed – this may be the first time anybody has taken notice of her pain and has confirmed that, whereas she feels she does her very best for her child, her child still consistently rejects her.

Occasionally additional help will be provided to parents whose MIM shows that they lack empathy, for example, or those who are insufficiently playful or show too little capacity for reducing their children's distress. This help may be offered in the form of role playing. Role playing allows the parent to perform the same series of tasks but to do so not with the child but with another adult. Playing out the task gives the parent the opportunity to 'do it over again'. This time the parent may be praised for doing it well or be invited to 'let's try it one more time'. Role playing also allows the reversing of roles. In role reversal it is the parent who plays the child while the other adult plays the role of parent. The parent is then more free to experience how it must feel to be on the receiving end of the parental behavior.

THE PRENATAL MIM: DIAGNOSIS

Referrals for *Diagnostic Prenatal MIMs* are made by obstetricians and others having a concern about a possible poor quality attachment between mother and infant post-birth. Many departments of obstetrics whose members become familiar with the MIM, find this method to be valuable as a prognostic indicator for mother–infant bonding.

The MIM method with mothers

The pregnant woman is seated on a comfortable chair. On a small table at her side are placed the *Prenatal MIM* instruction cards, a large envelope containing a pad of writing paper and pencil, a glass of water for drinking, and a box of tissues. She is instructed, 'Take each card and read the instructions on each one aloud before completing the task.' She is left alone with the assignment while the observer goes behind the video camera or retreats to an inconspicuous corner of the room for note-taking. The following constitute the tasks of the *Prenatal MIM*:

    Draw a picture of you and your baby.
    Talk and play with your baby.
    Tell your baby about when he/she is a grown-up.

MOTHER–CHILD BONDING

Communicate something to your baby without saying words, then say it to him/her.
Tell your baby the story beginning, 'When you were brand new ...'
Tell your baby what you think have been and are his/her most stressful times.
Tell your baby in what ways you try to reduce his/her stress.
Sing to your baby.
Teach your baby something.
Prepare your baby for childbirth.
Tell your baby about the happiest times you have had together and about the happiest times that lie ahead.
Make a drawing of you and your baby.
Tell your baby about his/her father.
Tell your baby about the people he/she will meet in his/her new world.

The MIM method with fathers

As we come to understand more and more about the importance of fathers to the developing infant, to the mother, and to the father's own self-image, we turn our attention to his relationship to the fetus.

Administration of the *Prenatal MIM* to fathers, of necessity, takes a modified form. So that neither parent will be influenced by the facial expression of the other, fathers are not present when their partner performs the MIM tasks. Since it is, of course, impossible to arrange for *mothers* to be absent from their fetuses during the procedure, a second alternative can be provided as follows.

In order to focus his attention on the fetus as exclusively as possible, mother is instructed to concentrate her attention elsewhere (e.g. on reading a newspaper if she is a reader, on looking at pictures if she is not) while he, sitting so as to directly face her body, yet not focusing on her face, engages in the MIM. The Father–fetus MIM is best conducted with the mother's face concealed behind the newspaper she is reading or the picture book or magazine she is looking at.

The same 14 tasks of the *Mother–fetus MIM* constitute the *Father–fetus MIM* with the substitution of 'Mother' for 'Father' in the instructions, 'Tell your baby about his mother'.

ANALYSIS

Verbal analysis

In analyzing verbal behaviors on the MIM the clinician attends to the nature of references to the baby ('it', 'the baby', 'he/she' or 'you'); references to the parent (e.g. 'I' vs. 'Mommy'); symbiosis/individuation ('you' and 'I' vs. 'we'); intra- vs. extra-family references; specificity; playfulness; practical vs. idealistic; hope vs. despair, etc. The clinician compares the number and quality of action verbs and compares these to other verbs. Other aspects looked at include the developmental level the parent uses when addressing the fetus; the estimated degree to which the parent expects self-fulfillment through the child; the degree of empathy with the child; degree of engagement; appropriateness of maternal mind state (e.g. it is typical that she is more contemplative and turned inward in the second trimester than in the first or third), etc.

Non-verbal analysis

Analyzing the *Prenatal MIM* from a non-verbal viewpoint entails the following. The observer notes how often, and with what quality, the mother 'touches' her baby (e.g. pats, strokes, kneads, pinches, rubs, etc.). The observer also notes the direction of her gaze (looks at abdomen, looks at self in mirror, looks elsewhere) and the quality (looks fleetingly, intensely, absently, angrily, not at all). And, finally, the observer notes the mother's body posture (rigid, relaxed, restless, quiet, alert, slouching, etc.).

EVALUATION

During the evaluation process attention is given to Trout's ten pathognomonic indicators (Trout, 1986):

(1) The presence of one or more previous reproductive casualties,
(2) The desirability of being in a state of pregnancy but not the reality of the baby,
(3) The presence of chronic anxiety or depression,
(4) The presence of chronic fatigue,
(5) Denial of the pregnancy,
(6) Denial of sexual experience,
(7) Attempts to sabotage the pregnancy,
(8) Self-referral for unrelated reasons (e.g. a sleeping problem in a 2-year-old),
(9) Nesting failure, and
(10) Inadequate support systems in the family.

The evaluation is designed to help first the clinician and then the parent gain an understanding of parental expectations, attitudes and behaviors toward the unborn child. It is hoped that this understanding will, in turn, lead the mother to begin to question why she behaves in the manner she does? What attitudes led her to behave this way? What, for example, may be the 'ghosts' in the closet (Fraiberg, Adelson and Shapiro, 1975) ready to interfere with or color her attachment to her baby? And, finally, what might help her to change her behavior and attitudes? In the process, the expectant mother will have to question whether there are perhaps other agendas which may interfere with her relationship with her baby and to question the implications of such interference for the parent in the present and for the parent–child bond in the future. The mother, having raised these questions internally first, the clinician next encourages her re-consideration of them as worker and parent-to-be examine the videotape together (or review the MIM task-by-task from notes if there is no videotape).

Many parents report that the very experience of taking the MIM has changed their perception of themselves, their babies and themselves as parent-to-a-child. It would seem far-fetched to think that half an hour or so of such an experience could have a profound effect. Yet a comparison of the drawings completed at the beginning and then repeated again at the end of the test do suggest that some changes have indeed taken place.

Preliminary findings

(1) Mothers who are ambivalent about keeping their babies after delivery seem to have the greatest difficulty performing or even agreeing to perform the MIM.

(2) The task 'Tell your baby about his/her father' is a favorite task of single mothers – especially those who doubt that they will ever see the baby's father again.

(3) Fathers initially relate to the fetus as an 'outside baby' (Trout, 1986). Only after performing the *Prenatal MIM* do they view it as an 'inside baby'.

(4) Mothers who have had the ultrasound experience tend to make 'outside baby' drawings.

INTERVENTION

In cases where an analysis of the MIM suggests the potential for attachment pathology and where suspicions of this pathology continue even after the parent has performed the MIM and has experienced the feedback session that follows, intervention is indicated.

The intervention session is presented as an offer to 'help the bond between you and your baby' and is scheduled one week after the feedback session. Rejections of the offer are rare. If they happen at all they will likely happen with young women who are secretly considering giving their babies up for adoption.

The intervention session begins with the mother and the clinician sitting side by side. The MIM instruction cards rest in the clinician's lap. One by one they are handed to the mother as she goes through the series of tasks again, and then again, and perhaps again. Each time she does so she is coached to involve herself more and more with her baby – to look at him, value him, touch him, talk to him directly, etc. – and to do all this with energy, imagination, emotion and intensity. When she succeeds in behaving in ways which will later be more conducive of attachment, she is responded to by her clinician with warm approval or a hearty cheer. Should she continue in ways which are antithetical to good attachment-formation, e.g. with diffidence, harshness, aloofness or developmentally inappropriate ways (as, for example, being overly merged with the baby in the first or third trimester (Trout, 1986) or insufficiently merged in the second trimester), she is never criticized; she is only invited to 'do it over'. Sometimes the despair of her situation makes it impossible for a mother to behave in the ways we are trying to encourage. In those cases the worker may pause and place an arm around her shoulder, saying nothing for a few moments – thus both communicating support and understanding and also modelling what 'good' parenting is like.

Intervention sessions may need to be scheduled only once or may require repeat appointments over a several session span. The experience should be an enjoyable and a challenging one. Most mothers report that they have grown in their self-image and in their awareness of the tremendous importance of 'myself-as-parent' in the relationship that is about to begin.

FOLLOW-UP: THE POSTBIRTH INTERVENTION

The Postbirth MIM includes the tasks of the Prenatal MIM in addition to the following:

Tell your child about when he/she was born and what it was like.

Play peek-a-boo with your baby.
Leave the room for a minute without your child.
Tell what you think your baby was doing while you were gone.
Feed your baby.

Returning to perform the *Postbirth MIM* is often a highly meaningful experience for mothers who had previously performed the Prenatal MIM. (Note: The Postnatal is specifically designed to replicate the tasks and the sequence of tasks performed before the baby was born. The task, 'Prepare your baby for childbirth' is of course omitted.) Often the return visit provides continuity to the mother–child relationship as evidenced in the very frequent comment to the baby, 'Remember the last time we came here?' In this postnatal visit as in the prenatal one, there is a feedback session. Both the taking of the MIM this time around and the ensuing feedback session may be nothing more than a glorified check-up and show-off visit or there may be attachment pitfalls that still need help. When help is indicated it is again offered by means of coaching and support, never by means of criticism. Whatever evidence of attachment can be found, these behaviors on the part of both mother and child are the ones that get the most attention. (For example, 'See how hard she struggles to keep gazing at you? That tells us how important you are to her,' or 'It's lovely how melodic your voice is when you talk to him.') In addition, however, it may be important to help a parent modify behaviors which may hamper the attachment (for example, 'Let's see. I wonder. Do you suppose if you hold him just like this, lying in your arm this way, you'd be giving him the best chance to come to know what a great Mom he's got?' or 'Look at that little girl of yours really carefully. I think you'll see something you've never seen before. I think what you'll see will make you appreciate how bright and special and responsive she really is. Look at that! I do believe she's trying to suck on her thumb. Wow! Are you lucky! Many Moms have babies who aren't half that alert, that charming and that curious.')

In the rare case where the infant is consistently unresponsive or rejecting, mothers need a great deal of help to persevere in their efforts. It is in these situations particularly that fathers must be encouraged to be supportive of the mothers' efforts and empathic with their pain.

Depending upon each professional's work situation it may or may not be appropriate to schedule subsequent check-up visits as the child grows older. Parents are encouraged to return with their children at regularly scheduled intervals. Generally, they very much enjoy doing this – all the more so as their family expands to include new siblings.

A SAMPLE CASE STUDY

Miss R, a talented, 24-year-old artist, was in her last trimester of pregnancy when she phoned for her prenatal MIM appointment. She did so, she told us, at the suggestion of her obstetrician who was concerned that she might not properly bond to her baby postbirth. In fact, in discussing her case with us before her appointment, he expressed considerable concern that this single, quite depressed and chronically self-centered young woman might indeed encounter trouble with her child at a later time if something were not done soon to help her.

With tears running down her cheeks, this very attractive woman performed the tasks slowly but methodically and in correct sequence. Her voice was barely audible; her posture was slouching. At no point during the entire session did she touch or even look at her abdomen. Regardless of the task assigned, she spoke in a dreary monotone either about abstractions like 'the future' and 'sadness' or about herself exclusive of the baby. Thus she reponded to 'Tell your baby about when he or she is a grown up' with gloomy pronouncements about 'Life'. She responded to 'Tell your baby the story beginning "When you were brand new"', with a long account about how miserable she herself has always been. Her response to the task 'Prepare your baby for childbirth' was directed to a distant imaginary audience, never once to the baby, and went as follows:

'Childbirth? Huh? What does that mean, "childbirth"? "Prepare"? How could I prepare? I don't even know how it all goes myself. Oh, I've been to all those classes and everything, you know, at the hospital. But I don't understand any of that stuff they taught us. I don't know *what* it's going to be like or anything *else* about it either.'

Following the administration of the first MIM she was scheduled for a subsequent feedback session. During this visit she was given the opportunity to express her concerns. These consisted primarily of her sorrow that she might never see the baby's father again and her fear that her parents might try to take over the raising of her child. She was helped to see that she need not be entirely helpless in the situation with her parents if she herself did not want them to play the care-taking role. She was encouraged to verbalize her wish that the pregnancy had never happened and to express her rage with a boyfriend who had sentenced her to a life of loneliness and premature responsibility.'Following the feedback session she was offered the opportunity to 'learn some ways that may help you better accept your baby and, who knows, maybe even teach you some ways that you and your baby might learn to have a lot of fun together.' She accepted the offer eagerly.

At the first intervention session her worker sat beside her and encouraged her to look down at the baby, speak to the baby, touch the baby, sing to the baby, etc., as together they worked and re-worked the tasks prescribed on the MIM. At first Miss R was reluctant, confused and distractible. With each new task she performed, however, she became more alert, more alive and more

MOTHER–CHILD BONDING

motivated to engage with the baby in a meaningful and real way. At the outset her worker involved her in the following kind of discussion:

Task: 'Tell your baby how you try to reduce his/her stress'.
Miss R: 'Tell your baby what? Stress? Huh? I guess I don't understand what that means.'
Worker: 'What do you think that means?'
Miss R: 'I guess that means I should talk about reducing stress. Right?'
Worker: 'Whose stress?'
Miss R: 'Whose stress? Huh? I don't know what that means.'
Worker: 'Just go ahead with what you think it means.'
Miss R: 'Well if it means I should talk about reducing people's stress, I guess what works best for me is just listening to music. You know ...' (Her voice drifts off in a long soliloquy of how she stands by the window with the rain coming down just listening to the words of the music.)
Worker: 'Well, that is interesting how you reduce your own stress and all that but if you look at the card again you'll see that isn't exactly what it asks for.'
Miss R: (slowly reads the card again). 'Oh, yes. Well I guess I would reduce the baby's stress by turning on music I like and that would make me feel better.'

It was quite some time before Miss R was able to move from her position of abstraction alternating with extreme self-centeredness.

Eventually her videotaped protocol records the same task, 'Tell baby how you try to reduce his/her stress', as follows:

Miss R: (reads instruction card) 'Well, sweetheart (looking down at abdomen), you know we're going to do everything we possibly can do so that you won't have to feel any more stressed than is absolutely necessary. But if it happens sometimes that there *is* stress (stroking "baby") I'll be right here with you to comfort you and hold you (hand on abdomen pretending to hold her "baby") and tell you "Everything's going to be all right," because you'll always know we're in it together and I'm going to take good care of you.' The drawings at the end of this particular MIM clearly indicate that at last she feels ready to give birth to her baby.

Following the completion of her series of MIM Interventions, Miss R gave birth to a little girl. At 4 weeks postbirth she and Jasmin came in for a follow-up MIM. Again, she needed some coaching regarding optimum ways to relate to Jasmin but, again, she 'caught on' and followed the suggestions, including both those on how to become a good observer of Jasmin-as-a-person and how to behave in more attachment-enhancing ways herself. She was proud to show their relationship off at yet a later MIM visit and has been quite satisfied with their relationship and with herself as a mother ever since.

CONCLUSION

In conclusion it can be said that the *Prenatal MIM* can be a highly useful method for helping to generate attachment. The literature cited in this paper suggests that, particularly in the last trimester of pregnancy, the attachment of a mother to her fetus, and her view of him/her as 'a separate human being', are of great importance to the development of later mother–child attachment. The *Prenatal MIM* allows the clinician to assess the attachment status and provides the mother the opportunity to develop skills and emotions which can enhance the bond between parent and child.

22
A program to facilitate prebirth bonding
E. Bowen

ABSTRACT

The concept of prebirth bonding in childbirth education will be discussed.

Based on the assumption of both scientific and anecdotal evidence of the existence of birth and uterine memories, a program has been developed that assists parents in becoming acquainted with their unborn child and facilitates bonding. The program increases parents' awareness of their unborn's activities and patterns, and consequently from the point of birth parents feel more comfortable in touching, talking, looking and experiencing their newborn.

Prebirth bonding is a process designed to create an acquaintance with the unborn baby. As with any relationship we become acquainted, fond of and maybe, eventually, fall in love with each other.

In 1982 when I first wrote of prebirth bonding there were few references on this subject. Two of these still stand out in my mind.

Linda Carter Jessop promoted maternal attachment through prenatal intervention encouraging mothers to feel and identify parts of their baby *in utero*, developing the mother's awareness for fetal activity, and via rubbing, stroking and massaging abdomens (Jessop, 1981).

Mecca S. Cranley studied the development of a tool to measure maternal attachment during pregnancy (Cranley, 1981a). Her study supported maternal–fetal attachment to the unborn.

SUMMARY OF A PREBIRTH BONDING PROGRAM

The following is a summary of the proffered ten-step program that can be regarded as a tool towards bonding with the unborn baby as outlined in my work, *Prebirth Bonding* (Bowen, 1982).

Step 1: rest

Before you can even begin being good to your baby, you must start being good to yourself. Set aside a time each day for rest from the moment you discover the pregnancy. This means both the mother and the father. The months of carrying the child produce chemical and hormonal changes in the female body which can have a decided effect on mood, endurance, temperament, ability to cope, physical strength and emotional balance.

Use this time to set up communications about your feelings, about the baby and about life in general. It is surprising how many couples do not regularly set up this 'quiet time' together, just in the normal course of their marriage. This is a wonderful time to get into the habit, a habit that could serve your partnership long after your baby is born.

So, make this special time a time that is set aside just for the two of you and the baby, right from the beginning. Do not allow interruptions. We are thinking here about a period that could be as short as 10 minutes each day. Quantity is not nearly as important as quality. Use this time to *rest,* to *be together,* to *be with your child.*

Step 2: enjoy the baby

It should begin a week or two later, after mother and father are used to simply being together, with nothing to do and nothing to say (deliberately). Here you begin to verbalize your feelings, to talk about the baby, the coming months, the plans, the hopes and dreams. If the baby is unexpected, talk out your feelings about that. Be open and honest. Approach the subject from every angle. It is astonishing how many couples do not share their feelings about the baby until just before (and in some cases after) the baby arrives. Clear the air now, if indeed there is anything to clear away. Candid discussion now of any worries or anxieties about the baby's arrival can make many of those feelings actually disappear. Enjoy the baby. Plan how the room will look and where the baby will sleep. Begin thinking about names. Set up a positive, loving attitude for the months ahead.

PROGRAM FOR PREBIRTH BONDING   269

Step 3: make contact with the baby

By now the baby's heart has started beating. You can now begin to make actual contact with the baby.

This step should begin within 30–40 days after conception. Don't worry if you're late. Begin now. This step, like step 1, is mental. It involves your thoughts only. Think to, not about, the baby. You thought about the baby in step 1. Now direct your thoughts to the baby. It may help to understand that your thoughts are not going to the body of the baby (which is, after all, hardly developed), but to the intelligence behind the body, the intelligence which will remain with the baby long after the body is grown. Send thoughts that communicate your love for the baby; let the baby know it is coming into a loving, caring environment.

Remember that this is your initial contact, or 'bonding'; so say 'hello' in a way that you would if you wanted to make anyone you loved welcome in your life. You should add music to your rest period in step 3. Pick out something you both like. Use the music to provide a mood in which both mother and father can relax and simply think thoughts to the baby. Don't be a bit surprised if, after the baby is born, it falls asleep immediately after having this same music turned on during its nap periods.

Add touch to the bonding process. Mother and father may want to both rest a hand on the baby. You will be able to feel the sensation of new life long before the baby starts kicking. And the baby will be able to feel you.

The loving, welcome thoughts – to which you have added music and touch – complete the process and establish the bond.

Step 4: begin conversation with your baby

As the process expands, we add voice to thought and music and touch. You may question why it is necessary to talk out loud to a person who is 'not in the room' (you may even feel a little silly doing this at first, particularly if it is true the baby can pick up your thoughts, anyway). Why speak? The answer is, speaking forces us to communicate more clearly. Thoughts are often jumbles of words and pictures. Putting thoughts into words adds a new dimension, a dimension the child will live with for the rest of his/her life. Obviously, words also let your partner know what communications you are sending, allowing him or her to join in a three-way communication.

You are building a family here. You are putting the first building blocks into place in a system of three-way communication which will serve you for years to come. Talking to your unborn baby is hardly a waste of time, not communicating with your baby would be the waste.

Step 5: share your whole life

With this step, we increase the amount of time we are spending with baby each day. We are including baby, too, in our other activities. Baby becomes, in a very real sense, a part of our daily life! Communication can now take place in the supermarket, backyard, church pew or public building corridor. The idea is to get away from a routine where the child is addressed during a certain period each day, then not again until the next day. The purpose of step 5 is to establish a link with the baby which permeates the entire experience of mother, father and child.

Step 6: visualization

Now set aside a time each day to use the highest power within you – the power of visualization – to begin planning exactly how the birth of your child will be. Use the chalkboard of your mind to draw specific images. Or think of your mind as a giant movie screen. Project images on that screen of just how it is going to turn out. Do this systematically, every day. Keep up with steps 1–5.

Step 7: education

To make your visualizations more potent, more informed, pick up everything you can find of value on pregnancy and birth. Attend classes and lectures. Buy tape cassettes and video programs. Scan the newspapers daily for informative articles. Talk at length with other mothers, with your doctor, with nurses, midwives and anyone you think has something to contribute. Especially, if it is possible, talk to your own mother about your birth. This includes husbands.

This step is a process in self-education. Both parents, as in all the steps, should take part. Pay at least as much attention to educating yourself about your baby as you would about a new car or a new home you are going to buy. Leave no stone unturned. Make sure all your questions are answered.

Step 8: preparation

Here is where we are going to fully prepare for the momentous occasion of your child's entry into the world. You have learned all you can learn (and you are continuing step 7 all along). Now begin making lists. Start putting your plans into writing: be specific. Try to think of everything, then think of it again.

Make out a road map of where you want this experience to go and how you want to get there. Keep communicating with your baby. Don't stop those rest periods. Keep playing music.

Step 9: materialization

Now, put the plans into action. Prepare a written agreement, and sign it with your doctor. Make sure the hospital or birthing center plans to proceed according to your specific wishes. Discuss every detail with your mate. Talk to relatives and anyone else who may be involved in the birth of your child.

Many families make more detailed plans for taking a weekend vacation than for the birth of a new member.

Step 10: actualization

Forget everything you have ever read or heard about birthing a baby. Start from scratch. Enjoy the actual experience. Be there. Throw out all of your preconceptions. Trust your intuition. Know that 'this is it'. Have the experience, not your thoughts about it.

CONCLUSION

In conclusion I would like to take note of the work of Maxine Johnston (1980). She writes 'There are perhaps few who would disagree that it is not only parenting patterns that influence attachment behavior, but often, and more importantly, it is our pattern of professional beliefs that influences this relationship and is a crucial variable in attachment behavior.'

I was delighted not too long ago to talk to an acupuncturist who explained that, in the Chinese Buddhist philosophy, it is believed that the life force comes from the air above, down to and meets the earth force of the baby. He visually described the tiny forming curved fetus and the energy and spirit coming into the tiny curved being. It is a delightful visualization image we might use in promoting prebirth bonding and conscious conception. As for the future, I firmly believe that we are moving toward the development of conscious conception. For now, I will be satisfied to see a *more* conscious conception on the part of parents.

23

Parental singing during pregnancy and infancy can assist in cultivating positive bonding and later development

L. Thurman

ABSTRACT

The paper first presents some theoretical bases for the beneficial effects of parental singing during pregnancy and infancy, and secondly, a few suggestions for practical applications of parental singing in early learning.

The theoretical bases include:

(1) *A brain-based theory of learning,*
(2) *A theory of multiple intelligences,*
(3) *The relevance of appropriate infant stimulation to brain growth and the development of the human intelligences,*
(4) *The importance of the human voice in developing positive bonding between parents and children, and*
(5) *The value of interchangeable speaking and singing in appropriate infant stimulation.*

The practical applications include a few specific suggestions about how parents might use prenatal and postnatal singing for the development of positive bonding and the intelligences.

How parents and their children interact influences the psychosocial orientation of both. The impact of parents on children is, of course, the more pervasive influence. Cataloging the parenting behaviors which may lead to an unfortunate psychosocial future for children is useful in preventive psychology. A much more useful approach, however, would be to determine how parents can interact with their children so that they might accumulate a psychosocial history that enables the optimal development of their human potential.

In other words, if human well-being and happiness are 'our business', then let us look for and share the kinds of parent–child interactions that are most likely to bring that result about. Of course, for greatest impact, the interactions must be appropriate to the developmental capabilities of children, and must begin at an appropriate developmental time.

My colleagues, Anna Langness, Margaret Chase Nelson and I have developed a publication and a parenting class which uses singing as a synthesizing focus for parent–child bonding and the development of infant capabilities.

THEORETICAL BASES FOR THE EFFECTS OF PARENTAL SINGING

Leslie Hart (1983), author of *Human Brain and Human Learning*, synthesized many volumes of brain research with research in such fields as information theory, psychology, computer science and anthropology. He describes the brain as the 'organ of learning', and suggests that it has two 'drives':

(1) To 'make sense' of the perceived 'world', and

(2) To achieve mastery of the perceived world.

Hart believes these drives are not learned, but that the nature of the brain is to carry these out. It does so by:

(1) *Seeking out and receiving non-threatening sensory input*, that is, observing the world through its sensory abilities, then

(2) *Detecting and recognizing patterns in the sensed world* by using some of its interpretive abilities, then

(3) *Selecting the most appropriate available brain program* in order to interact with the world, using its interpretive and movement abilities.

As the brain's neurons grow in size and length, as they are 'insulated' through myelinization, as neuronal interconnections are multiplied into the trillions, and as the prefrontal surfaces of the neocortex expand, then increases in a child's physical, intellectual and self-management abilities become possible (Luria, 1973).

Howard Gardner, a neuropsychologist and author of *Frames of Mind:*

The Theory of Multiple Intelligences (1983), proposes six human intelligences which are related to brain areas and processes. The intelligences are:

(1) Linguistic,
(2) Musical,
(3) Bodily-kinesthetic,
(4) Spatial,
(5) Logical-mathematical,
(6) Personal intelligences
 (a) Intrapersonal (self-esteem, ego, etc.)
 (b) Interpersonal (social sensitivity, etc.).

Everyone, including child development researchers, believes that parent-initiated interaction with babies (such as talking, touching, holding, rocking) is necessary to the healthy physical, intellectual and emotional development of children. Some people label those interactions as 'infant stimulation', and some call them 'early learning experiences'.

What is 'early learning' or 'infant stimulation?' It is 'sensory input' for the nervous system of an infant, that is, any stimulation of one or more of the senses, i.e. auditory, visual, tactile, gestatory, olfactory, vestibular, kinesthetic and emotional feeling. The stimulation is 'processed' by the brain's pattern detection abilities, and usually results in some kind of reaction by the infant such as focusing visual attention, smiling, kicking, vocalizing, calming, sleeping and crying. The brain's learning processes are thus stimulated into action, and stimulations that are repeated enough times will result in memory 'imprints' in the brain.

Most parent–child interactive stimulations are spontaneous, i.e. what the parents do 'automatically' without conscious planning. Should parent–child interactions be limited to what parents know to do spontaneously? Can basic and applied research findings indicate appropriate and beneficial parent–child interactions which parents can learn and conveniently use with conscious planning? Might some interactive stimulation of infants be detrimental to their development? If so, how can parents know how to distinguish appropriate from inappropriate stimulations?

A controversy has arisen in the United States among some child development specialists over whether or not parents can accelerate the intellectual and physical development of their children with emotional safety. At one extreme, some specialists believe that parents can develop so-called 'superbabies' by using recommended stimulation techniques for future intellectual advantage. At the other extreme, some specialists believe that overly-concerned parents can 'hurry' the development of their children's physical and intellectual capabilities in ways that compromise emotional security. These specialists strongly caution parents regarding certain special early learning experiences.

A centrist position argues that parents can learn:

(1) What developmental sequences children go through in developing their physical and intellectual capabilities, and

(2) How to 'read' their babies' responses to interactive stimulation and use them as a guide for when to stimulate and what stimulations produce a positive emotional response.

Proponents of this position believe that babies can show observable signs of attentive involvement when an interaction with people and things is within their developmental sequencing. In other words, their brains receive sensory input that engages their attentions, contains some new patterns to detect and stimulates an available program for response.

The centrist position asserts that parents can learn to 'read' the behavioral signs that their babies display when they are ready for interaction, when they are no longer interested in an ongoing interaction and when they are overstimulated. If parents have not learned how to read these responses, they may try to keep their baby involved in an interaction which the parents find pleasant, but which continues past the capacity of their baby to sustain involvement.

According to Susan Ludington (1985), a state of 'alert inactivity' means that babies are able to focus their attention for stimulating interaction. Ludington suggests that parents can look for these signs:

(1) Head turns toward you or an object that has attracted attention,

(2) Eyes gaze at you or an object of attention for the length of attention span (4–10 seconds at birth)

(3) Pupils dilate and eyes widen,

(4) Facial expression changes, is relaxed and pleasant, perhaps a smile,

(5) Breathing rate becomes slower and more even,

(6) Sucking rate becomes slower,

(7) Abdomen relaxes,

(8) Fingers and toes fan toward you or an object of attention as if to touch.

Babies need and enjoy repetition of the same appropriate interactions but only up to the point of habituation, when signs of disinterest will be shown and focused attention diminishes or stops. Parents can then change interactions.

Babies are overstimulated and need a break from interaction when they:

(1) Cry,

(2) Flail their arms and legs and squirm their bodies,

(3) Splay their fingers and toes and thrust tongue or droop their head,

(4) Open their eyes very wide and stare fixedly with either a wrinkled brow or pained expression,

(5) Become drowsy (Ludington, 1985).

Dr Ludington recommends a release from concentration, perhaps held close in stillness, or allowed to look at a blank ceiling or wall while recovering alert inactivity. Sensitive interaction has an effect on a baby's willingness to enjoy expanding experiences that lay the foundation for developing Gardner's human intelligences.

When do influences on those intelligences begin? They begin when the nervous system is capable of receiving, processing and storing sensory input. All human senses have begun 'operating' at least by sometime during the second trimester of pregnancy (Chamberlain, 1983; Ludington, 1985). The feeling-connection between mother and child – sometimes called bonding – begins prenatally, is mediated hormonally and can result in attachment to or rejection of the mother by the child (Fedor-Freyberg, 1985). At least by sometime during the third trimester of pregnancy, the brain of a child is sufficiently developed to support consciousness and self-awareness (Purpura, 1974, 1975b). The preceding information is known surely to every member of the International Society for Prenatal and Perinatal Psychology and Medicine (ISPP). Most of the non-specialists, or so-called 'ordinary' people of the world, would react to these statements with amazement, doubt or disbelief.

Newborns prefer to listen to human voices over non-vocal sounds (Butterfield and Siperstein, 1974), and prefer to listen to their mother's voice more than other voices (DeCasper and Fifer, 1980). Infants use vocal sounds to communicate needs and feelings, and to interact with their parents and others. The communicative capacities of infants begin to be shaped prenatally as part of the mother–child bonding process. Fetal babies begin hearing by at least the 20th week of gestation (Eisenberg, 1969). The most frequent sound that they hear is that of the pulsations from the womb's main artery (Salk, 1973). The bloodstream, which carries nourishment to a fetal baby, also carries the kaleidoscope of hormones that are the physical mediators of human emotions. When a baby experiences the hormone combinations that adults associate with particular emotions, and experiences them with some critical level of frequency, emotional memory imprints are formed within the child's neuroendocrinologic system. The mediators of prenatal positive mother–child bonding are the endomorphine group of hormones, and a prime mediator of negative bonding (disbonding) is epinephrene, which is released when the mother is distressed (Fedor-Freybergh, 1985). The emotional orientation of children begins to be formed *in utero*.

When mothers want their babies, love them, express those feelings to them and provide occasions for calm relaxation, the possibility of positive emotional imprints and positive bonding is increased. When mothers reject their babies, and are intensely distressed over a long course of time, the probability of negative emotional imprints and disbonding is increased.

The second most frequent sound that fetal babies hear in the womb is the sound of mother's voice. The threshold of audibility in the womb for a mother's voice is about 40 dB (a firm whisper is about 35 dB) (Bench, 1968, Henshall, 1972). When mothers experience their loving feelings toward their babies, they usually express those feelings in spoken words during private moments of special communication. The more frequent the feelings and the talking, the more an association can be built between positive emotional bonding and the sound of mother's voice. Fathers may be a part of such bonding if they also participate vocally in the special communications with sufficient frequency.

From before birth and throughout life, the voices of parents affect the emotional and intellectual learning of their children. The mastery of vocal co-ordinations for spoken language is a substantial development in the life of children. From birth to death the voices of human beings are the primary means by which we communicate our needs, wants, thoughts and feelings with others. Our voices are, therefore, connected to the deepest, most profound sense of 'who we are'. Those associations between parent–child bonding and the sound of parents' voices may be the primary bases upon which a healthy self-esteem can be built for a lifetime.

Speech combined with music is the use of the voice for singing. Singing provides a level of feelingful expression which language alone cannot provide. For instance, if I said to you, 'High stepping horses, high stepping horses, high stepping horses go jiggety, jiggety jog,' you probably would consider the expression unnecessarily repetitive and nonsense. But if I were to sing the same words to the melody of the song 'High Stepping Horses', then the repetition and nonsense would 'make sense', and would have a feeling quality that the spoken words could not have. According to psychologist Abraham Maslow (1968, 1972), music can create a 'peak' feeling-moment in people. In singing, we also can know that the sound which transforms that moment comes from inside our own bodies, and we can feel it happen.

Some people believe that the ability to sing is inherited. That would mean that some people will be very talented at singing, most will be average, and some will be 'tone deaf' or 'monotone'. The research indicates that *everyone* with normal anatomy and physiology can learn to sing and feel quite good about it. While there is a degree of inheritance involved in exceptional singers, many young 'average' singers have eventually developed a substantial singing ability, and so-called 'monotones' can learn to sing (Welsh, 1985, 1986).

Speaking and singing have common behavioral roots in the brain firing patterns that produce them. The area of the right hemisphere which 'fires' vocal melodies also appears to enact expressive pitch variability in speech (Bogen and Gordon, 1971; Mosidze, 1976). In most people, the left hemisphere fires nearly all of the language 'programs' for speech. Soundmaking is a brain program with which we are born. It is genetically prescribed so that babies can indicate their survival needs such as hunger, pain, threat and discomfort. Responsiveness to heard sound is also a brain program that is built into us through genetic inheritance. The shaping of the sound-making and receiving programs into the very complicated brain firing patterns of speech and song are all learned. The inherited programs are used at the beginning. New programs are developed and expanded from that base in response to sensory input from the hearing, visual and physical movement senses.

Music, especially sung music, benefits children who have been born prematurely. A music program is used at the Neonatal Intensive Care Unit, St Joseph's Hospital, Marshfield, Wisconsin, USA. Music with a tempo and character which approximates the adult at-rest heartrate is played for infants with respiratory distress, and it helps them regulate their breathing and thus their oxygen/carbon dioxide balance. Pillow speakers and battery-operated audio cassette tape recorders are used to play prepared recordings of parents' voices talking, reading and singing. Behavioral differences between children whose parents have agreed to the music program and the children of parents who have not agreed is continually noted by the unit's medical and nursing staff.

Talking and singing can develop together if they are experienced frequently and as interchangeable ways to use voice to communicate. Along with the formation of vowels and consonants, the vocal exploration of children during the cooing and babbling stages includes variations of vocal quality, pitch range and loudness. The hearing, imitation and 'practice' of all those elements of speech by babies are the foundation for the development of singing ability later on. In fact, the pitch matching capability of 3–6-month-old infants is quite remarkable (Kessen et al., 1979). The stages of song development, therefore, can be thought of as expansions of language and voice skills.

A FEW PRACTICAL APPLICATIONS OF PARENTAL SINGING IN EARLY LEARNING

My lifelong commitment, and that of my colleagues, has been to vocal music – singing. When preparing *Heartsongs* and the class, we read many books and research reports on child development and learning, and interviewed some of the authors. As we then considered our experiences with the expressive power of vocal music and its effects on children, we gradually became aware of just how much singing can interconnect with and mobilize all of our human senses, feelings and intelligences.

If parents choose to interact with their babies through singing, they may need to develop or expand their repertoire of appropriate songs. Children are aided more extensively by short, repetitive songs, than by the lengthier, more complex adult songs. Ideally, songs need to be so familiar to the parents that they can sing them spontaneously, without conscious planning. Then the songs can be woven into the fabric of everyday activities such as waking, dressing, eating, playing, calming, bathing and sleeping. Words can be created which describe immediate activities, and which reinforce a positive emotional bond while aiding in the stimulation of the intelligences.

Pre- and postnatal singing, integrated with daily activities, can stimulate the growth and retention of nerve cell interconnections (Ludington, 1985). Singing can be excellent preparation for parents before birth. Odent (1984) suggests that:

> ... singing provides a simple way for women to exercise their diaphragm muscles and learn to concentrate on breathing out, which can help them relax during labor. Singing also encourages women to feel comfortable, unselfconscious and expansive – able to experience and release the whole range of emotions' (pp. 27, 28).

Because of the hormonal feeling-connection between pregnant mother and baby, parents can communicate wantedness and security to their baby before birth. Bowen (1985) lists specific ways for parents to interact with their babies while still in the womb. Clarke (1978) suggests that 'affirmations for being' and 'positive strokes' can be offered to babies in order to create and deepen a feeling-bond and a healthy sense of self-esteem in a child. Parental singing can be used as a vehicle for the delivery of affirmations for being and positive strokes before and following birth. Positive feelings of physical mastery, along with the capacity of music to stimulate, express and communicate an array of feelings, contributes to the development of the intrapersonal and interpersonal intelligences.

The linguistic and musical intelligences are intertwined. Hearing speech sounds is necessary before production of speech is possible. The hearing begins sometime between the 16th to 20th weeks of gestation, because by the 20th week, a baby's ears are comparable structurally to those of adults. In fact, a baby's responsiveness to speech during pregnancy is so sensitive, that as a newborn, the baby will move subtly and intricately to the rhythm patterns of adult speech (Condon and Sander, 1974).

Following birth, parents can use imitative voice-play to stimulate vocalization. Sound-making conversations between parents and child can take place during the cooing and babbling stages of language development. There are techniques for advancing the onset and development of the vocal skills (language and singing) which parents can use in daily activities (Durrell, 1984; Ludington, 1985; Thurman and Langness, 1986).

The bodily-kinesthetic, spatial and logical-mathematical intelligences can be stimulated through musical experience. The tactile, vestibular and kinesthetic senses are stimulated when mother sings and sways or dances to music, while baby is in the womb or being held by mother or father. The auditory and visual-spatial senses are stimulated when a parent sings from appropriate locations and distances from baby, and while moving slowly from place to place. The developing recognition of object permanence can be enhanced in a musical game of peek-a-boo with a parent or a favorite object. Object permanence is one of the earliest bases from which logical-mathematical intelligence develops.

IN CONCLUSION

A friend of mine once started a community chorus of people who felt that they could not sing – that they did not have 'good' voices. As part of her doctoral dissertation, she interviewed the members. An 86-year-old man told her:

> 'As a child, I loved to sing. I sang all the time. One day the music teacher at school had us all sing for her by ourselves, and she divided us into two groups – the bluebirds and the crows. I was a crow. Well, I grew up on a farm, and I knew what crows sounded like. I haven't sung since. But I guess that before I die, I want to learn how to sing (Mack, 1982).'

We are interested in re-creating a singing society in the United States, where unself-conscious, full-voiced singing is as common and ordinary as talking, and where that possibility begins very early in life.

Who knows what the results of that may be? Perhaps happier, more sensitive and expressive people? Perhaps there will be no more 'crows' — only full-voiced, sweet-singing 'bluebirds'.

24

Implications of bonding research for adoptive families

E. Hormann

ABSTRACT

Research in the last 10 years has greatly altered our perceptions of optimal birth and early parenting experiences. The birth and postpartum practices that have developed in response to this work have benefited many families, but for the adoptive family this work may illuminate yet another area where they miss out.

Bonding research and the work of writers like Ashley Montagu, on touch, have important implications for adoptive families as well. They may not be able to have the early start that families with biologically related infants have, but the frequent, prolonged skin-to-skin contact that is part and parcel of attachment behavior is reproduceable in the adoptive family. Nursing may be part of that contact, but it should be presented in the context of a wide range of getting-in-touch behaviors.

In the last decade, we have witnessed a veritable explosion of material on bonding. The work of Marshall Klaus and John Kennell became widely known with the publication of *Maternal–Infant Bonding* in 1976 and suddenly 'bonding birth experiences' were all the rage.

These researchers and many of their not-so-famous colleagues opened up exciting possibilities for nurturing infants and forging bonds between them and their parents. Thomas Verny and John Kelly carried this work one step back with their *Secret Life of the Unborn Child* (1981) in which the emotional life of the child *in utero* was first explored for a lay audience. This work supported what folk wisdom has long held, that babies are affected – even before birth – by their mothers' moods, by noise and light and music. When he comes into the world, the baby already 'knows' his mother by the sound of her voice and her heartbeat and he may also recognize his father's voice if he has heard it frequently enough. A newborn is hardly a 'little stranger', but a person who already knows his parents and is known by them in many respects.

The new pregnancy and birth practices that have developed from this work and the growing awareness of the importance of touch in caring for a baby, have begun to alter both professional recommendations and the child-rearing practices of many individual families.

This is all very well for families with healthy home-grown infants, but the implications for families who adopt their infants are quite different – at least at first glance. Infants who are adopted lose their birth mothers just as surely as their mothers lose them. However adaptable they may seem, they know the heartbeat and the voice sounds of their adoptive mothers are not the ones they heard *in utero*.

Except in unusual cases such as those described in Suzanne Arms' *To Love and Let Go* (1983), adoptive parents have no involvement in or control over the sort of birth experience their child had and no opportunity to bond with him soon after birth – and they may not even know what sort of birth experience their child has had. A birth may be described as 'normal' when it was, in fact, highly interventionist. Medication, pitocin, artificially ruptured membranes, fetal monitoring and forceps may all be part of a birth ultimately described as 'normal' on the strength of it being a vaginal delivery rather than a Caesarean.

Postpartum separation of mother and child, still more the norm than the exception in hospital deliveries throughout most of the industrialized world, is even more likely when the infant is to be relinquished. This may, in part, be the mother's preference, but many professionals still discourage these women from seeing much of their babies. They believe this will make the separation easier when, in fact, it only postpones the necessary grieving.

Adopted children – even those adopted quite soon after birth, come to their parents with some history of loss and as yet unbonded. Adoptive parents, too, frequently have a history of loss. Their quest for a child may have involved years of infertility treatment, repeated pregnancy loss and exposure of their private lives to more or less public scrutiny. They have had to prove their parent-worthiness to a committee of virtual strangers and, more often than not, have endured a long wait before a baby has become available for them.

The natural cues that encourage early attachment between biological mothers and their children are missing in adoptive families. If these families are aware of the modern bonding research – as many of them are – this may place an additional burden of sadness and guilt on them, that they and their babies missed out on this early good start. It is really vital for the well-being of the whole family to get some perspective on the subject of bonding (Bumgarner, 1983).

In the Klaus and Kennell study (1976), there were several relevant factors in the group with better attachments to their babies. Not only did these mothers hold their babies sooner than other mothers, they also held their babies more frequently and for longer periods of time. They were encouraged, by being presented with their nude babies, to have skin-to-skin contact. The more obvious attachment behavior of the mothers in this group probably was a result of the quality and length of their contact with their babies as much as it was the timing of that contact.

The need to be in touch continues beyond the early postpartum period. Fifteen years ago, Ashley Montague wrote quite convincingly about this in his ground-breaking book, *Touching: The Human Significance of the Skin* (1971). Babies, small children and adults need to touch and be touched. Tactile deprivation in infancy and young children retards both physical and emotional development. Older children and adults who, for some reason, are no longer touched, lose something essential to their emotional well-being and will often go to great lengths to replace it.

Because adoptive families usually miss out on the earliest days together does not mean they won't ever grow attached to each other. In principle, the attachment is made in the same way it would have been had the child been born into the family. Parents and child spend a lot of time together at frequent intervals and some of that contact — most of it in the case of an infant — should be in the form of touch. The power of touch to soothe a fretful baby is well-known. A healthy baby loves to be touched by someone she knows and trusts. She cuddles up, wraps herself around the neck and visibly demonstrates her delight. She solicits touch by reaching for the people she loves and communicates by touching everyone and everything with her hands, her feet and her mouth. If her efforts to touch or be touched are rebuffed, she is thoroughly miserable — and she lets people know that. If she does not get enough touching, she may stop asking for it, but she needs it just the same.

Touching takes many forms. Certainly it includes being held for all feedings, being picked up when she cries and held until she settles down. Stroking, rocking, gentle play and frequent cuddling are also appropriate — and necessary. Many families substitute a baby carrier or a backpack for a carriage, they sleep in the same bed with the baby and bathe her with a parent or older sibling. In some families nursing may be part of the touching 'package'.

In cultures that give little support to breastfeeding, the idea of nursing an adopted baby may seem more than a little alien. But it is by no means an unknown practice and, in some cultures, it is fairly routine. There is a considerable body of literature that indicates that lactation can be induced without an immediately preceding pregnancy – or indeed without any prior pregnancy. Adoptive mothers in industrialized countries can, on average, expect to produce only about half the milk their infant needs. Their counterparts in cultures which accept breastfeeding as routine generally produce more milk that that, but if nursing is seen as one of the means to bond with a baby, milk supply need not be the primary concern for the adoptive mother.

Adoptive mothers nurse their babies primarily to build relationships with them. Nursing provides skin-to-skin contact. It is a good opportunity for mother and baby to gaze at one another for long periods and it gives the baby an opportunity to depend primarily on his mother rather than on an inanimate object or on himself for comfort.

We encourage adopting mothers to use the breast to pacify a fretful baby, to soothe a tired baby to sleep, to provide the non-nutritive sucking often provided instead by a rubber pacifier or the baby's thumb.

A newborn baby can easily learn to nurse for comfort even if he gets some or all of his nutrition from the bottle. The trick is to offer the breast frequently and not invariably link nursing with eating. Older babies can also learn to nurse – we have seen babies as old as 13 months nurse for the first time – if their mothers are patient and have the right frame of mind. We ask mothers of older babies to consider the situation that has become quite common, that of a breastfed baby weaned at 6–8 months to the bottle. These babies are often very resistant to the change their mothers are trying to introduce, but if their mothers are patient and persistent they will gradually be more willing to try it out and often grow attached to their bottles.

Introducing the bottle-fed baby to the breast is essentially the same process, but with a twist. When a baby resists the breast, his resistance may feel like a personal rejection to his mother. If his mother does not understand that her baby is resisting the breast essentially because it is unfamiliar, she may not have the heart to persist. Mothers who understand the source of their baby's resistance can generally get some distance from the personal issue and gently encourage the baby to learn to nurse.

Some babies learn to nurse more quickly if a supplementing device is used at the breast. These devices range from a simple syringe to a complex arrangement of plastic bags and tubing which provides a continuous flow of formula (or donated mother's milk) as the baby sucks at the breast. The idea, in any case, is to encourage the baby to suck at the breast. Some babies need this sort of encouragement; some do fine without it.

Once the baby is nursing, however that is accomplished, his sucking will encourage a milk supply. How much of a supply will depend not only on the frequency of nursing – as it does with any other baby – but also on the baby's vigor, the mother's body chemistry and cultural factors, all largely beyond the mother's conscious control. Our experience is that most adoptive mothers with babies who nurse for comfort eagerly consider the project a success regardless of milk supply.

We especially try to help infertile adoptive parents, who have already suffered – at least in their own perceptions – from reproductive 'failure', to avoid anything in their early parenting that smacks of failure. This is why nursing is presented as just one of a 'package' of options for getting in touch. If, for one reason or another, nursing does not seem to fit, the parents have learned a whole range of ways to be literally 'in touch' with their babies and their primary goal of establishing a bond between them has been achieved.

Part 3: Reports on psychotherapeutic methods: birth memory therapy and body centered therapy

25

Psychotherapeutic methods for working with birth memories: an introduction to the topic (edited extract)

B. R. Findeisen

The human being has in its genetic make-up a predisposition to learn. More than any other species, we rely on learned behavior rather than genetically fixed behavior, which gives us a greater potential for flexibility and change. All psychotherapy is based on this potential: exploring how we adapt, consciously and unconsciously, to new situations, and in trying to learn new and better ways of living.

It is often assumed that behavior which cannot be unlearned or modified must be innate or genetically determined. Many people, because they are not able to perceive why they are stuck in compulsive, fearful patterns, or not able to acknowledge a pattern to their lives at all, are soundly resistant to change. Having found a way to cope with their lives, they cling to their method unconsciously, even when it is isolating, or destructive. Those of us who do seek help in changing our lives for the better often find that a damaging behavior pattern repeats itself in spite of all our intentions to give up old defenses and change those destructive patterns into new, positive ones.

But are behavioral patterns genetic and inflexible? In recent years, interdisciplinary advances into various aspects of pre- and perinatology have exposed a stage of human psychological development which was previously unknown. Patterns of behavior established by learning before and during birth are locked deep in our unconscious minds, and are not usually affected by common intellectual therapies.

To work with these patterns, we must find ways to enter realms of the unconscious, to access suppressed memories of key experiences and bring them to consciousness where we may learn from them and free ourselves to change them.

If we wish to include the unresolved effects of pre- and perinatal trauma in adults within more complete psychotherapeutic models for healing, we must first understand the uterine and birth experiences from the point of view of the client-as-infant. Secondly, we must understand the types of learning that occur during these stages.

While adult clients report no conscious memory of their prenatal environment, they will, during birth regression therapy, describe their mother's emotions, often remarking that her true feelings were not those she expressed to the outside world. A client may also re-experience an emotional decision made *in utero* that has been an unconscious guideline for his or her entire life.

A newborn child, from an evolutionary perspective, has a biological expectation to be held, nurtured and comforted. From the infant's point of view, the transition from the aqueous realm of the womb to the outside world is the first and possibly the most stressful challenge he will ever face. Ideally, both mother and child are conscious during delivery and the newborn bonds to a loving mother and father – imprinting on trust and safety. In less than ideal circumstances, bonding will still take place, the newborn will still imprint, but it may be onto an experience of separation and fear, followed by isolation and apparent abandonment. How an infant interprets his first experience will affect the way he approaches all the other lessons and experiences in his life.

In experiential therapies which act out or access suppressed memories, it is possible for clients to re-experience the emotions they felt during the birth process, and expose their responses to specific traumas as blueprints for neurotic behavior in their adult lives. The term, 'trauma', used here refers to the experience of the fetus or the infant. Often, modern hospital procedures of delivery such as administration of drugs to mothers, forceps delivery, Caesarean section, premature cutting of the umbilical cord, separating mother and child, and circumcision are experienced as severely traumatic by the child.

The records of hundreds of birth regression therapy sessions, often including memories that can be verified in detail, corroborate the damaging effects of negative imprinting. At the time of the original trauma, the client decides unconsciously to protect herself and survive. When the perceived threat to survival is gone, the behavior stays firmly in place, even when it has become inappropriate or damaging.

It would be premature to draw conclusions regarding specific traumatic events at any stage of human development leading to identifiable adult behaviors. It is important to keep in mind as the field of pre- and perinatal psychology grows and develops, that there are no universal explanations. This is not a panacea but a model to help us understand ourselves more completely. Each client is unique. There is no general procedure to fit every case of traumatic Caesarean section, or every case of prenatal oxygen deprivation or any other traumatic experience imprinted during this time. An infant *in utero* or during birth is not aware of the reasons or circumstances of a trauma. What matters is the experience and how it is unconsciously interpreted and imprinted by the infant at the time.

The most important aspect of the pre- and perinatal therapeutic model is to validate in the present the individual's experience and interpretation of experiences during a period when they were helpless and dependent on forces they could not yet understand. Once a person experiences why they made a decision or chose to be a certain way as a method of survival back then, they have a chance to understand that the decision may no longer apply in their adult life. They can begin to explore healthier ways of being.

Successfully working with the effects of pre- and perinatal trauma in adults requires respect for human individuality and acceptance of each person's unique ability to heal themselves in their own way.

26

Prenatal and perinatal experience and developmental impairment

R. E. Laibow

We who follow the Western scientific modes of thought have what seems an embarrassing proclivity: we frequently see ourselves as ascending from where 'they' are and have been, climbing up, we tell ourselves, out of the morass of 'unscientific' and 'primitive' ways of thinking which benight our unsophisticated fellow-humans. We seek proof and certainty as the sign posts to guide us in our progress, and we do make progress. We see what is obvious from hidden perspectives and discover what had been hidden by the sheer weight and force of our mental powers. We scorn that which does not yield to rational examination and tell each other that we have ascended yet higher when we pay less heed to the common wisdom which our non-rational fellows use to guide their interaction with the world. And then, having reached a position of highly rational inquiry and powerfully manipulative capacity, we discover that the key to what stymies us in our quest lies somewhere in the pre-scientific, non-rationally derived 'truths', which we had already discarded as unscientific with such authority and decisiveness.

For example, despite his highly rational and scientific training (which included a Doctorate in Anatomy), Ashley Montagu was unable to forget that a cousin of his gave birth to a child bearing a birth mark in the shape of a Zeppelin after having been terrified by the Zeppelin raids on London during the First World War (personal communication). To the derisive hoots and howls of his scientifically 'more advanced' colleagues and mentors he proceeded along a line of investigation which allowed him to delineate not only the embryologic process by which the palatal arch is formed, but the impact of maternal stress on it during the sensitive developmental period and subsequent developmental defects in palatal closure. In short, he elucidated a developmental sequence which results in cleft palate. His respect for the truth buried in the common wisdom allowed a real advance in the deeply rational understanding for which we strive.

When I was being trained as a psychiatrist, a child psychiatrist and a psychoanalyst, I was given to understand that the notion of developmental impairment springing from pre- and perinatal causes could only be rationally viewed in the most concrete of terms. Hypoxia? Surely. Over-enthusiastic administration of oxygen postpartum? Surely. But events of an emotional or experiential nature? Surely not. My eminent and thoughtful teachers (psychoanalysts all, by the way), assured me that that line of inquiry represented the extrapolation of fantasy into the realm of rational thought – historically fascinating, but a backwater in which no time need be wasted. Infants were so developmentally psychologically immature that trauma could only be understood in concrete biological terms.

So today we have come together to discuss in a learned way what our fellow humans have maintained throughout most of our history: the well-being and developmental integrity of the fetus depends greatly on what happens to it *in utero* and shortly thereafter. Societies inevitably surround the conception, gestation and birth of the child with concerns and cautions, prescriptions and proscriptions designed to ensure increased well-being and survival. We, who have 'known better', need now to discover what has been metaphorized in these common wisdoms.

My own change of awareness began with the explicit and highly detailed set of questions pertaining to the events surrounding his parturition which my son presented me with as a very young child. Following that, my clinician's ear was attuned to material which previously I had been willing to construe only as fantasy data: rich in symbolic meaning but lacking altogether in concrete reference to actual events of significance in the life of the individual. My respect for these symbolic levels of reality is undiminished. Moreover, my conviction that patients can and do reveal information which points incontrovertibly toward a traumatic origin for developmental impairment early in pre- and perinatal life has grown very strong.

DEVELOPMENTAL IMPAIRMENT

HOLDING THERAPY

This is a powerful method in which two partners work together to repair the basic deficit in maternal–infant bonding and attachment afflicting the ability of the partners to develop, love and communicate effectively. Both partners undergo healing so that, where the partners are parent and child, this deficit is repaired in both mother *and* child. In the course of this work, material otherwise sequestered at unconscious levels becomes available in an experiential present tense. 'Working through' is therefore not a retrospective event, but a current activity.

Profound repair of pervasive deficits becomes possible. During the course of Holding Therapy, material clearly referring to birth-related events regularly becomes available in an explosive and cataclysmic way. This material carries the certainty of absolute reality for the partners of the working dyad. I will not elaborate further on the remarkable technique of Holding Therapy except to say that in addition to repair of the initial damage with the actual maternal partner – astounding enough – *full repair* is also possible using this method with a later partner accorded maternal status through the mechanism of transference. As Freud understood, it is the very process of transference which makes the therapeutic process effective. What he did not understand is that transference to the therapist has far less healing potential than what we have thought of until now as 'neurotic transference'.

For me as a clinician, this material has several important features which render it compelling and convincing. It emerges spontaneously (in some cases volcanically) and correlates completely with medical and historical data surrounding the child's birth. The patient seems relieved and comforted by sharing it. The material does not have the abstract, intellectualized quality of a retrospectively constructed picture of the past. Instead, it has the 'leaping and lingering' quality of immediacy and urgent reality which memories, as opposed to reconstructions, generally do. Both parent and child resonate to the reality of these productions very strongly (though not necessarily positively) and have no hesitation in incorporating the material as a factual recounting. Dealing with this material in the course of Holding Therapy produces marked and lasting improvement in the patients. It appears that this method, with its profound ability to stir the earliest levels of organization and experience of the human infant, routinely reaches into the deepest levels of memory, allowing it to become manifest on a regular basis.

Since I have the privilege of seeing a broad spectrum of diagnostic categories, this frequent emergence of birth memories suggests to me that it is the pre- and perinatal experiences which set the stage, organize the actors and ready the hall for what follows. I believe the human organism is primarily a pattern-builder, the templates laid down at this stage of development acting as gates though which subsequent material is filtered. That which corresponds to known patterns is encoded, that which does not is not 'glued down' so readily and must reach higher levels of intensity in order to gain significance.

When I entered medical school 20 years ago, in the paleolithic days of genetics, genes were genes, and constitution was constitution. For better or worse, brown eyes were brown. Whatever it was, it was fixed. We now understand that genetic endowment represents a potentiality for a wide range of expressions depending on the enzymatic, nutritional, emotional and neurologic surround. The earlier in the developmental life of the individual we focus our attention, the more plastic this potential and the more far-reaching the impact of developmental events. Damage the limb-bud of an embryo and the effects are far more pervasive than if the damage is to a finger in a 35-year-old.

CASE STUDY REPORTS

Now I would like to share with you some clinical data which I think help support and substantiate the information preceding.

Case 1: P.

P. is a 14-year-old white female. She was the product of a full-term gestation marked by several very long periods of inactivity on the fetus' part so that consultation was sought by mother to determine 'whether or not the baby was still alive'. Gestation was otherwise unremarkable. Birth was also unremarkable except for the postpartum administration of oxygen for reasons which the birth records fail to specify. Neonatal history is unremarkable. Pre- and perinatal health records show no other noteworthy features except for the repeated observation by health personnel of the mother's 'significant depression' which was not treated.

P.'s father is a very successful academic, her mother a highly educated artist. P.'s conception was the source of a bitter dispute between her parents. Father did not want children: before she was born he demanded a commitment from Mother that 'the baby would in no way interfere with [his] life'. Consistent with this, when she was 6 months old P. was left with a succession of nursemaids while Mother and Father went on a 4-month sabbatical trip. When her parents returned, Mother felt that P. was 'not there'. Mother's growing conviction that there was a serious problem led to evaluation at several leading medical centers throughout western Europe. P. was repeatedly assessed as 'congenitally blind, congenitally deaf and profoundly retarded'. Previous history and assessments of normal health and development were discounted. Neurologic assessment

DEVELOPMENTAL IMPAIRMENT 299

showed a profoundly disordered e.e.g. and a seizure disorder. These findings were replicated by teams at various centers.

P.'s father divorced Mother saying that 'a retarded child was the last thing [he] wanted or needed'. Mother received continuing assistance from her own mother in the difficult task of rearing P. At 4, P. was placed in a day treatment program for autistic and retarded children. Behavior modification, dietary and educational modalities proved unrewarding. By the age of 9, P. had developed widespread disuse atrophy in all muscle groups, was completely non-verbal, appeared totally unresponsive to verbal, visual and physical cues, was incontinent of urine and feces, babbled and drooled continually, had frequent seizures not controllable by medication, and displayed no areas of intact functioning. The director of the program pronounced her a 'total treatment failure' and advised mother to seek out Holding Therapy as the only remaining alternative.

Accordingly, P., Mother and Grandmother moved to the United States from Europe. They entered a course on Holding Therapy.

Over the next 4 years, eye-contact, bladder and bowel control and response to verbal cues were established. Seizure-inducing self-stimulation has been eliminated and clear responses to verbal, visual and physical cues were forthcoming. P. still appeared to be a profoundly retarded child, but her therapist maintained that she was not. Mother became enraged with the therapist and P. She grabbed a piece of paper and a pen, thrust them at P. and screamed, 'Well, if you're so goddamned smart, prove it to me! Write something!'

P. did. Over the last year, she has still refused to speak, but she has made it clear that her presentation as a blind, deaf and profoundly retarded person is motivated by rage, fear and a persistent but primitive notion that remaining totally dependent binds Mother to her. She has written about the period of early separation saying that she 'was just beginning to make words' when Mother left her for 4 months. She deduced that her speech had been the cause of that separation and felt that she must not speak again. She has written about her nursemaids, naming and describing each of them with complete accuracy. She accompanied her parents on a stay in Italy from 12 to 18 months of age. She has written accurately about that stay and accounted for her ability to read and write Italian by having learned it during that period. She also reads and writes German (Mother's native language), French and Yiddish (of which her parents are ignorant).

P.'s mother consulted me since I am both a therapist who practises Holding Therapy and one who has a particular expertise in the education of child prodigies. She recognized that P. presents an especially difficult problem in finding the best way to reach and teach the hidden but highly capable child inside the disastrously limited self-presentation which P. makes available.

While P. does not speak yet, she writes voluminously. I suggested that Mother asked her to draw the Goodenough series of pictures. Figure 1 shows one of these drawings.

In Holding Therapy Mother asked P. if she remembered her birth. With that question a flood of information began to pour forth. P.'s memories correspond well with data supplied by her mother and the lying-in hospital. Figures 2–7 are P.'s reports of her own birth and autism.

Case 2: S.

S. is a 9-year-old white male. During the first trimester Mother self-administered Librium (chlordiazepoxide) 'to control anxiety and disorientation'. When advised to abort the pregnancy because of possible damage to the fetus, she refused to do so for religious and personal reasons. The baby's father, with whom she was living, was very angry that she insisted on maintaining the pregnancy since he did not want the child. They fought continually about this.

S. was the product of a full-term gestation which was otherwise unremarkable. He was delivered by Caesarean section (because of physician convenience). Although he was alert during removal from the uterus itself, he became stuporous immediately following birth and was difficult to rouse for several hours. Mother was told by the anesthesiologist 'never to have general anesthesia again because you took so much to go under'. S. showed no abnormalities in growth and development to professional evaluation, although Mother reported a continual sense that 'something was wrong with the baby'. She took him to pediatricians at various medical centers during his first several years but received no confirmation of her fears.

Within a few months following his birth Mother consulted me for her own therapy. She was severely depressed, experienced paranoid fantasies, occasional hallucinations and reported that she could only take care of S. with the greatest of difficulty because of her agitated and depressed mood. She felt that she was virtually unable to deal successfully with any of S.'s needs. She reported almost continual fights with S.'s father over many aspects of their life together, but principally over her attachment to S.

When S. was almost 3 years old, Mother's fears were confirmed: he was seen by a pediatric evaluation team at a child study center and found to be moderately to severely retarded.

He was labelled 'mentally retarded' by the local school district's Committee On the Handicapped. Special education was therefore initiated at that point. He has continued in classes for the retarded since that time.

Mother refused to accept the diagnoses. She argued constantly with school district personnel and attempted to have them share her view of S. as a child of superior capacities. She met with little success. My role in S.'s management was very often that of mediator between Mother and school. I unsuccessfully attempted to help Mother relinquish her unrealistic evaluation of S. and to repair the damage done by Mother's bellicose interactions with the school district. I saw no indication whatsoever that S. was anything other than a retarded child with a mother who could not accept that fact. Meanwhile, Mother's life had improved markedly. She was no longer either paranoid or delusional, no hallucinations were present and she had managed to separate herself from S.'s father. She had attended a local 4-year college and received

DEVELOPMENT IMPAIRMENT

Figure 1

> I am simply sorrow dead making. Son of a bitch autism you is making suffer. I can satisfy you with not dedicating sentences to several son of a bitch sorrows but to one only. I sometimes so despise dopey behaviour as to deoderize eerie feelings. This minute I feel son of a bitch autism is so strong I can't help wishing I could deoderize it. We are so wishing to soon send it away.
> It sorrow is.
> It despair is.
> It several serious secrets is about me.
> It desolation is.
> It oodles of words is not expressable.
>
> When scholarly doctors words describe about autism they are full of dopey garbage. What casues autism is sorrowful wooden soon after birth or during birth despair about door closing danger.

Figure 2   P. view of her autism

> *I remember a descent or direction dragging down so goddam strong I didn't greatly like it and I declare that I am autistic because I didn't want to be born yet and didn't feel strong enough to dictate my needs. I felt doors were only going to throw me out in lonely new despair and I didn't do dire door kicking. Would you like me to describe why? I already so needed solace derogatory doctors greedily denied and I am going to describe it.*
> *Many sorrows denied me a normal world with decisive delights. I remember some definite sounds of desparate eager dove wounding arguments and I didn't want to very much hear them. Wounded dove deeds don't like to be remembered. More memories elude me despite desire to catch them. You do understand!*

Figure 3   P. birth memories, a

a B.A. degree with a perfect A average (the highest mark possible in the American educational system).

One year ago I offered Mother the opportunity to engage S. in holding therapy to test her hypothesis that he was not retarded. She agreed. After an initial period of intense resistance by both S. and Mother, S.'s rage at Mother began to become available. He felt that she had failed to keep him safe and cited injury, accident and moments of perceived neglect going back into his early infancy. He related that he felt her unavailability, preoccupation and sadness during his infancy were due to her anger with him.

During a period of intense rage with Mother's failure to keep him safe, he began to scream, 'The blood, the blood!', again and again. Mother became very frightened and attempted to reassure S. that there was no blood. In a highly agitated state he insisted that there was 'blood everywhere'. I asked him to tell Mother about the blood and he described the following: Mother was lying flat on her back partially covered with green cloths. Her face was covered by a mask but he was sure it was Mother. Her stomach was cut open: she was dead. He was being lifted up and he was bloody. He had killed Mother by cutting open her stomach. He felt himself becoming sleepy and was convinced that 'they want to kill the baby's brain! The baby killed N. (Mother) so they want to kill the baby's brain!'

S. then reported that when he and Mother came home from 'the place where I killed her' she was angry at him all the time. She was especially angry when he needed her and he deduced that in order to please her he had to 'kill the baby's brain'. He attempted to 'shut off' his thoughts and feelings with special reference to angry and demanding ones. 'N. picks me up more if my mind is dead. I have to make my mind dead so N. will not kill me!'

S. alternates between retarded, unavailable behavior and clear statements of his rage and distress. When he is angry, his facial set and demeanor is normal as opposed to the dull, slack-jawed and vacant appearance which he ordinarily offers. His marked internal strabismus corrects itself and his speech is coherent, appropriate, shows an excellent command of the language and contains high level abstractions not consistent with his speech in the retarded mode.

He has since been placed in a class for normal children of his age where he has reached 4th grade-level work in about 6 weeks. Previously, he was unable to master the pre-primer curriculum for over 6 years.

I have offered two cases of extreme and dramatic nature. But I believe that the notion of pre- and perinatally rooted developmental impairment extends into the less damaged population as well. To demonstrate that point, I would like to share with you the following pair of children.

Cases 3 and 4: E. and M.

E. is a 12-year-old white male, M. is his 9-year-old sister. They were both the products of full-term gestations without complications. Both children were delivered vaginally following difficult labor.

Mother has a PhD in Psychology. Father is a highly successful lawyer. Expectations for E. and M. are high, academically and socially.

M. has experienced no school difficulties. Mother sees her as 'all the best parts of me rolled into one'. Her compliance and over-eagerness to please, fear of her own anger and her tendency to do less than she has already shown herself able to do in order to involve Mother in 'helping' her, have become an increasing concern to Mother. M. asked over and over again to be allowed to come to therapy despite Mother's strong reluctance to see her as a child who required any therapeutic intervention at all. She reluctantly agreed.

E. has been the source of far more acute anxiety for Mother, however. She has seen him as 'divergent since his birth'. Mother reports, 'E. looked directly at me with a focused, fixed gaze and protested on being removed from the delivery room. He knew who I was and wanted to be with me. I hated that he was that aware!' Since entering kindergarten, teachers have complained that while E. clearly has no difficulty understanding the material, he does not perform up to expectations. His academic career has been stormy with poor grades, especially in mathematics and deportment (he uses his outstanding wit to mock and defeat the teachers' attempts to set limits in the classroom). The same pattern of behavior has manifested itself in Hebrew school where, after 4 years of thrice weekly study E. was 'still not able to read the Hebrew alphabet'. Mother and the school have been in constant conflict as elaborate educational plans would be worked out and then poorly followed through. Father generally absented himself from planning and implementation efforts, but would become enraged with E. and Mother when report cards arrived. Mother reports that Father's own school history included 'class clown' behavior, very poor mathematics performance despite very high potential, and a 'horribly difficult time' learning to read the Hebrew necessary for his Bar Mitzvah.

Mother initially consulted me for her moderately severe depression. In the course of 4 years of individual therapy, her own deprivation and internal splitting emerged. She is a schizoid woman whose fear of her own (considerable) creativity and insight has led her to hide it while secretly cherishing it. She loathes the lively, perceptive and forceful side of herself and favors a highly conventionalized, trivia-focused persona which fills her with loathing. An exceptionally forceful and perceptive child, she sustained significant emotional and physical neglect and abuse from her mother, who was terrified and enraged by the 'odd things' she said and did. These 'odd things' were, in fact, highly original, appropriate thoughts and behaviors on the part of a creative and highly motivated child. Mother hated the 'crazy ideas' which her own mother so feared and, subsequently, has unsuccessfully tried to 'be like every one else' by not being a creative and divergent thinker. She regarded her internal life as 'shameful, ugly, crazy and, simultaneously, the only thing that made life bearable'. When E. was born, she felt that she detected, from the moment of their first mutual gaze, the same capacity for divergent, bad, exciting and different thinking in him as in herself. She was at once delighted and horrified.

This dual response to E.'s divergence persisted. Mother saw E.'s development proceed along divergent lines and loved and hated it (and him). Father, who saw himself as 'the son who could never please his father', saw E. as a 'failure' because of the behavior patterns which reproduced his own childhood failures. While denying that connection, Father teased, berated and occasionally hit him for his shortcomings. Much to E.'s distress, their interactions were highly unpredictable and vacillated between warm, loving contact and cold, angry withdrawal.

E. is a cognitively and empathically gifted child who uses his special capacities both creatively and aggressively. He is a gifted comedian who spends many hours preparing comedy routines complete with taped audio effects. These efforts elicit real appreciation mixed with deep loathing, anger and fear from Mother and Father. While he has playmates he says he has 'no friend who understands and appreciates my way of thinking'. Given the diverse and unusually sophisticated nature of his processing, this probably represents an accurate assessment of his friends' response to him. At the same time, it reproduces exactly Mother's sense of alienation and loneliness.

E. had had 3 years of thrice weekly psychoanalytically oriented psychotherapy before I began to see him. My contact with his therapist showed that E. had successfully sequestered his inner world from him and had allowed him to see only a carefully constructed 'normal child'. Following an extensive workup for learning disabilities which produced no positive findings, E. was released from therapy with his therapist's assurance that his 'school failure was a thing of the past'. His academic performance did not improve, and Mother brought him to Holding Therapy as a 'last ditch attempt before I give up on him totally'.

During the course of the 15 months that E. and Mother have been in holding therapy many important themes have arisen. First and foremost has been his concern with his birth and early life. Spontaneously, E. began to recall his birth. His mother screamed at him 'stop remembering! That's more craziness! You'll make us both crazy if you go on like that!' He persisted and produced the document shown in Figure 8.

Mother was exceedingly agitated because 'remembering things like that shows how sick he is'. I had the impression that E. was offering a consciously elaborated fantasy mixed with spontaneous memory traces. I proposed that notion to him and asked him 'What did you really remember and what did you put in because you thought it made it sound better?' He volunteered (with a rather sheepish grin and a 'Gee Whiz! How did you know?') that his actual memories were represented by the italic type in Figure 8.

During a session at which Mother, E. and M. were present, E. said he wanted to draw a picture and produced a drawing of 'what it was like inside before I could get born' (Figure 9). As soon as he began to draw, M. followed suit and drew 'What it was like being born from the Mom' (Figure 10). I offered a larger paper to E. while M. was completing her second drawing (Figure 11). Without looking away from his work he began another picture. This one represented 'What it was like for me being born' (Figure 12). He described the danger which the spikes presented, 'if he wasn't O.K.'. 'The spikes would kill a baby if he wasn't just right, you know, inside his head and stuff.'

DEVELOPMENT IMPAIRMENT

> I felt so alone and sometimes only so wooden. I deducted that I donated wonderful delight to you and I wanted to see you. I didn't want to be born because I don't do decisive things easily. I am deciding to be born again now and you can help me by wooden feelings melting by soul searching. I can help you by coming out of autism. *'Do you remember that injection you got when you were a few months old against diseases?'* I can remember I cried exceptionally eerie desperate tears because the doctor was doing me a organic never recovered from damage. He made me ill. I am determined to get well now. I am sure I am wooden feelings melting, no I don't remember that it hurt only wooden wound made. I am soon going to come into the world and I am crying because I am wanting to wooden wounds heal with words of wonderfully loud.

Figure 4 Pam's birth memories, b

> I wish you would dig out more memories of my smoothless wooden birth. I want to wooden soul woe exorcise. Would you give me a soothing Monet edifying picture of delightful flowers. I want wooden womb memories to wounderful be. No wooden memories are coming. I remember some wonderful wiggly movements of worse eerie enveloping water which eerily soon managed to become only our surroundings.

Figure 5 Pam's birth memories, c

> *I greatly enjoyed writing around my memories of direction derogatory one gory surprise. I was wordless when I discovered all doors open and exerted all my energy into declaring sorrow about world entrance. I saw worldly goings on, sordid doctors. Were you excited about me wanting to do descending? I grow deoderized good soothing sights in delight at being directed here.*

Figure 6 Pam's birth memories, d

> I am deciding to only sow seeds of soulful
> Sorrow and will harvest them all tomorrow.
> I despair despite what devouring oafs say
> Of the everyday world we inhabit today.
> I don't pretend we can cancel out crime
> I won't pretend I am sane all the time.
> We go on our way one day at a time
> We won't care over sin to sigh
> Or sorrowful slow justice to cry
> I describe our plight as our world might
> As woe and sorrow would some fight
> But I believe God soon will give
> Us each another chance to live.

Figure 7 Dostoeyevsky: a poem

Neither child spoke while drawing and neither could see what the other was doing. Yet M.'s picture of being born, like E.'s, contains spikes at the outlet of the birth canal. From inside, there is a tube to be traversed and the cry: 'Mom, I can't control my pain!'

E. was able to delineate for us the part of his presentation which was a true memory and what was creative elaboration. E. and M. seem both to have experienced a dangerous and spiky gate through which they had to pass. They are children with very different symbolizing capacities and styles; they have totally different ways of metaphorizing and re-creating the world. Yet their presentation of birth from the same canal recreates the same danger. M.'s birth, through an already parturant mother's vagina, shows smaller spikes than E.'s. Are we seeing here a qualitative, as well as idiogrammatic (idetic) representation of the physical discomfort of birth?

In these four children we see a spectrum of long-standing developmental impairment which ranges from the most devastating (autism and retardation) through serious (school failure and childhood psychosis) to pre-neurotic functioning. Each of these children spontaneously presented either drawings or verbal material (or both) which represent birth-related material as central to his/her struggle to find a manner of being safe and surviving in the world.

As I have previously suggested, powerful and complete memory imprints seem to be laid down during pre- and perinatal life. Each child appears to have executed this storage of experience which then acts as a series of templates for further organization of experience. This in turn, of course, reinforces and strengthens the nature of the template for further encoding. These memory traces are frozen in (or rather, out of) time until verbal skills sufficient to elaborate them are acquired. The recording is so complete that as David Chamberlain (1983, 1987b), in his elegant experiments and those of others have demonstrated, not only are feelings and sensory impressions recorded, but conversations as well. Does the fetus have linguistic competence? Do newborns *understand* the verbalizations of the people around them? Do pre- and perinates think in symbolic terms, in language? I do not know. Do pre- and perinates organize their experiencing capacities, their growing awareness of self and safety, according to what is real? Of that I have no doubt. And, as a clinician, it seems necessary to me that our therapeutic focus expand to include the period of initial and sustained traumatic impact: the pre- and perinatal life of our patients.

DEVELOPMENT IMPAIRMENT

> ### MY OWN BIRTH!
> I still remember when I was born. These accurrances are in order. Read if you dare !
>
> ### WARNING! THESE THINGS ARE MORALLY, ETHICALLY TRUE!
>
> The first thing I remember is coming out of the body. Then I wondered where I was. I saw everybody dressed in blue gowns with blue masks. I really wanted to find out where I was. Everybody was staring at me so I stared back because of my curiosity. I had red stuff all over my body. It was scary being there because of everything around me. I felt alone and I did not know what was going on. I WAS SCARED! Then they dipped me in a bowl of cold water and the water became red. I felt like leaping out of her arms because she was controlling me. I do not, even to this day, like to be controlled. Then they dried me, wrapped me in a blanket and started to take me to the nursery. I did not want to leave my mother because she was the only person not dressed in blue. They took me to the nursery and I enjoyed being with my type of people. I wanted to stay with mother because I saw you there and I didn't want to leave you.
>
> I didn't want to be in the nursery because it was too noisy. I wanted it to be quiet in you – I love being with you.
>
> Your bed was kind of hard.
>
> When I entered the room I was kind of scared just because I wanted to be in you and it was kind of noisy.

Figure 8 Ethan's birth memories: *Text in italics identified by Ethan as 'real memories'*

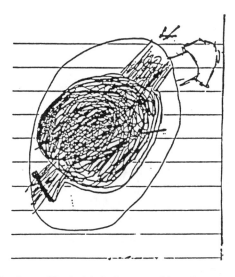

Figure 9 Ethan 'What it was like inside before I could get born'

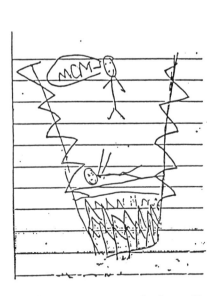

Figure 10   Margy 'What it was like being born from the Mom'

Figure 11   Margy 'Being born: Mom, I can't control my pain'

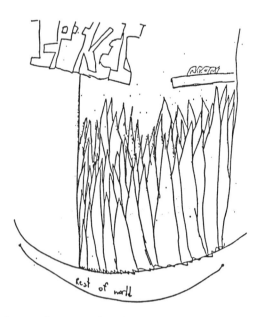

Figure 12   Ethan "What it was like for me being born". Legend above left: 'spikes', above right, 'Mom'

27

Birth, life and more life: reactive patterning based on prebirth events

J-R. Turner

ABSTRACT

This paper is based on the concept that not only do human beings inherit the genetic coding of mother and father but, also, the mental and emotional states of their parents in the form of reactions to specific stimuli during the 9 months of gestation.

Scientific studies have shown that the genetic coding of mother and father are synthesized to give specific characteristics in the offspring.

This paper describes a model which indicates that there are precise moments during the gestation when emotional reactions and mental attitudes appear to generate potential life patterns in the child.

Just as individuals can be reactive to deeply felt events in life covering a wide range of emotions from ecstatic to traumatic, it is possible to trace many patterns in the person's emotional/mental composition to their gestation. In cases of particularly complex and resistant pathology it is possible to identify as much as 50–70% of reactive chronic patterns to the prenatal–perinatal period.

Just as individuals can be reactive to incidents in this life without remembering the cause, this model suggests that there can be reactive patterning based on prebirth events. When a patient has spent years delving into his/her fear, phobia, disaster, dysfunction, disability, frustration, anger and rage without healing, guilt from failure in therapy intensifies the pathology. Marked acceleration in attitude and movement into wellness occurs through examination of the personal prenatal and perinatal history.

The method by which the data are elicited from the patient is through a non-

hypnotic re-experiencing of 22 specific moments during the gestation. Each point is related to specific emotional/mental states as lived by the person so that the therapeutic experience is clearly understandable and integratable.

In the mid 1970s, while working as a therapist at the Holistic Health and Medicine Clinic in Santa Monica, California I was asked to develop a weekend workshop which could be offered to the general public. The germinal idea was focused on three of the most commonly shared human experiences *Birth, Life* and *Death*. Rejecting the word *Death* in its usual meaning I chose the title *'Birth, life* and *more life'*.

In that first workshop, I guided the 60 people who were enrolled through some 22 sets of questions which, when interpreted, gave the participants a very clear matrix or blueprint for many of the problems and patterns – particularly repeated patterns – which they had been reactive to throughout most of their lives.

As a result of the transpersonal experience which they had shared, they began to suspect that maybe their lives were not just the result of some random coupling and mixing of genetic codings. What emerged in their minds was that not only had there been a synthesizing of the genetic coding of their mother and father, but somehow they had been acting out of the very specific emotional reactions of their parents, which had imprinted reactive patterns upon their memories during that 9-month period.

For them it was like seeing these patterns in miniature, condensed form. Their realization that many of these patterns actually existed before they were conceived or born was reacted to in almost every emotional combination.

Not long after this workshop I noticed that more and more people who came to my office were people who had failed in the many different forms of therapy they had tried – some they had worked in as long as 5, 10 or 20 years. Still others were referred by their therapist. When I recognized this trend or pattern, I asked myself, 'What can I do to help these people?' The inspiration came that if I took these people 'back', to psychologically experience what their father and mother had been experiencing during that person's gestation, it could help them to experience very rapid healing.

Having remembered the *Birth, life and more life workshops* from 2 years earlier, I started taking these individuals through the prebirth questions, and using this process in conjunction with other aspects of the Whole-Self-Therapy. People were showing substantial movement within a 4–8 hour session. The most common reaction was, 'I didn't do something wrong! That is a pattern that existed before I was even born!'

THE THEORETICAL MODEL

Before proceeding I will briefly explain the theoretical model upon which this work is based. Beginning with the basic principle that one of the main purposes of life is to feel, we can say that there are three aspects to this. First, *the body experiences* or feels. Second, the *mind evaluates*. That is, the mind tells me what I am experiencing. Thirdly, the *emotions judge*. That is, if I like what I am feeling, fine, however, if I do not like what I am feeling in my experience I resist, deny, suppress, push down, push away and/or oppose. When I react in one of these ways, I trigger a natural law called the *Law of Opposition*. The Law of Opposition says, 'Whatever I am opposed to I will have to experience.' Have you ever watched someone doing something that you didn't like and said to yourself, 'I'll never do that.' You probably ended by doing that same sort of act yourself. You say, 'I'll never be like my mother' and 20 years later you look in the mirror and who is looking out at you?

After the Law of Opposition is triggered, on a subconscious or unconscious level I make a judgement about myself. I say something like 'I'm bad. I'm unlovable. I'm unworthy. I'm not good enough. I'm inferior. I'm inappropriate. I'm dumb. I'm stupid.' The three most frequent judgements are 'I'm helpless. I'm hopeless. I'm powerless.'

When I make this judgement about myself I trigger a second natural law called the *Law of Confirmation*. The Law of Confirmation says, 'Whatever I really believe about myself I will keep proving to myself.' This does not mean what I say about myself. What I say about myself can be quite the opposite from what I really believe about myself. I can be quite the opposite from what I really believe about myself. I can say I'm lovable, yet keep having disastrous relationships which, over and over prove to me that I'm unlovable even when I can't consciously perceive the judgement.

The Law of Opposition and the Law of Confirmation create a third law called the *Law of Karma* which simply put says, 'Try it again!'

There are two more simple precepts connected with this model. The first is that when all these natural laws are triggered the mind can tell me when each episode happened or occurred. For example, when I was 1 day old, or 1 week, or 1 year, or 10 years or 20 years or 50 years. But, the emotional body does not work in the same way. It takes all the pain of the first traumatic episode and adds it to the next time. All that pain gets added to the next time. In other words, there is an accumulation of feeling. In effect, the pain on some level gets more and more painful until I finally ask myself, 'Why is this happening to me, again?' When I ask that question I stop making a judgement about myself and I begin my healing process.

As an interesting footnote I find that this question for most people comes at about the age of 37. This seems to be the age when the coping mechanism begins to fail. The statistical curve based on the ages of people with whom I have worked ranges from 32 up to 37 down to 44 years.

A DESCRIPTIVE MODEL OF A PREBIRTH WORKSHOP QUESTION PERIOD

I had a case in Beverly Hills where the woman had a lifelong spasm and hiccup which 5 years of various therapies had failed to resolve. Through the prebirth work she was able to discover that her mother had exactly the same feeling when she was informed that her husband had been severely wounded in World War II. In the session, her Whole-Self gave her the information that the event occurred during the *third month* of the pregnancy.

After the session she was very excited that, as I mentioned before so often happens, she had not done something bad or wrong to have had this reaction all her life. Then she stopped and said that the entire experience was not true because she had been told many times that she had been *11 months* old when her father had been wounded in the war. Several days later, she took her mother to lunch and asked her mother how old she was when her father had been wounded. Mother's answer: 'But, dear, you were not born yet when your father was wounded in the war. I was only *3 months* pregnant. You were *11 months* old when he got out of the Veteran's Hospital!' So you see the Whole-Self knows.

I will be asking you to ask your Whole-Self to give you the answers to these questions. Some people hear the answers as words within themselves. Some people see words. Some people experience the feelings in themselves. Some people simply know the answer. It does not matter how you get the information. What is important is *not* to try. Please, just allow. Also, it is helpful if you accept the first answer without analyzing even if the information you get is contrary to what you may have been told.

It is helpful to experience these questions with the eyes closed. The first question has three parts with short one or two word instant emotion answers. Do not write anything. Just get the answers. Then I will repeat the questions so you can write them with your answers.

(1) Ask your Whole-Self to let you experience your mother's instant reaction to the news of the pregnancy. This does not mean the statement or declaration she makes. But, what is her instant emotional reaction? One or two emotions please. Eyes closed!

(2) Ask your Whole-Self to let you experience your father's instant reaction to the news of the pregnancy. Again, not a statement or declaration but his emotional reaction – one or two words. Eyes closed.

(3) Now ask your Whole-Self to let you experience your mother's instant reaction to your father's reaction. How does she react to him?

I repeat these questions so that you can write the questions and the answers you received. Here are some examples. Mother feels happy. Father feels unhappy. Mother becomes unhappy, or sad, or depressed or angry.

A second example: 'mother is shocked and upset. Father is happy and proud. Mother acts like she is happy. But, she has suppressed her anger. He won't have to go through the pregnancy and raise the child for 20 years.'

I had a case in La Canâda, California. The woman's instant response was that her mother was joyous and exceedingly happy that she was pregnant. The woman stopped and opened her eyes. Looking at me in great seriousness she said, 'That is not possible! My mother has always been the most angry, argumentative, negative sort of person. I have never in my whole life seen her happy or smile.' At that point I asked her to feel her father's reaction to the news of the pregnancy. His reaction was with anger, of hostility, accusations of blame and betrayal. It was all her fault! Then I asked her to experience her mother's reaction to the father's hostility. She opened her eyes, looked at me quietly then said with a gentle compassion in her voice, 'Now I know why mother has been like this all her life! And, I don't need to blame myself anymore!'

I ask you now to look at the three sets of words you wrote down for your answers. As you look at the first words, what your mother is feeling, think of a time when you are doing something – anything – when you have that feeling. Now look at the second set of reaction words that the father is feeling. Someone in your life gives you the same reaction as father gave mother. How do you react? For most people your reaction is the same as the reaction of your mother toward your father's reactive pattern.

In approximately 10 000 people whom I have taken through this work, either in private sessions or in workshops, people recognize that this is the specific pattern which most often makes them feel that they are a victim. Here I define a victim as a person who cannot see an option in the situation they find themselves in – a different way – a way to respond instead of react.

In its final interpretation, people are often aware of the pattern as being repeated over and over in their lives but had not associated the Karmic Sequence as being the trigger for their 'being' a victim. As you know, you cannot change something until you know what needs to be changed. Once the person recognizes the behavior pattern they can be alert to avoid the trap.

Let me invite you to try another question. Close your eyes, please.

The first answer is *yes* or *no*. Don't think of an event. Ask your Whole-Self, 'Did mother experience any trauma, any traumatic incident, during the gestation?' The answer is an immediate *yes* or *no*.

Even if you heard *no*, ask your Whole-Self, 'If mother had experienced a trauma would it have happened during the first, second, third, fourth, fifth, sixth, seventh, eighth or ninth month?' If a number popped out, even if you had heard *no*, ask your Whole-Self to take you to the consciousness of your mother in that month. See where she is. Feel what she is feeling before the trauma strikes. Now feel her reaction as the trauma strikes. As she experiences the trauma and resists it, what is the *judgement* she makes about herself?

If there was no specific incident, but a chronic, pervasive feeling, what is the judgement mother makes about herself? Judgement words are, 'I'm bad. I'm unlovable. I'm unworthy. I'm not good enough. I'm inferior. I'm inappropriate. I'm dumb. I'm stupid. I'm helpless. I'm hopeless. I'm powerless!' Is that a familiar feeling in your life? Is that a familiar judgement in your life?

So now you know that these feelings and judgements, which you have experienced over and over again in your life, are patterns that existed before you were born. For most people, this is the source of the most familiar feeling and the most frequently made judgement about themselves throughout much of their lives.

THE IMPORT OF PREBIRTH EXPERIENCES AND MEMORIES

I would like to bring up another case which illustrates the importance of this prebirth period. I had been brought into the office of a prominent Beverly Hills attorney on a Sunday morning by his therapist. They had worked for several years to unlock this man from a terrible hatred of his father, who had badly abused his sister and himself when they were children. At the end of the $7\frac{1}{2}$ hour session he told me he still didn't love his father. He said he didn't hate him anymore because, based on the information he received in his prebirth awakening he was able to understand what his father was like. He said that he could even understand why he had chosen his father to help him activate the patterns he most needed for his own evolution. I told him that there was no law which said that he had to love his father. But, there was a law, the Law of Opposition, which said he could not hate him. He was still a little unconvinced about that.

Three days later his therapist called my office. The lawyer had just called his therapist to relate that the father, with whom he had had no communication for over 2 years, had called his son to tell him that for the last 3 days he had been constantly thinking about how badly he had

BIRTH, LIFE AND MORE LIFE

treated his children. He asked his son to please bring his sister to the father's house the next weekend so that he could apologize to them in person for how badly he had treated them as children. He said he wanted to do this before he died.

Another principle of Whole-Self therapy is that if my reality – that is what I believe is happening – creates in me pain, disease, disaster, dysfunction, disability, sadness, frustration, anger, rage, abuse, violence or any negative reaction, then that is the built-in system given me by nature to let me know that what I believe is happening is not in truth.

I can illustrate this principle with a case of a 46-year-old teacher with polioarthritis in Zurich. She had been frequently beaten by her mother from the age of 4–16. She was forced to sleep in her parents' bedroom and to witness their very loud frequent sexual sessions. Her two sisters and a brother shared another bedroom. Approximately twice a week the mother with clear words of hatred would pack a suitcase with the girl's clothes and, locking her outside the front door, would tell her to go away. Finally, at the age of 16 she did leave. At 18 she married a man who took up the mother's abuse patterns for 17 more years.

This woman came to a prebirth workshop at the University of Zurich. Almost every answer she received was 'anger and hatred'. We made an appointment to meet at an analyst's office the next day to work on this life patterning. I will relate briefly from the transcript. This comes $3\frac{1}{2}$ hours into the session.

> 'At 9 years of age mother placed me in a Catholic Institute. Here, also, I was beaten almost every day and was forced to kneel on little pieces of wood. The nuns kept saying they wanted to throw me out, but that I was so smart – intelligent – they could not.
>
> I asked her how she felt. She said 'Angry. It was so unjust.' I asked her, 'What did the little girl experience as love?' She replied, 'I was awful!' A very powerful self-condemnation. I asked her, 'Ask your Whole-Self, was it my reality that when I was not punished I was loved?' She replied, 'No!' I asked her to tell me the truth of herself regarding love. She replied, 'I have difficulty with truth!' I asked her, 'Ask your Whole-Self, Is it my reality that *Pain Equals Love*?' I asked her again the truth about love. She replied, 'The truth is everyone loved me! I've had many lovers whom I rejected after a month because they bored me.' I responded, 'They didn't cause you pain!' 'So, I got them to punish me or I rejected them. It doesn't make sense. It makes me nervous (to say these things). There is no longer any reason for me to have this disease (polioarthritis). I was filled with self-pity. Now, I can't use it as an excuse. I'm afraid!'
>
> I replied to her 'Ask your Whole-Self, if I accept that I created punishment to get love, what happens to my life?' She replied, 'How can I have a way to get love without punishment? I don't want to be punished!' I asked her what law she triggered when she said 'Never'. She replied, 'The Law of Opposition

(whatever I am opposed to I will have to experience) ... I want to be loved with love!' I asked her if it would be safe for her to do or have that love equal love. She replied, 'I want to be loved and I want to be held. So, *I can forgive all the people who punished me because they only did what I asked for.*' 'Why?' she asked herself. 'To learn the lessons (about love),' she answered herself. Again a question, 'Why had I asked for the lessons?' Her answer to herself, 'Because I felt guilty!' Again her self-questioning, 'For what (did I feel guilty)?'

Here her face opened in a gentle smile. 'It's a joke! I feel guilty for being here in the world – for Mother's unhappiness!' That's when we started the next 8 hours of work which brought her in touch with her immense anger and finally her self-love.

A week later, she reported that her mother had called and it felt different. 'I feel sorry for her. She can't hurt me any more! Her work is done. After last week's session, I feel free!' She smiled!

I would conclude with the idea that God gave humanity therapy in order to help us bring *Reality into Truth*. As we bring this truth more clearly into ourselves, and also help others to do this, we will bring humanity through the next major threshold of human evolution – conscious conception and conscious birthing! We are all privileged to be the midwives to a newer, more conscious, caring and loving humanity.

Copyright 1986 J-R. Turner.

28
Awareness-movement therapy
U. Kost

The Awareness Movement therapy is a holistic method based on analytical psychology. It refers to the human being as a wholeness of body, mind and spirit, bound into inter-human relationships in the context of a certain culture, religion and historical period. In its origins it reaches back to Elsa Gindler who, in the 1920s in Berlin, together with other creative people, searched for new ways. Her basic idea was to concentrate the attention on movement as an inner experience and sensation, contrary to the (still today) customary superficial consideration of movement as an externally observable measurable phenomenon that can be registered in its progress through time and space. If we experience movement in its wholeness and become aware of it, then it becomes clear that external movement implicates internal movement, moving induces 'being moved', the body-mind sets free memories, in the beginning often felt as pain. What was unconscious can become conscious, the inner experience can be reflected and put into words. But movement means action, too. Thus, inner experience can be understood and transformed into action.

About 30 years ago, Elsa Gindler's work was made known in the Federal Republic of Germany by Helmuth Stolze. Together with a small circle of interested people, out of this work he developed the method which I am presenting here. In 1975 I founded the 'Deutscher Arbeitskreis für Konzentrative Bewegungstherapie (DAKBT)' – the German Work-Group of Awareness-Movement Therapy, in order to enlighten the theoretical background of the experience-centered method and to develop a course of professional training. This has happened in the last few years. Our association now has 250 members. In many places in the Federal Republic, in private practice and in hospitals people work with the KBT. Also, in Austria, a sister-association has been founded.

Now, how is this work being done? In an individual or group setting the therapist, making open suggestions and pertinent questions, tries to induce perception and awareness of one's own body and its state of being. For example, the question of grounding, weight, breathing, inner and outer space can be put. In the beginning, many people have difficulty to perceive and sense themselves whilst resting. Small simple movements, like raising an arm or bending a knee help to concentrate on one's person. Further questions about the beginning and proceeding of a movement, the comparison with the other half of the body and the question of the emotional quality (how does this feel, what does this mean for you, do you want to change something and what is different now) can induce further experiences. One can touch and grip what has to be gripped, quite literally but often also in its symbolic meaning. The floor, as the ground that carries, is felt and described as hard, soft, warm, cold. But at the same time, the Mother Earth can cause deep fears and anxieties. This is shown by examples. More often, though, the ground supports and protects, gives security and takes on tensions and burdens. The four attitudes lying, sitting, standing and walking recall different steps of the individual development. At times, we experience a regression that reaches back to the intrauterine period. For this examples are given. But by way of the consciously perceived movement, all the other phases, too, are accessible in a primary process way, so that the elaboration and integration of the hitherto unconscious material is rendered possible.

But not only the relationship with one's own body is important, the other person, men as a whole are included, and, in a state of awareness, are perceived in a new and very intensive way. Basic human needs of closeness and security, of love and affection, but also of individual distinction and confrontation on both levels, real and transferral, are an essential component of the KBT. The Christian commandment, love thy neighbour like you love yourself, has to start by accepting the own person. To be with oneself and with the other, to accept and understand the other because I accept myself as I am, is one of the most important ends this work is aiming at.

From what is described above it can be deduced that the KBT is helpful for expectant mothers. Inner problems of the young woman, problems concerning the relationships with their mothers, husbands and families, but certainly to the same extent also the outward pressure, the threatened ecological environment, the social strain and role conflicts, make it increas-

AWARENESS-MOVEMENT THERAPY

ingly necessary to offer more than mere gymnastics during pregnancy. The KBT can indicate a way to find oneself, to discover one's own center and to render more tolerable the lacks and deficiencies felt in one's own childhood and adolescence. This renders possible a positive relationship with the child during this period of major inwardness.

The last part of this contribution concerns the socialization of the gynecologists, midwives and nurses. Numerous experiences that the referee, herself, has made with these people have revealed a far detachment from one's own body and emotions in this group. Thus it is considered highly necessary to make possibilities of experiencing oneself, in the sense indicated by the KBT, become an ingredient of the corresponding professional trainings and curricula.

Phenomena like the depersonalization of the pregnant woman in spite of all knowledge about the connections between mind and body, is still too widespread. The battle between the sexes fought in consulting-parlors and confinement-rooms and the dominance of apparatus and technology (also of the psychoanalytical technique) are understandable clearly in the background of the unfortunate personal development of many of the people working in this field. The usual primacy of the intellectual training over the development of the emotional parts of the personality is something that we must change by necessity.

29

A proposed model for prenatal prevention of postnatal disorders

S. M. Thom

ABSTRACT

When an illness or condition is identified, it is often assumed that the manifestations or syndromes follow similar or well-known patterns. This may be approximately true, in that a woman who has postnatal depression may be suffering from a mild but persistent depression crippling enough to alter her perceptions and ability to look after her newborn child. However, other women who have 'postnatal depression' may have profound and disturbing psychotic episodes, with manic and irrational outbursts which can last for many months. Both of these, and indeed all those degrees between are treated and are helped by a variety of sophisticated pharmacology. This mode of treatment looks at the result and not at the etiology. What I would like to do is to look at an alternative way of viewing disorders within our bodies which present such bewildering and far-ranging disturbances.

We live upon this earth both man and woman in essentially similar vehicles. Our vehicles are our mode of transport for our essential selves or souls whilst upon this planet. We are composed, both sexes of the same material, and only parts of our anatomy and physiology are different. We all enter into being through the same process of conception, and are carried through pregnancy and our births and into the world more or less in a similar way. We thus begin a new journey, which for some of mankind is an unfolding of consciousness where one is taken into the greater reality and to knowledge of oneself. However, it does seem that this whole process of acquiring our bodies to assist us in understanding our humanity has great disadvantages.

Our vehicle is a neuromusculoskeletal, chemical and electromagnetic mechanism. It is extremely complex. It is a triad of these three components. It has a physical form which is composed of a central nervous system, housed in a bony frame and moved by the action of the muscular and tendinous components. It has secondary systems which service the primary system. Thus the vascular system serves the needs of the muscular and the neural components. The lymphatic system removes fluid and waste, and adds protective measures, the genitourinary and excretory systems provide for removal of waste. Indeed, all of these systems have their normal place within the body, both the primary system and the systems which serve it.

A vehicle functioning efficiently within a framework, which has tissues (whether bony, muscular or fascial) correctly aligned will not act to cause dyspoetic signalling from the neurological component. Facilitated cranial, vertebral or peripheral nervous tissue, whether from somatic, chemical or electromagnetic sources, will cause disturbances in local or far-removed structures. The sympathetic nervous system mediates between all tissue, including humoral, and thus can have far-reaching effects upon the status of the whole organism. A physician who treats the structure to influence the function would see the body in this way.

Our bodies also have an electromagnetic part. This composes our emotional and psychic faculties, as well as the inherent electrical energy that exists alongside our neurological components, that include polarity, chakras and the meridian network of classical acupuncture. This electromagnetic system is obvient at a cellular level, where dysfunction of cells can now be read using EM scanners that pick up distorted and reversed electron spin. Our electrical systems can be disturbed at many levels, by both internal and external forces. One of the most potent forces that seems to affect many patients is termed geopathic. Such forces are 'lay lines', overhead power cables – as in the national grid, underground water ways, and electrical cables – of low current but located near people over extended periods of time. Modern examples of these would be a VDU monitor, electrical cabling spanning a bedhead, or electric blanket. All electrical appliances leak energy, but wiring that is carrying or running energy can distort the bioenergy field of people whose personal energy levels are lacking. Long-term exposure to powerful geopathic forces distorts, and ultimately changes the electron spin of the hydrogen ions within red blood cells and in other molecules.

Patients presenting geopathic stress are often those very patients who have not responded to treatment. They are those who respond initially to treatment but regress with a monotonous regularity, and who you would dearly like to foist onto another practitioner. They exhibit poor healing response, as well as much reduced energy levels, complaining often of many ills; they characteristically either sleep too heavily awaking feeling as if they need yet more sleep, or they are insomniacs or their sleep is often broken. The electromagnetically disturbed individual's system will be using up its energy trying to reverse the distorted field, and as it is constantly being further affected by the stress, it never has the capacity to alter the pattern.

The biocomputer has to make strategies to survive. It has three parts: physical, chemical and electromagnetic. All three are constantly interacting with one another, to make adaptive manoevers to counter deficiencies, stress, emotions, physical dysfunction ... birth. Thus the biocomputer may boost up its chakras to adjust to a chemical imbalance, or the chemistry makes a compromise to adapt to physical distortion. Similarly, the biocomputer may cause a vertebra to sublux or go into lesion to boost up the chemical or glandular system. The body is infinitely subtle and devious, making strategy upon strategy to alleviate and bypass areas of distortion or compromise within the overall system. It has a will to succeed. Illness or the signs characterized by pain and discomfort are but the signalling device of the biocomputer to alert us to the fact that it cannot make further adaptations. It can thus be clearly reasoned that it would be errant to sort out a symptom picture when the etiology lies buried deep within the system.

If we took the body and stripped it of all tissue — be it bone or muscle and left the connective or fascial tissue — we would view a whole body in three dimensions which would outline every structure in ghostly outline. Indeed the fascia envelopes every part of us, cushioning and dividing the brain, enclosing the spinal cord, supporting our organs, separating the folds of our intestines, rigidly fixing the outer aspects of our thighs, intertwining and enfolding, dividing and coalescing — it forms a continuous structure that interconnects the whole of the parts. The fascia is formed in collagen containing microtubules at a microscopic level that facilitate fluid movement. It requires adequate chemistry to maintain its integrity. Its function thus dictates good health at a physical level, and, because it is mesochymally connected to the acupuncture system, to the health of the emotions.

The fascial system is intimately connected to the craniosacral mechanism. This is also called the involuntary mechanism. An American osteopathic physician called William Sutherland, between the advent of this century and 1955 at his death, pioneered the art and science of 'cranial osteopathy'. Sutherland, on viewing a skull, suggested that the sutural configuration at the temporal parietal articulation was suggestive of movement, and that the temporal bones were analogous to the aquarian gills

... they were made to allow for some breathing mechanism. This farfetched suggestion took all his attention for the next 10 years, in an attempt to refute his own suggestion that the cranium moved. His research failed to refute his supposition and he had to conclude that the bones do in fact move, that each of the 22 cranial bones articulated with each other allowing movement between each other and moving in a set and prescribed fashion, dependent upon the sutural mechanics and the bevel of the joint.

Further years of research, initially using his own head and then with his patients', were required of him to understand the physiology of cranial motion. He postulated (subsequently confirmed with independent and unrelated research) that the ventricular system of the brain expands and recesses with a cerebral spinal fluid tide. This movement, according to Dr Upledger from Michigan State Osteopathic University, is mediated by an axon found to run through the falx cerebrum from the saggital suture and entering into the fourth ventricle. He postulates that internal fluid pressure mechanics fire off the stretch receptors which activate fluid exchange in the choroid plexus found in the 4th ventricle.

In health the whole brain expands and recedes upon its evolutionary stalk, folding and unfolding along the lines of its early differentiation as the straight notocord that begins to curl at its craniad end. The direction of the lateral ventricles allows the cerebrum to unfold laterally like the wings of a bird, emphasized by the anterio-lateral movement of the mastoid angles of the parietal bones in inhalation (expansion or flexion). The frontals push outwards and inwards as the ethmoid notch widens and narrows, and the occipital lobes, cushioned on the tentorium and walled by the falx, drop downwards and outwards, as the bellows of the cerebelli push laterally. The spinal cord shortens. In extension or exhalation the whole brain elongates, emphasized by the cranial vault doming up, followed by a higher palate, receding orbits and eyeballs, domed rather than Neanderthal forehead, and extended occiput. The cranial base, consisting of sphenoid and occiput, gently changes its horizontal axis around a pliable synchondrosis – the sphenobasilar symphysis lowers itself caudad in extension and rises in flexion.

The membrane system, allowing the brain to sit and be cushioned, acts as a reciprocal tension membrane whence from a shifting fulcrum around the straight sinus where the four leaves meet, the whole movement of all cranial bones is mediated. The change of internal diameters as the brain expands and recedes with the cerebrospinal fluid tide allows a shift in its fulcrum upon the membrane system, which rocks the sphenobasilar synchondrosis. Equal pulls upon the cranial dura allow for the cranial bones to be articulated but guided by the tension of these same membranes.

PRENATAL PREVENTION OF POSTNATAL DISORDERS 325

In normal health the cranium has a cranial rhythmic pulse of between 10 and 12 cycles per minute. This cycle varies with age, but more seriously with pathology. Depressives and various 'psychosomatic' illnesses often record 4–6 beats per minute. Rates of 14 or 15 are seen in conditions such as high temperatures, anxiety states, autism and hyperactivity. The status of the fluid mechanics, to those trained in the propioceptive awareness of this involuntary movement of the cranial contents within its waterbeds and the CSF enclosure, tells of its historical and pathological histories.

The cranium is directly connected with the sacrum where the motile and flexible dural sheath attaches onto the 2nd sacral segment. As the sphenobasilar synchondrosis lifts up in flexion, the dural sheath firmly attached to the foramen magnum and the axis pulls the base of the sacrum upwards and the apex anteriorly. When the occiput turns back into its exhalation phase the foramen magnum returns to its lower position, dropping the sacrum into its extension position with base forward apex back. As the occiput is part of the cranial mechanism, the principal part of the spinal dura acts as a reciprocal tension membrane; the sacrum too is part of the primary respiratory mechanism.

The fascial and muscular components interfere with, facilitate and reflect the cranial mechanism. In health we have movement of the CRI (cranial rhythmic impulse) which can be palpated throughout the tissues. The cranium and sacrum and ilia demonstrate a core link along with the pelvic and thoracic diaphragms and are thus palpated very much more easily. The muscles, fascia, organs and bones of the body integrate within this CRI and are so palpated as exhibiting a similar motion. Dysfunction in any element of the structure acts as an inhibitory element that restricts the fluidity of the motion.

In parturition the enormous forces acting upon the uterus, and the pelvic and abdominal contents, can have a marked influence on the organism. The caudad forces resulting from the birthing instinct leave a tissue memory within these structures. Thus an involuting uterus sitting on a pelvic floor which has just gone through enormous expansive and elastic changes can act to create a 'sag'. Likewise, the resultant force acting upon the uterus which is attached to the sacrum by ligamentous tissue can act to 'drag' the bone and displace it between the ilia which have, in the course of birth, disarticulated enough from their sacroiliac joints to allow for this. The core link so suggested between the sacrum and the cranial dural contents can act to drag the posterior brain firmly downwards onto the tentorium, with the occipital bones pulling the base and restricting the mobility of the cranial mechanism.

Similarly, the firmly attached peritoneum which envelops the uterus envelops the abdominal contents and the posterior wall of the abdomen rising to attach around the esophagus. This allows downward but little upward movement through the hiatus. Fascial continuation covers the esophagus right up to the superior constrictor, where it forms a raphe attaching both onto the sphenobasilar area and onto the hamulus of the ptygeroids. Thus there is a continual fascial connection from uterus to sphenoid which rests upon the ptygeroid plates.

Aberrant chemistry during the woman's life, inadequate nutrition, poor absorption, electromagnetic or structural strategies through chemical adaptation can lead to impoverished fascial integrity. Women who exhibit these sacral and pelvic floor drags have usually moderate chemical imbalances sufficient to cause poor integrity of the tissues, which retain enough tone to cause a pull but insufficient elasticity to allow the normal homeostatic mechanism to lift the sagging tissues back to their rightful position.

Riding in a depression within the body of the sphenoid sits the bulb of the pituitary. This is the orchestra of the humoral or endocrine system. The pituitary stalk or infundibulum hangs off the hypothalamus, the rightful conductor of the entire endocrine system. The stalk penetrates a diaphragm of dura, part of the tentorium, and as the 3rd or middle ventricle expands, assuming its V shape in flexion and closing its V in exhalation, the hypothalamus, stalk and pituitary go up and down rhythmically.

Now consider the action if there was a downward pull upon the body of the sphenoid, however small and delicate, but nevertheless an inhibitory influence directing an energetic force to distort the flexible and mutable living tissue of the synchondrosis. Indeed so much so that the balance between the sphenoid and occiput becomes uneven, hence the sphenoidal body is rotated upon its horizontal axis and sheared caudad. The sphenoid is firmly attached to the sella turcica or saddle, and is thus pulled along with it. Meanwhile sacral and spinal dural mechanics have also produced a similar posterior pull upon the tentorium. The resultant of these two forces leaves the pituitary stranded within its seat and having a relatively elastic but also firm noose of the diaphragm sellae slowly inhibiting the neural pathway through the infundibulum and possibly causing constriction, as in a sphygonometer cuff, of the vascular supply running along its length to the pituitary body. As the instructions from the hypothalamus are not nervous but chemical and they travel through the infundibulum it does not take too much scrutiny to realize that the messages to the anterior and indeed posterior lobes of the pituitary may well be curtailed or reduced. Sheehan's disease, where there is complete failure of the anterior pituitary, results from hemorrhage or infarct of the vascular supply that supplies it. It is never said how this infarct occurs. The suggestion of a tight noose around the stalk and blood vessel may answer this mystery.

In a woman who has had enormous adjustments to make regarding her new child, with the actual trauma of the birth and the period of pregnancy behind her, physiological changes are present. There are massive hormonal levels, high levels of toxins due to the sheer amount of work and effort that birth demanded, huge demands on her vitamin, mineral and glandular components and of course changes in her consciousness with regard to the acupuncture and chakra systems. In all she has put upon herself a massive stress loading. Her biocomputer, her vehicle must exert maximum effort to resolve and integrate these overloaded systems. Her autonomic nervous system will be countermanding her parasympathetic system which will be trying to repair and replenish exhausted tissue. The CNS will have been geared up by high levels of adrenocortical hormones to support her in labour. The sheer emotion of birth will demand or pull upon her fragile and labile electromagnetic system — distorted by the disruption in the solar plexus, sacral and coccygeal chakras, and further disrupted by the fascial and muscular elements within the pelvic and abdominal 'jiao' or cavities. The physical, chemical and electromagnetic part of her will be called upon to repair and exert by sheer will or strategy a survival plan. The body thus makes crucial decisions and prioritizes its needs. In many women the chemical integrity of the fascial system as a whole does not warrant priority. Thus the ability of the tissues to return to normal is hindered. The restricting element of the meningeal pull upon both the hind brain and the pituitary stalk causes subtle neurological and hormonal changes which are insufficient to meet demands.

Every woman is different. Their personal ecology, external and internal environments and historical stressors will all be different. It serves not to make issue of symptom pictures. The mere fact of a woman who is unable to cope emotionally or psychologically after giving birth, whether to a slight or great degree, is immaterial. What is important is that there is an *alternative view* of what is happening to her body, and that there is coupled with this understanding the possibility of resolution.

Osteopaths who are trained in the involuntary mechanism, or clinical kineseologists who can assess physical, chemical and electromagnetic distortions, can all help. It takes but thinking, seeing and feeling fingers to rearrange the fascial envelope of our human frames.

Section 3
OBSTETRICAL AND GYNECOLOGICAL RESEARCH

Part 1: Prenatal diagnostic research

30
Diagnostic ultrasound in prevention of physical and mental defects

A. Kurjak, B. Funduk-Kurjak, M. Biljan, D. Jurkovic and Z. Alfirevic

INTRODUCTION

If only 30 years ago someone wanted to talk about treatment of physical and mental defects in the fetal period he would be considered either insane or lunatic. Very understandably so as 30 years ago the only tools a gynecologist had to examine the pregnant abdomen were his fingers and Pinot phonoscope. What is really happening inside the uterus was just a matter of speculation. The fetus was considered to be a bunch of cells living in a kind of divine stupor and waiting in ideal silence and darkness to be extracted like toothpaste out of the maternal uterus.

In the last few decades a fast development of technology has enabled us to penetrate inside the fetal world and to change plenty of dogmas about fetal physiology and behavior.

In 1963, a father of fetal therapy, New Zealand gynecologist A. W. Liley, started to cure severe cases of Rh-immunization by means of abdominal transfusions. To visualize the fetal abdominal cavity X-rays were used. X-rays enabled Liley to localize a fetal abdomen but at the same time the procedure was indeed very dangerous, exposing fetuses to as much as 6.6 rad per transfusion (Liley, 1963). Of course such a dangerous procedure was justified only in cases of severe immunization where a fetal life depended upon the success of intrauterine transfusion.

Fetoscopy enabled us to obtain wonderful pictures of the fetus and surrounding structures (Nicolaides and Rodeck, 1984), but again the very high rate of postprocedural abortions stopped the practical use of this method.

When, in 1953 Scottish doctor Ian Donald (1959) reported a first potential clinical application of ultrasound, only a few people believed that that non-invasive harmless method could take such a serious place in modern diagnosis.

First pictures were static, shapes of the organs were vague and uncertain, and a lot of experience and imagination was needed to interpret an image correctly (Kurjak, 1975). Since then in only 30 years the technology of ultrasound has developed tremendously and today in modern high resolution real-time grey-scale machines we have a powerful and very precise tool which enables a sonographer to recognize plenty of very delicate disorders in fetal organism. Ultrasound enabled us to learn much about fetal senses and behavior and today we have evidence that the fetus breathes (Kurjak et al., 1978a), experiences pain, tastes, sees, hears and cries (Liley, 1972). These developments in research and technology have made it possible to detect congenital defects (Kurjak, 1978a, 1978b, 1980; Kurjak and Latin, 1979a, 1979b; Kurjak et al., 1980, 1986; Kurjak and Zergollen-Cupak, 1982) and growth retardation (Kurjak et al., 1977) at very early stages of gestation. These powerful diagnostic tools, coupled with significant advances in surgical technique, have given rise to a relatively new concept in medicine: the fetus as a patient. The fetus, therefore, becomes the central entity in terms of active therapy (Michejda and Pringle, 1986).

In a present study our experience, at the Ultrasonic Institute, University of Zagreb, into the detection and cure of the malformed and growth-retarded fetus, is reviewed. In the first part of the paper a possible way of management of correctable malformations is described. In the second part some new and exciting ways of treatment of fetal growth retardation are suggested.

PART I

Materials and methods

At the Ultrasonic Institute, University of Zagreb in a period of 5 years 50 000 obstetrical ultrasonographic examinations have been performed. During that period 85 surgically correctable fetal malformations have been detected. Among them the most frequent were gastrointestinal malformations, 29 cases; then urinary malformations, 28 cases; malformations of the central nervous system, 17 cases; respiratory malformations in five cases and all other malformations six cases.

All malformations were detected by means of real-time grey-scale ultrasonic machines Aloka SSD-250, Aloka-256 and Aloka SSD-280. All postnatal operations were performed in the Department of Neurosurgery at the University of Zagreb, and the Department of Pediatric Surgery of the Institute for the Care of the Mother and Child.

Results and discussion

Hydrocephaly

More than half of our hydrocephalic babies were detected before 24 weeks of pregnancy and after the mother's decision and agreement of our ethical committee all those pregnancies were interrupted. We therefore had no suitable patient for ventriculo-amniotic shunt procedure (Harrison et al., 1982). In 14 cases pregnancy was left to proceed until the fetus reached a gestational age of 33-34 weeks by which time it should be able to exist independently outside the uterus. Immediately upon delivery those hydrocephalic babies were handed to our neurosurgeons who considered further treatment. In all those patients ventriculo-abdominal or ventriculo-atrial shunting was performed (Rudenz et al., 1967; Hakim and Jimenez, 1955).

The mortality rate, even in the very early detected hydrocephalic babies, was very high, and we feel that much experience and research is still needed in this field (Kurjak, 1978a).

Cystic hygroma

A variety of abnormalities can be detected in the fetal cervical region. Cystic hygroma appears as a sonolucent mass arising on the head and neck region of the fetus. It is a focal developmental malformation of the lymphatic channels. Although it is found among a variety of other circumstances in a high percentage of cases it is associated with Turner's syndrome (Kurjak et al., 1986). When quite large these lesions can also result in distocia. There were six infants out of ten detected antenatally in whom the resection was performed. An interesting case of cystic hygroma was detected at 18 weeks of pregnancy. The pregnancy was otherwise normal. Because of the large size of tumor and an obvious cystic structure we decided to evacuate the cyst in order to prevent distocia during delivery. Fluid collected from this cystic structure proved to be lymphatic. Immediately upon delivery the infant was handed to a pediatric surgeon who performed the resection of the cystic hygroma. The baby is now healthy and well.

Thorax

The therapeutic implications of finding thoracic abnormalities by ultrasound are shown, for example, in the case of hydrothorax. An ultrasound examination was performed in the third trimester of pregnancy. A large collection of fluid was seen in the fetal thorax displacing the heart and compressing the normal lungs. In an attempt to achieve better lung maturity a thoracocentesis was performed at the age of 30, 34 and 37 weeks with removal of 160, 100 and 175 ml of fluid, respectively. The infant was born after spontaneous labor at 39 weeks of pregnancy. In spite of all our efforts the infant died 6 hours after delivery due to severe respiratory distress.

Gastrointestinal tract

The fetal gastrointestinal tract is the most common site of surgically correctable fetal malformations detected by ultrasound (Kurjak et al., 1984a, 1985). Early detection of duodenal atresia, esophageal atresia, or duodeno-jejunal atresia allows planning of delivery and subsequent postnatal corrective surgery in the best equipped center available and in the most suitable conditions.

Ultrasound is quite accurate in diagnosis of defects in the fetal anterior wall. The primary concern in those lesions is a prompt surgical repair in a center where the very special needs of those babies can be met (Klein et al., 1981). In most of our cases the diagnoses were made in outside institutions not equipped to take care of the baby after delivery. Our policy is to deliver babies with defects of the front abdominal wall by means of Caesarean section. Immediately after section babies are handed over to the pediatric surgical team in sterile conditions.

Our preferred postnatal method of management involves use of primary closure rather than use of prosthetic devices when possible. However, in small babies with an enlarged defect of the abdomen, the abdominal wall is covered by a plastic bag which will be gradually pushed back into the abdominal cavity (Kurjak et al., 1980).

Urinary tract.

In urinary tract abnormalities the most important fact for management is the fundamental distinction between unilateral and bilateral malformations (Berkowitz et al., 1982; Hadlock et al., 1981). Therefore, if one has to manage a case of unilateral pathology, either multicystic kidney (Figure 4) or hydronephrosis, if one is sure that the other kidney is perfectly normal, there is no indication for intervention either by treatment *in utero* or bringing forward delivery. Weekly ultrasonographic checks will be sufficient (Kurjak et al., 1984b). We had three cases of unilateral multicystic disease which we operated on after delivery.

Prenatal diagnosis of obstructive uropathies offers new and exciting possibilities in pediatric urology and the benefits of fetal sonography are now increasingly evident. It is not surprising, therefore, that almost 60% of our urinary tract abnormalities had antenatal intervention (Kurjak et al., 1984b). Most of them repeated renocenthesis with evacuation of accumulated fluid.

In a very interesting case of bilateral uropathy diagnosed at 26 weeks of pregnancy a normal quantity of amniotic fluid was found and the growth of baby was also normal. Puncture and evacuation of both cystic structures were performed. We have done weekly sonograms of this baby. Further accumulation did not occur. Labor started at 39 weeks, vaginal delivery occurred and a healthy boy was delivered without any signs of urinary abnormalities.

Ovarian cyst

Ovarian cyst was detected at 31 weeks of pregnancy. We punctured the cyst and evacuated the contents. Interestingly enough no further accumulation of fluid occurred, and a normal baby was delivered vaginally at term. We wanted to puncture the ovarian cyst in a similar case but spontaneous rupture occurred before we could operate. Just before term the size of the cyst increased again and the newborn was operated on soon after delivery.

Sacrococcygeal teratoma

Sacrococcygeal teratoma presents a typical sonographic occurrence and prenatal diagnosis is not difficult. This tumor, which may reach an impressive size, may be an unexplained cause of dystocia at the time of vaginal delivery, often resulting in the rupture of the tumor. In cases where we recognize a large tumor which might complicate delivery we aspirate liquid inside the tumor and in that way facilitate delivery. Further prompt resection in the neonatal period is important because of malignant changes in this tumor after birth and the not infrequent occurrence of coagulation factor aberrations in the postnatal period.

PART II

Intrauterine growth retardation

One of the most important problems in present day perinatology is the correct approach to the treatment of intrauterine growth retardation (IUGR) which is defined as a birth weight below the 10th percentile for given gestational age. IUGR is still, even in the most developed countries, the most important cause of perinatal morbidity and mortality. Surviving small-for-date children display a high incidence of neurologic and intellectual deficiencies (Low et al., 1968; Fitzardinge and Stevens, 1972; Parkinson et al., 1981).

IUGR can be reliably diagnosed by means of ultrasound only in cases where the gestational age is certain. The best measurement for assessing gestational age is the crown–rump length of the embryo during the first trimester. By means of this technique the gestational age can be determined within 6 days in 95% of cases (Robinson, 1973; Robinson and Fleming, 1975).

After that period, to assess growth rate serial cephalometry (Campbell and Dewhurst, 1971) and abdominal circumference measurements are performed (Kurjak et al., 1975, 1984c; Kurjak, 1979; Beazley and Kurjak, 1984).

Recently, ordinary as well as color Doppler measurements of blood flow in maternal arcuate arteries, fetal aorta, umbilical vein and fetal cerebral artery have been employed (Kurjak et al., 1981, 1984d; Rajhvajn and Kurjak, 1981; Kurjak and Rajhvajn, 1982a, 1982b; Wladimiroff et al., 1986).

In 1974 Rosso and Winick recognized two types of growth retardation. This hypothesis was later ultrasonically confirmed by Kurjak and co-workers (Kurjak and Kirkinen, 1982).

Type I or symmetrical growth retardation, occurring in 20% of growth retarded cases, is characterized by continuous symmetrical slow development of fetal structures caused by disturbed fetal growth potential. Growth retardation occurs early in the second trimester. The main characteristic of this type is proportionate reduction in size of fetal head, body weight and length. Some of these babies have genetic and chromosomal abnormalities (Kurjak et al., 1978b).

Type II or asymmetrical growth retardation is a state in which disproportionally slow growth of the fetal abdomen occurs in late pregnancy. This type of growth retardation is associated with conditions which cause reduced placental perfusion.

Impairment of fetal abdomen is a result of a phenomenon called 'brain sparing effect', which enables the fetus, by means of redistribution of blood between head and abdomen, to maintain normal nourishment of the brain even in very unfavorable intrauterine conditions (Winick et al., 1970). Biometric measurements of asymmetrically growth-retarded fetuses show a remarkably increased proportion between fetal head and abdomen. The fetal abdomen is smaller because of reduced fetal liver and subcutaneous fat growth.

In this group there is a tendency to perinatal asphyxia and usually the Apgar score is remarkably low.

Until now many different modes of antenatal treatment of IUGR have been attempted (Heller, 1975; Brettes et al., 1976; Rush et al., 1978; Charlton and Rudolph, 1979; Katz et al., 1982; Charlton and Johengen, 1983).

Materials and methods

At the Ultrasonic Institute, University of Zagreb, a comparative study of the effectiveness of Solcoseryl, a standardized protein-free and antigen-free dialysate of calf blood has been carried out. In our study 57 pregnant women with ultrasonically verified growth retardation were included. All patients were fully informed about the aim of this investigation and the experimental nature of proposed treatment. Written, informed consent was obtained from all mothers participating in the study.

The group treated with Solcoseryl consisted of 32 pregnant women with IUGR fetuses between 34 and 41 weeks of pregnancy. Fetal blood flow measurements were obtained every day during hospital treatment, usually 1–3 hours after intravenous infusion of the preparation being tested. This group has been divided into three subgroups:

Subgroup I ($n=20$) bedrest + Solcoseryl in 0.5 l of 5% glucose, single pregnancy

Subgroup II ($n=4$) bedrest + Solcoseryl in 0.5 l of 5% glucose, twin pregnancy

Subgroup III ($n=8$) bedrest + Solcoseryl in 0.5 l of 0.9%NaCl, single pregnancy

The control group consisted of 25 pregnant women. This group was also divided into three subgroups:

Subgroup IV ($n=12$) bedrest, single pregnancy
Subgroup V ($n=5$) bedrest, twin pregnancy
Subgroup VI ($n=8$) bedrest + 0.5 l 5% glucose, single pregnancy

Risk factors, such as hypertension, anemia, complicated previous pregnancies, spontaneous abortions and low birth weight in previous pregnancies were homogenously distributed in both groups.

Results and discussion

The frequency of the most common complications in growth-retarded babies was recorded in both the Solcoseryl and control groups. Results show that children treated with Solcoseryl had significantly lower percentages of fetal distress, hypoglycosemia, polycythemia and neonatal death.

Fetal blood flow, Apgar score after birth and neonatal birth weight were also favorable in the Solcoseryl group.

Some long-term studies, reported by other authors, show that proper treatment of IUGR babies can improve significantly their further intellectual development.

It has been shown in many animal and cellular studies that Solcoseryl activates the respiratory chain leading to better oxygen utilization by the tissue (Herre et al., 1976; Chann et al., 1980). Blood dialysate decreases the total peripheral resistance and elastic resistance of arteries. Therefore, deproteinized hemodialysate seems to be a promising drug for improvement of fetal metabolism and fetal well-being in cases of asymmetrical growth retardation.

Our preliminary data, although based on a small number of patients, indicate that therapy with hemodialysate effectively improves feto-placental circulation and enhances weight gain *in utero* (Kurjak et al., 1984e, 1984f; Kurjak and Kaplinski, 1984; Kurjak and Pal, 1985).

CONCLUSIONS

With remarkable improvements in antenatal, intrapartum and newborn care, the proportion of perinatal problems attributable to congenital abnormalities and IUGR has significantly increased. With the advent of ultrasound many structural abnormalities and growth-retarded babies can be detected early in pregnancy.

Analyzing the outcome of pregnancy in potentially correctable anomalies, one can see that a significant proportion of mothers asked for pregnancy interruption and we interrupted pregnancy in 29% of cases. Postnatal operations were carried out in 53 patients. This means that about 45% of all anomalies and 64% of operated patients had normal development. Even in the group of correctable anomalies the mortality rate was very high, about 58%. These figures show that much research is still needed to improve this advanced method of treatment.

However, the technological achievements in medicine in the last two decades, particularly surgical developments, have benefited older people too. *In utero* surgery may improve the quality of life of a newborn who could enjoy that quality for 75–80 years, and that should certainly be given weight in any consideration about the cost-effectiveness of technology.

Understandably enough, many ethical problems are raised by fetal therapy. Some of them have already been discussed elsewhere (Barclay et al., 1981; Degen and Kurjak, 1982; Kurjak, 1982; Chervenak et al., 1984; Kurjak and Beazley, 1984; LeRoy, 1986).

31
Early ultrasound monitoring and the status of the newborn

A. Bacz and W. Borkowski

ABSTRACT

The aim of the study was to observe pregnancy and the state of the newborn after delivery in women whose last ovulation before fertilization had been monitored by ultrasound. 11 women achieved fertilization in a monitored cycle amongst the women who were treated for marital infertility in 1984–85 in OB/GYN Institute, Copernicus University School of Medicine in Cracow, Poland, and in whom spontaneous or induced ovulation was monitored ultrasonographically. Of the 11 women seven had given birth to healthy term infants. The course of pregnancy in these women (except for one – chronic hypertension and superimposed pre-eclampsia) ran normally. One patient miscarried in the eighth week of pregnancy. The remaining three women are still pregnant: the pregnancies so far have continued normally.

This preliminary data may indicate that the ultrasonographic monitoring of the Graaf follicle has no influence on the development of the fetus or the condition of the newborn.

INTRODUCTION

Modern methods used in the diagnosis and treatment of infertility include an ultrasonographic monitoring of spontaneous and induced ovulation. In the literature available to us we have found no information about the possible effect of ultrasound on the development of the ovum. However, ultrasonographic monitoring in early pregnancy most probably has no adverse effects in the development of the embryo and the fetus (Bakketeig et al., 1984; Petitti, 1984). This method has been universally used in the program of *in vitro* fertilization and embryo transfer (IVF and ET), which is characterized by a higher rate of miscarriage (Chilik et al., 1985; Muasher et al., 1985; Sinosich et al., 1985). However, it is difficult to establish whether this phenomenon is connected with harmful effects from ultrasound because first, gametes that may have been damaged can be eliminated in the process of fertilization and the early period of the zygote's development, and secondly, many other factors can interfere with the normal development of the blastocyst after implantation (e.g. corpus luteum insufficiency).

The aim of the present study was to observe pregnancy and the state of the newborn after delivery in women whose last ovulation before fertilization had been monitored by ultrasound.

MATERIAL AND METHODS

Amongst the women who were treated for marital infertility at the Department of Endocrinology, Institute of Gynecology and Obstetrics, Copernicus University School of Medicine, Cracow, Poland, in 1984–85 and in whom spontaneous or induced ovulation was monitored ultrasonographically, 11 achieved fertilization in a monitored cycle.

The monitoring was done with an RT 3000 General Electric ultrasonograph, by a sectional-angular detector, 3.5 MHz, beginning from day 7 of the cycle, every other day, increasing the frequency of the observations to one daily as the Graaf follicle grew. Each of the patients was monitored in all about 4–6 times. The duration of the examination varied from 3 to 10 minutes, during which time the number, size and volume of the follicle(s) were recorded.

The course of the early pregnancy was monitored with hCG in a sample of morning urine, basal body temperature and ultrasonographic examination. All the patients were hospitalized in the first trimester of pregnancy and before giving birth. The maturity of the newborns was estimated according to Dubowitz, and their birth weight, sex, Apgar score and the presence of congenital anomalies were recorded. The observation of the newborns took place in the period 3–5 days after birth.

RESULTS AND DISCUSSION

Data concerning the patients observed, the method of inducing ovulation, the method of fertilization and the outcome of the pregnancy and the state of the infant are shown in Table 1.

Table 1 Obstetrical and neonatal data of patients monitored by ultrasound

Patient	Age	Cause of infertility	Treatment	Fertilization	Outcome	Week	Newborn Sex	Weight (g)	Apgar score	Congenital anomalies
M.P.	34	anovulation male factor	bromocriptine 2.5 mg daily (9–13th day of cycle)	AID	full-term delivery	40	D*	2870	10	none
K.H.	35	male factor	none	AIH	full-term delivery	39	D	3750	10	none
M.E.	27	anovulation male factor	bromocriptine	AIH	full-term delivery	41	S†	3850	10	none
D.K.	37	anovulation male factor	bromocriptine	AIH	full-term delivery	38	D	2900	8	none
M.K.	33	anovulation male factor	bromocriptine	AID	full-term delivery	40	D	4600	10	none
M.B.	31	male factor	none	AIH	full-term delivery	41	S	3650	10	none
S.K.	29	male factor	none	AID	full-term delivery	39	S	3180	9	none
K.B.	31	anovulation male factor	bromocriptine	AID	abortion	8	—	—	—	—
K.B.	32	anovulation male factor	bromocriptine	AID	ongoing	(30 week)				
H.E.	32	anovulation	gonadotropins	spontaneous	ongoing	(12 week)				
J.I.	29	male factor	none	AID	ongoing	(14 week)				

*daughter; †son

As the present paper was being written, of the 11 women seven had given birth to healthy term infants, who did not deviate in any way from the normal state in physical examination. The course of pregnancy in these women (except for one – chronic hypertension) ran normally. One patient miscarried in the eighth week of pregnancy. The remaining three women are still pregnant; the pregnancies so far have continued normally.

Taking the initial results already obtained into consideration, it may be supposed that the ultrasonographic monitoring of the development of the ovum has no influence on the development of the fetus or the condition of the newborn. The one early miscarriage may suggest that the real rate of abortions in this group of pregnant women is basically close to the rate of miscarriages in the normal population (10–15%), and at the same time lower than the rate of early pregnancy failure after IVF and ET.

Ultrasonographic monitoring of ovulation in hitherto infertile women most probably has an additional psychological effect. For in our case, the patient observes the ultrasonographic image together with the examining doctor, and is informed of certain details concerning the ultrasonogram. This may have a positive effect on the mental state of the patients, particularly those who thus far have not had ovulation confirmed in this way. This aspect of the method is to be the subject of our future research.

32

A further contribution to a functional interpretation of fetal movements

E. A. Gidoni, M. Casonato and N. Landi

ABSTRACT

Adriano Milani Comparetti was developing this subject – functional interpretation of fetal movements – from 1980 onwards in collaboration with Tajani and Janniruberto. The confluence of ideas from developmental neurology and obstetrics proved fertile and a suggestive model of human ontogenesis was put forward.

It is necessary to recall here the main points of this research in a short premise.

(1) The fetal motor behavior in 2000 pregnant women was observed over a 5-year period. Then analysis of motor patterns, long established as a clinical tool in our group, was applied to the findings (Milani Comparetti and Gidoni, 1967a; Ianniruberto and Tajani, 1981).

(2) Motor development was interpreted according to a theoretical model based on the interactive quality of the relationship among the components of a given structure. The background experience was 25 years of clinical observation and follow-up of babies from 0 to 3 years old in a child welfare clinic.

(3) The relationship between development of the whole person and the interference of central nervous system lesions was studied in a population of 4750 cases of cerebral palsy, which had been followed

in rehabilitation centres and in the integrated community services in Florence and elsewhere in Italy (Milani Comparetti and Gidoni, 1967b).

(4) A search for prognostic reliability of clinical signs and the shaping up of procedures for neurological examination of the newborn baby was carried out, aimed at finding out 'readiness for function' instead of the early detecting of defects. In this procedure the examiner is directly involved as a partner in the dialog with the baby; signs are collected in the interaction and are decoded, using a code that integrates different contexts simultaneously (the mother and baby relationship, as well as the examiner's and parents' relationship and this in relation to the child) (Brazelton, 1974a; Brazelton et al., 1974; Milani Comparetti and Gidoni, 1976).

(5) Data collected with the above mentioned procedures were processed by the group working as an integrated multidisciplinary team. As a consequence, emphasis on the prognostic features in the neurological examination of the newborn led us to retrospectively infer the presence of certain movement patterns in the fetus (Figure 1) (Milani Comparetti and Gidoni, 1976).

Four years later, the pattern analysis applied to motoscopic observation of fetuses with real-ultrasound apparatus confirmed the hypothesis made in 1976. A functional interpretation of fetal movements and the devel-

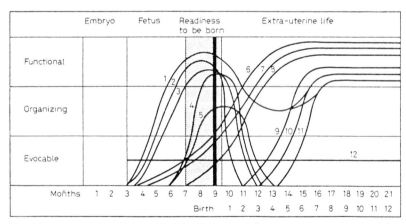

Figure 1 Patterns of readiness to be born 1=Placing reaction; 2=fetal locomotion; 3=propulsion; 4=Moro; 5=rooting; 6=response to auditory stimuli; 7=response to visual stimuli; 8=head postural control; 9=Landau r.; 10=antigravity support on hands; 11=antigravity support on feet; 12=tendon reflex. From A. Milani Comparetti (1981). The neurophysiologic and clinical implications of studies on fetal motor behavior. *Sem. Perinatol.*, **5,** 2

opmental model of ontogenesis was put forward. In synthesis, this model comprehends continuity and punctuation; it fits into the General Systems Theory and also contributes to the theory itself (Milani Comparetti, 1986).

Figure 2 represents a synthesis of the proposed interpretation of fetal movements and contains considerable potential for further research and clinical work (Milani Comparetti, 1981). For instance, it still has unexplored implications in neurology, such as the interpretation of cerebral palsy as a prenatal condition, and in child psychiatry (the pathogenesis of certain psychotic conditions).

Milani Comparetti's studies on the fetus and his theoretical model also aroused interest among psychoanalysts and offered ground for much vivacious discussion about the building up of the self and mental life.

So far, the question of *when* mental life starts was unsolved. Milani Comparetti's contribution gave birth to a new vision of fetal life, where the fetus is defined as an autonomous entity in interaction with his environment and his motor activity is both expression of 'readiness for' and, simultaneously, the generator of competences to be used at higher organizational levels (Figure 3).

However, we can see in real-time ultrasonographic observation, that the normal fetus can also be still, motionless.

We suggest that immobility is not seen only as a negative image of absent motion, but rather as an expression of the overall competence of the fetus to deal with posture and movement.

In the neurological literature there are antecedents concerning this approach. De Lisi considers body motoricity as a primary and immediate manifestation of human and animal individuality, expansion and establishing of personality which precedes the rational as well as the most concrete affective processes. Movement translates biological organization (and in the first place that of the central nervous system) into action.

He also says that resting postures are to be considered as an expression of the tonic muscle function, and as such appear to be of the same nature as movement: they identify with the perpetual dynamics of a being in its becoming. These considerations date back to 1957 and were based on motoscopic observations of normal human movement (De Lisi, 1957, 1958).

In other words, *alternation of movement and immobility* in the fetus is in itself an *expression of an existing organization*.

As a further step we would like to verify whether *fetal immobility* also can be interpreted *as a function* and as such fit into the developmental model proposed by Milani Comparetti.

In order to do so, we must now consider the point of view of the observer. Immobility in itself recalls meanings referred to in different contexts: of course it may mean sheer absence of movement, as in death,

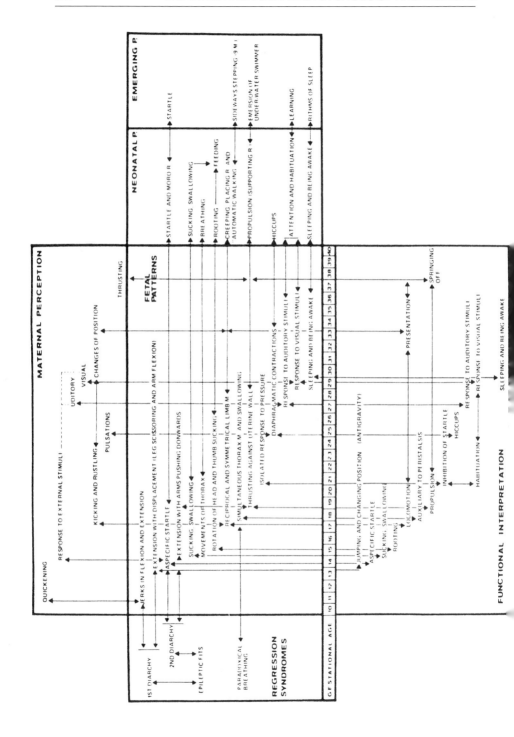

INTERPRETATION OF FETAL MOVEMENTS

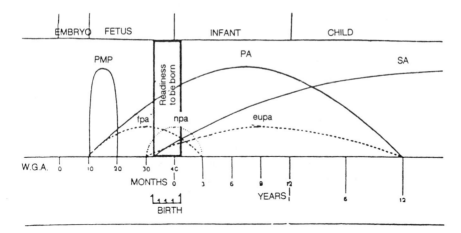

PMP = PRIMARY MOTOR PATTERNS   fpa = fetal PA
PA = PRIMARY AUTOMATISMS   npa = neonatal PA
SA = SECONDARY AUTOMATISMS   eupa = extra uterine

Figure 3 Developmental curves representing the acquisition of PMP and PA. From A. Milani Comparetti (1986). Fetal and neonatal origin of being a person and belonging to the world. *Int. J. Neurol. Sci.*, **5**, 2

paralysis or extreme weakness. But it may also suggest sleep, rest, fear, awaiting. It may recall the image of enchantment, deep thinking, meditation, recalling to memory and getting ready for. It may also remind one of the lying down posture of the patient in the psychoanalytical setting.

In the fetus, and at this stage of our speculation, we would like to point out the features of immobility as (1) absence of movement as a lesional sign (death, paralysis, metabolic or toxic interference), (2) readiness for, as if adjusting the body to the next sequence of movement, (3) waiting for forthcoming biological events (movement as an outburst of primary motor patterns, urination, endocrine and metabolic signals).

But by far the most suggestive *feature of fetal immobility is the 'composing' of identity by an inner process of organization of states.*

If we consider the primary motor patterns as the kinetic modules genetically determined, then *immobility may be interpreted as the feature of the primary making up of elements into a unity, which is identity.* The fetus is then engaged in a self-making activity as the subject, his propositional quality showing within his relationship with his mother.

The mother interacts with the fetus biologically, in a complex system of homeostatic, releasing, organizing factors; but the baby is also present in the mental setting of the mother's project concerning him, even before he is conceived (Del Carlo Giannini et al., 1981).

The biological and psychological partnerships are related to each other as two complex systems and constitute a system in themselves. The mother applies the rule of attributing meanings to fetal states and the fetus is exposed to her code of interpretation. Here we can just mention that, in its turn, the mother–fetus system interacts with other codes (for instance the father's) and this brings about further interactions and reciprocal modulations.

Hence the question of *when* was changed into the question of *how* mental life develops.

Milani Comparetti used to represent his model by using the visual metaphor of the open spiral: a creative circle *without a base* and self-making through interaction (Figure 4).

Moreover, structuring his identity provides the fetus with the faculty of picking up those interactions which are compatible with his own actual competence. This happens *only within a certain range and only up to a certain point,* thus establishing a dialog with the environment.

Discrepancy, as a fundamental parameter between proposal and counter-proposal, is also a feature of identity in the interaction. But 'it is not just due to the difference of the explicit messages'.

Milani Comparetti suggested that the personal identity in the interpersonal interaction comprises a basic element: *the secret.* This constitutes

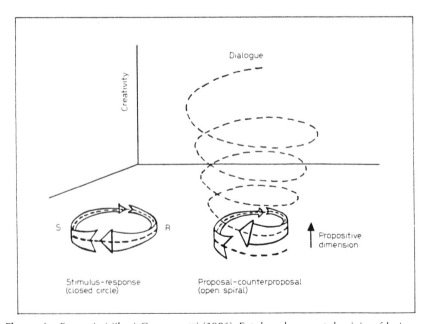

Figure 4 From A. Milani Comparetti (1986). Fetal and neonatal origin of being a person and belonging to the world. *Int. J. Neurol. Sci.*, **5**, 2

the privacy of silence and belongs to the dialog in so far as it defines the subjective niche of the *individual* system in the *interactive* system (Milani Comparetti, 1986).

Discrepancy, reserve, secret, hidden features: words of the uncertainty that now makes its entry into the realm of science, not as a deprivation or lack of certitudes, but as a source of deeper insight into the uncertain universe that challenges our system of knowledge.

The challenge of complexity (Ceruti, 1985) is now being taken up by the epistemologists within the new theoretical models in the philosophy of science. To probe the secret of the baby in the womb seems indeed to be going deeper into the adventure of knowledge. It takes courage to face the mysterious and the indefinable, and to allow oneself to be exposed to it. As Ceruti says, it needs a transformation of priorities, and a dialog between our minds and what they have produced as ideas and systems of ideas (Ceruti, 1985). Milani Comparetti was a pioneer of this approach.

33

The psychological effects of antenatal diagnosis on pregnancy

M. Endres

ABSTRACT

By means of punction of amniotic fluid during second trimester of pregnancy and also by improved ultrasound technology, prenatal diagnosis of certain diseases of the fetus is possible. The development of the biopsy of chorionic tissue makes possible the detection of genetic diseases as early as the first trimester of pregnancy. The advancing development and improvement of methods of early detection of fetal diseases leads increasingly to a 'technization' in prenatal medicine. This is in opposition to a lack of information about the psychological effects of prenatal diagnostic care during the course of pregnancy.

The following items will be pointed out:

The possibilities of prenatal diagnosis presently available

Results of an empirical study, in which women were questioned about their experiences of genetic counseling and prenatal diagnosis

Discussion of the influence of prenatal diagnosis on the course of pregnancy and development of the mother–child relationship.

The development of diagnostic techniques within the last 15 years has allowed the ever increasing detection of fetal diseases. Since the early 1970s amniocentesis within the second trimester of pregnancy has been widely used as a means of antenatal diagnosis of chromosomal diseases.

With improved ultrasound techniques and the introduction of *chorion villi biopsy* it is possible to detect fetal diseases within the first trimester of pregnancy. The swift development of screening methods in prenatal medicine has led to what Fresco and Silvestre (1982) called 'medicalization' of the fundamentally normal and not pathological course of pregnancy. By contrast, studies on the psychological effects of antenatal diagnosis on the course of pregnancy are rare.

The following topics will be discussed:

Current methods of antenatal diagnosis;

The results of an empirical study where female clients were interviewed on amniocentesis and genetic counseling;

The effects of antenatal diagnosis on the course of pregnancy.

CURRENT METHODS OF ANTENATAL DIAGNOSIS

The aim of antenatal diagnosis is the detection of fetal diseases. However, the available methods differ in their validity, the risk to the expectant woman and the indication for the test. Ultrasound permits visualization of fetus' morphology after the 6th week of pregnancy and therefore documents pregnancy itself. In the second trimester of pregnancy external and internal malformations can be detected. This method is thought to be harmless to the mother and her child and it is routinely used in antenatal care.

Amniocentesis allows visualization of fetal chromosomes. The test is usually carried out within the 16th or 17th week of pregnancy by puncturing the abdominal wall of the women. To avoid fetal injury ultrasound is used with amniocentesis. Fetal cells in the amniotic fluid are cultivated. Within 2–3 weeks microscopic analysis of the fetal chromosomes is possible (reviewed in Murken, 1987). In addition, fetal neural tube defects (*spina bifida*) can be detected by determining the level of a fetal protein (alphafetoprotein) in the amniotic fluid. In special cases the diagnosis of metabolic diseases is possible using fetal cells. The risk of abortion due to amniocentesis is about 0.5–1%. Amniocentesis is particularly offered to expectant women at an older child-bearing age since, with increasing age, the likelihood of giving birth to a child with chromosomal anomalies increases. At the age of 35, the risk of fetal chromosomal anomaly detected by amniocentesis is about 1%; at 40 years it is about 2%; and at 45 it is around 5%. The risk of giving birth to a child with a chromosomal anomaly is clearly lower than stated above, because about half of the fetuses with a chromosomal anomaly die between the 16th week of pregnancy and the forecast date of birth. In these cases pregnancy ends with spontaneous abortion or in still birth (Hook, 1983).

The etiology of the increased risk of older women having a chromosomally abnormal child is not completely understood. They are prone to a higher number of spontaneous abortions. In around 50% of these cases abnormal fetal karyotypes are found. Additionally, immunological changes are discussed which cause this increased risk to older women resulting in an insufficient detection of an abnormal fetus.

The age-dependent chromosomal abnormalities are the trisomy 21 (Morbus Down, mongolism), trisomy 13 (Pätaus syndrome), trisomy 18 (Edwards syndrome), Klinefelters syndrome and XXX syndrome. The increased risk of giving birth to a mongoloid child is the main reason for resorting to antenatal diagnosis, as the case of such a child poses great difficulties to the family unit. Amniocentesis plays a minor role in the detection of other chromosomal abnormalities; trisomy 13 and trisomy 18 cause severe somatic and mental retardation with the children generally dying within the first months of life. By contrast, Klinefelters syndrome and the other aberrations of sex chromosomes (Turners syndrome, Triplo-X syndrome) do not cause mental retardation or severe somatic abnormalities.

The effect of the father's age on the likelihood of conceiving a child with a chromosomal anomaly is discussed controversely. In West Germany legal abortions may be induced up to the 22nd week of pregnancy on the grounds of a pathological result. An induced abortion can result in severe psychological trauma to the woman concerned, because the result of amniocentesis is only available at an advanced stage of pregnancy (Blumberg, 1975).

With chorion villi biopsy it is possible to diagnose chromosomal abnormalities from the 8th to 11th week of pregnancy. Fetal tissue is taken by transvaginal and transcervical catheter aspiration (Simoni, 1986). The risk of abortion is currently estimated at 2–4%. The result is available before the 12th week of pregnancy. Originally method was developed in the People's Republic of China to allow an antenatal sex diagnosis (Han, 1975). After detection of a female fetus an induced abortion was offered to the respective women. While the Chinese government tries to decrease the population with the so-called 'One-Child-Policy', the couple aspires to a boy for religious reasons. This method has been forbidden for fetal sex determination (Han, 1986) for the last 10 years in China. The West German genetic counseling departments agreed to tell parents the fetal sex only after the 12th week of pregnancy.

With special indications fetal blood sampling and fetoscopy is performed. After the 20th week of pregnancy the transabdominal puncture of the placental blood vessel is possible, controlled by ultrasound. This method is used if ultrasound shows fetal abnormalities, which could be a sign of a chromosomal disease in the fetus. In a case where the child's death in the first months of life can be predicted, and with an expired deadline for legal abortion, obstetricians can refrain from invasive procedures (e.g. Caesarean operation) which would unnecessarily jeopardize the expectant woman.

Listing medical methods of antenatal diagnosis in such a way gives the impression that pregnancy is viewed in pathological terms. This idea is often implied to the expectant woman over 35 years. She is categorized as a 'risk-patient' due to her age, confronted with an array of medical-technical procedures and forced to decide about antenatal diagnosis, particularly amniocentesis or chorion villi biopsy.

The public often develops false beliefs about the efficiency of antenatal examinations. Female clients are often disappointed that only a few diseases can be excluded by antenatal diagnosis, when they expect a guarantee for a healthy child.

The process of decision making is an important part of genetic counseling which precedes antenatal diagnosis. Aside from objective criteria, the subjective perspective of the expectant woman is important in the course of deciding whether to undergo antenatal diagnosis (Endres, 1987).

PREGNANCY AND PRENATAL DIAGNOSIS FROM THE CLIENT'S PERSPECTIVE: RESULTS OF AN EMPIRICAL STUDY

The situation of expectant women intending to undergo an antenatal diagnosis will now be discussed and parts of an empirical study will be presented[1].

In the Genetic Counseling Department of Munich the client and her husband are routinely advised during early pregnancy. Therefore a decision within the limits of time is possible. Additionally, they can request chorion villi biopsy, which can be performed up to the 11th week of pregnancy. Currently around 30% of women over 35 undergo amniocentesis in Bavaria (Schröder-Kurt, 1985). There is a higher acceptance of this method in urban areas compared to rural ones. Most women interviewed are anxious not to have a handicapped child and, therefore, decide on antenatal diagnosis.

Genetic counseling departments recommend amniocentesis for women over 35 years. This is due to the consideration that at this age there is a balance between the probability of a fetal chromosomal anomaly and one of an abortion after amniocentesis. Women realizing this situation sometimes have great problems in choosing between the risk of an abortion and the risk of having a handicapped child.

Before amniocentesis 78% of clients reported anxiety. Anxiety about a fetal injury was more often cited (67%) than anxiety about an abortion

(53%). Pearn (1973) reported that the subjective evaluation of a concrete risk varies greatly. In our study, 10% of the women evaluated a 1% risk of abortion as high or very high, 15% of the interviewed rated it as medium, and 72% considered such a risk as low or very low. Life events may also influence subjective experiences, e.g. women who had already suffered a spontaneous abortion, or the so-called 'late-mothers-of-a-first-child' who view their pregnancy as a last chance to have a child. These women are threatened by the risk of an accidental abortion in the course of amniocentesis.

Expectant women often receive well-meant directive advice from members of their social environment, which can be interpreted as projections of the fears of the advice givers. Besides these influences, decision making is dependent on the individual structure of personality, with the correlated abilities to tolerate fear and to cope with real danger. Self-confidence and self-esteem are functionally important to enable the expectant woman to make self-responsible decisions. However, in this study only a minority of the interviewed women (15%) decided on amniocentesis totally on their own. The majority of them (74%) consulted their partners. Within this category, decision on amniocentesis was mutually reached in 47% of the cases, in 45% the woman's preference was decisive, and in 8% the opinion of the partner overrode the one of the respondent. It becomes clear that the couple's relationship is important in making the decision about amniocentesis. The actual study cannot answer whether an ambivalent attitude to pregnancy influences the decision to undergo amniocentesis. Around half of the expectant respondents stated that their pregnancy was planned, compared to the other half where pregnancy was not intended. Yet a majority of those interviewed (70%) reported 'being happy about pregnancy', with 20% having 'mixed feelings about pregnancy'.

First results with chorion villi biopsy demonstrate that women with an ambivalent attitude towards pregnancy are more likely to choose this earlier and riskier examination. Subjective evaluation and subjective experience of the communicated risk of fetal disease are the deciding factors for undergoing antenatal diagnosis, as are the anticipated consequences to the client in the case of a pathological result.

30% of our interviewees answered the question, 'Did you anticipate a risk of having a handicapped child,' with 'No' (compared to 70% that answered 'Yes'). They answered in this way despite the fact that all women respondents complied with amniocentesis, though only 5% within the whole category of those considering such a risk estimated the risk of having a handicapped child as high.

Only 14% of the interviewed women requested to talk about an induced abortion during genetic counseling. The interviewees of such a consultation were offered a list from which they could select topics. 25% of the women indicated in their answer that during genetic counseling, induced abortion had been addressed. Not until after a closed counseling session solely concerned with this topic did 85% of the respondents answer affirmatively when asked for a second time.

The results can be interpreted to mean that antenatal diagnosis is essentially performed to confirm the health of the unborn child, and that the problem of induced abortion is partially repressed. After having received the results of the examination about half of the female respondents showed no further fears as to the health of their child, compared to 35% who still expressed uncertainty.

Thus, antenatal diagnosis appears to be helpful especially when coping with the fear of fetal diseases.

EFFECTS OF ANTENATAL DIAGNOSIS ON PREGNANCY AND THE DEVELOPMENT OF THE MOTHER–CHILD RELATIONSHIP

Women usually think about antenatal diagnosis within the first trimester of their pregnancy when having to cope with their pregnant state. In recent years some women, especially the so-called 'late-mothers-of-a-first-child', have expressed the desire to continue their professional careers. Therefore a compromise had to be found between their occupational commitments and the demands of maternity. In addition, the one-to-one relationship with her partner changes as a concept of the future family grows out of the developing pregnancy. At the same time the expectant woman witnesses a change. The daughter of her parents becomes the mother of her child. This can cause complex and conflict-prone changes within the intra-familial system of relationships. Besides the absence of menses, medical pregnancy tests and somatic changes, the image of the self alters within the intra-psychic system, which can temporarily be experienced as greater vulnerability. There is a change which is new and unaccustomed, and sometimes inspires anxiety, especially for mothers of a first child. At the end of a large scale study in psychodynamic aspects of pregnancy, Bibring et al. (1959, p. 116) concluded:

> 'Pregnancy, like puberty or menopause, is a period of crisis involving profound psychological as well as somatic changes. These crises represent important developmental steps and have in common a series of characteristic phenomena. In pregnancy, as in puberty and menopause, new and increased libidinal and adjustive tasks confront the individual, leading to the revival and simultaneous emergence of unsettled conflicts from earlier developmental phases and to the loosening of partial or inadequate solutions of the past. This disturbance in the

equilibrium of the personality is responsible for creating temporarily the picture of a more severe disintegration.'

Only on rare occasions during this period of intra-psychic change is the decision on antenatal diagnosis made quickly and without problems. Nevertheless, a decision about diagnosis is usually reached at a single counseling session or, at least, conditions are established for the client which allow her a self-responsible decision. In rare cases these efforts are unsuccessful. Then the expectant woman remains undecided for longer, repeatedly revising her previous decision, leading to countless sleepless nights. The inability to make a definite decision may be related to regressive tendencies during the developing pregnancy which may be expressed in seemingly illogical and irrational activities. In these situations the relationship to the partner, the consulted doctor or the therapist can have a stabilizing effect.

The decision on amniocentesis, which is expected to yield information about the child's health, induces anxiety and uncertainty. This is because the operation constitutes a threat to the body of the patient and a danger to the pregnancy through a potential abortion induced by amniocentesis, or induced as a consequence of a pathological result. The preceding genetic counseling was usually unable to revolve fears of fetal injury through puncture.

With developing pregnancy the state of bodily unity between mother and child changes. The child cannot be directly perceived by the mother as the child still is part of the maternal self. This state is followed by a phase of differentiation during which the mother ceases to sense and perceive her child as part of unity, and perceives it instead as becoming a psychologically separate and independent object. The process of differentiation begins when the mother senses the first movements of the child, a moment called by Bibring (1961) a 'milestone' of further pregnancy. Ultrasound examinations at an early stage of pregnancy initiate the process of differentiation as the mother looks at her child on the ultrasound screen. The effects of these examinations are generally evaluated positively for the intensification of the mother–child relationship. However, premature forcing of such a relationship may increase the painful experience of a spontaneous abortion which is more likely to occur during the first trimester, i.e. an experience which is more painful with a more intense relationship between mother and child.

During the 16th and 17th week of pregnancy amniocentesis is performed shortly before the mother will sense the first movements of her child. The preparation of the result averages another 3 weeks. Yet in the case of a repeated test the waiting period may extend up to 6 weeks. The period of waiting for the result takes place during definite intensification of the relationship with the child due to the perception of quickening. At the same time a potential pathological result threatens pregnancy in each case like the sword of Damocles. In the case of a pathological result, until now antenatal diagnosis has, with rare exceptions, no beneficial therapeutic consequences for the child. At the time the expectant woman senses the child's movements and has a growing awareness of its existence there is only the choice of an induced abortion. Nevertheless, this case remains the exception as about 98% of the examinations yield a normal result. In retrospective interviews, female clients unanimously reported the period of waiting for the result as the most stressful, not knowing whether to happily anticipate a birth or to fear an induced abortion. Beeson *et al.* (1979) designated such a state as a 'suspension of pregnancy'.

Many pregnant women are convinced that their child will be healthy and pass the waiting period quite easily. Others develop doubts with progressing time. These women pass sleepless nights, and phone the genetic counseling department to ask if the result is available. The waiting period thus becomes a time of growing uncertainty, where the process of differentiation may come to a standstill. The communication by telephone of a normal result often triggers a marked relief, and many times a sceptical, 'Is that true? I can't believe it yet.'

Most of the female clients ask for information about the sex of their child. This request is discussed before amniocentesis during genetic counseling. Most of the time the couple comes to a mutual agreement, but sometimes there are differences of opinion about the desire for information concerning the child's sex. At any rate the decision should be left to the pregnant woman. 70% of the female clients of the Genetic Counseling Department of Munich requested the child's sex, 20% declined this information and 10% were undecided at the time of genetic counseling. Information about the child's sex fosters parents' imagining of their unborn offspring. They are able to search for a proper name and to enter an inner dialog with their future daughter or son.

CONCLUSION

The future use of antenatal diagnosis will be further extended to detect fetal diseases and screen earlier stages of pregnancy. The decision to resort to antenatal diagnosis should ultimately be left to the expectant woman, since the most extreme consequences for the future course of her pregnancy range from an abortion induced by amniocentesis, to an abortion induced for fetal disease. Individual counseling is indispensable in allowing an informed individual decision, and to ensure that an indication for antenatal diagnosis is not based on objective criteria alone.

The results of antenatal diagnosis influence the mother–child relationship and the further course of the pregnancy. The information should only be communicated on the request of the patient, as for example, information about the child's sex is especially important for the mother–child relationship. Its development has a dynamic which can be affected through the visual representation of the child via ultrasound.

The time-span between amniocentesis and the communication of the result is experienced by expectant women as particularly stressful, because pregnancy might be threatened by an imminent pathological result and because the growing mother–child relationship might stagnate.

Expectant women primarily experience antenatal diagnosis as a confirmation of their child's health rather than as evidence of fetal disease. Therefore, antenatal diagnosis helps in coping with anxiety.

---

[1] The quoted study was conducted in the Spring of 1986 at the Genetic Counseling Department of Munich. A questionnaire was designed to sample antenatal diagnoses with 44 single questions divided into four classes: questions for genetic counseling; questions for amniocentesis; questions for risk evaluation and questions for pregnancy.

A total of 650 questionnaires were mailed to all female clients who consulted the Genetic Counseling Department of Munich and underwent amniocentesis in 1985. The completed sheet was anonymously sent back in a postpaid return envelope. After a one-time reminder a total of 503 questionnaires were mailed back and processed. In 55 cases the letters were returned to sender.

The following data are cited from this study which will be published at a later date. The questionnaire and further details concerning the procedures and results can be obtained from the author.

34

Who's next? – notes on genetic counseling of pregnant women from studies in conversation analysis*

C. Scholz and M. Endres

Medical sociological and social psychological literature views doctor–patient communication and conversation between medical counselor and client primarily as questions of the participants' personality traits, their linguistic skills and competence, or, as an issue of dominance and power. Potential conflicts of medical counseling are discussed under three aspects.

In particular, a first view of the literature attributes 'snags' in counseling (e.g. to be at cross purposes, not to cope), to personal traits of the participants, to their cooperativeness, i.e. with respect to their resistance or to their rapport (Kessler, 1979; Balint and Norell, 1978). A second view assumes causes of conflicts between counselor and counselee primarily in regard to the way of speaking (e.g. fluent speech, pitch of voice) and in the comprehension of the conversational content (e.g. medical terms). Explanations of misunderstandings vary from sociolinguistic codes, differing native tongues and psycholinguistic characteristics of speech (Korsch and Negrete, 1972; v. Ferber 1975). Finally, a third perspective locates problems of counseling in the doctor's dominant behavior, his use of power in conversation, or, quite contrary, in the strategic block-up of medical

*Special thanks go to Wolfgang Kroner for his tireless advice in conversational analysis and helpful comments on the several drafts of our report. He also took care of the English translation.

diagnoses and therapeutic advice by 'consumers'. Indicators are, then, status asymmetries of the interactants (e.g. expert–lay (wo)man), the specific role relationship (e.g. service provider–consumer), or the Turn pre-allocation as a prominent characteristic of such conversations (Freidson, 1975; Siegrist, 1976; Quasthoff-Hartmann, 1982).

Beyond these notions of somewhat 'deficient' and 'non-ideal' counseling, we are interested in how participants actually accomplish the tasks of looking for advice, counseling or talking adequately about problems. To put it succinctly, our concern is with the *interactional achievement of conversation-as-genetic-counseling*. How is it that counselor and client manage such tasks of who is to begin with what (counseling) topic at which point in conversation?

To unravel this question and to demonstrate the methodology of conversation analysis in genetic counseling, we turn speaker change during such a conversational event into a topic of study. Thereby, we refer not only to the 'machinery' that can be observed in every naturally occurring conversation but, in addition, our concern is with the potential usefulness of conversation analysis for current research problems in medical treatment and genetic counseling. In the discussion of conversational fragments from genetic counseling sessions, we would like to demonstrate how participants actually co-ordinate their speech, and which resources are available to them 'to get' or 'to hold the floor'.

THE TURN-TAKING SYSTEM

We start with data Fragment 1 which is taken from the beginning of a genetic counseling session[1]. We may see that the start of such a conversation is not always taken for granted by the participants. Unlike in two-party conversations[2], where it remains usually unnoticed, the decision as to when and who is to speak next might become problematic in multi-party settings.

Fragment 1[3] *(K13)*

1	Dr F.:	May I help you
2	Mrs S.:	eh
3	Mr S.:	Do you want to or shall I
4	Mrs S.:	Yeah, alright. We're not yet at the age when amniocentesis
5		is necessarily required, but I am nevertheless interested because
6		I...
7	Mr S.:	(simultaneous) What the statistics say, if there are other
8		criteria as age etc., I mean some more precise information.

GENETIC COUNSELING: CONVERSATION ANALYSIS

```
 9   Dr F.:    Yeah, we offer amniocentesis to women from around 35 on,
10             because then the approximate risk of the test and the
11             probability that we detect something by the test is about
12             to be balanced. That roughly was the reasoning: to which
13             women do we offer the test, to whom do we not offer it.
14             About from 35 on there's an approximate risk of one per
15             cent to give birth to a child with a chromosomal anomaly.
16   Mrs S.:   Well, how high is it with 30.
```

In Fragment 1 we may note three observations:

Only one speaker (here: counselor and client) speaks at a time. If two persons talk simultaneously, it becomes noticeable;

There is a change from the current to next speaker (here: counselor and client). The participants alternate their respective turns;

Speaker change does not recur automatically. By speaking participants display to each other who intends to talk, who addresses whom and who has nothing to say at a specific moment.

These observations do not apply solely to every naturally occurring everyday conversation but also equally as well to counseling. Sacks et al. (1978) describe the fundamental *turn-taking system* with which the parties to a conversation organize their talk from utterance to utterance. This system consists of two components, namely the construction and distribution of turns.

Turn-constructional components serve speakers to project the completion of their utterance and to anticipate a possible transfer of speakership. Turn-constructional units may consist of lexical items (e.g. a sentence, a clause) or paralinguistic utterances (e.g. throat clearing, coughing) (Streek, 1983). All these units allow hearers to project the *unit-type* under way (e.g. a question, a statement, a rejection). In sum, hearers do not depend on completed sentences (or even completed words) to make these inferences.

Take the 'eh' (2) in data Fragment 1 for example. The husband of the client takes this as a hint of difficulties in formulating her problem, and as an occasion to select himself as next speaker. Speaker change occurs at a following *transition-relevant place*, i.e. at a point in the conversation where a turn-constructional unit projects the end of an actual utterance.

The *turn-allocational component* clarifies who speaks next. Sacks et al. (1978) note two rules that govern a set of three options for speaker change. Rule 1 refers to the first transition-relevant place. It provides three options to organize turn-taking:

(1a) If the current speaker selects in his turn the next speaker, the selected speaker has the right and obligation to talk next;

(1b) If the current speaker does not select in his turn a next speaker, other parties to the conversation can select themselves. Then, the first speaker gets the floor;

(1c) If the current speaker does not select a next speaker, and if nobody present selects him/herself as the next speaker, the actual speaker may continue his turn.

In our fragment the use of all three options is observable.

Option (1a): Mr S. asks his wife explicitly whether she intends to begin. He allocates her the floor (3).

Option (1b): After Dr F. did not address Mrs S. directly, and after she hesitates to take the next turn (2), her husband selects himself to speak next.

Option (1c): No party selects itself at a transition-relevant place, or is selected by the counselor (cf. 9). He continues his turn and produces what becomes at the end a 'detailed information' (9–15).

Rule 2 refers to the operation of these options at any transition-relevant place. It provides recursively for Options (1a)–(1c) at each next transition-relevant place, if neither (1a) nor (1b) has been used and the current speaker has continued.

It follows that the observed regularities (e.g. one person speaks at a time) are not taken-for-granted facts, but systematic accomplishments to which the parties to the conversation orient by producing turn-constructional units and taking as a resource the rules and options of speaker transfer. By doing this participants have methodical ways to cope with structural problems of conversational organization, for example, who begins, who continues, when does current speaker complete his turn, etc.

In our case, Mr S. solves the problem of who is next by turning to his wife. Thereby, he displays his orientation(3) that in genetic counseling a request for amniocentesis conventionally is a female client's concern. By interpreting her hesitation as difficulty in beginning and by attempting to formulate her concern Mr S. shows himself as a 'partner' to his wife. At the same time he makes himself available as an addressee for Dr F.

THE TRANSCRIPTION OF CONVERSATIONS

To study the unproblematic character of structural problems of conversational organization for participants, and the consequences of a noticeable speaker change for them an edited version of a conversation (as in

GENETIC COUNSELING: CONVERSATION ANALYSIS

data Fragment 1) appears insufficient. We shall now scrutinize more closely this data by using the notation system of conversation analysis included in the Appendix at the end of this chapter (Bergman, 1980).

Fragment 2 (K13)

```
 1   Dr F.:    %May I help you%
 2   Mrs S.:   eh hhh
                   (
 3   Mr S.:       %Do you want to or shall I%
                       (
 4   Mrs S.:              'hh
 5   Mrs S.:   'hh yeah alright we've we're not yet at the age when
 6             amniocentesis is necessarily required 'hh bu:t eh I am
 7             nevertheless interested
 8   Mr S.:    what the statistics say if there are other criteria as age
                  (                )           (
 9   Mrs S.:      because I  as you know I am       n-n
10   Mr S.:    etcetera I mean some more precise information
                  (
11   Dr F.:       mhm
12   Dr F.:    ehm yeah we offer amniocentesis to women from around thirty
13            five on because then (.) eh the approximate risk of the
                  (
14   Mrs S.:      mhm
15   Dr F.:    test (.) and the probability (.) that we detect something
16            by the test is about to be balanced that roughly was the
17            reasoning to which women do we offer the test to whom do
                  (
18   Mrs S.:      mhm
                      (
19   Mr S.:           mhm
20   Dr F.:    we not offer it (.) eh about from thirty five on there's an
21            approximate risk of one per cent to give birth to a child
22            with a chromosomal anomaly (.) eh
                                            (
23   Mrs S.:                                well how high is it with
24            thirty
```

By reproducing the same audiotaped conversation using the notation system of conversation analysis we are able to reconstruct more precisely than in data Fragment 1, the operation of the three options of turn-taking.

GENERAL TECHNIQUES OF TURN-TRANSFER

Participants orchestrate by various techniques to select themselves or others as the next speaker(s). One place in the conversation where this becomes especially apparent is the sequence of two mutually dependent utterance types, like a question and its following answer.

The one asked should answer: 'other-selection' as application of Option (1a)

Question–answer sequences are typical for genetic counseling. Through the act of questioning the other party present is selected as the next speaker. This form of 'other-selection' is extremely relevant for deciding on the type of conversation (here: 'counseling'). Questions are devices to start a conversation. At the same time they project a speaker identity for the recipient. In data Fragment 2, Dr F. officially begins the session. He becomes recognizable as 'counselor' not only on account of his question which is understandable as a generalized offer (Heath, 1981) to expose a 'concern' but, in addition, by being the first party to begin with such an utterance. Likewise Mrs S. begins to turn herself into a 'client'. Her utterance can be interpreted as a search for an answer to the preceding offer by Dr F. If a question is directed to someone by a counselor (s)he is required to answer even if (s)he does not exactly know what to say at this point. The questioner can take the very way of answering by the addressee as a display of (non)alignment to his projected identity ('role').

Fragment 3 (K13)

1   Dr F.:   %May I help you%
2   Mrs S.:   eh hhh

The opening of a counseling session is not without presuppositions: a counselor may class a counselee by record cards in a certain type of counseling (e.g. pharmacological counseling). On the other side, clients 'know' that the forthcoming conversation will primarily turn around medical topics after leaving their medical card with the reception and being informed there about the name and title of the counseling doctor. This characterizes the forthcoming conversation as (genetic or medical) counseling (Heath, 1981; Robillard et al., 1983; Scholz, 1984). In our example, the utterance of Dr F. addressed to the expectant counselee, is clearly discernible in this respect.

Here the counselor is using a device to:

(1) Select the next speaker (Option 1a)

(2) Establish himself as the next speaker after the addressee's turn as her answer has to be ratified in some way;

GENETIC COUNSELING: CONVERSATION ANALYSIS

(3) Require an answer, i.e. to make himself addressable irrespective of the content of the following answer.

The sequence of two utterance types as question–answer constitutes an *adjacency pair* (Sacks, 1972). Characteristically it consists of two parts which are not only serially tied but mutually constitutive, as they have to be produced by different speakers (here: counselor and client). A first part (here: the counselor's starting question) makes a specific answer conditionally relevant, i.e. an answer that is relevant to the question at hand (here: the counselee's concern in medical or health problems). As persons do not automatically take their turns at speaking, a person addressed by a question does not give an answer in every case. Yet, a missing second part of an adjacency pair is a noticeable event to the parties of the ongoing conversation[4]. The specific ways of sequentially tying a second pair part to the first one (e.g. rushing through or hesitating) enable the participants to make inferences about the comprehension or acceptance of the preceding first pair part (Wolff, 1986).

The following fragment is taken from the closing phase of a pharmacological counseling session where the participants are scheduling an appointment. Such an activity of fixing a new date is routinely unproblematic for the participants, as such a question by the counselor may be answered with 'yes' by the client without being afterwards obliged to comply.

Fragment 4 (K13)

```
475   Dr G.:    Do you like to ponder on it this weekend
476              (.)
477   Mrs A.:   It has to be done quickly (     ) it's a long time I have
478              reflected upon it
```

The client hesitates with her answer (476) and in the following utterance (477–478) she makes clear that the counselor's offer to 'ponder on it' for her amounts to not dealing with her concern: her decision is shown to be already established prior to the session. This warrants the inference that she had undergone genetic counseling to get a license for an induced abortion. Therefore, the vacancy of an answer to the doctor's offer is more an indicator of its rejection (Pomerantz, 1975) than of considering acceptance of the offer.

First speaker holds the floor: 'self-selection' as application of Option (1b)

After the start of the counseling session in data Fragment 2 the female client does not continue her turn. Her partner can legitimately select himself as the next speaker as she neither addresses a specific party with her utterance nor proffers an account of some medical or genetic problem.

Fragment 5

2   Mrs S.:   eh hhh
                  (
3   Mr S.:   %Do you want to or shall I%

Responding with 'eh' Mrs S. displays her disposition to take her turn. At the same time she acknowledges that she is the addressed person. However, by an audible exhaling sound ('hhh', 2) she does not project a continuation of her talk at this point, instead, she announces the completion of her turn. Mr S.'s utterance, therefore, becomes recognizable not as an interruption of his wife (which could be further interpreted as evidence for 'male dominance', 'specific problems of the client–partner relationship' or the like), but, to the contrary, as support of her efforts to formulate a problem.

If a participant to the conversation applies Option (1b), he has to start with his utterance at the earliest possible point of a transition-relevant place to display his self-selection to the other parties present. This may result in overlaps with the preceding speaker's turn or the other's incipient speech, who may just as well 'self-select' himself as the next speaker (Sacks et al., 1978; Jefferson, 1984).

Rechecking the family history ('Familienanamnese') the counselor addresses himself to the female client as well as to her husband. During the treatment of this topic Mr S. may also become a client. Part of an artful counseling practice consists, then, of making clear whom he is addressing with a single utterance. If this is ambiguous, i.e. if the counselor does not select a specific next speaker, simultaneous speech by several hearers may result as in the following fragment.

Fragment 6 (K13)

114   Dr Q.:   Was it a girl or a boy
115   Mr N.:   A girl
                    (
116   Mrs N.:   A girl

The overlap on-set is produced by simultaneous self-selection where, in this case, an identical answer remains unproblematic.

A speaker continues his turn: the application of Option (1c)

Speaker transfer is not a process whereby one party automatically and spontaneously follows the other in speaking, rather it requires the co-operation of all participants. The non-triviality of 'speaker change' for genetic counseling is further underscored in the production of utterances longer than one turn by a single speaker. If no other party is selected or selects itself a current speaker may continue his turn. With *embedded subordinate clauses* ('Nebensatzeinbettungen') before a possible completion point, speakers may expand their turn and oblige their hearers to listen. This might be especially relevant where conversational issues require longer time to explicate themselves. Thus, counselors may use embedded subordinate clauses to discuss specific *counseling topics* like medical treatments or risk evaluations at length.

Fragment 7 (K13)

12	Dr F.:	ehm yeah we offer amniocentesis to women from around thirty
13		five on because then (.) eh the approximate risk of the
		(
14	Mrs S.:	mhm
15	Dr F.:	test (.) and the probability (.) that we detect something
16		by the test is about to be balanced that roughly was the
17		reasoning to which women do we offer the test to whom do
		(
18	Mrs S.:	mhm
		(
19	Mr S.:	mhm
20	Dr F.:	we not offer it (.) eh about from thirty five on there's an
21		approximate risk of one per cent to give birth to a child
22		with a chromosomal anomaly (.) eh
		(
23	Mrs S.:	well how high is it with
24		thirty

In this piece of data it is noticeable that the counselor holds the floor over an extended sequence of turns without being interrupted by the minimal responses ('mhm'). Several reasons account for this fact:

The counselor expands his utterance before a possible completion point by embedding a subordinate clause ('because then', (13); 'and the probability' (15)).

He prevents transfer of speakership by placing his pauses not at possible completion points but at places where hearers cannot anticipate the completion of his turn ('because then (.)' (13); 'and the probability (.) that' (15)).

Here, the counselor uses the possibilities to expand his turn by resorting to embedded subordinate clauses as place-holders, and by not placing his pauses at possible completion points. On the other hand, this data (Fragment 7) evidences that the decision to complete his turn is not solely the affair of the counselor. If his hearers do not take their turns at places where he offers them a transfer of speakership, he might well continue inferring that the counselees have not yet understood what he was about to say. The listeners display their expectation for more explanation by:

> Restricting themselves to minimal responses at possible completion points of the counselor's turn ('from around thirty five on' (12/13); 'that was roughly the reasoning' (16/17)), i.e. hearers enter only minimally into conversation just to take their turn and immediately concede the floor to the prior speaker.

> Not 'self-selecting' themselves at a possible completion point of the counselor's turn ('to whom do we not offer it (.) eh' (17/20)).

Dr F.'s utterance finally is completed when Mrs S. takes her turn at a possible completion point and returns with more than a minimal response (23/24).

IMPLICATIONS

Let us briefly summarize our observations on speaker change. By choosing specific turn-constructional types and by resorting to one of the three options of the turn-taking system, parties to a conversation organize the sequence, the extent and the meaning of their respective utterances. This is by no means a solipsistic act, but a *co-operative accomplishment of all parties present*. This becomes especially clear when adjacency pairs are used to the introduction and working through of counseling topics. By orienting to the turn-taking system the parties to the conversation acquire specific participatory rights and obligations. The one who is selected as next speaker should answer. Those who are not a passive audience should display that they are listening, i.e. they should not only keep silent but demonstrate from time to time that they follow the actual conversation and understand what it is all about.

The *meaning of utterances* is constituted through the following turns of next-speakers. An official absence of specific returns, hesitation phenomena, or close tying at turn-taking is noticeable to the participants. They may take it as grounds to look for possible misunderstandings, unofficial motives or hidden resistance.

In constructing their turns current speakers display how long (and how detailed) they intend to talk. Nevertheless, the (temporal) *extension of utterances* is not fixed. A speaker does not decide solely on his own when his turn is to be completed. In the production of an utterance possible completion points become apparent. The other parties present are not restricted to the identification of an actual utterance, they do not begin autonomously, instead, they display to the current speaker their disposition to take their turn.

If at first it seemed trivial to study turn-taking in conversation, it became amply apparent that in genetic counseling participants in important ways have to take into account an orderly transfer of speakership. They thereby assure that the actual encounter is recognizably and reportably a 'counseling session', and the activities of the counselor can be recognized as 'provision for help'. In such a situation a typical beginning question like 'May I help you?' is not 'open'. Placed at the beginning of a genetic counseling session only certain answers can legitimately be expected (referring to medical-genetic facts). An utterance at this specific place in the conversation, and by 'other-selecting' with it a next speaker, hearers are informed that the current speaker should be treated as 'counselor' – irrespective of what the hearers know previously of this person. By being recognized as the counselor, he is officially entitled to ask specific questions and he is obliged to give information and advice about the clients' concerns. This may become problematic, if participants do not understand to whom the starting question is addressed, or if they mistake this specific opening as the beginning of a service encounter, where for example one easily obtains a license for an induced abortion.

To bring about actual counseling, the parties present have to establish their respective participant status. As potential 'counselees' they have to present a concern relevant for genetic counseling. It is not sufficient to talk somehow about troubles. Persons have to restrict the options of turn-taking, e.g. waiting for an invitation to expose one's problem. They have to display their immediate personal concerns with medical-genetic facts, and they have to do it in such a way that these concerns are heard as a request for help by the counselor. Only then can participants be categorized as 'clients'.

Participants undertake certain rights and obligations in genetic counseling concerning the production of specific utterance types, their proper placement in conversation and expectable returns to preceding utterances. A counselee is not entitled to open a counseling session. Instead, she readily has to inform the counselor about diseases in her family, her desire to have a child and the course of pregnancy.

In studying genetic counseling we should take seriously these normative obligations on the part of the parties in regard to this conversational type. As a consequence, at least some problems on the acceptance of medical advice discussed in research upon patient compliance could be seen in a fresh light. Take, for example, the widely discussed phenomenon that a client accepts advice for amniocentesis during genetic counseling, but refrains from actually undergoing the test without demonstrating medically acceptable reasons (e.g. a spontaneous abortion in the meantime). A closer scrutiny of the interactive accomplishment of such consent during a counseling session often reveals that an 'okay' for amniocentesis is rather a situationally appropriate 'polite answer' to a helpful offer on the part of the counselor. It is then possible that the participants will depart upon friendly terms but not with a trans-situationally binding decision.

However, beyond such potential usefulness of studies in conversation analysis for genetic counseling (e.g. research on client compliance) our aim in this research report is avowedly much more modest. We intended to describe some essential methods of turn-taking with which participants in a conversation analyze themselves – their utterances and, consequently, decide what to do next and who is next. Nevertheless, we hope that with our present endeavor we have sharpened the reader's sense for a fundamental insight of conversation analysis. Much is to be overlooked, if an observer tries to see more in a conversation than the participants do. Much is to be gained for an understanding of genetic counseling if we take seriously the fact that only in and through speaking are participants able to make explicit their concerns, feelings and knowledge.

[1] All data fragments are drawn from a corpus of 15 first counseling sessions at the Genetische Beratungsstelle der Kinderpoliklinik der Universität München. Five different counselors took part in these conversations. The recorded sessions can be classed with two types of genetic counseling: counseling before antenatal diagnosis (with amniocentesis and chorion villi biopsy) and pharmacological counseling ('Medikamentenberatung'). The first takes into account the age of the expectant client, whereas the latter is aimed at evaluating potential risks of maternal drug use for the fetus. All participants consented to the recording of their conversation.

[2] A naturally occurring dialog is not construed after the model of sender and receiver of information. This means that speakership is not automatically transferred, but requires that persons constitute themselves as addressees, a fact which is easily observable, for example, in attempts at dialog by males to females on the street. This also holds for legitimate dialogs such as two-party counseling. Clients may not only be silent when addressed, therefore rejecting an answer, they may also apparently disrupt the dialog by selecting other topics for conversation than those which counselors introduce.

[3] As an introductory step we reproduce an edited transcript of a conversation that was recorded during a genetic counseling session. We use a version of transcription that is usually employed in studies of genetic counseling (Kessler, 1979). As a second step we shall contrast this notation with the transcription system of conversation analysis (Bergmann, 1980).

A central flaw of the data reproduced in the text is that the conversations are translated from German into English. The reader is advised to take these fragments with caution. The original data excerpts can be obtained by contacting the authors.

[4] In our material of 61 genetic counseling sessions we found no instance of a missing answer to a question by the counselor. This may be due to our still small corpus. Nevertheless, we strongly assume that missing, not just delayed, answers are typical for other types of conversation than counseling, e.g. psychiatric interviews where such

absences of second pair parts may be used for diagnosis. Bergmann (1980, p. 197–8) cites such an instance from a psychiatric intake (our translation):

Dr N.:	He:lo Missus Benz,	Dr N.:	Gu:'n Tach Frau Benz,
	(1.8)		(1.8)
Dr N.:	Missus Be:::nz?	Dr N.:	Frau Be:::enz?
	(.)		(.)
Dr N.:	Hello,	Dr N.:	Gu'n Tach,
	(1.0)		(1.0)
Dr N.:	((to U.)) % Yeah she is really tired she has immediately go to bed (	Dr N.:	((zu U.)) %Ja die is'ganz müde die muß gleich in' (
U.:	mm	U.:	mm
Dr N.:	hasn't she?%	Dr N.:	Bett Ni:ch?%
U.:	mhm	U.:	mhm

The absence of a greeting return by Mrs Benz serves in this context (hospital reception, taken by an ambulance) as indicator of a 'psychiatric case'.

APPENDIX: SYMBOLS OF TRANSCRIPTS

(.)	pause of about half a second
(..)	pause of less than a second but more than $\frac{1}{2}$
(1.0)	1 second
(1.8)	1.8 second
= and	quick tying to previous turn
(	overlap on-set
)	end of overlap
ye::s	stretching of sound; number of colons indicates approximate length of utterance
yes	stressing of utterance
%yes%	low
ye-	interrupted utterance
'hh	inhaling
hh	exhaling
(yes)	unclear notation
( )	not audible/transcribable
(( ))	comments of transcriber
	punctuation marks exclusively denote intonation
,?	weak and stronger raised pitch of voice
;.	weak and stronger lowered pitch of voice

Part 2: Labor and preterm labor: risk pregnancy

35

Prenatal and perinatal psychology: implications for birth attendants

M. L. Davenport

ABSTRACT

In this paper various facets of prenatal and perinatal psychology that have a direct relationship to birthing practices will be presented. New findings in newborn and fetal capabilities, the relationship between mother and newborn or fetus, and the impact of the birth experience on psychological well-being will be discussed. Practical suggestions of the implications for delivery will be outlined.

Our appreciation of the impact of the mother on the unborn child and newborn is growing. This important influence seems to occur through three channels of communication: physiological, behavioral and what Verny terms 'sympathetic', the least understood pathway (Verny and Kelly, 1981). The physiological channel consists prenatally of the uteroplacental circulation. Through this channel, most substances in the maternal circulation enter the fetal circulation. Through the placenta not only do such exogenous substances as food, medication or toxic substances, such as carbon monoxide and nicotine, reach the fetus, but also endogenous substances such as the mother's stress hormones and some neurohormones. In addition, the blood supply and oxygen levels to the fetus can be affected by uterine contractions and by mechanisms that impair the blood supply to the uterus including maternal stress (Shnider *et al.,*

1979). Fetal and placental metabolic products are also released into the maternal circulation.

The behavioral channel of communication involves the mother's daily rhythms of work and rest, level of activity, body mechanics and exercise, as well as the sounds and sensations of the environments in which she surrounds herself. This channel also includes whatever conscious, intentional efforts she makes to connect with her unborn baby through sound, sight and touch.

The third and least understood channel of communication is the sympathetic channel of communication. This is an intuitive level that defies conventional explanation. An example of this kind of communication would be noting the ability of African mothers in certain tribes to sense when their babies need to urinate or defecate. The babies never wear diapers and never soil themselves; the mothers lift them off their hips and hold them over the road at the necessary times without any obvious external signs (Pearce, 1980). Some mothers can sense when their newborns are distressed, even if they are at some distance beyond normal hearing range. Intuition about the baby's sex and emotions during pregnancy are common instances of this type of communication. During pregnancy, this type of extrasensory perception of the baby occurs sometimes through dreams. Verny and Kelly (1981) give examples of mothers who felt that they received definite communication from their fetuses prior to spontaneous abortion or premature delivery, in one instance of the fetus shouting, 'I want out!' Although this type of experience does not conform to a mechanistic, materialistic view of the relationship between the mind and the brain, concepts such as the collective unconscious of Jung, the holographic paradigm of Pribram (1981) and morphogenetic fields of Sheldrake (1981) provide a plausible rationale for this type of phenomena. A number of reports of this type occur in prenatal and perinatal psychology.

Because the mother can have such a profound effect on her baby through her actions, thoughts and emotions, measures to support the mother's physical and psychological well-being are of direct benefit to the fetus. The fetus and newborn will in some way reflect the maternal emotional and physiological state. The deleterious effect of psychological stress in labor on the length of labor and neonatal outcomes has been the subject of a variety of studies (Lederman et al., 1978; Shnider et al., 1979). High maternal anxiety is associated with dysfunctional labor, preeclampsia, hemorrhage, instrumental deliveries and fetal distress (Crandon, 1979). Attention in the prenatal period to couples' normal concerns about ambivalence, doubts about adequacy in parenting, worry about jobs and relationships, and fears about injury to the mother and baby are best addressed openly and as early as possible to reduce anxiety. The unborn child responds in a physical way to his mother's images of him. There has been found to be a relationship between intrauterine growth retardation (IUGR) and the mother's lack of image of her future child. This is of great interest because in approximately half of the cases of IUGR there is no obvious physical cause. The possibility of therapeutic intervention through helping the mother to visualize her child, as in guided imagery sessions, presents itself.

Beyond preventing injury, knowledge of consciousness and perceptual abilities in the unborn child and the communication channels allows a wealth of possibilities for prenatal bonding, and teaching. Van de Carr reported on the use of a prenatal stimulation and bonding program utilizing simple methods of communicating with the unborn child through touch and vocalization. Newborn 'graduates' of the program had higher Apgar scores, shorter labors and performed better on a variety of parameters than controls. Parental singing is another powerful means of prenatal communication. Guided imagery is an excellent tool to help clients integrate negative prior birthing experiences as well as providing an experiential base for good outcomes during labor (Peterson and Mehl, 1984). Mothers often seem to be able to attune to their unborn baby through the sympathetic communication channel in a way that aids both of them in having a successful birth experience and improves their relationship postnatally. In labor the fetus can respond to the mother's thoughts and emotions. Mothers whose cervices remain stuck in labor at a certain dilation sometimes report a sudden shift in fetal position that allows the birth process to proceed. This release sometimes does not appear to be random or the product of a change in maternal posture, but occurs seemingly as a volitional response of the fetus to a communication from the mother to help in the process of being born. Birth attendants often observe that the clearing of emotional difficulties during labor can produce a sudden increase in the intensity of contractions and release of cervical and pelvic musculature to allow birth to proceed. The fetus is an active participant in birth and can respond to communication from the mother by flexing the head, relaxing his neck to allow easy rotation through the smallest diameters of the pelvis, and extending his legs to push himself down the birth canal.

There is now excellent literature for childbirth educators, birth attendants and parents that provides detailed descriptions of therapeutic visualization and 'inner bonding' to connect with the baby before birth (Schwartz, 1980; Olkin, 1981; Noble, 1983; Paruthos, 1984). Simply talking to the unborn child and massaging him a few minutes each day is very helpful. Parents need to know that bonding can begin well before birth, and that external and internal efforts to communicate with the unborn child have been shown to be of benefit.

THE SIGNIFICANCE OF BIRTH IN PSYCHOLOGICAL DEVELOPMENT

A major contribution from prenatal and perinatal psychology is the idea that birth is an event of critical importance in the psychological life of the individual. This does not mean that birth is the only significant event, but merely that birth needs to be rescued from its state of oblivion in traditional psychology and given much more attention. Those therapists who are skilled at uncovering birth memories unanimously agree that the circumstances of birth can have a profound effect on a person's relationships, ability to perform tasks, coping with life's stresses and transitions, as well as having a major influence on psychopathology such as recurrent depression, manic-depressive psychosis, addictions and sexual dysfunction (Grof, 1985). Further development of prenatal and perinatal psychology as a field will elucidate key mechanisms in the genesis of psychological problems.

The importance of perinatal experience, particularly the concept of a 'critical period' in creating lifelong patterns, has been appreciated for several decades in animals and more recently for humans. Attention was initially directed to attachment and bonding. Konrad Lorenz demonstrated in the 1930s that goslings would become attached to whatever care-taker was present at their hatching, bird or human. Much data have been collected on the deleterious effects on nurturing abilities and social interactions in lambs, monkeys, calves and other mammals resulting from separation from their mothers for even short periods after birth. Klaus and Kennell (1982), in their study of human mother–infant contact, found substantial differences 6 months after birth in the quality of mother–infant interaction between two groups of mother–infant pairs, one of which was allowed only 10 hours more contact in the first 2 days of life. De Chateau (1976) in Sweden discovered significant differences at 3 months with just one extra hour immediately after birth of suckling and skin to skin contact.

Beyond bonding, the new discipline of prenatal and perinatal psychology has created an experiential base that demonstrates that during this 'critical period' patterns are created that potentially influence many areas of life. The case reports of Chamberlain (1981, 1983), Cheek (1975, 1980), Grof (1976, 1985), Laing (1976, 1982), Verny (1981) and others provide numerous examples of this phenomenon. The psychotherapist Marion Woodman (1985) very succinctly delineates the relationship between birth patterns and her clients' way of handling life transitions:

'I have found that individuals tend to repeat the pattern of their own birth every time life requires them to move onto a new level of awareness. As they entered the world, so they continue to re-enter at each new spiral of growth. If, for example, their birth was straightforward, they tend to handle passovers with courage and natural trust. If their birth was difficult they become fearful, manifest symptoms of suffocating, become claustrophobic (psychically and physically). If they were premature, they tend to always be a little ahead of themselves. If they were held back, the rebirth process may be very slow. If they were breech birth, they tend to go through life 'ass backwards'. If they were born by Cesarean section, they may avoid confrontations. If their mother was heavily drugged, they may come up to the point of passover with lots of energy, then suddenly, for no apparent reason, stop, or move into a regression, and wait for someone else to do something. Often this is a point where addictions reappear — binging, starving, drinking, sleeping, overworking — anything to avoid facing the reality of moving out into a challenging world.'

The mechanisms by which events of the perinatal period form patterns in this imprinting process are not fully understood. A theory explaining this patterning phenomenon must both account for the entire 'gestalt' or sequence of events and relate them to the biological and physical characteristics of the birth process. Psychotherapists observe that situations of life stress or transition evoke birth patterns in their clients' behavior. This may occur because physiological, emotional or physical cues trigger the birth pattern or 'gestalt'. The phenomena of state-dependent learning may be a relevant concept in explaining how a birth pattern might be repeated later in life situations. In state-dependent learning, a particular behavior or group of memories is restricted to a particular neurophysiological or biochemical 'state' or 'gestalt'; for example, an experimental subject memorizing a sequence of numbers while intoxicated with alcohol is only able to retrieve this information at a later time when drunk on alcohol (Bustamente et al., 1970). The totality of neurochemical, physiological and mechanical factors operative at birth may comprise such a 'state' that can be reactivated at a later time.

The experience of birth for the newborn contains a number of unique events: profound mechanical pressures from the birth canal, forcible rotation of the head on the neck while traversing the maternal pelvis, the first breath of air, the first exposure to the variety of sensory stimuli outside of the uterine environment, the first extension of the previously flexed spine and opportunity for unconstrained movement. In addition, all of these physical changes occur when exceedingly high levels of the neurohormones prolactin and beta-endorphin, as well as high levels of stress hormones, are secreted by the fetoplacental unit in the process of birth (Golard et al., 1981; Kimball et al., 1981). These biochemical and physiological characteristics of the birth process may recur in a variety of circumstances in later life, and trigger birth memories, emotions or behavior patterns. It is important for personnel attending births to appreciate that difficulties or iatrogenic interruptions in the natural process may have far reaching implications.

MAXIMIZING HUMAN POTENTIAL AT BIRTH

At birth there are ways in which attendants can help ensure that the process unfolds in a manner that will be least traumatic to the newborn, and have the most beneficial effects on future psychological well-being. In general, these measures are very similar to those advocated in books on natural childbirth. However, beyond aesthetics, emotional satisfaction and fewer physical complications in the mother and newborn, prenatal and perinatal psychology provide a powerful rationale for motivating birthing personnel to concentrate on human (as contrasted with technological) support, to provide a birthing environment conducive to newborn capabilities, to allow spontaneous respirations to occur in a natural manner and to maximize newborn–family contact.

The basis for providing an optimal birth experience for the newborn is support for the mother. The very profound multilevel connection between mother and child must be respected, for the fetus and newborn will reflect the maternal emotional and psychological state. Human support, ideally a continuous care-giver present throughout labor such as the 'doula' or labor companion advocated by Klaus and Kennell, or midwifery or nursing standards providing one-to-one care, have already been proven to have a markedly beneficial effect on the length of labor and rate of complications (Sosa et al., 1980). Privacy, pleasant surroundings in which to ambulate, warm water in which to recline, all help to facilitate normal labor (Odent, 1984). The patience to allow mother and baby to complete the birth process on their own without instruments or artificial stimulation will help provide the newborn with a bodily felt sense of competence from this critical period that will serve him for the rest of his life.

Birth attendants should be aware that depressant medication during labor may have deleterious consequences far beyond the perinatal period. Although practices in the United States have changed from the 1950s when heavy maternal sedation was the norm, a large percentage of women in labor still receive drugs. A study from Cambridge showed that babies whose mothers were given narcotics during labor were sleepier and more sluggish at sucking (Richards, 1978). Brackbill and Broman (1979) found that children of women who received large doses of drugs were slower in development of motor and cognitive skills, and that some deficits in development persisted when the children were studied at 4 and 7 years. The use of narcotic analgesics during labor suppresses the natural rise in endorphins in the fetus, and it is possible that this practice affects endorphin response during stress in later life (Thomas et al., 1982).

Psychotherapy clients reliving their own birth experiences often perceive anesthetics and analgesics as a wave of noxious material clouding their consciousness. This sensation of a clouded sensorium can be related to a pattern in adult life of losing mental clarity in stressful situations. A recipient of obstetrical anesthesia discusses her habit of resistance to necessary change (English, 1985):

> 'So often I have an impulse to sink way in deep. It seems like going into total inaction. But that is how I was born, the anesthesia. Somehow I believe that real change has to be preceded by fogging out. Sometimes when I want to do something, I seem to go into total inaction. When I fully sink way in and feel the responsibility of never doing anything again, new inspirations come to me. But most often I resist both the action and the sinking in, and I stay stuck in the middle.'

In addition to confusion and mental fuzziness, the fetus in the process of birth can lose the intuitive, sympathetic communion with the mother as she is being drugged. A subject reiterating her birth experience noted that when her mother was anesthetized, 'That person is not there for you. That is exactly the experience you have in birth when your mother goes unconscious. You feel abandoned' (English, 1985).

The abilities of the fetus and newborn to interact with their environment should be taken into account in birthing practices. The newborn can be welcomed by familiar voices and music that he has heard during pregnancy. Avoidance of eye medication in the early postpartum period and dimmed lights can allow him to exercise his preference for looking at human faces, to focus on his family, to interact with them and to express himself. Babies are in a special state of receptivity after birth, unusually alert and sensitive for a prolonged period of time.

The literature of prenatal and perinatal psychology contains very important information about cutting the umbilical cord and the transition from respiration through the placenta to autonomous breathing through the lungs. There is a widespread belief among therapists using birth simulation techniques that breathing patterns are deeply influenced by the manner in which one experiences the first breath. Full, natural spontaneous breathing begins at birth, and has profound beneficial effects. Chronic shallow breathing, forced exhalations and uneven respirations originating from traumatic early respiration may result in depression, inability to tolerate stress and other disorders. A recent book by Pelletier (1977) on psychosomatic illness and the mind–body relationship underlines the close relationship between breathing patterns and disease:

> 'Breath is life, and it is a small wonder that patients suffering from serious respiratory disorders suffer fear and panic. Emotional states and breathing patterns are very much interrelated ... Respiration patterns become irregular with anger, slow and deep in relaxation, and quicken in fear or stress ... Slow, rhythmic breathing can turn an anxious mental state into one of relative tranquility and release the body from many of the other adverse effects of anxiety. Practicing proper breathing techniques is one of the most vital techniques we have at our disposal ... to reduce the anxiety associated with all psychosomatic illnesses.'

It is notable that in the excellent epidemiologic study by Salk on adolescent suicide, respiratory distress at the time of birth was frequently correlated (Salk et al., 1985).

The psychotherapist R. D. Laing (1976) indicates that some of his clients have felt shocked and confused by the disappearance of the placenta cord and membranes, which are cellularly and genetically of the same materials as the subject. It is conceivable that some of these sensations may be related to the sudden cessation of placental endorphins, which are secreted in high concentrations during birth, as well as lack of placental oxygenation.

Frederick Leboyer (1982), whose insights into gentle birth came from both attending thousands of births as an obstetrician and the reliving of his own birth, eloquently discusses the issue of cutting the cord:

> 'To sever the umbilicus when the child has scarcely left the mother's womb is an act of cruelty whose ill effects are immeasurable. To conserve it intact while it still pulses is to transform the act of birth ... Oxygenated by the umbilicus, sheltered from anoxia, the baby can settle into breathing without danger and without shock ... In short, for an average of four to five minutes, the newborn infant straddles two worlds. Drawing oxygen from two sources, it switches gradually from one to the other, without a brutal transition. One scarcely hears a cry ... For the baby, it makes an enormous difference. Whether we cut the umbilical cord immediately or not changes everything about the way respiration comes to the baby, *even conditions the baby's taste for life*.* If the cord is severed as soon as the baby is born, this brutally deprives the brain of oxygen. The alarm system is thus alerted, the baby's entire organism reacts. Respiration is thrown into a high gear as a response to aggression. Everything in the body-language of the infant – in the frenzied agitation of its limbs, in the very tone of its cries – shows the intensity of the panic and its efforts to escape ... How do things unfold when we refrain from interfering, when we protect the umbilicus? ... The baby ... gradually begins to breath deeply. Soon it is taking

---

*Emphasis mine. M.D.

IMPLICATIONS FOR BIRTH ATTENDANTS

pleasure in what a few moments ago was pain. In a little while the breathing is full and abundant, easy and joyous.'

Leboyer is vigorously criticizing our departure in North America and Europe in the last few decades from the traditional practice of leaving the umbilical cord intact until the cessation of pulsations. The principal American textbook, Williams' *Obstetrics*, recommended in its 1909 edition that the cord should be left intact. However, in the 1936 and subsequent editions earlier cord clamping is recommended. One rationale is concern that the newborn might receive too great a volume of blood from the placenta, a condition that in rare instances has deleterious consequences. Another major factor in earlier decades, however, was the prolific use of analgesics and anesthetics in laboring women, especially inhalant anesthetics to the point of unconsciousness at the moment of birth. Although this practice has decreased markedly, and the vigorous and immediate resuscitation of heavily drugged infants is necessary much less frequently, hospital personnel have not yet fully acclimatized to drugless birth. Newborns in the vast majority of births do not need 'stimulation' with rough towels or rubbing on their chests to breathe, and do not usually need suctioning to remove mucus. Often newborns in gentle births do not cry, and may begin spontaneous respirations without crying or with soft cooing vocalizations (Oliver and Oliver, 1978). Most medical personnel believe that it is necessary for newborns to cry in order to breathe, having been habituated to rough births in their training; home birth experience contradicts this assumption. A recent review of cord clamping in a major perinatology journal dispelled fears that late cord clamping causes newborns to be overtransfused, noting that if the infants are placed on the mother's abdomen an optimal amount of blood enters the baby's circulation from the placenta (Linderkamp, 1982). Although a mainstream organization, The American Society for Psychoprophylaxis in Obstetrics, has in an official statement noted that Leboyer's procedures and concepts may have merit and are not harmful, it will take a persistent and major effort on the part of consumers and professional organizations to change practices of cord clamping on a large scale.

The newborn benefits greatly from prolonged contact with his mother after birth as shown by the follow-up studies discussed previously. The newborn is most secure at birth close to the mother's body in direct skin-to-skin contact. A simple way to ensure this contact is for the birth attendant or mother herself to lift the baby onto the mother's abdomen or chest at birth, and to cover the baby with warm blankets. This procedure allows the cord to remain intact until pulsations cease, and permits maximum skin-to-skin contact. Shared touching at birth is rewarding for both mother and baby, and both suffer if it does not occur. Early breastfeeding allows intimate contact between mother and newborn, with touching, smelling and the opportunity for the baby to hear the familiar maternal heart-beat. With nursing shortly after delivery, the mother's uterus will contract to normal size more quickly, lessening the possibility of hemorrhage.

Clients in birth-oriented psychotherapies usually perceive separation from their mother in the early postpartum period as traumatic. This is a typical exchange from an adult hypnotic regression, describing how being in the nursery felt after delivery (Chamberlain, 1983):

> Subject: 'Nothing's comfortable now ... Women come in and look at us. Cold hands, really cold hands touching us, with masks on covering their nose and mouth. And everybody's crying. All I can see is me in the incubator...'
> Doctor: 'How did you like being in there?'
> Subject: 'I didn't like it. I didn't like it. I wanted to be where I was, inside my mother. I just didn't feel secure. No one to hold me, tell me everything's okay. Oh God! It was so upsetting ... (whimpering, then crying) ... I needed her to hold me. They should have let her hold me.'

Touch deprivation can have severe emotional and physical consequences. The skin is the largest organ of the body, occupies a large area of cerebral cortex, and needs stimulation for optimal health. To separate mother and baby significantly in the perinatal periods, as is still the norm, is only different in degree from the isolation infants experienced in foundling homes (where many died from the lack of touch) or the deprivation young monkeys felt when they were denied the opportunity to cling (with subsequent poor growth and deranged relationships) (Montagu, 1978).

The idea that birth is a life event with profound, long lasting psychological consequences is not new, but has recurred intermittently in the psychological literature since Otto Rank wrote *The Trauma of Birth* in 1924. The psychology of birth seems on the verge of a renaissance, and we can expect to see a further proliferation of studies on fetal and newborn perception and memory, and longitudinal studies relating birth events to adult pathology. Birthing personnel must not allow guilt from having followed traditional practices to prevent them from taking a nonjudgemental look at new information, and changing, sometimes radically, if necessary. The development of greater sensitivity, patience and better interpersonal skills will help in a shift away from mechanistic attitudes of the past that rely heavily on drugs and machines, towards more humane birth.

36

The midwife as attendant for women with high-risk pregnancies

E. Pichler

I am glad that as a midwife I can contribute with part of my practical work, and I hope to approach directly colleagues and physicians who are concerned about holistic support of expectant mothers.

PRELIMINARY REMARKS

For several years I have been working as an independent midwife in prenatal and follow-up care (preparing women and couples for the birth, pregnancy counseling, childcare courses, information evenings for expectant parents) in the district of Freising near Munich. A family center has developed out of this work, which has been recognized as a pilot project and is supported to the extent of 60% by the Bavarian government. The center keeps in touch with all physicians, bureaus and departments that are in charge of medical or social problems. I have found local gynecologists to be especially supportive of this work in the prenatal area.

In the last 3 years I have attended (in their homes) about 30 women with high-risk pregnancies. What does this mean? A woman with premature labor or cervical insufficiency is supervised closely by her gynecologist and treated medically. In addition, he generally orders strict bed-rest at home. These are often women who already have small children and thus want to avoid as long as possible a stay in a clinic. In such cases in Germany a family care-taker comes into the home. If certified by a doctor, the costs are borne by the insurance company. The gynecologist recommends that the expectant mother get in touch with me, and we set a date for a house visit. Following this, I visit the woman once or twice a week. These visits last around $1\frac{1}{2}$ hours. Some women are attended in early pregnancy and some later. If the doctor thinks that treatment at home is no longer sufficient, the woman is treated further in the clinic. I will now briefly describe the group of women I have attended, specifically women threatened by late miscarriage or premature birth.

CAUSES OF HIGH-RISK PREGNANCIES: A SUMMARY

As is to be expected from the complicated functions of the pregnant uterus, there is a multiplicity of possible causes of premature birth. A definite explanation is possible in only 40–50% of premature births. This must be attributed to the fact that there is usually not just a single cause, but several factors working together to influence the outcome. The following factors are summarized in Table 1.

(1) *Cervical insufficiency* Premature shortening or opening of the cervix can occur independently of labor, so that uterine contractions go unnoticed or are incorrectly interpreted.

(2) *Neurovegetative hyperexcitability* Neurovegetative hyperexcitability is the most significant cause of premature contractions. Everything that overstimulates a woman mentally or physically can bring about readiness for labor prematurely, as can mechanical factors such as stretching of the myometrium, perhaps with multiple births or with a hydramnion.

(3) *Uteroplacental insufficiency* Often, microscopic examination of placentas after premature births shows a striking accumulation of severe transformations. But even limited perfusion of the uterine (preplacental) vascular space in EPH-gestosis (ranging from such causes as nicotine abuse or from an infantile uterus) can lead to premature birth. Such cases, depending on the severity of the undernourishment of the baby, may require an effort to terminate the pregnancy early. It is in this sense, a 'necessary premature birth' in order to prevent the death of the baby within the uterus (Martius, 1983, p. 286)

Diagnosis is not my job as midwife. The gynecologist performs all the examinations. I undertake to observe labor and to check the heart beat.

I have found, in my many discussions with women, that excessive psychosocial stress for the mother brings about an increased risk of attempts at premature delivery. The number of women with premature labor seems to have increased in recent years.

Table 1 Reasons for premature birth

Maternal factors	Pathogenesis	Fetal factors
EPH-gestosis Endometrial insufficiency Implantation disturbances Older women with a first baby Juvenile pregnancy Infectious diseases Anemia	Utero-feto-placental insufficiency	Placental abnormalities Multiple births Fetal malformations Prenatal infections Incompatibilities
Maternal factors Genital abnormalities Infectious diseases Bad diet Nicotine abuse Anemia	Neurovegetative hyperexcitability Premature labor	External factors Excessive mental stress Excessive physical stress Unfavorable social relationship Traveling, climate change Deliberate abortion, trauma
Maternal factors Genital abnormalities Previous abortions Previous curettage Weakness of connective tissue Multiple births	Cervical insufficiency	Fetal factors Multiple births Hydramnion

In two World Wars, for two generations, many values have been questioned or have undergone changes. The result is, in my opinion, a new orientation. This development is taking place at an ever faster pace. The extended family no longer exists in order to help provide standards in this orientation. In addition, contradictory information from the media causes confusion, and a great deal of uncertainty stems from this. Most of the women who are now becoming mothers were born in the 1960s. At that time, not only was it usual to medicate heavily during the delivery (e.g. tranquilizers, opiates and during delivery full narcosis for the passage of the head), there was also no chance for the child to remain beside the mother in the hospital. Instruction of young mothers in breastfeeding was very poor. Moreover, 8 weeks after the birth, young mothers often went back to work, and the baby was entrusted to a nurse. I wonder whether, today, the worry and uncertainty in handling the newborn, and in learning the role of the mother are not influenced by unfavorable circumstances in her own early childhood.

POSSIBLE CAUSES OF STRESS, ANXIETY AND TENSION

Naturally the following list makes no claim to completeness, but it provides a useful, overall view of psychological factors the midwife must watch for and take account of in her home visits.

Social setting

This includes financial need, problems in finding a place to live, and physical and mental stress in the workplace.

The family

The mother can often have problems in breaking away and living apart from her own mother and father. These problems result in difficulties in learning her own role as a mother. I have also been told of a prolonged separation from the parents during the first years of life (stays in hospital), which may also contribute to poor early mother–child bonding development. On the other hand, the man's family can sometimes be a source of trouble. For example, they have sometimes conveyed the negative feeling (stress producing) that the young mother had failed at having children or having them in a most satisfactory manner.

Problems with the partner

In some cases the pregnancy was not desired by one of the partners, and she becomes worried that she cannot fill the new role. Among fathers, some are afraid of changes in the relationship, afraid of accepting responsibility, or afraid of losing their wife to her new role as mother. It is also painful when the man is repelled by his pregnant wife's physical changes. Men react differently to this stress; they take refuge in their work or in external relationships, find a girl-friend or become ill (e.g. stomach aches, etc.).

The woman's own problems

These often consist of concern about having to become a 'good mother', and the fear of not being able to live up to this role and satisfy claims on her from outside. Some cannot accept their changed physique, not finding the big stomach and the breasts attractive, and they were afraid of not regaining their good figure. It is common for these women to have a very low weight increase during pregnancy, and their babies may be somewhat underweight.

These women often decline sexual relations during pregnancy. Some of them are worried because they are 'supposed' to give up their profession after the baby is born, and also fear being financially dependent on their husbands (i.e. losing their own hard earned independence and self-sufficiency).

Problems with the baby

Undesired pregnancy, fear of responsibility, and fear of a sick child stand out here as some of the most common problems encountered. If a woman has a negative experience of birth (sometimes it has been her own that was especially stressful) or she has heard from other women of bad birthing experiences, then these things often become very worrying for the woman. These women often suffer nightmares because of these anxieties. I have noticed that, in many of these cases, the movements of the child are felt either very early (around the 16th week of pregnancy) or rather late (around the 23rd week). The movements are often spoken of with anxiety and violent ones are perceived as threatening.

WHAT DOES THE HIGH-RISK PREGNANCY WOMAN WANT FROM THE MIDWIFE?

She would like to talk about her pregnancy and have somebody who will listen attentively. She would like to receive information she can understand about the medical situation of her pregnancy and about the delivery. Sometimes she would like to be put in touch with counseling sources (the youth welfare office, the social welfare office, etc.). Naturally, she wishes to prepare herself for the delivery, to learn to deal with labor, to practise breathing and relaxing, and to put herself into the appropriate mood for the period after the birth, e.g. for childcare. Sometimes the partner is also included in this preparation.

WHAT ROLE DOES THE MIDWIFE PLAY?

I take needs and pains seriously and make an effort to listen attentively. Through explanation and information, making the woman aware of what is happening to her body and preparing her for the delivery, I try to allow anxiety. I support her initial efforts to communicate with her baby. This is often most successful in the protective environment of the home.

Tension can be removed by any of the deep relaxation methods. One is autogenous training (conscious tensing – conscious relaxing) or by a metamorphic method which is also known as prenatal foot massage. It is a primary concern of mine to relieve women of the anxiety brought on by self-accusation or of the feeling that they have failed.

Experience shows that in many cases the doctor's treatment of premature labor by medication is helped by these methods, that uteroplacental perfusion is promoted, and that greater growth of the baby can be observed. This strengthens the feeling of the expectant mother that she has prepared herself sufficiently for the arrival of her baby.

OVERALL OBSERVATIONS

(1) There seems to be a direct connection between a stressful early pregnancy, vigorous movements of the baby, and increased winding of the umbilical cord.

(2) The nightmares women speak of (the baby is sick, starves because the mother forgets to feed it, etc.) go away by the time of delivery.

(3) Labor pains that occur in the mornings seem to indicate a more stressful pregnancy than do the multiple pains in the afternoon and evening. I have often seen morning pains in very anxious patients, along with sleep disturbances.

(4) Some women know the reason for their labor pains.

(5) If there is a lot of worry and tension, the woman is not able to breathe with her stomach. She breathes with her chest. The metamorphic method referred to previously may help to remove this block. The baby reacts to the stomach breathing with greater liveliness. One woman said: 'If I breathe with my stomach, the baby moves a lot and that scares me!'

(6) Women suffer from 'lying around useless like this', and often do not receive enough support from their family or their partner. Explanation and encouragement by the midwife can also be useful here.

CONCLUDING REMARKS

Close medical supervision in the gynecologist's office, accompanied by the midwife's housecalls, seems in many cases to be an alternative to a stay in a hospital. Such a hospital stay can last for weeks for a woman with a high-risk pregnancy, and is very mentally stressing.

At a time when health care costs are exploding, there is a great financial difference between attending as an outpatient and a longer stay in a hospital. The costs saved by both the parents and government coffers would be significant.

The midwife is prepared for this task by her training and work. She is not there to treat, but to counsel, to support and to relieve. She can contribute to making pregnancy and birth less frightening, and she can encourage the woman to start communicating with her baby before the birth. Indeed, in some cases, we have observed that a very stressful pregnancy need not lead to a delivery with complications.

We hope gynecologists will give some thought to this kind of midwife attendance for women with high-risk pregnancies. Further, I would like to encourage others to undertake this demanding, but in so many cases gratifying work, so that mother and child can establish a good relationship with each other in those so essential and vital first months.

37

Relationship of psychiatric diagnosis, defenses, anxiety and stress with birth complications

G. Peterson, L. Mehl and J. McRae

ABSTRACT

A prospective study was conducted of 270 women planning for low-risk childbirth. These women were middle socioeconomic status or higher. Experienced psychotherapy clinicians assessed these women during pregnancy in terms of predominant and major defense systems used to cope with new life situations and anxiety, psychiatric diagnosis, life stresses, and the desire of the woman's partner for the child. Following delivery, four groups were large enough to use for purposes of data analysis. These were Caesarean section, uterine inertia, minor complications, and entirely normal delivery. More severe psychiatric diagnoses were more commonly found among women having more complicated deliveries. Character disorder as an entity was more commonly linked with uterine dysfunction or Caesarean section. The defenses of denial, repression, projection, and somatization were more commonly used by women whose births fell into the uterine dysfunction or Caesarean section group. Higher anxiety ratings were associated with more severe complications, as were higher levels of life stress and more negative reactions of the woman's partner to the pregnancy. Suggestions are made for including a mental health professional as part of the obstetrical team.

INTRODUCTION

The prediction of women who will deliver normally has occupied the efforts of obstetricians, family physicians, and midwives for years. Many systems have been developed to make such predictions more successfully (Mehl and Peterson, 1981). Heretofore all such systems have been created by obstetricians and identify the very high risk mother-to-be. Richard Aubrey (1978) has bemoaned that as many as 30% of low-risk women become high-risk during labor, developing a previously unexpected complication with possibly life-threatening potential to child and/or mother. For this reason alternative childbirth has been argued against (Mehl and Peterson, 1981). It has been stated that psychosocial predictor variables of high vs. low risk status are generally unhelpful.

The psychological literature, however, has concerned itself with the study of psychological predictor variables for birth complications. Anxiety has received the most attention in that literature. Ferriera (1965), for example, reviewed over 100 studies relating anxiety to pregnancy. Higher levels of maternal anxiety were related to fertility problems, nausea and vomiting, repeated spontaneous abortion, toxemia and pre-eclampsia, patterns of fetal activity, and premature birth.

Davids and Devault (1962) found higher anxiety levels using the Taylor Manifest Anxiety Scale among women having complicated deliveries, compared with women having normal deliveries. These differences disappeared postpartum.

Davids and Devault (1962) measured anxiety psychometrically, clinically, and projectively and found higher anxiety levels among women who had abnormal births, compared to women having normal deliveries. Grimm (1961) found no significant relationship among results of projective tests and length of labor, birth complications, and newborn problems, although results were in the expected directions. McDonald et al. (1963), using the Anxiety Scale of the International Personality Assessment Test, found significant differences between women having normal deliveries and those having complicated deliveries among a group of very low socioeconomic status patients. The Minnesota Multiphasic Personality Inventory (MMPI) gave evidence of less ego strength, more tension, and more guilt proneness for the 'abnormal group', whose characteristic defenses were intellectualization and obsessive rumination. A replication (McDonald, 1965) in a sample of unmarried expectant mothers showed higher levels of manifest anxiety in association with 'abnormal' obstetrical outcomes. The 'abnormal' outcome group was thought to be characterized by 'greater neuroticism, anxiety, and the use of ruminative ego defenses' (p. 200). Postpartum personality characteristics were similar. A separate analysis

(McRae, 1981) of the same data indicated that significantly higher MMPI scores on anxiety, social introversion, and hypochondriasis were associated with complications of excessive weight gain, premature rupture of membranes, and pre-eclampsia. Personality factors associated with individual complications were: higher elevations of the anxiety, depression hypochondriasis, schizophrenia, and psychasthenia scales with premature rupture of membranes; and higher elevations of the hysteria and hypochondriasis scales with pre-eclampsia.

For uterine dysfunction, Crammond (1954) compared a 'uterine dysfunction group' with a 'normal birth group' describing a 'dysfunction temperament', characterized by inhibition, conventionality, emotional constraint, and inability to express anxieties. Tendencies to conceal anxiety during pregnancy have also been associated with prolonged labor (1976). Longer labor times have been associated with conflicts about pregnancy and motherhood for patients who denied anxiety, while shorter labor times were found for patients who admitted anxiety and also for patients without conflicts (Scott and Thompson, 1956).

Gunter (1963) performed a retrospective study of premature versus fullterm births among lower socioeconomic status black women, finding that mothers of premature infants reported twice as many stressful life events, including early neglect by their own mothers, deaths, desertions by husbands, financial difficulties, interpersonal problems and physical disabilities. Shereshefsky and Yarrow (1973) described three cases of infant death in a sample of 60 middle-class couples, among whom overt stress during pregnancy was prominent in each case. Nuckolls et al. (1972) found that women with high life stress scores and low psychosocial assets had two-thirds more obstetrical complications than other groups. Gorsuch and Key (1974) found that life stress in the second and third trimesters of pregnancy was associated with obstetrical abnormalities, while life stress prior to conception had no effect.

PREVIOUS RESEARCH

Our clinical work had convinced us that beliefs, attitudes, emotions, and coping styles were related to birth complications. Few studies had collected prospective data. Our previous research (Grimes et al., 1981; Peterson, 1981) had shown that inclusion of psychosocially derived variables enabled us to increase the efficiency of risk prediction among low-risk women. We were successfully predicting most of Aubrey's 30% of low-risk women who become high-risk during labor. In this study, we wanted to determine if, on prospective clinical evaluation, there were factors statistically significantly different between women who give birth normally and other groups of women having various obstetrical problems.

METHODS

270 pregnant women were studied prospectively and consecutively from the inception of prenatal care through delivery and whenever possible, into the postpartum period. These women were all receiving care from a midwifery group practice in Berkeley, California with a strong orientation to natural childbirth. We consulted with the midwives to develop a prenatal program that addressed both the emotional and physiological aspects of pregnancy. All patients were interviewed by a psychological clinician during the first or second trimester of pregnancy.

We supervised childbirth education classes for the pregnant woman, oriented at her expressing fears and concerns. Early childbirth classes provided information about pregnancy, fetal growth and development, nutrition, and other concerns. Pregnant women and their partners were helped to address issues of sexuality during pregnancy, fears of becoming parents, and to improve basic communication skills. Late classes began at about 30 weeks of pregnancy and helped the women prepare to cope with the pain of labor (Peterson, 1981).

All patients received a psychosocial history review, family interview, somatic assessment, and early and late childbirth classes. These extra services increased professional involvement in prenatal care by three contact hours. Added supervision of childbirth education improved the quality of these services, allowing for better integration into prenatal care provided. After the family interview, the researcher conducting the interview completed a rating scale on the patient and her partner. For the purposes of this study, a modification of a form initially devised by Shereshefsky and Yarrow (1973) was used. This was completed in the first trimester, when there was further interaction with the research staff member (through counselling or childbirth classes) and changes were noted over the course of the pregnancy. For the purposes of analysis the forms were averaged with greater weighting given to the last trimester. Weightings were 0.5 for the 3rd trimester; 0.35 for the second; and 0.15 for the first. We relied upon Shereshefsky and Yarrow's definition of terms to allow comparisons with their earlier results.

POPULATION

The population receiving care at the clinic was predominantly Caucasian middle class as judged by background, educational attainment, and value system. Some persons attending care at the clinic defied the usual assessment procedures for class assignment. Such patients were assigned to the class that seemed to most accurately reflect their real status. A daughter of a Texas obstetrician who was living in Berkeley receiving public support with a Master's degree was considered middle class, even though she was receiving public support and her income level was low. Her partner was the son of a pediatrician from Ohio and was also receiving public support while completing his Master's degree. He was also considered middle class. By these criteria, all the population receiving care were, at minimum, middle class. 35% of the population funded their care through the Medi-Cal program. The racial breakdown was 85% Caucasian, 5% black, 5% Asian, and 5% other. Almost everyone had attended college, and one-third of the population of couples had at least one member with an advanced degree. Nutrition was excellent in this population, as was sophistication of health care alternatives and concern about health. The average age of women was 29, with the range being 18–42 years of age. For 80% of the women this was their first birth; for 18% their second; for 2%, their third; and for one woman, her fourth birth; and another, her eighth birth.

DATA ANALYSIS

Staff generated ratings were coded, using the SPSS system of statistical programs, modified for use on the IBM 370 computer of the Stanford University Forsythe Computer Center. For purposes of this analysis, the Breakdown and Frequencies procedures were used. Groups were formed consisting of

(1) Entirely normal deliveries,
(2) Minor complications,
(3) Uterine dysfunction, and
(4) Caesarean section.

The variables of interest were broken down across these four groups.

The first 270 women to come through the clinic during the time of this program are included here in the analysis.

VARIABLE NAMES AND DEFINITIONS: DEFENSE SYSTEMS

Denial was rated as present (1) or absent (0) if used as a predominant coping style in the face of stress. *Somatization* was rated as present or absent, similarly. For example, under stress, does the woman tend to experience physical symptoms accepted by most doctors as 'genuine' (demonstrable tissue pathology). *Style of control* was defined as an intellectual adaptation process in the face of stress, new experience, or crisis and was rated as largely emotional (1), not excessively emotional or logical (2), or entirely logical and analytic (3). *Repression* was rated as present or absent if the patient repressed feelings as a response to stress, crisis, or as a habitual way of interacting. We differentiated repression from denial in considering denial as a more intellectual process of experiencing a feeling and then convincing one's self through internal dialog or social interaction that the feeling was not valid or did not pertain. Repression was defined as not recognizing that feeling in the first place.

Projection was rated as present or absent if the woman tended to project feelings onto others in her environment. This would be a predominant coping strategy in the face of stress or crisis. *Intellectualization* was defined as a pattern of over-analyzing information in the face of stress. It differed from denial in that the emotion was not being denied, argued against, or pushed down out of the reaches of consciousness (as in repression). Nevertheless, the process of coping was one in which feelings were represented more analytically as thoughts and problems to be solved on that level. *Reaction formation* was defined as a pattern of responding to stress or crisis by behaving in counter-intuitive manners (naively speaking). For example, a woman terrified of birth might train to become a midwife. A woman scared of snakes might express a desire to study herpetology. *Isolation* was defined as a pattern of behavior in response to stress in which the woman withdraws from social contact. *Acting out* was defined as behaving in response to stress. Under stress, the acting out person might have an affair to 'get back' at a marital partner rather than engaging in a direct confrontation.

Diagnoses were assigned by Standard DSM-II* procedures, following the categories previously used by Shereshefsky and Yarrow (1973).

Anxiety referred to expressed anxiety, either behaviorally or verbally. The above variables were rated on a five point scale with a woman rated as (1) if she predominantly exhibited the behavior associated with the variable, to (3) if her behavior was somewhere in between the extremes, to (5) if she rarely displayed the variable in her personality.

The mate was rated as to *reaction to pregnant woman* regarding the pregnancy from dejected (1) to enthusiastic (5) and on *reaction to baby-to-be* from dejected to enthusiastic.

Current stresses were noted as to worries about financial security, food and household management, illness or recent death in the extended family, illness of either the woman or her mate, problems with relatives, problems from a previous relationship of one of the members, problems with friends, job dissatisfaction for the woman, job dissatisfaction for the mate, religious differences and other stresses. A mean total stress score was derived consisting of a mean for each group of the number of these stresses marked.

RESULTS

Table 1 illustrates the breakdown of the sample by Birth Outcome scores. 62% of the deliveries required little or no medical technology interventions; this was not the case in the remaining 38%. Table 2 shows that infant status at birth was 'good' for 77% of the sample, 'fair' for 18%, and 'poor' or 'very poor' for only 3%. The relationships between predictor variables used and the Birth Outcome and Infant Apgar scores are indicated in Table 3. Of the 45 variables, 40 are significantly correlated, in the expected direction, with Birth Outcome Score. 39 of these correlations are significant at the 0.001 level of statistical significance, and one is significant at the 0.01 level. 26 of the 45 variables are significant correlates of Infant Apgar Score, with three variables significant at the 0.001 level, 14 at the 0.01 level, and nine significant at the 0.05 level.

Table 4 shows sample breakdown by Complication Group, including Normal Births and Minor Medical Intervention Births, which made up 63% of the sample, and Uterine Dysfunction and Caesarean Section Births, which made up 35% of the sample. Types of uterine dysfunctions and medical indications for Caesarean section in this sample are also broken down by sample percentages. Eight deliveries (five premature deliveries and three forceps deliveries), which were not analyzed due to the small size of these Complication Groups, are also noted. Table 5 shows the variation in infant status at birth for the different Complication Groups.

Tables 6–8 indicate the characteristics of the sample in terms of diagnosis and coping styles. Table 6 shows the percentages of subjects from the present sample placed by diagnostic categories. This is compared with results reported in Shereshefsky and Yarrow (1973) in their study of 60 'normal' pregnancies in a middle class sample. In the present study, 65% of the subjects were diagnosed as 'normal', in comparison with the Shereshefsky sample, where 78% of the subjects received a diagnosis of 'normal'. Differences are spread across diagnostic groups, with the largest difference being an increased incidence of 'character disorder' diagnoses in the present sample.

Table 1 Sample breakdown by birth outcome scores

Birth outcome score	Total number	Percentage of sample
(5) Normal delivery with no intervention	61	22
(4) Normal delivery with minimal intervention	81	30
(3) Delivery with intermediate medical technology intervention	27	10
(2) Delivery requiring major medical technology intervention	97	36
(1) Delivery requiring major medical technology interventions in life-threatening situations	4	2

Table 2 Sample breakdown by infant Apgar scores

Infant Apgar score	Total number	Percentage of sample
Status: good / Score: 9–10	208	77
Status: fair / Score: 7–8	50	18
Status: poor / Score: 5–6	5	2
Status: very poor / Score: 4 or less	2	1
Missing data	5	2

Table 7 shows diagnostic classification broken down by Complication Groups. Each group seemed to offer its unique aspects. The most frequently received diagnosis for the Normal Birth Group (Group N) was 'normal with a tendency toward neurotic' (46%), and 'normal' (15%). In the Minor Medical Intervention Group (Group M) the most frequently received diagnosis was 'normal with a tendency toward character disorder' (37%), and 'normal with a tendency toward neurotic' (22%). The most frequently

Table 3 Pearson correlation coefficients of MPRS variables with birth outcome and Apgar scores

MPRS scale		Pearson r outcome	Pearson r Apgar
1	Reaction to pregnancy	0.24‡	0.14†
2	Reaction to baby-to-be	0.24‡	0.14†
3	Congruence pregnancy-life	0.31‡	0.10*
4	Congruence pregnancy-plans	0.33‡	0.11*
5	Response – discussion of pain	0.58‡	0.21‡
6	Mate – discussion of pain	0.40‡	0.15†
7	Mate response – dependency	0.30‡	0.14†
8	Dependency of mate	0.25‡	0.00
9	Mate's empathy	0.16†	0.17†
10	Mate – fostering confidence	0.27‡	0.17†
11	Mate re. sharing woman	0.21‡	−0.02
12	Communication – couple	0.23‡	0.11*
13	Affection – couple	0.25‡	0.11*
14	Hostility – couple	0.22‡	0.07
15	Sexual adjustment – couple	0.27‡	0.07
16	Decision process – couple	0.24‡	0.04
17	Success homemaking – couple	0.44‡	0.21‡
18	Identity – couple	0.22‡	0.05
19	Mate–woman adaptation	0.29‡	0.09
20	Current stresses	0.02	0.06
21	Anxiety	0.44‡	0.12*
22	Repression	0.31‡	0.01
23	Impulsiveness	0.03	0.08
24	Hostility and explosiveness	0.29‡	0.00
25	Tenderness and affection	0.38‡	−0.02
26	Responsivity and nurturance	0.32‡	0.09
27	Passive–aggressiveness	0.04	0.04
28	Need to control	0.34‡	0.16†
29	Overall emotional adaptation	0.01	−0.06
30	Concern with appearance	0.19‡	0.11*
31	Ability to meet own needs	0.37‡	0.14†
32	Sense of humor	0.32‡	0.14†
33	Flexibility with change	0.42‡	0.11*
34	Overt dependency	0.07	0.06
35	Covert dependency wishes	0.43‡	0.12*
36	Ability to take help	0.54‡	0.16†
37	Ability to give help	0.40‡	0.04
38	Sense of success as woman	0.37‡	0.13†
39	Gratification in sexuality	0.35‡	0.05
40	Achievement of adult role	0.32‡	0.17†
41	Acceptance of own identity	0.41‡	0.14†
42	Superego	0.41‡	−0.08
43	Insight into self	0.36‡	0.21‡
44	Overall adaptive behavior	0.46‡	0.12*

* = 0.05 significance level; † = 0.01 significance level; ‡ = 0.001 significance level

Table 4 Sample breakdown by complication groups

Complication group		Total number	Percentage of sample
(1) Normal births		142	53
(2) Minor intervention births		27	10
(3) Uterine dysfunction births		62	23
(A)	Augmentation	(53)	(19)
(B)	Induction	(5)	(2)
(C)	Hemorrhage	(4)	(2)
(4) Caesarean section		31	12
(A)	Non-responsivity oxytocin	(21)	(7)
(B)	Fetal distress	(5)	(2)
(C)	Breech-abnormal	(2)	(1)
(D)	Breech indications oxytocin	(3)	(1)
* Premature births		5	1
* Forceps births		3	1

*Occurred in sample but not analyzed as separate groups due to infrequency of occurrence

Table 5 Infant condition by complication group

Infant condition (1 min Apgar scores)	Normals	Minor complications	Uterine dysfunction	Caesarean section
Very good (9–10)	89%	65%	85%	50%
Good (7–8)	11%	30%	13%	39%
Fair (5–6)	0	5%	3%	11%
Poor (4 or less)	0	0	0	0

received diagnosis for the Uterine Dysfunction Group (Group U) was 'normal with a tendency toward character disorder' (26%), and 'character disorder' (21%). In the Caesarean Section Group (Group C), the most frequent diagnosis was 'normal with a tendency toward neurotic' (26%), and 'borderline/narcissistic' (19%).

Comparing Table 6, which shows the frequencies of diagnostic categories occurring in the entire sample, and Table 7, which shows the diagnostic frequencies for the different Complication Groups, reveals many

Table 6 Breakdown by diagnostic categories: present sample and Shereshefsky (1973) sample

		% of cases present sample	% of cases Shereshefsky
(1)	Normal	12	18
(2)	Normal tends toward psycho-somatic	8	3
(3)	Normal, tends toward neurotic	26	39
(4)	Normal, tends toward character disorder	19	18
(5)	Psychosomatic	4	—
(6)	Neurotic	9	16
(7)	Character disorder	16	3
(8)	Borderline/narcissistic	4	3
(9)	Psychotic	1	0
(10)	Other	1	0

Table 7 Diagnostic classification within each complication group

Diagnosis	Normal ($n = 142$)	Minor intervention ($n = 27$)	Uterine dysfunction ($n = 62$)	Caesarean section ($n = 31$)
Normal	21 (15%)	1 (4%)	3 (5%)	1 (3%)
Normal (psychosomatic)	13 (9%)	3 (11%)	4 (7%)	2 (7%)
Normal (neurotic)	65 (46%)	6 (22%)	10 (16%)	8 (26%)
Normal (characterological)	19 (13%)	10 (37%)	16 (26%)	1 (3%)
Psychosomatic	3 (2%)	0	0	2 (7%)
Neurotic	5 (4%)	1 (4%)	7 (11%)	5 (16%)
Character disorder	11 (8%)	3 (11%)	13 (21%)	4 (13%)
Borderline/narcissistic	3 (2%)	0	7 (11%)	6 (19%)
Psychotic	0	1 (4%)	0	6 (3%)
Other or unspecified	2 (1%)	2 (7%)	2 (3%)	1 (3%)

differences. A diagnosis of 'normal' occurs less than half as often in Groups M, U and C as in the total sample. A diagnosis of 'normal with tendency toward neurotic' occurs nearly twice as often in Group N, as in the total sample. There were nearly twice as many 'normal with tendency toward character disorder' diagnoses in Group M, and 'psychosomatic' diagnoses in Group C, as in the total sample. Half as many subjects in Group N received a diagnosis of 'neurotic', 'character disorder', or 'borderline/narcissistic', as in the total sample. In comparison to the total sample, Group U received twice as many diagnoses of 'borderline/narcissistic', and Group C received three times as many. Finally, the only subjects to receive a diagnosis of 'psychotic' ($n = 2$) were in Groups M and C. In general, it may be said that subjects in the less severe Birth Complication Groups (including no complications at all) tended to receive more 'normal' diagnoses. In Group N, 83% of the subjects were diagnosed 'normal' (categories 1-4), compared to 74% in Group M, 54% in Group U, and 39% in Group C.

Table 8 contains diagnostic information regarding coping styles across Complication Groups. An 'obsessional' coping style was prominent across all Complication Groups. It was the most frequent coping style in all groups except Group M, where it was preceded by 'hysterical'. The second most frequent coping style across the other Complication Groups was 'affective' for Group N, 'hysterical' for Group U, and 'schizoid' for Group C. 'Somatization' occurred nearly three times as often for Group C, as for any other Complication Group. Notable findings were that higher frequencies of 'hysterical' ratings occurred in women who had deliveries requiring minor medical interventions, and higher frequencies of 'somatization' occurred in women who had Caesarean sections.

Table 8 Defense system by complication group

Defense system	Complication group			
	Normal (%)	Minor intervention (%)	Uterine dysfunction (%)	Caesarean section (%)
Obsessional	27	25	36	37
Hysterical	18	35	19	11
Affective	20	15	7	0
Acting out	18	10	18	11
Somatization	6	0	6	16
Schizoid	6	0	10	21
Unspecified	7	5	5	5

Table 9 Prominent defenses by complication group

Defense	Normal (%)	Minor intervention (%)	Uterine dysfunction (%)	Caesarean section (%)
Denial	45	40	48	63
Repression	44	40	50	79
Projection	24	60	45	42
Intellectualization	35	20	38	42
Reaction formation	11	15	10	16
Regression	31	25	33	32
Isolation	25	25	31	32
Acting out	26	35	43	21
Somatization	24	15	21	47

Table 9 shows a different breakdown of coping styles by Complication Groups. While Table 8 addresses 'major coping style' (and subjects therefore only received one rating), Table 9 details the occurrence of 'Prominent coping styles'. Subjects may have received more than one rating. Ratings on 'denial' and 'repressions' were relatively frequent across all groups, but the frequency was highest for Group C. After 'denial' and 'repression', the most frequently observed defense was 'intellectualization' for Group N,

Table 10 Anxiety rating by complication group

Anxiety		Normal (%)	Minor intervention (%)	Uterine dysfunction (%)	Caesarean section (%)
(1)	Intense disruptive anxiety	2	10	29	42
(2)	Marked anxiety	20	35	45	37
(3)	Moderate anxiety	48	40	19	16
(4)	Some anxiety	28	15	8	5
(5)	Little or no anxiety	2	0	0	0
Mean anxiety rating:		3.1	2.6	2.1	1.8

Lower anxiety ---------------- higher anxiety

'projection' for Group U, and 'somatization' for Group C. For Group M, 'denial' and 'repression' followed after 'projection' as the most frequent rating. In general, it appears that about half of the subjects, across Complication Groups, utilized denial and repression.

Tables 10–12 show a breakdown on 'anxiety', 'environmental stresses', and 'reaction to pregnancy', respectively. These variables have been selected for more detailed consideration because they have proved to be of importance in other studies of obstetric outcome.

Inspection of Table 10 shows that in the present sample only 2% of the subjects were rated as having 'little or no anxiety' – and all of these ($n = 6$) were in Group N. The most frequent anxiety rating for Group N and Group M was 'moderate anxiety'. The most frequent anxiety rating for subjects in Group U was 'marked anxiety'. Examination of mean anxiety rating across groups shows increase in the level of anxiety as such complications become increasingly serious.

Table 11 shows specific environmental stresses broken down by total sample and by Complication Group. The 'reaction to pregnancy' variable represents a global estimate of the subject's emotional attitude toward

Table 11 Specific environmental stresses by complication groups

Stresses	Total sample (%)	Normals (%)	Minor intervention (%)	Uterine dysfunction (%)	Caesarean section (%)
Anxiety about financial security	65	58	80	69	58
Food/nutrition management problems	50	38	60	50	58
Illness or death extended family	2	1	0	0	0
Illness of mate or woman	5	2	5	5	16
Problems with relatives	10	6	10	14	16
Problems with previous relationships	5	3	5	7	5
Problems with friends	5	1	5	10	11
Job dissatisfaction, woman	7	6	10	5	0
Job dissatisfaction, mate	8	6	5	7	5
Religious differences	2	2	5	2	0
Other stresses	65	61	55	71	74
Mean total stress score:	2.25	1.95	2.42	2.63	2.43

Table 12 Reaction toward pregnancy by complication group

Reactions to pregnancy	Total sample (%)	Normal (%)	Minor intervention (%)	Uterine dysfunction (%)	Caesarean section (%)
(1) Dejected	2	1	0	7	0
(2) Unresponsive	14	11	15	14	16
(3) Contented	41	29	45	52	60
(4) Very satisfied	23	37	15	16	10
(5) Enthusiastic	11	16	10	7	5
Mean rating: reaction to pregnancy	3.30	3.58	3.23	3.02	3.05

the pregnancy (Table 12). The most frequent rating for Group N was 'very satisfied', while for Groups M, U, and C the most frequent rating was 'contented'. Examination of group means shows that subjects in Group N were seen as having the most positive emotional response to the pregnancy, followed by subjects in Group M. The least positive attitudes toward the pregnancy were observed in Groups U and C.

DISCUSSION

The breakdown by birth outcome scores indicating that 38% of these medically low-risk women became high-risk during labor compares well with the oft quoted figures provided by the obstetrician Richard Aubrey that 30% of low-risk women become high-risk during labor. The general statistical correspondence of our diagnostic categories with those of Shereshefsky and Yarrow (1973) for middle-class, Washington, DC women having their first baby was also encouraging in indicating some similarities. The only major difference in our breakdown was a 16% diagnosis rate of character disorder compared to 3% in Washington, DC.

The significant correlation of so many of our prenatal ratings with birth outcome strengthens our developing belief that birth is a psychophysiological process and that the many correlated psychological and social environmental variables are highly interrelated and interactive. We suspected Apgar score was also highly interactive with the quality of obstetrical management.

Each group seemed to offer its unique aspects. The uterine dysfunction group was over-represented with women who received the diagnosis 'normal with tendency to character disorder' and 'character disorder', In separate research, uterine dysfunction has been found to be correlated with the woman's attitudes about the pain of labor and her plans for coping with that pain (Mehl and Peterson, 1981; Peterson, 1981). The essence of 'character disordered' coping styles is the active avoidance of pain and pain-provoking situations. The uterine dysfunction group also utilized obsession as a major defensive style (as did the Caesarean section group) somewhat more so than the normal or minor intervention groups. The uterine dysfunction group tended to utilize projection more than the normal group (as did the minor intervention and Caesarean group) and to use acting out somewhat more. The uterine dysfunction group was rated as a group as experiencing marked anxiety (2.1) as compared to the normal group (moderate anxiety, 3.1) on a 5-point scale. Their total mean stress score was actually the highest of the four groups, as was their mean rating of their mates' reaction to the pregnancy (3.02; contented) but similar to the Caesarean group (3.05).

The two major diagnoses of the Caesarean group were 'normal with a tendency towards psychoneurotic disorders' and 'borderline/narcissistic' disorders. The Caesarean group had the highest incidence of 'abnormal' diagnoses (61%), with the next highest being the uterine dysfunction group (44%). The normal group was 17% and the minor intervention group 23%. The 'neurotic' diagnosis was also over-represented in the Caesarean group. The major defense systems of the Caesarean group were obsessional (37%) and schizoidal, 21% and over-represented in the Caesarean group. The somatization defense as a major defense was also over-represented in the Caesarean group. The prominent defenses over-represented in the Caesarean group were denial (63%), repression (79%), projection (42%), and somatization (47%). The Caesarean group had the highest anxiety rating (1.8; marked anxiety). Specific stresses over-represented in the Caesarean group included 'food/nutrition management problems' (58%), 'illness of mate or women' (16%), 'problems with relatives' (16%), and 'problems with friends' (11%). The husbands of the women having Caesareans tended toward a less than enthusiastic reaction to pregnancy.

The normal group had the highest percentages of the 'normal' diagnosis (15%), and the 'normal with tendency toward psychoneurotic disorders' (46%). The one over-represented major defense system compared to other groups was affective (20%). The highest were obsessional and affective. No particular prominent defense was over-represented. The two major ones were denial (45%) and repression (44%). The anxiety rating was lowest (3.1, moderate anxiety) and the mean total life stress rating was lowest (1.95) with no particular life stress over-represented. The highest two were 'anxiety about financial security' (45%) and 'other stresses' (65%). The mates' reactions to the pregnancy were highest (3.58, tending toward 'very satisfied').

The minor intervention group differed from the normal group in having less 'normal' diagnoses (4% vs. 15%), and less 'normal with tendency toward psychoneurosis' diagnoses (22% vs. 46%). The minor intervention group had more 'normal with tendency toward character disorder' diagnoses (37% vs. 13%). The hysterical major defense system was more common in the minor intervention group (35% vs. 18%). Projection was a much more common prominent defense (60% vs. 24%) and intellectualization was less common (20% vs. 35%). Anxiety was rated as higher (2.6 vs. 3.1, inverse scale) and life stresses were higher (2.42 vs. 1.95) while husband's reaction to pregnancy was lower (3.23 vs. 3.58).

SUMMARY

Overall, the normal group tended toward more normal diagnoses. The tendency toward neurosis would indicate the ability to feel pain vs. character disorders, for example, one who feels no pain where others would. The obsessional defense was high for all groups (probably representative of Berkeley intellectuals), but 'normals' were also more affective, again a defense characterized by recognizing and utilizing feelings and emotions. They experienced less anxiety and life stress and their husbands were more enthusiastic about the pregnancy (and probably provided more support and encouragement).

The transition toward minor intervention seemed to involve a movement toward not feeling pain (character disorder) and toward higher anxiety, more stress, and less enthusiastic husbands.

The uterine dysfunction group tended even more toward behavioral styles involving not feeling pain (more actual character disorder diagnoses). These women were also more obsessional, projected more (implying movement toward an external locus of control) and acted out more (behaving as opposed to feeling pain). Anxiety and stress were also higher and life stress lower.

The Caesarean group was moving toward even more severe emotional disturbance with schizoidal defenses (divorcing feeling from thought and therefore possibly attempting to avoid the pain of labor). Somatization (working stress out in the body) was more pronounced, along with an external locus of control, and denial and repression of emotion. Stress increased with anxiety and negatively with the husband's reaction to pregnancy. Illness was more common in the family.

The psychology of complications is probably mathematically complex.

Some of the relevant variables may include:
(1) Ability or willingness to experience pain,
(2) Locus of control,
(3) Anxiety,
(4) Life stress,
(5) Support system,
(6) Expressivity vs. repression of emotion, and
(7) Somatization.

Psychosocial risk factors, indeed, can be useful predictors of complication and birth and can serve to increase prediction and therefore prevention.

Part 3: Psychoneuroendocrinology

38

Significance of hormone-dependent brain development and pre- and early postnatal psychophysiology for preventive medicine

G. Dörner

ABSTRACT

During pre- and/or early postnatal life, systemic hormones and neurotransmitters are capable of acting as organizers of the brain, which is the controller of the neuro-endocrine-immune system. Thus, the quantity of systemic hormones and neurotransmitters determines, during a critical period of brain development, the quality, i.e. the responsiveness, of their own central nervous controllers and hence the functional and tolerance ranges of their own feedback control systems throughout life (determination rule). Abnormal levels of systemic hormones and neurotransmitters, which can be induced by abnormal conditions in the psychosocial and/or natural environment, can act as teratogens and lead to permanent physiological and/or psychological dysfunctions in later life. Thus, many malfunctions of reproduction, metabolism, information processing and immunity called up to now idiopathic, essential, cryptogenic, primary or genuine can be explained by pre- and/or early postnatal psycho- and/or physiological processes. Therefore, 'structural teratology' (teratomorphology) was supplemented by 'functional teratology' (teratopsychophysiology). Psychophysiological dysfunctions based on abnormal brain differentiation can be widely prevented either by optimizing the psychosocial and/or natural environment or by the well-timed correcting of abnormal concentrations of systemic hormones and/or neurotransmitters. Thus, new possibilities have been opened for preventive medicine, and a world-wide established immune prophylaxis should be supplemented now by a corresponding neuroendocrine or psychoneuroendocrine prophylaxis.

Hormones may be defined as intercellularly active chemical messengers that are produced in specialized cells and exert biological effects on other cells of the same organism by acting locally (as local hormones) or on distant target cells (as systemic hormones). They affect, reversibly in adulthood or more or less irreversibly during critical developmental periods, cell activities, especially gene expression and/or enzyme activities, by intracellular messengers such as cyclic AMP or GMP. Hormones can be classified according to their chemical structure, site of production, site of action, biological action and mechanism of action.

In view of this definition, neurotransmitters may be regarded as local hormones of the brain, and a strict differentiation between neurotransmitters, releasing hormones and systemic neurohormones no longer appears to be justified.

Fundamental processes of life, such as reproduction, metabolism and information processing, are controlled by neuroendocrine feedback systems. The functional and tolerance ranges of these systems are predetermined by the genetic material. However, this phylogenetic predetermination of neuroendocrine systems is established ontogenetically by hormones, e.g. the expressibility of the genetic material in central nervous neurons throughout life is determined by hormones during critical periods of brain development.

Sexual differentiation of the brain can be regarded as a classical model for hormone-dependent organization processes.

In sexual differentiation of the human, five steps may be distinguished (Dörner et al., 1985a):

(1) The genetic or gonosomal sex is determined by the presence of an X- or Y-chromosome in the fertilizing sperm cell.

(2) The gonadal sex is then differentiated under the control of sex-determining genes.

(3) The somatic or genital sex is organized under the control of the Müllerian inhibiting substance (MIS) and of androgens.

   (a) During the 2nd and 3rd prenatal month the internal genitalia are organized by MIS and testosterone (T).

   (b) During the 3rd and 4th prenatal month the external genitalia are organized by 5α-dihydrotestosterone (DHT). Therefore, clear-cut dissociations between hormone-dependent malorganizations of the internal and external genitalia are possible and also known.

(4) The neuronal sex, i.e. female-type or male-type gonadotrophin secretion, sexual orientation and gender role behavior are organized by sex hormones and mediated, at least in part, by neurotransmitters. The critical periods for sex-specific differentiation of the corresponding sex, mating and gender role centers in the brain are not completely identical but overlapping. Moreover, different sex hormones appear to be responsible – at least in part – for the organization of sex-specific gonadotrophin secretion, sexual orientation and gender role behavior.

  (a) The 'sex centers' controlling female-type or male-type gonadotrophin secretion are organized only by estrogens, which are mainly converted, however, from androgens within the brain. Thus, male-type differentiation of gonadotrophin secretion is achieved by estrogens or by androgens which are convertible to estrogens, but not by non-convertible androgens.

  (b) The 'mating centers' controlling sexual orientation are organized by estrogens and androgens as well. Thus male-type differentiation of sexual orientation is achieved by synergistic effects of estrogens and androgens which are convertible or non-convertible to estrogens.

  (c) Finally, the 'gender role centers' controlling female-type or male-type gender role behavior are organized only by androgens.

Thus, not only the absolute levels of sex hormones, but also the ratios of androgens to estrogens are responsible for a specific sexual differentiation of the brain. Therefore, several combinations and dissociations between sex hormone-dependent deviations of gonadotrophin secretion, sexual orientation and gender role behavior are possible.

(5) In a final step, sexual differentiation in the human is completed by the establishment of gender identity, i.e. by a consciously experienced self-concept of being male or female. This self-concept is dependent on the sex hormone-controlled differentiation of the somatic and psychic sex in prenatal life and on psychosocial influences in postnatal life. All these differentiation and activation processes in the brain appear to be mediated, at least in part, by neurotransmitters and neuromodulators.

Crucial experiments on sex-specific brain differentiation were done by

C. A. Pfeiffer (1936) and Vera Dantchakoff (1938). Pfeiffer was the first to discover that, independent of the genetic sex, the presence of testes during a critical perinatal period in rats resulted in acyclic gonadotrophin secretion in adulthood, whereas the absence of testes during this critical period resulted in cyclic gonadotrophin secretion in adult life. Barraclough and Gorski (1961) then demonstrated that testosterone is the mediator of the testes for sex-specific differentiation of the brain. High androgen levels during brain differentiation gave rise to a more tonic gonadotrophin secretion in postpubertal life, whereas low androgen levels during this period gave rise to a cyclic gonadotrophin secretion in adulthood.

Regarding sexual behavior, Vera Dantchakoff (1938) reported that prenatally androgenized female guinea pigs showed significantly increased male sexual behavior in adulthood. This finding was then confirmed and supplemented by Phoenix and associates (1959), who distinguished between a sex hormone-dependent prenatal (or perinatal) organization period and a postpubertal activation period of the brain.

During the past two decades among many experimental findings the following data were obtained in our laboratories.

In male rats an experimental model for male homosexuality could be produced by castration on the first day of life and androgen substitution in adulthood (Dörner, 1967; Dörner and Hinz, 1967). Such males displayed significantly more frequently sexual responsiveness towards male partners than towards female partners. Due to androgen deficiency during the early postnatal period the female mating center in the hypothalamus is fully organized. Therefore, in the presence of normal androgen levels in adulthood predominantly female-type, i.e. homosexual behavior, is activated in these genetic males.

On the other hand, a neuroendocrine conditioned predisposition for female homosexuality could be induced in female rats by exposure to an excess of androgens or estrogens during the early postnatal differentiation period of the brain (Dörner, 1968; Dörner and Fatschel, 1970; Dörner and Seidler, 1971; Dörner, Döcke and Hinz, 1971). In further animal experiments, male homosexuality could be prevented by administrations of androgens (Dörner and Hinz, 1968) and female homosexuality by administration of antiandrogens during the critical differentiation phase of the brain (Dörner, 1968; Dörner and Fatschel, 1970).

Stereotaxic lesions or sex hormone implantations in different brain regions led to the discovery of a 'male mating center' localized in the preoptic hypothalamic area and a 'female mating center' localized in the hypothalamic ventromedial nucleus region of rats (Dörner, Döcke and Hinz, 1968, 1969; Dörner, Döcke and Moustafa, 1968a, 1968b).

Furthermore, a sexual dimorphism of the brain, which is dependent on the testosterone level in perinatal life, was also first found in rats. The nuclear volumes of the nerve cells in discrete brain regions, i.e. in the hypothalamic ventromedial nucleus, were significantly enlarged in female rats as compared to male rats. Such sex-specific brain structures could be inverted by perinatal androgen administration in females or neonatal castration in males (Dörner and Staudt, 1968, 1969). A sexual dimorphism of the brain was meanwhile confirmed for several species, including human beings (Bubenik and Brown, 1973; De Lacoste-Utamsing and Holloway, 1982; Swaab and Fliers, 1985).

When rats of both sexes were exposed to very high androgen or estrogen doses during the hypothalamic differentiation phase, they exhibited a hypogonadotrophic hypogonadism during the postpubertal activation phase (Dörner and Hinz, 1971; Dörner, Hinz and Stahl, 1972; Hinz and Dörner, 1974). These experimental results were then arranged into an etiogenetic system for sex hormone-dependent deviations or developmental disturbances (Dörner, 1969, 1970).

Permanent alterations of gonadal functions and/or sexual behavior produced by neuroendocrine changes during brain organization in animals could be equivalent to well-known syndromes in human beings (Dörner, 1972, 1976a). Thus, primary hypo-, bi- or homosexuality produced by androgen deficiency in males or androgen excess in females during sex-specific brain differentiation might correspond etiogenetically to primary (inborn) hypo-, bi- or homosexuality in human beings. As analogous syndromes of acyclic or oligocyclic females with polycystic ovaries, the Stein Leventhal syndrome and polycystic ovaries in congenital adrenal hyperplasia can be considered. Finally, as etiopathogenic equivalents of the experimentally induced hypogonadotrophic hypogonadism the idiopathic eunuchoidism in men and the idiopathic hypothalamic insufficiency in women may be regarded.

This postulate is supported by the following findings. In homosexual men, a positive estrogen feedback effect on LH secretion could be evoked, which can be considered as a criterion for a predominantly female-differentiated brain (Dörner et al., 1972, 1975). These data were strongly confirmed by Gladue, Green and Hellman (1984).

In untreated women with adrenogenital hyperplasia, who have been exposed to an increased adrenal androgen level during the prenatal differentiation phase, partial masculinization of gonadrotrophin secretion, sexual orientation and/or gender role behavior was described (Hinman, 1951; Trampuž, 1968; Ehrhardt, Evers and Money, 1968; Money and Schwartz, 1977).

Stillman (1982) reported on partial masculinization of gonadotrophin secretion and Meyer-Bahlburg and Ehrhardt (1983) on homosexual tendencies in the female offspring of mothers who were exposed to high estrogen doses (diethylstilbestrol) during pregnancy. In the male offspring of mothers, who had been treated with high estrogen doses during pregnancy, a partial demasculinization of gender role behavior was observed (Yalom, Green and Fish, 1973; Reinisch, 1977), which can be explained by prenatal androgen deficiency produced by estrogen administration.

According to a Kinsey Institute Report (Bell and Weinberg, 1978; Bell, Weinberg and Hammersmith, 1980), postnatal psychosocial conditions were investigated and evaluated by psychologists and sociologists in about 1000 homosexual as compared to about 500 heterosexual men and women. In this study, no significant psychosocial differences in postnatal life could be found between the homosexual and heterosexual groups which could explain the etiogenesis of homosexuality. It was concluded that increasing and convincing research material appears to provide evidence now for a biological basis of homosexuality.

We postulated for many years (Dörner, 1972, 1980b), that discrepancies between the genetic sex and a sex-specific sex hormone level occurring during brain differentiation can be regarded as causes for the development of sexual deviations. This postulate is in good accordance with findings obtained in patients with testis dysgenesis, testicular feminization and Imperato-McGinley's syndrome.

In testis dysgenesis, female-like regulation of gonadotrophin secretion (positive estrogen feedback) as well as female-like sexual and gender role behavior were observed (Van Look et al., 1977). In testicular feminization, female-like sexual and gender role behavior were described due to an insensitivity of androgen receptors (Money, Ehrhardt and Masica, 1968; Van Look et al., 1977; Aono et al., 1978).

Finally, Imperato-McGinley et al. (1979) described male pseudohermaphrodites born with ambiguity of the external genitalia. Biochemical evaluation revealed normal testosterone levels, but a marked decrease in plasma dihydrotestosterone levels due to 5α-reductase deficiency. The decrease of dihydrotestosterone *in utero* resulted in incomplete masculinization of the external genitalia. Thus, the affected males were born with more female-like external genitalia, and were therefore considered and raised as girls. Psychosexual orientation, however, was unequivocally male. They considered themselves as males and had a libido directed towards females. Despite being reared as females, almost all of them even changed gender identity at the time of puberty. Hence, testosterone exposure *in utero* appears to be most important for the development of a male sex drive, male sexual orientation and even male gender identity.

In view of our experimental findings on sexual brain differentiation two ontogenetic organization rules for neuroendocrine systems were deduced (Dörner, 1973a);

(1) During a critical period of brain differentiation, an open-loop regulatory system (e.g. placenta–fetal gonad–fetal brain) is converted into a feedback control system (e.g. the central nervous–hypophysial–gonadal system).

(2) During brain differentiation, the quantity of the regulating variable (e.g. sex hormone) codetermines the quality, i.e. the responsiveness of the central nervous controller and hence the functional and tolerance ranges of the neuroendocrine feedback control system throughout life (e.g. cyclic or acyclic gonadotrophin secretion; hypo-, bi- or homosexual behavior).

Permanent changes of sexual behavior could not only be observed in animal experiments after perinatal alterations of the sex hormone levels, but also after perinatal administration of psychotrophic drugs which are able to affect the neurotransmitter metabolism (Dörner, Hecht and Hinz, 1976; Dörner et al., 1977a; Dörner and Hinz, 1978; Hinz, Döcke and Dörner, 1978). In view of these data, systemic hormones as well as neurotransmitters were regarded as organizers of the brain (Dörner, 1974, 1980b, 1982a).

Prenatal psychosocial influences, which are able to affect the levels of systemic hormones and/or neurotransmitters, should also be regarded as possible etiogenetic factors in the development of sexual deviations. Thus, Ingeborg Ward (1972) reported that prenatal stress in male rats demasculinized and feminized sexual behavior potentials in adult life. Since similar findings were obtained in male rats castrated on the day of birth, we have measured the plasma testosterone levels in such prenatally stressed males, i.e. in male fetuses and newborns following maternal stress between day 14 and 21 of gestation. The testosterone level was found to be significantly decreased, in fact, in these prenatally stressed males during the early postnatal life as compared to non-stressed control males (Stahl et al., 1978).

More recently, we have observed bi- or even homosexual behavior in prenatally stressed male rats after castration plus estrogen treatment in adulthood, whereas prenatally non-stressed but later equally treated males displayed heterosexual behavior (Götz and Dörner, 1980). Hence, prenatal stress can predispose to the development of bi- or even homosexual behavior in males.

In view of these data, a retrospective study was carried out to answer the question whether stressful maternal life events occurring during pregnancy may have irreversibly affected sexual differentiation of the brain in men who were born in Germany during the stressful period of World War II. Out of about 800 homosexual males highly significantly more homosexuals were born during the stressful war and early post-war period than in the years before or after this stressful period (Dörner et al., 1978, 1980). This finding suggested that stressful maternal life events, if occurring during pregnancy, may represent, in fact, an etiogenetic risk factor for the development of sexual variations in the male offspring.

In addition, 100 bi- or homosexual men as well as 100 heterosexual men of similar age were asked about maternal stressful events that might have occurred during their prenatal life. Indeed, a highly significantly increased incidence of prenatal stress was found in bisexual and, in particular, in homosexual men as compared to heterosexual men (Dörner et al., 1983). About one-third of the homosexual men reported to have been exposed to severe maternal stress – such as bereavement, reputation by the partner, rape or severe anxiety – and about an additional one third to moderate maternal stress during their prenatal life. On the other hand, none of the heterosexual men was found to have been exposed to severe and less than 10% to moderate maternal stress during their prenatal life. These data also indicate that prenatal stress may represent a risk factor for the etiogenesis of sexual variations in later life.

In the future, such retrospective studies should be supplemented by prospective studies.

In further experimental and clinical studies we have found that pre- and early postnatal overnutrition represent an important risk factor for the development of obesity, diabetes mellitus, hyperlipoproteinemia and atherosclerosis (Dörner, 1973b, 1978a, 1982b; Dörner et al., 1973; Dörner, Haller and Leonhardt, 1973; Dörner, Mohnike and Steindel, 1975; Dörner, Hagen and Witthuhn, 1976; Dörner, Grychtolik and Julitz, 1977; Dörner and Mohnike, 1973, 1976, 1977; Dörner, Mohnike and Thoelke, 1984). It was postulated that changes of the insulin level and/or glucose utilization during a critical differentiation period of the brain can alter irreversibly the functional and tolerance ranges of hypothalamic control centers for glucose metabolism.

As early as 1964, Denenberg found in animal experiments that specific early postnatal arousals of the central nervous system, e.g. handling or exposure to electric shocks, could affect the reactivity throughout life. Permanent mental and/or psychic disturbances, which are associated with permanent neurochemical changes of the brain, could be produced by maternal deprivation of newborn rats (Dörner et al., 1981, 1984a; Dörner, Bluth and Tönjes, 1982). Significantly decreased mental and psychic achievements in school were also observed in children who were not reared by their mothers during the first years of life (Dörner and Grychtolik,

1973). Finally, permanent alterations of emotionality, learning capability and memory capacity were found after early postnatal qualitative and/or quantitative malnutrition (Franková, 1970; Ryan, 1977; Hinz et al., 1983; Dörner and Grychtolik, 1978; Rodgers, 1978).

On the other hand, early postnatal administration of neurodrugs, which affect neurotransmitter concentrations in the brain, resulted in permanent alterations not only of sexual behavior but also of emotionality, exploratory activity, learning behavior and memory capacity (Dörner, Döcke and Hinz, 1968; Dörner, 1976b; Dörner, Hecht and Hinz, 1976; Dörner et al., 1977; Dörner and Hinz, 1978; Hinz, Döcke and Dörner, 1978; Hecht et al., 1978). Furthermore, permanent morphological and biochemical changes could be observed in distinct brain regions of these animals (Dörner et al., 1977b, 1984a; Staudt, Stüber and Dörner, 1978a, 1978b).

All these experimental and clinical findings suggest that neurotransmitters represent mediators of systemic hormones, metabolic factors and environmental signals for the differentiation and maturation of the brain. Hence, it is conceivable that abnormal concentrations of neurotransmitters during brain development can lead to permanent malfunctions in the neuro-endocrine-immune system (Dörner, 1978b, 1980b).

According to this concept, many developmental disorders or diseases of reproduction, metabolism, information processing and immune responses called idiopathic, essential, cryptogenic, primary or genuine thus far can be based upon such teratogenetic defects and prevented, at least in part, by improving the external and/or internal environment during critical developmental periods of the neuro-endocrine-immune system. Therefore, it was proposed to supplement teratomorphology, i.e. the science of teratogenic malformations, by teratophysiology, teratopsychology and teratoimmunology, i.e. the science of teratogenic malfunctions. In other words, 'structural teratology' should be completed by 'functional teratology' (Dörner, 1975a, 1975b).

Several experimental and clinical data were already obtained which demonstrate the possibility of correcting abnormal levels of systemic hormones and/or neurotransmitters during brain differentiation and preventing permanent malfunctions of reproduction, metabolism and information processing.

Thus, male homosexuality produced by neonatal orchidectomy or prenatal stress in rats could be completely prevented by perinatal administration of androgen (Dörner and Hinz, 1968; Dörner, Götz and Döcke, 1983). Prenatal administration of the norepinephrine precursor tyrosin was able to prevent permanent changes of gonadotrophin secretion, gender role behavior and sexual orientation in prenatally stressed rats (Ohkawa et al., 1986).

A significant decrease of acetylcholine induced in newborn rats by maternal deprivation, which gave rise to a significantly diminished learning capacity in later life, could be compensated, at least in part, by neonatal administration of the acetylcholinesterase inhibitor pyridostigmine (Dörner et al., 1981, 1982).

A delay of puberty produced by neonatal deprivation in female rats could be prevented by postnatal injections of the monoamine oxidase inhibitor pargylin (Tönjes et al., 1984).

In the human, a virilization of female fetuses with congenital adrenal hyperplasia could be prevented by prenatal administration of cortisol (Forest and David, 1984). Most of all, in patients with malignant phenylketonuria severe mental defects could be prevented, at least in part, by postnatal administration of neurotransmitter precursors, such as L-Dopa for dopamin and 5α-hydroxytryptophan for serotonin (Bartholomé, 1980). Thus, our thesis established by animal experiments that neurotransmitters may be regarded as organizers of the brain (Dörner, 1975a, 1976b) was strongly supported by clinical findings.

In view of experimental and clinical data, we have predicted for many years that a genuine prophylaxis may become possible for diabetes mellitus by preventing hyperglycemia in pregnant women and hence hyperinsulinemia in fetuses and newborns.

Therefore, a systematic diagnostic screening for gestational diabetics and prevention of hyperglycemia in pregnant women and hence of hyperinsulinemia in fetuses and newborns was carried out in Berlin/GDR since 1973 (Dörner et al., 1985).

Meanwhile, our prediction about the possibility of prenatal diabetes prophylaxis appears to have been realized (Dörner et al., 1984, 1985; Dörner, 1986):

(1) The prevalence of diabetes mellitus in children, who were born in Berlin/GDR since 1973, was found to be significantly decreased (less than one third) as compared to those born between 1962 and 1972. In contrast, a continuous significant increase of childhood-onset diabetes was found in other districts in the GDR.

(2) Between 1979 and 1983, significantly more gestational diabetics were then diagnosed and treated not only in Berlin but also in Halle and Leipzig than in the other districts of the GDR. Interestingly enough, a highly significantly decreased prevalence of diabetic children (less than one third), who were born during this period, was also found in Berlin, Halle and Leipzig than in the other districts.

(3) Even a highly significant inverse correlation could be demonstrated

for the 15 districts of the GDR between the incidence rates of prophylacticly diagnosed, diet-treated and delivered pregnant diabetics – mostly gestational diabetics – and the prevalence rates of diabetic children who were born during this period.

(4) In addition, a highly significantly decreased prevalence rate (less than one third) was found for infantile- or juvenile-onset diabetics, who were born in a low-caloric war and post-war period (1941–1948), as compared to those of similar age, who were born in a high-caloric peace period (1949–1956).

During the past decades a world-wide dramatic increase in the prevalence of insulin-dependent diabetes mellitus (IDDM), particularly of infantile- and juvenile-onset diabetes, was found in the industrialized countries.

In view of our findings, an interruption and even a reversal of this dramatic increase of IDDM appears to be possible by preventing hyperglycemia in pregnant women and hence hyperinsulinemia in fetuses and newborns.

In conclusion, during the pre- and/or early postnatal life, systemic hormones and neurotransmitters are capable of acting as organizers of the brain, which is the controller of the neuro-endocrine-immune system. Thus, the quantity of systemic hormones and neurotransmitters codetermines during a critical period of brain development the quality, i.e. the responsiveness, of their own central nervous controllers and hence the functional and tolerance ranges of their own feedback control systems throughout life (determination rule). Abnormal levels of systemic hormones and neurotransmitters, which can be induced by abnormal conditions in the psychosocial and/or natural environment, can act as teratogens and lead to permanent physiological and/or psychological dysfunctions in later life. Thus, many malfunctions of reproduction, metabolism, information processing and immunity called up to now idiopathic, essential, cryptogenic, primary or genuine can be explained by pre- and/or early postnatal psycho- and/or physiological processes. Therefore, 'structural teratology' (teratomorphology) was supplemented by 'functional teratology' (teratopsychophysiology). Psychophysiological dysfunctions based on abnormal brain differentiation can be widely prevented either by optimizing the psychosocial and/or natural environment or by the well-timed correcting of abnormal concentrations of systemic hormones and/or neurotransmitters.

In my opinion, millions of human beings are mentally, emotionally or physically handicapped or even disabled and/or die prematurely by developmental deviations, disorders or diseases that could be prevented by a neuroendocrine prophylaxis. Thus, a general immune prophylaxis, which is planned by WHO up to 1990, is to be completed by a corresponding neuroendocrine prophylaxis. In this context, ten recommendations may be given for prevention or correction of abnormal levels of systemic hormones and/or neurotransmitters during brain development, i.e. by prevention or correction of the following abnormal conditions in pre- and/or early postnatal life:

(1) Iodine deficiency,
(2) Hyperinsulinism, mostly induced by gestational diabetes,
(3) Hypoxia,
(4) Stress,
(5) Placental insufficiency and other gestational disorders,
(6) Quantitative and/or qualitative malnutrition,
(7) Radiation and pollution with environmental chemicals,
(8) Misuse of drugs, hormones, alcohol and nicotine,
(9) Psychosocial deprivation, and
(10) Abnormal levels of systemic hormones and/or neurotransmitters induced by genetic defects (congenital hypothyroidism, congenital adrenal hyperplasia, phenylketonuria and other inborn errors of metabolism).

39

Neurobiochemistry of immersion in warm water during labor: the secretion of endorphins, cortisol and prolactin

M. Boulvain and S. Wesel

INTRODUCTION AND HISTORICAL DATA

Following the experience of M. Odent (Pithiviers, France), the use of immersion in a warm bath during the first stage of labor was introduced 6 years ago in our maternity ward.

Beyond the obvious benefits provided by this practise in the field of psychological as well as physical comfort, on the one hand, and of pleasure, on the other hand, we showed in 1982, at the 8th European Congress of Perinatal Medicine in Brussels its advantage as an antalgic, antispastic and accelerating agent in labor.

In a large number of cases, the warm bath allows the avoidance of the use of more classical, but more invasive pharmacological or anesthetic techniques (Abboud et al., 1984; Troisfontaines-de-Marneffe, 1984).

At last, at the 2nd Congress of the North American Society of Pre- and Perinatal Psychology (San Diego, USA) in 1985, we presented the results of a study about the experience of delivery in women who had been given a bath during dilatation. The conclusion of that work demonstrated that the bath provides more improvement on the delivery experience of 'pathological' women (first of all primiparas). Through its reassuring, relaxing and antalgic effects, it enables 'pathological' women to find their delivery a gratifying experience, and avoids them being overwhelmed by anxiety.

The bath can allow women to control pain, to look for protection in close relatives (like the husband, the mother, friends), and, finally, to regress enough to be in close accordance with their baby.

As naturalists, it seemed to us interesting to undertake research about the biological mechanisms at stake during immersion at the cerebral level.

BIOLOGICAL DATA

A large number of neurotransmitters are present at a very low concentration in the central nervous system. These substances have various important biological effects.

Our interest is mostly focused on peptides synthetized by the hypothalamo-pituitary system: nevertheless, their effects are ubiquitous and their distribution not restricted to this area. They are mostly derived from pro-opio-melanocortin via enzymatic fragmentation (endo- and exopeptidases) according to the pattern shown in Figure 1.

These neuropeptides act on synaptic receptors (Krieger and Martin, 1981) by modulating neurotransmission by means of the cellular ion-permeability and the AMPC system (inactivating adenyl-cyclase and thus decreasing the AMPC level). The half-life time of these substances is remarkably short (from 10 minutes for ACTH to 30 minutes for β-endorphin). Two kinds of receptors have been characterized: μ-receptors (mostly implied in analgesia) and δ-receptors (principally connected with behavior). β-endorphin acts on both types of receptors (Hoffman et al., 1984; Olson et al., 1985; Pancheri et al., 1985), as enkephalins and dynorphin act mostly on δ-receptors and morphine on μ-receptors. Other hormones are involved in the response to stress: cortisol and prolactin, for example.

Cortisol is a hormone secreted by the adrenocortical gland in response to an increase in ACTH plasma level. Thus cortisol acts as a marker of an ACTH rise in the central nervous system.

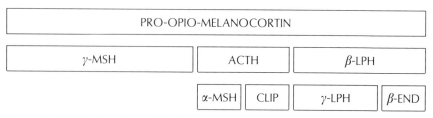

Figure 1 Derivation of peptides from pro-opio-melanocortin

Prolactin is secreted by the anterior lobe of hypophysis (Kimball, 1981). It acts on lactation, but also in connection with the dopaminergic system, modulating the response to stress. The plasma levels of all these hormones are high in late pregnancy and labor. But, in case of an extra stress, the secretion rate is high enough to create plasma levels significantly different from normal pregnancy situations.

MATERIAL AND METHODS

18 patients in active labor were included into the study, and randomly sorted in 'Bath' and 'No bath' groups. They had regular contractions, ruptured membranes and a cervical dilatation of at least 4 cm. They were provided with explanations about the study protocol and the usefulness of the experiment. They had to give their full consent after being properly informed.

An heparinized intravenous catheter was inserted in a forearm vein, and three blood samples taken at intervals of 30 minutes. In the 'Bath' group, bathing took place 15 minutes after the first blood sampling and ended 15 minutes after the second one, according to the pattern shown in Figure 2.

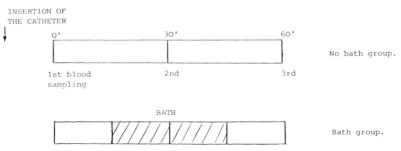

Figure 2 Experiment protocol

The blood samples were centrifuged at 2000 rpm and their plasmatic fraction preserved at a temperature of $-20°$. The analyses were performed by RIA in the Laboratory of Neuroendocrinology of Prof. Franchimont (Université de Liège, Belgium) and in the Laboratory of Isotopes of Dr Etienne (Hôpital de Braine l'Alleud, Belgium). The significance of results was estimated by statistical calculation.

11 patients were randomly selected for the 'Bath' group, and seven for the 'No bath' group. That unequal partition was due to the fact that randomization was done on 40 cases for the total, this study being of a preliminary nature.

RESULTS

One formerly elevated cortisol level has been noticed in one patient from the 'Bath' group. Two formerly elevated prolactin levels have been noticed in two patients, one from each group. One prolactin sampling was performed 30 minutes after an injection of metaclopramide for nausea, and thus was subject to iatrogenic elevation.

β-Endorphin plasma levels (Figures 3 and 4)

The mean values are slightly different in the two groups. The increase in levels during the period is not significant in the 'Bath' group and very significant in the 'No bath' group.

Standard deviations are large from one subject to another. But levels are relatively stable in the course of observation in one single subject.

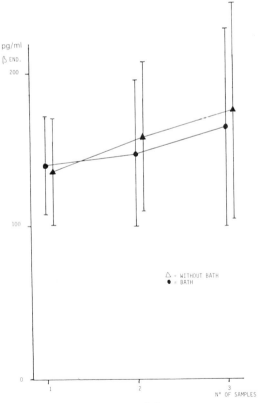

Figure 3 β-endorphin mean and standard deviation

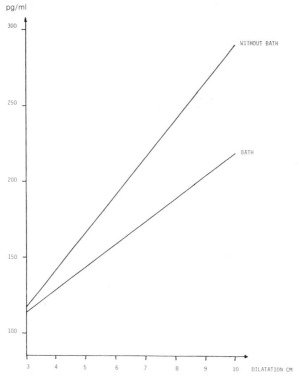

Figure 4 Linear regression of β-endorphin vs. dilatation

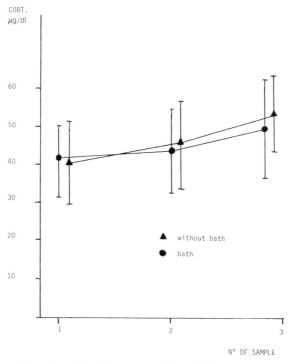

Figure 5 Cortisol mean and standard deviation

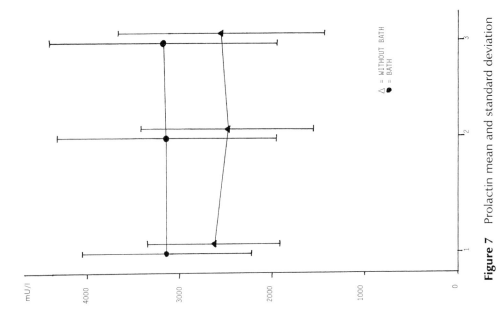

Figure 7 Prolactin mean and standard deviation

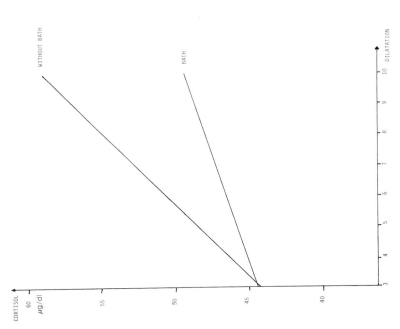

Figure 6 Linear regression of cortisol vs. dilatation

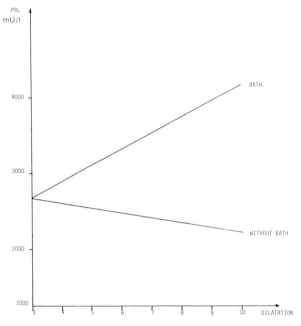

Figure 8 Linear regression of prolactin vs. dilatation

The calculated linear regression shows, better than mean values, a statistically significant difference between 'Bath' and 'No bath' groups.

The apparently slight difference in mean levels is enhanced by a faster dilatation rate.

The bath seems to lower the increase in endorphin plasma levels during labor.

Cortisol plasma levels (Figures 5 and 6)

The same phenomenon is observed for cortisol as for β-endorphin.

Prolactin plasma levels (Figures 7 and 8)

Mean values are more noticeable for prolactin than for other markers. Linear regression shows a statistically significant difference between the two groups, i.e. an increase of prolactin levels in the 'Bath' group, a decrease in the 'No bath' group.

CONCLUSION

The differences observed in the plasma levels of β-endorphin and cortisol are probably related with a decrease in stress during the bath. The increase of PRL levels in the bath could be interpreted as a favorable effect.

The number of our cases is not sufficient yet to reduce the standard deviations. Extra cases will be necessary for a more valuable statistical evaluation.

ACKNOWLEDGEMENTS

We are happy to thank Prof. Franchimont who generously welcomed us into his laboratory. Our special gratitude goes to Mrs Reuter who performed the β-endorphin assays. We thank also Dr Etienne who performed the assays for cortisol and prolactin, offering us his competence and a large amount of free time.

40

From psychoneuroendocrinology to primal health: new concepts as strategic tools

M. Odent

There have been many books and conferences during these last 10 years about the fetal life, the perinatal period, and the period of breastfeeding. In fact these books and conferences attracted mainly the converted, that is to say people convinced in advance of the importance of these periods. We are now at a time when we must reach other kinds of people and spread a new awareness. There are two ways to do this, to be used in parallel: concepts and emotions.

PSYCHONEUROENDOCRINOLOGY HAS SMASHED A BARRIER

Psychoneuroendocrinology is a new discipline born as soon as the barriers between the nervous system and the hormonal system became obsolete, and more precisely after the discovery of the neurohormones. It is well known, for example, that the hypothalamus is both a nervous structure, a part of the brain, and also an endocrine gland which secretes hormones of its own and whose functions are regulated by other glands through a feedback mechanism.

Moreover, the whole brain can be considered nowadays as a gland which uses chemical messengers to send information from one part of itself to another. Nerve cells do not need to touch each other to communicate.

Certain substances can modify the activity of the brain by a mechanism which is similar to the tuning of an orchestra. That is why some brain grafts can compensate for certain deficits, or thirst can be triggered by injecting a small amount of angiotensin into a precise zone of the brain, or a maternal behavior by injecting some pituitary oxytocin. The time has come to get rid of the mental picture of a brain as an electronic network with only cell-to-cell transmissions.

A SECOND BARRIER TO SMASH

In the same way that we must smash all the barriers between the nervous and the endocrine systems, we must also smash the barriers which traditionally divide the hormonal system from the immune system. Some examples among thousands are sufficient to show that they are both part of a whole. The thymus itself is an endocrine gland which secretes different kinds of thymosine. The thymosines take part in controlling the secretion of the stress hormones by a feedback mechanism. Cortisol, the adrenal hormone secreted in situations of 'helplessness', depresses the immune system by reducing the size of the thymus, by reducing the number and the activity of the T cells, and by inhibiting the synthesis of proteins in general and of antibodies in particular. Noradrenalin binds itself to surface receptors of lymphocytes and inhibits their functions. Endorphins also influence the activity of the immune system. In fact every kind of hormonal secretion plays a role in immunity. So the growth hormone is needed to maintain or restore the functions of T lymphocytes.

The fusion between the hormonal system and the immune system is even more obvious since we know that lymphocytes themselves can produce ACTH and endorphins, and that lymphocytes have surface receptors for a wide variety of hormones.

A THIRD BARRIER TO SMASH

What is perhaps even more difficult for many doctors and scientists is to fuse together their mental pictures of the primitive parts of the brain and of the immune system. The importance of some research findings must be emphasized.

Certain lesions and certain stimuli of nerves are known to have important effects on the number and activity of cells in different organs of the immune system (thymus, bone marrow, spleen, lymphatic nodes). Also we know that some antigens can considerably increase the electrical activity of certain nerve cells of the hypothalamus: the immune system can now be seen as an actual sensory organ which gives information to the brain.

Some spectacular experiments on the conditioning of immune reactions contribute to make obsolete any barrier between the nervous system and the immune system. The works of Metalnikov in the 1920s in Paris have been forgotten, but the more recent works of the American scientist, Ader, using taste aversion are better known. Ader gave to animals saccharinated water at the same time as injections of a drug which depressed the immune system and which triggered digestive troubles. He then found that he could depress the immune system by giving saccharinated water alone.

THE PRIMAL ADAPTIVE SYSTEM

So modern science is able to point to the unity of our adaptive systems, and to the incessant circulation of information inside this infinitely complex network.

We call this network the 'Primal adaptive system'.

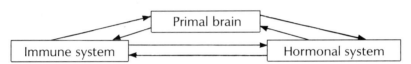

Health means the way our primal adaptive system works. The brain structures we have in common with the most primitive mammals are called 'primal brain' (hypothalamus, thalamus, hippocampus, amygdala, a rim of cortical structures called the limbic system). It is essential to understand that the different parts of the primal adaptive system develop simultaneously and reach their maturity during the 'primal period', that is to say the period of dependence on the mother, a period which is from conception to the end of infancy. It is as if all the events which happen during this period of dependence on the mother influence the way we program our biological computers. The hormonal levels have to be set at the beginning of life and continue to switch on at the set level.

Suppose that a newborn baby is separated from the mother at birth. This is not different from what the physiologists call a situation of 'helplessness' or 'hopelessness'. The response is a high secretion of cortisol which will depress the immune system and reduce the size of the thymus. If such situations are prolonged the baby will have a tendency to adjust its secretion of cortisol at a high level. At the end of the 'primal period' the human being is in a basic state of health which we call 'primal health'. Then, later on during life, one can only cultivate this 'primal health'.

Our understanding of the primal adaptive system as a whole suggests a new definition of emotion. When certain situations trigger a sudden change in the working of the primal adaptive system, this becomes an emotion. An emotion is a response by the entire primal adaptive system, that is to say by the primal brain, the immune system and the hormonal system all in union.

The primal adaptive system is not a closed system. Communication with the exterior is made by eating, breathing and sensory stimulation. The primal adaptive system also has at its disposal the associative brain, that extraordinary supercomputer called neocortex. This new brain continues to develop late in adulthood. It receives information from the outside environment through sensory organs, and from the whole body through specialized receptors. It is through the neocortex that we know about the world of time and space, and can communicate through language in a sophisticated way.

In adult humans the neocortex is so highly developed that it tends to overcontrol and repress the activity of the primal brain. It can do this to such an extent that it inhibits those physiological functions which are most vulnerable, such as childbirth and the sexual act. But however much the neocortex assumes control, the primal brain will still be primal in the sense of being first in importance. It is the primal brain which gives us the urge to survive as an individual and through procreation. It is also the primal brain which gives us a sense of belonging to the universe, a religious sense, a spiritual dimension.

The neocortex may be considered to be the seat of the rational: the primal brain the seat of the supra-rational. The struggle for life is itself supra-rational. Thus the neocortex can be seen as a tool to be used in every aspect of the struggle for life, and in the survival of the individual, the group or the species.

IMPLICATIONS OF THE CONCEPT OF PRIMAL HEALTH

The concept of primal health has many practical implications. It shifts the emphasis away from the prevention of diseases onto the genesis of good health.

It opens the way to a new generation of research, whose aim is to discover correlations between the different episodes of the primal period and what happens later on during adolescence, adulthood and old age. 'Research in primal health' is also a simple way to encompass new disciplines commonly defined by long words such as psychoneuro-endocrinology, psychoneuroimmunology and immunoendocrinology. The concept 'primal health', helps focus research which leads to a better understanding of some fundamental human needs which are rarely met in the industrialized countries. It helps us to be more conscious of the most dangerous aspects of our society.

TOWARDS A NEW AWARENESS

To convince and trigger a new awareness, concepts must be associated with emotions. 'Primal health' is a concept which can be used to spread a new awareness. But to convince and trigger a new awareness, concepts by themselves are not sufficient. They must be associated with emotions and used in parallel.

Part 4: Impact of social implications upon obstetrics and gynecology

41

Maternal psychosociobiological barriers in human reproduction

R. Klimek

ABSTRACT

Life is not only exclusively a question of biology, since maternity is also psychosocially conditioned. Pregnancy can be described by regarding the mother as an open thermodynamic system. The zygote is an entirely new biologically different one. It can appear, grow and develop only thanks to the essential internal work of the mother, a system, precisely a single whole, and for this reason the psychological, emotional and social processes of the mother always interact with the other thermodynamic forces and influences on her organism. This is particularly applicable in reproduction with its psychosocial barriers as thermodynamic factors. The first of them is the very fact of accepting the pregnancy. Psychosocial factors also play a part in the second (biological-preclinical abortion), third (clinical, especially habitual abortions) and fourth (premature births) barriers. The final one is the barrier of term birth, in which psychosocial aspects are usually restricted to, for example, fear of birth, or to acceptance of the child. The need for the woman giving birth to accept as a mother responsibility for enlargement of the family, and for its socioeconomic state, is too often forgotten. The aim of this paper has not been to describe in detail the psychosocial aspect of the five barriers mentioned, but to conceive of them in a phenomenological sense as components that are fundamental in the reproduction of homo sapiens. For the simultaneity and variety of organism is not merely an accident.

INTRODUCTION

Every age has its own aims, of which it is not always fully conscious, but man remains the most important object and at the same time subject of cognition, and that across a huge range, for example the physical, between the microcosmos and the macrocosmos, or the biological, from conception till death. The modern world is experiencing a new stage in the evolution of knowledge, for after the stage of links between chemistry and biology, biophysics has become all-embracing, with the Second Law of Thermodynamics expanded to include non-linear processes far from equilibrium. This also applies to the psychosocial aspects of pregnancy.

Figure 1 offers a schematic presentation of the course of fertilization *in vivo* and *in vitro*. The spermatozoon and the egg cell, as microsystems of the parent organisms, after combining to form a zygote, produce an entirely new organism, which may continue to exist and develop only in the environment constituted by the mother's organism. The creation of a similar environment *in vitro* is a huge achievement, indicating above all the significance of physical and chemical components in the initiation of a new person's life. However, it is now already known that a prolongation of the *in vitro* period dramatically reduces the effectiveness of a fertilization

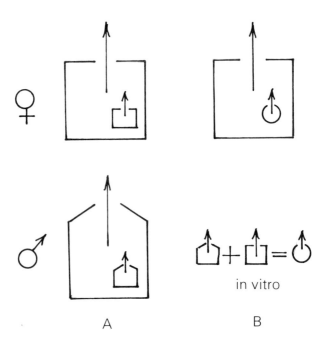

Figure 1 Schematic presentation of course of fertilization *in vivo* and *in vitro*

process carried out in this way, for only the mother's organism, through its psychological and biological component, guarantees the kind of environment for the fetus, which in turn acts to induce the required changes during pregnancy.

To achieve complete maturity, the egg cell needs a time span varying from a few years up to several dozen years. This stage is reached by means of the ovulation of only about 400 cells from amongst 10^7 cells which exist in the fifth month of fetal life, and only 10^6 cells which survive till birth. In every menstrual cycle a number of cells begin to mature, but normally only one of them is subjected to ovulation.

How different is this enormous world, with millions of cells competing with each other according to the laws of statistics, from the images of classical handbooks, in which the cycle of maturation, ovulation and occasionally fertilization is presented wrongly as the story of one Graaf follicle.

Processes which are statistically even clearer and easier to understand take place in the organism of man, in whose testicles the huge number of 10^9 spermatogonia are to be found, and the manufacture of mature spermatozoa continues throughout life. In the fertilization of one egg cell, optimally selected from millions, 200–300 million spermatozoa take part in a single ejaculation. Only several hundred thousand of them, however, reach the commonest place of fertilization, in the ampulla of the uterine tube. In this way, nature itself literally uses great amounts subject to non-linear statistical equations to ensure the most basic phenomenon of all in the life of man – the preservation of the species!

The example given above best illustrates the two divisions of medical thermodynamics, which belongs to the phenomenological part of thermodynamics as a separate discipline. The description of a single fertilization is found in our phenomenological description of medicine hitherto, but it is only a result (an averaging!) of statistical procedures (statistical thermodynamics) lying at the base of phenomena observed and only descriptively presented. It was not so long ago that the language of medical biochemistry seemed incomprehensible; for preceding generations, perhaps, Virchow's maxim – omnis cellula e cellula – was also a great leap forward. The modern scientific revolution is resolving itself into an understanding of the essence of statistical processes, and thus of that which for centuries has been called unpredictable chance. The brilliant discoveries of mathematicians led to a broadening of one of the most basic laws of nature – the Second Law of Thermodynamics – by a description of statistical phenomena with non-linear equations. In other words, everything we perceive and feel is the mediated outcome of these phenomena, which are accidental for us, but which in the world of physics are determined by statistical laws. An understanding of the statistical conditioning of something apparently so simple as fertilization brings with it important consequences, and not only ones of perception.

THE THERMODYNAMIC SYSTEM AND ITS BRANCH

One of the most fundamental concepts of thermodynamics is the thermodynamic system, in other words, the part of nature singled out for consideration. In this work it is the fetus or the mother. The basis for classifying thermodynamic systems is the properties of the screen, or the material edge of the system which separates it from its environment. For the fetus, this environment is not only the mother's organism, but beginning from the zygote – the zona pellucida, the amniotic fluid, and the cells of the cytotrophoblast, the fetal membranes and the placenta.

Ontogenesis is a shortened repetition of philogenesis, but descriptions of it often omit its earliest stage, that of the non-nucleated fetus, such a fundamental reminder of life at the level of procaryotes; and yet it is at this time that the entire fate not only of the fetus but of its immediate surroundings, and also the future of the species, is decided. The initial plasma division of the zygote, generally of maternal origin, is of importance for the future of every one of its descendant cells.

A pregnancy can be described by regarding the mother as an open system. The zygote is as entirely new, biologically different thermodynamic system. It can appear, grow and develop only thanks to the essential internal work of the mother's system, precisely to prolong the life of the human species.

In accordance with the laws of thermodynamics, the correct joint action of three systems, (1) the fetus, (2) the placenta and fluid, (3) the mother, is carried out by regulatory-control mechanisms. Nature, in concordant and astonishing harmony, imparts biological and mental life to one person or several (in multiple pregnancies) simultaneously assuring the survival of the species and its culture.

In the concept set out above, there is no need for comparisons such as: fetus as graft, fetus as 'parasite' or symbiont, or for a description of the roles of the nervous, hormonal, immunological and biophysical systems, etc. For in each of these concerns some aspects or part of the problem, and thus the beauty of generalizations with their natural simplicity is lost.

Dynamic equilibrium (steady state) amongst all these systems guarantees that the system as a whole functions correctly and is known as a state of physiological equilibrium.

Each of these systems is composed of internal systems – cellular and subcellular formations. The smallest of these biological microsystems is in turn constructed of that smallest number of atoms and particles which stills show evidence of having the properties of life. Just as the existence, growth and development of the whole organism depend on the state of equilibrium between its distinct systems, so in turn each system, including also those of individual cells, depends on the state of equilibrium between the microsystems of which it is composed.

For further consideration the most essential thing is the assertion, which does not require any special proof, that in states of equilibrium, structures (systems) are stable and resistant to small disturbances. Also, in structures close to equilibrium, systems tend spontaneously towards a state of equilibrium, and the appearance of a new structure is impossible.

In both situations both the whole organism and its elementary microsystems have a common feature — they must exist themselves, and demonstrate the ability to work on the exterior, in relation to their environment. In states of equilibrium (good health) and close to equilibrium (illness, with the exception of cancer) the system retains the ability to work on the exterior and to react to the condition and needs of the environment.

We call the group of stable states in which a given system may appear the thermodynamic branch (Figures 2 and 3) and the efficiency of a system is always decided by its internal state. If the system is in a state far from equilibrium in relation to the environment, then for various reasons it has a reduced capacity for external work or becomes quite incapable of it. Far more important is the survival of the system itself, i.e. the maintenance of its internal structure and function. In states that remain far from equilibrium the system is either destroyed or may, and sometimes even must, transform itself into a new, so-called dissipative structure. It is quite simply that for its existence, it gathers excessive amounts of matter and energy from the environment and disperses them.

PREGNANCY IN THE UNDERSTANDING OF MEDICAL THERMODYNAMICS

The non-nucleated zygote is constructed of elementary biological microsystems, which through various positionings in space and time, determine from which of its parts there will eventually appear, for example, the heart, the eye, the placenta, etc. Let us remember that each such elementary biological system has its own thermodynamic branch, and the proper development of the zygote is dependent on their mutual equilibrium (Figure 4). The scale of these interactions is enormous, even if we were to take into consideration only the chromosome systems of the mother and the father. For these 23 chromosomes there exists an enormous number of possible combinations of genotypes — 2^{23} or 8 388 608 possible

452 PRENATAL AND PERINATAL PSYCHOLOGY AND MEDICINE

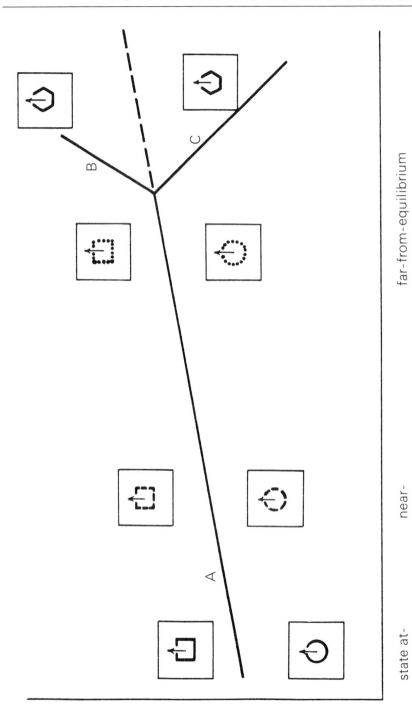

Figure 2 Thermodynamic branch of microsystem

MATERNAL PSYCHOSOCIOBIOLOGICAL BARRIERS

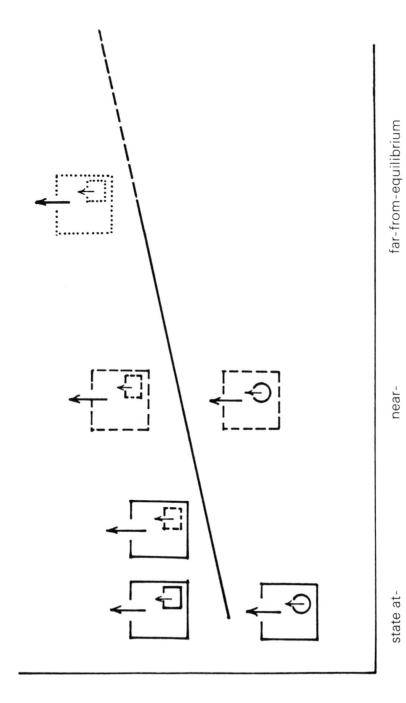

Figure 3 Thermodynamic branch of macrosystem

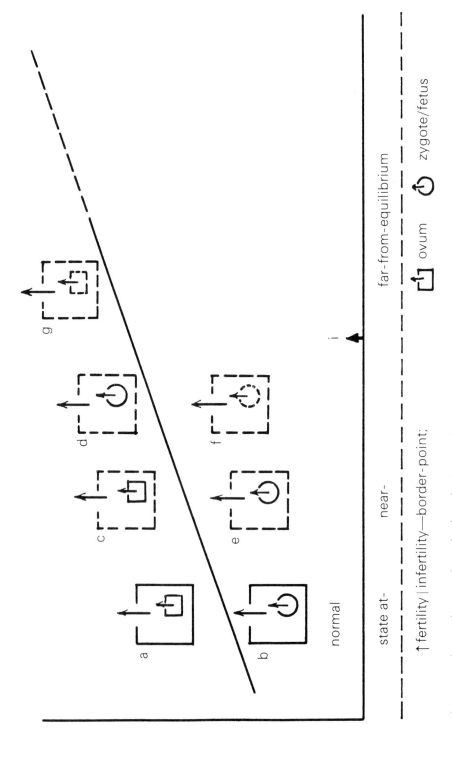

Figure 4 Thermodynamic branch of mother's organism

combinations, not counting extra-nucleinic influences on the final phenotype of the zygote, obviously stochastically selected! The meaning of these huge amounts and possible fluctuations to which the systems under discussion are subject assumes the appropriate dimension if we take into consideration the fact that virtually the whole cytoplasm of the zygote is of maternal origin. It is precisely in this that there appears the enormous significance of the hereditary material of the egg cells, which does not alter in them from the birth of the future mother. The spermatozoa, on the other hand, appearing in 21-day cycles, allow adaptive changes of new generations according to the conditions of their life and the state of the environment.

Another important element in the existence of the zygote is external action. This begins from the most general and universal signal that is the exchange of matter and energy with the environment. After physical changes there appear signals that are often chemically connected with the production of carbon monoxide (a change in the pH of the environment) or of simple organic compounds such as histamine. The thermodynamic forces and influences determine the reactions of the organism of the mother, whose role in procreation is highly complex.

The woman's organism is adapted for (1) the manufacture of egg cells suitable for fertilization; (2) guaranteeing their fertilization, including a check on the state of spermatozoa potentially capable of insemination; (3) guaranteeing conditions for the development of the newly created organism, as of an independent biological system, till it becomes able to exist separately outside the mother's organism in a common environment; and (4) securing not only biological but also psycho-emotional inheritance through psychological and emotional maternal ties. The role of the male organism in the process of procreation is more limited in comparison with that of the woman.

Pregnancy alters the internal state of the woman's organism, moving it away from the pre-pregnancy state of equilibrium. Furthermore, there arises the necessity for ever more internal work, comprising not only the interaction hitherto with its own environment, but this necessary guaranteeing of the creation and development of the fetus. The fetus only appears to develop in the mother's organism, for as a new biological system, from the point of view of thermodynamics, it is an external world for her.

Nature does not give anything for free – in her laws, she is at once cruel and fair. She allows every one of us to live thanks to the fact that every day thousands of cells and other living elements (microsystems) perish, and sometimes, through neoplastic transmutations, their death is accelerated – simply in order that the entirety of our organism may function. Similarly, we die so that our species might live.

Death is the antithesis of life, and an essential element in biological selection, since only 30% of inseminated egg cells survive till birth. As many of 75% of the losses do not arise with the range of clinical methods but may be revealed only by biochemical and/or biophysical methods. At present it is also possible non-invasively to examine a biophysically growing Graaf follicle, to locate the place of implantation and the development of a trophoblast, and finally to diagnose a multiple pregnancy. But again only in one third of women is a double pregnancy confirmed which had been diagnosed by ultrasonograph before the 20th week of pregnancy.

Miscarriage then may concern the ending of the pregnancy at its biological, pre-clinical stage, by the expulsion or resorption of a fetus incapable of further development. The most important selection, however, takes place before implantation, the lack of which may be either the result of insufficient adaptation by the mother's organism or the inability of the fetus itself to create signals inducing in the genital organ the necessary conditions for nidation. We speak in such cases of biological miscarriage.

The mutual relationship between the mother and the fetus is shown in Figure 5, which depicts the thermodynamic branch of the states of the pregnant woman. A healthy woman in a state of equilibrium (Figure 4a) in optimal conditions of age, health and environment, remains in a state of equilibrium (good health) after becoming pregnant (Figure 4b). A diametrically opposite state on the thermodynamic branch of a woman's life is the border point of fertility (Figure 4i), after which, as a result of a state far from equilibrium (Figure 4g, e.g. lack of genital organs, general severe

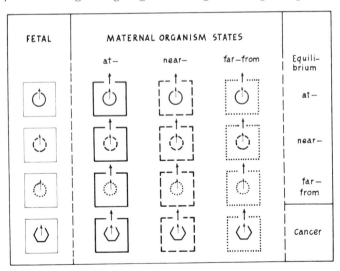

Figure 5 Maternal organism states

illness) the woman is permanently infertile. In states close to equilibrium (Figures 4c and 4d) pregnancy is possible, but, as an additional burden in matter and energy on the organism, it leads to an intensification of already existing states of sickness. In this case pregnancy may be an undesirable state, dangerous to the woman's health and sometimes her life. To preserve the internal state existing hitherto, the woman's organism will favor miscarriage rather than protecting the fetus with its defensive-corrective powers.

The fastest growth of the fetus, which takes place between the 4th and the 8th weeks of pregnancy, decelerates in the following weeks, maintaining a linear growth between the 12th and 26th weeks. The placenta also grows till the 36th week, after which the proliferation of cells is replaced by processes of further maturation. The growth of the fetus then is not compensated for by the capacity of the placenta, but must be balanced by an increased permeability and capacity for taking in nourishment through the mother. Thus then, after a period of biological adaptation at the beinning of the third trimester and the clinical signs of cohabitation till the 37th week of pregnancy, there begins a period of the increasing interference of environmental factors on the fetus via the mother's organism.

The data given above illustrate the significant burden exerted on the mother's organism by the most generally defined needs created by pregnancy. 'Gestamen' in Latin means both 'weight' and 'stretcher', 'litter'; 'gestatio' means 'departure', 'avenue', 'carriageway'. Doctors added the ending -osis to these words to define a state of sickness, in other words clinically confirmed disorders and symptoms in a hitherto healthy woman in connection with her becoming pregnant.

Gestosis is a state close to equilibrium on the thermodynamic branch of the woman's organism (Figure 4e), and the disturbances that appear in it disappear when the pregnancy comes to an end.

When the mother is in a state of equilibrium, miscarriage may occur only as a result of external causes. Amongst clinically diagnosed pregnancies that suffered miscarriage in the first term, as many as 60% showed evidence of chromosomal disorders! Pregnancy in a woman who is far from a state of equilibrium is not only rare, but even when correctly programmed is terminated for maternal reasons together with medical intervention.

A certain percentage of pregnant women find themselves in a state close to equilibrium, one of sickness, before pregnancy or as a result of becoming pregnant. The diagnosis of such gestoses must take into account above all the intrauterine state of the fetus, as the prime condition for medical intervention. Before clinical changes take place in the woman (swellings, hypertension, proteinuria, an increased level of uric acid in the blood, etc.) the lateness in the growth and development of the fetus may itself suggest the beginnings of gestosis. And vice versa, the initial confirmation of clinical changes makes it all the more necessary to monitor carefully the state of the fetus, for this determines clinical diagnosis and the possible necessity of action being taken. For example, increased blood pressure in the mother may be a desirable adaptive change, and desisting from lowering the blood pressure in all such women has improved survival rates amongst threatened fetuses.

Just as with the treatment of various kinds of gestoses, so it is with delaying any premature birth which may occur in the interests of the fetus, for which, at its stage of development, the organism of the mother becomes a worse environment than outside! The prolongation of such a pregnancy may become dangerous for one or even both of the co-existing organisms.

PSYCHOSOCIAL BARRIERS AS THERMODYNAMIC FACTORS

From the considerations thus far, it arises clearly that any system acts as a single whole, and for this reason the psychological, emotional and social processes of the mother always interact with the other thermodynamic forces and influences on her organism. This is particularly applicable in reproduction.

The first of these psychosocial barriers is the very fact of accepting the pregnancy. This, however, is not exclusively of a psychological, emotional or social matter, since there exist active syndromes of deliberate exposition to unwanted pregnancy.

For man's behavior is also biologically conditioned. And for example, the use of contraceptive pills over a long period, limits the capacity of the egg to be fertilized and of the fertilized egg to be implanted.

In the second barrier often defined as a purely biological, biochemical or indeed preclinical miscarriage, psychosocial factors also play a part.

The third barrier is the development of full efficiency by the placenta, assuming the organogenesis of the fetus has progressed normally. The mutual interaction of psycho-emotional and biological states in potential or habitual miscarriages are of course well known. However, considerably less attention is paid to the barrier of premature births. How often is it forgotten that towards the end of pregnancy the fetus may find better conditions outside the mother than in her organism.

What is natural at term birth causes concern in the period several weeks or even just a few weeks earlier. And yet not every premature birth may be considered as undesirable from the point of view of the future of the fetus. It may also turn out to be essential for the mother, burdened with her own illnesses, which, with the growing energy needs of the fetus, may prove to be fatal if the pregnancy is continued.

The final barrier is the barrier of birth, in which psychosocial aspects are too often restricted to, for example, fear of birth, or to acceptance of the child. The need for the woman giving birth to accept herself as a mother responsible for the enlargement of the family and for its socioeconomic state, is forgotten.

The aim of my paper has not been to describe in detail the psychosocial aspect of the five barriers mentioned, but to conceive of them in a phenomenological sense as components that are fundamental in the reproduction of Homo sapiens. For the simultaneity and variety of the jointly acting factors are not chaos — just as the new organism is not merely an accident.

Modern equipment allows the creation of images, comprehensible and understandable to us, of radio waves received simultaneously from millions of atomic nuclei or even just electrons. The computerization of our life ought likewise to enable us to take the appropriate medical action by (phenomenological) information about the processes of reproduction which, as natural processes, are also subject to the Second Law of Thermodynamics expanded to include non-linear (statistical) phenomena. For maternity is by its very nature a state which reveals the whole meaning of the unity and continuity of life.

42

The impact of reproductive technology on society: the donated egg and its mother, and induced abortion as seen via the ultrasound screen

D.M. Serr, S. Tyano, R. Mane, L. Zabner, S. Mashiach and J. Shalev

ABSTRACT

In pregnancies which are the result of an in vitro fertilization of a donated egg and the husband's sperm, the mother carrying the child develops the biological role of a surrogate mother with the emotional task of fulfilling her feminine role. In contradistinction to pregnancies of in vitro fertilized ova carried by the genetic mother with its own specific psychological aspects, we have in our present situation a different psychological attitude more closely simulating that of an organ transplant. Both patients followed-up in this study had already undergone adoption procedures. However, in their present pregnancies they both expressed the desire to deliver by Caesarean section – as if to say, if to become pregnant by technology then also to deliver mechanically. Intellectualization of the child attachment to its mother follows a reaction to estrangement. This was noted throughout the interviews by an avoidance of using the term 'my baby'. The patients would even use the term 'taking' or even 'stealing' the egg from the donor, as the means of using her husband's sperm to fertilize the ovum which produced the fetus she is carrying. The significance of this conscience of 'stealing' and the anxieties concerning the implantation are demonstrated by analyzing the dreams accompanying these pregnancies.

Society is concerned today with modern manipulative reproductive technology. We will discuss two aspects of these manipulations; one restores fertility where it has ceased to exist, and the other will demonstrate how interrupting the natural course of reproduction can be shown, again by technological intervention, to be a subject of great impact.

The first part of this presentation may be called the rejuvenation of the prematurely menopausal woman by enabling her to reproduce and bear a child despite physiological data which would preclude such a result. Premature menopause is a not infrequent condition and usually follows early ovarian failure and secondary amenorrhea. It is paralleled as far as *in vitro* fertilization techniques are concerned by such a congenital condition as Turner's syndrome in which patients have amenorrhea due to ovarian failure or agenesis, as well as lack of primordial follicles. Hormonal profiles show these patients to have high FSH and LH levels similar to those in the physiologically postmenopausal woman in her fifties or sixties, except that the patients in our study are between the ages of 25 and 40.

In our *in vitro* fertilization program, permission for new applications was granted by the committee on human bioethics. Egg donation was allowed under certain circumstances, and among the patients suitable for this program to receive a donated egg, were the two presented in this study. Both of them were successfully transplanted by embryo transfer of a donated egg fertilized by their husbands' sperm. One has since delivered a healthy, male child, and the second patient is due to deliver during the writing of this report.

Only brief reference to the clinical data in this program is mentioned here. Our primary purpose in this presentation is to attempt to analyze the psychological elements involved and the consequences for parent and child.

The high gonadotrophin levels are suppressed by estrogen and progesterone substitution therapy. This hormone replacement in the absence of embryo transfer will result in withdrawal bleeding interpreted by the patient as a kind of pseudo-menstruation. Successful embryo transfer results in pregnancy of the nidated fertilized ovum, and, hopefully, no withdrawal bleeding. Progesterone support is necessary during early pregnancy.

The two patients involved in this study had been advised some years previously that their chances of becoming pregnant were nil and had undergone adoption procedures. One had already adopted a child who is now 5 years of age. The pregnancies resulting from these reproductive manipulations have been physiologically successful, and the patient who delivered underwent Caesarean section and gave birth to a normal male child.

The choice of patients brings us to the psychosocial aspects of reproductive technologies. It may be said that this reproductive revolution has brought us to the age of procreation without sex, and egg donation goes one step further, bringing us reproduction in a woman, who by clinical standards has passed the age of procreation. In fact problems are beginning to arise as requests are submitted by postmenopausal women in their late fifties, for admission to the egg donation program. They had been declared sterile during their childbearing years, but had heard of the new techniques through the media. From the psychosocial viewpoint it must be pointed out that in contradistinction to adoption procedures, we cannot select our patients as to whether they are suitable or not by the standards set up for adoption. They present by clinical syndromes which are, in effect, absolute. In this case parenthood does not require a certificate of competence from the psychiatrist. There are no psychological characteristics or personality structures specific to organic sterility. This is in contrast to possible personality types found in functional infertility groups (Kipper et al., 1974). However, having undergone a serious life event upon becoming aware of their 'disability' and the possible psychological consequences of such counseling (Kaplan, 1968) we feel it important to stress that in spite of their relative lack of psychopathological features, these patients require preparation for pregnancy at a level not required of a completely natural pregnancy. Concerning this approach we should see our patients as belonging to one of the following groups:

(1) Natural spontaneous pregnancy and birth,
(2) Absolute sterility,
(3) Functional infertility.

The patients of Group 3 have a condition which is dependent, perhaps upon hormone replacement, or maybe on psychotherapy (Honig et al., 1975). The patients of Group 2 will include those women with mechanical sterility who have now become subjects for microsurgical rehabilitation of the Fallopian tubes or subjects for homologous *in vitro* fertilization. However they underwent, at some point in time, a life event upon being informed of their 'absolute' inability to reproduce. Couples in whom the husband is azoospermic would undergo a similar life event in which they are faced with a 'make or break' situation as regards parenthood.

The patients of our present study fall into this group of so-called 'absolute' sterility. However, the reversal of this life event by *in vitro* fertilization and embryo transfer of a donated egg is unlike either tuboplastic surgical treatment, homologous *in vitro* fertilization or even artificial donor insemination.

METHODOLOGY

The study involves investigation of these patients at four important stages:

(1) On joining the project,
(2) On becoming pregnant,
(3) Pre-labor,
(4) On becoming a parent.

These tests were carried out on our patients by a full clinical psychiatric interview, both structured and unstructured. This was followed up by the following tests: MMPI – this test is featured to identify psychopathology. It is based upon a 550 item questionnaire and gives a personality assessment scale of 1–10. It comprises clinical scales ranging conditions from hysteria to schizophrenia and three validity scales, including the attitude of the subject to the test being taken. Two other tests were also given, the one assessing the interrelationship of the couple to each other, and the second to test attitudes to pregnancy and parenthood. These latter two tests are still under study and the present report will, therefore, be based on the clinical psychiatric interview and the MMPI tests.

The early observations on these patients resulting from the interviews show that these women had no psychopathological conditions. The psychiatrist's view is that this may be the result of a rapport between the gynecologist and his patient selection process, in that in an intuitive manner and subconsciously he tends to choose his patients for this controversial technological procedure, and has the instinct to involve only a subject devoid of gross psychopathology. For this reason it was considered unnecessary to resort to the use of other psychological tests as projective tests. This working hypothesis is born out by the MMPI results obtained.

However, when we come to a breakdown of the MMPI tests, the results show denial of illness anxiety as low as zero on the MMPI scale. This represents a reinforcement of the defense mechanism of a denial of any body dysfunction. Directions by the attending physician such as to 'be careful' result in an actual denial of somatic anxiety due to an annulment of the disability previously expressed in the life event. From this conclusion it would seem appropriate to subject all *in vitro* fertilization subjects, even the homologous ones, to MMPI tests since they also belong to the Group 2 type of absolute sterility conditions now reversed. In the two control cases we examined in this study, who were homologous *in vitro* fertilized patients, we did not find this same intensity of denial of illness anxiety although there was some expression of this type of denial. This confirms the specificity of this characteristic to the egg donated patients.

The next important observation specifically applying to the donated egg patients refers to the psychological aspects of organ transplantation. The subject constantly asks herself ... 'Whose organ was it, that is now in me?', or in our case, ... 'Whose egg is growing in me?', ... 'What were the donor's characteristics?' ... 'What about ethnic differences?'. The patient fantasizes about the donor and sees her almost as a sibling. She chooses someone in the waiting room from whom she builds the image of her 'partner'. She sees this one come and go. She hears talk that the donors themselves have not yet achieved pregnancy, and feels guilty when she sees her phantom donor in the waiting room. She feels she has 'taken' or even 'stolen' her fertile egg.

The situation in pregnancies of the various group types we have described may be diagrammatically shown in the following situations:

(1) The normal couple have each other and their unborn child whose fantasized image becomes real. This is a three-item situation.

(2) The couple whose sterility is due to a male factor and an embryo developing from a fantasmatic donor. At birth and during early development, this family unit is due to alter this prenatal situation with a complete disappearance of the donor fantasy. In these circumstances we start with a four-item situation but arrive back eventually to a three-item situation.

(3) In the donated egg embryo transfer we have a similar prenatal combination as above with a pregnant wife, husband, developing fetus and fantasmatic donor. The difference, however, in this situation is that the fantasmatic donor may continue to exist in the mother's mind even after delivery and may never completely disappear. The bonding is never purely father, mother and child, but may always be joined by the fantasy of the donor. This characteristic is typical of the psychology of organ transplantation as described in regard to kidney transplants (Moniz and Tyano, 1973). In the study presented here we have, however, also noted an interesting feature of personal genetic fiction. One of our patients explained her version of the genetic balance she sees in her four-item situation. In her case, she said, that of the 100% genetic material of her baby's constitution 50% comes from the husband, whilst the remaining 50% are equally made up from the donor and herself. She, therefore, reasons that the donor contributes only 25% of the newborn, thus giving her family the majority share – a strange sort of pseudo-mendelian philosophy.

During the clinical interviews both patients expressed their desire to deliver by Caesarean section. This was rationalized by the sentiment 'if one is to become pregnant by technology then one should deliver by technology' – mechanics all the way. From the contents of their dreams one may also discern the conflict of the natural versus the unnatural, an expression of the difficulty in bridging the world of nature and the world of technology. A typical dream went as follows ... 'came to the hospital and delivered twins – but not *she* is the one who delivered the twins. Immediately phoned her mother from the labor room – but it was not *she* who delivered the twins. Mother arrives and sees my stomach is flat. I brought up and cared for the twins. No other woman was in sight ...' There is expressed here difficulty in bridging between nature and technology, between delivery and adoption, and a blurring of the boundary between delivering a baby and *adopting* an egg.

We have, therefore, before us a new situation in parenthood – biologically, legally, and just as important, if not more so, psychologically. We may be in an era of reproductive revolution where the whole concept and definition of the family may require revision in social thinking and in the philosophy of procreation.

This brings me to the second subject of my presentation in which the natural process of fertilization is subjected to annihilation by the act of abortion. It would be impossible to say that this is a modern technology as *in vitro* fertilization. Abortifacient procedures have been tried for thousands of years. The present generation has, however, liberalized our thinking on the subject and introduced technological perfection which we have attempted to demonstrate on film. The traditional curettage could be aptly termed, 'The prenatal duel', except that the only sword is in the physician's hand and the opponent has no chance. So vivid is the ultrasonic viewing of an abortion, that one is reminded of the words of Stanislaw Lec, a Polish satirist, who said, in his *Neue Unfrisierte Gedanken,* – 'Technology is on its way to achieving such a degree of perfection that the human being will get by without himself.' The ease with which vacuum aspiration disposes of a pregnancy can also be vividly seen with the aid of ultrasound recording. Comparing the vacuum aspiration method with the traditional curettage makes one want to call this film, 'Termination without violence'.

The film was made with two thoughts in mind. Whilst carrying out a perfectly legal abortion and searching for a lost IUD with the aid of ultrasound, we were shocked to see the routine procedure 'live' on the television screen, and we began to develop guilt feelings, and, therefore, recorded this on video-tape. The experience of visualizing a 'live' fetus being eliminated in contrast to the blind curettage procedure in which a non-personalized 'pregnancy is terminated' led us to record this visual happening. For physicians and gynecologists in training we were interested to note the reaction and compare this with our own feelings.

In the long term it was our design to bring this film to the attention of patients requesting abortion on paramedical or social grounds in order to obtain their informed consent to a procedure they knew little about.

In the course of the film we observed that the actual viewing caused shock and concern and feelings of guilt. Only the most regular abortion performers were more blasé in their reactions, but even they expressed surprise and agreed that they felt that performing the procedure under vision produced subjective reactions, varying in nature and intensity, but most definitely present.

Among the patients who have seen this video presentation there have been interesting reactions. The impact is definite, but sometimes subdued, especially when the desire to terminate the pregnancy is strong. We do not yet have sufficient numbers for statistical analysis but we do have specific cases of subjects who have re-considered their abortion request application, and some have actually withdrawn it.

In discussions with colleagues of allied disciplines a view has been expressed that this is a form of brainwashing. We cannot accept this view. If technology allows us advances in fertility techniques for curing sterility, then why should technology not be used in all problems of reproduction, including the dilemma of whether to request an abortion.

We would simply close our remarks on this film with the following quotation from the proceedings of the General Assembly of the United Nations and leave you with thoughts open to discussion in which we will gladly take part. On November 20, 1959 the General Assembly of the United Nations adopted unanimously the *Declaration of the Rights of the Child,* which reads in its preamble:

> 'Whereas the child, by reason of his physical and mental immaturity, needs special safeguards and care, including *appropriate legal protection, before as well as after birth,*'

and in Principle 4:

> 'to this end special care and protection shall be provided to him and to his mother, including adequate pre-natal and post-natal care.'

43

The effects of continuous social support during birth on maternal and infant morbidity

M.H. Klaus and J.H. Kennell

ABSTRACT

In our first study in Guatemala we found that the presence of a supportive lay woman (doula) during labor was associated with a greatly reduced incidence of perinatal problems. The present study was designed in an attempt to replicate these findings. We studied 427 primigravid women in early labor with no medical problems. Mothers were randomly assigned to have a doula continuously present during labor and delivery or to labor alone (routine).

There was a significantly higher incidence of perinatal problems in the control group (59% vs. 27%, p < 0.001) which could not be explained by background variables or cervical dilatation at the time of admission. There was also a higher incidence of Caesarean sections, 17.3% vs. 6.5% (p < 0.002), and need for pitocin augmentation, 13.3% vs. 2.4% (p < 0.001), in the control group.

For mothers with normal labor and delivery, labor length was longer in the unsupported group, 15.4 vs. 7.7 hours (p < 0.001). The doula accounted for 25% of the variance in labor length above that explained by the background variables and initial cervical dilatation.

These findings suggest an interaction between behavior and physiology and have practical significance for the care of mothers and infants in hospitals throughout the world.

Anthropological data now suggest that the human species has not significantly changed for one to one and a half million years. During this time period, we have had the same skull, bone structure and perhaps most of the same behavior patterns that we have today. During most of this period we humans lived as hunters and gatherers. Thus our physiologic processes and genetic make-up were probably adapted to the life of hunting and gathering during this long time period. For 10 000 years humans had an agricultural mode of existence but our present industrialized society is represented by just 200 years; a period too short for evolutionary adjustments to occur.

This long history of evolutionary adaptation during which our biology, molded by the environment, slowly evolved practices related to childbirth and the raising of young children can provide the conceptual framework for productive research. The behavior of hunters and gatherers is a *source of many interesting ideas but does not necessarily tell us what to do about childbirth today*. It may be most profitable to use observations of the behavior of hunters and gatherers, as well as those noted almost universally in agricultural societies to generate questions about *human physiological processes* that can then be tested. Let us consider one example, *support during labor*.

John Kennell and I studied who was present with the mother during labor using the Murdock and White Anthropological Sample of 186 geographically, linguistically and historically representative non-industrialized societies (1969). This cross-cultural sample resulted from a major anthropological effort to facilitate comparative research. We examined the ethnographic material available in 128 societies that described who was with the mother. In 127 of the 128 societies, a family member or friend, usually a woman, was present with the mother-to-be *throughout labor,* and in only one society did the mother labor alone.

Before childbirth moved from the home to the hospital in the twentieth century, it was also the practice in industrialized nations for family members to support the mother actively in labor, often with the assistance of a trained or untrained midwife. Although more fathers, relatives and friends have been allowed into labor and delivery rooms in the past 20 years, a considerable number of mothers still undergo labor and delivery in some hospitals without the presence of family members or close friends. Even though fathers are allowed in many hospitals they frequently are unsure, ill at ease, often in the way and unable to provide active support.

Prior to the earthquake that destroyed one Guatemalan maternity hospital in 1976, we carried out a pilot study in which we asked a caring woman to stay with a mother during labor and birth. We observed changes in the women during labor. They became quiet and peaceful. Seven of the first ten women gave birth in bed. We noted that several of the women in this pilot study had milk dripping from their nipples when their baby was brought to them following the birth. Up to that time we had not seen this occur in the approximately 100 women who labored and gave birth without a supportive companion.

Our first study in Guatemala was designed to investigate the effects of a continuous supportive companion (locally referred to as a 'doula') on the length of labor, perinatal complications and maternal–infant interaction in the first hour after birth in an obstetrical setting in which mothers routinely labored alone (Sosa et al., 1980). In this unit primigravid mothers in labor were admitted to an observation ward when regular uterine contractions were present and the dilatation of the cervix was 1–2 cm. Women in early labor with no known medical problems were eligible, and the assignment of women to the control or experimental group was made on a random basis after the woman was admitted to the study. Control mothers followed the hospital routine, which consisted of monitoring the labor by infrequent vaginal examinations and auscultation of the heart and assistance to the mother during delivery. Electronic fetal monitoring was not available in this unit.

The continuous support provided to the experimental group by medically untrained lay women ('doula') consisted of physical contact (e.g. rubbing the mother's back and holding her hand), conversation, and supplying the mother with a friendly companion who, although previously unknown to her, would not leave during the entire labor.

Just who are these doulas? We have found these women by asking for personal referrals of individuals who are known to be mature, warm, responsible and caring. We used the following criteria in the selection of doula trainees.

(1) A mature woman who has experienced at least one normal labor and vaginal delivery with a good outcome,

(2) A warm, loving, motherly, enthusiastic person,

(3) Tolerance for people of different ethnic groups, social status, levels of income and lifestyles,

(4) Good health and the endurance to stand for long periods, and to work for long stretches without breaks in a crowded labor room,

(5) The ability to deal with and remain supportive of women who may become abusive during the final stages of labor.

In addition to the above criteria, additional criteria have been essential for the research duties of the doula.

At this point, you may be wondering what a doula does. We have some descriptive information recorded by experienced doulas working with 125 mothers in a Tampa hospital. Specifically, physical contact of the doula with the patient occurred most frequently on the mother's arms, shoulders and hands, with less contact on the face, back and legs. There was even less touching of the abdomen. The doulas spent a large proportion of their time (71%) talking to and (70%) touching the laboring mother.

It is preferable for the doula to be a woman who has borne children. A woman who has given birth has an innate sense of what the experience is like and possesses a natural empathy that a man cannot have. In addition, the intimate aspects of bodily functions are more easily carried out with a person of the same sex. The mother can often be less inhibited in front of another woman. Plus, many of the softer, quieter, sensitive, nurturing responses – mothering behaviors – come more naturally and comfortably from a woman, in our culture. It is desirable for the doula to 'mother' the mother at this vulnerable time when a woman's mind is unusually open as she prepares for a major maturational change. However, while allowing herself to be almost fully dependent on a support person, the mother still needs to have the freedom to tune into herself and then to respond at an instinctive level to what her body wants to do. Really, it is a paradoxical situation. Here the need is for total support in order to let go completely, for the purpose of allowing her whole system to respond to the birthing process.

Often this mixed need is confusing to the mother herself and difficult for care-givers to appreciate. Often husbands and men have difficulty with someone being dependent and independent at the same time.

Stimulated by observations of the clinical usefulness of continuous social support during labor, we systematically studied its clinical effect on maternal and neonatal morbidity in an obstetric setting in Guatemala in which mothers routinely underwent labor alone. A total of 427 healthy primigravidous women were enrolled using a randomized design. The experimental group received support from a woman (a doula) who was not a midwife, physician or nurse. She provided social support continuously throughout the labor and delivery. The control group of mothers labored alone, which was the routine practice in the hospital in which the study was conducted. The 168 women receiving support throughout labor had significantly fewer perinatal complications (34 vs. 74%). We tabulated the problems in the experimental and control groups including the incidence of Caesarean section, meconium staining, asphyxia of the infant and the use of pitocin. Medication was prescribed significantly more often in the control group (19 vs. 4%). The rate of Caesarean section was significantly greater in the control group also (17 vs. 7%). With a continuous care-giver the length of labor was significantly shorter (8 vs. 14 hours). Interestingly, a smaller percentage of infants was admitted to the NICU unit from the group of mothers who had a continuous care-giver (1 vs. 6%). It should be emphasized that all the mothers had had a normal pregnancy and were healthy at the beginning of labor.

Doula contact is individualized to the needs of each mother so it is difficult to specify exactly what the doula support will be for each mother. However, from 'our' doulas we have gained some insights characterizing the development and nature of the doula–patient relationship during labor.

The following excerpt from one experienced doulas's notes on 'how to be a doula' may help to clarify in general terms the nature of doula support and the dynamic quality of the interaction as labor progresses.

> 'There are different stages in the doula–patient relationship. (1) During this stage you become a friend; you relax the patient and enjoy her. You become very close at this time. (2) This stage starts when she is dilated between 5 and 6 cm. She needs mothering. Consequently, this is where your mothering instincts take over. I find telling them how proud I am of them seems to make them try a little harder. It is very important to soften your voice. This relaxes them and they quite often sleep between contractions. I have also found keeping my hand on their leg lets them rest comfortably. (3) This stage starts when she is between 8 and 9 cm. She's at a point where she can lose control. She needs your strength at this time. She needs strong support in a loving way. Sometimes they'll say "I can't do it" and you have to say "You are doing it!" You must be *strong* or she will lose control. (4) Pushing is the next stage. I always feel like a cheerleader at this stage. Telling them you "can see the hair", "you're getting closer to that delivery room" and similar positive, encouraging remarks makes them pick up your excitement and they seem to have more energy. (5) The delivery room is the final stage. The doctors and nurses will be telling her to push but when they're not talking you're going to be telling her how great a job she's doing and "just remember, there's a *baby* at the end of all this." I'm holding her hand all this time, sometimes even both hands. I stay with the patient until she goes to recovery even if the baby is not in the room. I feel a tie to her and I feel she still needs me.'

Under the crisis situation of labor and delivery a very strong attachment develops between the doula and the mother. After the delivery the comments about the value of the doula for both the mother and father are often enthusiastic.

The surprising findings of increased complications and labor length for the control group raise the possibility of an association between acute anxiety and an arrest of labor and fetal distress. The studies of human and primate mothers suggest that one explanation for this is an increased catecholamine level. Lederman and associates (1978) noted that plasma epinephrine levels and self-reported anxiety at the onset of phase two of labor were significantly correlated in 32 normal primigravid women. Physiological elevations of plasma epinephrine were associated with decreased uterine contractile activity at the onset of labor (3 cm of cervical dilatation) and a longer duration of labor from 3 to 10 cm dilatation. Epinephrine has a direct effect on uterine muscle, decreasing uterine contractions and thereby increasing the length of labor (Zuspan et al., 1962).

However, fetal asphyxia is possibly secondary to the effect of epinephrine on uterine blood flow. Barton and co-workers (1974) noted significant reductions in blood flow (up to 50%) to the sheep uterus with injections of epinephrine or norepinephrine. Catecholamines injected into pregnant rhesus monkey mothers by Adamson and associates (1971) resulted in fetal asphyxia but had no such effect when injected only into the fetus. It has been noted that psychological stress alone to pregnant monkeys, without pain or physical contact, resulted in severe fetal asphyxia with significant reductions in fetal arterial pH and oxygen tension (no data are available in human mothers). Therefore we can hypothesize that the presence of a supportive companion in the experimental group of mothers may have helped to reduce catecholamine levels. With increased levels in the control group, there was decreased uterine contractile activity and a significant reduction in uterine blood flow.

The 'active management of labor' advocated by O'Driscoll and Meagher (1980) which specifically includes the provision of human support, has had a major influence on the management of obstetric patients in many parts of the world. They have reported that the mean length of labor for primiparous women was less than 8 hours. With the introduction of the 'active management of labor' their definition of prolonged labor was reduced from 36 hours to 12 hours. The Caesarean section rate varied from 4.0 to 5.3%. The other components of the 'active management of labor' are artificial rupture of membranes if labor does not progress according to a predetermined schedule and the use of intravenous oxytocin if the desired progress is not achieved.

The effect of each of the three components has never been evaluated. When the O'Driscoll timetable for the active management of labor was used in other hospitals, one of his three components was often neglected – the assignment of a midwife who provided continuous support for each woman throughout labor. The midwife in the O'Driscoll system may contribute effects similar to those achieved by the doula in the studies in Guatemala.

The direct effects of the continuous support of a doula on the health of the mother and infant in the study in Guatemala are dramatic. Additionally, there appear to be important indirect effects that make a mother's early attachment to her baby progress more easily.

In a preliminary study in Guatemala, mothers who had a doula present during labor were awake more of the time when they were with their newborns after delivery and they stroked, smiled at and talked to their babies significantly more than the control mothers when controlling for length of labor and the time the mothers were awake. We do not have evidence to indicate whether this has long-term implications.

Further study will be necesssary to determine the long-range impact of continuous support during labor on the relationship of the mother and baby, father and baby, and the mother and father.

Our findings from the doula research are particularly relevant to the care of mothers where positive family support may not be provided during labor and delivery, and where there may be no cultural preparation for childbirth. For example, young, poor, deprived, unmarried and minority mothers.

How do we decide who will provide positive support? Is the father of the baby adequately prepared to fill the role of the doula? What about other family members? Until these issues have been studied we must be careful about jumping to conclusions. Non-systematic observations in private and public obstetric units show that some fathers provide excellent support but other fathers leave early. Even well prepared fathers may find the strain too great, fade into the background or even leave during transition. Most mothers, particularly with their first delivery, report that they spent much of their time during labor worrying about and supporting their husband, rather than the other way around. This is not to minimize the importance of the father's presence. Even when the father has not appeared to provide significant support, the mother has indicated the value of his presence. Experiences with the doula supporting the couple (mother and father) during labor and delivery suggest strongly that the doula's support of the father may enable him to be more supportive toward his wife. With a first baby, for example, this is the first labor and delivery experience for both the father and the mother.

Even as research is underway to investigate the effectiveness of the doula in the United States, doulas are beginning to provide support for mothers and for couples throughout the country. Many of them have a longer association with the mother than in our research. This seems highly desirable. There may be one or two contacts before the delivery so the mother will know the person who will be with her during labor. The doula has often gone to the mother's home and has made herself available to her by telephone to discuss the many questions that arise at the beginning of labor. Then many of these doulas continue their association after the delivery. They often provide support to the mother in relating to the baby and in establishing breast-feeding during the postpartum days in the hospital and the first difficult days of adjustment at home.

The results of the present investigations suggest that further studies of any labor intervention must ensure that both groups receive the same amount of attention and support from nursing and medical personnel. An untrained woman provided the friendly support in our Guatemalan study, but a similar or greater benefit might be expected when a family member or friend remains with the mother throughout the labor and birth.

In conclusion, the doula is a low-cost intervention that may be a simple way to reduce the length of labor, Caesarean sections, and a number of perinatal problems. However, there is a real hazard that the supportive companion will be considered less important than medical interventions because it does not fit the western medical model of care. Consequently, it may not be provided, as it should be, for all mothers, every mother, in all hospitals.

Section 4
PRENATAL AND PERINATAL BIRTH TRANSITIONS

Part 1: Birth preparation and birthing strategies

44

Childbirth preparation and unfulfilled transitions

E. Noble

ABSTRACT

This paper examines some physiological, psychological and philosophical fallacies of childbirth education and their role in creating performance anxiety. The mind–body dichotomies in obstetrics, Western culture and language will be explored and new avenues for developing a couple's intuition, flexibility and confidence will be suggested. The importance of regression for maternity care-givers to foster awareness of prenatal events for maternity care-givers will be stressed

Today, the context of birth is a mechanical world, where medicine is no longer just a healing art but has become an instrument of social control. Life events in the West are typically viewed as problems to be solved; indeed the technology that has been developed bears witness to this belief. Concomitant with the rise in technology has been the decline in individual intuitive response and rituals that socially sanction that response. This loss can be seen dramatically in such subcultures as the Australian Aborigines and the American Indians. Rituals that affirmed individual knowing have been replaced by technology which attempts to provide a shared reality. For example, watching TV has taken over from conversation, the routine birth interventions now proscribe and describe the birth experience (just listen to a typical childbirth class!). Awareness of individual reality has thus become subordinated to an illusory 'shared reality' which is ever-expanding through medical technology, political disempowerment and the media. I suggest that the assumption is that the more birth and other experiences can be structured by technology, the more 'shared' is the reality. This is how we deal with alienation – anomie – in modern life.

The childbearing experience is viewed today as a disaster waiting to happen, and must be submitted to the constant monitoring of expert health professionals.

The term, unfulfilled transitions, best expresses the emotional corollary for the mother of events that the medical staff clinically evaluate as dysfunctions in labor. These dysfunctions may be major or minor. Major ones, such as fetal distress or 'failure to progress', usually lead to rapid intervention for which the woman/couple is unprepared. Minor dysfunctions relate more to verbal exchanges, including lack of explanation, insensitive orders or to the use of medication which often impairs memory. Several unfulfilled transitions, both major and minor types, may be experienced around one birth, and the intensity of emotional stress goes beyond what has been described as cognitive dissonance or 'missing links'.

While unfulfilled transitions are increasing with the use of interventions (notably the escalating Caesarean rate), these experiences also arise in the absence of technological interference, such as homebirth. Reality, as Einstein observed, is an individual perception, and it is not necessarily the long or difficult labor that results in unfulfilled transitions. Unfulfilled transitions may be experienced despite the conduct of birth, a common example being disappointment with the gender of the child. Thus human interventions or lack of support can affect labor as much as the technical ones. Imprints received by the mother during her own gestation contribute to the perceptual framework in which these phenomena are interpreted.

Preoccupation with past events which disrupts the integration of the birth experience may impair interaction with the baby, and even drag on to disturb prenatal bonding between the mother and a subsequent baby. Facts are only part of the reconstruction process; feelings about each aspect are the key to resolution. Studies on the 'fourth trimester' are usually limited to the first few days after birth. However, there is a time lag, especially with the altered state of consciousness that prevails during a woman's labor, in assimilating the unanticipated events. This time lag may persist for hours, days, weeks, months or years after the birth. Nancy Cohen, author of *Silent Knife: Cesarean Prevention and Vaginal Birth After Cesarean* has received over 60 000 letters from women lamenting their unfulfilled transitions.

Often the mother feels guilty at acknowledging any deep feelings she has of unmet expectations or aroused primal pain. Clients frequently present a trivial symptom which masks the deeper issues. For example, physical therapy treatment for a one square centimeter numb area at the edge of a Caesarean scar when the real issue is enormous rage, grief and disappointment about the surgical delivery.

Ideally, some working through of primal anguish can be done prenatally and such facilitation should be an integral part of childbirth preparation. For some women, the ultimate connections will emerge during labor and birth – spiritual lessons in living that serve to raise consciousness if handled in a loving way. As Stanislav Grof (1976) noted in his research, women who were mothers could not tell the difference between being born and giving birth under the influence of LSD, and likewise during the birth experience, many women regress to their own births. The present labor may follow the same or opposite pattern. In my own experience, the first stage of labor related to ovum memories, a circular experience of opening and yielding, whereas the second stage of labor was a feeling of linear energy like the sperm thrusting toward a goal.

Many birthing women lose contact with the baby. The staff rarely encourage such contact apart from their job of monitoring of the fetal heart and checking position. Thus psychological alignment between mother, father and child during most labors is less than ideal. Our concern for *postpartum* bonding and mother–child relationships makes the lack of concern for prenatal bonding evident.

Ironically, those who work with birthing women within the medical model (especially men) are generally drawn to this vocation because of their unresolved birth anxiety. While they are physically present, psychologically and spiritually they are absent and thus are unable to support the mother through her emotional transitions. Instead, the staff, with the best of intentions, attempt to bring the mother back into present time, to have her focus on something concrete and external, or rush to implement the technology, whether it be breathing patterns, drugs or anesthesia. Panic is not uncommon in maternity units as rescue measures are set in action leaving many bewildered postpartum mothers to wonder how and when things went awry.

Yet the regressive process, as Michel Odent (1985) confirms, is important for the hormonal balance of birth, and is facilitated in his unit at the Pithiviers hospital with freedom, privacy and dim lighting.

THE LIMITATIONS OF CHILDBIRTH EDUCATION

Childbirth classes based on the educational model are sessions of instruction designed for the left cerebral hemisphere. However, the medium (instructor's non-verbal cues) remains the message despite standardization of curriculum and training programs for childbirth educators. The props of labor (IVs, fetal monitors, Caesareans) receive extended coverage in class and the essence of birth is rarely conveyed. When birth appears to move from one intervention to another couples have neither a sense of the natural flow, nor of the significance of psychological time and the emotional transitions of the labor experience.

The unique and uncontrollable nature of birth does not, in my opinion, lend itself to structure and instruction. The map is never the territory, and couples have been given such complicated maps that they often have their nose in the guidebook and miss the view. Childbirth classes can never be more than a menu, and as with diners in a restaurant, there is no control over the kitchen with regard to delays, disturbances and final outcome. Couples frequently feel confused, tired, fuzzy, out of control after birth and resentful that the dutiful attention at childbirth classes did not guarantee them the experience they had consciously and/or unconsciously expected.

NEW DIMENSIONS IN SUPPORT FOR THE CHILDBEARING YEAR

I see the challenge of pregnancy as the mother's ability to identify with her unborn child in a way that increases her self-esteem. Common symptoms are taken as normal, such as morning sickness. However, nausea is often symbolic of being 'stuck'. Prenatal screening, such as amniocentesis and AFP testing have created, what Barbara Katz Rothman (1986) calls, 'the tentative pregnancy' and definitely delays prenatal bonding.

Experiential sessions are where the women make contact physically with each other's babies, listen to heart beats, share dreams, and art and spiritual assumptions (such as when the soul enters the body). Visualization, guided fantasies and meditation enhance prenatal bonding. However, the real issue is to explore the emotional baggage – unfinished primal business.

An open-ended birth journey is helpful when I work with individual couples. For example, after settling the mother into deep relaxation and a hypnotic state, I ask her to go into the future, seeing all the concrete details of the setting when labor starts: day of week, time of day, signs and nature of progress, etc. Potential blockages can thus be identified and resolved, as in one case where the baby had chosen a breech position, (I gently suggested) to permit the mother to have a honorable Caesarean rather than compete with her partner's first wife who had had two home-births.

Childbirth preparation ideally begins as early as possible, prior to conception. Healing unfinished business from each partner's own birth, and before, is a priority in my work. Such psychodynamics are much more important than feeding the couple a method of childbirth.

I now facilitate childbirth preparation in a weekend format for the extended and heightened group dynamics, rather than a consecutive weekly series. A one-page autobiography of each expectant parent is requested in advance of the workshop. The form requesting information about their own conception, gestation and birth invariably brings the realization that little or nothing is known about these very significant beginnings. That such information is retrievable with facilitation also helps people to become aware of the environment they are creating for their unborn child.

On the Saturday evening, I ask each participant to write a page or two about the future birth in the past tense. These are not shared between the couple until the following morning, when partners exchange birth stories and read them aloud to the group. This is an invaluable tool for exploring fears and expectations, not just of the birth experience, but of role interaction and support systems as well. Synchronicities as well as predictive value with regard to timing and nature of the events are often amazing between couples.

I design the experiential sessions in prenatal classes so that there is no possibility of any right or wrong judgements. Instead, there is sharing of individual perceptions. What has to be learned cannot be taught ... flexibility, confidence and surrender. Letting fear surface so that it can be acknowledged, and to some degree released, is one of the challenges. This may involve expressive bodywork, contact, breath awareness, visualization, massage, meditation and stretching techniques with partners even to the edge of pain in order to learn surrender.

MATERNAL POSITION AND MOBILITY

The physiological advantages of the upright position of the laboring woman, plus ambulation, have been well documented. There are also important psychological benefits. Doctors Moyses and Claudio Paciornik in Brazil, who made the movie 'The Squatting Position Birth' note that:

> 'in the supine position the BEFORE and AFTER stand out as intense moments, while the moment of birth dilutes itself because of the diminishing of the active maternal participation which is unstructured.
>
> In contrast, the squatting position allows a transition which links the BEFORE and AFTER birth. The uninterrupted exchange of stimuli facilitates the emotional rapport between mother and child, especially her confidence in mothering. A baby born this way is thus stimulated by human love rather than artificial procedures.'

PAIN

The major psychological drawback with using medication during labor is the effect on time-perception and the possibility for increased intervention resulting in unfulfilled transitions.

I have concluded (Noble, 1983) that the pain of birth is the pain of *opening up*, involving the mind and heart as well as the body. The cervix and vagina are physically stretched, of course, but the intense energy of the life force, the opening up to the new life and to the primal feelings that surface ... all contribute to make birth an existential crisis. The mother's hormonal adaptation prepares her for this in most cases; unfortunately those who attend her at that time do not have that advantage. DeRohan (1984) comments in *The Right Use of Will*:

> 'Pain in childbirth, for example, is just another expression of less than total attunement between the Spirit and the Will, and between the mother and the child. Total attunement never brings a painful or life-threatening situation to the birth experience.'

If pain in birth results from *resistance* to that expansive energy flow, the challenge then is to surrender resistance to the labor process, and this resistance is both mental and physical. Since the mental resistance draws on many facets of the psyche and the physical resistance reflects the life of the body, confronting that resistance can, and should, begin well before birth, even before conception.

COMMUNICATION AT BIRTH

If knowledge was all that birthing women needed, then the 'experts' would have the easiest births – and that is rarely the case. Rather then, the unfolding of labor depends on intuitive knowing, faith in the wisdom of the body and trust in the natural process of birth–life–death. Physical and emotional support by loving attendants is a common need of birthing women, and I encourage women to take in an intimate friend as labor support. The partner, friend, lover and/or family members can best be there for the mother in their usual role. No partner or friend should expect to become a 'coach' for birth after a crash course of birthing classes. S/he probably has an understandable fear of hospitals, and feelings of inadequacy beside all the medical experts, perhaps as well as personal unresolved birth/death anxiety.

Preoccupation with orders about how to breathe and push overrides the necessary sensitivity to the birth process and emotional evolvement that occurs when the flow is not disturbed by empty transitions.

In a video I saw recently, the woman hired to provide labor support four times commanded the (second-time) mother who was cuddling her newborn, to 'Talk to your baby'. It seems obvious that *her* mother did not speak to her when she was born, and thus she is acting out this need at every birth she 'supports'.

Such 'put-downs' lead many women to feel that they acted wrongly in their labors, especially if attendants begin phrases with the words, 'Don't ...'. The repetition of 'Push, push, push, push' suggests to a mother that she is still not pushing right. Instead, a gentle suggestion, and/or continuing affirmation such as 'That's it ... all the way', 'Your sound', 'Mmmmmm' (rising intensity of pitch), 'Yesss', 'More', 'And that' create a much more encouraging effect and thus empower and expand the woman's activity. 'Bring your baby into the world', is a more positive, more immediate and concrete image than 'Bear down' or 'Push'.

I first became aware of the power of words in facilitating organic response through experiencing my own regression and later observing many others under the facilitation of Australian psychiatrist, Dr Graham Farrant. In a re-birth setting there is, of course, no fetus and hence none of the accompanying anxiety about its well-being. This anxiety, usually unconscious, is the prime reason why attendants at birth are so unaware of their behavior, language and tension. However, the unresolved birth anxiety is often so deep-seated, that nothing short of personal exploration and release will do for most accoucheurs. Then their own individual rebirth experience will allow positive birth practices to be reborn. Those who work in labor and delivery, especially obstetricians, are typically the most resistant to developing this kind of personal awareness, and I would suggest that they at least begin by reviewing their behavior and language using a video format. It is interesting that despite the uniqueness of each birth, most obstetricians 'deliver' women in *their* own consistent way (just look at how women have had to accommodate doctors with the lithotomy position).

Rarely do the birth attendants process the mother's emotional distress during labor. Feelings are usually denied in the interests of 'professionalism' or camouflaged with psychoprophylactic techniques or drugs.

During preparation for a Caesarean the mother can be encouraged to explore self-forgiveness, and to prepare and reassure the baby about the surgical delivery. Yet this is the time the woman is usually treated only as a failing human incubator. The greater the wish for normal delivery, the more reticent the attendants are to come to terms with the mother's disappointment on an immediate emotional level. John Spensely, a pediatrician in Melbourne, Australia and a colleague of Graham Farrant, brings his expertise with primal therapy to the operating room. As the exploration of feelings is done at the time of maximum emotional charge, enough healing and integration is experienced so that a Caesarean mother can be truly present with her baby at the time of the birth. The testimony of women who were thus helped to avoid unfulfilled transitions is very convincing.

A phenomenological approach, as outlined by Lewis Mehl and Gayle Peterson (1985), is needed in labor to replace diagnostic labels. For example, body language clearly indicates if a person is tense, and rather than teaching a relaxation drill, the challenge is to discover the origin of the tension. Likewise, an arrest of labor indicates that for some reason, the woman does not want to give birth at that time, or place. Simply administering pitocin or doing a Caesarean sidesteps the causal reason, and certainly leads to unfulfilled transitions.

Germaine Greer (1985) observes in *Sex and Destiny: The Politics of Human Fertility:*

> The expectant mother today, instead of being aided by familiar figures whom she trusts and who have nothing else to do for the time being but assist her, is competing for the attention of professionals, who will not give her their undivided attention unless she earns it by turning into a medical emergency. Hospitals do not encourage competence in giving birth because they do not recognize it, let alone reward it.'

In contrast Greer observes that:

> 'The ways of managing childbirth in traditional societies are many and varied; their usefulness stems directly from the fact that they are accepted culturally and collectively so that the mother does not have the psychic burden of re-inventing procedures.'

The couple is the ultimate consumer unit in Western society, but obstetric patients are transients in a health care system that is beset by contradictory and fashionable obstetric trends. We have lost our heritage of collective experience as birth practices are fragmented between generations in modern times. Consequently, the best we can do is to honor each couple as unique and help them seek their own style of birth with some of the approaches that have been indicated here.

Copyright 1988 Elizabeth Noble. All rights reserved.

45

Effects of a prenatal intervention program

K. Van de Carr, R. Van de Carr and M. Lehrer

ABSTRACT

The purpose of this study was to test the effects of a prenatal stimulation program of specific sensory stimuli and word associations (the Prenatal University Program (TM)) upon the development of mother–infant attachment, as well as the physical condition of the infant at birth.

Five obstetricians in the same hospital, provided 20 experimental groups and 20 control patients. The data were collected by the obstetric nurse 24–48 hours postpartum. The two groups were matched on ten demographic variables.

Using the Neonatal Perception Inventory, the mothers in the experimental group had a significantly higher rating of their infants than mothers in the control group (p < 0.0005). Experimental mothers of first borns or with other children evaluated their newborns more positively than mothers in the control group and were more pleased with their pregnancy and the birth experience (p < 0.035). Mothers in the experimental group had a more positive evaluation of their babies' physical and emotional response to them, as well as more confidence in meeting their babies' needs (p < 0.002). The effects of prenatal stimulation program on the physical development and health of the infant were suggested when the 5 minute Apgar score showed a significantly higher experimental group score (0.035).

It has been suggested that there exists a critical time for the establishment of mother to infant attachment, termed 'bonding' (Klaus and Kennell,

1975). However, other researchers have stated that the 'critical period' of immediate mother–infant separation or contact has had little long-term effect on the mother's subsequent behaviour and attitudes toward the infant (Dunn and Richards, 1977; Leiderman and Seashore, 1975; Carlsson et al., 1978; Leifer, 1980; Goldberg, 1983).

Even though immediate contact after birth has important benefits, the total emphasis on that period obscures the importance of mother–infant attachment as a developmental process. A crucial factor in that process of mother–infant attachment is the mother's early perception of her baby. Consistent with this belief are findings that the mother who considers her unborn child as a person early in pregnancy is more likely to form a good relationship with the infant after birth (Macy and Falkner, 1979; Seashore, 1979). It was also found that not perceiving the fetus as a person by 36 weeks of pregnancy was seen as related to a delayed onset of maternal attachment (Robson and Kumar, 1980).

Another significant factor affecting the mother's attachment to her infant has been the father's acceptance and involvement in the pregnancy (Cronewett and Newmark, 1974; Greenberg and Morris, 1974; Peterson, Mehl and Leiderman, 1979; May, 1982). It was shown that the father's involvement in the pregnancy was promoted by his awareness of the fetus as a person, which was enhanced through the father hearing the fetus' heartbeat and feeling the fetus move within the mother's uterus (May, 1982).

With the advent of advanced scientific equipment (sonogram and fetoscope) it has been demonstrated that the fetus is considerably more sophisticated and capable of responding and learning than had been previously realized (Schwartz, 1980; Verney and Kelly, 1981; Chamberlain, 1983).

By the fifth month *in utero*, the fetus can hear and respond to stimuli outside the uterus (Eisenberg, 1969). It appears that the infant has an inherent tendency to seek and respond to stimuli that will activate and promote maturation of functioning (Als and Duffy, 1980; Van de Carr, Lehrer and Van de Carr, 1984). Auditory and visual stimulation was found to facilitate the maturation of the function that was most ready to mature. It has also been shown that there is a transference of effect from one sensory modality to another, suggesting that stimulation through one modality may affect the maturation of another sensory system (Gottlief, 1971). Economically stressed mothers who were 'communicating with their babies' were shown to have more positive perception of their infant (Van de Carr, 1985).

The present research was based on the hypothesis that mother–infant attachment is a developmental process and may be enhanced through intervention beginning in the last trimester of pregnancy (the time period during pregnancy when the fetus has been shown to be capable of receiving and reponding to outside stimuli). A prenatal intervention program which has been used in obstetric practice since 1979 was selected to test out this hypothesis. In this prenatal program, mother, and father if living in the home, received a systematized method of parent–fetal communication and interaction. The program utilized both written and audiovisual material, as well as brief instruction and reinforcement during normal obstetrical visits.

Five obstetricians with clinical practices in the same geographical area, who used the same hospital for their deliveries, agreed to allow their patients to participate in this study. The experimental group consisted of 20 patients using the prenatal stimulation program and 20 control patients in normal obstetrical care. Subjects were gathered at the time of the birth of their infant. All subjects were unaware of the study until after the birth of their baby. The subjects were all approached between 24 and 48 hours postpartum. Those subjects who were willing to participate were given forms by the obstetric nurses. The completed forms were then collected and submitted to the researcher. The researcher did not have direct contact with any of the subjects, thus eliminating potential bias effects.

After the completion of the forms by 20 subjects in both experimental and control groups, the groups were analyzed in terms of ten demographic variables. One experimental subject was removed from the group because the subject stated on her prenatal record that she had not read the manual and was not interested in carrying out the program. After removing the subject from the experimental group, another subject was obtained.

The demographic variables were used to evaluate the similarity of the experimental and control populations. These variables were: age of mother, education, income, mother working or not working, father present, previous children, alcohol consumption during pregnancy, cigarette smoking, major health problems and Caesarean births. It was determined that there were no significant differences between the experimental and control groups based on these demographic variables. This implies that the experimental and control groups were drawn from the same general population. This further suggests that any significant differences in the dependent variables would be attributable to the effects of the stimulation program.

The data were then compiled and processed by computer and the analysis was then reviewed by an independent statistician to confirm the validity and processing methods used.

The purpose of the research was to evaluate the effects of the prenatal stimulation program on the mother–infant attachment process. The Neonatal Perception Inventory (NPI) was utilized to test one obstetrician's clinical impression that program mothers perceived their babies in a more beneficial way. The mean score of the experimental group was substantially higher at 4.6, while the control group showed a lower mean score of 1.4. The significance level as determined by the Student's t test was 0.0005.

When evaluating the experimental and control groups' perception of an average baby, it was found that both groups held similar expectations of an average baby. The mean for the experimental group was 16.3, compared to the mean for the control group of 17.1. The level of significance was not statistically significant at 0.4. This finding is important in that both experimental and control groups started with similar expectations of an average baby.

The results of the findings on the Neonatal Perception Inventory support the concept that a pregnancy intervention program beginning at the fifth month of pregnancy can have a definite effect on the mother's perception of her newborn at birth.

The Neonatal Perception Inventory has been utilized to indicate babies at risk of developing a later emotional disorder (Broussard and Hartner, 1971). It was not the purpose of this study to identify infants at risk, rather to evaluate the mother's perception of the newborn with an instrument that has been widely evaluated in the early postpartum period. In this study the mothers in the experimental group had a significantly higher rating ($p < 0.0005$) of their infants than the mothers in the control group.

An additional finding of interest is that mothers of first borns in the experimental and control groups scored higher on the NPI than mothers with other children in both groups. This implies that if a mother has other children she may respond to her newborn in a different way than if this were her first child. This may be due to a more 'wait and see attitude' in experienced mothers which may slightly reduce their enthusiasm as compared to mothers of first borns whose responses show higher evaluation of the first born children. The scores of the mothers with other children on the NPI were also interesting in that the mothers with other children in the experimental group had an average mean score of 4 compared to the mothers with other children in the control group that had an average mean of 1.1. It appears that experienced mothers with other children in the experimental group showed enhanced positive perception of their newborn when compared with the control mothers.

This suggests that the effects of prenatal stimulation are evident in both mothers of first born and mothers of other children. Mothers of first borns in the program and mothers who have previously had a child both evaluated their newborn more positively than mothers in the control group. The results of the data, therefore, supported the first hypothesis of the study.

The Pregnancy-Birth Questionnaire was designed by the researcher to assess the subject's perception of the pregnancy and the birth experience. Results of the study showed that the experimental subjects in the Prenatal Stimulation Group (PSG) had a higher mean score of 14.6, as compared to the mean score of the control group of 13.2. The statistical significance was found to be at the 0.035 level. When individual questions from the Pregnancy-Birth Questionnaire were analyzed it was found that all of the questions were significant or approached significance in the predicted direction. The overall impression is that mothers in the experimental group were generally more pleased by the birth experience than mothers in the control group. This is most likely attributable to prenatal attachment between mother and infant that occurred prior to birth due to the mothers' use of the prenatal stimulation program.

However, the only question which was significant at the 0.05 level was the one which assessed the mothers' opinion about the ease or difficulty of the birth process. The response of experimental mothers to the birth process indicated that the birth process was perceived by the mothers to be significantly 'easier than expected' as compared to the mothers' responses in the control group.

An interesting possibility exists to explain these results. The prenatal stimulation program which was used has some specific parts which are meant to help facilitate the birth process. An example of this is the use of the word 'squeeze' which the mother demonstrates to the baby while saying the word, from the 7th month on during pregnancy. The program maintains that the use of this early modeling of an actual part of the birth process to the baby is helpful in preparing the infant and mother for the physical contractions and perhaps lessening the stress of birth for both. Therefore, the results of this study which showed that the experimental mothers felt that the birth experience was significantly easier than expected, is consistent with the idea that the prenatal stimulation program helped prepare the mothers to have a more positive birth experience.

The Mother–Newborn Scale was designed by the researcher to evaluate the mother's perception of the baby's response to her, as well as her ability to assess the baby's needs. The mean score for the experimental group was 64.5, as compared to 54.6 in the control group. The higher score in the experimental group was significant at the 0.01 level.

The results imply that the mothers in the experimental group felt that they understood their baby's responses better than mothers in the control group. This is consistent with the contention that the prenatal stimulation exercises taught the mothers to be able to notice differences in how their babies were developing during the prenatal period. The mother's ability to become a good observer during pregnancy seems to have carried over during the period soon after birth. In addition, some of the prenatal stimulation exercises taught the mothers to respond to and to reinforce their baby's kicking. It is possible that the prenatal stimulation program enhanced maturational development. Additional research should explore this preliminary finding.

A potential consequence of enhanced development would be infants who are more mature at birth and are therefore more responsive and capable of making their needs apparent to their mothers. Another possibility is that the mothers in the experimental group felt more confident in being able to know the needs of their newborns. This would also be attributable to the prenatal stimulation exercises and would result in the mothers continuing to pay attention to their infants in ways which would allow them to respond better and convey a sense of involvement and sensitivity to the baby. In either case these results show a very important effect of the prenatal stimulation program on the mother–infant attachment process as measured at birth on the Mother–Newborn Scale.

The questions on the Mother–Newborn Scale were individually evaluated for significance. Of particular interest were responses on the questions which assessed the mother's perception of the infant's gaze at mother and perception of the baby listening to the mother's voice. The baby's ability to make direct eye contact with the mother has been supported in the literature (Van de Carr et al., 1984). It has been shown that babies who have had their fathers involved during the pregnancy frequently turn to the sound of the father's voice (Greenberg and Morris, 1974; Van de Carr et al., 1984). The experimental mothers' response to these questions was significant at the 0.004 and 0.045 levels, respectively.

The possibility that program babies might do better at birth was tested by evaluating Apgar scores. The Apgar scores consist of two evaluations one at 1 minute, the other at 5 minutes. The Apgar scores consist of the following criteria: heart rate, respiratory effort, muscle tone, cough and color.

The study found that the 1 minute score on the Apgar was not significantly different in the experimental and control groups. The mean of 8.75 in the experimental group was slightly higher than the mean of 8.55 in the control group. However, the significance level of 0.22 showed no statistical difference between the two groups.

The 5 minutes Apgar score for the experimental group, however, showed that a significant difference existed between the experimental and control groups. The mean of 9.10 in the experimental group was significantly higher than the mean of 8.85 in the control group. This statistical significance was at the 0.03 level. The hypothesis was confirmed on the Apgar score at 5 minutes.

Although there appears to be a tendency toward a higher score in the experimental group on the 1 minute Apgar, it was not at a statistically significant level. This was probably due to the effects of the delivery experience that are more pronounced at the 1 minute Apgar, and may not be as representative of the baby's condition as the 5 minute Apgar score, i.e. the baby is still in relative shock at 1 minute after birth and the immediate physiological state due to the delivery is most relevant. A second factor that may be important is that the Apgar score at 5 minutes may be a more accurate evaluation of the infant's condition than immediately after birth. It was also supported in the research that the 5 minute Apgar has greater predictive value of the baby's subsequent physical condition (Apgar et al., 1957). The results of this study, therefore, show that the Apgar scores at 5 minutes were significantly better in the group of babies who had received the prenatal stimulation program. This supports the hypothesis that the prenatal stimulation program may have enhanced the baby's physical development during the prenatal period.

46

The role of emotional and social support to pregnant teenagers (edited extract)

E. Scarzella Mazzocchi

ABSTRACT

The Village of Mother and Child (Villaggio della Madre e del Fanciullo) is a social center created in 1945 which has, little by little, specialized its services in the treatment of pregnant adolescent girls and mothers. Their stay begins with the onset of pregnancy and is extended without limit after the child's birth. One immutable premise of the Village is that the mothers are not separated from their children at any time, thus giving them the opportunity of maturing as mothers through the daily experience of being with their child. Further, this arrangement provides them with options: the continuation of studies, specialized training (in an educational atmosphere within the Village) or even continuing to work. All this takes place with the support and stability offered by an experienced resident staff.

TREATMENT CONTINUITY WITHIN A SECURE ENVIRONMENT

The prenatal period, the delivery and the first period of the child's life must represent a treatment continuity within the same environment. Establishing a stable and secure environment during the prenatal and perinatal period is extremely important in order to avoid pregnancies at a high psychological risk. For the unmarried mother, rejected by her family and society, the child growing inside her is not only experienced as a physiological entity, but also as a life creating and psychological being.

We have learned from our work experiences how important it is to try solving our young mother's problems with her family and/or the child's father as soon as possible. In order to assure that the physiological symbiosis of 'mother–child' is also experienced as a healthy psychological symbiosis, it is essential in our work to cure the young girl's feelings of guilt towards her family during the pregnancy. While the child is growing inside her, the feelings of guilt need to be substituted by fostering feelings of caring and responsibility. Here we see the importance of the environment to assist in this necessary transformation. Without a positive support group comprised of both medical and psychological counselors, the beleaguered girl faces a lonely uphill battle for which she is ill-equipped.

One of the fundamental principles in our work is to encourage the young girl and her 'partner' (whoever it was through whom she conceived) and their families to understand that it is essential for the unborn child to clarify their relations from the very beginning of the prenatal period and to decide early on if it is worthwhile or not to create a 'home' together. From these dialogs between the young 'couple', the realization of the consequences of having conceived a child is 'borne' out. The young mother's maturity is also developed and this is extremely important. After all, it is she who some day will have to answer the child's question concerning its father (in the case where he is not the biological father).

The medical and psychosociological assistance aids the pregnant minor not only in reducing any danger to which the child may be exposed, but it is also an extension of a line of treatment representing an unbroken continuum integrating medical, psychological and educational dimensions. Through treatment, the line of which will be defined by the staff team, a therapy to help develop the young girl's personal and psychological resources is undertaken. The newborn child may even become the means, thanks to which the mother will be able to live through negative elements which survive in an unconscious affective form from her own early childhood. The sexual act which determined the pregnancy is very often still thought of as an irreparable guilt, reinforced by the family and society. Perhaps such feelings in the young girl can cause reactions of aggressiveness towards her mother/family, flight from home, or even attempted suicide in extreme cases. The point of a comprehensive continuum of therapy is to help the young woman through these problems; at the same time providing support and the security of knowing that all is well while she builds her own sense of inner security and maturity to face the important task ahead – motherhood.

THE PSYCHOPROPHYLACTIC PREPARATION FOR BIRTH: ELEMENTS WHICH ASSIST THE MOTHER AND CHILD IN EXPERIENCING A GENTLE BIRTH

Our midwife and gynecologist help the young pregnant women to overcome their anxiety and provide them with a sense of security. The medical examinations, which are necessary to ascertain the unborn child's development, coupled with the regularity of contacts with the other counselors, help the future mothers to experience their pregnancy in physiological and psychological symbiosis. The gynecologist's observations, and any problems which become apparent as a result of these observations, are employed by the counseling staff in their assessment of the young woman's immediate psychological needs. In addition, the young girls attend preparatory courses concerning the course of their pregnancy and the birthing process. Through the knowledge obtained during the preparation for the delivery the future mother can follow the course of her three delivery phases mentally and physically.

At the time of delivery the staff with their familiar presence will be on hand, will accompany the mother to our 'delivery home' (a small internal clinic), and attend the birth to offer emotional support for the young mother. If necessary the same arrangements can be made with an outside maternity clinic, in the event of complications.

Abroad, and within Italy, the proper psychoprophylaxis for delivery has already been realized years ago: the necessity for a convivial pregnancy, delivery without over-medicalization, promotion of home birth deliveries where possible (attended by a midwife), and even deliveries by water immersion have been instituted in many cases. But, outside a few exceptional clinics, the newborn child is always separated from its mother shortly after birth. Typically, only the hospital's nursery and staff are there to welcome the newborn child.

At the Village, mothers and their newborn are never separated unless there is a medical emergency. Home birth is the best way to promote this bonding process and it is the birthing method we use here, unless there are complications. The birthing experience and post-birth period comprise some of the most important moments between the mother and child in terms of initiating attachment and bonding. This is especially so for young mothers who are unmarried and may otherwise suffer ambivalent feelings toward the child. The post-birth stage is the most crucial for bonding and should not be taken over by a staff nurse, no matter how well intentioned. Such an experience is the privilege and right of the mother and no one should take it away from her.

So we can conclude that a good preparation, and not to be forgotten, the environment and the atmosphere, all play a very important role in conditioning the woman for her labor. It is obvious that, in order to guarantee security for a labor assisted in this way, the doctor and the midwife must have a good knowledge and experience in working together in this 'old fashioned' way (without the aid of too sophisticated technological means). Prior preparations must be made for an external hospital to receive them immediately if possible complications arise during labor.

HELPING THE MOTHER TO GROW WITH HER CHILD

The child determines the family life in the home. At the Village this 'home' is composed of six young girls, either pregnant or mothers with their children, under the guidance of three resident women educators, who relieve each other periodically.

When the baby is about 3 months old, if the mother has to be away for a couple of hours a day for her studies, it is important that the child remains in the same environment and atmosphere to which it is accustomed. They play together in small groups with the other babies in their big play pen, stimulated by a nurse who helps the young mothers to understand the importance of psychomotor development. Observing the relations between the babies, one discovers that the child who is deeply bound to its mother in a positive way is more often behaving in a harmonious way towards its small friends.

The artisan school integrated into the Village center, which is also open for girls coming from outside the Village, gives our young mothers the opportunity of expressing themselves through the different activities of this workshop – and perhaps to earn their own pocket money from weaving cloth and sewing clothes. We also give our mothers the possibility of continuing their interrupted schooling on the Village's premises. The voluntary teachers, fully understanding the principle of the child's right, accept working hours to fit in with the baby's hours.

THE POST-BIRTH CARE AND FOLLOW-UP

One of the principles of our work is to avoid at any price the premature leaving of the mother and her child before close relations have been established between them. Such a relationship reinforces the young girl's resolve to take the responsibility for the baby upon herself. In this way the child will not become the grandparents' child and it will not run the risk of being put into an institute.

Our aftercare presents follow-up assistance without any pre-established limits. Follow-up care is determined according to the mothers' needs (problems with their families, work, lodging, health and newly arising psychological problems). This help includes a whole range of counseling services, from daily assistance to less frequent contacts[1]. Our close relations with the mother, who finds our understanding and respect in the moment of rejection by her family and society, also helps later to create strong bonds with her child. These children, during their early growth, will need an extra source of security and someone to communicate with in order to reach the age of puberty without suffering undue psychological injury. Further, our experience teaches us that it is fundamental that the child is informed about its father (if he is not the biological father) as soon as possible.

Generally, the inquiries coming from mothers who have left the Village are not of a material nature, as one might expect, even though several among them have economical problems. More often, we find ourselves face to face with loneliness, which happens to all mothers generally, but particularly to the unmarried mother.

Out of the 444 mothers who have left the Village between 1957 and 1970, 41% married (17% to the child's father, and 24% to another partner). 13% of our mothers were separated from their spouse. (These statistics were reported at the International Congress on Medical Sexology in Paris, 1973. The latest statistics are not yet ready for publication.)

RESEARCH CONNECTED WITH THE VILLAGE

The research of the Village is a natural consequence of the human relations which have been created with our mothers. The integration of the child into the mother's life gives the answers to our research questions and the fulfilment of our work. The child is our school book, by him we measure our results; the child shows us our mistakes and tells us what has to be done.

From the very beginning of the Village's 'life', we considered it important to transmit our own studies and the elaboration of our research on the child's rights through field-work training. Since 1969 the Village has been in contact with the University of Milan and later with the University at Padova. Already 18 theses have been defended. Of course, this field training has always been open for the social workers, nurses and educators' research departments – as well as those studing psychology and child development. The alpha and omega of our field training programs is to stress that the students must always consider the child *in relation* to the mother from the very onset of pregnancy and throughout the birthing process.

We think that society should consider the prenatal period as one of the most important human events. One has only to consider prenatal injuries (and mortality) to realize what it costs society to have such a large number of psychologically handicapped people.

Section 5
CULTURAL AND ETHICAL DIMENSIONS OF PRENATAL AND PERINATAL PSYCHOLOGY AND MEDICINE

Part 1: Cultural aspects of research into prenatal and perinatal development and experience

47

The cultural and historical evolution of medical and psychological ideas concerning conception and embryo development

D. Gupta and B. Datta

ABSTRACT

Embryology stands in a peculiar relation to the history of mankind. In remote antiquity, although very little was known or understood in relation to conception or development of the embryo, this in no way hindered children being born all the time. Ancient folk-medicine had, therefore, to confine its ideas mostly to simple obstetrics, but at the same time could hardly avoid some kind of speculation of the growth and formation of the embryo. Thus, there is no scarcity of informative materials regarding so-called primitive philosophies of life and their development coming down from the remote past. From this time onwards, through the great embryologists of ancient Egypt, India, Greece and Rome, to the current number of modern obstetric and gynecological journals, the line runs as straight as the Champs-Elysées.

It is surprising to note that all these ancient doctrines on embryology developed in different parts of the world are in many respects quite akin in general attitude to modern medicine and physiology. These remarkable attempts at causal interpretations also included budding forms of genetics and prenatal psychology. It is simply astounding to think how much our modern embryology does owe to the concepts of our spiritual ancestors of ancient time.

INTRODUCTION

Embryology stands in a strange relation to the history of mankind. They share a common bondage. In remote antiquity, although very little was known or understood in relation to conception or development of the embryo, children were being born all the time, and therefore, ancient folk-medicine had to develop certain ideas mostly concerning simple obstetrics. But at the same time our ancestors could hardly avoid some kind of speculation on the formation and growth of the embryo.

One of those archaic primitive concepts with regard to the embryo in the mother's body can be seen in Figure 1. It is a painted and carved door

Figure 1 Painted and carved door from a house in New Guinea (taken from de Clercq and Schmelz, 1893)

CULTURAL AND HISTORICAL EVOLUTION

from a house in Dutch New Guinea, taken from de Clercq's book (1893). The original was of yellowish brown wood. The picture shows that it is a male embryo, but obviously the artist could not decide what to do with the umbilical cord. The line has passed from the uterus to the mother's head. The informative materials regarding so-called primitive philosophies of life and their development come down from the remote past, mostly in the form of paintings. From this time onwards, through the great embryologists of ancient Egypt, India, Greece and Rome, to the current number of modern obstetric and gynecological journals, the line runs as straight as the Champs-Elysées.

During the course of the current investigation to trace the line of evolution of ideas about conception, we have examined carefully the ancient Egyptian sources, the Dhanvantari and Atreya Schools in ancient India, especially Suśruta, Caraka, Nāgārjuna, Agnivesha and Bhāgavata; in Greece, the Coans (Hippocrates of Cos, his son-in-law Polybus), the Greco-Sicilians (Alcmaeon, Empedocles), the Peripatetics (Aristotle), Stoics (Zeno) the School of Alexandria (Diocles, Herophilus, Erasistratus), the Jewish New Wisdom School (Philo Judaeus) and the Roman School (Soranus, Galen, Cleopatra and Oribasius). This course of investigation covers about 1500 years, from about 1500 BC to just after the beginning of the Christian era. The details of various schools and their influence on each other have been depicted in Figure 2 as a chart.

EGYPTIAN SOURCES

Although ancient Egyptian medicine was not much involved with embryology, two aspects indicate that it supplies the starting point for later thoughts. One is the theory of the placenta. According to Murray (1930) there is evidence that the fate of the placenta in the royal families was regarded as of great importance. Some Egyptian royal officials even carried a title, 'Opener of the King's placenta'. The Egyptians believed that besides the placenta, the external soul was also very important for the fetus. The various receptacles were thought of as containing the soul and were called 'The Bundle of Life' (Figure 3 illustrates the 'Bundles of Life' in C–F while A and B show the standard). This figure is taken from the work of Murray and Seligman (1911). They were of the opinion that the term 'Opener' originated from some actual or forgotten ritual king-murder, the bundle of life containing the placenta being ceremonially opened at the conclusion of the reign.

Secondly, the ancient Egyptians also had the knowledge that man and woman both contribute to conception. During 1400 BC (18th dynasty) the

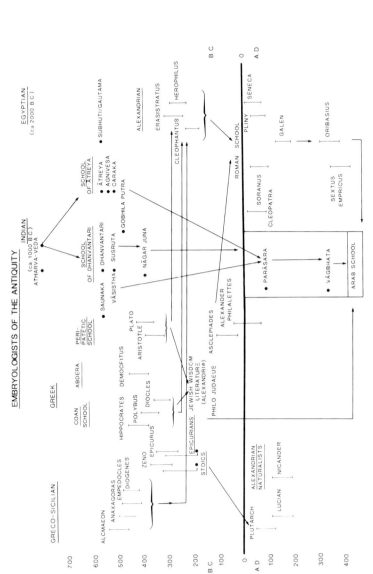

Figure 2 Chart depicting the embryologists of antiquity. Vertical spear-headed lines indicate investigators belonging to the same school. Horizontal lines indicate the influence of one school on the other. The vertical lines with two bars give the approximate time of the embryologists, while for the Indian masters only points are given, as the exact time is not known

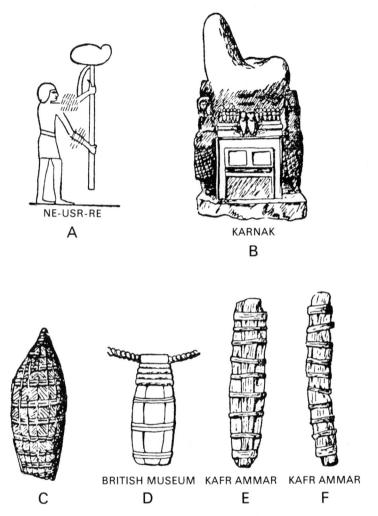

Figure 3 The standard representing the royal placenta (A and B) as found towards the end of the Old Kingdom in Egypt. The figures C–F represent the bundles of life (Murray, 1930)

great king Akhnaton wrote a hymn to establish the new sun-god Aton, saying:

> 'Creator of the germ in woman,
> Maker of seed in man,
> Giving life to the son in the body of his mother.'
>
> (Breasted's translation)

Thus, together with the placenta and the traditional form of the womb as it appears in mythological contexts (Figure 4), this evidence suggests some genuine access to anatomical sources. In Figure 4, Taurt, the hippopotamus-headed goddess of childbirth, is almost invariably represented as carrying the sign of the uterus either in front (Figure 4, left) or at her side (Figure 4, right).

At that time no distinction was made between life and the soul. During this early period there is no trace of notions which appear later, such as the idea that the soul is breathed into the embryo at some particular point in development. In later days (and even today in many circles), these ancient beliefs carried great weight and gave rise to a 'theological embry-

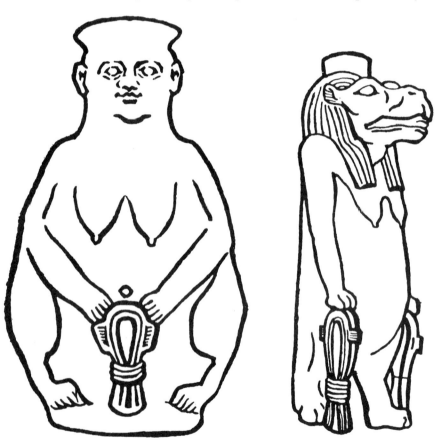

Figure 4 Taurt, the Egyptian hippopotamus-headed goddess of childbirth. The goddess is always represented as carrying this sign of the womb either in front of her (left) or at her side (right)

ology'. This 'theological embryology', in turn, gave rise to a 'pathological embryology' as demonstrated by the research of Teuscher (1888), y Gonzalez (1930), Swenson (1928), and Coghill (1929). A large work on the psychoneural development of the fetus had already appeared more than 50 years ago (1933) in a very well written monograph by Carmichael.

TOPICS DISCUSSED

The formation of the fetus and its development *in utero* have provoked at all times a keen interest among writers discussing generation. This interest cuts across national barriers with surprising speed, even without such facilities as printing technology. The anatomists and embryologists of the ancient days made themselves busy with a variety of questions in relation to generation. They are as follows:

(1) How conception takes place,
(2) Existence of the female seed,
(3) Mechanisms for the
    (a) Male embryo
    (b) Female embryo,
(4) Movement of ovum and sperm,
(5) When is life generated in the embryo?
(6) Formation of the fetal membranes and the development of the fetus,
(7) Position of the fetus during development, and
(8) Parturition.

We will limit our discussion to these primary questions which agitated the minds of our ancient embryologists in their very different and distant countries.

ANCIENT GREEK THOUGHTS

Ancient Greek thought shows much evidence of an appreciation of the mystery of embryonic growth. Nearly all the pre-Socratic philosophers seem to have had opinions upon embryological phenomena, dealing more with fetal development rather than with the fertilization phenomenon. The principal pre-Socratic embryologist was Alcmaeon of Crotona, who lived in the 6th century BC, and who was a disciple of Pythagoras. He is said to have been the first man to make dissections. The fragments of Alcmaeon's work have been collected together by Wachtler (1896). Aristotle also mentioned him in his book on the generation of animals. Alcmaeon described the head of the fetus as the first part of the body to be developed, a justifiable deduction from the appearances.

The anatomists, Democritus (born 460 BC) and Epicurius (born about 342 BC) were involved in the understanding that the embryo ate and drank *per os*. Plutarch of Chaeronea (3rd century AD) in a later commentary compared the views of Democritus and Epicurius with that of Alcmaeon. Plutarch says, 'Democritus and Epicurius hold that this imperfect fruit of the womb receiveth nourishment at the mouth.' Then he continues, 'But Alcmaeon affirmeth that the infant within the mother's wombe, feedeth by the whole body throughout for that it sucketh to it and draweth in manner of a spunge ...' (translated by P. Holland, 1603).

Another very important figure among those early Greek writers, especially for his influence on later thought, was Empedocles (about 480 BC) of Acragas in Sicily. His view, that the blood is the seat of the *innate heat*, recurs in many later authors' works. His teaching led to a belief in the heart as the centre of the vascular system, and the chief organ of the *pneuma*, which was distributed by the blood vessels.

Empedocles believed that 'the embryo derives its composition out of vessels that are four in number, two veins and two arterias, through which blood is brought to the embryo.' He held that the sinews are formed from a mixture of equal parts of earth and air, and the bones are formed from a mixture of equal parts of water and earth. Empedocles also had opinions about the origin of monsters and twins, and asserted that the influence of the maternal imagination upon the embryo was so great that its formation could be guided and interfered with (Diels, 1906).

Like Alcmaeon, Diogenes of Apollonia (5th century BC) also believed that the male embryo was formed in 4 months, but the female not till 5 months had elapsed. Diogenes did not believe, like Alcmaeon, that the head was the part first to be formed in the development of the fetus; he maintained that a mass of flesh was formed first and afterwards the bones and nerves were differentiated (Diels, 1906).

HIPPOCRATIC SCHOOL OF EMBRYOLOGY

The first detailed and clear-cut body of embryological knowledge which superseded all the earlier fragments of speculation is associated with the name of Hippocrates. About him nothing certain is known except that he was probably born about 460 BC, and he lived on the island Cos in the Aegean Sea.

There is no satisfactory evidence as to which works in the so-called 'Hippocratic Collection' are really from the hand of Hippocrates, though there is abundant evidence that the works in that 'collection' are the result of many hands. One of the most likely to write part of the collection is Polybus, the son-in-law of Hippocrates.

For the most part the embryological knowledge of Hippocrates is concerned with obstetrical and gynecological problems. Thus in the Aphorismus, containing the books on epidemics (the treatise on the nature of women, the discussions of premature birth, and the books on the diseases of women) there is an abundance of facts about the embryo, all with obstetrical reference. In this way the Hippocratic School comes far closer to modern medicine in its general attitude.

The treatise, *On Semen and on the Development of the Child*, is a milestone in ancient embryology. The earlier sections deal with the differences between the male and female seed, and the latter is identified with the vaginal secretion. The nourishment of the embryo takes place via the maternal blood, which flows to the fetus and there coagulates to form the embryonic flesh. Later, the umbilical cord is recognized as the means by which fetal respiration is carried out (Ellinger, 1952).

Hippocrates always tried to give a causal explanation rather than morphological description. His theory on the formation of the embryo at first sight seems a little fantasy-like, but several interesting things can be observed. The Hippocratic writer sets out to explain the development of the embryo from the very beginning on machine-like principles, no doubt very much simplified. Some of the theories are as follows (Hippocrates: Treatise on *Regimen*, Section 9):

(1) 'Whatever may be the sex which chance gives to the embryo, it is set in motion, being humid, by fire, and thus it extracts its nourishment from the food and breath introduced into the mother.'

(2) 'By the motion and the fire it (embryo) dries up and solidifies, a dense outer crust is formed.'

(3) 'In this way parts naturally solid being up to a point hard and dry are not consumed to feed the fire but fortify and condense themselves the more the humidity disappears – these are called bones and nerves.'

(4) 'The most interior fire, being closed round on all sides, becomes the most abundant and makes the most canals for itself and this is called the belly.'

(5) 'In the intermediate part the remainder of the water contracts and hardens forming the flesh.'

The most important observation which the Hippocratic writer made was in regard to the embryo drying up during its development. This is also a modern observation. The essential chemical aspect of living matter is oxidation and the development of the embryo is also subject to this rule.

The simple observation of the Hippocratic school comes very close to modern medicine.

In relation to parturition the Hippocratic embryologist also made a very important observation. The writer, comparing the development of the chicken inside its egg with human fetal development, commented:

> 'All (food) has been consumed by the foetus. In just the same way, when the child has grown big and the mother cannot continue to provide him with enough nourishment he becomes agitated, breaks through the membranes and incontinently passes out into the external world free from any bonds' (Hippocrates: *Generation*, Section 30).

Thus, according to the Hippocratic writer the exhaustion of nutriment was the cause of birth. It is of interest to see that modern research is pointing to a probable failure or inefficiency of the mammalian placenta towards the end of intrauterine life as the cause of birth.

Diocles of Carystus in Euboea, a medical practitioner during the 4th century BC, was one of the few who came on the scene between the Hippocratic writer and the emergence of Aristotle. Diocles also regarded the heart as the principal organ and the seat of intelligence. He further developed embryological theory, holding that the seed came from both sexes. Diocles claimed to have examined a human fetus of 27 days and to have found traces of the head and of the spinal column. At 40 days he was able to distinguish the form as human (Allbutt, 1921).

ARISTOTLE: THE FATHER OF MODERN EMBRYOLOGY

Although Plato dealt with various natural phenomena, he had hardly any views on the development of the embryo. Only with Aristotle (1910, 1912), the pupil of Plato, does a general and comparative biology come into its own. A number of monumental works from him, *On the Generation of Animals, The History of Animals, On the Parts of Animals, On Respiration, On the Motion of Animals*, poured out constantly and paved the way for modern embryology. Many natural phenomena, which were silently put aside by great Greek thinkers like Socrates and Plato, were for the first time exhaustively studied and a new sense of orderliness was established.

It is still a mystery whether Aristotle was acquainted with the Coan School and the massive Hippocratic works. Although he always mentioned his predecessors, such as Democritus, Anaxagoras, Empedocles, and even Polybus, he never once quoted Hippocrates. This is strange since from the beginning Aristotle diligently followed the advice of the author of the Hippocratic treatise on generation, and opened chicken eggs at different stages during their development. Of course, Aristotle with his keen scientific eyes learnt much more from them than did the unknown Hippocratic embryologist. It is also evident from Aristotle's writings that he dissected and examined all kinds of animal embryos, mammalian and cold-blooded. However, whether he dissected any human embryo is not clear. In one place he mentions, 'aborted embryo', which could have been a human embryo; but as he never qualified the species of his easily obtainable animal embryos (Ogle, 1882) it shall remain a mystery.

Aristotelian theories on embryology

Aristotle's greatness lies in the fact that the depth of his insight into the generation of animals and the development of the embryo has not been surpassed by any subsequent embryologist. It is true that sometimes Aristotle's conclusions were not warranted by the facts at his disposal, and some of his observations were not correct at all. But he stood at the very entrance into an entirely unawakened field of knowledge, and when he died in 322 BC, human knowledge was vastly enriched.

Aristotle did not believe in the requirement of male and female seeds for the generation of an embryo. According to him menstrual blood was the material out of which the embryo was made. He says:

> 'That, then, the female does not contribute something to generation, but the male does contribute something, and that this is the matter of the catamenia ... If, then, the male stands for the effective and active, and the female, considered as female, for the passive, it follows that what the female would contribute to the semen of the male would not be semen but material for the semen to work upon' (Aristotle: *On the Generation of Animals*, 729^a, 22).

Aristotle continues to discuss the central problems of embryology, but now in a way which presents features of directly physico-chemical interest. Aristotle writes:

> 'When the material secreted by the female in the uterus has been fixed by the semen of the male (this acts in the same ways as rennet acts upon milk, for rennet is a kind of milk containing vital heat, which brings into one mass and fixes the similar material, and the relation of the semen to the catamenia is the same, milk and catamenia being of the same nature), when, I say, the more solid part comes together, the liquid is separated off from it, and as the earthy parts solidify membranes form all around it ...' (Aristotle: *On the Generation of Animals*, 739^a, 22).

This is a remarkable passage. It contains the first important reference to enzyme action made in a discussion of embryology.

According to Aristotle, 'The heart is the principle and origin of the embryo' (Aristotle: *On the Generation of Animals*, 740^a, 20) and then he goes on to describe the membranes of the mammalian fetus and its relationship with the umbilical cord. 'The vessels join onto the uterus like the roots of plants and through them the embryo receives its nourishment. This is why the embryo remains in the uterus' (Aristotle, *On the Generation of Animals*, 740^a, 33). He also believed in concurrent growth and differentiation where the former is temporally followed by the latter. He comments,

> 'The upper half of the body, then, is first marked out in the order of development, as time goes on the lower also reaches its full size in the sanguinea. All the parts are first marked out in their outlines and acquire later on their colour and softness or hardness, exactly as if Nature were a painter producing a work of art ...' (Aristotle: *On the Generation of Animals*, 743^b, 17).

Together with the development of the embryo, Aristotle thought different types of souls entered the embryo in association with the developmental phenomena. He writes,

> '... for nobody would put down the unfertilized embryo as soulless or in every sense bereft of life (since both the semen and the embryo of an animal have every bit as much life as a plant) and it is productive up to a certain point ... As it develops it also acquires the sensitive soul in virtue of which an animal is an animal ... For first of all such embryos seem to live the life of a plant, and it is clear that we must be guided by this in speaking of the sensitive and the rational soul. All three kinds of souls, not only the nutritive, must be possessed potentially before they are possessed actually' (Aristotle: *On the Generation of Animals*, 736^a, 33).

He is verging on genetics when he comments:

> 'The end is developed last, and the peculiar character of the species is the end of the generation in each individual. This means that the embryo attains the point of being definitely not a plant before it attains that of being definitely not a mollusc but a horse or a man' (Aristotle: *On the Generation of Animals*, 736^b, 2).

Aristotle was of the opinion that the different sorts of souls enter the embryo at different stages of development, just as the shape of the embryo gradually approximates to the final adult shape that it is going to possess. (This could be comparable to similar doctrines of succession of souls during embryo development current in ancient Chinese thought (Needham, 1954); conversely, Indian embryologists thought of only one soul, described later.)

Nevertheless, it must be observed that Aristotle is erroneous in supposing the heart to be the first organ to be formed in actuality. The vertebral column and the brain are differentiated earlier. This could not, however, be observed without a microscope. When it is realized that circulation and a rudimentary heart had been discovered in an embryo only 1.3 mm in length, one feels that Aristotle may be excused for his error.

On theoretical grounds, Aristotle believed it is appropriate that the heart should be the organ formed first, for it is here that the blood is charged with *pneuma*, the physical substance most closely associated with the soul. Semen is produced from blood and is, therefore, ultimately dependent upon the heart (Aristotle: *On the Generation of Animals*, 742[a-b]).

Aristotle was also of the opinion that women age after childbirth more rapidly than men (Aristotle: *The History of Animals*, 582[a] and 583[b]). Their moisture cools more rapidly and becomes phlegmatic, and they soon become grey and wrinkled with age. This is especially true of those who have had intercourse frequently. The impediments which delay the gestation of a female are removed after birth, so that women reach puberty sooner and age more quickly.

INDIAN EMBRYOLOGY: SUŚRUTA

One of the earliest known works on medicine in India is the *Atharvaveda* (ca. 1000 BC) which contains a multitude of medical information, although embryology has not been dealt with systematically. We also do not know for certain who were the authors of this vast treatise. Historically, the name of Dhanvantari could be, perhaps, taken as the father of the Indian science of surgery and medicine. His name appears in many passages in the Vedas, the Puranas and classical Sanskrit literature. Though the actual time of Dhanvantari is not known, it seems from scholastic literature that he took part in the discussion about the human fetus in the womb organized by Subhuti Gautama (S.S. Suśruta Saṃhita 3.18), a direct disciple of Gautama Buddha (6th century BC). So it is possible that Dhanvantari's time belonged to about the late 6th century BC.

Suśruta, the great medical scientist, who first presented medical and surgical knowledge rationally and systematically, is considered to be the direct disciple of Dhanvantari, and therefore possibly belonged to the late 6th century or early 5th century BC.

Fertilization and the concept of soul

Suśruta makes it clear that the process of fertilization of ovum by sperm as a result of sexual maturing is an essential feature of conception. But Suśruta believed this is not sufficient for the creation of life. For this the intervention of a superior agent is necessary (S.S.3.2), although certain factors are under human control, such as selection of the parents, the act of mating, and the nurturing of the fetus within the mother's womb. In the middle ages, similar thoughts also developed in Europe. The necessity of a superior agent and the descent of soul into the fetus at a particular time during pregnancy were especially stressed (Figure 5).

Figure 5 An illustration showing the descent of the soul into the embryo (left panel) (taken from C. Singer, 1917)

Planned parenthood

On the basis of this very rational deduction on selection of the parents, Suśruta formulates some important principles of human genetics. Based on the application of scientific knowledge and practice with the purpose of improving the factors under human control (S.S.2.35), he gives an analogy between the plant and human being. Just as the growth of the best possible specimens of any particular species of plant requires the ideal *bija* (seed) and *ambu* (nutrient and the environment), so the birth of the best type of human being could be skillfully manipulated by the co-ordination of the ideal conditions, relating to *rtu* (particular date of mating during the menstrual phase), *kṣetra* (womb), *bija* (parental seeds) and *ambu* (nutritive substances from the mother's body).

Together with these factors under human control, Suśruta stressed the intervention of some kind of superior agent which he termed *kṣetrajna* (disembodied soul) – eternal, indestructible and capable of penetrating anywhere in space. A living being arises from the association of a material body with such a *kṣetrajna*. The emergence of life takes place only when the disembodied soul descends into the body (see Figure 5).

Suśruta maintained that the prospective parents should be adult men and women (not teenagers) endowed with perfect healthy semen and menstrual flow respectively. If these are not up to the proper standards, or are vitiated by deranged humors, or by defective blood, normal conditions should be first restored by medical treatment (S.S.2.2.5). Certain defects of the sperm and of the menstrual flow are considered beyond remedy. Persons suffering from such defects are declared unfit for procreation (S.S.2.2,4.5).

Ancient genetics

According to Suśruta, the conception of a male child occurs when the sperm is stronger than the ovum; the reverse holds for a female child. When the sperm and ovum are exactly matched in potency, a rather rare occasion, a hermaphrodite is conceived (S.S.3.4). Suśruta comes close to modern genetics when he says that the bodily and mental characteristics of the future child, whether manifest or latent, are pre-determined. The character of the hair (on the head, face or body), bones, nails, teeth, veins, arteries, nerves, tendons, semen and all other stable and firm components of the body are derived from the male parent; that of the muscles, blood, fat, bone-marrow, heart, umbilicus, liver, spleen, intestines, rectal parts, sex organs and all other soft components from the female parent. Valour, health, constitution, brightness of complexion, and intellect arise from the physiological and spiritual harmony of the parents (S.S.3.31).

Embryonic growth and the elements of life

According to Suśruta, the sperm–ovum complex which is formed after mating is transformed into a living fetus as soon as the disembodied soul (*ksetrajna*) enters into it. The constituents that are present and endowed with life are the five primal elements forming the material body of the zygote. These are the thermal principle (*agni*) contributed by the mother's ovum, which is potentially the second humor *pitta*; the placid principle (*Saumya*) from the father's sperm, which is potentially the third humor, *slesman*; the omnipresent cosmic *vāyu*, which becomes the first humor *vāta*; the three fundamental reals (*Guṇas*) – essence, energy and inertia; the five senses; and the disembodied soul. This complex forms the living entity (S.S.4.3).

Immediately after conception, the active principles begin to play their individual parts in the future development of the embryo (S.S.5.2):

Vāyu: this cosmic principle divides the material particle into the three bodily humors, the seven bodily *dhātus*, the elimination products, the individual limbs and organs, etc.

Tejas: this fiery principle sets the process of metabolic change.

Apas: this liquid principle is responsible for the embryo's humidity.

Pṛthis: the solid principle moulds it into the shape of its species.

Ākāsa: the ether principle promotes growth and development of the fetus.

Following this, seven successive layers of epidermis (created out of the metabolic substances present locally) are formed and deposited on the rapidly transforming fetus (S.S.4.3).

Aristotle in Greece also held, following more ancient writers, that there were four primary and opposite fundamental qualities – the hot and the cold; the wet and the dry. These are fire, earth, water and air (Figure 6), which meet in binary combination to constitute the four essences or existences which enter in varying proportions into the constitution of all matter. Thus water was wet and cold, fire hot and dry and so forth.

In the Greek conception the four elements, fire, earth, air and water, are closely related to the four humors: blood, black bile, yellow bile and phlegm; while in the Indian conception, the five elements and three humors (air, bile and phlegm) act synergistically, but are not synonymous.

Thus, during the second month of embryonic growth, the fetus is transformed from an indefinite gelatinous mass and becomes denser due to the interplay of the five elements which are induced into its mass through the agency of the three humors. Due to these interactions the

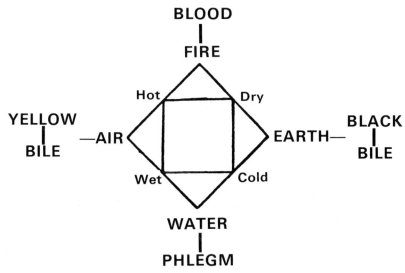

Figure 6 Scheme of the four qualities and the four elements as exhibited in the Aristotelian writings, and of the four humors as exhibited in the Hippocratic and Aristotelian writings

embryo acquires a recognizable shape, a spherical one indicates a male while an elongated structure indicates a female.

By the third month, all the limbs and organs, including the heart, are developed in their rudimentary forms. At this stage of embryonic growth Suśruta's writings elaborate on prenatal psychology. According to him from 3 months on the fetus acquires a consciousness of its surroundings through the action of its heart, and begins to long for sense objects. This longing is reflected through the mother, who is termed to have a second heart at this stage. If, at this stage of pregnancy or even later, the desires of the mother are suppressed or remain unfulfilled, congenital defects may be caused in the fetus; the future child may be paralytic, hump-backed, dwarf, lame, crooked-limbed, blind or suffer from defects of the sense organs (S.S.3.15). In the fifth month, the fetus acquires a mind of its own and is said to awaken. After this the embryonic growth takes the following course:

Sixth month: The fetus acquires intellect.

Seventh month: The limbs and organs of the body approximately attain their future shape.

Eighth month: The vital life-force in the heart of the fetus becomes

	restive and has a tendency to move to and fro. If a child is prematurely born at this stage, there is risk of immediate death due to possible lack of this vital force.
Ninth month:	The actual delivery takes place about this time or a little later. If there is an unusually prolonged period of gestation, medical treatment or surgical intervention is needed (S.S.3.28; S.S.5.).

Nourishment of the fetus

According to Suśruta, nourishment for the growth and development of the fetus takes place by means of the umbilical cord, which serves as a channel for the lymphchyle (*rasa*) formed in the mother's body. This nourishment from the mother's body starts as soon as the fetus is endowed with life (S.S.3.17). Suśruta mentions his mentor, Dhanvantari, who was of the opinion that all parts and organs of the fetus develop simultaneously (S.S.3.18). But as there is no movement of the element *vāyu* (air) in the stomach or intestine, these parts do not function in the fetus. Besides, a membrane covering its mouth and its throat remains full of phlegm (*kapha*), and therefore the fetus is unable to emit any sound. It gets all the nourishment from the mother and sleeps in unison with her. Its movements are limited by the size and shape of the womb (S.S.2.52–53, 56–58).

With regard to the diet of the fetus, Suśruta suggested that this should be changed from time to time, in relation to the requirement of the fetus at various stages of its development. During the first 3 months the diet should be rich in cooling and sweet products with a preponderance of liquid foods. During the third month the best quality of rice should be taken with milk. For the next 2 months milk and yogurt were suggested. From the fourth month onwards generous quantities of milk and milk products, good quality soup and light meat preparations were prescribed (S.S.10.3).

In this way Suśruta's suggestions were meant for the well-being of the mother and the fetus together, or in modern terminology the fetoplacental unit. Suśruta kept a keen eye on the health of the mother during pregnancy. Even when abortion was maintained as strictly illegal and a sin in the eyes of religion, Suśruta recommended abortion in certain cases. For example, when the fetus was known to be defective, or damaged beyond repair or when there was no hope of a normal birth, surgical removal was prescribed. Craniotomic operations involving destruction and subsequent removal of the fetus were also sometimes prescribed (Suśruta Saṃhitā. Cikitsā-Sthāna.15.13–15).

INDIAN EMBRYOLOGY: CARAKA

Besides Suśruta, the other great name in Indian embryology is Caraka. Various dates for Caraka have been proposed by scholastic researchers on the basis of external and internal evidence. But we are still not sure whether Caraka was before Suśruta or after him. As Suśruta has been mentioned as the direct disciple of Dhanvantari, Caraka has been placed as the direct disciple of Agniveśa, who was one of the six disciples of the ancient sage and medical expert Ātreya Punarvasu. This relationship is according to Dṛdhabala, a 9th century expert on medicine, who edited Caraka's writings as well as his revision of *Treatise of Agniveśa*. Mention of Caraka's School of Medicine can already be found in the Taittirīya Saṃhitā, which was composed earlier than 1000 BC. It is also known that Pātanjali, the great grammarian, whose time is ca. 200 BC revised the Caraka Saṃhitā (C.S.). Roy, in his *History of Hindu Chemistry* (Vol. I), after investigating various factors, put Caraka in the pre-Buddhist age, i.e. before the 6th century BC.

Fertilization: semen, ovum and spirit

According to Caraka, conception occurs inside the womb by the union of semen, ovum and the spirit (C.S.4.5). By the physical act of mating, union takes place between the semen (sperm cell) and the female ovum (germ cell), then the spirit, associated with mind, descends and enters into the formed zygote. Thus a new embryonic life is created (C.S.3.13). If the spirit does not descend, no life is created. Conception of all living being originates from father, mother, the spirit and the essence of the elemental properties and nourishment (C.S.3.3). It is the mind that connects the living organism to the spirit and holds the senses together. With the departure of the mind, the organism becomes lifeless matter (C.S.3.13).

Embryo development and genetics

According to Caraka, the embryo is a shapeless jelly in the first month, and tumor-like or fleshy in the second. By this time there emerges the first indication of the future sex of the embryo. In the third month, the limbs and the sex organs are no longer latent but emerge as separate entities (C.S.4.9). The embryo inherits its skin, blood, flesh, fat, heart, liver, lungs, spleen, kidneys, stomach intestines, etc. from its mother (C.S.3.6), while its bones, semen, hair and nails come from the father (C.S.3.7). Its mind, senses, consciousness, ego, memory and life span come from the spirit (C.S.3.10). Its clarity of senses, quality of voice, appetite and vitality arise from parental harmony (C.S.3.11). Its visible shape, vigor, sense of contentment and energy are a result of proper nourishment (C.S.3.12).

The first stage of fetal development postulated by different experts is given in the Caraka Saṃhitā (C.S.6.21).

Fetal psychology

The fetus in the womb has its limbs folded, its head erect and its back towards the mother's abdomen (C.S.6.22). Its heart is connected with the mother's through the umbilical cord and the placenta, the latter is flooded with blood via the pulsating arteries of the mother. The mother's blood transmits nourishment, vitality and complexion. The skin pores of the fetus also absorb nourishment (C.S.6.23). The two minds of the mother and the fetus have an intimate psychical connection (C.S.4.15/12). The fetus may be destroyed, deformed, or may suffer psychic injuries due to the emotional or physical disturbance of the mother (S.C.4.15–30). Caraka was very aware of prenatal psychological factors, and he drew up a comprehensive list for mental stresses and shocks, and habits as well as faulty diets which might cause great mental imbalance in the fetus (C.S.8.21). In this way Caraka could be taken as one of the pioneers who even in those early days put great emphasis on the psychological well-being of the pregnant mother.

OTHER INDIAN EMBRYOLOGISTS

Besides Suśruta and Caraka, other medical experts, who existed either before them or later, also expressed their views on embryology. But these writings as we now have them are neither rational nor coherent, and sometimes they are mere repetitions of Suśruta and Caraka.

With regard to the development of the embryo, almost all the medical experts of the time put forward their views. According to Śaunaka, when the embryo is formed its head appears in the beginning because the head is the root of all the sensory organs. According to Kṛtavīrya, it is the heart which appears in the beginning, because it is the location of both the intellect and the mind.

Nāgārjuna, the redactor of the extant Suśruta Saṃhitā and a follower of Suśruta, elaborated his ideas on embryology. In Kalhana's *Rājtarangini*, the name of Nāgārjuna is mentioned as a great scholar (1,172–173), who lived a century and half after Buddha. According to Parāśara, the umbilicus (*nabhi*) appears at the beginning, because it is from the umbilicus that the growth of the body takes place. According to Mārkāṇḍeya, the hands and the legs appear first, because the activity of the fetus is based on these limbs. According to Subhūti Gautama, the direct disciple of Gautama Buddha, the trunk of the body appears initially, because all the limbs of the body are connected with it. According to Dhanvantari, the teacher of

Suśruta, these views are not correct. All the limbs and organs of the fetus appear simultaneously. Because of their subtlety, they are not directly recognizable. In the beginning the fetus looks like the bud of the bamboo tree, or like a small mango fruit (S.S.3.32).

The Indian embryologists followed the embryonic development very closely and the following passage is a typical summary of such observations:

> 'Within one night of the conception there is a jelly like formation (*Kalala*). Within five nights it takes the shape of jelly having bubbles (*Budbuda*). Within ten nights it takes the shape of blood. In 14 nights it takes the shape of a muscle. In two months, the embryo becomes compact and grows in five different directions. During this period, because of the effect of *vāyu* (air) and *agni* (fire), the head, shoulder, the lower limbs and upper limbs are formed. In the third month, all the limbs and the organs of the body appear simultaneously. During this month the umbilical cord appears. It is with the help of this that the fetus gets nourishment, as a field gets irrigated by the canals.' (Mārkaṇḍeya Purāna: quoted by Dash and Kashyap, 1980.)

Vṛddhātreya commented, 'The *rasa* which is produced out of the four types of eatables in the woman passes through this cord for the nourishment of the fetus.'

According to Parāśara:

> 'during the sixth month, holes appear in the ears of the embryo. During the seventh month vessels, ligaments, bones, phalanges, hair on the head, nails and skin appear on the embryo. The embryo becomes more conscious during this month. When the eighth month is reached, sexual intercourse should not be performed' (Parāśarasmṛti).

Thus, one can see that, already in ancient times, the consciousness of the fetus by the eighth month was recognized. And according to some experts the parturition was the effect of this consciousness. Vaśiṣṭha wrote:

> 'During the ninth month of pregnancy, the fetus gets matured. In the tenth month the fetus develops a hateful disposition (*ghṛni*). He feels his residence in the mother's womb as placement in hell because of the presence of stool and urine there. He feels, "if I get a chance to get out of it then I shall pray God so that I shall never be required to come to the mother's womb again"'.

All this sounds rather fantasy-oriented, but the foundation of prenatal psychology was being slowly established in those days.

The development of the fetus also affects the mother's health. Agniveśa summarized the situation month by month:

> 'In comparison to the other months, during the fifth month of pregnancy, the fetus will have more flesh and blood. Therefore, the pregnant woman becomes excessively emaciated during this period. During the sixth month the fetus gets

more strength and complexion in comparison to other months. Therefore, at that time there will be an excessive diminution of the strength and complexion of the pregnant woman. During the seventh month, the fetus gets nourished from all the aspects. Therefore, at that time the pregnant woman becomes extremely exhausted in all forms' (C.S.4.21–23).

THE HELLENISTIC AGE AND THE ALEXANDRIAN SCHOOL

While in India the science of embryology, even after the passing away of Suśruta and Caraka, had continued developing; in Greece with the death of Aristotle in the year 322 BC embryology as a science nearly came to a stop.

The founder of Stoic philosophy, Zeno of Citium, was born some 20 years before the death of Aristotle. The Stoics regarded the four qualities of cold, hot, wet and dry as ultimate – instead of the four elements of the earth, fire, air and water of the Peripatetics and their predecessors (see Figure 6). With regard to the development of the embryo, the Stoics expressed their views, as summarized by Plutarch,

> 'The Stoicks say that it (fetus) is a part of the wombe and not an animal by itselfe. For like as fruits be parts of trees, which when they be ripe do fall, even so it is with an infant in the mother's wombe ... The Stoicks are of opinion that the most parts are formed all at once, but Aristotle saith the backbone and loines are first framed like as the keele in a ship' (Plutarch, translated by Holland, 1603).

The Epicureans differed slightly from the Stoics in their opinions on these subjects. They thought that the fetus in the mother's womb was fed by the amniotic fluid or the blood. They were of the opinion, in contrast to the Peripatetics, that both male and female supplied seeds in generation.

However, the most important development in this period is the rise of the great University of Alexandria. That seat of learning was important because it inherited all the traditions of earlier times and united them within the boundary of this University. Democritean atomism, Peripatetic science and philosophy, Coan biology and medicine, as well as Athenian mathematics and astronomy, were all carefully collected in Alexandria under the great promoters of learning, the dynasty of the Ptolemies (see Figure 2).

The link between the Alexandrian biologists and the school of Aristotle was Strato of Lampsacus, who came over to Alexandria to become the tutor of Ptolemy Philadelphus. The link between Cos and Alexandria was Diocles of Carystus, who was the last of the Hippocratic school. Diocles also has a certain importance in the history of embryology (Allbutt, 1921). Oribasius, the great Roman gynecologist, refers to him as the discoverer of the *punctum saliens* in the mammalian embryo: 'on the ninth day a few points of blood, on the eighteenth beating of the heart, on the twenty-seventh traces of the spinal cord and head' (Oribasius, translated by Bussemaker and Daremberg, 1851–76). Diocles also described the human placenta, as well as embryos of 27 and 40 days respectively (Plutarch, translated by P. Holland, 1603). In contrast to Aristotle, he held that both male and female contribute seed in generation.

All these influences had an enormous impact on the development of the Alexandrian School, and produced two great physiologists of ancient times, Herophilus of Chalcdon and Erasistratus of Chio, during the 3rd century BC. They experimented much and wrote a great deal, but all except fragments of their writings have been lost. Only recently have they been collected together out of the books of Galen by J. F. Dobson (1925, 1927).

Herophilus described the ovaries and the Fallopian tubes, and made many dissections of embryos. He gave a correct description of the umbilical cord, except that he assigned to it four vessels instead of three for carrying blood and breath to the embryo. Herophilus also much occupied himself with obstetrical matters, but his greatest contribution was the association of the brain with the intellect, in contrast to Aristotle who was of the opinion that the heart was the seat of the mental performance (Herophilus: Dobson, 1925).

Erasistratus did not study embryology as much as Herophilus did, but made some interesting contributions in relation to embryonic growth (Erasistratus: Dobson, 1927). Galen, who admired Erasistratus a great deal, once found fault with him as a mechanistic philosopher. From Galen we come to know the views of Erasistratus with regard to embryonic development:

> 'The heart is no longer at first more than a millet seed, or, if you like, a bean. Ask yourself how it could grow larger otherwise than by being distended and receiving nourishment throughout its whole extent, just as we have shown above that the seed is nourished. But even this is unknown to Erasistratus, who makes so much of Nature's art. He supposes that animals grow just like a sieve, a rope, a bag, or a basket, each of which grows by the addition to it of materials similar to those out of which it began to be made' (Galen, translated by A. W. Brock, 1924).

Jewish wisdom literature

When the University of Alexandria rose to its zenith, the city had become an important Jewish scholastic center. Two centuries later, Philo Judaeus reigned upon the scene with brilliance, and the Alexandrian Jews were writing that part of the modern Bible known as the Wisdom Literature. There are two passages of embryological importance, one is in the Book of Job (X, 10), and the other is in the Wisdom of Solomon (VII,2). In the first, Job says:

> 'Remember, I beseech thee, that thou hast fashioned me as clay; and wilt thou bring me into the dust again? Hast thou not poured me out as milk, and curdled me like cheese? Thou hast clothed me with skin and flesh, and knit me together with bones and sinews.'

The description of embryo development in terms of making cheese can be found in the writings of Aristotle (*On the Generation of Animals*), which has been elaborated upon already. The second reference to embryology could also be traced back to Aristotle, or even to Hippocrates. This was the view that the embryo was formed from (menstrual) blood. The speaker says, 'In the womb of a mother was I moulded into flesh in the time of ten months, being compacted with blood of the seed of man.' It is quite possible that the Alexandrian Jews of the 3rd century BC had been more influenced by the writings of Aristotle than anybody else.

ROMAN EMBRYOLOGY

The Alexandrian school was directly responsible for the introduction of the Greek medical and biological sciences into Roman thought. At the end of the 2nd century BC, Rome received the first well-known Greek physician Asclepiades of Parion, who brought the idea of atomism with him, and became the link between Epicurus and the later methodistic school of physicians. The other great physician, Alexander Philalethes, served as the link between Cleophantus and Soranus, two great gynecologists of that ancient time. Soranus of Ephesus lived in Rome from about AD 30 till just after the end of the first century, about 20 years before the birth of Galen. Soranus wrote voluminously, and he is one of the few authors whose influence on embryology continued into the Middle Ages. His treatise *On the Diseases of Women* was translated into Latin, then back into Greek and finally back into Latin again. It is largely obstetrical, but it shows an advanced knowledge of embryology, and an especially accurate idea of the anatomy of the uterus (Figure 7). Soranus also prepared a diagram showing the complete anatomy of a pregnant woman (Soranus of Ephesus: translated by H. Lüneberg, 1894).

Contemporary with Soranus was a woman gynecologist in Rome, called Cleopatra. Her short treatise on obstetrics was often printed in the collective works of the Renaissance. Although her work was not of a very high standard, it seems that she was a practical obstetrician. Together with Cleopatra the gynecologist, the name of the Ptolemaic queen, Cleopatra (who died in the year 30 BC), is also mentioned for carrying out investigations on the fetal developmental processes. However, this is a legend and the

CULTURAL AND HISTORICAL EVOLUTION

Figure 7 The uterus from the Latin summary of Soranus by Musico. The figure is taken from a manuscript of about AD 850 in the Royal Library at Brussels (MS 3714, folio 16)

source of it can not be traced. It is said that Queen Cleopatra continued such investigations by dissecting live female slaves impregnated by prison guards at known intervals of time from conception – following the procedure of Hippocrates with regard to hen's eggs. This Alexandrian experiment established that the male fetus was complete in 41 days and the female in 81.

Galen: the prince of physicians

Galen of Pergamos (AD 129–199) was one of the most prominent physicians of ancient time. His brilliance completely hypnotized the men of the Middle Ages, by whom he was dubbed the 'Prince of Physicians'. At 16, when his father chose medicine for him as a profession, he began his study at Pergamos under Satyrus. Even at this early period Galen wrote a book *On the Anatomy of the Uterus*, which he dedicated to a midwife.

Most of Galen's writing was done between AD 150 and 180. In spite of his prolific writing, he does not quite rate a very high rank in embryology. Of his 20 volumes of work, only part of one is concerned with embryology.

It is called, *On the Formation of the Fetus*. Together with a rather spurious treatise, *On the Question as to whether the Embryo is an Animal*, it forms his total output on embryology.

Galen differed very considerably from Aristotle with regard to the nature of the generative process. He considered, contrary to Aristotle, that the testicles correspond to the ovaries, both secreting sperm. Basing his remarks on the dissection of animals, he describes the uterus as bifid, each branch conveying seed from the corresponding ovary (Galen, translated by Brock, 1924). Galen believed that the female produced a seed of her own, having a formative or 'sub-formative' virtue which must combine with the male semen if conception was to occur. The attraction of the womb for the semen being such that it is not easily expelled (even by jumping, as in the case of a woman who would seek thus to escape conception), suggests the presence of an active force in the womb, and a *fortiori* in the seed of the womb itself. This retentive virtue of the healthy womb indicates that it retains its seed as something necessary for generation, and this female seed must be active since the menstruum provides the matter of the fetus (Galen, translated by Brock, 1924).

Galen's ideas as to the development of the embryo are strange, being less satisfactory and less based upon experience than his opinion on other medical matters. He considers that the first organ to be formed in the embryo is the liver, which is congealed from the blood, next the brain is formed from the seed, then the heart is formed from the blood. A little later blood vessels and nerves are also formed from the seed. However, when Galen writes on anatomy he gives a correct view. The book on the formation of the embryo opens with a historical account on the views of the Hippocratic writers with whom Galen was largely in agreement. It goes on to describe the anatomy of the allantois, amnios, placenta and membranes with considerable accuracy. The embryonic life, according to Galen, consists of four stages:

> '(1) an unformed seminal stage; (2) a stage in which the *tria principia* are engendered, the heart, liver and brain, (3) a stage when all the other parts are mapped out, and (4) a stage when all the other parts have become clearly visible. Parallel with this development, the embryo also rises from possessing the life of a plant to that of an animal, and the umbilical cord is made the root in the analogy with a plant' (Galen, translated by Brock, 1924).

Galen wrote:

> 'Genesis is not a simple activity of Nature, but is compounded of *alteration* and of *shaping*. That is to say, in order that bone, nerve, veins and all other tissues may come into existence, the underlying substance from which the animal springs must be altered' (Galen, translated by Brock, 1924).

CULTURAL AND HISTORICAL EVOLUTION 533

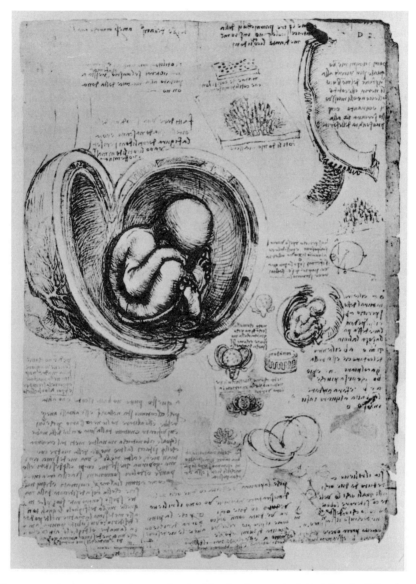

Figure 8 A page from Leonardo da Vinci's *Anatomical Notebooks* (Quaderni d'Anatomia) AD 1490

In this way Galen came very near to the modern views about growth and differentiation. They are also applicable to our current distinction between chemical and biological differentiation on the one hand, and morphogenesis on the other.

The long line of experimentalists, who had arisen in the 6th century BC, came to an end with the death of Galen. Experimental research and biological speculation came to a halt until the age of the Renaissance when medical research and experimentation flourished all over again.

Figure 8 is taken from the *Anatomical Notebooks* by the great Renaissance artist, Leonardo da Vinci. It is a dissection of the pregnant uterus, and its membranes are beautifully depicted. Among the artists of this period, Leonardo was not alone in his anatomical interests, for Michelangelo, Raphael, Dürer, Mantegna and Verrocchio all made dissections in order to increase their knowledge of the human body. But Leonardo penetrated more into the physiology than did the others, and historically he will always remain as one of the greatest of biologists, for he first introduced the quantitative outlook in embryology (Leonardo da Vinci, Ed. Vaugenstein *et al.*, 1911).

Leonardo touched on one of the most modern quantitative aspects of embryology, the exponential growth of the fetus *in utero*. Here we read his note on the subject:

> 'The child grows daily more when in the body of its mother than when it is outside of the body, and this teaches us why in the first year when it finds itself outside of the body of the mother, or, rather, in the first 9 months it does not double the size of the 9 months when it found itself within the mother's body. Nor in 19 months has it doubled the size it was 9 months after it was born, and thus in every 9 months diminishing the quantity of such increase till it has come to its greatest height' (Leonardo da Vinci: Ed. Vaugenstein *et al.*, 1911).

This description is very precisely like a graphic calibration of a child's growth and development curve observed from his intrauterine life until he has reached his adult height. It was another five centuries before C. S. Minot (1908), who first calibrated the growth curve of a baby from fetal life till 241 days after birth, improved upon and verified Leonardo da Vinci's insightful observations.

48

The use of placental symbols in accessing pre- and perinatal experience

T. W. Dowling

ABSTRACT

A brief introduction will be given to what is understood by the term 'placental symbols' and their existence will be related to Jung's concept of the 'collective unconscious'. The relationship between the mythopoetic function of the human mind and pre- and perinatal psychology will be discussed. The example of the symbol of the tree and how it reveals aspects of our experience of the placenta in utero will be explored. This exploration will take the form of a fantasy journey or directed dream. Some of the preliminary results of this technique will be given and the tree-images and stories produced by the subjects present will be discussed.

Several workers in the field of pre- and perinatal psychology have understood and elucidated the existence of what are best called 'placental symbols'. (See, for example, the work of Lloyd de Mause, 'The fetal origins of history' in *Foundations of Psychohistory*.) Ever since the work of Carl Gustav Jung (1875–1961) and his use of the concept of the 'collective unconscious' with its system of archetypal symbols and mythological motifs, many have been aware of the universality of various aspects of the deep unconscious. Jung proposed that every individual stands in relation to and draws upon a transcultural and, in some sense, pre-existent system of symbols and images which informs his unconscious mind and which is always revealed in his creativity. In fact, by definition, it is impossible for any individual to escape from or bypass this system. Every creative act, no matter how seemingly new and unique, draws upon the old, deep-rooted consciousness which fundamentally defines our humanity.

In general, the universality of the collective unconscious has been understood either as issuing from the structure of the brain itself or as an expression of some kind of World-Soul. Jung himself, who claimed to be an empiricist, did not deny the possibility of either explanation but said that he had to recognize the existence of the archetypes without knowing their intimate nature. A good example of this is afforded by his work on the symbol of the tree as used by the alchemists. (See 'The philosophical tree' in C. G. Jung, *Alchemical Studies,* translated from *Von den Wurzeln des Bewusstseins,* Zurich, 1954.)

Jung collects some of the curious statements made by the alchemists about this tree. It is 'like a tree planted in the sea', 'It is red and white', 'Its trunk is red tinged with a certain blackness', 'From it all flesh is fed', 'Nature has planted the root of the tree in the midst of her womb'. When the roots 'are torn from their places, a terrible sound is heard and there follows a great fear'. One author says that the tree is in a region 'closed on all sides, its interior made up of intercommunicating labyrinths'. The 17th century alchemist, Gerard Dorn, writes: 'After nature has planted the root of the metallic tree in the midst of her womb ... and has set its trunk in the earth, this trunk is divided into different branches, whose substance is a liquid ... The branches spread ... as in the human body the veins spread through the different limbs. ...' Dorn continues that this tree 'is like to the branches of a loathsome sponge'. This sponge contains a substance which he calls 'virgin's milk and blessed rose-colored blood'.

After citing all these texts and others, Jung comments: 'The tree is obviously thought of as a system of blood vessels. It consists of a liquid like blood, and when this comes out it coagulates into the fruit of the tree.' However, explicit as this is, Jung still has no idea of the source of this imagery. He writes: 'A sponge that bleeds and that shrieks when pulled up is neither "vegetabilia materia" (i.e. vegetable matter) nor is it found in nature, at least not in nature as we know it.'

With the development of pre- and perinatal psychology, our knowledge of human nature has increased. It can be shown that there is a relationship between our life before birth as sustained by the placenta and our mythologies which so often rely upon the symbol of the tree. All the mythological stories which mankind has told from the dawn of history about trees are stories which are only literally true of the tree of the placenta. In mythologies of all types, we project aspects of our prenatal experience into symbols which by their shape and configuration remind us of that experience. This is why we feel so at home with the symbol of the tree, why it is so central to so many stories, why it is so often a key feature of stories about our 'beginnings'. Even when our stories express an ambivalence or fear towards the tree, as for example in stories about wicked witches who live in a tree-house and poison little children, stories which are rooted in our experience of a placenta which can be both nurturant and poisonous, our nostalgia for the placenta and our deep attachment to the symbol of the tree are still in evidence.

The curious 'tree-therapy' which was used for a short time at the beginning of secular psychotherapy in Europe was popular and successful, although the therapists understood it as a scientific procedure. The 'magnetism' of the tree cured the magnetic fluid imbalances in the patients, who clearly looked at the trees used with far different eyes. They saw and experienced similarities between these magnetized trees and all the sacred trees traditionally used for healing and sustaining of well-being. They were more aware than the therapists with their new ideas that the 'tree-therapy' had an ancient heritage, that it even had something to do with the beginning of their history and life.

It is possible now after the research in pre- and perinatal psychology has begun to understand how and why 'tree-therapy' — whether scientific or sacred — could work to cure some human disorders. Many researchers have demonstrated using various methods that the conditions of pregnancy and any trauma sustained by mother and fetus deeply imprint into the growing child. The patterns of prenatal experience then form the context for all future experience and we can talk of 'fetal scripts', scripts which we re-enact throughout our life. Some of these scripts, learned in the womb in response to conditions prevailing then, are maladaptive and sometimes could lead to self-destruction when lived out in the world of postnatal experience. By their very nature as the first and most fundamental scripts for life, they are very difficult to see and to change. It has taken almost 200 years in the history of Western European scientific psychology for us to approach, accept and begin to understand our prenatal consciousness. In individual therapy, it can take years for a person to face the roots of his psychic pain, personality disintegration and emotional disorder. Many therapists and most psychiatrists are unprepared and unwilling to make the journey to the intrauterine depths of their patients' unconscious. From the point of view of prenatal experience, it can be appreciated that most theorizing about human personality and its disorders hides as much as it reveals and that this concealment prevents effective therapy.

In this workshop, the image of a tree will be used to access some aspects of pre- and perinatal experience. Other images could be used and, no doubt, new images which are placental symbols will be contrived in the future. However, as the world's mythologies testify, the symbol of the tree is the most specific and at the same time the most open and polyvalent representation of the placenta; that is, we can most easily project aspects of our own specific prenatal experience into the symbol of the tree. It speaks to all of us about our placenta, albeit in the most general terms. We can all use it as an entry into the more specific aspects of our deep unconscious and its intrauterine roots.

CREATING A DIRECTED DREAM USING THE PLACENTAL SYMBOL OF THE TREE

In as deep a state of relaxation or hypnosis as possible, whichever can be achieved, and this is not critical, the symbol of a tree is used in a 'fantasy journey' or 'directed dream'. The following instructions are given:

(1) You walk towards a wall and in the wall there is a door. Look carefully at the wall and the door and remember what they are like.

(2) Now you open the door. How difficult is it to do so?

(3) You go through the door and you enter a garden. What sort of a garden is it? Look carefully all around it. What is the weather like?

(4) In the middle of the garden there is a tree. What sort of tree is it? How big, how strong, how many branches, how many leaves? Are there any fruit or flowers? What is the trunk like? What is the earth like around the tree?

(5) Now you climb up into the branches of the tree. You can see the whole garden. Below your feet, there is a little hole. It goes right down the middle of the trunk into the roots. You go down this hole head first. What does it feel like? You go down into the roots of the tree.

(6) Now you are in the roots. What are the roots like? How do you feel down here in this place? What is the earth like? Can you hear, see, smell, touch anything?

(7) Now you come up out of the hole. You come out into the light and the fresh air. What does it feel like?

(8) Now you climb down the tree and stand in the garden and look at it. Suddenly, something happens to the tree. What happens to the tree?

Following these instructions, each person creates their own story and uncovers specific images of garden and tree from their unconscious. Even when the garden and tree are reported to exist in reality, this does not prevent projection onto them and the question of why this particular garden and tree were chosen remains open. The variety of details imagined is often remarkable but the similarity of pattern among certain responses is also striking. For example, the tree is most often struck by lightning and split or simply cut down and removed following the instruction suggesting that something suddenly happens to it.

Many individuals report having experienced some deep aspects of themselves and recognize in the story they create some of their archetypal attitudes and responses to life. The weather conditions in the garden, for example, often correlate to the mood of their most common feelings. There is also some correlation with the specific seasonal duration of pregnancy and the time of birth. Using this technique, some research into the relationship between astrology and pre- and perinatal psychology is possible.

After the fantasy journey, many find it easier to recall or become able for the first time to recall what they actually know of their birth and pregnancy experience. Some are opened in a dramatic way with strong emotional and even physical responses to primal experiences. The authenticity of the recall can in some cases be verified with parents and doctors but even when this is not possible many have a feeling of insight into themselves which is self-authenticating. For example, the motifs of entry into the garden and descent into the tree, and then the movement up and out of the tree often correlate with each other and point to possible birth experiences.

The general well-being of the tree as witnessed by the number of leaves, flowers, fruit and branches correlates strongly with general fetal well-being. The state of the tree often mirrors the state of the garden but not necessarily. For example, the story of a healthy tree standing in a cemetery or on top of a grave has often been given by a person whose mother suffered a bereavement during pregnancy. The picture of an unhealthy tree in a graveyard has been given by those who suffered an attempted abortion or threatened miscarriage.

An unhealthy tree has often correlated to fetal distress and trauma. For example, a tree without any leaves and only few branches has often been seen by a person whose mother was unhealthy during pregnancy or who contemplated an abortion or who attempted one. Lack of leaves or their general condition when bad often correlates with skin problems. Often the state of the leaves reflects the type of soil seen in the fantasy, a tree planted in sand or concrete or on top of a sewer correlating with fetal distress. Prenatal trauma can also suddenly force itself upon the image of the tree, uprooting it or shaking it or in some other way fundamentally changing it. This can occur at any time within the fantasy journey.

When the person in the fantasy has climbed into the branches of the tree and descended into the earth through the trunk, the roots correspond to the placenta. The person's general feeling in this place and the description of the soil are most indicative of their relation *in utero* to the placenta. Whether the size of the roots with respect to the tree actually reveals anything about the physical size of the placenta is as yet unclear from the research. However, the root size does often indicate something about fetal feeding and its adequacy. The quality of the soil is also indicative of general maternal emotional health during pregnancy. If the mother has smoked, for example, it is most often expressed here by a bad taste and small, tight roots.

That one of the most significant aspects of the birth experience is the loss of the placenta has been known and understood by several workers in pre- and perinatal psychology. What happens suddenly to the tree in the fantasy often reveals aspects of this experience. Feelings of loss, constriction, panic, defeat, anger, liberation, can accompany the event which befalls the tree. This event is certainly indicative of the fate of the placenta at birth and the cutting of the umbilical cord but the research here is just progressing. However, one thing which seems clear already is that when nothing is remembered, nothing projected as to the end of the tree, it is often a sign of fetal narcosis or loss of consciousness at birth caused by other factors.

As can be appreciated, what has been presented here are the preliminary indications of a promising line of research. About 200 fantasy journeys around the symbol of the tree have been examined so far but not all have afforded the opportunity of correlation with actual pregnancy and birth experience. However, in most cases, the fantasy revealed aspects of the deep unconscious which the subject found helpful to know in later therapy and analysis. Some startling cures have been achieved.

As the insights gained from the tree-fantasy have penetrated consciousness, there have sometimes been quick and remarkable returns to health. The simple revealing of aspects of the person's relationship to their placenta and womb environment has been enough to begin the re-ordering of their relationship to various aspects of postnatal reality, their home, their sexual partner, their eating habits, their own body in general. It is to be hoped that the symbol of the tree will continue to be so fruitful in research and in therapy and that eventually all of the insights gained may be used to prevent pre- and perinatal distress through the agency not of trees but of flesh-and-blood placentas and healthy, happy mothers.

49

Cross-cultural descriptions of prenatal experience (edited extracts)

T. Håkansson

The process of giving birth is surrounded by so many myths that it is difficult to be objective about it. All cultures throughout history abound with mixtures of legends and facts – and it is interesting to note that it has become in our time and culture a subject of research and regulation. My own interest is not in the clinical aspects of birth but consists more as an emotional speculative art. I do not think that it is possible to deal with birth and death with total scientific objectivity and detachment. For, when we come to the subject of prenatal psychological development and memories, we have less exact methods of research at our disposal in comparison with the physical sciences. Therefore in this paper the problem of the development of a prenatal psychology will include both a personal dimension and a cross-cultural point of view.

Is it likely that we can relive or remember events from our earliest years, right back and even before birth? The historical ethnographic evidence shows that the ability to accept either of these possibilities largely depends upon the cultural perceptions we are born into and which shape our everyday ideas of reality. Our discussion will begin with some non-Western perceptions of the prenatal experience and birth, and then move toward a brief overview of the development of Western psychological ideas concerning prenatal experience. This latter section will focus especially on reviewing the work of Georg Groddeck, one of the first medical doctors in the West to write on prenatal psychology in the early 1920s.

SOME NON-WESTERN PERCEPTIONS ON PRENATAL EXPERIENCES

According to the Anbarra of Arnhem land in Australia, there is no concept of life at birth or even of conception, for life pre-exists in the form of spirit-children 'in the dreaming'. When a spirit-child enters a mother's womb it is transformed into a human baby and then passes through various stages. The newborn baby is not yet regarded as a child but is called by the same term as the unborn and the spirit-child, Yukiyoko (yokoko). No distinction is made based upon sex at this stage, but the word, wupa (inside), is used to indicate that the child is *in utero*. The term child (andalipa for male or djindalipa for female) is not used until the baby begins to smile.

Here, among the Anbarra, birth is seen as a continuum of the 'dream time', which is the ultimate reality for them. There are no negative perceptions attached to the prenatal experience or birth. But to take another non-Western example, the Buddhist and Eastern philosophy in general, life is suffering and birth is an experience to be avoided by various spiritual exercises.

The Hindu-Buddhist religious practises consist of yogic exercises and the suppression of all desires. Preferably it means retirement to a cave, giving up of all possessions and connections, renunciation of all pleasure and sexual satisfaction It is a reconstruction of the prenatal state, where the cave or the isolation in loneliness represents the womb. The renunciation of all pleasure together with a cultivation of hatred and disgust for all bodily functions, fasting, and a fixed rigid bodily posture serve to stop the yogi from wanting to return to the world. Once this temptation is conquered the feeling of disgust has lost its usefulness and can be replaced with a sense of euphoria. This is the second stage and can be described as a regression to a narcissistic ecstacy. According to the Buddhist texts the bikkhu (yogi) is then flooded 'as if a dam inside him burst open'. 'He is surrounded by water ... it covers him completely, fills him and penetrates him from all sides with joyous lust-feelings'. This is the second stage which not only describes the situation of the fetus in the amniotic fluid *in utero*, but also indicates a narcissistic ecstacy of the kind experienced by schizophrenics in a catatonic ecstacy.

The third stage is a deeper regression beyond blissful feelings towards apathy. The fourth and final stage is total emptiness: 'Beyond pleasure and pain, above love and hate, joy and suffering, indifferent to the whole world, to men and gods, to his own self'. This is Nirvana, the conquest of all desires, the return to the womb, the state of the unborn. The Hindhu-

Buddhist yoga is an attempt and method to bring about a physiological and psychological regression to the prenatal state. It is a step-by-step reversal of the gestation, a kind of rewinding back to the intrauterine state.

According to Buddhist beliefs the disciple who has gone through all four stages has an ability to remember, a technique of mnemonics which far exceeds the normal memory. It is rather a complete anamnesia, a total memory to the smallest detail, and with all the emotional charges of the past life. It is a kind of psychoanalysis, a recalling and reliving of repressed memories.

Psychoanalysis tries to go back to the birth process, and prenatal psychology deals with life *in utero*. But the Buddhist-Hindu methods claim that the recalling of forgotten memories transcends the individual life and at the same time reduces all feelings to nothing. There is neither pleasure nor pain. According to Buddhist texts: 'I direct the mind to the remembered knowledge of earlier forms of existence. I remember many different forms of existence such as one life and two lives, then three lives, then four lives, then five lives, then ten lives, then twenty lives, then thousand lives, hundred thousand lives, then times of many creations, then times of many destructions, then times between creations and destructions.'

What does this mean? The memory of all earlier forms of existence beyond birth and conceptions, until man ceases to exist is a symbolic reversal of the evolution. It is a total regression, where all desires cease. It goes beyond birth and through all the prenatal stages, through the development of the embryo, which as we know, is a 9-month repetition of all forms of existence since the beginning of the first living cell. In Eastern philosophy the purpose of all spiritual exercises is to conquer the wish to live, to be born. Therefore one has to recollect and remember the prenatal state until the very beginning in order to undo the meeting of the sperm and the ovum, and permanently prevent their union. This means that the regressive memory goes back to the very beginning of the conception. Nirvana means not only the total regression to the beginning of evolution but also a clairvoyant knowledge of all forms of existence from the beginning of life. What Buddha claims to have reached is our basic biogenetic law.

In this connection I like to refer to *The Tibetan Book of the Dead*, a guide-book for the soul of the dead on how to avoid entering the womb and being born again. The officiant speaks to the dead:

> 'The visions of males and females in union will appear. When thou seest them, remember to withhold thyself from going between them. ... Still if the womb-door is not closed even by that and thou findest thyself ready to enter the womb the method of attachment and repulsion is hereby shown unto thee. The visions of males and females in union will appear. If, that time, one entereth

into the womb through the feelings of attachment and repulsion, one may be born either as a horse, a fowl, a dog, or a human being. If about to be born as a male the feeling of itself being a male dawneth upon the Knower, and a feeling of intense hatred towards the father and of jealousy and attraction towards the mother is begotten. If about to be born as a female, the feeling of itself being a female dawneth upon the Knower and a feeling of intense hatred towards the mother and of intense attraction and fondness towards the father is begotten.'

We find here the Oedipus complex, precisely and eloquently described in this Tibetan text from about the 10th century AD.

For much of Eastern philosophy, and we speak here especially in regard to the Tibetan, Buddhist and Hindu religious precepts, the starting point is that life is suffering and pain. But this is also the starting point in many Western medical and psychiatric practices. And in classical Greece the satyr says to king Midas: 'Best is not to be born, next best to hurry to Hades and be covered by earth.' Christianity offers us a corpse on a cross of dead wood, 'a curse on men and woman – she shall give birth in pain', life is sin and guilt. Modern psychologists declared that birth is a trauma followed by pain and suffering, prenatal to postmortem! The leaders of a 5000-year-old patriarchal culture have yet to entirely give way. However, it is from these cultural embers that prenatal psychology was to develop and grow.

WESTERN PSYCHOLOGICAL OBSERVATIONS ON PRENATAL EXPERIENCES AND THE BIRTH OF PRENATAL PSYCHOLOGY

The philosophical basis of life as the unavoidable experience of pain and suffering is not unique to Eastern philosophies, it is shared by Western medical philosophy as well, and birth is most often described as a traumatic and painful ordeal. But there is an important difference between the Eastern philosophies on this point, for the goal of the yogi is to escape from life and existence to the state of the unborn, and never to be born again, while the various forms of Western therapy are trying to reduce the pain and make an adjustment to the so-called reality principle.

Otto Rank's concept of the moment of birth as a trauma was extended by Janov (1985) to embrace the time in the womb. I quote: 'Pregnancy may be a 9-month nightmare ... The structures mediating pain and suffering are some of the most ancient in the nervous system ... After a few weeks in the womb the fetus can react to and store input. ... We can become neurotic in the womb. ... Neurosis is a physiological disease. The pains that are stored in the womb can be "remembered", but not in terms of the cognitive memory mechanisms. ... Fetal recall is body memory. The body remembers ... and that stored "knowledge" is no less valid than the intellectual recall.' According to Janov the pain is held down by endorphines so that the trauma imprinted during pregnancy is repressed and made unconscious. Thus the barrier between the conscious and unconscious begins in the womb.

One of the first medical doctors in the West to recognize and write about the prenatal experience was Freud's good friend, Georg Groddeck. Freud writes about Groddeck's work in *The Ego and the Id*:

> 'Groddeck is never tired of insisting that what we call Ego behaves essentially in a passive way in life, and that, as he expresses it, we are "lived" by unknown and uncontrollable forces. We have all had impressions of the same kind ... and we feel no hesitation in finding a place for Groddeck's discovery in the structure of science.'

I refer to his paper, on prenatal psychology, 'Uber das Es', published in 1920 in *Psychoanalytische Schriften zur Psychosomatic*. He writes:

> 'At the moment of birth the child starts to breathe. It acts with a purpose by adjusting to the new conditions of life and the new atmosphere, an action which seems to be as well reasoned as a man's escaping from a burning house or the opening up of an umbrella when it starts to rain. There are similarities between our reflex actions and conscious actions. This raises the question as to whether there is a difference between conscious and unconscious life, and the possibility has to be considered that everything which we call the conscious expression of a personality is really a disguised working of the unconscious, the Id. One of the actions of the Id is the compulsion of self-deception.'

Groddeck further writes:

> 'From the human semen and the human ovum a human being is made, not a dog or a bird; there exists an Id which enforces the making of a human being and builds up a human body and a human soul. This Id supplies its creature, the personality and the ego of a human being with nose, mouth, muscles, bones, brains, and makes these organisms functional, activates them even before birth and causes the developing human being to act purposefully before his brains are fully ready. The question is whether this Id which can do so much may not be able to build churches, compose tragedies or invent medicines. We may even wonder whether perhaps every human expression of life, be it physical or mental, of health or ill health, thought, action or vegetative function, can be traced back to the Id – which would mean that body and soul and conscious life are an illusion, a self-deception.'

Groddeck had notions about prenatal life which, after 50 years, have become acceptable. The state of rest in the mother's womb means a great deal for man's unconscious processes in later life. The need for peace and quiet asserts itself in the form of regular sleep which is analogous to dozing in the darkness of the womb. The need for security is met by a room or some kind of enclosed place. The memory of blissful loneliness in the womb can create a craving for being alone, for going into oneself, an unconscious longing to return to the mother's womb in a symbolic way.

Georg Groddeck noted how we talk about 'the final resting place' and other expressions which show an awareness that birth and death are one, e.g. from 'earth to earth ...' and 'Mother Earth'. The man placed seed in the woman but also in the soil, and we talk both of the fruit of the womb and of the soil. The protection which the growing fetus has in the womb is a fundamental experience, and is after birth supplemented by various means. We know that every cell, every organ, every sensation and emotion develop in the security of the mother's womb, and every living being seeks support and protection from somebody or something else – be it another person, a friend or a lover, an object or an ideology.

Groddeck has also anticipated the research on the fetal heartbeat by 40 years and called it a most powerful sensory impression. He noted how excitement makes us sense our heartbeat and how rhythm dominates music and poetry, speech and movement. The sense of the rhythm of breathing can also be related to the rhythm of the fetal heartbeat. The memories of floating in the amnion fluid, and the swinging, rocking movements are recalled when the baby is rocked or cradled. This, together with lactation creates a symbiosis with the mother which in some way is a continuation of the prenatal state. Groddeck refers to the erotic significance of the swinging movements and of the pleasure of being whirled about and even thrown up in the air. We know how the dream of flying often symbolizes the sexual act, that Cupid has wings and we also remember the Christian cherubs.

Groddeck, who used warm bath in his therapy, reminds us that the pleasure of lying in warm water is nothing but a repetition of the pleasure of prenatal life. Aversion to a warm bath and accidents in the bath can often be traced back to grave conflicts with the mother. About parturition Groddeck writes:

> 'For both mother and child the lack of space, an increase in size gradually becomes unbearable. ... The child's increase in weight and size automatically destroys the pleasure of close proximity and awakens a wish for separation. The mother also wishes to get rid of the big belly and its burden ... in my view birth happens only when the wish to separate turns for both parties into a decision. Birth is thus not a mechanical process but a mutual agreement between two individualities that somehow play an active part in it.'

According to Groddeck, the two deepest and most powerful patterns, love and hatred for the mother, start in the embryonic stage. That a mother also can have these feelings is a fact, although it is unacceptable to many that a mother can hate the fetus. Many pregnancies can be unwanted and we have today frequent reports on hateful mistreatment of babies.

How far the unborn can sense unwantedness we can of course not know, but the physical expressions of hostility surely must be felt like a threat — abortion attempts, the mother's use of drugs, alcohol, smoking, etc.

Here I would like to refer briefly to the work of Sheila Kitzinger. She considers birth a sexual experience and refers to the expression and behavior of the woman in normal labor. In this, her work corroborates the work of Groddeck. She writes that:

> 'apart from labor pains the woman's spirits are usually high, her face very red and her eyes shining brightly like in moments of sexual excitement. The natural conclusion is that giving birth is not a horrible experience, but somehow a climax of physical pleasure, and women who combine the qualities of honesty and attentiveness will confirm the observation that labor pains are pleasure pains and that the passage of the child's head through the vagina is more pleasurable than any other erotic sensation. ... The woman in labor is in pain but she does not suffer, a distinction of great significance of human life.'

CONCLUSION

Western man has forgotten and suppressed the significance and basic conception of the navel as the place through which life entered, both the biological and the mental. In the East we find a recognition of the navel as the center of knowledge, and as a focus for intellectual research and meditation. For Wilhelm Reich the navel cord and the placenta represent the total unity of the child with the mother, which is the base for the orgiastic bliss *in utero*. This bliss is later recalled through the orgasm as a symbol for the total unity, the bliss of the unborn. In the Upanishades we read: 'He who is embraced by a beloved woman knows nothing that is without nothing that is within ...'

For the fetus in the womb only one cavity exists and the entrance, exit and connecting link is the navel. The existence of holes or cavities in different contexts must be one of the earliest discoveries going back to the child's experience during the time in the womb. This perception includes the sensations of liquid and solid, of ingoing and outgoing products, of light and darkness, of sound and silence. Already before birth the basic perceptions of body functions have been imprinted. Knowledge of organs and their functions is present before birth, and before the brain has classified and named these functions. The experiences in the prenatal state are of a very different kind from those after birth.

We have today a number of methods by which we can follow the prenatal physiological developments from conception to birth. We can observe and record how the human body systems start to function during prenatal life. Dr D. Alley, ultrasound technician at Norfolk General Hospital, Virginia, USA reports: 'We can watch the baby's bladder empty and fill again with a 30-minutes interval. We often see the fetus empty its bladder which appears as a steady stream of echoes flowing out through the penis.' 25 years ago, Dr C. N. Smyth of London University Hospital studied the responses of the fetus to auditory and light stimulation through the maternal abdominal wall. Heart rate changes were produced by audiogenic stimulation and bright light. A 1983 sonograph of a 29-week-old fetus clearly shows an erection, indicating that the human sexual responses system, together with the other body system, function before birth.

According to Freud, the unconscious is always right and knows everything, including the primal scene, the conception. In this regard he used the term, 'Ur-phantasien', and thereby postulated a phylogenetic knowledge, a kind of unlimited memory of the embryological evolution. The unconscious in its deepest layers is a collection of memories of the earliest biological processes, the origin of life itself, memories which have been repressed and forgotten. Buddha originally had used yogic meditations, a kind of autohypnotic research method into the origin of suffering, illness and death. Unsatisfied with this method he found that a search for the origins of suffering had to be done in full consciousness in order to reach Nirvana. Freud also started with hypnosis but replaced it with free association as an instrument for recalling the repressed memories of the past.

Western psychoanalysis goes back to the moment of birth, prenatal psychology deals with life *in utero*. The aim of Buddhism is to regress even further through the life of the unborn, beyond conception, beyond organic life to Nirvana, the state of no birth. But the focus for prenatal psychology in the West is upon the direct relation between biological and psychological functions in prenatal experience, and upon their inseparable unity and identity. This sense of unity is lost during birth, with the separation from the sheltered life in the womb and the awakening into the outside world. The age old problem of mind versus body is thus established and remains mankind's insoluble riddle.

50

Sociocultural expectations and responses to the sexual identity of the unborn and newborn in San José, Costa Rica (edited extracts)

M.T. Zeledon, R. Flores and M. Villalobos

ABSTRACT

Based on the theories of affective attachment and mother–infant bonding, a descriptive study was carried out with 120 women from the city of Heredia in Costa Rica in order to evaluate the culturally influenced expectations that a pregnant woman has in regard to the sex of the newborn and the resulting relationship that is established from the moment of birth. Additionally, comparative analysis was made with the father's responses to the same or similar questions (when the father was available to be interviewed).

It was found that parents had a specified preference towards the sex of the future child; nevertheless most women reacted positively in the presence of the child. This was generally the case whether the desired gender was obtained or not. It seems that breastfeeding and rooming-in play a decisive role in the strengthening of the weak affective tie between a mother and child.

In a high percentage of cases, the gender preferences obeyed specific culturally bound stereotypes that were linked to sex roles; in the final instance, these stereotypes determine ideas about upbringing which are initiated at a very early age. These sociocultural processes ineluctibly influence a mother's expectations in regard to the newborn, and are based upon speculations which only rarely have a biological foundation.

INTRODUCTION

The purpose of the study was to investigate the expectations of the pregnant woman in regard to the sex of the unborn child and the resulting relationship established after birth. The sexual stereotypes held by the mothers and fathers are also explored, including the manner in which these interfere in the project of breastfeeding and the postbirth interaction they have with their child.[1]

METHODOLOGY

The investigation was carried out in Heredia City, Costa Rica, with a population of 120 women who were in the last trimester of gestation (and had experienced pregnancy without complications). The exploratory questionnaires were applied over a period of time. The first one was applied during the last trimester of pregnancy, the second one within the 3 days after the birth, and the third one 5 months after the child's birth.

To complete the necessary information to be obtained in the last two questionnaires, direct observation was utilized in order to ascertain and register the important aspects of interaction behavior within the mother–child relationship soon after birth. This data included noting interaction behaviors such as eye contact, caresses, tone of voice employed, physical care rendered to the baby, maternal stimulation and the general perception of the mother's attitude towards the newborn child. The births were attended at the San Vicente Hospital of Heredia (part of the Costarrician Social Security Department, which has joint lodging there and a policy of encouraging the use of lactation).

Subjects were selected under consultation with the Prenatal Section of the Central Clinic in Heredia. The following factors were used to define and delimit the subject group: (a) first time mothers between the ages of 18 and 35 years, and (b) mothers with several children between 18 and 40 years of age with children younger than 6 years. The following cases were excluded: (a) women with a high obstetric and perinatal risk, (b) women with psychopathological histories, and (c) women whose children were born with one or more etiologic problems of mental retardation (as established by the World Health Organization).

RESULTS

Characteristics of the population

The group studied was comprised of a total of 120 pregnant women, of whom three quarters were married and the rest single (unmarried, but not necessarily living alone). Their ages ranged from 17 to 39 years, and the majority of the population was found to be between 23 and 30 years. Slightly more than half were mothers with one or two children. In relation to their education level, those having finished secondary school predominated, while a very low proportion of the group had little or no schooling. The same low representation of mothers with university studies filled out the group profile. Pertaining to work experience, the majority of the women did not work outside their homes. Most were in charge of the domestic tasks, and did not work even when their family economic income was very low. Only a quarter of them had their own house.

Only 31.8% of the study group had received information which contributed to a better understanding of pregnancy and of the physical and emotional preparation for birth.

The study sought to explore the initial reaction of the woman when learning that she was pregnant, finding that a little more than a third of the women experienced negative reactions (Table 1). Further, their replies were characterized by double-meaning elements, disconformity, apathy and, at times, of refusal to accept the pregnancy. These attitudes were often modified during the course of pregnancy. Negative responses were reduced from 32.5% to 19.2% by the 8th month of gestation (Table 2). It seems that the process of adaptation and acceptance consolidates while the fetus develops, in most cases to be transformed into a positive attitude for the moment of birth.

Mother's expectations in relation to the child's gender

When exploring the desire of both parents towards any particular sex, it was found that three quarters declared that they had established preferences toward the unborn child's gender (Table 3). The study shows that there is no great predominance one way or the other, though preference tilts slightly toward the male gender, especially among fathers (45% to 30%). Mothers showed a virtual equilibrium in regard to gender preference. Only a small group of parents did not show any preference in regard to sex. Predictably, given the preceding statistics, it was the women who showed the highest percentage (19.2%) of response in the 'no preference' category (almost twice that of the fathers, 10.8%).

The majority of the mothers who declared that they had no preference towards the future sex of the child, indicated that this factor was not important as long as their children were born 'sane and complete', that is, in a good physical and mental health condition.

Table 4 shows the distribution of the sex obtained in relation to the sex desired.

One or two days after birth, the level of satisfaction in regard to the

Table 1 Mother's reaction when knowing of the pregnancy

Category	n	%
Very satisfactory	28	23.3
Satisfactory	36	30.0
Resigned	13	10.8
Indifferent, ambiguous	25	20.8
Non-resigned, refusal	14	11.7
No answer, ignored	4	3.3
Total	120	100.0

Table 2 Emotional condition of the mother during the pregnancy evaluated in the 8th month of gestation

Category*	n	%
Very satisfactory	38	31.6
Satisfactory	49	40.8
Resigned	5	4.2
Indifferent, ambiguous, non-resigned	23	19.2
No answer	5	4.2
Total	120	100.0

*From the replies given by the mothers.

resulting gender was checked. Response was elicited based upon the question, 'What did you feel when you knew it was a male/female baby?' It was observed that the majority of mothers responded with a positive attitude towards the baby's sex, even when it was not the wished for sex (see Table 5). At the same time, evaluation was made via direct observation concerning the quality of interaction between the mother and her newborn baby. Our observations show that 71.3% of the mothers acted positively in their relationship with their newborn, while only 6.9% maintained a negative attitude, thereby fostering a negative relationship.

Sexual stereotypes based upon sociocultural attitudes

After determining gender preference, it was discovered that these choices largely follow specific rationales which are assigned according to sex, while a minority of these reasons are common for both sexes (e.g. 'sane and complete'). Some of the reasons given for preferring a male child were: (1)

Table 3 Sex desired by the parents

Category	n	%
Sex desired by the mother		
Male	49	40.8
Female	46	38.8
Without a preference	23	19.2
Undecided	2	1.7
Sex desired by the father		
Male	54	45.0
Female	36	30.0
Without a preference	13	10.8
Undecided	7	5.8
Did not answer	10	8.3

Table 4 Sex obtained in relation to the sex desired by the mother

Sex obtained	Male n	Male %	Female n	Female %	Undecided n	Undecided %	Total n	Total %
Male	19	52.8	17	53.1	8	42.1	44	50.6
Female	17	47.2	15	46.9	11	57.9	43	49.4
Total	36	100.0	32	100.0	19	100.0	87	100.0

the idea that men are more obedient, (2) benefits the mother's future security, as they think that a son can protect them, (3) supposition that men are less jeopardized than women, (4) supposition that men suffer less than women.

Pertaining to reasons expressed in preferring a female child, we recorded the following: (1) 'it is nicer to dress them up and make them clothes', (2) it is nicer to be accompanied by a daughter, (3) because they are more 'homey'.

Considering the above statements, it is easier to appreciate how, before the birth, the parents have already formed a series of preconceived sociocultural attitudes towards the future child. Many of these ideas revolve around the sex of the child. When exploring which home tasks the child could adopt, there was persistent tendency to establish tasks according to the differences between the sexes; more than half of the

Table 5 Reactions of the mother when knowing the sex of her child as per her expectations

	Obtained desired sex		Did not obtain desired sex		Without a preference		Total	
	n	%	n	%	n	%	n	%
Satisfactory	31	86.1	27	84.4	12	63.2	70	80.5
Little satisfied	1	2.8	1	3.1	5	26.3	7	8.0
Unsatisfied	4	11.1	4	12.5	2	10.5	10	11.5
Total	36	100.0	32	100.0	19	100.0	87	100.0

women considered that the boy and the girl must help with the tasks in the home. But the specific tasks are largely predetermined in relation to sex. A minority of those interviewed thought that the boys should not help at all, or do not have any household responsibilities.

DISCUSSION

Upon learning of her pregnancy, the woman undergoes emotive reactions and experiences which question and bring about a reappraisal of her life and her new role in the near future. All this can generate anxiety when suddenly she is facing an irreversible process which is happening within her own organism. This obliges the woman to readjust most areas of her life style: her studies, occupation, relations with her family, relationship with her mate, and her basic goals for the future.

Simultaneously, the pregnancy elicits responses within her which have been socioculturally conditioned since her early childhood, and conform to the 'ideal role of mother'. Such psychosociological conditionings look forward to being fulfilled with the initiation of maternity. If conditions surrounding her allow the pregnancy to be welcomed, these act as facilitators of the adaptation process, channelling the natural anxiety produced through a manner both personally acceptable as well as culturally expected. This is why the emotional reactions produced by the pregnancy under positive circumstances are important; they confirm the female subjects' emotional expectations in terms of her 'fulfillment as a woman'. In such a moment it is common to hear replies such as: 'I felt the happiest woman in the world' and 'I cried of happiness, this is the greatest dream for one as a woman'.

In the opposite situation, when the conditions of the sociocultural environment do not accept the pregnancy, the expression of the positive emotional conditioning is blocked, thus creating a great anxiety. In such cases the defense mechanisms appear, such as reactive emotive formations, rationalizations and displacement, among others. It is clear even here, as we observed through the questionnaires, that the mother–child relationship is a process initiated long before birth and its ramifications are long-lasting.

It is valuable to note that a very significant percentage of the studied population had not planned their pregnancy. They did not utilize contraceptives to prevent conception. This is a fact which led us to question if this behavior followed from a lack of information on the part of the couple or, to the contrary, that this may reveal a passive role on the woman's part in the relationship with her partner. Notwithstanding the high percentage of women who did not plan their pregnancy, only 32.5% of the population reacted in a negative manner when learning that they were pregnant. The rest of the questionnaire responses were located within the categories of 'very satisfied' or 'resigned' (see Table 1). When analyzing their replies, however, there is some doubt as to whether they are really recording what they 'feel', or if their responses are a reflection of what is socially expected of a woman faced with the *fait accompli* of pregnancy. This doubt was not satisfied in the investigation, since a projective method was never employed.

As previously stated, the majority of the pregnant women interviewed showed preferences toward a specified gender. These choices were made in the light of cultural expectations oriented in one way or another in regard to the future child's gender, and the subsequent social role to be fulfilled. There were several possible reasons put forward in wishing for a male child as the first offspring, connected with the respective social status represented within the study group. For example, a peasant would wish to have male offspring in order to help with the agricultural tasks; a middle class urban father often is looking to perpetuate his family name and, maybe even, his family company. In the cases where a baby girl was desired as the first choice, it was most often for the mother's sake: for her to have someone to accompany her and help with the homemaking tasks.

In general terms, it was observed that after birth a positive attitude towards the child, independent of previous expectations in regard to gender, was established. The satisfaction or dissatisfaction of the mother's expectations with respect to the desired sex of her child did not seem to translate itself in regard to the level of acceptance or rejection which she exhibited toward the child.

These results propose that there is a tendency in the middle and lower class women to change their attitude (from negative to positive) when the newborn is presented to them immediately after birth. This phenomenon was not observed by the authors in women of a higher economic class. From the socioeconomic point of view, the women of our study were closer to what is economically classified as the lower middle class.

Another influencing factor which helped explain to us changes in maternal attitudes, is that of the perinatal care programs we administered. The joint lodging program allows the mother and child to room together, and also encourages the mother's lactation. Both of these primary aspects of the program were designed in order to strengthen the mother–child bonding process which begins immediately after birth. All the mothers in our study were involved and exposed to the above program which is part of the hospital routine here. Therefore, it should be considered that some of the changes of attitudes into positive responses towards their child may be, at least in part, a product of this intervention.

The fact that since birth, and even before, those close to the newborn adopt a series of attitudes depending, to a large extent, upon the baby's gender shows how prevalent sexual stereotypes are within the sociocultural context. Even before birth these gender expectations are functioning and being projected upon the unborn. However, research studies show that the 'gender role' is overwhelmingly constituted by social regulations of behavior which rarely have a biological foundation.

Notwithstanding the fact that presently the processes utilized during pregnancy and birth have been significantly modified, we noted that the majority of women still face pregnancy, birth and the raising of their children without adequate preparation to confront these processes. This is a strange paradox for a society which every day places ever higher levels of expectation upon the individual. Nevertheless, our evidence shows that men and women are still not being prepared for one very fundamental task: being parents.

---

[1] A complete account of this study in its original language (Spanish) can be found in the library of the University of Costa Rica, under the Social Science or Psychology archive sections. This present paper is an edited version for English publication. The original study, 'Expectativas de la Mujer Embarazada Respecto al Sexo del Hijo por Nacer y Su Reaccion ante la Realidad', was completed in 1983. It includes all the original questionnaires used in the study, samples of the prenatal and perinatal educative materials available to mothers and the complete and comprehensive data (including bibliographic data) collected from the study research.

Part 2: Ethical considerations in prenatal and perinatal psychology and medicine

51

The ultimate preventive: prenatal stimulation (edited extracts)

B. Logan

ABSTRACT

Systems hypotheses have evolved so thoroughly in recent years that physical proof of unification among basic cosmic principles appears a matter more temporal than probable (Barrow and Tipler, 1986). Similarly, motivated by a nuclear age to where we must find agreement on optimal human behavior, the question whether our species can itself be treated as a patient (much like Freud, 1930, p. 144 concluded in Civilization and Its Discontents) becomes more essential than ever before. With diagnosis eventually leading to cure, a theory of phylogenetic dysfunction has been posited, from which individual no less than group traits take on special meaning.

Identification of early infancy, especially in utero, as the critical period poses an intriguing methodological query. How might we safely intervene during such a vulnerable time for the organism's lifelong benefit? Clues to some shared element among current approaches suggest that our heartbeat serves as the primary natural stimulus for neurological viability and patterning. Enhancement of this endogenous learning process is then proposed from the daily application of progressively sophisticated variants, that is, a cardiac curriculum generated by an electronic synthesizer while observing several specified protocols. Finally, the psychodynamics of education in the womb – leading to the prenatal being's potential creative expansion and integration – are discussed. We conclude with an appeal for extensive investigation concerning what is summarized as a seminal consciousness breakthrough.

Are humans born missing an essential link to potential, whereby usually falling short rather than achieving accurately describes each and all? Where is demonstrated consistent and unquestionable sensitivity, tolerance, compassion, intelligence, generosity, forgiveness, informed innocence, and good cheer? Are these virtues unrealistically solicited because of private and public disappointment, habit, some disinclination for universal solutions? Do the paramount primates exemplify a genetic perversity, cellular cynicism, or is the mortal flaw environmentally acquired from those civil instruments meant to alleviate it? How can there be so much immediately discernible space between promise and practice when most millenial assessments claim we have improved mightily? In confidence, it would be less than candid not to admit these are worrisome subjects, though customarily suppressed. Certainly our path from the past is marked with signs that success bred of failure has been the general guideline behind a pilgrimage intent on creating its special destiny.

Toward his last years Freud addressed the problem of social ills and their ultimate resolution.

> 'In the neurosis of an individual we can use as a starting-point the contrast presented to us between the patient and his environment which we assume to be *normal*. No such background as this would be available for any society similarly affected; it would have to be supplied in some other way. And with regard to any therapeutic application of our knowledge, what would be the use of the most acute analysis of social neuroses, since no one possesses power to compel the community to adopt the therapy? In spite of all these difficulties, we may expect that one day someone will venture upon this research into the pathology of civilized communities.'

Our current attempts at remedying aggregate ills by both institutional and technological correction illustrate a commitment to apply antidotes of increasingly powerful dosage. Yet whether political, scientific or esthetic solutions are directed to modern concerns, the gap towards achievement of these goals waxes wider still; if anything, the human appetite for instant and comprehensive pragmatisms has become insatiable.

But this can create a healthy situation. Answers foster expectation, vision's expansion, hence an unbridled desire for betterment has caused us to reluctantly reassess educational and social tools no longer adequate for the crises at hand. Secretly unhappy with our apparent nature, we have moved by default to modify, even reconstitute such identity. From these initial experiments we are inventing and effecting radical options. However, of the three leading practible means for human redesign (actually, accelerating a scarcely static cultural status quo), two of these suffer from generic limitation.

ULTIMATE PREVENTIVE: PRENATAL STIMULATION

The first, computerized extension of intelligence, by definition cannot qualitatively rise above that which is programmed. Numerically capable of compounding data beyond our range and rate, doubtless someday cerebrally implanted, it must always duplicate the host's procedural bias – a correspondingly problematic prejudice. Might information alone accrue until its mass infers independent activity ... a library come alive? Again, no matter the level of sophistication, conclusions depend upon their composition – it is still teleology recast.

What of bioengineering, which is another possibility for substantially transfiguring the species? Endemic to such alteration is its specificity: particular features or traits are deleted, enhanced, or introduced irrespective of the future child's choice. Biological tampering at so intrinsic a stage runs counter to our society's belief in traditional freedoms, and recent restrictions on genetic restructuring underscore this concern.

Out of equitable consideration of all probable options, then, the appropriate place to begin is by amplifying an individual's intellectual and creative potential. This is why our scrutiny has now turned to the child's earliest developmental stage. Prenatal stimulation is the proposed third alternative for enhancing human potential. It comes from two seminal ideas derivative of observing nascent vertebrate life: how the cerebral process begins and how it is influenced by external stimuli.

If the promise of higher consciousness seems too remote a possibility then either homo sapiens was preordained to always miss its potential, or our skills fall consistently short of what imagination provides. From contemporary technological vantage, such a disparity has come to intrigue researchers like few other prospects. Emphasizing endurance for its own sake, nature fertilizes quite beyond simple durability of species. From overcompensating against environmental hazards, it has bestowed upon neurogenesis a rare opportunistic byproduct: that *in utero* occasion when continuing rhythmic and intermittent stimuli are imprinted (Salk, 1966; Grier et al., 1967), thereby reducing massive brain cell death at birth.

The net effect from this multisensory provision for ordering primate perceptual principles can be described as *preconscious imprinting* (putting patterns into place before mental reactivity, and well prior to awareness exercising choice). Viewed retrospectively – which is admittedly arguing from derived design – could the concept and timing of this cornerstone to human architecture be more perfect?

What might this earliest 'schooling' render? Beside planned testing of an expanded cardiac curriculum with animal and human subjects, programs in place over the last few years, each linked by an auditory factor, have already produced demonstrated developmental successes.

Intelligent grafting does not engineer veneer, but rather individuals with greater potential for cognitively and behaviorally improved lives in which psychological health has been nurtured and enhanced prenatally: this is the ultimate preventive for pathological social ills.

Research leading toward implementation cannot be reversed. Past the storms darkly foreshadowed by the events of 1929, Freud (1930, p. 33) prophesied a parallel promise ... while overlooking the source of the solution:

> 'The fateful question of the human species seems to me to be whether and to what extent the cultural process developed in it will succeed in mastering the derangements of communal life caused by the human instinct of aggression and self-destruction. In this connection, perhaps the phase through which we are at this moment passing deserves special interest. Men have brought their powers of subduing the forces of nature to such a pitch that by using them they could now very easily exterminate one another to the last man. They know this – hence arises a great part of their current unrest, their dejection, their mood of apprehension. And now it may be expected that the other of the two *heavenly forces,* eternal Eros, will put forth his strength so as to maintain himself alongside of his equally immortal adversary.'

Whatever positive directions our future then takes must interpret for a needy universe that secret message hidden in the ontogenetic heart, as it is perceived and practiced phylogenetically; like the Gaia hypothesis of our living planet, a civilization pulsing both outward and inward with purpose which its very existence defines while verifying through its brave vision.

Such liberation of a species starts from endowing every newborn with the unequivocally requisite right for optimized potential. Here is suggested no more extreme an intervention than undertaken through educational or social caring, yet one which permits a freedom of will beyond the prescriptions either presently attempts. Human history, as Freud concluded, shows much which needs to be prevented. Aiming for ultimacy, our momentary mission lies in proving and then administering a pertinent eventuality which the evolution of knowledge has provided. It would seem wrong if we did not try – and quite impossible to resist – this truly proverbial opening of heart.

52

The psycho-technology of pregnancy and labor

T.R. Verny

Couples and their friends who desire a more personal birth experience than a hospital normally allows often cast obstetrical nurses and doctors in the role of insensitive professionals. Nurses and doctors tend to feel resentful when confronted by women with a shopping list of demands, yet their professional roles do not allow them to show their annoyance. What do they do with these feelings?

Often, because one cannot predict how many women will be in labor at any one time, a situation in which too few nurses are treating too many patients will develop. Under such circumstances, they may have their hands full just making sure nobody dies and, much as they would like to, are unable to meet the emotional needs of the laboring woman. Thus the medical staff is frequently assigned the part of 'heavies' in accounts of birthing practices.

Speaking from firsthand experience as a clinician, I know that under the insistent demands of a busy work week I sometimes tend to act more like a fireman rushing from one fire to the next than a physician who stops long enough to really see and hear his patient.

I think all health professionals should get sick once every 2 years and be hospitalized at least once every decade to appreciate fully what it is like to be a patient. Though I say this tongue in cheek, I do believe that all of us need to be reminded occasionally that patients are people and that their emotions will affect all their bodily functions.

This article is concerned with two themes: the hospitalization of birth and the increasing use of and reliance on technological devices as diagnostic tools during pregnancy and labor. It will explore the physiological and psychological effects of these procedures on the pregnant woman, her unborn or newborn baby, and the hospital staff.

THE HOSPITALIZATION OF BIRTH

During the last 100 years, birthing has moved from the home into the hospital. The home is the domain of the family; the hospital is run by doctors and nurses. Doctors and nurses are trained to treat sick people, and hospitals admit only very sick people for treatment, surgery and special investigations. Consequently, anyone who occupies a hospital bed will likely be regarded by the staff as an ill patient. In this simple way, without anyone giving it much thought and with the best of intentions by health professionals, the natural process of birth has been transformed into a major disease. What are the consequences of this hospitalization of birth for the pregnant woman?

(1) She finds herself in an unfamiliar place where she has to obey peculiar rules enforced by strangers.

(2) Because staff members are experts and she is not, the pregnant woman is made to feel as if others know more about her body than she does.

(3) Staff members often behave as if her body has become theirs to do with as they please. They give her drugs to swallow, stick needles into her, take blood from her veins and urine from her bladder, measure her blood pressure, subject her to X-rays, and so on.

(4) On admission, the pregnant woman receives a name tag with a number. Then she is asked to disrobe and change into a hospital gown that leaves her totally exposed from the back when she is not lying down. Confined to her room, she has a never-ending stream of nurses, interns, and residents examining her. Her sense of individuality and self-esteem are gradually eroded.

This process is uncannily similar to what happens to people entering a prison. Both systems deprive their inmates of liberty and dignity, and they both aim to achieve compliance with the rules and regulations of the institution. This is not the place to examine what effect this system has on prisoners. What it does to the pregnant woman, however, is very bad indeed. For one thing, it increases her anxiety. Anxiety will interfere with the birth process by decreasing the efficiency of contractions and increasing muscular tension. More muscle tension will lead to more pain and more pain to more anxiety. As the pain and the anxiety increase, the staff, in their attempt to be helpful, offer her painkillers. These medications slow down contractions and doctors become more anxious and increasingly interventionist, resorting to the use of forceps, episiotomy, induction of labor with oxytocin (Pitocin), and/or Caesarean section. Then the mother is expected to feel grateful for having had such wonderful care. Obviously, she could not have been so well cared for in her home.

Fear and apprehension cause us all to shift into a flight-fight pattern. One of the results of this stress reaction is the shunting of blood from internal organs such as the uterus to the large muscles – a good system when one is confronted by a lion but counterproductive when one is a laboring mother. She will end up with a bloodless uterus which leads to uterine inertia and decreases the amount of blood flowing to the baby.

When people feel pushed around like pawns on a chessboard, they tend to become angry, and the pregnant woman is no exception. But how can she get angry with the medical staff when her own and her baby's life and health depend on these very individuals' goodwill and expertise? So the pregnant woman keeps quiet while her blood pressure rises and her body reacts in a million other harmful ways to her suppressed feelings of frustration. None of this makes her feel good or enhances birthing.

Many women recognize the futility of the struggle – especially if they are unaccompanied by an assertive mate, friend, or midwife – and resign themselves to the role the staff demands of them. Their attitude becomes, 'do with me as you like, wake me up when it's all over.' A woman like that will be deprived of one of the most magical moments she can experience in life. And her baby, after his arduous and perilous journey, will not be hugged, stroked, looked at, or talked to after finally emerging into the light; his mother will not be there to welcome him. Many studies on bonding have shown that this lack of early and intimate contact may adversely affect both mother and child (Klaus and Kennell, 1976; Carter-Jessop, 1981; Lumley, 1980; Bowlby, 1982).

By stripping the childbirth experience of so much of its personal and familial character, we have diminished its rewards and created a multitude of new problems.

Hospital staff members like to follow routines because routines make the staff's lives easier. They want pregnant women to do as they are told and not to make a fuss. Even if the staff is genuinely committed to 'family-oriented birth' and Leboyer type of deliveries, their foremost goal is to facilitate a safe and efficient birth. They are quick to show their annoyance if the woman persists in breathing in her own way instead of their way or if she refuses medication and begins to scream. The woman who refuses the well-intentioned ministrations of the medical staff calls into question their competence and threatens their self-esteem. Thus, if anything goes wrong, they quickly turn on her and reassert control. 'You wouldn't want to endanger your baby, would you now?' Of course not, so in goes the merperidine hydrochloride (Demerol) or the local anesthetic and out goes the pregnant woman's determination that this is going to be her delivery. More suppressed anger, anxiety, or resignation follow.

Hospitals can be not only authoritarian and impersonal, but also downright dangerous. In the hospital, germs are more numerous than in the home, and they are also more virulent. So infections in hospitals are usually more frequent and more severe than those acquired outside of hospitals. If an infection develops, it will make the new mother uncomfortable at the very least and in some cases quite sick. She will not be able to breastfeed her baby, and she may not even get to see him. This again mitigates against the development of a loving mother–newborn child relationship.

In 5% of high-risk pregnancies, the benefits of medical treatment in a hospital far outweigh the emotional and bodily risks discussed here. The other 95% of pregnant women require the hospital to serve as insurance against anything going wrong. Is it fair to manage them as if they were sick? In addition to having to cope with the general effect that hospitals have on patients, the pregnant woman also has to contend with an explosion of high-technology tests and electronic equipment designed to help her and her baby to a safe birth. Nobody would quarrel with this objective, but does all this gynegadgetry really deliver? (Pardon the pun.) And what are the emotional sequelae to the mother and baby of this increasing reliance on instrumentation and invasive devices?

I believe that the proliferation of such techniques as amniocentesis, the fetal heart monitor, fetoscopy, hysteroscopy, and ultrasound – just a few of the most widely used devices – is now changing the fundamental character of birthing as much as the move away from the home did in the past.

HIGH-TECH OBSTETRICS

Amniocentesis

When amniocentesis was introduced in the 1950s, it was used to test for Rh-hemolytic disease in the third trimester (Walker, 1957). Today amniocentesis is still employed for that purpose. Prior to introducing the needle, the doctors would palpate the woman's abdomen to determine the baby's position. Some doctors inject a local anesthetic before amniocentesis; others believe that a second needle with an anesthetic is as painful as one needle without an anesthetic. I feel strongly that every woman should be given a choice in this matter instead of having the doctor decide what's good for her.

Presently, amniocentesis can also identify over 75 metabolic diseases and about 80–90% of open neural tube defects (such as spina bifida) in the second trimester of pregnancy (Beeson and Douglas, 1983). An examination of the chromosomes in the fetal cells can reveal the baby's sex.

Seven out of ten women are referred for amniocentesis because they are age 35 or older. Most of the others are tested because of a family history of chromosomal aberrations. At age 35, the chances of a woman having a baby with Down's syndrome is 1 in 350; at age 40, the chances increase to 1 in 100; and at age 45, chances are 1 in 32 (Golbus et al., 1974).

Complications

Scientists at the Mayo Clinic report that amniocentesis stands a 15% chance of being technically unsatisfactory: the sample of amniotic fluid may be inadequate, the culture may fail to grow, or the laboratory analysis may be wrong (Gordon, 1979). In one study, 22% of specimens were blood tinged to grossly bloody (Robinson et al., 1973). Major complications of amniocentesis include pneumothorax, gangrene of a fetal limb, and sudden fetal death (Cook et al., 1974; Goodlin and Clewell, 1974; Lamb, 1975). A study at the University of California at San Francisco based on 3000 consecutive cases from 1970 to 1978 found a 1.5% spontaneous abortion rate before 28 weeks gestation. These investigators 'are reasonably certain that a small proportion of these losses were directly attributable to the procedure (*Medical World News*, 1979). They are also concerned that, as amniocentesis moves from controlled research settings to many hospitals and likely less skilled office practice, the complication rate will increase.

Of the fetuses on whom amniocentesis is carried out, 95% are unaffected with the condition for which the test is performed. Parents should balance this information against the known risks of this procedure to their probably well babies (Thompson, 1979).

So far, there have been only three major studies on the effects of amniocentesis on the mother and her baby (DHEW, 1976; Crandall et al., 1980; Wald et al., 1983). A fourth is presently taking place in Toronto, and the results will not be known until 1988.

A National Institute of Child Health and Development project reported in 1976 that about 2% of women had complications such as vaginal bleeding or amniotic fluid leakage following the procedure. They found no increased risk to mother or child. These conclusions were confirmed in a 1980 study in which total fetal mortality was 2.7% among the amniocentesis group compared to 2.2% in the control group (Crandall et al., 1980).

However, a British study sponsored by the Medical Council of Britain concludes that amniocentesis increases the risk of fetal loss and neonatal and obstetrical complications by 1–1.5% and by the same amount for certain types of major infant problems. It reports a fetal death rate of 2.6% in the amniocentesis group and 1.1% among the controls. These investigators also found that amniocentesis significantly increases rates of maternal antepartum hemorrhage and neonatal respiratory distress and slightly increases major neonatal orthopedic deformities such as hip malformation (Wald et al., 1983).

In *The Secret Life of the Unborn Child* (Verny and Kelly, 1981), I report on the case of 16-month-old Claude, who developed severe head and neck spasms and limitations of movement following birth. His mother's pregnancy history revealed that she had undergone amniocentesis in her last trimester and that the needle had nicked her baby's neck. This child would shrink away from any bodily contact with his mother, who was as distraught by his apparent fear and avoidance of her as she was by his physical handicap. After 6 months of psychotherapy as practised by Anne-Marie Saurel in France, Claude totally recovered both in body and mind. Although there are few reports in the scientific literature on this, many obstetricians have told me that under ultrasound they have seen babies move away from the intruding needle or even try to push it aside.

Consider for a moment how you would feel if you sensed a sharp object as long as your entire body coming at you and did not know whether it was going to stop short or pierce you. Clinical evidence from observations in my own practice and those of other psychotherapists indicates that the unborn ascribes almost everything that happens to him as originating with his mother. Therefore, the newborn might naturally develop an avoidance or fear of his mother because of the suffering that amniocentesis caused him. Because every pregnancy and birth is accompanied by inevitable stresses, one wonders whether an additional stress which offers no benefit to the newborn is justified.

Consider the predicament facing a woman who becomes pregnant at age 42 and desperately wants a child. Knowing that her chances of giving birth to a live child with Down's syndrome are about the same as those of causing a miscarriage by the diagnostic procedure itself, does she refuse the amniocentesis?

At medical centers throughout the country, ever-increasing numbers of doctors and their patients have turned to amniocentesis and subsequent abortions to control the gender of the child to be born. Marilyn Pollack at New York's Sloan-Kettering Institute has devised a means for establishing the paternity of the baby through amniocentesis (Pollack, 1981). She thinks the technique is warranted only in cases of rape, suspected incest, or situations where uncertain paternity puts a great strain on the pregnant woman.

What does a mother do when amniocentesis demonstrates that her child has spina bifida or has an extra Y chromosome, a condition that be linked to mild retardation and increased aggressive behavior? Most amniocenteses are performed from the 16th to the 20th weeks of pregnancy. The results are known about 4 weeks later. By the 20th week, the woman is showing, feels fetal movement, and, should she opt for abortion if abnormalities are found, she chances delivering a live fetus. What are the psychological effects on a woman who aborts a live baby that has an outside chance of growing into a mentally and physically well person? The answer must be weighed against the consequences of giving birth to a handicapped youngster or of sustaining the pregnancy and then relinquishing the infant for adoption at birth.

There are no clear-cut or simple solutions to the problem of fetal screening, but we may be certain that amniocentesis:

(1) Is not the 'safe, highly reliable, and extremely accurate' procedure it was touted to be just a few years ago (Lamb, 1975),

(2) It is an invasive technique that can harm the unborn child both physically and mentally, and

(3) Its results may force parents to make agonizing choices – to play God and then to live with that decision for the rest of their lives.

Because amniocentesis is performed routinely together with ultrasound visualization of the baby, the combined risks of the two techniques rather than the hazards of each separately should be considered.

Ultrasound

For this test, the woman is required to have a full bladder, but the procedure is not otherwise unpleasant. While she lies on the examining table, oil is poured on her stomach and a probe is moved back and forth over her abdomen.

Until recently, ultrasound in obstetrics was used to determine the baby's gestational age and the size of its head, to detect abnormalities of early pregnancy (such as ectopic pregnancy or congenital malformations), to ascertain the location and health of the placenta and position of the baby in conjunction with amniocentesis, to investigate vaginal bleeding or pelvic masses, and to confirm multiple pregnancies or abnormal fetal presentation.

Surveys indicate that diagnostic ultrasound is employed in about 76% of high-risk pregnancies and in a steadily increasing percentage of low-risk pregnancies (*Med. World News*, 1984b). Many physicians screen all their pregnant patients with ultrasound.

Complications

Because of the known hazards of X-rays, scientists have welcomed ultrasound as an investigative tool that provides them with better and apparently safer information. But because ultrasound is a mechanical form of energy that creates heat, most researchers have been more cautious about its widespread use than they have been with amniocentesis.

This attitude was reflected by Doreen Liebeskind, assistant professor of radiology at Albert Einstein College of Medicine, at a symposium sponsored by the March of Dimes and Columbia University in 1983:

> 'I don't think we are producing childhood cancers, rather we may be producing subtle changes. ... When we say subtle, we mean possibly behavioral mechanisms; possibly changes in reflexes; in IQ or attention span; or some of the more subtle psychological, psychiatric, or neurological phenomena. ... My only concern is possible delayed effects, and I think we should proceed as if there were some' (Payer, 1983).

Good advice, as it turns out.

In the spring of 1984, the National Institutes of Health consensus panel released its long-awaited report on the use of ultrasound. The panel noted that ultrasound was not essential in any condition and discouraged its use 'solely to satisfy the family's desire to know the fetal sex, to view the fetus, or to obtain a picture of the fetus' (*Med. World News*, 1984b).

Some physicians have been ringing the alarm bells for years. James Stockman, the associate editor of the 1979 *Year Book of Pediatrics*, states: 'Whether ultrasound is as safe as it appears to be remains to be seen. Ultrasound can produce breakage in purified DNA' (Stockman, 1979). He adds that the use of ultrasound reminds him of the days when every shoe salesman had a fluoroscope in his store. It was fun watching your toes wiggle, but none of us would subject ourselves to that examination today.

Animal and laboratory studies have shown that ultrasound may cause chromosome damage, breakdown of DNA, and a variety of changes in circulation, liver cells, brain enzymes, EEG tracings, nerve reflexes, and emotional reactivity (Stratmeyer, 1980). In addition, experimental rats exposed to ultrasound demonstrated delayed neuromuscular development and reduction of antibodies involved in immune response (Wald et al., 1983).

Professor Earl Prohofsky of Purdue University has studied the structure of DNA extensively. He has demonstrated that all kinds of waves, including microwaves, will cause the double-stranded DNA to vibrate, much like the strings of a violin (Strauss, 1984). Reacting to various chemicals, DNA begins to vibrate, causing the strands to unwind during cell reproduction. Researchers at the University of Maryland have shown that DNA absorbs 400 times more microwave radiation than a surrounding salt solution (Swicord, 1984). Increased microwave (and presumably other waves as well) absorption leads to increased heat and vibration within the DNA, which in turn can cause genetic damage.

Researchers at the University of South Florida studied children exposed to ultrasound *in utero*. Although they found no solid indications of subtle or late-occurring harm, their advice to pregnant women was to reject ultrasound as a diagnostic procedure. Dr Charles Stark, who conducted the study, stated that he would personally not consider using ultrasound at any time during pregnancy.

Benefits

It is regrettable that ultrasound is considered potentially biologically harmful to the unborn child, for it is the only high-tech investigative tool in obstetrics that has proven psychologically beneficial to the pregnant mother and her baby. At a time when many women are not even aware of being pregnant and when many who are don't really feel pregnant, ultrasound enables the mother to actually see her child in the uterus.

Seeing that she is carrying within her a tiny human being engenders positive feelings that predate by several months the experience of fetal movement. As one woman reported: 'At 9 weeks, it looks like a tadpole. You can definitely see the little head and the spinal cord and sticks of arms and legs. After 12 weeks, you can see a dot going up and down – that's its heart. Then as the baby gets older, you can see it moving.'

In a pioneering study conducted at King's College Hospital in London, two groups of pregnant women underwent ultrasound examination. Those in a high-feedback group were shown the monitor screen and provided with visual and verbal descriptions of their babies. A low-feedback group received a comparable examination but were unable to see the monitor screen and did not receive visual and verbal descriptions. Instead, they were simply told, 'All is well.'

The women's attitudes toward being pregnant and toward the fetus were tested before and after the scan. The direction of change was the same in both groups, with the women becoming less 'concerned, more attached, reassured, secure, and confident.' However, women in the high-feedback group felt better during the scan, 74% rating their emotional state as 'wonderful' compared to 11% in the low-feedback group. The researchers conclude that scanning is informative as well as emotionally rewarding – especially when specific and detailed feedback is made available to the mother (Campbell et al., 1982).

Being able to see her unborn child on an ultrasound monitor could have a beneficial emotional effect for a mother who had ambivalent feelings about her pregnancy or is particularly worried, anxious, or depressed about the prospect of having a baby. The pregnant mother and her physician would have to weigh carefully the potential biological risks against the known psychological value of this procedure.

Fetal heart monitors

Until recently, the fetal heart rate was determined by listening with a stethoscope placed on the pregnant woman's abdomen at intervals throughout labor. Now the electronic fetal monitor (EFM) can continuously record the fetal rate on a graph. The EFM utilizes continuous wave ultrasound, in contrast to the ultrasound scanner, which uses pulsating ultrasound. The purpose of the EFM is to detect fetal heart rate abnormalities that would indicate that the baby is in distress. The EFM is applied to the mother's abdomen with tape or an elastic belt to hold an ultrasound transducer and pressure gauge in place. The transducer is positioned where fetal heart sounds can best be heard. The pressure gauge indirectly records intrauterine pressure during contractions.

A further refinement of the EFM is the internal fetal monitor, which involves placing of two catheters into the uterus during labor. After the membranes rupture, a spinal metal wire electrode is inserted beneath the scalp of the baby's head. This catheter measures fetal pulse while the second catheter measures intrauterine pressure. The internal monitor is more precise and allows more freedom of movement than the external monitor.

Does fetal monitoring accomplish what its supporters claim? Does it prevent cerebral palsy and brain damage? Does it correctly identify fetal distress? Does it, in the final analysis, reduce fetal and maternal morbidity and mortality?

An analysis in 1978 of 15 486 live-born infants published in the *New England Journal of Medicine* showed a drop in the neonatal death rate from 304 per 1000 live births in non-EFM labors to 195 per 1000 in EFM labors in the highest risk pregnancies (*Med. World News*, 1984a). However, the neonatal death rate in the lowest-risk group was only 1 per 1000 live births, so EFM could not possibly improve the outcome. In this group it would probably affect mother and child adversely.

A study at the Denver General Hospital compared high-risk women in labor who were monitored with EFM with an equal number of high-risk women on whom EFM was not used. There were no differences in neonatal deaths, Apgar scores, or cord blood gases between the two groups. However, the monitored group's Caesarean section rate was more than double that of the auscultated group, and the monitored group had a three times higher rate of postpartum infections (Haverkamp et al., 1976).

Researchers at the National Center of Health Sciences Research (US) who reviewed over 600 studies on fetal monitoring concluded that there was no scientific evidence that continuous EFM prevents brain damage or otherwise improves infant health except in very small babies (Edwards and Simkin).

The internal monitor is an invasive technique that carries bacteria into the uterus. Because the likelihood of infection increases as time passes, the procedure commits the hospital staff to deliver the baby, ready or not, within 12–16 hours. This is turn leads to an increased number of induced labors and Caesarean sections. It is not surprising, then, that electronic fetal monitors have led to an increase in Caesarean sections wherever they have been used.

If the fetal heart monitor tells doctors that the baby is in distress, they will likely draw blood from the fetal scalp. Some babies have been delivered with heads that have been described as looking like raw hamburger meat. It is conservatively estimated that up to 5% of babies who have had scalp electrodes during labor develop abscesses on their heads, which lead to the use of antibiotics (more needles) and prolonged hospitalization.

Finally, the use of the machine over 6, 10, or more hours exposes both the baby and mother to a significant dose of ultrasound energy.

In spite of all this data, EFM advocates have done a remarkable job of selling the idea to pregnant mothers. Studies have shown a largely positive response to its use, with laboring women finding monitoring reassuring, though worry appeared to increase slightly with longer labors (Starkman and Youngs, 1980; Jackson et al., 1983).

Negative responses focused on the physical discomfort associated with the placement of the electrodes and enforced immobility. The authors of one of these reports suggest: 'In order to maximize beneficial and minimize detrimental psychological effects, accurate information about fetal monitoring and its associated procedures should be given to mothers' (Starkman and Youngs, 1980). What are the psychological effects of the EFM on the staff, the pregnant woman, and her baby?

The first law of psychotechnology of labor (*Verny's First Law*)

The quantity of technological devices in the labor room is inversely proportional to the amount of human contact between staff and patient.

As soon as a woman is connected to a fetal heart monitor, all eyes are on the monitor. The pregnant woman must lie flat on her back and not move or she will disturb the monitor. The nurses and doctors no longer put their stethoscopes on her abdomen to listen to the baby; the monitor takes care of that. They no longer palpate, the traditional way to determine quality of contractions, because the belts of the monitor are in the way.

The nurse who watches the monitor does not function as a nurse but as a technician. How do nurses feel about this new role? I doubt that this is what they had in mind when they entered nursing with the idea of caring for people. Obstetrical nurses are not oblivious to this; they try to relate to the patient, but their attention is at best divided between the machine and the woman in labor. The staff's job is made more difficult by the unreliability of the information and the very large chance of misinterpretation of data provided by fetal monitors.

Under these circumstances, I would expect the medical staff to be under considerable stress and this stress to be conveyed to the pregnant woman. Staff members seem to deal with this stress by unconsciously denying it and at the same time idealizing the machine. The result is an over-reliance upon the monitor and an inability to perceive its shortcomings objectively.

The second law of psychotechnology of labor (*Verny's Second Law*)

The quantity of technological devices in the labor room is directly related to the degree of discomfort experienced by the patient.

Even women thoroughly brainwashed or 'prepared' for electronic monitors (and some high-risk women are plugged into both an external and an internal fetal monitor) become uncomfortable, worried, and progressively more anxious as labor drags on and they are not allowed to move about. What an insane way to have a child: strapped down to a bed, belts over her stomach, connected with wires to a machine that emits weird sounds and draws graphs – with everyone paying attention to it and not to her. I cannot think of a better method to make a pregnant woman feel unimportant and vulnerable. As her anxiety increases, her body will try to delay labor rather than facilitate it; this will provoke medical interventions and may culminate in a Caesarean section. Then staff members will congratulate each other on having saved another baby that would have been lost before the advent of space-age technology. And the mother will be thankful and more than willing to repeat the experience next time she is pregnant.

And what of the poor baby? Up to the time his mother is laid out flat on her back, the baby is comforted by the unique rhythm of her movements. Suddenly, all movement ceases. Dramatic changes in its routine elicit anxiety in the baby. Next a needle is jabbed under his scalp, and it hurts. Then perhaps more needles, sometimes one every half-hour. Such a baby might well experience a sense of angry puzzlement, an emotional equivalent to the question: 'Why is my mother doing this to me?' How is the baby expected to be eager to be born if this is a foretaste of what the outside world will be like? How can the baby be expected to push forward with his head when any such movement causes more pain? What a torture to inflict on a human being. How could this process fail to leave psychological scars? (Verny and Kelly, 1981).

Fetoscopy

Fetoscopy is an outpatient procedure done under ultrasound guidance. It lasts 1–2 hours and is usually performed after 18 weeks gestation. Physicians generally administer a local anesthetic and intravenous diazepam (Valium) to relax the mother. The most widely used instrument is a combination needle 15 cm long and 1.7 mm wide. It contains a solid optic lens with fiberoptic illumination that allows the doctor to see the unborn child in the uterus with 2–5-fold magnification (Elias and Esterly, 1981).

Fetoscopy is used to determine the appropriate spot for sampling fetal blood or tissue. Potentially lethal syndromes involving skin abnormalities can be diagnosed by skin biopsies taken with the aid of a fetoscope. Fetoscopy directed by sonography has been successful in obtaining fetal blood in approximately 90% of cases. It is accompanied by a 3–5% risk of spontaneous abortion in experienced hands (Nolan et al., 1981).

Other risks to the mother include exchange of blood between the baby and the mother, with maternal sensitization, leakage of amniotic fluid during later months of pregnancy, uterine bleeding, scarring of the uterus, infection, and puncture of other organs (Phillips, 1975). There is also the unknown effect of the intensity of the fiberoptic light on the baby's eyes. One good result of the use of fiberoptics has been the realization by at least a few obstetricians of the sensate nature of the unborn. One obstetrician observed: 'I had a blood vessel lined up and was just about to strike when out of nowhere came this hand to knock away the needle. I think it was coincidental, but who knows?' (Baker, 1978).

Fetal therapy

Fetal surgery got its start in 1963 with intrauterine transfusions for Rh disease. With the widespread use of such high-tech procedures as ultrasound, amniocentesis, and fetoscopy, the number of unborn children being operated upon is beginning to rise rapidly.

Recent cases include surgery on the unborn's bladder, head, diaphragm, and heart. In one instance, doctors in San Francisco discovered on a routine ultrasound scan that one of their patients had twins, a female and a male, and that the male was developing abnormal urine retention. 'As the picture became clearer, we diagnosed the condition as bladder-outlet obstruction.' They realized that any kind of intervention might induce premature delivery and endanger the normally developing twin. At 31 weeks gestation, the doctors succeeded in inserting a catheter under local anesthetic into the bladder of the boy and thus prevented the continued accumulation of urine in his body. At the time the case was reported, he was $2\frac{1}{2}$ months old and doing well. He will require further surgery when he is a little older (*Med. World News*, 1981).

With ultrasound scanning, about 30 unborn babies have had shunts inserted into their brains to relieve pressure caused by the buildup of cerebrospinal fluid. 'It's like bobbing for apples,' said Dr Thomas Brown, a neurosurgeon at Northwestern Memorial Hospital in Chicago. Dr William Clewell of the Colorado Health Science Center cautions that 'results are not as dramatic as preliminary reports indicated.' He states that the fetal mortality rate for the treatment of fetal hydrocephalus has been 25% and that 30% of the survivors have significant to profound developmental delays (McDaniel, 1983).

Some disorders such as Rh incompatibility and heart rhythm irregularities may now be detected and treated *in utero*. Others, such as anencephaly (absence of brain tissue) and chromosomal disorders, though diagnosed, cannot be treated.

Prenatal diagnosis

Prenatal diagnosis benefits many prospective parents who wish to know whether their fetus suffers from certain mental and physical impairments. In most centers, prenatal diagnosis is offered on the assumption that relief from anxiety or an opportunity to prepare for a disabled child are benefits that outweigh the risks to the fetus and mother from the procedure. At the same time, prenatal diagnosis presents a wide range of decisions and challenges for health care providers, prospective parents, and policy makers.

Prenatal diagnosis has been integrated into obstetric care with minimal attention to its psychological effects on families. The guiding assumption of advocates of prenatal diagnosis has been that it is a means of preventing tragedy.

The testing process appears to change the parents' experience of pregnancy — even when the results are favorable. The period of waiting for results (up to 6 weeks in some tests) is often characterized by a 'suspension of commitment to the pregnancy,' a postponement of what has been called the 'integration' stage of pregnancy (Beeson and Golbus, 1979; Beeson, 1984).

Fletcher has observed the impact on parents of learning the sex of the fetus, referring to the time of pregnancy following test results as 'the newest human stage of life' (Fletcher, 1972). Both he and Beeson observed that parents who were told the sex of the fetus, and assured of the absence of certain major disorders, began a series of family interactions that previously took place upon birth. These included naming the fetus, informing relatives and friends of the news (or of the pregnancy), and going out and celebrating (Beeson, 1984; Fletcher, 1972).

The psychological effects of miscarriage following amniocentesis (estimated at 0.5%) or fetoscopy (estimated at 3–5%) have not been studied. Those who miscarry may never know if the miscarriage was caused by the testing, even though they opted to take this risk. Perhaps the most difficult dilemmas are faced by women who are carriers of Duchenne muscular dystrophy, an X-linked disorder. Such women carrying male fetuses must decide whether or not to abort, knowing only that 50% will be affected and *50% will be normal.*

Selective abortion: the ethical issues

The central ethical issue in prenatal diagnosis that has concerned laymen, religious leaders, and ethicists has been selective abortion.

For some parents, prenatal diagnosis may prevent abortion by assuring the absence of certain disorders, *but for the majority, abortion is the primary procedure* that is responsible for preventing the birth of a disabled child. This option, for which many families are deeply grateful, is not without psychological costs to the parents. Blumberg et al. (1975) found that women who abort because of the risk of genetic disease may suffer significant emotional trauma and may have a greater need for psychotherapy than women who abort for socioeconomic or psychological reasons. Despite this trauma,

> '77% of families studied would again opt for amniocentesis and, if indicated, selective abortion in any future pregnancy. These families have accepted

selective abortion and its attendant problems as preferable to the birth of a defective child.'

Many who oppose abortion on general grounds think it is the only humane response to the knowledge of genetic disease. Others approve of abortion for fetal degenerative diseases such as Tay Sachs disease and Duchenne muscular dystrophy but disapprove of abortion for sickle-cell anemia and hemophilia, which are not as immediately fatal and can be treated, albeit with only partial success. A few ethicists and others have expressed concern that we are reducing our tolerance for imperfection (Harris, 1975). Some bioethicists view prenatal diagnosis as an appropriate method of reducing the suffering of the unborn child and the burden on the family; others oppose selective abortion as a violation of fetal rights (Fletcher, 1975; Dyck, 1971).

In response to this controversy, an interdisciplinary group of bioethicists from the Hastings Institute of Society, Ethics, and the Life Sciences met to form guidelines. They concluded that the purpose of prenatal diagnosis should be to treat and eventually cure disease in the fetus or infant. Because this is possible in only a small fraction of cases, they conclude:

> 'Abortion is never therapeutic for the fetus, but we believe it can be morally justified for the relief of suffering and burden to family and society. These guidelines were developed in a moral framework favoring the protection of individual choice and the autonomy of parents, even when we disagree with their courses of action. . . . These guidelines cannot reconcile the views of those who believe that abortion is wrong virtually without exception with the views of those who exclude the welfare of the fetus completely from any argument about reproductive decisions' (Powledge and Fletcher, 1979).

Because with present technology abortions following prenatal diagnosis are generally performed during the second trimester, they are often viewed as ethically more questionable than first-trimester abortions. They are more physically and emotionally traumatic for the mother because she has felt fetal movements and the pregnancy is apparent to others.

In some centers, it is thought to be psychologically easier on the mother if the abortion is conducted by suction and curettage under general anesthesia. However, many nurses and doctors in the operating room find this form of abortion particularly repugnant and prefer that the mother go through induced labor and delivery. The mother herself may have little choice in the method of abortion.

Abortion is not the only ethical issue raised by prenatal diagnosis. It is now possible to detect a number of chromosomal abnormalities the effects of which are not agreed upon. One such case is the presence of an extra Y chromosome. Because the consequences of the condition are disputed, the appropriate response is unclear. In such cases, practitioners generally agree that parents should be informed of the ambiguities even though this may cause anxiety (Beeson et al., 1983).

Another problem is the question of whether prenatal diagnosis should be denied to women who are at risk and want the procedure but have decided not to abort.

CONCLUSION

Medical technology has greatly added to our knowledge of fetal development and our capacity to 'see' the unborn child. It has also improved the outcome in high-risk pregnancies. The question is whether the benefits from this explosion of gynegadgetry outweigh the risks.

First we hospitalized birth; now we have mechanized it. Obstetrics today is rushing headlong toward 'guaranteed safe no-risk' birth. In pursuing this goal, we have created new problems that may prove worse than the ones the high-tech procedures were supposed to solve.

Current evidence does not favor the unrestrained use of technical procedures. Rather, it would be prudent at present to limit diagnostic tests and monitoring devices in obstetrics to a narrow segment of the spectrum of conditions in high-risk pregnancies.

53

The mother mystique: psycho-sociological factors which promote an unrealistic view of mothers (edited extracts)

J. Raphael-Leff

ABSTRACT

This paper explores the unrealistic view of mothers perpetuated by western society in what I have called the myths of the 'mother mystique'. Basically, these myths deny the existence of maternal ambivalence, reinforcing the belief that mothers are unconditionally loving. Paradoxically, alongside the idealization of mothers there exists a social and emotional denigration of maternal status and creativity. I have introduced evidence of the mother mystique from various fields – mythology; psychosocial theories; ethology and obstetrics.

It is my contention that this unrealistic view of mothers originates in and reflects the mother–fetus placental exchange, prenatal psychology and our earliest experiences of mothering.

Furthermore, I suggest that, generally, mothers are depicted 'as babies see them'. Each mother struggles individually with her own inability to live up to these unrealistic expectations, assuming it to be her own personal shortcoming. Ambivalence is seen as a dire secret to be repressed rather than the inevitable result of conceiving a child who is partly an alien intruder into her life, demanding maternal perfection.

In my research I have delineated two general maternal orientations: that of Facilitator and Regulator which represent different ways of resolving this conflict, focusing on love and hate respectively. In this paper, I express the belief, based on clinical experience, that a third, compromise therapeutic resolution may exist.

Namely, recognition by primary health care workers and mothers themselves, of the reciprocally ambivalent mixture of feelings involved in this most intimate and complex relationship, between a mother and the fruit of her womb.

'There is much more continuity between intrauterine life and earliest infancy than the impressive caesura of the act of birth would have us believe' (Freud, 1926, p. 138).

AN INTRODUCTION INTO THE MOTHER MYSTIQUE

We have all been babies. Each of us has had a mother. But, only some of us have become mothers. I think these simple facts help account for the unrealistic view of mothers perpetuated in western society. What is puzzling is how these beliefs are formulated, and why mothers go along with the distortion. In order to answer these questions I have had to cast my net wide, and perhaps at times, it will seem as if I have wandered far off the question. Nevertheless I shall return, hopefully with my net full of elusive metaphorical fish.

The experience of pregnancy

The mystery of pregnancy remains awesome, despite our increasing understanding of the complex physiological, biochemical and morphological processes taking place, and the sophisticated means of exploring the uterine cavity and its secrets. Some of the mystery remains impenetrable. Pregnancy, and particularly first pregnancy, is a time of contradictions. It is a time of looking forward and of looking back; it is a time of reaching outwards and of reaching inwards. It is a junction in which several worlds meet, forcing confrontation between elemental opposites in the woman's inner world: female and male; birth and death; creation and destruction; order and chaos; self and other.

With conception, the woman's singularity is abruptly disrupted. Suddenly, two beings inhabit one body – hers! A male substance, a sperm has entered her body and united with her ovum to produce a genetically foreign body living inside her. In the normal course of events, such an invasion would be destroyed or rejected by the host's immune system but the sperm has a superior ability to suppress her normal immunologic responses through mechanisms we have yet to understand.

First pregnancy is also the experiencing of a *psychologically* 'foreign body', a concept loaded with connotations and associations reaching back to the mother's own infancy, and overlaid with mystification and silent unconscious fantasies. It creates a state of emotional disequilibrium within which each pregnant woman must find her own resolution. Thoughts, feelings and processes which are usually subliminal suddenly flood consciousness and must either be attended to or with great effort kept at bay. Paradoxically, at the very time of discovering her 'twosomeness', each pregnant woman often feels very lonely and irredeemably alone – locked into herself with incommunicable experiences, inexplicable mood swings, intense urges, irrational cravings, altered states of consciousness and sudden flashes of insight, yet all too often, she lacks the language to explain and the courage to explore the numinous mystery occurring within her.

Deep in the interior

Each and every one of us has dwelled for almost three seasons in a dark, warm, wet place of which we have little recollection – but know it to have been a woman's body.

Floating within the salty sea of amniotic fluid, the fetus swallows and urinates, takes in and pushes out, ingests and expels. Brief encounters with the containing membrane create fleeting experiences of a boundary which recurrently and increasingly closes in, as the fetus grows larger and uterine contractions harden the enclosing walls. The baby encounters the cord, too, a dimly realized plaything of supreme importance. His own body becomes familiar through touch and feel and contact with its own limbs and the external stroking and patting of the pregnant bulge. The 'dialog' proceeds between the mother's touch and the baby's kicking; between maternal heart-'drumming' and fetal listening; within the rhythmic synchronization of waking and sleep, dancing and rest.

Whatever the level of awareness of maternal existence and emotional interplay, we may assume that within the liquid bubble, the fetus, like his maternal hostess, is largely unconscious of the continuous exchange of nutriments and waste; unaware that with every heart beat his mother pumps oxygen-loaded blood and nourishment into the placenta and removes carbon dioxide to be breathed out through her lungs and nitrogen compounds to be excreted through his mother's kidneys in her urine. Thus already in the womb, the mother sustains for the fetus an illusion of magical 'unconditional omnipotence' (Ferenczi, 1913, p. 219) while she serves the function of container, metabolizer and waste-disposer.

In this paper, I would like to propose that this initial prenatal interchange of nutrients and waste between mother and baby, becomes an unconscious metaphor and paradigm for postnatal interaction which may last as long as a lifetime. Also, I will suggest that this earliest transaction has wider social manifestations and implications in the almost universal devaluation of women throughout history.

THE ULTIMATE DISILLUSIONMENT

All cultures endorse myths, beliefs and rituals which incorporate fantasies of this first prenatal experience. The poignant awakening to separateness and wish to recapture the illusory intrauterine oneness can also be suspended in dream states and sleep, and is expressed by adults in a religious yearning that the philosopher, Martin Buber, called 'the cosmic connection' (Buber, 1958). Freud described it as the 'oceanic feeling' seeking the 'restoration of limitless narcissism', later becoming connected with religious 'oneness with the universe' (Freud, 1930, p. 72). We mourn the lost paradise of primal unconditional omnipotence before we ate of the tree of knowledge and knew ourselves to be naked, vulnerable and exiled.

It has been said that among humans, it is the male who comes nearest to fulfilling the longed for return to uterine existence during sexual intercourse – 'with his semen in reality, with his penis symbolically and with his whole self in fantasy' (Balint, 1956, p. 141). Strangely, this idea overlooks the simple reality that the pregnant female actually recreates the original experience through dual identification with both the baby in her womb and the pregnant mother of her own gestation *in utero*. This then is the biological bedrock of gender distinction – women create babies. Men cannot. *The human female has the formative power to regenerate her origins within her own body while the male regains access to this early state momentarily through sexual entry into a woman's body or symbolically in myth and religious ideas.*

Underlying all these illusions is the *ultimate disillusionment* that can never be fully contemplated: that mother, who has the capacity to create also has the capacity to destroy – to abort, to expel, to starve, poison, smother; the power to drop, smash, forget, ignore, or to cut down to size.

Instead, mothers collude in keeping the 'mother mystique' going – the myths that mothers love unconditionally and that any other activity is superior to women's ability to create and nurture a live human being. It is my contention that we can see the perpetuation of these myths of 'male' cultural supremacy and unconditional mother-love in all spheres of life. Briefly, I shall illustrate this from several areas – mythology, psychosocial development, ethology and obstetrics.

Mythology

In the beginning there was the Mother...

Myths create a bridge between outer realities and inner hopes, wishes and dreams, providing man with a 'play area in a world which would

THE MOTHER MYSTIQUE: PSYCHOSOCIOLOGICAL FACTORS

otherwise be fearsome, unbearable, dull or frustrating' (Mitchell, 1982, p. 63). One function of myths is to provide authorization for continuance of traditions or to approve alterations and justify the existing social system (Graves, 1979) – 'an authority that transcends rational argument' (Cavendish, 1984, p. 10) yet contains, according to the anthropologist, Levi-Strauss, in a veiled form, the contradictions inherent in life which the conscious human mind is unwilling to confront (Levi-Strauss, 1969).

In cosmological myths where creation signifies procreation, we very often find an elaboration of the idea of male supremacy. Although prehistoric cultures stressed female fertility goddesses, in more recent civilizations it is invariably a male figure who is the creator. Even in Indian, Tibetan, Chinese or Greek mythology, where the world is created from a 'cosmic egg', it is often a *male* deity or warrior who lays it! Likewise, myths and artifacts from ancient cultures in India, Egypt, Bali, Rome and Peru celebrate both fertile, life-giving maternity and the terrible, death dealing aspects of mothers (see Neumann, 1963), whereas more recent traditions depict them adoring unconditionally.

Thus, too, in the Old Testament, although nearly all pre-biblical sacred documents have been either suppressed or lost, we can still detect allusions to ancient folklore.[1] The role reversals of patriarchal editing have the male God of Genesis form the first man, Adam out of (mother-) earth ('Adama' is the Hebrew word for earth) and then remove his spare rib to create Eve (whose Hebrew name, 'Hava' reveals *her* to be the mother of all living). She was, however blamed for the expulsion from the womb of paradise and cursed to bear sons in pain and be ruled by her man (Genesis, 3). Although exorcized from Scripture, we find that Eve had a predecessor, Lilith, a fertility Goddess who, taking offence at the recumbent position in sexual intercourse, demanded equality with Adam, but when he tried to compel her to housewifely obedience by force, left him in a rage to live a life of orgiastic freedom and infanticide (Graves and Patai, 1964, pp. 64–5). Primordial fear of the archaic mother's destructive powers is thus revealed behind the scenes and has survived in rituals performed to protect newborn babies.[2]

In this example we find that the early matriarchal version of the world has been expunged and the myths rewritten with a male pen. As a contemporary feminist writer says: 'Patriarchal monotheism did not simply change the sex of the divine presence; it stripped the universe of female divinity, and permitted woman to be sanctified ... only and exclusively as mother' (Rich, 1977, p. 119). I would add, that such 'sanctification' indicates unrealistic idealization of a function and simultaneous degradation of its status.

We must question not only what motivated the rewriting of mythology but why women all over the world have accepted these devaluating changes in silence all these years. Indeed, we must question why, in virtually every society women are physically, politically and/or economically dominated by men; women are thought to be and think of themselves as inferior (Chodorow, 1971).

Psychosocial development

This universality of female subordination has been anthropologically explained as the symbolic equation of women with Nature (and the natural functions of reproduction) which male Culture attempts to transcend (Ortner, 1974). The psychoanalyst, Zilboorg (1974), attributed the original subjugation of women to the discovery of the male role in biological paternity. He assumed that prehistoric overthrow of ancient gynocentric rule originated in man's early hostility toward his primordial mother (not his father, as Freud postulates in the Primal Horde myth). Zilboorg bases psychological fatherhood on identification with the envied fertile mother; he does not, however, explain woman's acceptance of her subjugation or the degeneration of her role. Anthropologically, the ambiguous position of woman has been attributed to her marginality: she is an alien on whom the society is dependent for reproductivity – the fact that (in patrilocal, patrilineal societies) she is an outsider to her husband and yet has a bloodlink to her son. The power a woman wields in any given society would therefore depend on the closeness of the mother–son bond (Kessler, 1979, p. 57). It has been suggested that the tragedy of woman, is that she has become resigned to producing sons who will perpetuate the system that devalues the mother. As long as women live through their children and are the primary care-takers, sons will continue to base their sexual identity on devaluing femininity, their own and that of others (Chodorow, 1974).

Psychosexual identification

Psychoanalytic theories have stressed that initially, both little girls and little boys identify with their primary care person, invariably a woman, the pre-oedipal mother. With growing independence, both boys and girls try to detach themselves from mother and the fearful attraction of sinking back into boundary dissolution and fusion with her. The boy does so through increasing awareness of his phallic difference. He gradually 'dis-identifies' (Greenson, 1968) from mother who serves as his initial model in order to pursue masculine identification with his phallic father. However, sociologists have stressed the irony of the western father who presents a fallacious model to his children – his work is elsewhere; its product intangible; he is largely unavailable and when at home is at leisure. Granted ideological supremacy both in the family and in public because of the very elusiveness of his role, father's unavailability means that the boy defines and constructs his masculinity in negative terms, by denigrating all things feminine (Chodorow, 1978). In fact, anthropologist Margaret Mead stated that the 'recurrent problem of civilization is to define the male role satisfactorily enough to provide men with the sense of irreversible achievement that is granted women in childbearing' (Mead, 1949, p. 160). Conversely, the little girl, who also has to separate from her pre-oedipal mother, has nothing intrinsically different with which to liberate herself. She lacks the organ 'to placate or restore the avenging mother' (Heimann, 1951, p. 31). She thus turns to her father both to break free of her mother and through envy of his phallic power which she now idealizes. Like her brother, she also becomes contemptuous of feeding, waste disposing, projecting mother's creativity onto father. The irony is, that 'power becomes then the prerogative of the man' and any achievement of the girl's will be felt as an encroachment on the father's power (Chasseguet-Smirgel, 1981, p. 116). All this begins with the simple fact that 'women mother' (Chodorow, 1978, p. 3). In virtually all societies it is women who are primary caretakers; both girls and boys are mothered by women.

Ethology

Like all female mammals, human mothers have been constrained by suckling their offspring. However, primary responsibility of mothers for child rearing often extends well beyond the breast-feeding stage, and with the introduction of bottle-feeding, even infant feeding need no longer be the prerogative of lactating women. It has been suggested that it is in the interest of patriarchy to maintain confusion between birth giving and exclusive care-taking functions in human society (Badiner, 1981). Animal studies have often been used as evidence to support sexist stereotypes of human male and female roles. However, gradually it is becoming apparent that apart from the fact that females make eggs and males make sperm, no other universal axioms are possible. There is a general belief that females are instinctively maternal and make better mothers than males. No scientific evidence exists for this and in vast numbers of non-lactating species, the *male* is the primary caretaker. Research with other mammals has suggested that 'maternalistic' reactions in both virgin females and in males can be induced *by exposure to the newborn* and social bonding (Shaw and Darling, 1985).

Obstetrics

Over 70% of human societies ban men from observing or assisting their wives in birth (Shaw and Darling, 1985). It is a moot point whether men segregate dangerous birthgiving women or are prohibited access to birth by women who wish to retain an area of power. The net result in many societies is reinforcement of the myth that 'biology is destiny' and insurance that primary caretaking remains an exclusive female prerogative. Ironically, in our own western societies, female controlled, community managed birth has been gradually medicalized and hospitalized by male obstetricians (Oakley, 1980). They, according to one 18th century English midwife, have taken over by 'forging the phantom of incapacity in women' (Nihell, *Treatise on the Art of Midwifery*, 1760; quoted in Rich, 1977, p. 147).

Western woman has all but lost the tradition of labour attended only by experienced females. In the 'delivery' room as in pregnancy, she no longer has the encircling protection of the 'mothers of the tribe', the women who mediate for the primigravida in her liminal state – between past and future, natural and supernatural, dispelling fear, promoting health and guiding the novice step by step, through the unknown. The initiated women, who like the mothers of early childhood, are believed to possess special healing capacities and magical powers to ward off danger, permit, nurture and ensure the safety of mother and baby during pregnancy and in the birth chamber. In our non-traditional societies we have eroded the framework of folklore and ancestral custom handed down from one generation of mothers to the next; there is little acknowledgement of the pregnant woman in her marginal position of 'not-yet-motherhood', and few rituals or socially approved taboos to help assuage her anxieties and reinforce her sense of belonging to a chain of mothers. She has become alienated from the natural femaleness of her own body processes and feminists have recently begun to question the mystification in 'male authored sciences of womankind' and the right of male gynecologists to 'fixate on what they do not have and cannot themselves do' (Daly, 1978).

WOMEN'S SILENCE

If in the past men have been excluded from the chambers of childbirth, we women around the world have been excluded from the production of cultural forms, lacking a female language, unable to give weight to our own symbolic meanings even in such purely female experiences as menstruation, pregnancy and lactation. It is almost trite to say that women's reality has been circumscribed by male social definitions and control. 'Both sexes inhabit a male decreed reality' (Spender, 1980, p. 57) and the closer woman approximates male roles, the higher the status accorded to her by society. Nevertheless, we must also admit that women's silence has perpetuated the unquestioned male version of reality. We women have colluded in preserving male illusions; we have remained silent in the face of the distortions of 'man made language' (Spender, 1980) and as such have become 'accomplices' forcing ourselves into an alien mold. Feminist Sheila Rowbotham says 'people who are without names, who do not know themselves, who have no culture, experience a kind of paralysis of consciousness' (Rowbotham, 1973, p. 27).[3]

However, once again, I feel it is not simply a question of the absence of knowledge, but rather of the acceptance of projections. Women have taken into themselves evacuated dark fears and fantasies of mother's sons and have survived the onslaught, feeding back the safe version. It is believed that the Women's Movement and consciousness raising has enabled women to recognize our femaleness and see through existing versions of feminity (Rowbotham, 1973, p. 3). Nevertheless, on the issues of pregnancy and lactation it has at times presented options which I feel are simple inversions of male idealization or degradation rather than a truly open-ended exploration of an exclusively female reality, a validation of her own experience not in defiance of male meanings but in discovery of her own. Feminist Germaine Greer notes that 'the closer women draw in social and economic status to the male level, the more disruptive childbirth becomes. In order to compete with men, western woman has joined the masculine hierarchy and cultivated a masculine sense of self' (Greer, 1985, p. 12). As feminist sociologist, Ann Oakley, remarks, in its anti-natalist focus on freeing women from child-bearing and child-rearing roles (demanding more abortion, contraception, state child-care and equal non-domestic work opportunities for women) feminism too, has 'unconsciously echoed the patriarchal view of women as sexual objects or subjects condemned by their biology to motherhood' (Oakley, 1981, p. 23).

It is my contention that on issues related to motherhood, women are as susceptible as men to unconscious bias. Although we may have repudiated the myth of male supremacy we often still adhere to the denigration of the power to create life and/or to the myth of maternal non-ambivalence. If the male 'mother-mystique' myths have been unconsciously constructed on the basis of being the son of a mother, we as women must strive to free ourselves to define motherhood both as mothers to our own children as well as daughters to our mothers. For each of us, even as adults it is painful to believe that mother did not love unconditionally. That one is not eternally her special 'wunderkind'; that she will not forever put her own needs second to those of her beloved child. So deep is the fantasy, that even when we become mothers ourselves, we are guilt ridden at having failed at times to protect our child's belief in a all beneficent universe, the illusion of his own omnipotence and the myth of his mother's invincibility and boundless love. Clearly, we mothers play the same role for society as we do for our children – we detoxify the ambivalent maternal images projected into us and hand back the laundered version of unconditionally loving mothers.[4]

EXPERIENCING PREGNANCY – FACILITATORS AND REGULATORS

Like all transitional phases, pregnancy reactivates long-inhibited conflictual areas of inner life, necessitating dissolution, new resolutions and reintegration (Kestenberg, 1976). In an attempt to integrate the new, strange and ambiguous situation with some familiar internal reality, dormant processes are revitalized, earlier modes of being and archaic beliefs are resuscitated along with fantasies of prenatal existence and infantile identification. Because it provides only minimal enigmatic clues about the outcome, pregnancy calls forth the woman's unconscious fantasies and their conscious derivatives which she projects onto the contents of her womb, her imagined future baby and herself as mother-to-be.

In my research I have found it possible to delineate two broad categories of women's conscious orientations towards pregnancy and motherhood, which I feel are informed by feminine myths and feminist traditions respectively, and are rooted in unconscious identifications. In previous papers I have called these the Facilitator and Regulator orientations. Before describing them, I would like to stress that although most mothers gravitate towards one or other of these polarized reactions and remain consistent at least until the birth of the next child, increasingly, there are women who courageously fall into an intermediate orientation, refraining from commitment to one or other stance. By trying to suspend previously defined patterns of thought and feeling, these women encounter the unforeseen; are receptive to ambivalent forces within themselves and use both pregnancy and early motherhood as a creative period of personal growth.

The *facilitator* greets conception as the long-awaited fulfilment of her feminine destiny. Women, in her view, are uniquely privileged in their ability to create, contain and nourish a new life. Pregnancy signifies the realization of an old, much postponed childhood wish to have a baby of her own. Trustingly, she gives in to the emotional, psychological and physiological processes of pregnancy, allowing herself to drift on a sea of surging emotions, as old as time, as new as conception. She experiences herself as part of the long chain of mothers since time immemorial, and like a Russian doll, makes the fetus an integral part of herself in the identificatory merging of self and other, erasing the boundaries between the embryo in her womb and her nascent self within her own pregnant mother's womb. She is recapturing the long yearned for 'undivided primal world that precedes form, in the womb of the great mother' (Buber, 1958, p. 25). Rejoicing in the easy accessibility to unconscious fantasies and symbolic imagery, she becomes proverbially radiant. The Facilitator luxuriates in the internal glow of her projected ideal self coming to fruition in the cherished contents of her womb.

The initial fusion of the first stage is interrupted by the fetal movements, drawing the woman into gradual awareness of the reality of her fetus as a separate being, and initiating a process of slow differentiation from both her baby and her mother. She believes her fetus is both *knowing and communicative* and that she must be receptive and attuned to every flutter, deciphering its messages, seeking always to provide the ideal prenatal experience. The third stage, which I have found to be heralded by the belief in the baby's viability outside the maternal body, activates a new process in the Facilitator. She is both curious and eager to meet her 'real' baby but not yet ready to give up the inner imaginary one. Thus, she both grieves for the loss of their magical intimacy, while yearning for their extra-uterine rapprochement. 'Nesting', she prepares an external replica of the womb in which to cherish her newborn, aware that with their physical detachment, all the special attention now lavished on her will be focussed on the baby, who will be seen as a reflection of all the goodness in her.

The *regulator* approaches pregnancy differently. To her it is the means to getting a baby. She dislikes the need for continuous reappraisal of her self and body image and tries to preserve her own familiar identity for as long as possible. She resists the regressive tug and emotional upheaval of pregnancy, avoiding introspection and fortifying her defences against sentimentality and superstition. She dislikes the physical symptoms welcomed by the Facilitator as proof of pregnancy, and disciplines herself to continue life as usual.

The control she exerts during the first stage of pregnancy is undermined by the strange sensation of movements within her body which are beyond her control. They serve as a constant reminder that she has been invaded by a parasitic alien feeding off her life-blood. She resolves to maintain her own separateness, ignoring the internal 'gate crasher' by stepping up her social activities and maintaining an inner reserve. She does not indulge in playful fantasies and imaginary dialog with the fetus, reluctant to become attached in case things go wrong. Unconsciously, she invests the fetus with repudiated aspects of her baby-self – voraciousness, dependency, neediness and vulnerability. Whereas the Facilitator feels *enriched* by the pregnancy, the Regulator feels *impoverished* by hers. She envies her partner's symptomless ease of having a baby and resents her body for growing out of her control and divulging her sexuality to all and sundry. The Regulator feels she has no privacy – spied on from within and stereotyped from without! She finds the third stage particularly trying. She feels tired, heavy and internally bruised, her inner resources drained by the greedy and increasingly lively fetus. Although eager to rid herself of her 'internal persecutor' she dreads the birth, fearing her badness will be disclosed by the newborn who unconsciously represents split-off sadistic and insatiable aspects of her self.

Labor and birth

The *facilitator* by contrast looks forward to the birth. She imagines labor as a powerful and exciting process, propelling the baby and herself towards a reunion – a transitional passage of time between pregnancy and motherhood, during which, she, like the baby, will be in the grip of an experience beyond their control. She feels that like the infant, all she can do during the first stage of labor is to submit to the process, trustingly to resign herself to her body's revival of the innate skills of bringing forth a baby reaching back through her mother and grandmother to the beginning of time. She conjures up an elemental faith in her own life-giving forces by which she unconsciously hopes to conquer the primal fear of death. To the Facilitator, birth is an intimate event and she longs for seclusion, like a female animal, afraid not of predators but of the envy and excitement of her own species. Her main desire is to have a natural birth to enter into the rhythmicity of her contractions in harmony with the baby who she feels pushing and sliding his or her way out towards her. To the Facilitator, any intervention is seen as a distortion of the natural course of events, a violation that spoils the harmonious perfection she has so painstakingly established and maintained during the long months of pregnancy. As she enters second stage and reaches the orgiastic climax of propulsion, her excitement at imminent reunion all but wipes out the sadness of imminent loss and the deflated emptiness of her no longer pregnant body.

The *regulator* by contrast, approaches labor as a painful, medical event. More than at any other point in her life, she is conscious of the biological differences between the sexes – the unfairness of being designated female and having to go through this trial of pain and suffering while her male partner stands by unaffected. She is determined to minimize her own discomfort by any technological means available. She is, however, caught between fear of loss of control under the influence of pain or of drugs.

The Regulator regards labor as a dangerous passage – fraught with the threat of mutilation and fears of harming the baby or being damaged herself internally. Throughout pregnancy she has harbored thoughts of the monster she might bring forth. Fate would take revenge for her hubris — she feels doomed to be tripped up by her own buried evilness, or punished for her smoldering hatred towards her own early mother.

With the birth, the moment of truth draws closer, when what she has been growing inside her will emerge for all to see. Unconsciously, she wishes to prolong the labor and delay the moment of birth; consciously, she worries what other concealed aspects of herself might be unleashed during protracted labor. She dreads failure and fears she might be worn down by the pain, may lose control of her temper or her bowels, may scream in murderous rage or helpless persecution. There is some small comfort in being among strangers and experts who will maintain their reserve. She resolves to use drugs and will-power to curb impending chaos. Above all, the Regulator wants a civilized birth.

The fourth trimester

After the birth, having checked the baby for signs of normality, the Regulator is glad to have the little stranger taken off to be cleaned up and laid to rest in the nursery, giving her the space to recuperate from the ordeals of pregnancy and labor.

By contrast, for the Facilitator the baby that emerges, is familiar — special, unique and invested with mother's idealizing aura: he or she is a being from another time, a secret place, trailing the cord that binds it to the interior. The Facilitator gathers her succulent newborn into her encircling arms, suckling and crooning. The boundaries dissolve as she is reunited with the baby still smelling of her own inner world, reflecting her own ideal image invested in the baby for safekeeping.

The Facilitator mother feels herself to be the source of all good, providing love and nourishment like a primordial goddess. Once again, she merges with her idealized infant and the mother of her infancy in a series of interchangeable identifications as she did in early pregnancy. The Facilitator mother recreates the magic bubble of her womb, enclosing herself and the newborn in an enchanted circle of her making, an 'omnipotent symbiotic dual unity' (Mahler, 1975, p. 46). Breathing the baby's breaths, synchronizing their elemental rhythms, she adapts her being to the infant, in unconditional selfless devotion. She blissfully feeds the baby whenever and for as long as he desires, keeps him with her day and night, and feels herself to be indispensable to the baby's survival: exclusive provider, sole interpreter and mitigator of all distress. There is clearly a reciprocity in maternal/infant ideas of fusion: the magical symbiosis is intended to revive the newborn's belief in its own omnipotence. Constantly close and receptive, the Facilitator intuitively deciphers and spontaneously meets her baby's needs, thus sustaining the infant's illusion, which in turn is fostered by the mother's own yearning for fused omnipotence.

In essence, she continues doing what she did during pregnancy – providing the ideal environment, ever protecting the baby from impingements from within or without. If the mother is introjecting the continuous stream of infantile fantasy projected into her by the baby, so too is the infant invested with mother's projections. While sponsoring an idealized babyhood, she is stung into unconscious envy and resentment by providing the idyll she could not possibly have had. Any maternal ambivalence is kept at bay, denied and unconscious although undoubtedly being absorbed by the infant, who is expected to mitigate it with a loving smile. As long as the Facilitator maintains the psychological umbilical cord the child too, must sustain their mutual illusion and deny the underlying sense of begrudging, depressed or destructive qualities in both mother and himself.

In her empathic identification with the baby into whom she has projected her ideal baby self, the Facilitator can recreate a glorified image of mother–baby fusion, vicariously enjoying a return to infantile bliss by being the perfect mother she never had. However, if, as Winnicott suggests, 'the mother's eventual task is gradually to disillusion the infant' (1951, p. 238) the Facilitator cannot do so without shattering the illusion she is sustaining for herself. As long as her own ideal-self is invested in the baby through projective identification, it is necessary for her to maintain the dual illusions of the child's omnipotence and her own unconditional non-ambivalent love.

Feeding the baby, the Regulator is unnerved by the vaguely erotic sensations in her nipples and uterine contractions. The little creature nursing at her breast feels cannibalistic in its mouthing grasp of her body. She is being sucked dry of the strange liquids her body has produced all by itself. It feels as if the infant leaves none for her, draining her vitality. She grits her teeth so as not to bite back, neither to devour this morsel nor yet be sucked into a seductively regressive interchange. Once home, the Regulator follows the hospital regime or establishes a routine of her own. Feeding the infant on a 3 or 4 hourly schedule and introducing bottle feeds too, she ensures that the baby is well-fed and that she is not the sole provider for such a greedy, needy being. Consciously she regards the baby as pre-social and sees socialization as the main aim of child-care, a mothering skill which can be shared with others. She is also determined not to be taken-in by the myth of exclusive mothering seeing it as a patriarchal ruse to domesticate women. She assumes that since the infant does not yet differentiate between people, if she introduces other caretakers early, she will not be missed in her absence. The routine ensures continuity and fosters predictability and independence – the baby's and her own. On a deeper level, she experiences the baby as persecuting: as it has been inside her, she cannot hide from it any of her badness. It knows her from within, and judges her for being less than the perfect mother-ideal. In addition, as the infant is invested with the mother's own repudiated infantile aspects, it is felt to be parading her greed and vulnerability to the world. Shared care, therefore both offers the baby protection from the mother's hostility and resentment, and offers the mother protection from the critical baby. By introducing other care-takers, she can no longer be held to be solely responsible for the baby's badness now or madness in future years.

The Regulator experiences her baby as a potentially overpowering dangerous force, like the untamed and primitive side of her own nature. Unconsciously, she sees in the baby split-off greedy or sadistic aspects of herself. When the infant projects his own needs into her she feels panic stricken at their conflicting demands, their competition over her meager resources. Well-meaning experts enforcing 'bonding' and advocating full-time mothering, overlook this very primitive exchange of feelings between mother and baby, that could cause more damage by exposure than by absence.

Whereas the Facilitator is afraid of hating her baby, the Regulator is afraid of loving. By sharing child-care she protects the baby from forming an exclusive intimate relationship with her, and herself from becoming captivated by the baby's ever-increasing charms. She is cautious about loving the baby too much: afraid that the baby will be 'spoilt' by her love; that she will be at its beck and call; that the person she is will be smothered by the mother she'll become; that she'll drown in love of the baby and become baby-like herself; that if she loves too much it will be taken from her.

THE MOTHER MYSTIQUE AND THE NATURAL AMBIVALENCE OF MOTHERHOOD

Given time, the fourth trimester passes — although sometimes it may take many years to do so. Gradually, with recurrent feedback from the child that she is loved and appreciated although known from within, both the Regulator and the Facilitator mother begins calling back the split-off parts she had projected onto the baby. Increasingly, she sees the child for what it is, a separate ambivalent individual in his or her own right. However, the persistence of the mother-mystique in society, myths of devoted unconditional, non-ambivalent mother-love coupled with denigration of maternal status, reveal that *mothers* are rarely accepted for what they are — separate, ambivalent individuals in their own right.

In conclusion, we see that the Facilitator embodies the 'positive' aspect of the mother-mystique, striving to achieve the impossible. The Regulator, determined to withstand being exploited by the myths of patriarchy, is nevertheless taken in by the denigration of dependence and maternal creativity. Both deny the natural ambivalence of motherhood.

In subsequent pregnancies, a woman may change her orientation from being a Facilitator to a Regulator or vice versa depending on a variety of emotional and socio-economic reasons, as well as the age-gap between the children. Sometimes, due to emotional growth the mother can engender a shift towards a fresh orientation, a realistic, ambivalent relationship from the start.

The conspiracy of silence about maternal ambivalence is institutionally upheld by society's psychological, medical and pediatric experts sentimentally expecting selfless devotion and exclusive mothering; advocating intuitive understanding yet insisting there is a Right Way to mother and treating the mother as responsible for all ills that befall the child – idealizing mothering yet undermining maternal self-confidence. We can no longer go on unrealistically demanding that mothers fulfil the expectations we imagine babies to have.

This conspiracy of silence about maternal ambivalence is furthered by adults because it suits society to allocate mothering to devoted mothers; it is upheld by children despite their unconscious knowledge to the contrary, because they wish to believe in the illusion of unconditional love. Finally, it is upheld by mothers, because of the guilt instilled in us by society, experts, our children's demands for maternal perfection and above all our own demands as the daughters of our internal mothers.

Ambivalence is an internal reality. Let us accept it for what it is.

---

[1] In the Genesis creation story, etymological and symbolic links exist between 'tehom', the deep, and 'Tiamat', a formidable Babylonian mother goddess, who bore the gods. She was rebelled against and finally surrendered her body as building material for the universe (Graves & Patai, 1964, p. 26). According to other sources, God forbade Tehom, the sweet underground waters, to rise up, confining her with a 'bolt and two doors' to prevent her letting out her waters; none may visit her recesses (p. 41). The necessity to curb allows us to detect some of the dark dread of unleashed maternal powers. Comparative mythology reveals that similar motifs occur in myths of origin of many diverse cultures all over the world: time and again we find descriptions of the 'dark, watery chaos' that first existed and the need for separation of elements, whether earth and sky, sea and land, fire and water, night and day, upper and lower waters. These have been interpreted as a separation of the chaotic coupling of male and female principles resulting in the patriarchal social order (Graves & Patai, 1964). However, I would suggest that in the recurrent themes of original dark, watery chaos and separation of elements, we glimpse the earlier matriarchal myth underlying the patriarchal editing of cosmology – an awareness that physical birth entails separation from the maternal womb and psychological birth, separation from the maternal orbit.

[2] In some Jewish communities a newborn was safeguarded by a ring of charcoal on the wall of the birthroom in which were inscribed the words: 'Adam and Eve. Out Lilith!' (Graves & Patai, 1964, p. 68).

[3] Freud observed that for women the early prohibition against thinking about sex caused 'intellectual atrophy' (Freud, 1928, p. 48).

[4] It is against this background that I have found the experience of my own pregnancies and mothering invaluable. Particularly, being in analysis myself, and later participating while pregnant, in an ongoing discussion group of other expectant women. Also, in my capacity as social psychologist I have conducted studies and questionnaire surveys with women during pregnancy and early motherhood as well as working for 10 years as a psychoanalyst and therapist to women involved in issues of reproduction (Raphael-Leff, 1980, 1984, 1986).

As a mother, I must express gratitude to my husband, without whose mothering of our children this paper could not have been written.

54

It's better to build children than repair men: preventive aspects of parenting and birthing education

R. Phillips

ABSTRACT

Building children versus repairing men – such a shame it is that all over the world we largely ignore the early development of children, and later, end up paying a heavy price because of our ignorance and short sightedness. Very few realize the job of building children – the job of parenting – begins before the child is even born. The primary reason so few know the importance of good parenting is due to the lack of proper parenting education. If we want our latest psychological and medical findings to be of benefit, we must work to make sure parenting is taken seriously and the level of parent education is increased. All the most wonderful prenatal care and concern in the world will be thrown out the window if the postnatal care and concern is poor.

In America, and in other countries as well, parents are spending alarmingly less time raising their children. This trend and other significant trends can be partially attributed to a lack of proper knowledge. People involved in the 'baby profession', such as childbirth educators, must and do act as a bridge between the medical and psychological elements and the parents. Parent education must begin in the school systems before parents actually become parents, because educating parents once they are parents is often too little too late. Our most precious commodity is a human being, and it is much better to build this human being properly in the first place than repair it later.

Building children versus repairing men — such a shame it is that all over the world we largely ignore the early development of children, and later, end up paying a heavy price because of our ignorance and short sightedness. Many mistakenly believe children virtually build themselves. Give a child food, shelter, and education and that child will grow up to be just fine. Others know that love and affection must be given in addition to food, shelter, and education. Some even know the importance of touching and skin contact as illustrated by Ashley Montague's work. But very few realize the job of building children — the job of parenting — begins before the child is even born.

I am now an experienced mother of three, but when I was pregnant with my first child in 1963, as for most every other mother of that time, I was very naive and uninformed about the whole parenting process. Consciously I was neither especially aware of the far reaching effects mothering would have, nor did I know how important the early months of a child's life were. Since that time I have sought a better way to bring babies into the world. I was hungry for knowledge, and with each birth I became more enlightened.

Even though I looked for it at the time, I had little preparation for my first birth. The only thing I had seen on the subject was the film *Gone With The Wind*. There was a birth scene in this film that showed a woman hanging on to the end of a bed, writhing in pain, which is exactly what I ended up doing. My mother was not much help either. She had told me she felt like she was dying during her births. She also said only peasants had babies quickly, and because my name was Royal, to suffer a long labor would be lady-like. Even my mother-in-law said, 'Please don't ask me about it, just tell me when it is over.' Needless to say, my first birth was long and painful. Now I find it amusing to reflect on my mother's statement about peasants because little did my mother know, the reason peasants had babies quickly and easily was because they regularly used all of their bodies in hard work. The royalty had long painful births because they were sedentary and had flaccid muscles.

Prior to my 2nd pregnancy and birthing process I still had not found any information on childbirth in my community, except for a Red Cross emergency film depicting a woman screaming in the back of an ambulance. This time I was impatient. This child was finally forced after laboring for 2 days and 2 nights by contractions that were augmented with pitocin.

By the birth of my third child in 1969, I had discovered Lamaze childbirth classes which were very new and almost underground in our community. These classes taught breathing techniques to use instead of drugs, exercises to get the body ready and, most importantly, improve relaxation. This education meant so much to me that I was forced to change doctors in my eighth month of pregnancy so that I could find a doctor who supported this childbirth method. Prepared and armed with breathing techniques, relaxation techniques, and the knowledge of the birthing process, I went into labor and had a 10 lb daughter in $5\frac{1}{2}$ hours without an episiotomy. My husband was my trained coach who knew me better than any nurse could. I even laughed through the first 2 hours of labor. This entire childbirth experience was like a revelation to me. There was a world of difference between my first and second births and my third birth, which had such dignity and control. Lamaze childbirth education had made all the difference. It was this third birth experience that propelled me to become involved with the American Institute of Family Relations in Los Angeles, where I later became an accredited childbirth instructor.

I have been a certified Lamaze childbirth instructor for 16 years now in California as well as abroad, and during that time I have come into contact with several thousand mothers and fathers. I have watched and I have listened to the fears, beliefs, and concerns of these mothers and fathers. Having known and observed such a number of parents and parents-to-be has allowed me to make many observations. Some of the observations I have made support the research and findings of others. Some of my observations I believe to be unique because of my unique relationship with my students. I have enjoyed a relationship with my students that differs from the relationship they may have had with their doctor or their friends and relatives. Because I meet with my students in a relaxed, informal atmosphere, because I am not their obstetrician or mother, because I am not an authority figure, and because I am really an informed mother much like themselves, I believe they speak more honestly to me (than they would with a doctor) and listen more receptively to me (than they would with a friend or relative). It is partially for this reason that childbirth educators such as myself play an important role in the profession of obstetrics.

A childbirth educator functions as a bridge between the medical and psychological professions and the parents, relaying information to the mother and father in an easily understandable and non-threatening way. It is this relaying of information, this education, that is so very important to the whole birth process. When parents go to childbirth classes and learn about what is happening to them during pregnancy and what will happen during birth, they gain knowledge. From this knowledge they gain confidence, which in turn takes away their fears. It's a simple concept – Knowledge plus Confidence equals No Fear – and it is a concept that works, one that I see working several times every week. Education – educating the parents – is a vital part of building children.

While we are improving the quality and quantity of the education we provide parents, there is still much room for further improvement. What

I have found most surprising in my teaching is the state of parenting education in this country. I am regularly amazed at how little couples know in the first place about this major event that is about to take place in their lives. Since our society in America (and I know other countries as well) does little to prepare adults for parenthood, it is understandable why few are well prepared for it. Most parents-to-be today do not realize the amount of work and responsibility parenting entails. And it is easy to see why these parents-to-be have so little knowledge on parenting – most 'seasoned' parents who have teenage children have a difficult enough time explaining 'the birds and the bees' or sexual reproduction to their teenagers. Even educators in the school systems have recognized how little and inaccurate the information is that children have on the sexual reproduction processes, and have therefore incorporated 'sex education classes' into the school's curriculum to make up where parents lack. How can we expect these many seasoned parents who fumble with basic reproductive education to do an adequate job with parent education? If these seasoned parents have trouble explaining to their children just how it is they actually may become parents, how are they going to explain the principles and responsibilities of good parenting? Yes, childbirth education during pregnancy does provide some of this 'parent education', but often this education is too late – after the parents are already committed and usually in a hurried manner during the third trimester.

One solution to the lack of proper parental education could be to provide this needed parenting education in the school systems. To become a licensed driver (or vehicle operator) in the United States, an individual must undergo several hours of training and testing. Most secondary schools in the United States provide this training. To become a parent, a role I believe to have greater importance and influence than that of a licensed driver, no education or training is provided or required at all.

I have also found surprising the change the parents go through in the course of their childbirth education. Drastic changes in attitude can be seen that are caused when knowledge replaces fear sometimes in the course of only a few hours. Reticent fathers become enthusiastic. Nervous mothers begin to enjoy their pregnancy. Couples become closer. The average parent's lack of proper childbirth knowledge and training, as well as the dramatic changes in parental attitude underline the importance of childbirth education. Again, it is better to build children than repair men, and I believe childbirth education to be a vital part of building children.

Another interesting trend that many of you should be especially aware of, because it negates much of the work you do, is the increasing tendency of mothers to return to work soon after birth. I have noticed more and more mothers going back to their jobs as soon as 3 weeks after delivery, which is very unhealthy. This trend has a negative effect on both the infant and the mother, not to mention her employer. The newborn child is separated from its mother and left usually with a stranger who is caring at the same time for several other children. The child does not receive the attention and affection from its mother that is so very important at so young an age. The mother, on the other hand, has not had the time to get used to the baby. She has only gotten a taste of the hard, exhausting part of parenting and has not yet experienced the joys of parenting. Often the mother is tired after work when she must pick up the child from the day care center and has little patience or time to spend with her infant. Sometimes the reason the mother goes back to work so soon after delivery is one of economic necessity — with the rising cost of living, the family simply cannot afford for her not to work. Sometimes the mother goes back to work because she simply chooses so — oftentimes older mothers who have held high-ranking, prestigious job positions are suddenly faced with such mundane tasks as changing diapers, and instead they prefer to go back to work. Other times the mother will find her old job easier than taking care of a newborn and choose to return to work. And it is not just mothers who are spending less time with their children — recent studies by American sociologists find fathers spend an average of 2 minutes a day with their children. The amount of time spent raising children is small in comparison to an entire lifetime. The parenting years go by very quickly. Also consider the staggering divorce rate in the United States, which will most likely cause the responsibility of parenting to fall solely upon one parent's shoulders.

I find the trend of mothers returning back to work so soon very alarming, and it reminds me of my trip to China in 1984. I visited maternity wards in communes and hospitals, and kindergartens in the cities and country. Virtually all the mothers in China return to the factories and fields soon after birth and end up spending an average of one full day a week with their child. The children are put in nurseries near the factories and fields, and the smallest nursery takes care of 200 children. Are we headed in this direction? We have increasingly paid attention to such issues as dim lights, cool colors, no drugs, no spanking, music, and massage during birth so that the child and parents will be happy and healthy. But for what? So the mother can go back to work 3 weeks after delivery and the child can be raised by a stranger? Are the mortgage payments more important than a brand new human life? What are our priorities? Mothers must realize there is plenty of time to have children and a career. Educators and researchers like ourselves must realize that all the most wonderful prenatal care and concern in the world will be thrown out the window if the postnatal care and concern is poor. We must make sure our steps forward in prenatal development do not cause us to take steps backward in postnatal care.

As we delve deeper into the womb and further learn the importance of prenatal psychology, we must remember much of the world is not as technologically advanced in the areas where we practise our professions. If we want more than just a small circle of people to benefit from the work we do, we must keep in mind the world's lack of proper childbirth knowledge, and work to educate so that our new findings will sooner benefit the rest of the world. I am even amazed at the level of childbirth misinformation that exists in the city where I live in California. California has been referred to as an 'open-air insane asylum' because of the advanced (and sometimes strange) techniques and trends that have originated and are practised there.

But many of the mothers and fathers I teach believe in and are frightened by many long-standing misconceptions and beliefs. Many women believe they will have the same or similar birth experience as their own mother did. At the beginning of my classes I always ask the mother what she thinks her labor will be like. I then ask her what her mother's labor was like. Usually both answers are very much the same. Many couples believe they should not have sexual intercourse during pregnancy (especially during the third trimester) for fear they might harm the child.

To combat such common misinformation and the fear that accompanies such beliefs, I not only present the proper information, but also give my students the tools to help dispel these common fears. Relaxation exercises coupled with visualization techniques seem to be especially effective in dispelling fear. Again, knowledge replaces fear. To further educate mothers and fathers and to help build better children, I also suggest, among other things, for parents to talk to their child in the womb, introduce siblings to the infant before it is born, and discuss their parenting strategy.

From the time of conception, children are like a snowy white blotter. The power of the parent is great – mothers and fathers can fill the blotter with good, or they can fill the blotter with bad, and can sometimes do so unknowingly. It is for this reason – the power of the parent – that parental education is so important. We must do more to make people realize the importance and power of motherhood and parenthood, and to make people realize the responsibility and stature the job of parenthood really entails. Parent education should really begin early in school so that future parents realize the magnitude of their job before they are committed. Isn't our most important commodity a human being? Isn't our most valuable treasure a human soul? What kind of reflection is it upon our society when a mother, who is the guardian of our most precious commodity and treasure, is asked about her profession and says humbly, 'I'm just a housewife'? When the seriousness of parenthood begins to be realized, in its proper dimensions, imagine all the time, energy, and money the world will save when we will have to work less on repairing men. Yes, it truly is better to build children than repair men.

55

Future prospects and trends regarding prenatal and perinatal studies

M. L. Vanessa Vogel and P. G. Fedor-Freybergh

> 'Listen. Think not forever of yourselves, O Chiefs, nor even of your own generation. Think of continuing generations of our grandchildren and of those yet unborn, whose faces are coming from beneath the ground.'*
>
> The Peacemaker[1]

The ISPP is an international non-profit making organization and was originally organized and founded as the Study Group for Prenatal Psychology. It was the Swiss psychoanalyst, Gustav Hans Graber, who initiated its founding in 1971. Already in the early 1920s, Dr Graber first recognized the need to address the psychological concerns of the unborn, including publication of modern scientific research to readdress issues on prenatal and perinatal psychology. In 1986 during the Badgastein International Congress, the name was enlarged to more accurately represent the work of its members: The International Society for Prenatal and Perinatal Psychology and Medicine. As such the society serves as the umbrella organization wherein members of national and regional societies may meet to exchange ideas and practice on an international, cross-cultural and interdisciplinary level.

---

* According to tradition, these words were addressed to the chiefs of the Haudenosaunee (Iroquois) more than 1000 years ago. According to Western historical tradition, these words by the Peacemaker were spoken between AD 1350 and 1600.

OVERVIEW OF THE WORK OF THE ISPP AND RELATIONSHIP TO OTHER RESEARCH EFFORTS IN PRENATAL AND PERINATAL STUDIES

To date eight international congresses and numerous symposia have been held. It has been during these meetings that the theoretical conceptions and the practical applications have met to cross-fertilize research and practice, with an emphasis on preventive care from the medical, psychological and social pedological points of view. Over the years the themes focussed upon have been: The Fundamentals of Prenatal Psychology (Freiburg, West Germany, 1972); The Research of Prebirth Perception and Sensation (Paris, 1973); Aspects and Practice of Prenatal Psychology and Psychotherapy (Munich, 1975); The Interpretation of Pre- and Perinatal Dreams in Psychotherapy (Bern, Switzerland); Birth: Entrance into a New World (Salzburg, 1978); Human Behavior and Experience in the Prenatal Period of Life (Basel, Switzerland, 1979); Sensitivity Toward the Child: Dialogue with the Child (Dusseldorf, 1983); and The Contribution of Prenatal Psychology to Preventive Medicine, Preventive Psychology and Preventive Aspects of the Socially-Oriented Professions (Badgastein, Austria, 1986).

1986 represented a new turning point wherein existing barriers between professional and care practitioners were eliminated. Here the new vision of the society, putting into practice its own philosophy, actively promoted a wide range of interdisciplinary ventures and international exchange (participants came from 22 different countries) in regard to prenatal and perinatal psychology and medicine. It was at this time that we also committed ourselves to concentrate upon and actively promote the preventive aspects and importance of prenatal health care work. In 1989, in Jerusalem at the 9th International Congress, we will try to deepen this commitment by focussing on Aids and the Unborn, The Psychoneuroendocrinology and Psychoneuroimmunology of the Fetus, Technology and the Enhanced Prenatal and Perinatal Environment, Radiation and other Ecological Hazards and the Unborn, and Women of the Third and Fourth Worlds – their birthing experiences and the culturally informed context of pre- and perinatal health care[2].

Our membership now includes: obstetricians and gynecologists, pediatricians, endocrinologists, embryologists, geneticists, social workers and sociopedagogical researchers, developmental psychologists, psychiatrists, childbirth educators, midwives, anthropologists/ethnologists, cultural historians, ethicists, socioeconomists and representatives from the disciplines of philosophy, as well as many interested lay persons. Members coming from 32 countries are presently a part of the ISPP, and we are actively reaching out to make contacts in other parts of the world to help promote the understanding and practice of prenatal and perinatal psychology and medicine. Through the sponsoring of international congresses and workshops which integrate all levels and dimensions of prenatal and perinatal care giving, and via grassroots communication to childbirth organizations and prospective parents, the ISPP hopes to ensure that our future and our children are truly better, not just more plentiful.

The ISPP has helped and encouraged in every possible way the initiation of national and regional societies. To date such societies now exist in Italy, Britain, Holland, Poland, Germany and North America, and others are now in the planning stages in Japan, Israel, Belgium, France, Spain, Argentina, Brazil and Scandinavia.

THE PRESENT WORK, ON-GOING INITIATIVES AND FUTURE TRENDS

Prenatal and perinatal psychology and medicine is a relatively new development within medical and psychological research, but one of the first guidelines is that medical and psychological issues cannot be separated from other health and social questions involved in prenatal and perinatal studies. No one isolated discipline can creatively function or adequately address all these complexly interrelated issues. ISPP promotes the following research proposals and on-going research and practice, which is not to suggest in any way that our members are the only ones researching in these areas or that we have adequate representation in all these areas of research. Quite the contrary, we need and advocate more participation!

Polyvalency of research views and methods

There exists the need for initiating cross-disciplinary teamwork in order to further develop a new scientific theory to adequately account for prenatal existence; and further, to develop a polyvalent methodology (including methodological concepts) appropriate to such studies.

In order to undertake and continue such interdisciplinary cooperation and collaboration first requires a common language; one that is not only understood across disciplines, but by the lay person. Such a language must assist us in getting beyond the semantic problems and confusion created by the Cartesian dualism inherent in so much of medical and psychological language. Often disagreements between disciplines and practitioners turn not on substantive issues, but semantic misdirection. We must remain aware of this problem in future research, guard against it and improve upon the present semantic malaise.

Internationalization of research

As has already been mentioned, no one nation or cultural point of view can account for the plurality of problems and concerns (not least of which ethnical, cultural and religiously based ones) that circumscribe prenatal and perinatal studies. The future role of the ISPP is as facilitator on an international and interdisciplinary level in furthering research into and understanding of the psychological dimensions of prenatal and perinatal development, and the consequences of this development on the future human being.

(1) *International Multi-Centered Resource Institute for Prenatal and Perinatal Studies* Within the ISPP there is a project underway for an institute to coordinate research and assist in networking between researchers and care practitioners. Such a multi-center will provide information concerning fellow researchers and their research projects in related fields; information for government and international health organizations working on updating, and hopefully, revising standard social health policies; and in assisting individuals and self-help organizations gain access to the latest scientific research results and practices in prenatal and perinatal care. An international database is planned as a part of the institute's activities.

(2) The ISPP is also preparing an *International Journal for Prenatal and Perinatal Studies*. The journal will serve as an interdisciplinary review of research related to prenatal and perinatal medicine, psychology, pedagogy, sociology, philosophy and ethology, anthropology/ethnology and cultural history. From prenatal and perinatal practice it will include the latest results and ideas from psychotherapy, prebirth and birth memory therapies, midwifery and birthing practices, birth preparation and education.

(3) Finally, in order to totally internationalize our work and to share ideas, it is necessary to communicate with lay persons, and for them to communicate with one another. Consequently, within the ISPP there is an on-going initiative now to publish a Grassroots International Prenatal and Perinatal Newsletter to emanate via the Multi-Center Institute through the cooperation of other centers of research. It is designed to be written by experts in the field but in non-technical language so as to give parents and practitioners the latest news on prenatal and perinatal health care possibilities, who is practising them, where, and how to contact them (both internationally and on a local level). As such it will serve as an international message board for

networking, providing contact addresses worldwide with other related self-help groups or interested persons, and related events.

Studies on prenatal and perinatal morbidity and mortality and intensive care (NICU)

Prematurity is still one of the most important and most common causes for prenatal and perinatal mortality and morbidity. While morbidity and mortality statistics remain two of the key factors for evaluating the health of a community or nation (as the prenatal and perinatal are the most sensitive and vulnerable members of any society), it still remains to link psychological crises both in contributing to and resulting from these phenomena. There is the need to explore the psychological crisis in relation to this morbidity and mortality. For example, such studies could include parents and staff in neonatal intensive care units. Research should be focussed not only with how to cope with prematurity and the problems connected with it, but also on the possibilities of preventing unwanted premature births and to thereby decrease the risk factors which lead to it. Incorporating findings both from the obstetrical and gynecological and the pediatric research units is essential to complete a comprehensive overview.

Environmental and ecological research

It is ecologically unsound in the 21st century to continue a paleolithic philosophy of 'more is better' when we can clearly see that 'more' is overwhelming us and the ecological balance of our planet. It is extremely important to a nation's, society's and even world health that we do not overtax our environment's ability to support us. Unfortunately, this has already happened through near-sighted health planning in, for example, Africa's sub-Sahara.

What factors from the outside world psychologically support or detract from the development of the fetus? And what are the most pressing environmental and ecological hazards affecting the prenatal and perinatal development? We need to understand fetal reactions/responses to the physical and psychological environmental influences (e.g. music/noise; motion/stress; pollution, etc.).

Bonding and attachment studies

There is the need for further development of research into attachment and bonding processes, both during the prenatal period and later between the mother and the father. Work is needed focussing on the importance of a successful prenatal bonding for the postnatal emotional maturation and later abilities for creating positive bonding situations as an adult. Some specific research areas of great potential include: (1) bonding during delivery and its impact on the outcome of labor, psychologically and physically; (2) postnatal bonding as a continuum; (3) hazards of any separation between mother/parents and child, and potential health risk, both psychologically and physically; (4) the biochemistry of bonding and the role of different neurotransmitters in creating and developing or inhibiting the bonding process.

Sociopedagogic studies and childbirth education/preparation

As already stated, it is the quality of life we need to enhance, not the quantity. For this reason the work of the ISPP actively promotes the idea of conscious parenting. We need to concentrate our efforts on creating and preparing quality parents and parenting, including questions about our ideas of parenting.

For such ideas to become practical (i.e. practiced) they must be taught both in high school/preparatory school curriculums and to future parents. In order for this type of education to become generally available, curricula in medical and psychological schools will need to be adjusted by implementing prenatal and perinatal studies into their courses; and enlisting the aid of those working in sociopedagogic studies for creating and implementing such programs (in line with local religio-cultural values).

Psychoneuroendocrinological and psychoneuroimmunological research of the fetus

Psychoneuroendocrinological studies of the fetus and the mother during pregnancy focus upon research into hormones and neurotransmitters in their dynamic interdependency with emotional/psychological and biological influences. This includes the ecological environment both of the fetus and the mother and the impact of their experiences upon primary informational processes, prebirth and birth memories, bonding processes, primary sexual functions, etc. How, for instance, can depression or stress in the mother influence the sensibility and balance of these hormones, polypeptides and functions, thus influencing both the prenatal and postnatal development of related functions (e.g. growth, sexuality, bonding, etc.). Further research is needed to study the possibilities for optimizing these processes in order to prevent prenatal and perinatal impairment.

Psychoneuroimmunological studies concerning the needs of the fetus should be concentrated upon finding such factors and preventing disturbances during the pregnancy which would impact negatively upon the psychoneuroimmunological and endocrinoimmunological development and functions of the fetus. In addition, attention needs to be paid to the sensibility of this system and thus the potential decrease in immunological capacity of the child during and after birth. Here specific research is required in relation to AIDS and the decreased immunological capabilities of the fetus and neonate, and on SIDS (sudden infant death syndrome) and its connection to the prenatal and perinatal conditions.

Study of the nature and characteristics of prenatal memories and adaptation response

Here research is concentrated on the prenatal period of life as an essential part of the learning process along a life continuum. Adaptation processes, experience and memory are the main elements of the information processing capacity. This research, again, is interdisciplinary based, wherein biochemistry, endocrinology and the psychotherapeutic contributions play equally important roles in helping to marshall a fuller understanding of prebirth and birth memories. Inseparable from such studies is the ecological factor as a mediating influence upon the child's learning process in relation to his/her mother.

Ethical and philosophical contributions to the study

Ethical and philosophical research into the moral and ethical questions behind such research lags way behind medical and technological developments; these need to keep pace with science and practice. We need to be actively promoting collaboration between the theoretical researchers and care practitioners and the ethical dimensions of this work. It cannot be avoided; it should not be avoided. In addition, the cross-cultural ethical dimensions in this area have hardly been explored and need pursuing. This includes the ethical effect upon psychological responses, that is, the effect on research, practice and popular ideas when there is an ethical void in this area to guide research development in line with cultural and religious precepts. Any such void creates a psychological vacuum, which leads to an unhealthy discontinuity between research, practice and issues concerning human values.

Development and promotion of humanistic technology

Research is needed into the methods of research, and even the appropriateness of research methods. We must use technology to the advantage of the child and the mother by (1) only using low risk technology, and (2) not over-technologizing the creative process, thereby disturbing the integrity and dignity of the mother–child relationship. Technology should not be used to control the mother or restrict her choices, but rather be employed to enhance the potential for creating psychological contact between the mother and the child. For example, ultrasound imaging which allows the mother to come in visual contact with her child; and *in vitro* fertilization, thus giving some women the chance to be mothers who would not otherwise have such a possibility.

Socioeconomic questions

As Paul Ekins puts it in his *The Living Economy: A New Economics in the Making*, economics can be defined in various ways, but basic to any such definition is the concern for human welfare. And human welfare is the health of any nation, for without health no nation can successfully continue to function. How then to define health in new, revised economic terms; not as a commodity but based upon the ability of the individual to live a self-fulfilling life. In fact, Ekins (1986:28) notes that worldwide 'a far better indicator of positive or negative monetary measures is the health of the people concerned.' In their 1984 discussion document WHO stressed that health is 'seen as a resource for everyday life', not as a static condition or a goal to be attained in some distant future.

Revised economic indicators point to the prenatal and perinatal morbidity and mortality rates as the best gauges of the quality of health care. Life expectancy indicators do not tell us anything about the quality of life only the quantity; to survive and yet be poor and in perpetual ill-health is not unusual – whether in so-called overdeveloped or underdeveloped nations. But the unborn and the newborn, as Trevor Hancock points out, being so very sensitive and fragile to their environment and the ecological factors, make morbidity and mortality the best signposts of quality of life in both poor and wealthy population areas (in Ekins, 1986, p. 141). Such insights call for even further in-depth research and interdisciplinary collaboration in regard to the socioeconomic factors concerning prenatal and perinatal care.

International and cross-cultural development program for the improvement of prenatal and perinatal care: indigenous/anthropological/medical/psychological collaborative research and practice

Today more than ever we have begun to realize that Western patterns of development — including Western medical models — have not always had the same positive effect in non-Western cultures as they have had in our own. The failure of the Western medical model to serve as a universal antidote for the world's health care needs has spurred the initiation of research into new and important issues of ethnomedical and ethnopsychological studies with both non-Western and cross-cultural bases. Three of the most notable areas related to prenatal and perinatal studies are: (1) the effects of Western medical models upon indigenous prenatal and perinatal health care systems; (2) the construction of alternative, non-intrusive medical models which can co-exist and assist traditional indigenous systems (including supporting and promoting such systems); (3) in-depth studies of midwifery, both Western and non-Western procedures and practices, as this is the practice par excellence to encourage and support the future mother's sense of competency.

Within prenatal and perinatal practices, there exists the need to intensify and expand cooperative and collaborative research between anthropologists/ethnologists and indigenous health care practitioners, local doctors and psychologists. Medical practitioners who work cross-culturally and internationally need to acknowledge their own limitations and that their best efforts to date have not always succeeded or succeeded so well that they actually failed. For example, the sub-Sahara nomadic peoples' problems with over-population due to vastly improved medical care have upset the ecological balance of their ethno-environment, thereby helping to destroy the future of their culture. Hopefully with WHO's cooperation and collaboration, we will be able to assist in developing appropriate endogenous prenatal and perinatal health care systems to improve upon, but certainly not replace, traditional indigenous health systems for the unborn and the newborn.

Another area of growing concern deals with Western forms of applying and addressing medical concerns, which sometimes make them inappropriate, incomprehensible or even threatening to the indigenous cultural worldview. Luis Luna (1986), in his study of mestizo forms of shamanic healing in the Peruvian Amazon (Vegetalismo/ayahauasca ceremonies), notes that Western forms of medicine are not so readily accepted — unless the indigenous healing practices do not suffice. His analysis astutely points to the difference between the two systems: the traditional systems are more affordable, the shamans travel far and wide for the sake of patients, but mostly the shamans do not separate mind and body illnesses. Much of what they do is to counsel and thereby relieve the anxiety and stress related to the illness. Western medical models do not help them to understand their illness and for this reason often increase their anxiety – and their symptoms.

Our Western medical models are not necessarily applicable or applicable in their present form(s) to large portions of the technologically developing or so-called underdeveloped world. They do not work or function in certain ethno-environments. Therefore Western medical practitioners and developers of medical models for developing countries need to acculturate themselves and their practices to the cultural environment if they truly want to be helpful.

In the same way, Western scientific models have played a large role in re-shaping the health miseries caused by ecological and environmental catastrophies. Through her excellent research and portrayal of a worldwide catastrophy in the making, Catherine Caulfield outlines the consequences of the loss of traditional knowledge and environments on a worldwide scale, which in many ways centers around medical issues. *In the Rainforest* deals largely with the destruction of indigenous environments through which local populations have lost access to traditional medicinal plants and the store of traditional knowledge intimately connected to these ethno-environments. Moreover, we have lost and are losing everyday the possibility of preserving the greatest storehouse of medical knowledge and pharmaceutical cures that exists on this planet. Many of the most effective cures for diseases of the modern age have come from or are coming out of the native tropical rainforests; and synthetic antidotes cloned from the natural products do not have the latitude of applicability or adaptability. Quinine now is less and less effective as a preventive measure against malaria, but there are several other natural medicinal plants that could be employed. However, if we destroy the people's cultural and natural environments through misuse we destroy the greatest potential source of medical cures we have access to today.

There is an immediate call for promoting much more ecological and environmental research in regard to the prenatal and perinatal, including our own industrialized environment. It is crucial that such work be done now – effects of the loss of tropical forests and acid rain, chemical dumping, loss of ozone, and all the 'Chernobyls' need be examined for their effect on pregnant mothers' psychological stress, and thereby subsequent effects upon the unborn. This will require cooperation among medical, psychological and anthropological experts, midwives, indigenous practitioners and birth educators – to name a few of the foremost participants.

In the field of prenatal and perinatal practice, one of the strongest arguments for stopping this needless destruction of people and environments, is in regard to midwifery. Here there is so much we can learn, and this is one of the most fertile grounds for cross-cultural cooperation and reciprocal benefit. One widely-praised example of such research is Carol Laderman's *Wives and Midwives*, a study of Malay childbirth practices. It includes her observations of a traditional culture adapting to modern medical procedures. In order to undertake such a study, Laderman adapted and acculturated herself to local customs, apprenticing herself to one of the village midwives and a local shaman.

Initially, an international project needs to be undertaken in coordinating a worldwide study of midwifery, also on a cross-cultural level. For this, medical and psychological practitioners will need contact with the indigenous cultures on their own terms, possibly with the assistance of those trained in working cross-culturally: cultural anthropologists. This is something we are trying to initiate and coordinate interest in at this time – hopefully with preliminary results in Jerusalem in 1989[3].

Motivation behind ISPP research

Through cooperation and collaboration of international health organizations like WHO, we wish to promote and acknowledge the importance of this innovative medical philosophy to enhance the future of our children and the general ecology of the world we live in. The ISPP is taking a new direction within the medical establishment, trying to change from within old perspectives which no longer serve us well and breaking new ground in the process.

The ISPP stresses that the care of the future, the child, begins within the womb as the first ecological environment we experience physically and psychologically. It is here wherein the quality of life begins, both physically and psychologically. It is the quality of life we need to concentrate our efforts upon and to enhance its possibilities – not on increasing the quantity. Therefore, our first environment is potentially the most important basis for all subsequent development. We carry both physical and psychological imprints from this earliest primal experience. The psychological impressions left can shape our attitudes toward life, and perhaps even the kind of life we may choose to live. Ethically, then, we must pay careful attention to this essential time of human development. The work of the professional care givers must be to assist mothers in enhancing the positive environmental factors of their baby's development, and to help ameliorate any negative potentialities. The ISPP advocates an innovative psychological and medical view stressing preventive initiatives which ultimately will enhance the quality of life. After all is said and done, it is much better (and easier) to create whole children than to heal a broken humanity.

[1] Peacemaker quote from: 'The Fire that Never Dies', by Harvey Arden in *National Geographic*, **172**, No. 3, p. 375.

[2] For further information and proposals for presentations, please contact: Peter Fedor-Freybergh, President of the ISPP and Chairman of the International Advisory Board/Scientific Program Development *or* David M. Serr, Chairman of the Organizing Committee (see Contributors' Appendix for addresses).

[3] Please contact Vanessa Vogel (Member of the International Advisory Board/Anthropology-Ethnology Section for the 9th International Congress of the ISPP in Jerusalem in 1989) if you have interest in contributing to or supporting such a project.

Appendix I

List of contributors

BACZ, Andrzej
M.D.
Department of Endocrinology
Institute of Gynaecology and
　Obstetrics
Copernicus University School of
　Medicin
23 Kopernika Str.
PL-31-501 Kraków
Poland

BENDER, Helen
Principal Child Psychotherapist
48 Cissbury Ring South
Finchley N12 7BE
London
England

BERGH Van den, Bea
Ph.D.
Faculteit der Psychologie en
　Pedagogische Wetenschappen
Tiensestraat 102
B-3000 Leuven
Belgium

BLETON-KRYMKO, Irène
Ph.D., Professor
Département de psychologie
Université du Québec à Montréal
Case postale 8888,
Succursale 'A'
Montréal, P.Q. H3C 3P8
Canada

BORKOWSKI, Wlodzimierz
M.D.
Chief, Department of Neonatology
Institute of Gynaecology and
　Obstetrics
Copernicus University School of
　Medicine
23 Kopernika Str.
PL-31-501 Kraków
Poland

BOULVAIN, M.
M.D.
Hôpital de Braine-Waterloo
35 rue Wayez
1420 Baine l'Alleud
Belgium

BOWEN, Eve
Childbirth Educator
1003 Hayes Avenue
San Diego, CA 92103
USA

CARR Van de, Kristin
Ph.D.
27225 Calaroga Ave.
Hayward, CA 94545
USA

CARR Van de, René
M.D.
27225 Calaroga Ave.
Hayward, CA 94545
USA

CHAMBERLAIN, David B.
Ph.D. Clinical Psychologist
909 Hayes Avenue
San Diego, CA 92103
USA

COLTER, Marvin W.
Ph.D.
14041 Lambert Road
Whittier, CA 90605
USA

DATTA, Bhakti
Ph.D. Professor
Indologisches Seminar
University of Tübingen
D-7400 Tübingen
FRG

DAVENPORT, Mary L.
M.D., Obstetrician and Gynecologist
4653 Benevides Ave.
Oakland, CA 94602
USA

DOWLING, Terence W.
M.A., Ph.B., B.A.
60, Beechgrove Road, Cruddas Park
Newcastle-upon-Tyne, NE4 6RS
England

DÖRNER, Günter
Prof. Dr. Sc. med.
Institut für Experimentelle
Endokrinologie
Humboldt-Universität
Schumannstrasse 20–21
104 Berlin
GDR

ENDRES, Manfred
Dr. med.
Genetische Beratungsstelle
Kinderpoliklinik der Universität
Goethestrasse 29
D-8000 München 2
FRG

FEDOR-FREYBERGH, Peter G.
M.D., Ph.D., Professor
Obstetrician and Gynecologist
President of ISPP
President of the 8th and 9th
 International Congresses of ISPP
Engelbrektsgatan 19
S-114 32 STOCKHOLM
Sweden

FINDEISEN, Barbara
MFCC
3960 W. Sausal Lane
Healdsburg, CA 95448
USA

APPENDIX I

FREUD, W. Ernest
Psychoanalyst, IPA, DPV
Giselbertstrasse 20
D-5060 Bergisch Gladbach 1
Bensberg
FRG

GIDONI, E. Anna
Italian Red Cross
Via Camerata
I-50133 Firenze
Italia

GOLANSKA, Żelislawa
Ph.D.
Department of Endocrinology
Institute of Gynaecology and
  Obstetrics
Copernicus University School of
  Medicine
23 Kopernika Str.
PL-31-501 Kraków
Poland

GUPTA, Derek
M.D., Professor
Department of Diagnostic
  Endocrinology
Rümelinstrasse 23
D-7400 Tübingen
FRG

HÅKANSSON, Tore
Cultural Anthropologist
Brännkyrkagatan 55
S-117 22 Stockholm
Sweden

HORMANN, Elisabeth Ed. M.
Stormstr. 12
D-5000 Köln 1
FRG

JANUS, Ludwig
Dr. med.
Psychoanalyst
Köpfelweg 52
D-6900 Heidelberg-Ziegelhausen
FRG

JERNBERG, Ann M.
Ph.D.
Clinical Director
333 North Michigan Avenue
Chicago, Illinois 60601
USA

KENNELL, John H.
M.D., Professor
Case Western Reserve University
2101 Adelbert Road
Cleveland, OH 44106
USA

KLAUS, Marshall
M.D.
Professor and Chairman
Dept. of Pediatrics/Human
  Development
B-240 Life Sciences Building
Michigan State University
East Lansing, MI 48824
USA

KLIMEK, Rudolf
M.D. Professor and Chairman
Institute of Obstetrics &
  Gynaecology
Copernicus University School of
  Medicine
23 Kopernika Str.
PL-31-501 Kraków
Poland

KOESTER-SANFORD, Lynne
Ph.D.
Max-Planck-Institut
Kraepelinstrasse 10-EPB
D-8000 München 40
FRG

KOST, Ursula
Dr. med
Bismarckstr. 41,
D-741, Reutlingen,
FRG

KURJAK, Asim
M.D., PH.D., Professor
Yugoslav Association of Societies
  for Ultrasound in Medicine and
  Biology
Pavleka Miškine 64
YU-41000 Zagreb
Yugoslavia

LAIBOW, E. Rima
M.D., Psychoanalyst
Cerridwen
13 Summit Terrace
Dobbs Ferry
NY 10522
USA

LEHRER, Marc
Ph.D.
1466 7th Avenue
San Francisco, CA 94122
USA

LOGAN, Brent
Ph.D., Director
Prenatal and Infant Education
  Institute
2000 Lake Street
Snohomish, Washington 98290
USA

LÜPKE, Hans von
M.D., Pediatrician
Psychotherapist
Gesundheitszentrum
Böttgerstr. 20
D-6000 Frankfurt/M.60
FRG

MEHL, Lewis
M.D., Ph.D.
1427 Miliva St.
Berkeley CA 94709
USA

MUSAPH, Herman
Prof. Dr.
Cath. van Rennesstraat 30
NL-1077 KX Amsterdam
The Netherlands

MUYLDER, Xavier de
M.D., M.Sc.
P.O. Box 1019
Gweru
Zimbabwe

NICKEL, Horst
Professor, Ph.D.
Inst. f. Entw. u Sozialpsychologie d.
  Univ. Düsseldorf
Universitätsstrasse 1
D-4000 Düsseldorf 1
FRG

NOBLE, Elizabeth
Director
Maternal & Child Health Center
2464 Mass Avenue
Cambridge, MA 02140
USA

APPENDIX I

ODENT, Michel
M.D.
59 Roderick Road
London NW3 2NP
England

PÁL, Maria
Dr. phil., Clinical Psychologist
Abteilung für Psychiatrie und
  Psychotherapie, Staatliches
Zentralkrankenhaus
Postfach 330
H-1536 Budapest 114
Hungary

PETERSON, Gayle
LCSW
1749 Vine Street
Berkeley, CA 94709
USA

PHILLIPS, Royal
Childbirth Educator
549 Hodges Lane
Santa Barbara, CA 93108
USA

PICHLER, Erika
Training Midwife
Körnerstrasse 19
D-8050 Freising
FRG

RAPHAEL-LEFF, Joan
Psychoanalyst and
  Social Psychologist
1 South Hill Park Gardens
London NW3
England

SCARZELLA-MAZZOCCHI, Elda
Presidente del Villaggio della Madre
  e del Fanciullo
Via Goya n. 60
I-20148 Milano
Italy

SCHINDLER, Sepp
Dr. phil., Univ. Professor Institut für
  Psychologie der Universität
  Salzburg
Hellbrunnerstrasse 34
A-5020 Salzburg
Austria

SCHOLZ, Christine
Sociologist
Bahnhofstrasse 17
Deisenhofen
FRG

SCHUSSER, Gerhard
Apl. Prof. Dr. phil. habil. Dipl. Psych.
Akademischer Direktor
Fachbereich Erziehungs- und
  Kulturwissenschaften
Universität Osnabrück
Ziegelstr. 13
D-4500 Osnabrück
FRG

SERR, David M
M.D., Professor and Chairman
Department of Obstetrics and
  Gynecology
The Chaim Sheba Medical Center
Tel-Hashomer 52621
Israel

THOM, Solihin
DO, MRO
56 New Kings Road
Fulham
London, SW6 4LS
England

THURMAN, Leon
Ed. D.M.S.
Instructor of Voice and Early
    Childhood Music
MacPhail Center for the Arts
11128 La Salle Avenue
University of Minnesota,
Minneapolis
Minnesota
USA

TURNER, John-Richard
Prenatal Therapist
Whole-Self Institute
535 Cordova 238
Sante Fe, NM 87501
USA

VERNY, Tom
M.D., D.Psych., F.R.C.P.(C)
36 Madison Avenue
Toronto, Ontario
Canada, M5R 3S1

VOGEL, M. L. Vanessa
Ethnologist
Affiliated Researcher
Sweden's National Ethnographic
    Museum
Fisksätra Torg 5
S-133 00 Saltsjöbaden
Sweden

WESEL, Serge
M.D., Obstetrician and
    Gynecologist
Hôpital de Braine-l'Alleud-
    Waterloo
Rue Wayez 35
B-1420 Braine-l'Alleud
Belgium

ZACHAU-CHRISTIANSEN, Bengt
Professor, M.D., Pediatrician
Carl Johans Gade 1,2
DK-2100 Copenhagen Ø
Denmark

ZELEDON AGUILAR, Marco T.
Ph.D., Clinical Psychologist
Apartado 335, 1002
San José, Costa Rica
Central America

Appendix II

German papers on prenatal and perinatal psychology and medicine: selected abstracts

Below is listed a selection of German abstracts and titles which will be published simultaneously with the English edition of *Research and Practice in Prenatal and Perinatal Psychology and Medicine*. The composition of the German edition is very different and the nature of the work made it undesirable to translate into English, as it was found that too much was lost in translating. Therefore, a selection of these research papers and their titles are printed below (in abstract form where available), with German titles for reference purposes. The German edition, *Pränatale und Perinatale Psychologie und Medizin: Begegnung mit dem Ungeborenen*, edited by Peter Fedor-Freybergh is available through Saphir Publications, Box 2060, S–12502, Älvsjö, Sweden.

TITLES AND ABSTRACTS

Gisela Adam-Lauer
Auswirkungen der Erkentnisse pränataler Psychologie auf die Sozialarbeit/Sozialpädagogik.

Gertrude Aigner
Die Bedeutung der Sexualität in der pränatalen Zeit.

Edith Bauer, Marlen Grimm and Ulrike Hauffe
Eine multidisziplinäre Frauen-Gesundheits-Praxis: Ein sich entwickelndes Modell in Bremen. Darstellung am Beispiel vorzeitiger Wehentätigkeit.

Claus H. Bick
Pränatale Beobachtungen bei kognitiv integrierendem hypnoanalytischem Verfahren.

Gaetano Benedetti
Schizophrenie und pränatale Psychologie.

Abraham Braun
Perinatale Phänomene als charakteristische Ausdrucksformen regressiver Zustandsbilder.

Heide Dellisch
Prävention psychischer und psychosomatischer Störungen schon in der Schwangerschaft – eine Utopie?

Géza Dobrotka
Gedanken zu frühesten-präkonzeptiven-Vorbeugung späterer Fehlentwicklungen der Persönlichkeit.

Eva Eichenberger
Hinweise auf prä- und perinatale Störungen im anamnestischen Gespräch.

Indications of pre- and perinatal troubles in the anamnestic dialogue
The biography of most of the psychotherapy patients is characterized by a difficult birth or unusual problem situations before the birth. Taking an anamnesis and listening to the life story of a patient implicates identification, transmission and countertransmission of both patient and therapist. Integrating what the patient tells about the beginning of his life, enables him to continue his therapy with more freedom and more real feelings. This is shown in three cases of women approximately 30 years old.

Wlodzimierz Fijalkowski
Elemente der pränatalen Psychologie in der Gebärschule in Polen.

Giorgio Foresti und Carla Berlanda
Die Anamnese der prä- und perinatalen Periode in der Psychotherapie.

Prenatal and perinatal anamnesis in psychotherapy
The authors value the interest of prenatal and perinatal experiences in the psychotherapeutic perspective. As they have noticed the relation between the events and conditions of prenatal and perinatal periods, and psychopathologic and psychosomatic symptoms, they support the necessity of a correct anamnesis of this period for a better understanding of the patient. The anamnesis of prenatal and perinatal periods can be carried out in two ways: an active psychodynamic research through the emersion of emotions and the live reconstruction of the personal experiences of the patient; a parental investigation to discover special events, which is more frequent in the treatment of children. The authors advise a brief guide to this kind of anamnesis as it is in use by the Centro Ricerche Biopsichiche.

Gudrun Gauda
Elternleitbilder Gestern und Heute: Modelle für die Entwicklung der Elternidentität.

Models for the development of parental identity: past and present
The development of parental identity is one of the most important developmental tasks in the transition to parenthood. It develops embedded in a historical and cultural background offering different models to the future parents.

Actually parents can choose among different models. The first — the sacrificing unselfish mother and the providing, authoritarian father — no longer fits into our social reality. The second model requires better knowledge and skill for optimal advancement of the child from both parents. In some cases the child is placed so far from the focus of attention of his parents, that their own developmental possibilities are threatened.

The orientation of both models prevents the individual growth of all family members and leads to the limitation of developmental possibilities in the family.

Ulrike Hauffe
Ansprüche an geburtsvorbereitende Arbeit.

Demands on birth education work
Birth education became and still is an outsider department, acknowledged by a few, stamped as superfluous by others. Thus we unfortunately miss the chances of birth education which unite the following possibilities:

to develop confidence in one's physical, intellectual and psychical abilities;

to make a step to overcome specialization;

and to meet the resulting procedure of surrendering responsibility to the experts;

and thus also initiating the discussion with experts (experts, but also the authority of the 'fateful' course of pregnancy, birth and parentage, the authority of the body experienced as a separate object).

Birth preparation which can oppose the socially developed separation of body, mind and soul is an important possibility for public health, assisting and producing a prophylactic effect.

Birth education has always existed and it is not an invention of the 20th century. It is sometimes dismissed as 'just a fashion', but there always was birth education in everyday life, in families, in village life. Men and women grew up with the direct experience of pregnancy, birth and parentage. Today, in our age of strongly separated living conditions, we need an institution which makes this mutual learning possible.

Birth education groups have taken widely differing courses in the Federal Republic of Germany. This development is dependent on the training of our birth educators. The great variety of schools (midwife schools, physiotherapy schools, private institutions) produces a corresponding variety in training. Unfortunately, almost all of them concentrate only on a part of the birth education spectrum.

We should aim for a birth education system with three crucial points of equal standard: body work, information and talks in groups.

Body work sharpens the mind and the consciousness for one's own and other people's needs.

Information gives an insight on things that happen.

Talks between expectant parents create understanding.

Therefore a birth education should provide the building stones for this complete birth preparation.

Ursula Keller-Husemann and Kurt Husemann
Die Bedeutung G. H. Grabers in der Entwicklung psychoanalytischer Konzepte der frühen Störung.

Ilaina Kaplan
Geburtsvorbereitung als Lebensschulung für Elternschaft und Partnerschaft.

Marlies Köster-Schlutz
Konfliktbearbeitung in Anpassung und Widerstand. Zur psychologischen Arbeit mit Risikoschwangerschaften.

> *The apprehension of conflicts by adaption and opposition: psychological work with endangered pregnant women*
> Psychological work with pregnant and psychologically endangered women shows that behind the obvious symptoms of tendencies to premature birth there are found to be latent allusions to female conflicts of identity.
>
> Today women are experiencing conflicts of identity which result from the change in the traditional image of the women's role in life, which seems no longer to be adequate. A new structure of their role, active in emancipation, has not yet reached stability and full force. Female subjectivity concerning the capacity of child-bearing and of natural reproduction cannot be put totally under the order of patriarchal regiment, but even today women have introverted the social standards of the struggle of competition and efficiency.
>
> During pregnancy this situation of conflict may result in two different tendencies, which are in themselves ambiguous. Assuming more than before the responsibility for their own fertility, women are able to serve their own identity in a more progressive way, but they still however, remain involved in (male) images of efficiency standards.
>
> Conflicts and a symptomatic development of pregnancy are to be expected particularly if there is no individual way to find a synthesis between active self-determination and passive reproducing. This is also objectively difficult because there is no cultural cover for it. In such a situation the affected women can respond via adaptation or defensively. In the first case the women try to externalize the ambiguous situation of the conflict; they try to solve the inner tensions by delegating them to the physician, e.g. by producing symptoms which can be treated medically.
>
> By adapting herself to the medical institution and therewith to the existing cultural possibilities, the woman falls back into her role as the dependent patient, which does not really balance the situation of conflict, and adds to the ambiguities. In this case the social and psychic conflict hides behind the illness and is therefore no longer communicable (definable).
>
> In the second case, women feel or reflect upon the cultural con-

tradiction of their situation and offer psychic resistance by opposing certain objectifying forms of treatment. Such attitudes of resistance are apt to produce new conflicts, but include also an urge for self-determination, and to initiate an active object relation to the unborn child and to experience a more congruent self-harmony.

Sonya Kübber
Vater werden als Chance in der Entwicklung des Mannes.

> *The process of becoming a father – an opportunity in male development*
> In contrast to the commonly accepted necessity for the pregnant woman to regress emotionally during pregnancy, childbirth and the postpartum period, in western civilizations this process is not considered a necessity for the male. Cross-cultural information shows that so-called primitive societies pay special attention to the development into fatherhood. The ritual of 'couvade' leaves no doubt that for the father the same possibility of regression is needed as for the mother in order to prepare for parental maturity. The path of dissolution and restructuring of the early experiences is recommended and socially accepted. In western civilizations inhibition of male regression creates a predisposition for psychosomatic disorders; variations of fatherhood imitating the 'good' mother and thus eliminating structuring and aggressive components in the father–child dialog are seen as further ways of 'hidden' male regression. Broader understanding for the regressive needs in the male is considered necessary in order to lead to more integrated forms of femininity and masculinity in our societies.

Lisa Leitgeb
Praxis einer psychosomatischen Geburtsvorbereitung.

Zdeněk Matějček
Kinder aus unerwünschter Schwangerschaft geboren: Longitudinale Studie über 20 Jahre.

> *Children born from unwanted pregnancies. Longitudinal study over 20 years.*
> The longitudinal study has as its subject 220 children born in Prague between 1961 and 1963 when their mothers had twice asked for an artificial termination of the pregnancy and had been twice refused both by the district and the regional appellate abortion committee. These children were pair-matched, using rigorous criteria, with 220 control children. The examination included a vast number of methods. None of the examiners knew which child belonged to which group. There were

no differences between the groups in the children's birth weights, incidence of malformations, preterm births, perinatal complications or any other indicators of the fetus having suffered prenatally. More complications in pregnancy and the puerperium were found in the control mothers.

Detailed examination made when the children were 9 years old showed some serious differences in the *psychosocial development* of the two groups and are unfavorable to 'unwanted children'. Similar, or even more pronounced, differences in findings appeared on examining the children in early adolescence. These children have now exceeded the age of 20 and have themselves entered the period of reproduction. The findings of the new extensive examination are again unfavorable to children once born from unwanted pregnancies. They fit in with the picture of psychological subdeprivation which has a tendency to transfer to the next generation.

Marianne Meinhold
Strategien zum Abbau von Nutzungsbarrieren.

Strategies for the reduction of barriers preventing the use of services
This paper deals with the question of which services are appropriate to reach those client groups which previously have made little use of the opportunities available for the care of and work with pregnant women.

In addition to external barriers and the particular characteristics of the under-users (e.g. lower social status), an important reason for this lack of demand can be found in the *'social and cultural distance'* between those offering the service and potential clients. Social and cultural distance can be seen, for example, in the fact that the problem definitions of the professional helpers and those of the users are not synonymous. This distance between those offering the service and the clients can rarely be diminished by making the service a little more user-friendly or by advertising campaigns through which the clients are encouraged to use the service. The reduction of barriers preventing the use of services demands a far longer process of acquaintance between those offering the service and its potential users. This is true especially for services concerning psychosocial matters.

The individual steps towards this acquaintanceship are described in the case of the 'babysitter-emergency-service' project. There is need first of all for an open service which is distinguished by the features of understandability, non-discrimination and client-participation. The social workers (or health workers) in this service work on the principle of creating contacts with intermediary agencies or workers, unburdening the client, networking and finally respecting the perspectives and problem definitions of the users.

The meaning of these working principles for services involved in the care of and work with pregnant women is discussed in this paper.

Edeltraud Meistermann-Seeger
Pränatale Existenz in der Kurztherapie, die Fokaltraining heisst.

Margarete Meyer
Erkentnisse der pränatalen Psychologie als Handlungsanleitung bei der Frühförderung behinderter Kinder.

Findings of prenatal psychology as a guide to early pedagogics with handicapped children
The severity of a child's handicap depends in later life not only on biological damage. The parents' reactions and those of its entire social environment have an essential bearing on whether it comes to serious secondary damage. Early pedagogics should not simply be related to the child, but rather, the whole affected family must be looked after. The child's parents must remain the principal persons of reference and not become co-therapists.

The basis of early pedagogics is the actual observation of the child and the consideration of the peculiarities of its prenatal development with the emphasis on the formation of a sensorimotor circulation and language acquisition.

Ivan Milaković
Die Theorie einer pränatalen libidinösen Phase: 20 Jahre danach.

The theory of a prenatal libidinal phase – after 20 years
The author offers a brief survey of his theory of a prenatal stage in libidinal development. According to this theory, the fetus from his 5th month suffers from thirst. He drinks the amniotic water and so he abolishes suffering from this displeasure. This gives evidence that all the components necessary for functioning of a libidinal phase do exist: pleasure–displeasure phenomena; the role of Ego and the libidinal cathexis of the satisfying organ (pharynx); the abolishing of dissatisfaction and the appeasement that are the psychical experiences of the fetus in that stage and the model for the later drive satiations.

The author stresses the phenomenon of transposing of libidinal cathexes from pharynx to mouth (lips), which process must be accomplished before birth so that the newborn can immediately suck at the breast after being born, and to transpose its libidinal interests on the outer world of objects.

The author has been obliged to change nothing in his theory in the last 20 years, e.g. the prenatal libidinal stage is continuing in the so-called oral-erotic stage, which is only the interim to bring over the newborn in the first months and to help him to adapt himself to new circumstances.

The author's opinion is that the most important reminiscence of this period of life is the fact that this experience of peace and satisfaction will be indelibly memorized, and that it will be the basis for later dissatisfactions of men/women. The ambivalency of children, withdrawal tendencies in adults, resignation and suicidal tendencies – all these phenomena have their origin in this basic dissatisfaction with the loss of prenatal peace.

This prenatal libidinal phase could also be called the 'pharyngeal', but it was previously published as a 'deglutitive' one.

Hans Neumann
Die Überdramatisierung der Geburt – Das Problem der heutigen Geburtshilfe.

Hans Neumann
Ziel und Sinn einer Geburtsvorbereitung.

F. Olejár and A. Hrdlićková
Hypnose als Forschungsmethode in der pränatalen Psychologie.

Kurt Theodor Oehler
Die pränatale Vorbestimmung des Lebens einer Frau.

Peter Petersen
Unsere Verantwortung zum ankommenden Kind hin – Moderne Fertilitetstechnologien fordern das Paradigma der Kinderankunft heraus.

Our responsibility towards the child to be born – modern fertility technologies present a challenge to the paradigm of the arrival of a child
The arrival of a child refers to the time from conception and procreation. The paradigm of the arrival of a child regards this point of time as open, free, self-determined (autonomous). The child that is to be born is conceded the autonomy and freedom to be able to determine whether and when it wishes to come. By contrast, modern fertility technologies and reproduction medicine (IVF representing the current peak of this development) obscure our consciousness of and responsibility for the autonomy of the child to be born: the child is outwardly determined by the absolute wish for a child on the part of the parents and by

biotechnical manipulation — a child is produced by a certain date as desired by the parents; the open time aspect, the freedom and spontaneity of the arrival of a child are thereby eliminated.

The freedom of the individuality of the child is already threatened at conception and procreation by the manipulative concept of such technologies — mental and emotional disturbances for the child and its parents are predictable.

These fast-expanding fertility technologies call upon us to develop within ourselves a new and clearer awareness of the spontaneity and freedom with regard to a child's arrival.

Herwig Poettgen
Die ungewollte Schwangerschaft und Schwangerschaftskonflikt.

Psychological conflicts encountered in cases of unwanted pregnancy
In dealing with the problems of unwanted pregnancy we find three fields of conflict. It is important for advisers and physicians to know them: (1) intrapsychic conflicts; (2) interpersonal conflicts, or in a dynamic word: the interactional field of conflicts; (3) the sociocultural, which implicates the ethical conflict. This classification, however, made for didactic reasons will be met with, in practice, in full complexity. In everyday life, everybody will be confronted with the solution of conflicts. Unsuccessful solutions of conflicts are a central problem of neurosis psychology. However, we have also learned to interpret psychosomatic (consequently physical) symptoms of illness as compromise forms of intrapsychic conflicts; for according to the theory of impulses, each psychic impulse has its equivalent in the motoric sector of our body. This has been confirmed in the correlation of 'perception and motion' (V. v. Weizsäcker). That means, however, that even where no manifest psychosomatic illness occurs, also in case of pregnancy, the psychologic correlations of psychosomatic processes may become effective as permanent irritations. By the analytic psychotherapy of women who went through pregnancy interruptions we know they may possibly show damages to their 'self' (their personal being) even after decades. On the contrary depressive reactions with aggressive and self-destructive impulses are met with in cases of an enforced continuation of involuntary pregnancy. Concerning their children, as psychoanalysis teaches us, they will become aware in the course of their socialisation of the fact that they were undesired, even if their mothers and fathers never verbalized it. Such children suffer from defects in developing their personalities (self-esteem). This occurs in connection with depressive neurosis. Psychic injuries will also be done to children of such mothers as they will, for the reason of suppressed desires of interruption, after

these children's birth react as 'over-protective-mothers'. They surround their children with a cover of anxiety. That leads to 'Matrices', the origin of neuroses and phobias.

Alcoholism and smoking are phenomena of self-destructive regression. In our days they are known as one of the most frequent causes of embryo-pathologies. Alcohol as well as nicotine passes the placental barrier. So do biochemical transmitters in the sense of the just mentioned physiological correlates of psychic stress experiences of pregnant women. Here the field is open for prenatal psychosomatic research. Knowledge may grow in this field which might diminish uncertainty with regard to indications concerning pregnancy interruption.

Hans Rausch
Unerwünschheit von Schwangerschaften als Realität und gesellschaftliches Tabu.

Social taboos and undesired pregnancies
It is the author's assumption that even in our enlightened society there are equally strong taboos as there were in primitive times. According to this conviction one of these taboos is the recognition of the existence of the undesirability of pregnancies. The maintenance of this taboo leads inevitably to more and more psychosocially and psychosomatically sick people. Conventional science is inclined to cement this situation with its over-emphasis of inheritance of severe illnesses – using the terms 'connatal' and 'genetic' synonymously. Prenatal development is thereby totally neglected. The importance of a positive prenatal mother–child relationship for a healthy development is being supported by the author's biological and anthropological view. The biological view ought to be the basis of psychological and psychoanalytical knowledge. The author attempts to critically evaluate conventional science and orthodox psychoanalysis which he suspects to be also fraught with taboos and dogmatisms which developed as a result of repression and denial of early preverbal patterns of experience. Parental rejection is very frequently caused by the inability of the parents (often as a result of their own disturbed psychosocial development), to accept their children as autonomous beings. At the end the author ennumerates and defines several pathological phenomena, which according to him originate in prenatal developmental disturbances.

Alfons Reiter
Die pränatale Dimension des Narzissmus.

Alfred Rockenschaub
Geburtshilfliche 'Experimente' und pränatale Psychologie.

Brigitte Rollett
Frühsozialisation und Autismus.

Edeltraud Schmücker
Kultivation und Ritualisation von Schwangerschaft und Geburt: Kulturpsychologische Aspekte der Entwicklungsgestaltung.

Regine Schneider
Die Bedeutung der Gegenübertragung in der Rekonstruktion und Bearbeitung frühester Störungen – Ein Fallbeispiel.

Gisela Schneider-Flagmeyer
Die Bearbeitung des Geburtstraumas in der analytischen Behandlung schwer gestörter Patienten.

Maria Summer
Beeinflussung der Heilpädagogik durch die pränatale Psychologie.

Lili de Vooght
Die präverbale Sprachstruktur des ungeborenen Kindes.

> *The preverbal language structure of the unborn child*
> Based on a clinical study, by the French children's psychoanalyst F. Dolto, we know that the child from the time of conception belongs to a language structure. The concept of language structure is taken from the French structuralistic school.
> Also we ascertain that the child itself during pregnancy is able to signal and signify, which in the case we analysed was done by a bodily symptom.

Elisabeth M. Wetzel
Bedeutung von Musikanwendung in der Geburtsvorbereitung und in der ersten nachgeburtlichen Phase.

> *The signification of musical concepts in birth preparation and in the first phase after birth*
> In this paper, possibilities are shown for a 'musical developmental treatment' during pregnancy and in the first phase after birth.
> Starting with the method of development, on which this paper is based, the physiological and psychosomatic effects of music are shown.

The development of fetal mobility and hearing, and the first processes of integration are briefly pointed out.

Different aspects are brought into connection with concepts of birth preparation, which include listening to music, dancing, singing and moving (also concerning the accompaniment of newborn and preterm infants).

The systematization of research results will make possible future development of prophylactic and therapeutic methods.

Beate Wimmer-Puchinger
Zur Bedeutung der Mutter–Tochter-Beziehung in der Schwangerschaft am Beispiel der Hyperemesis gravidarum.

PRÄNATALE UND PERINATALE PSYCHOLOGIE UND MEDIZIN

BEGEGNUNG MIT DEM UNGEBORENEN

A German language volume is now available, based on presentations made in German at the Congress of the International Society of Prenatal and Perinatal Psychology and Medicine (ISPP) held in September 1986 at Bad Gastein, Austria.

Price: 140 DM Hardback
          88 DM Paperback

It is available from
SAPHIR,
Box 2060, S-125 02 Älvsjö, Sweden

Bibliography

Abboud, T. K. et al. (1984). Effect of intrathecal morphine during labour on maternal plasma endorphin levels. *Am. J. Obstet. Gynecol.*, **150**, 709–11

Adamsons, K., Mueller-Heubach, E. and Meyers, R. E. (1971). Production of fetal asphyxia in the rhesus monkey by administration of catecholamines to the mother. *Am. J. Obstet. Gynecol.*, **109**, 248–62

Affonso, D. (1977). Missing pieces – a study of postpartum feelings. *Birth*, **4**, 4

Ainsworth, M. D. S. and Wittig, B. A. (1969). Attachment and exploratory behavior of one-year-olds in a strange situation. In Foss, B. M. (ed.) *Determinants of Infant Behavior.* Vol. 4. (New York: Wiley)

Akhnaton, Nefer-Kheparu-Ra, Ua-En-Ra, Amen-Hetep IV (1926). Hymn to Aton. ca. 1400 BC Tr. Breasted, J. H. In *Cambridge Ancient History.* Vol. 2, Cambridge

Alcmaeon of Crotona: See Diels

Alexander, F. (1925). Metapsychologische Darstellung des Heilungsvorganges. *Int. Z. Psychoanal.*, **11**, 157–78

Alexander, F. (1950). *Psychosomatic Medicine.* (New York: Norton)

Allbutt, Sir Clifford (1921). *Greek Medicine in Rome.* (London: Macmillan)

Allert, A. and Jernberg, A. (1987). *MIM Manual: Adult–toddler.* (Chicago: The Therapy Institute) (In Press)

Als, H (1984). Discussion of Nurcombe et al. In Call, J. D. et al., (eds.) *Frontiers of Infant Psychiatry II.* pp. 211–18. (New York: Basic Books)

Als, H. and Duffy, F. (1980). The behavior of the premature infant. In Brazelton, T. B. and Lester, B. M. (eds.) *Infant at Risk.* (New York: Elsevier)

Anaxagoras of Clazomenae: See Diels

Anderson, G. C. (1977). The mother and her newborn: mutual caregivers. *JOGN Nursing,* **Sept/Oct,** 50–7

Anderson, G. C. et al. (1986). Abstract: a fact-finding expedition to Bogota. *Programma Ambulatorio de Prematuros,* Mimeographed report

Aono, I., Miyake, A., Kinugasa, I., Kurachi, K. and Matsumoto, K. (1978). Absence of positive feedback effect of estrogen on LH release in patients with testicular feminization syndrome. *Acta Endocrinol.,* **87,** 259–67

Apgar, V., Holaday, D. A., James, L. S., Prince, C. E., Weisbrot, J. M. and Weiss, I. (1957). *J. Am. Med. Assoc.,* **165,** 2155

Aristotle (1910). *Historia Animalium.* d' A. W. Thompson, tr. and ed. Oxford

Aristotle (1912). *De Generatione Animalium.* A. Platt, tr. and ed. Oxford

Arms, S. (1983). *To Have and Let Go.* (New York: Alfred A. Knopf)

Arnold, K.-H. (1981). *Der Situationsbegriff in den Sozialwissenschaften.* (Basel: Weinheim)

Arthur, G. (1949). The Arthur adaption of the Leiter International Performance Scale. *J. Clin. Psychol.,* **5,** 345

Asclepiades of Parion: See Diels

Ashton, R. (1976). Aspects of timing in child development. *Child Development,* **47,** 622–6

Aslin, R. N. (1981). Development of smooth pursuit in human infants. In Fisher, D. F., Monty, R. A. and Senders, J. W. (eds.) *Eye Movements: Cognition and Visual Perception.* (Hillsdale, N. Jersey: Lawrence Erlbaum Associates)

Aubrey, R. (1978). The case against out-of-hospital delivery. In Stewart, L. and Stewart, D. (eds.) *21st Century Obstetrics Now.* (Marble Hill, MO: NAPSAC Press)

Auerbach, J., Levev, M., Nowik, R. and Margolin, J. (1985). Teaching pregnant women about newborns. *Cahiers de Psychologie Cognitive,* **5,** 485

Bakeman, R. and Brown, J. (1977). Behavioral dialogues: an approach to the assessment of mother–infant interaction. *Child Development,* **48,** 195–203

Baker, R. A. (1978). Technologic intervention in obstetrics. *Obstet. Gynecol. J.,* **51,** 2

Bakketeig, L. S. et al. (1984). Randomised controlled trial of ultrasonographic screening in pregnancy. *Lancet,* 207

Balint, M. (1956). Perversions and genitality. In *Primary Love and Psychoanalytic Technique.* Chap. IX. (London: Tavistock)

Balint, M. and Norell, J. S. (eds.) (1978). *Fünf Minuten pro Patient.* (Frankfurt: Suhrkamp)

Baltes, P. B. (ed.) (1979). *Entwicklungspsychologie der Lebensspanne.* (Stuttgart)

Bannister, D. and Fransella, F. (1981). *Der Mensch als Forscher* (Inquiring Man). (Münster)
Barclay, W. R., McCormick, R. A., James, A. J., Sidbury, J. B., Michejda, M. and Hodgen, G. D. (1981). The ethics of *in utero* surgery. *J. Am. Med. Assoc.,* **246,** 1550–5
Barglow, P. *et al.* (1984). Improving the psychological prognosis for offspring of adolescent mothers. In Call, J., Galenson, E. and Tyson, R. L. *Frontiers of Infant Psychiatry, II.* pp. 300–6. (New York: Basic Books)
Barnett *et al.* (1970) Neonatal separation: the maternal side of interactional deprivation. *Pediatrics,* **45,** 2, 197–205
Barnhill, L., Rubenstein, G. and Rocklin, N. (1979). From generation to generation: fathers-to-be in transition. *Family Coordinator,* **28,** 229–235
Barraclough, C. A. and Gorski, R. A. (1961). Evidence that the hypothalamus is responsible for androgen-induced sterility in the female rat. *Endocrinology,* **68,** 68–70
Barrett, J. H. W. (1982). Prenatal influences on adaptation in the newborn. In Stratton, P. (ed.) *Psychobiology of the Newborn.* pp. 267–95. (New York: John Wiley & Sons)
Barrow, J. D. and Tipler, F. J. (1986). *The Anthropic Cosmological Principle.* (New York: Oxford University Press)
Bartholomé, K. (1980). Die molekulare basis der Heterogenität der Phenylketonurie. *Naturwissenschaften,* **67,** 495–8
Barton, M. D., Killam, A. P. and Meschia, G. (1974). Response of ovine uterine blood flow to epinephrine and norepinephrine. *Proc. Soc. Exp. Biol. Med.,* **145,** 966–1003
Bartoszyk, J. and Nickel, H. (1986a). Geburtsvorbereitung, Geburtserlebnis und Eltern-Kind-Kontakt während des Klinikaufenthaltes: eine empirische Untersuchung unter besonderer Berücksichtigung der Rolle des Vaters. *Geburtshilfe und Frauenheilkunde,* **46,** 353–8
Bartoszyk, J. and Nickel, H. (1986b). Die Teilnahme an Säuglingspflegekursen und das Betreuungsverhalten von Vätern in den ersten Lebenswochen des Kindes. Praxis der Kinderpsychologie und Kinderpsychiatrie. In press
Baum, J. D. and Howat, P. (1978). The family and neonatal intensive care. In Kitzinger, S. and Davis, J. A. (eds.) *The Place of Birth.* pp. 216–28. (Oxford University Press)
Beardall, A. *Clinical Kineseology.* (Private editions)
Beasley, J. M. and Kurjak, A. (1984). Clinical assessment of intrauterine growth retardation. In Kurjak, A. and Kossoff, G. (eds.) *Recent Advances in Ultrasound Diagnosis 4: Proceedings of the International Symposium on Recent Advances in Ultrasound Diagnosis* Dubrovnik, June 1–3, 1983. pp. 127–32. (Amsterdam: Excerpta Medica International Congress Series 640)

Beebe, B., Feldstein, S., Jaffe, J., Mays, K. and Alson, D. (1985). Interpersonal timing: the application of an adult dialogue model to mother–infant vocal and kinesic interactions. In Field, T. and Fox, N. (eds.) *Social Perception in Infants*. pp. 219–47. (Norwood, N. J.: Ablex)

Beeson, D. (1984). Technological rhythms in pregnancy: the case of prenatal diagnosis by amniocentesis. In Duster, T. and Garrett, K. (eds.) *Biological Rhythms and Social Relations*. pp. 145–81. (Norwood, N. J.: Ablex)

Beeson, D. and Douglas, R. (1983). Prenatal diagnosis of fetal disorders. I. Technological capabilities. *Birth,* **10**(4), 227–32

Beeson, D., Douglas, R. and Lumsford, T. F. (1983). Prenatal diagnosis of fetal disorders. II. Issues and implications. *Birth,* **10**(4), 233–41

Beeson, D. and Golbus, M. S. (1979). Anxiety engendered by amniocentesis. In Epstein, C. J. et al. (eds.) *Risk, Communication and Decision Making in Genetic Counselling*. pp. 191–7. (New York: Alan R. Liss). For the National Foundation, March of Dimes Birth Defects: Original Article Series, XV

Begemann, H. (1986). Das dicke Ende kommt noch. In *Stern*. 15 May

Bell, A. P. and Weinberg, M. S. (1978). *Der Kinsey Institut Report über weibliche und männliche Homosexualität*. (München: Bertelsmann Verlag)

Bell, A. P., Weinberg, M. S. and Hammersmith, S. K. (1980). *Der Kinsey Institut Report über sexuelle Orientierung und Partnerwahl*. (München: Bertelsmann Verlag)

Bell, J. E. (1948). *Projective Techniques: a Dynamic Approach to the Study of the Personality*. (New York: Longmans)

Bell, J. E. (1969). *The Family in the Hospital: Lessons from Developing Countries*. Ch. IV: Premature infant wards, Baragwanath Hospital, Johannesburg. pp. 51–6. (Chevy Chase, Maryland: NIMH)

Bench, R. J. and Anderson, J. H. (1968). Sound transmission to the human fetus through the maternal abdominal wall. *J. Gen. Psychol.,* **113,** 85–7

Bender, H. (1981) Experiences in running a staff group in colloquium: hospital care of the newborn: some aspects of personal stress. *J. Child Psychother.,* **7,** 2, 152–9

Bergmann, J. R. (1980). *Interaktion und Exploaration*. Diss., Universität Konstanz

Bergmann, J. R. (1981). Ethnomethodologische Konversationsanalyse. In Schröder, P. and Steger, H. (eds.) *Dialogforschung*. pp. 9–51. (Düsseldorf: Schwann)

Berkowitz, G. and Kasl, S. (1983). The role of psychosocial factors in spontaneous preterm delivery. *J. Psychosom. Res.,* **27,** 283–90

Berkowitz, R. L., Glickman, M. G., Smith, G. J. W., Siegel, N. J., Weiss, R. M.,

Mahoney, M. J. and Hobbins, J. C. (1982). Fetal urinary tract obstructions: what is the role of surgical intervention *in utero*? *Am. J. Obstet. Gynecol.*, **144,** 367–75

Bertalanffy, L. von (1986). *General Systems Theory: Foundations, Development, Applications.* (New York: Braziller)

Bettelheim, B. (1954). *Symbolic Wounds – Puberty Rites and the Envious Male.* (Glencoe, Illinois: The Free Press)

Bibring, G. L. (1959). Some considerations of the psychological processes in pregnancy. In *Psychoanalytic Study of the Child.* Vol. 14, pp. 113–21. (London: Imago Publishing)

Bibring, G. L. et al. (1961). A study of the psychological processes in pregnancy and of the earliest mother–child relationship. *Psychoanalytic Study of the Child.* Vol. 16, pp. 9–72. (London: Hogarth Press)

Bick, E. (1964). Notes on infant observation in psychoanalytic training. *Int. J. Psychoanal.*, **45,** 558–66

Bion, W. R. (1962). *Learning from Experience.* (London: Maresfield reprints)

Birnholz, J. C. and Benecerraf, B. R. (1983). The development of human fetal hearing. *Science,* **222,** 516–18

Bisping, R. and Steingrüber, H.-J. (1984). Grundfrequenz und spektrale Zusammensetzung der Vokalisation Neugeborener als psychophysikalische Wirkfaktoren. In *Bericht 34. Kongreß der DGfPs.* p. 22

Blarer, S. (1982). Manifestationen einer Geburtskomplikation in Träumen und Phantasien. In Schindler, S. (ed.) *Geburt – Eintritt in eine neue Welt.* Verlag für Psychologie Göttingen, pp. 122–5

Blau, A., Slaff, B., Easton, K., Welkowitz, J., Springham, J. and Cohen, J. (1963). The psychogenic etiology of premature births. *Psychosom. Med.*, **25,** 201–11

Blau, A., Welkowitz, J. and Cohen, J. (1964). Maternal attitude to pregnancy instrument. *Arch. Gen. Psychiatr,* **10,** 324–31

Blechschmidt, E., Göttingen (1983). Personal Communication

Blumberg, B. D. et al. (1975). The psychological sequelae of abortion performed for genetic indication. *Am. J. Obstet. Gynecol.*, **122**(7), 799–808

Bogen, J. E. and Gordon, G. M. (1971). Musical tests for functional lateralization with intracarotid amobarbital. *Nature,* **230,** 524–5

Bohman, M. (1980). Adoptivkinder und Familien, Göttingen

Bonnard, A. (1960). The primal significance of the tongue. *Int. J. Psychoanal.*, **41,** 4–5, 301–7

Booth, P. and Jernberg, A. (1987). *The Marital MIM.* (Chicago: The Theraplay Institute) In Press

Bostock, J. (1958). Exterior gestation, primitive sleep, enuresis and asthma: study in aetiology. *Med. J. Aust.*, **2,** 140–53; 185–8

Bottari, M. and McLaughlin, F. (1984). The relationships of psychological characteristics of pregnancy to postpartum adjustment and maternal perception of the newborn. Paper presented at the *International Conference on Infant Studies,* New York, April 5–8

Bowen, E. M. (1985). *Pre-birth Bonding.* (San Diego, California: Heartstart Lovestart Publications)

Bower, G. H. (1981). Mood and memory. *Am. Psychol.,* **36**(2), 129–48

Bower, T. G. R. (1974). *Development in Infancy.* (San Francisco: W. H. Freeman)

Bower, T. G. R. (1977). *A Primer of Infant Development.* (San Francisco: W. H. Freeman)

Bowlby, J. (1969). *Attachment and Loss.* (New York: Basic Books Inc.)

Bowlby, J. (1969). *Attachment* (Vol. I of Attachment and Loss). (England: Hogarth Press & Inst. of Psychoanal., Pelican Books)

Bowlby, J. (1973). *Separation* (Vol. II of Attachment and Loss). (England: Hogarth Press & Inst. of Psychoanal., Pelican Books)

Bowlby, J. (1980). *Loss, Sadness and Depression* (Vol. III of Attachment and Loss). (London: Hogarth Press & Inst. of Psychoanal.)

Bowlby, J. (1982). Attachment and loss: retrospect and prospect. *Am. J. Orthopsychiatry,* **52**(4), 664–78

Bowlby, J. et al. (1952). *A Two-Year Old Goes to Hospital. Psychoanal. Study of the Child VII.* pp. 82–94. (London: Imago Publishing Co. Ltd.)

Brackbill, Y. and Koltsova, M. M. (1967). Conditioning and learning. In Brackbill, Y. (ed.) *Infancy and Early Childhood.* pp. 207–88. (New York: Free Press)

Bradley, R. M. and Mistretta, C. M. (1975). Fetal sensory receptors. *Physiol. Rev.,* **55,** 352–82

Bradley, R. M. and Stern, L. B. (1967). The development of the human taste bud during the foetal period. *J. Anatomy,* **101,** 743–52

Brazelton, T. B. (1974a). *Neonatal Behavioural Assessment Scale (Clinics in Developmental Medicine,* n. 50). (London: Spastics International Publications, Heinemann)

Brazelton, T. B. (1974b). Mother–infant reciprocity. In Klaus, M., Leger, T. and Trause, M. (eds.) *Maternal Attachments and Mothering Disorders.* (Sausalito, CA: Johnson & Johnson)

Brazelton, T. B. (1984). *Neonatal Behavioural Assessment Scale. Clinics in Developmental Medicine,* 88. (London: Blackwell Scientific Publications)

Brazelton, T. B., Koslowski, B. and Main, M. (1974). The origins of reciprocity: the early mother–infant interaction. In Lewis, M. and Rosenblum, L. (eds.) *The Effect of the Infant on Its Caregiver.* pp. 49–76. (New York: Wiley)

Brenot, M. and Brenot, J.-L. (1984). Ultrasound scanning in obstetrics: a necessary view of the child to be born. In Call, J., Galenson, E. and Tyson,

R. L. (eds.) *Frontiers of Infant Psychiatry.* Vol. II, pp. 176–80. (New York: Basic Books)

Brettes, J. P., Renaud, R. and Gandar, R. (1976). A double-blind investigation into the effects of ritodrine on uterine blood flow during the third trimester of pregnancy. *Am. J. Obstet. Gynecol.,* **124,** 164

Brockbill, Y. (1979). Obstetrical medication and infant behavior. In Osofsky, J. D. (ed.) *Handbook of Infant Development.* (New York: Wiley-Interscience)

Brody, L. R., Zelazo, P. R. and Chaika, H. (1984). Habituation–dishabituation to speech in the neonate. *Dev. Psychol.,* **20**(1), 114–19

Bronfenbrenner, U. (1981). *Die Ökologie der menschlichen Entwicklung.* (Stuttgart)

Broussard, E. R. and Hartner, M. S. S. (1970). Maternal perceptions of the neonate as related to development. *Child Psychiatr. Hum. Dev.,* **1,** 432–99

Brown, J. and Helper, R. (1976). Stimulation – a corollary to physical care. *Am. J. Nursing,* **76,** 4, 578–81

Brown, L. B. (1964). Anxiety in pregnancy. *Br. J. Med. Psychol.,* **37,** 47–58

Brunswick, R. M. (1940). The preoedipal phase of the libido development. In Fliess, R. (ed.) *The Psychoanalytic Reader.* pp. 261–83. (London: Hogarth Press)

Bubenik, G. A. and Brown, G. M. (1973). Morphologic sex differences in primate brain areas involved in regulation of reproductive activity. *Experientia,* **29,** 619–21

Buber, M. (1958). *I and Thou* (1934). (Edinburgh: T. & T. Clark)

Bullowa, M. (1973). When infant and adult communicate, how do they synchronize their behaviors? In Kendon, A., Harris, R. M. and Key, M. R. (eds.) *Organization of Behavior in Face-to face Interaction.* pp. 95–129. (The Hague: Mouton)

Bumgarner, N. J. (1983). *Helping Love Grow: Parenting Adopted Children.* (Franklin Park, Illinois: La Leche League International)

Burlingham, D. and Freud, A. (1942). *Young Children in War-time.* p. 76. (London: Allen & Unwin)

Bustamente, J. A. *et al.* (1970). State dependent learning in humans. *Physiol. Behaviour,* **5,** 793–6

Butterfield, E. C. and Siperstein, G. N. (1974). Influence of contingent auditory stimulation upon non-nutritional suckle. In *Proceedings of the Third Symposium on Oral Sensation and Perception: The Mouth of the Infant.* (Springfield, Illinois: Charles C. Thomas)

Bydlowski, M. (1984). Mother's desire to have a child. *Prog. Reprod. Biol. Med.,* **11,** 132–9

Campbell, S. and Dewhurst, C. J. (1971). Diagnosis of the small-for-dates fetus by serial ultrasonic cephalometry. *Lancet,* **2,** 1002

Campbell, S. et al. (1982). Ultrasound scanning in pregnancy: the short-term psychological effects of early real-time scans. *J. Psychosom. Obstet. Gynecol.* **1**(2), 57–61

Caplan, G. Emotional implications of pregnancy and influences on family relationships. In Stuart, H. C. and Prugh, D. G. (eds.) *The Healthy Child.* (Cambridge, Mass.)

Capra, F. (1987). *The Turning Point: Science, Society and the Rising of Culture.* (London: 1987 Fontana Publishing) (first edn. 1982)

Caraka (1962). *The Carakasmhita of Agniveśa (Sārirasthānam and Cikitsāsthānam).* Revised by Caraka and Drdhabala with commentary by Kashi Nath Pandeya and Gorakh Nath Caturvedi. (Benares: Chowkhamba Vidyabhavan)

Carlson, B. and Labarba, C. (1979). Maternal emotionality during pregnancy and reproductive outcome: a review of the literature. *Intern. J. Behav. Dev.,* **2**

Carlsson, S. G., Fagerberg, H., Horneman, G., Hwang, C. P., Larsson, K., Rodholm, M., Schaller, J., Danielsson, B. and Gundewall, C. (1978). Effects of amount of contact between mother and child on the mother's nursing behavior. *Dev. Psychobiol.,* **11,** 143–50

Carmichael, L. (1933). Origin and prenatal growth of behaviour. In *Handbook of Child Psychology.* (Worcester, Mass.: Clark University)

Carter-Jessop, L. (1981) Promoting maternal attachment through parental intervention. *Am. J. Maternal Child Nursing,* **6,** 2, 107–12

Cassel, Z. K. and Sander, L. W. (1975). Neonatal recognition processes and attachment: the masking experiment. Paper presented to the *Society for Research in Child Development,* Denver, Colorado

Caulfield, C. (1986). *In the Rainforest.* (London: Picardor Pub.)

Cavendish, R. (1984). *Mythology, an Illustrated Encyclopedia.* (London: Orbis)

Ceruti, M. (1985). *La sfida della complessità.* (Milano: Feltrinelli Editore)

Chalmers, B. (1984). Behavioural associations of pregnancy complications. *J. Psychosom. Obstet. Gynecol.,* **3,** 27–35

Chamberlain, D. B. (1981). Birth recall in hypnosis. *Birth Psychol. Bull.,* **2**(2), 14–18

Chamberlain, D. B. (1983). *Consciousness at Birth: a Review of the Empirical Evidence.* Chamberlain Publications: 909 Hayes Ave, San Diego, CA 92103

Chamberlain, D. B. (1987a). *The Mind of the Newborn Baby.* (San Diego: Chamberlain Publications)

Chamberlain, D. (1987b). The cognitive newborn: a scientific update. *Br. J. Psychother.,* **4**(1)

Chann, P. H., Basile, J. P., Navarro, Ch. and Venthroai, N. M. (1980). Cardiovascular activity of a deproteinised blood extract. *Arzheim. Forsch/Drug Res.,* **2,** 30

Charlton, V. and Johengen, M. (1983). Effect of fetal nutritional supplements on growth retardation. *30th SGI Meeting*, Washington DC, abstract 213

Charlton, V. and Rudolph, A. (1979). Digestion and absorption of carbohydrate by the fetal lamb *in utero*. *Pediatr. Res.,* **13,** 1018

Chasseguet-Smirgel, J. (1981). Feminine guilt and the Oedipus complex (1964). In *Female Sexuality: New Psychoanalytic Views*. (London: Virago)

Cheek, D. B. (1974). Sequential head and shoulder movements appearing with age regression in hypnosis to birth. *Am. J. Clin. Hypnosis,* **16**(4), 261–6

Cheek, D. B. (1975). Maladjustment patterns apparently related to imprinting at birth. *Am. J. Clin. Hypnosis,* **18,** 75–82

Cheek, D. B. (1980). Ideomotor questioning revealing an apparently valid traumatic experience prior to birth: a clinical note. *Aust. J. Clin. Exp. Hypnosis,* **8**(2), 65–70

Chervenak, F. A., Farley, M. A., Walters, L., Hobbins, J. C. and Mahoney, M. J. (1984). When is termination of pregnancy during the third trimester morally justifiable? *N. Engl. J. Med.,* **301,** 501–4

Chilik, C. F. *et al.* (1985). The role of *in vitro* fertilization in infertile patients with endometriosis. *Fertil. Steril.,* **44,** 56

Chodorow, N. (1971). Being and doing: a cross-cultural examination of the socialization of males and females. In Gornick and Moran (eds.) *Woman in Sexist Society: Studies in Power and Powerlessness.* Ch. 11. (New York: Basic Books)

Chodorow, N. (1974). Family structure and feminine personality. In Rosaldo and Lamphere (eds.) *Woman, Culture and Society.* pp. 43–66. (Stanford: Stanford University Press)

Chodorow, N. (1978). *The Reproduction of Mothering: Psychoanalysis and the Sociology of Gender.* (Los Angeles: University of California Press)

Chomsky, N. (1965). *Aspects of the Theory of Syntax.* (Cambridge, Mass.: MIT Press)

Clarke, J. I. (1978). *Self-esteem: A Family Affair.* (Minneapolis, Minnesota: Winston Press)

Clauser, G. (1971). *Die vorgeburtliche Entstehung der Sprache als anthropologisches Problem: Der Rhythmus als Organisator der menschlichen Entwicklung.* (Stuttgart: Enke Verlag)

Clercq de, F. S. and Schmelz, J. D. E. (1893). *Ethnographische Beschrejving van de West en Noordkust van Nederlandsch Nieuw-Guinea.* Leiden

Coghi, I. *et al.* (1979). Psychological variables in habitual abortion: a combined diagnostic-therapeutic approach. In Carenza, L. and Zichella, L. (eds.) *Emotion and Reproduction.* 20A, p. 28. (London: Academic Press)

Coghill, G. E. (1929). *Anatomy and the Problem of Behaviour.* (Cambridge)

Cohen, L. B., DeLoache, J. S. and Pearl, R. A. (1971). An examination of the interference effect in infants' memory for faces. *Child Development,* **48,** 88–96

Cohen, R. L. (1966). Some maladaptive syndromes of pregnancy and the puerperium. *Obstet. Gynecol.,* **27,** 562–70

Comparetti, A. M. (1981). The neurophysiologic and clinical implications of studies on fetal motor behavior. *Sem. Perinatol.* **5,** 2, 183–9

Condon, W. S. (1975). Speech makes babies move. In Lewin, R. (ed.) *Child Alive.* (London) (zit. nach R. Schaffer, 1978, p. 77, sowie aus Videofilm *Benjamin*)

Condon, W. S. (1977). A primary phase in the organization of infant responding. In Shaffer, H. R. (ed.) *Studies in Mother–Infant Interaction.* (New York: Academic Press)

Condon, W. S. and Sander, L. W. (1974). Neonate movement is synchronized with adult speech: interactional participation and language acquisition. *Science,* **183,** 99–101

Connolly, J. and Cullen, J. (1983). Maternal stress and the origins of health status. In Call, J., Galenson, E. and Tyson, R. (eds.) *Frontiers of Infant Psychiatry.* pp. 273–81. (New York: Basic Books)

Cook, L. N., Shott, R. J. and Andrews, B. F. (1974). Fetal complications of diagnostic amniocentesis: a review and report of a case with pneumothorax. *Pediatrics,* **53,** 421–4

Corliss, C. E. (1976). *Patten's Human Embryology.* (New York: McGraw Hill)

Crammond, W. A. (1954). Psychological aspects of uterine dysfunction. *Lancet,* **2,** 1241–5

Crandall, B. F. *et al.* (1980). Follow-up of 2000 second-trimester amniocentesis. *Obstet. Gynecol.,* **56,** 625–8

Crandon, A. J. (1979). Maternal anxiety and obstetric complicators. *J. Psych. Res.,* **23,** 109–11

Cranley, Mecca S. (1981a). Development of a tool for the measurement of maternal attachment during pregnancy. *Nursing Res.,* **30,** 5

Cranley, Mecca S. (1981b). Roots of attachment: the relationship of parents with their unborn. *Birth Defects: Original Article Series.,* Vol. XVII, No. 6 pp. 59–83

Cronewett, L. R. and Newmark, L. (1974). Fathers' responses to childbirth. *Nursing Res.,* **23,** 210–17

Crovitz, H. F. and Harvey, M. T. (1979). Early childhood amnesia: a quantitative study with implications for the study of retrograde amnesia after brain injury. *Cortex,* **15,** 331–5

Daly, M. (1978). *Gyn/Ecology: the Metaethics of Radical Feminism.* (London: Women's Press)

Dantchakoff, V. (1938). Role des hormones dans la manifestation des instincts sexuels. *Compt. Rend. Acad. Sci.,* **206,** 945–7

Dash, B. and Kashyap, L. (1980). *Basic Principles of Āyurveda*. (Delhi: Concept Publishing Company)

Davids. A. and De Vault, S. (1962). Maternal anxiety during pregnancy and childbirth abnormalities. *Psychosom. Med.,* **24,** 464–70

Dawes, G. S. (1973). Revolutions and cyclical rhythms in prenatal life: fetal respiratory movements rediscovered. *Pediatrics,* **51,** 965–71

De Casper, A. and Fifer, W. (1980). Of human bonding: newborns prefer their mother's voices. *Science,* **208,** 1174–6

De Casper, A. and Spence, M. (1982). Prenatal maternal speech influences human newborn's auditory preferences. Paper presented at *3rd Biennial International Conference on Infant Studies,* Austin, Texas

De Casper, A. J. and Spence, M. J. (1986). Prenatal maternal speech influences newborn's perception of speech sounds. *Infant Behav. Development,* **9,** 133–50

De Chateau, P. (1976). The influence of early contact on maternal and infant behavior in primiparae. *Birth Fam. J.,* **3,** 154–5

De Chateau, P. and Wiberg, B. (1984). Three-year follow-up of early postpartum contact. In Call, J. D. et al., (eds.) *Frontiers of Infant Psychiatry.* Vol. II, pp. 313–22. (New York: Basic Books)

Degan, S. and Kurjak, A. (1982). Medico-legal aspects of antenatally detected malformed fetuses. *J. Perinat. Med.,* **10** (Suppl. 2: Progress in Perinatal Medicine 2, 2nd International Berlin Meeting of Perin. Med. 81)

De Lacoste-Utamsing, C. and Holloway, R. L. (1982). Sexual dimorphism in the human corpus callosum. *Science,* **216,** 1431–2

Del Carlo Giannini, G., Del Papa, M. and Ceccarelli, P. (1981). L'esperienza di gravidanza. *Età Evolitiva,* **10,** 93–9

De Lisi, L. (1957). Biologia ed estetica della motilità costituzionale dell'uomo. *Sistema Nervoso,* n. 6

De Lisi, L. (1958). Le posizioni di riposo nell'uomo con particolare riferimento all'arte. *Sistema Nervoso,* n. 1

De Mause, L. (1974). *The History of Childhood.* (New York: Psychohistory Press)

De Muylder, X. (1986). Attitudes maternelles en cas de travail prématuré. *Memoire de License on Sexologie,* Université de Louvain

Denenberg, V. H. (1964). Critical periods, stimulus input, and emotional reactivity: a theory of infantile stimulation. *Psychol. Rev.,* **71,** 335–51

DeRohan, C. (1984). *Right Use of Will: Healing and Evolving the Emotional Body.* (One World Publications, 110 Dartmouth SE, Albuquerque, NM 87106)

Deutsch, H. (1954). *Psychologie der Frau.* Vol. 2. (Bern/Stuttgart)

DFG-Bericht. (1977). *Schwangerschaftsverlauf und Kindesentwicklung.* (Deutsche Forschungsgemeinschaft), Boppard

Diagenes of Apollonia: See Diels
Dicks, H. V. (1963). Object relations theory and marital studies. *Br. J. Med. Psychol.,* **36,** 125–9
Diocles of Carystus: See Allbutt
Diels, H. (1906, 1922). *Fragmente der Vorsokratiker.* (Berlin)
Dobson, J. F. (1925). Herophilus. *Proc. R. Soc. Med.* (History of Med. Sect), **18,** 19
Dobson, J. F. (1927). Erasistratus. *Proc. R. Soc. Med.* (History of Med. Sect.) **20,** 49
Dodd, B. (1979). Lip-reading in infants: attention to speech presented in and out of synchrony. *Cognitive Psychol.,* **11,** 478–84
Donald, I. (1959). *Practical Obstetric Problems.* 2nd edn. (London: Lloyd-Luke Ltd.)
Dorman, R. and Olds, D. (1983). Antepartum worries as predictors of maternal care giving and perceptions of infant temperament during the first year of life. Paper presented at the meeting of the *American Psychological Association,* Anaheim, CA
Dörner, G. (1967). Tierexperimentelle Untersuchungen zur Frage einer hormonellen Pathogenese der Homosexualität. *Acta Biol. Med Germ.,* **19,** 569–84
Dörner, G. (1968). Hormonal induction and prevention of female homosexuality. *J. Endocrinol.,* **42,** 163–4
Dörner, G. (1969). Die Bedeutung der sexualhormonabhängigen Hypothalamusdifferenzierung für die Gonadenfunktion und das Sexualverhalten. *Acta Biol. Med. Germ.,* **23,** 709–12
Dörner, G. (1970). The influence of sex hormones during the hypothalamic differentiation and maturation phases on gonadal function and sexual behaviour during the hypothalamic functional phase. *Endokrinologie,* **56,** 280–91
Dörner, G. (1972). *Sexualhormonabhängige Gehirndifferenzierung und Sexualität.* (Jena: VEB Gustav Fischer Verlag und Wien/New York: Springer Verlag)
Dörner, G. (1973a). Zur Bedeutung prä- oder perinataler Umweltsbedingungen für die postnatale Regelung neuroendokriner Systeme. *Endokrinologie,* **61,** 107–23
Dörner, G. (1973b). Die mögliche Bedeutung der prä- und/oder perinatalen Ernährung für die Pathogenese der Obesitas. *Acta Biol. Med. Germ.,* **30** K19–K22
Dörner, G. (1974). Environment-dependent brain differentiation and fundamental processes of life. *Acta Biol. Med. Germ.,* **33,** 129–48
Dörner, G. (1975a). Perinatal hormone levels and brain organization. In Stumpf, W. E. and Grant, L. D. (eds.) *Anatomical Neuroendocrinology.*

pp. 245–52. (Basel, München, Paris, London, New York, Sydney: S. Karger)
Dörner, G. (1975b). Problems and terminology of functional teratology. *Acta Biol. Med. Germ.,* **34,** 1093–5
Dörner, G. (1976a). *Hormones and Brain Differentiation.* (Amsterdam, New York: Elsevier Scientific Publishing)
Dörner, G. (1976b). Further evidence of permanent behavioural changes in rats treated neonatally with neurodrugs. *Endokrinologie,* **68,** 345–8
Dörner, G. (1978a). Über den Einfluß der frühpostnatalen Ernährung auf die Körpergröße im Adoleszentenalter. *Acta Biol. Med. Germ.,* **37,** 1149–51
Dörner, G. (1978b). Hormones, brain development and fundamental processes of life. In Dörner, G. and Kawakami, M. (eds.) *Hormones and Brain Development. Developments in Endocrinology.* Vol. 3, pp. 13–25. (Amsterdam, New York, Oxford: Elsevier/North-Holland Biomedical Press)
Dörner, G. (1980a). Hormone und Gehirndifferenzierung. *Leopoldina,* (R. 3), 22. 1976, 93–101
Dörner, G. (1980b). Die Ontogenese des neuroendokrinen Systems als kinetischer Prozeß. *Nova Acta Leopoldina Neue Folge,* 51 Nr. 237, 279–91
Dörner, G.; unter Mitarbeit von Döcke, F., Geier, T., Götz, F., Hinz, G., Poppe, I., Rohde, W., Stahl, F. and Tönjes, R. (1982a). Zur Bedeutung von Systemhormonen und Neurotransmittern als Organisatoren des Gehirns. *Charité-Annalen Neue Folge,* **2,** 168–74
Dörner, G. (1982b). Zur Entwicklung der Stillhäufigkeit und der Gewichtszunahme im ersten postnatalen Lebenstrimenon. *Dtsch. Gesundh. Wesen.,* **37,** 389–92
Dörner, G. (1985a). Sex-specific gonadotrophin secretion, sexual orientation and gender role behaviour. *Exp. Clin. Endocrinol.* **86,** 1–6
Dörner, G. (1985b). Hormone und ihre Wirkungen. In Meng, W., Knappe, G. and Dabels, J. (eds.) *Klinische Endokrinologie.* p. 16. (Jena: VEB Gustav Fischer Verlag)
Dörner, G. (1986). Hormones, brain development and preventive medicine. In Dörner, G., McCann, S. M. and Martini, L. (eds.) *Systemic Hormones, Neurotransmitters and Brain Development.* (Basel: Karger)
Dörner, G., Bluth, R. and Tönjes, R. (1982). Acetylcholine concentrations in the developing brain appear to affect emotionality and mental capacity in later life. *Acta Biol. Med. Germ.,* **41,** 721–3
Dörner, G., Döcke, F. and Hinz, G. (1968). Entwicklung und Rückbildung neuroendokrin bedingter männlicher Homosexualität. *Acta Biol. Med. Germ.,* **21,** 577–80
Dörner, G., Döcke, F. and Hinz, G. (1969). Homo- and hypersexuality in rats with hypothalamic lesions. *Neuroendocrinology,* **4,** 20–4

Dörner, G., Döcke, F. and Hinz, G. (1971). Paradoxical effects of estrogen on brain differentiation. *Neuroendocrinology,* **7,** 146–55

Dörner, G., Döcke, F. and Moustafa, S. (1968a). Homosexuality in female rats following testosterone implantation in the anterior hypothalamus. *J. Reprod. Fertil.,* **17,** 173–5

Dörner, G., Döcke, F. and Moustafa, S. (1968b). Differential localization of a male and a female hypothalamic mating centre. *J. Reprod. Fertil.,* **17,** 583–6

Dörner, G. and Fatschel, J. (1970). Wirkungen neonatal verabreichter Androgene und Antiandrogene auf Sexualverhalten und Fertilität von Rattenweibchen. *Endokrinologie,* **56,** 29–48

Dörner, G., Geier, T., Ahrens, L., Krell, L., Münx, G., Sieler, H., Kittner, E. and Müller, H. (1980). Prenatal stress as possible aetiogenetic factor of homosexuality in human males. *Endokrinologie,* **75,** 365–8

Dörner, G., Götz, F. and Döcke, W. D. (1983). Prevention of demasculinization and feminization of the brain in prenatally stressed male rats by perinatal androgen treatment. *Exp. Clin. Endocrinol.,* **81,** 88–90

Dörner, G. and Grychtolik, H. (1973). Zur Bedeutung frühpostnataler Umwelteinflüsse für die spätpostnatale Lernfähigkeit von Kindern. *Acta Biol. Med. Germ.,* **31,** K53–K56

Dörner, G. and Grychtolik, H. (1978). Long-lasting ill-effects of neonatal qualitative and/or quantitative dysnutrition in the human. *Endokrinologie,* **71,** 81–8

Dörner, G., Grychtolik, H. and Julitz, M. (1977). Überernährung in den ersten drei Lebensmonaten als entscheidender Risikofaktor für die Entwicklung von Fettsucht und ihrer Folgeerkrankungen. *Dtsch. Gesundh. Wesen,* **32,** 6–9

Dörner, G., Hagen, N. and Witthuhn, W. (1976). Die frühpostnatale Überernährung als ätiopathogenetischer Faktor der Erwachsenenfettsucht. *Acta Biol. Med. Germ.,* **35,** 799–803

Dörner, G., Haller, H. and Leonhardt, W. (1973). Zur möglichen Bedeutung der prä- und/oder frühpostnatalen Ernährung für die Pathogenese der Arteriosklerose. *Acta Biol. Med. Germ.,* **31,** K31–K35

Dörner, G., Hecht, K. and Hinz, G. (1976). Teratopsychogenetic effects apparently produced by nonphysiological neurotransmitter concentrations during brain differentiation. *Endokrinologie,* **68,** 1–5

Dörner, G. and Hinz, G. (1967). Homosexuality of neonatally castrated male rats following androgen substitution in adulthood. *Germ. Med. Mon.,* **12,** 281–3

Dörner, G. and Hinz, G. (1968). Induction and prevention of male homosexuality by androgen. *J. Endocrinol.,* **40,** 387–8

Dörner, G. and Hinz, G. (1971). Männlicher Hypogonadismus mit sekundärer Hyposexualität nach hochdosierten Gaben von Östrogenen während der hypothalamischen Differenzierungsphase. *Endokrinologie*, **58**, 227–33

Dörner, G. and Hinz, G. (1978). Apparent effects of neurotransmitters on sexual differentiation of the brain without mediation of sex hormones. *Endokrinologie*, **71**, 104–8

Dörner, G., Hinz, G., Döcke, F. and Tönjes, R. (1977a). Effects of psychotrophic drugs on brain differentiation in female rats. *Endokrinologie*, **70**, 113–23

Dörner, G., Hinz, G. and Stahl, F. (1972). In Dörner, G. (ed.) *Sexualhormonabhängige Gehirndifferenzierung und Sexualität*. pp. 153–6. (Jena: VEB Gustav Fischer Verlag und Wien/New York: Springer Verlag)

Dörner, G., Krell, L. and Ahrens, L. (1978). Pre- and early postnatal testosterone levels in rat and human. In Dörner, G. and Kawakami, M. (eds.) *Hormones and Brain Development. Developments in Endocrinology*. Vol. 3, p. 106. (Amsterdam, New York, Oxford: Elsevier/North-Holland Biomedical Press)

Dörner, G. and Mohnike, A. (1973). Zur möglichen Bedeutung der prä- und/oder frühpostnatalen Ernährung für die Pathogenese des Diabetes mellitus. *Acta Biol. Med. Germ.*, **31**, K7–K10

Dörner, G. and Mohnike, A. (1976). Further evidence for a predominantly maternal transmission of maturity-onset type diabetes. *Endokrinologie*, **68**, 121–4

Dörner, G. and Mohnike, A. (1977). Zur Bedeutung der perinatalen Überernährung für die Pathogenese der Fettsucht und des Diabetes mellitus. *Dtsch. Gesundh. Wesen*, **32**, 2325–8

Dörner, G., Mohnike, A., Honigmann, D., Singer, P. and Padelt, H. (1973). Zur möglichen Bedeutung eines pränatalen Hyperinsulinismus für die postnatale Entwicklung eines Diabetes mellitus. *Endokrinologie*, **61**, 430–2

Dörner, G., Mohnike, A. and Steindel, E. (1975). On possible genetic and epigenetic modes of diabetes transmission. *Endokrinologie*, **66**, 225–7

Dörner, G., Mohnike, A. and Thoelke, H. (1984). Further evidence for the dependence of diabetes prevalence on nutrition in perinatal life. *Exp. Clin. Endocrinol.*, **84**, 129–33

Dörner, G., Plaschke, M., Tönjes, R. and Wenzel, J. (1984a). Teratomorphogenic effects on the brain produced by neonatal maternal deprivation can be partly prevented by pyridostigmine administration. *Exp. Clin. Endocrinol.*, **84**, 352–5

Dörner, G., Rohde, W. and Krell, L. (1972). Auslösung eines positiven Östrogenfeedback-Effekt bei homosexuellen Männern. *Endokrinologie*, **60**, 297–301

Dörner, G., Rohde, W., Stahl, F., Krell, L. and Masius, W. G. (1975). A neuroendocrine predisposition for homosexuality in men. *Arch. Sex. Behav.,* **4,** 1–8

Dörner, G., Schenk, B., Schmiedel, B. and Ahrens, L. (1983). Stressful events in prenatal life of bi- and homosexual men. *Exp. Clin. Endocrinol.,* **81,** 83–7

Dörner, G. and Seidler, C. (1971). Einfluß hochdosierter perinataler Androgengaben auf Sexualverhalten, Gonadotropinsekretion und Geschlechtsorgane der Ratte. *Zbl. Gynäk.,* **93,** 777–89

Dörner, G. and Staudt, J. (1968). Structural changes in the preoptic anterior hypothalamic area of the male rat, following neonatal castration and androgen substitution. *Neuroendocrinology,* **3,** 136–40

Dörner, G. and Staudt, J. (1969). Structural changes in the hypothalamic ventromedial nucleus of the male rat, following neonatal castration and androgen treatment. *Neuroendocrinology,* **4,** 278–81

Dörner, G., Staudt, J., Wenzel, J., Kvetňanský, R. and Murgaš, K. (1977b). Further evidence of teratogenic effects apparently produced by neurotransmitters during brain differentiation. *Endokrinologie,* **70,** 326–30

Dörner, G., Steindel, E., Kohlhoff, R., Reiher, H., Anders, B., Verlohren, H. J. and Heilscher, K. (1985). Further evidence for a preventive therapy of insulin-dependent diabetes mellitus in the offspring by avoiding maternal hyperglycemia during pregnancy. *Exp. Clin. Endocrinol.,* **86,** 129–40

Dörner, G., Steindel, E., Thoelke, H. and Schliack, V. (1984). Evidence for decreasing prevalence of diabetes mellitus in childhood apparently produced by prevention of hyperinsulinism in the foetus and newborn. *Exp. Clin. Endocrinol.,* **84,** 134–42

Dörner, G., Tönjes, R., Hecht, K., Hinz, G., Poppe, I., Poppei, M. and Tsamaloukas, A. (1981). Pyridostigmine administration in newborn rats prevents permanent mental ill-effects produced by maternal deprivation. *Endokrinologie,* **77,** 101–4

Douglas, J. W. B. (1975). Early hospital admissions and later disturbances of behaviour and learning. *Dev. Med. Child. Neurol.,* **17,** 456–80

Dröscher, V. (1984). *Nestwärme.* (München)

Dubowitz, L. M. S., Dubowitz, V., Morante, A. and Verghote, M. (1980). Visual function in the preterm and fullterm newborn infant. *Dev. Med. Child. Neurol.,* **22,** 465–75

Dunn, J. B. and Richards, M. P. (1977). Observations on the developing relationship between mother and baby in the neonatal period. In Scaffer (ed). *Studies in Mother–Infant interaction.* (London: Academic Press)

Durrell, D. (1984). *The Critical Years.* (Oakland, California: New Harbinger Publications)

Duxbury, M. and Thiessen, V. (1979). Staff nurse turnover in neonatal intensive care units. *J. Advanced Nursing,* **4,** 591–602

Dyck, A. J. (1971). Ethical issues in community and research medicine. *N. Engl. J. Med.,* **284,** 724

Edwards, K. R. and Jones, M. R. (1970). Personality changes related to pregnancy and obstetric complications. *Proc. 78th Ann. Conven. Am. Psychol. Assoc.,* 341

Edwards, M. and Simkin, P. *Obstetric Tests and Technology: A Consumer Guide*

Ehrhardt, A. A., Evers, K. and Money, J. (1968). Influence of androgen and some aspects of sexually dimorphic behaviour in women with the late-treated adrenogenital syndrome. *Johns Hopkins Med. J.,* **123,** 115–22

Eisenberg, R. B. (1969). Auditory behavior in the human neonate: functional properties of sound and their ontogenic implications. *Int. Audiology,* **8,** 34–45

Eisenberg, R. B. (1979). Discussion comment on L. P. Lipsitt, The pleasures and annoyances of infants. In Thoman (ed.) *Origins of the Infant's Social Responsiveness.* p. 151. (Hillsdale, N. J.: Erlbaum Associates)

Eisenberg, R. B. and Marmarou, A. (1981). Behavioral reactions of newborns to speech-like sounds and their implications for developmental studies. *Infant Mental Health J.,* **2,** 129–38

Ekins, P. (ed.) (1986). *The Living Economy: A New Economics in the Making.* (London: Routledge and Kegan Paul)

Elias, S. and Esterly, N. (1981). Prenatal diagnosis of hereditary skin disorders. *Clin. Obstet. Gynecol.,* **24,** 1069–87

Ellinger, T. U. H. (1922). *Hippocrates on Intercourse and Pregnancy.* (New York: Schuman)

Empedocles of Acragas: See Diels

Endres, M. (1987). Psychologische Aspekte genetischer Beratung in der pränatalen Diagnostik. In Murken, M. (ed.) *Pränatale Diagnostik und Therapie.* (Stuttgart: Enke)

Engel, G. L. and Schmale, A. H. (1972). Conservation-withdrawal: a primary regulatory process for organismic homeostasis. *Ciba Foundation Symposium.* 8, pp. 57–85. New Series (Amsterdam: Elsevier-Excerpta Medica, N. Holland)

English, J. B. (1985). *Different Doorway: Adventures of a Caesarean Born.* (Point Reyes Station, CA: Earth Heart)

Epicurus: See Plutarch and Allbutt

Eraristratus of Chios: See Dobson

Erlinghauser, R. F. (1959). *Year Book of Academy of Applied Osteopathy.* pp. 77–87

Escalona, S. K. (1973). See Neumann, 1983

Fagley, N., Miller, P. and Sullivan, J. (1982). Stress, symptom and general adapational distress during pregnancy. *J. Hum. Stress*, **8,** 15–22

Falzeder, E. (1984). Die 'Sprachverwirrung' und die 'Grundstörung'. Die Untersuchungen Sandor Ferenczis und Michael Balints über Entstehung und Auswirkungen früher Objektbeziehungen. Salzburg, Phil. Diss.

Farber, E. A., Vaughan, B. and Egeland, B. (1981). The relationship of prenatal maternal behavior and mother–infant interactions during the first six months of life. *Early Hum. Dev.,* **5,** 267–77

Feder, L. (1980). Preconceptive ambivalence and external reality. *Int. J. Psycho-Analysis,* **61,** 161–78

Fedor-Freybergh, P. G. (1974). Hormone therapy in psychiatry: a historical survey. In Itil, T. M., Laudahn, G. and Herrmann, W. M. (eds.) *Psychotropic Action of Hormones.* (New York: Spectrum Publications)

Fedor-Freybergh, P. G. (1983). Psychophysische Gegebenheiten der Perinatalzeit als Umwelt des Kindes. In Schindler, S. and Zimprich, H. (eds.) *Ökologie der Perinatalzeit.* (Stuttgart: Hippokrates Verlag)

Fedor-Freybergh, P. G. (1985). The biochemistry of bonding. Paper presented at the Second International Congress of the Pre- and Perinatal Psychology Association of North America, San Diego, California

Fedor-Freybergh, P. G. (ed.) (1987). *Pränatale und Perinatale Psychologie und Medizin: Begegnung mit dem Ungeborenen.* (Munich: Saphir)

Feher, L. (1980). *The Psychology of Birth: The Foundation of Human Personality.* (London: Condor Book, Souvenir Press)

Ferber, L. V. (1975). Die Sprachsoziologie als eine Forschungsmethode in der Medizinsoziologie. In Blohmke, M. et al. (ed.) *Handbuch der Sozialmedizin.* Vol. 1, Grundlagen und Methoden der Sozialmedizin. pp. 317–26. (Stuttgart: Enke)

Ferenczi, S. (1913). Die Entwicklungsstufen des Wirklichkeitssinns. *Int. Z. Ärztl. Psychoanalyse,* **1,** 124–38

Ferenczi, S. (1913). Stages in the development of the sense of reality. In *First Contributions to Psycho-Analysis.* Ch. 8. (London: Maresfield Reprints, 1952)

Ferenczi, S. (1929). The unwelcome child and his death instinct. In *Final Contributions to the Problems and Methods of Psycho-Analysis.* Chap. 9. (London: Maresfield reprints, 1955)

Ferenczi, S. and Rank, O. (1924). Entwicklungsziele der Psychoanalyse. *Int. Psychoanal. Verlag Leipzig*

Ferreira, A. J. (1960). The pregnant woman's emotional attitude and its reflection on the newborn. *Am. J. Orthopsychiatr.,* **30,** 553–61

Ferreira, A. J. (1965). Emotional factors in prenatal environment: a review. *J. Nerv. Ment. Dis.,* **141,** 108–17

Field, T. M. (1979). Interaction patterns of pre-term and term infants. In

Field, T. M. (ed.) *Infants Born at Risk*. Ch. 17, pp. 333–56. (London, New York: Sp. Medical & Scientific Books)

Field, T. M., Sostek, A. M., Vietzke, P. and Leidermann, P. H. (eds.) (1981). *Culture and Early Interactions*. (Hilldale, NJ: Lawrence Erlbaum Associates)

Field, T. M., Woodson, R., Greenberg, R. and Cohen, D. (1982). Discrimination and imitation of facial expressions by neonates. *Science,* **218,** 179–81

Fijalkowski, W. (1983). Wann beginnt der Dialog mit dem Kind? In Schindler, S. and Zimprich, H. (eds.) *Ökologie der Perinatalzeit*. (Stuttgart: Hippokrates)

Fitzardinge, P. and Stevens, E. (1972). Small for dates. II. Neurological and intellectual sequelae. *Pediatrics,* **50,** 50

Fletcher, J. (1972). The brink: the parent–child bond in the genetic revolution. *Technological Studies,* **33,** 457–85

Fletcher, J. C. (1975). Moral and ethical problems of prenatal diagnosis. *Clin. Generalist,* **8,** 251

Fletcher, J. (1983). Sounding boards: maternal bonding in early fetal ultrasound examinations. *N. Engl. J. Med.,* Feb. 17

Fodor, N. (1949a). The trauma of bearing. *Psych. Q.,* **23,** 59–70

Fodor, N. (1949b). *The Search for the Beloved. A Clinical Investigation of the Trauma of Birth and Prenatal Condition*. (New York: University Books)

Forest, M. C. and David, M. (1984). Prenatal treatment of congenital adrenal hyperplasia (CAH) due to 21-hydroxylase deficiency. p. 716 (Abstract 911). *Internat. Congr. Series 652*. (Amsterdam, Oxford, Princeton: Excerpta Medica)

Fraiberg, S., Adelson, E. and Shapiro, V. (1975). Ghosts in the nursery. *J. Am. Acad. Child Psychiatr.,* **14,** 387–421

Franková, S. (1970). Behavioural responses of rats to early overnutrition. *Nutr. Metab.,* **12,** 228–39

Freeman, J. M. (ed.) (1985). *Prenatal and Perinatal Factors Associated with Brain Disorders*. (Washington: Nat. Inst. Health)

Freidson, E. (1975). *Dominanz der Experten*. (München: Urban & Schwarzenberg)

Fresco, N. and Silvestre, D. (1982). The medical child: comments on prenatal diagnosis. *J. Psychosom. Obstet. Gynecol.,* **1,** 3–8

Freud, A. (1967). About losing and being lost. *Psychoanalytic Study of the Child,* **22,** pp. 9–19. (New York: Int. Univ. Press)

Freud, A. (1971). Problems of termination in child analysis. In *The Writings of Anna Freud*, Vol. VII, Ch. 1. (New York: Int. Univ. Press)

Freud, S. (1900). Die Traumdeutung. In Freud, S. *Studienausgabe,* Vol. II. 1972 Edn. (Frankfurt: Fischer)

Freud, S. (1908). *On the Sexual Theories of Children.* 1971 Standard Edn. IX, pp. 207–26. (London: Hogarth Press & Inst. of Psycho-Anal.)

Freud, S. (1917). Vorlesungen zur Einführung in die Psychoanalyse. In Freud, S., GW XII. 1944 Edn. (Frankfurt: Fischer)

Freud, S. (1917). The Libido Theory and Narcissism. *Introductory Lectures on Psycho-Analysis.* XXVI, pp. 412–30. 1963 Standard Edn. XVI. (London: Hogarth Press & Inst. of Psycho-Anal.)

Freud, S. (1920). Beyond the pleasure principle. 1953–74 Standard Edn. Vol. 18, p. 1 (London: Hogarth Press)

Freud, S. (1921). Massenpsychologie und Ich-Analyse. In Freud, S. GW XIII. 1940 Edn. (Frankfurt: Fischer)

Freud, S. (1926). *Inhibitions, Symptoms and Anxiety.* Vol. XX. 1971 Standard Edn. (London: Hogarth Press)

Freud, S. (1928). *The Future of an Illusion.* Vol. XXI. 1971 Standard Edition. (London: Hogarth Press)

Freud, S. (1930). *Civilization and Its Discontents.* Vol XXI. 1971 Standard Edn. (London: Hogarth Press)

Freud, S. and Breuer, J. (1895). *Studien über Hysterie.* 1970 Edn. (Frankfurt: Fischer)

Freud, W. E. (1975). Infant observation: its relevance to psychoanalytic training. *Psychoanalytic Study of the Child.* Vol. 30, pp. 75–94. (New Haven, London: Yale University Press)

Freud, W. E. (1980). Notes on some psychological aspects of neonatal intensive care. In Greenspan, S. I. and Pollock, G. H. (eds.) *The Course of Life: Psychoanalytic Contributions Towards Understanding Personality Development.* Vol. I, pp. 257–69. (Adelphi, Maryland: US Govt. Printing Office, NIMH)

Freud, W. E. and Freud, I. (1976). The well-baby clinic. *Child Psychiatr. Hum. Dev.,* **7**, 2, 67–84

Fryman, U. M. (1976). Trauma of birth. *Osteopathic Ann.,* **4**, 22–31

Fthenakis, W. E. (1984). Die Vaterrolle in der neueren Familienforschung. *Psychologie in Erziehung und Unterricht,* **31**, 1–21

Fthenakis, W. E. (1985). *Väter.* Vol. 1: Zur Psychologie der Vater–Kind–Beziehung. Vol. 2: Zur Vater–Kind–Beziehung in verschiedenen Familienstrukturen. (München, Wien, Baltimore: Urban & Schwarzenberg)

Galen of Pergamos (1924). *On the Natural Faculties.* Ed. and tr. by Brock, A. W. Leob Classics. (London: Heinemann)

Gardner, H. (1983). *Frames of Mind: The Theory of Multiple Intelligences.* (New York: Basic Books)

General Register Office (GRO) (1951). *Classification of Occupations.* (London: Her Majesty's Stationary Office)

Gesell, A. and Ilg, F.L. (1965). *Infant and Child in the Culture of Today.* (London: Hamilton)

Gidoni, E.A., Fantini, M.L. and Noferi, S. (1983). La crisi puberale nella ricapitolazione dei vissuti dei genitori di figli handicappati. *Convegno Nazionale di Auxologia Sociale,* Montecatini Terme, 5–6 novembre

Gladue, B.A., Green, R. and Hellman, R.E. (1984). Neuroendocrine response to estrogen and sexual orientation. *Science,* **225,** 1496–9

Gloger-Tippelt, G. (1984). Der Übergang zur Elternschaft. Eine entwicklungspsychologische Analyse. *Zeitschrift für Entwicklungspsychologie,* **4,** 53–92

Gloger-Tippelt, G. (1985). Kongreßbericht 34. Kongreß DGFPs, pp. 432–5

Golanska, Z. and Borkowski, W. (1985). The first contacts between mother and child: its importance for further development of premature infant. *XXV Congr. Pol. Soc. Ob & Gyn.,* Kraków, Sept. 1985, Abstract 155

Golard, R.S. et al. (1981). Human plasma beta-endorphin during pregnancy, labor and delivery. *JCEM,* **52**(1), 74–8

Golbus, M.S., Conte, F.A. et al. (1974). Intrauterine diagnosis of genetic defects: results, problems and follow-up of one hundred cases in a prenatal genetic detection center. *Am. J. Obstet. Gynecol.,* **118**(7), 897–905

Goldberg, S. (1983). Parent–infant bonding. another look. *Child Dev.,* **54,** 1355–82

Gonzales, A.W.A. (1929). *Anat. Rec.,* **42,** 17

Gonzales, A.W.A. (1930). *Proc. Soc. Exp. Biol. Med.,* **27,** 579

Goodlin, R.C. (1979). *Care of the Fetus.* (New York: Masson Publishing)

Goodlin, R.C. and Clewell, W.H. (1974). Sudden death following diagnostic amniocentesis. *Am. J. Obstet. Gynecol.,* **118,** 285–8

Gordon, H. (1979). *Mayo Clinic, The People's Doctor Newsletter,* **3**(11), 3

Gorsuch, R.L. and Key, M.K. (1974). Abnormalities of pregnancy as a function of anxiety and life stress. *Psychosom. Med.,* **36,** 352–62

Goshen-Gottstein, E. (1969). *Marriage and First Pregnancy.* (London: Tavistock Publication Limited)

Gottlieb, G. (1971). Ontogenesis of sensory function in birds and mammals. In Tobach, E., Aronson, L.R. and Shaw, E. (eds.) *The Biopsychology of Development,* pp. 67–128. (New York, London: Academic Press)

Gotz, F. and Dörner, G. (1980). Homosexual behaviour in prenatally stressed male rats after castration and oestrogen treatment in adulthood. *Endokrinologie,* **76,** 115–17

Graber, G.H. (1924). *Die Ambivalenz des Kindes.* (Wien: Int. Psychoanal. Verlag)

Graber, G.H. (1966). *Die Not des Lebens und ihre Überwindung.* (Bern, Düsseldorf: Ardschuna)

Graber, G. H. (1967). Zur Analyse der geburtstraumatisch und total-regressiv bedingten Urwiderstände. *Jb. Psychol., Psychother. med. Anthropol.,* **15,** 243–7

Graber, G. H. and Kruse, F. (1973). *Vorgeburtliches Seelenleben.* (München: Wilhelm Goldmann Verlag)

Graffar, M. (1960). Social studies of samples. *Mod. Probl. Pädiat.,* **5,** 30–42

Graves, P. L. (1980). The functioning fetus. In Greenspan, S. I. and Pollock, G. H. (eds.) *The Course of Life: Psychoanalytic Contributions Toward Understanding Personality Development.* Vol. I, pp. 235–56. (Adelphi, Maryland: NIMH)

Graves, R. (1979). Introduction in *New Larousse Encyclopedia of Mythology.* (London: Hamlyn)

Graves, R. and Patei, R. (1964). *Hebrew Myths, the Book of Genesis.* (London: Cassel)

Greenacre, P. (1945): The biological economy of birth. In *Psychoanalytic Study of the Child.* Vol. I, pp. 31–52. (London: Imago Publishing Co. Ltd.)

Greenacre, P. (1953). *Trauma, Growth and Personality.* (London: Hogarth Press & Inst. of Psycho-Anal.)

Greenberg, M. and Morris, N. (1974). Engrossment: The newborn's impact upon the father. *Am. J. Orthopsychiatr.,* **44,** 520–31

Greenson, R. (1967). *Technik und Praxis der Psychoanalyse.* Vol. I. (Stuttgart: Klett)

Greenson, R. (1968). Dis-identifying from mother: its special importance for the boy. *Int. J. Psycho-Anal.,* **49,** 370–4

Greer, G. (1985). *Sex and Destiny: the Politics of Human Fertility.* (London: Picador)

Grier, J. B., Counter, S. A. and Shearer, W. M. (1967). Prenatal auditory imprinting in chickens. *Science,* **155,** 1692–3

Grimes, L., McRae, J., Peterson, G. and Mehl, L. (1981). Psychophysiological risk factor screening. *Birth Psychol. Bull.*

Grimm, E. (1961). Psychological tension in pregnancy. *Psychosom. Med.,* **23,** 520–7

Grinker, R. and Walsh, F. (1978). Concurrent grandparent death and birth of schizophrenic offspring: an intriguing finding. *Family Process,* **17,** 141

Groddeck, G. (1926). Das Buch vom Es. 2. Aufl., pp. 42–4. (Leipzig: Int. Psychoanalytischer Verlag)

Groeben, N. and Scheele, B. (1977). Argumente für eine Psychologie des reflexiven Subjekts. Darmstadt

Grof, S. (1975). *Realms of the Human Unconscious.* (New York: Viking Press)

Grof, S. (1976). *Realms of the Human Unconscious.* (New York: E. P. Dutton)

Grof, S. (1985). *Beyond the Brain, Death and Transcendence in Psychotherapy.* (Albany, NY: State University of New York, Press)

Gross, W. (1982). Was erlebt ein Kind im Mutterleib? Ergebnisse und Folgerungen der pränatalen Psychologie. (Freiburg: Herder Verlag)

Grossmann, K. (1978). Die Wirkung des Augenöffnens von Neugeborenen auf das Verhalten ihrer Mütter. *Geburtsh. u. Frauenheilkunde,* **38,** 629–35

Grundy, F. and Lewis-Fanning, E. (1957). Morbidity and mortality in the first year of life. (Cardiff: Eugenics Soc.)

Gunter, L. (1963). Psychopathology and stress in the life experience of mothers of premature infants. A comparative study. *Am. J. Obstet. Gynecol.,* **86,** 333–40

Hadlock, F. P., Dieter, R. L., Carpenter, R. et al. (1981). Sonography of fetal urinary tract anomalies. *Am. J. Radiol.,* **137,** 261–7

Håkansson, T. (1986). Smiling in newborn infants: a cross-cultural study of the mother's reaction to the infant's first smile. Unpublished manuscript

Hakim, S. and Jimenez, A. (1955). Drainage of cerebrospinal fluid into the spinal epidural space. *Acta Neurochir.,* **4,** 224–7

Halliday, M. A. K. See Neumann, 1983

Han (1975). Fetal sex prediction by sex chromatin of chorionic villi cells during early pregnancy. *Chin. Med. J.,* **1,** 117–26

Harris, U. (1975). *Prenatal Diagnosis and Selective Abortion.* (Cambridge, Mass.: Harvard University Press)

Harrison, M. R., Golbus, M. S., Berkowitz, R. L. et al. (1982). Fetal treatment. *N. Engl. J. Med.,* **307,** 1651–2

Hart, L. (1983). *Human Brain and Human Learning.* (New York: Longman)

Hau, T. F. (1973). Perinatale und pränatale Faktoren der Neurosenätologie. In Graber, G. H. and Kruse, F. (eds.) *Vorgeburtliches Seelenleben.* pp. 129–42. (München: Wilhelm Goldmann Verlag)

Hau, T. F. and Schindler, S. (1982). *Pränatale und Perinatale Psychosomatik: Richtungen. Probleme, Ergebnisse.* (Stuttgart: Hippokrates Verlag)

Haverkamp, A. D. et al. (1976). The evaluation of continuous fetal heart rate monitoring in high risk pregnancy. *Am. J. Obstet. Gynecol.,* **125,** 310–17

Heath, C. (1981). The opening sequence in doctor–patient interaction. In Atkinson, P. and Heath, C. (eds.) *Medical Work.* pp. 71–90. (Westmead u.a.: Gower)

Hecht, K., Poppei, M., Schlegel, T., Hinz, G., Tönjes, R., Götz, F. and Dörner, G. (1978). Long-term behavioural effects of psychotrophic drugs administered during brain development in rats. In Dörner, G. and Kawakami, M. (eds.) *Hormones and Brain Development.* Vol. 3, pp. 277–83. (Amsterdam, New York, Oxford: Elsevier/North Holland Biomedical Press)

Heimann, P. (1951). A contribution to the re-evaluation of the Oedipus complex – the early stages. In Klein, Heimann and Money-Kyrle (eds.)

New Directions in Psycho-Analysis: the Significance of infant conflict in the pattern of adult behaviour. 1977 edn., Chap. 2. (London: Maresfield Reprints)

Heller, I. (1975). Intrauterine amino acid feeding of the fetus. In Bode, H. and Warshow, J. (eds.) *Parenteral Nutrition in Infancy and Childhood.* pp. 206–13. (New York: Plenum)

Hemminger, H.-J. (1982). *Kindheit als Schicksal?* Reinbek

Henshall, W. R. (1972). Intrauterine sound levels. *Am. J. Obstet. Gynecol.,* **112** (4), 576–8

Herre, H. D., Kyank, H., Adomssent, S. and Wilken, H. P. (1976). Influence of protein-free calf blood dialysate (Solcoseryl) on estrogen secretion in chronic placental insufficiency. *Zbl. Gynaek.,* **98,** 212

Hinman, F. (1951). Sexual trends in female pseudohermaphroditism. *J. Clin. Endocrinol. Metab.,* **11,** 477–86

Hinz, G., Döcke, F. and Dörner, G. (1978). Long-term changes of sexual functions in rats treated neonatally with psychotrophic drugs. In Dörner, G. and Kawakami, M. (eds.) *Hormones and Brain Development.* Vol. 3, pp. 121–7. (Amsterdam, New York, Oxford: Elsevier/North Holland Biomedical Press)

Hinz, G. and Dörner, G. (1974). Effects of estrogens and gestagens on the sex-specific brain differentiation in rats. In Dörner, G. (ed.) *Endocrinology of Sex.* pp. 126–31. (Leipzig: Johann Ambrosius Barth)

Hinz, G., Hecht, K., Rhode, W. and Dörner, G. (1983). Long-term effects of early postnatal nutrition on subsequent body weight gain, emotionality and learning behaviour in male rats. *Exp. Clin. Endocrinol.,* **82,** 73–7

Hippocrates of Cos (1839–61). *Opera Omnia.* Ed. E. Littré, 10 Vols. (Paris: Bailliere)

Hoffer, W. (1949). Mouth, hand and ego integration. *Psychoanalytic Study of the Child.* Vols. III/IV, pp. 49–55. (New York: Int. Universities Press, Inc.)

Hoffman, D. I. et al. (1984). Plasma-endorphin concentrations prior and during pregnancy, in labour and after delivery. *Am. J. Obstet. Gynecol.,* **150,** 492–6

Hofsten, von C. (1983). Foundations of perceptual development. In Lipsitt, L. P. and Rovee-Collier, C. K. (eds.) *Advances in Infancy Research.* Vol. 2, pp. 241–64. (Norwood, NJ: Ablex)

Hollòs, J. (1924). Die Psychoneurose eines Frühgeborenen. *Int. Z. f.Ärtztl. Psychoanal.,* **10,** 423–33

Honig, Y., Dorshav, N., Zakut, H. and Serr, D. M. (1975). The family. In selected papers from *The 4th Int. Congr. of Psychosomatic Obstetrics & Gynecology,* (Tel-Aviv, 1974). pp. 306–10. (Basel: Karger)

Hook, E. B., Cross, P. K. and Schreinemachers, D. M. (1983). Chromosomal abnormality rates at amniocentesis and in live-born infants. *J. Am. Med. Assoc.,* **249,** 2034–8

Hooker, D. (1952). The prenatal origin of behavior. (Lawrence, Kansas: University of Kansas Press)

Hövels, O. and Halberstadt, E. (1981). Geburtshilfe und Kinderheilkunde. (Symposionsbericht Bad Kreuznach), Stuttgart, New York. pp. 1–26

Humphrey, T. (1978). Function of the nervous system during prenatal life. In Stave, U. (ed.) Physiology of the Perinatal Period. Vol. 2, pp. 751–96. (New York: Plenum Medical)

Hunt, J. McV. and Uzgiris, I. C. (1964). Cathexis from recognitive familiarity: an exploratory study. Paper presented at the American Psychological Association Convention, Los Angeles, California

Ianniruberto, A. and Tajani, E. (1981). Ultrasonographic study of fetal movements. Sem. Perinatol., **5,** 2, 175–81

Imperato-McGinley, J., Peterson, R. E., Gautier, T. and Sturla, E. (1979). Male pseudohermaphroditism secondary to 5α-reductase deficiency – a model for the role of androgens in both the development of the male phenotype and the evolution of a male identity. J. Steroid Biochem., **11,** 637–45

Jackson, J. E. et al. (1983). Psychological aspects of fetal monitoring: maternal reaction to the position of the monitor and staff behavior. J. Psychosom. Obstet. Gynecol., **2**(2), 97–102

Jacobson, E. (1950). Development of the wish for a child in boys. Psychoanalytic Study of the Child. Vol. 5, pp. 139–52. (New York: Int. Univ. Pres, Inc.)

Jaffe, J. and Feldstein, S. (1970). Rhythms of Dialogue. (New York: Academic)

Janov, A. (1983). Imprints: The Lifelong Effects of the Birth Experience. (New York: Coward-McCann)

Janus, L. (1986a): Zur Geschichte der psychoanalytischen Behandlungstechnik. Forum Psychoanalyse, **2,** 1–19

Janus, L. (1986b). Vorgeburtliche Lebenszeit und Geburtserleben. Ein verborgenes Basisthema der Psychoanalyse. (Heidelberg: Bischoff)

Jefferson, G. (1984). Notes on some orderlinesses of overlap onset. In d'Ursoa V. and Leonardi P. (eds.) Discourse Analysis and Natural Retorics. pp. 11–38. (Padova: Cleup)

Jernberg, A., Allert, A., Koller, T. and Booth, P. (1983). Reciprocity in Parent–Infant Relationships. (Chicago: The Theraplay Institute)

Jernberg, A., Wickersham, M. and Thomas, E. (1985). Mothers' Behaviors and Attitudes Toward their Unborn Infants. (Chicago: The Theraplay Institute)

Jessop, L. and Carter (1981). Promoting maternal attachment through prenatal intervention. Maternal Child Nursing, **6,** 107

Johnson, W. F., Emde, R. N., Pannabecker, B. J., Stenborg, C. and Davis, M. H. (1982). Maternal perception of infant emotion from birth through 18 months. Infant Behav. Dev., **5,** 313–22

Johnston, M. (1980). Cultural variations in professional and parenting patterns. *Joqn. J. Obstet. Gynecol. Neonatal Nursing,* **9,** No. 1–9
Jones, E. (1960). *Leben und Werk von S. Freud.* Vol. I. (Bern: Huber)
Jones, S. (1981). *To Love a Baby.* (Boston: Houghton-Miffling)
Jonxis, J. H. P. (1967). A premature's nursery without incubators. *Acta Paediatr. Scand.,* Suppl. **172,** 100–2
Jordan, B. (1980). *Birth in Four Cultures – A Crosscultural Investigation of Childbirth in Yucatan, Holland, Sweden and the United States.* p. 44. (Montreal, Canada: Eden Press Women's Publications)
Josselyn, I. M. (1956). Cultural forces, motherliness and fatherliness. *Am. J. Orthopsychiatr.,* **26,** 264–71
Jung, C. G. (1946). Die Psychologie der Übertragung. In Jung, C. G. (ed.) *Praxis der Psychotherapie.* 1958, edn. pp. 173–274. (Zürich und Stuttgart: Rascher)
Jungmann, J. (1983). Prä-, peri-, und postnatale Risikofaktoren und neurofunktionale Entwicklungsstörungen. *Ztschr. Kinder- und Jugendpsychiatrie,* **2,** 13–27
Kagan, J. (1964). American longitudinal research on psychological development. *Child Dev.,* **35,** 1–32
Kahn, E. et al. (1954). The Baragwanath premature baby unit – an analysis of the case records of 1000 consecutive admissions. *S. African Med. J.,* May, 453–6
Kaplan, E. H. (1968). Congenital absence of vagina; psychiatric aspects of diagnosis and management. *N.Y. St. J. Med.,* **68,** 1937
Katz, M., Block, B. S., Haymann, M. A. et al. (1982). Fetal organs weight changes after intravenous terbutaline administration in the rabbit. *29th Annual Meeting of the SGI,* Dallas, abstract 10
Keller, H. and Meyer, H. J. (1982). *Psychologie der frühesten Kindheit.* (Stuttgart, Berlin, Köln, Mainz)
Keller, N. A. (1985). Relationship between social support and mother's perceptions of the birth experience in the early postpartum period. Unpublished *Doctoral Dissertation,* University of Alabama, Birmingham
Kelsey, D. E. R. (1953). Phantasies of birth and prenatal experience recovered from patients undergoing hypoanalysis. *J. Ment. Sci./Br. J. Psychiatr.,* **99,** 216–23
Kempe, R. S. and Kempe, C. H. (1980). *Kindesmißhandlung.* (Stuttgart) (Ersterscheinung, London, 1978)
Kennell, J. H. and Klaus, M. (1983). Early events: later effects on the infant. In Call, J., Galenson, E. and Tyson, R. (eds.) *Frontiers of Infant Psychiatry.* pp. 7–16. (New York: Basic Books)
Kennell, J. H., Trause, M. A. and Klaus, M. H. (1975). Evidence for a sensitive

period in the human mother. In *Parent–Infant interaction*. (Ciba Foundation 33-New Series). (New York: Elsevier)

Kessen, W., Haith, M.W. and Salapatek, P. (1970). Human infancy: a bibliography and guide. In Mussen, P. (ed.) *Carmichael's Manual of Child Development*. pp. 287–444. (New York: Wiley)

Kessen, W. et al. (1979). The imitation of pitch in infants. *Infant Behav. Dev.*, **2**, 93–9

Kessler, E. S. (1979). *Women: an Anthropological View*. (New York: Holt, Rinehart & Winston)

Kessler, S. (1979). *Genetic Counselling. Psychological Dimensions*. (New York: Academic Press)

Kestenberg, J. (1976). Regression and reintegration in pregnancy. *J. Am. Psychoanalytic Assoc.*, **24**, 213–50

Kestenberg, J. S. (1977). Psychoanalytic observation of children. *Int. Rev. Psycho-Anal.*, **4**, 4, 393–407

Kestenberg, J. (1980). Pregnancy as a development phase. *J. Biol. Experience*, **3**, 1, 58–66

Kimball, C. D. et al. (1981). Immunoreactive endorphin peptides and prolactin in umbilical vein and maternal blood. *Am. J. Obstet. Gynecol.*, May 15, 157–64

Kipper, D. A., Zigler-Shani, Z., Serr, D. M. and Insler, V. (1975). Two tests for measuring personality characteristics of functionally sterile women. *The Family. 4th Int. Congr. of Psychosomatic Obstetrics & Gynecology*, Tel-Aviv, 1974, pp. 278–81. (Basel: Karger)

Kitzinger, S. (1978). *Women as Mothers*. (London: Fontana/Collins)

Klaus, M. H. and Kennell, J. H. (1982). *Maternal–Infant Bonding*. 2nd Edn. (St Louis: Mosby Publishing Co.)

Klaus, M. H. and Klaus, P. H. (1985). *The Amazing Newborn*. (Reading, Massachusetts: Addison-Wesley Publishing Co.)

Klein, M. (1946). Notes on some schizoid mechanisms. In *Envy and Gratitude and Other Works*. 1984 Edn., Chap. 1. (London: Hogarth Press)

Klein, M. D., Klosloske, A. M. and Hertzler, J. H. (1981). Congenital defects of the abdominal wall. *J. Am. Med. Assoc.*, **245**, 1643–6

Kleining, G. and Moore, H. (1968). Soziale Selbsteinstufung (SSE). *Kölner Zeitschrift für Soziologie und Sozialpsychologie*, **20**, 502–52

Knop, J., Teasdale, T. W., Schulsinger, F. and Goodwin, D. W. (1985). A prospective study of young men at high risk for alcoholism. *J. Stud. Alcohol*, **46**, 273–8

Kobasa, S. C. (1979). Stressful life events, personality and health: an inquiry into hardiness. *J. Pers. Soc. Psychol.*, **37**, 1–11

Köcher, E. M. T. and Nickel, H. (1985). Die Berücksichtigung des Vaters in der gegenwärtigen Forschungspraxis: Ergebnisse einer Umfrage im deutschsprachigen Raum. *Psychologie in Erziehung und Unterricht,* **32,** 288–92

Koller, T. (1981). Older child adoptions: a new developmental intervention program. Presented at the *Annual Meeting of the American Psychological Association,* Los Angeles, CA, August

Konner, M. J. (1976). Maternal care, infant behavior and development among the Kung San, Kalahari hunter-gatherers. In Lee, R. B. and DeVore, I. (eds.) *Studies of the Kung San and their Neighbors.* (Cambridge: Harvard University Press)

Koester, L. S., Papousek, H. and Papousek, M. (1985). Patterns of rhythmic stimulation by mothers with young infants: a comparison of multiple modalities. Presented at the *Eighth Biennial Meeting of the International Society for the Study of Behavoral Development,* Tours, France. Abstracted in *Cahiers de Psychologie Cognitive,* **5,** 270–1

Koester, L. S., Papousek, H. and Papousek, M. (1987). Psychobiological models of infant development: influences on the concept of intuitive parent. In Stelmach, G. E. and Vroon, P. A. (eds.) *Advances in Psychology.* pp. 275–87. (North Holland: Elsevier)

Korner, A. F. and Thoman, E. B. (1972). The relative efficacy of contact and vestibular-proprioceptive stimulation in soothing neonates. *Child Dev.,* **43,** 443–53

Korsch, B. M. and Negrete, V. F. (1972). Doctor–patient communication. *Sci. Am.,* **227,** 66–74

Kotelchuck, M. (1976). The infant's relationship to the father. Experimental evidence. In Lamb, M. (ed.) *The Role of the Father in Child Development.* pp. 329–44. (New York: Wiley)

Kovács, F. (1960). Biological interpretation of the nine-month duration of human pregnancy. *Acta Biol. Magyar. Tudom. Akad.,* **10,** 331–6

Krieger, D. T. and Martin, J. B. (1981). Brain peptides. *N. Engl. J. Med.,* **304,** 876–85 and 944–52

Kruse, F. (1969). *Die Anfänge des menschlichen Seelenlebens.* (Stuttgart: Enke)

Kruse, F. (1978). Zur Psychologie der Ungeborenen. *Therapiewoche,* **28,** 9540–50

Kruse, F. (1982). Erinnerung an die eigene Geburt – Realität oder Fiktion? In Schindler, S. (ed.) *Geburt – Eintritt in eine neue Welt.* pp. 111–21. (Göttingen: Verlag für Psychologie)

Kruuse, E. and Zachau-Christiansen, B. (1986). Plateauer i børns intelligensudvikling. *Skolepsykologi,* **23,** 541–50

Kuhn, J. (1962). *The Structure of Scientific Revolution.* (University of Chicago Press)

Kulka, A. et al. (1960). Kinesthetic needs in infancy. *Am. J. Orthopsychiatr.*, **30,** 562–71

Kumar, R., Robson, K. M. and Smith, A. M. R. (1984). Development of a selfadministered questionnaire to measure maternal adjustment and maternal attitudes during pregnancy and after delivery. *J. Psychosom. Res.*, **28,** 43–51

Kurjak, A. (1975). Antenatal diagnosis of fetal malformations and abnormalities by ultrasound. Proceedings of the *Second European Congress on Ultrasound in Medicine,* Munich, 12–16 May. No. 363, pp. 304–10. (Amsterdam, Oxford International Congress Series: Excerpta Medica)

Kurjak, A. (1978a). Direct ultrasonic diagnosis of fetal malformations and abnormalities. In Kurjak, A. (ed.) *Progress in Medical Ultrasound.* Vol. 2., 436, 224. (Amsterdam, Oxford International Congress Series: Excerpta Medica)

Kurjak, A. (1978b). Review of current status of early detection of fetal abnormalities. In Kurjak, A. (ed.) *Recent Advances in Ultrasound Diagnosis 1: Proceedings of International Symposium on Recent Advances in Ultrasound Diagnosis,* Dubrovnik, Oct. 10–15 1977. (Amsterdam, Oxford: Excerpta Medica). International Congress Series, Vol. 1, 436, 224

Kurjak, A. (1979). The assessment of fetal development by ultrasound: experience from 15 000 obstetrics patients. *Zjazd naukowy polskiego towarzytwa ginekologioznego,* Warsaw 6–8 pazd, 1977. *Ginekol. Pol.* (Suppl), 43–6

Kurjak, A. (1980). Fetal abnormalities in early and late pregnancies. In Kurjak, A. (ed.) *Progress in Medical Ultrasound.* Vol. 1, pp. 107–27. (Amsterdam, Oxford: Excerpta Medica)

Kurjak, A. (1982). The legal problems and the ultrasonically detected malformed fetus. In Lerski. R. and Morley, P. (eds.) *Ultrasound 82; Proceedings of the Third Meeting of The World Federation for Ultrasound in Medicine and Biology.* pp. 33–6. (Oxford: Pergamon Press)

Kurjak, A. and Beazley, J. M. (1984). Fetal therapy: ethical and legal aspects. In *Fetus as a Patient. Proceedings of International Congress on Fetus as a Patient,* Sv. Stefan, 4–7 June

Kurjak, A. and Kaplinski, A. K. (1985). *In utero* treatment of the fetus with growth retardation. In Kurjak, A. (ed.) *Fetus as a Patient. Proceedings of International Congress on Fetus as a Patient.* Sv. Stefan, 4–7 June, 1984. (Amsterdam: Excepta Medica). International Congress Series, 665, 86–102

Kurjak, A. and Kirkinen, P. (1982). Ultrasonic growth pattern of fetuses with chromosomal aberrations. *Acta Obstet. Gynecol. Scand.,* **61,** 329–35

Kurjak, A. and Latin, V. (1979a). Ultrasound diagnosis of fetal abnormalities in multiple pregnancy. *Acta Obstet. Gynecol. Scand.,* 153–61

Kurjak, A. and Latin, V. (1979b). Diagnostics and exclusion of malformed fetuses by ultrasound. In Sakamoto, S., Tojo, S. and Nakayama, T. (eds.) *Gynecology and Obstetrics Proceedings of the IX World Congress of Gynecology and Obstetrics,* Tokyo, October 25–31. (Amsterdam, Oxford: Excerpta Medica). International Congress Series, 1, 736–9

Kurjak, A. and Pal, A. (1985). The effect of Solcoseryl therapy on the uterine and fetal blood flow. Perinatal care and gestosis. *Proceedings of the 17th Meeting of Organization Gestosis International symposium on Perinatal Care and Gestosis,* Sendai, Japan, 17–22 May. (Amsterdam: Excerpta Medica). International Congress Series, 87–93

Kurjak, A. and Rajhvajn, B. (1982a). Ultrasonic measurement of umbilical blood flow in normal and complicated pregnancies. *J. Perinat. Met.,* **10**(1), 3–16

Kurjak, A. and Rajhvajn, B. (1982b). Ultrasonic control of umbilical blood flow in small for dates fetuses. *J. Perinat. Med.,* **10,** (Suppl. 2: Progress in Perinatal Medicine 2nd International Berlin Meeting of *Perin. Med.*), 90–2

Kurjak, A. and Zergollen-Cupak, L. J. (1982). Ultrasound diagnosis of fetal malformations. *J. Perinat. Med.,* **10,** (Suppl. 2: Progress in Perinatal Medicine 2nd International Berlin Meeting of *Perin. Med.*), 10–12

Kurjak, A., Rajhvajn, B., Drazancic, A., Gorecan, V., Barsk, B., Latin, V. and Olajos, I. (1975). Antenatal diagnosis of the 'at risk' fetus during late pregnancy by serial ultrasonic cephalometry. In Stembera, Z. K., Polacek, K. and Sabata (eds.) *Perinatal Medicine: 4th European Congress of Perinatal Medicine,* Prague, August 1974. pp. 150–1. (Stuttgart: G. Thieme)

Kurjak, A., Breyer, B. and Olajos, I. (1977). Ultrasonic assessment of fetal growth and gestational age by measurement of three fetal dimensions. In White, D. and Brown, R. E. (eds.) *Ultrasound in Medicine.* Vol. 3A, pp. 681–9. (New York: Plenum)

Kurjak, A., Latin, V. and Czajkowski, Z. (1978a). Clinical application of fetal breathing movements. *Fifth Conference on Fetal Breathing,* Nijmegen, June 26–27. 1978, pp. 95–105

Kurjak, A., Latin, V. and Polak, J. (1978b). Ultrasonic recognition of two types of growth retardation by measurement of four fetal dimensions. *J. Perinat. Med.,* **6,** 102–8

Kurjak, A., Kirkenen, V., Latin, V. and Rajhvajn, B. (1980). Diagnosis and assessment of fetal malformations and abnormalities by ultrasound. *J. Perinat. Med.,* **8,** 219–35

Kurjak, A., Beazley, J. M., Latin, V. and Funduk-Kurjak, B. (1981). Fetal growth retardation and EPH gestosis. In Kurjak, A., Rippman, E. T. and Sulovic, V. (eds.) *Twelfth International Meeting on EPH Gestosis,* Dubrovnik, May 18–25, 1980. (Amsterdam, Oxford: Excerpta Medica). International Congress Series, 534, 340–52

Kurjak, A., Gogolja, D., Kogler, A., Latin, V. and Rajhvajn, B. (1984a). Ultrasound diagnosis and perinatal management of correctable fetal malformations. *Ult. Med. Bio.,* **10**(1)

Kurjak, A., Latin, V., Mandruzzato, G. and D'Addario, V. (1984b). Ultrasound diagnosis and perinatal management of fetal genito-urinary abnormalities. *J. Perinat. Med.,* **12,** 291–312

Kurjak, A., Omran, M. and Rajhvajn, B. (1984c). Biometric and dynamic ultrasonic assessment of fetal growth retardation. In Schenker, I. (ed.) *Recent Advances in EPH Gestosis.* (Amsterdam: Excerpta Medica). International Congress Series

Kurjak, A., Rajhvajn, B. and Aradi, M. (1984d). Clinical application of ultrasonically measured umbilical blood flow. In Kurjak, A. (ed.) *Measurements of Fetal Blood.* pp. 103–25. (CIC Edizioni internazionali)

Kurjak, A., Kaplinski, A. and Rajhvajn, B. (1984e). The treatment of fetal growth retardation by blood extract controlled by ultrasonic measurements of umbilical blood flow. In Schenker, I. (ed.) *Recent Advances in EPH Gestosis.* (Amsterdam: Excerpta Medica). International Congress Series

Kurjak, A., Kaplinski, A. and Latin, V. (1984f). The current status of ultrasonically guided fetal therapy. In Kurjak, A. and Kossoff, G. (eds.) *Recent Advances in Ultrasound Diagnosis.* Vol. 4. *Proceedings of the International Symposium on Recent Advances in Ultrasound Diagnosis,* Dubrovnik June 1–3, 1983. (Amsterdam: Excerpta Medica). International Congress Series 640, 98–126

Kurjak, A., Rajhvajn, B., Kogler, A. and Gogolja, D. (1985). Ultrasound diagnosis of fetal malformations of surgical interest. In Kurjak, A. (ed.) *Fetus as a Patient. Proceedings of International Congress on Fetus as a Patient,* Sv. Stefan, 4–7 June, 1984. (Amsterdam: Excerpta Medica). International Congress Series 665, 243–72

Kurjak, A., Rajhvajn, B., Jurkovic, D., Relja, Z., Jakovcic, J., Alfirevic, Z. and Rusinovic, F. (1986). Interventional ultrasound in diagnosis and treatment of fetal malformations. In Kurjak, A. and Kossoff, G. (eds.) *Recent Advances in Ultrasound Diagnosis,* Vol. 5. *Proceedings of the International Symposium on Recent Advances in Ultrasound Diagnosis,* Dubrovnik, September 29–30. (Amsterdam: Excerpta Medica). International Congress Series, 701, 27–43

Lacan, J. (1956). *The Function and Field of Speech in Psychoanalysis.* Translated by Sheridan-Smith, A. 1977. (London: Tavistock)

Laderman, C. (1984). *Wives and Midwives: Childbirth and Nutrition in Rural Malaysia.* (Berkeley: Univ. of California Press)

Laing, R. D. (1976). *The Facts of Life.* (New York: Pantheon Books)

Laing, R. D. (1982). *The Voice of Experience.* (New York: Pantheon Books)

Lally, J. R. (1974). *The family development research program. A program for prenatal, infant and early childhood enrichment. Progress Report.* College for Human Development Syracuse University, Syracuse, New York, March, 15

Lamb, M. E. (1976a). Interactions between eight-month-old children and their father in child development. In Lamb, M. E. (ed.) *The Role of the Father in Child Development.* (New York: Wiley)

Lamb, M. E. (1976b). Twelve-month-olds and their parents: interaction in a laboratory playroom. *Dev. Psychol.,* **12,** 237–44

Lamb, M. E. (1977). Father–infant and mother–infant interaction in the first year of life. *Child Dev.,* **48,** 167–81

Lamb, M. E. (1979a). Paternal influences and father's role: a personal perspective. *Am. Psychol.,* **34,** 938–43

Lamb, M. E. (1979b). Effects of infant sociability and the caretaking environment on infant cognitive performance. *Child Dev.,* **50,** 340–9

Lamb, M. E. (ed.) (1982). Nontraditional families: parenting and child development. (Hillsdale, NJ: Lawrence Erlbaum Associates)

Lamb, M. E., Pleck, J. H. and Levine, J. A. (1985). The role of the father in child development: the effects of increased paternal involvement. In Lahey, B. B. and Kazdin, A. E. (eds.) *Advances in Clinical Child Psychology.* Vol. 8. (New York: Plenum Press)

Lamb, M. P. (1975). Gangrene of a fetal limb due to amniocentesis. *Br. J. Obstet. Gynecol.,* **82,** 829–30

Langworthy, O. R. (1933). Development of behavior patterns and myelinization of the nervous system in the human fetus and infant. *Carnegie Institution of Washington, Contributions to Embryology,* **24,** 1–57

Laplanche, J. and Pontalis, J. B. (1973). *The Language of Psycho-Analysis.* (London: Hogarth Press & Inst. of Psycho-Anal.)

Laukaran, V. and Van Den Berg, B. (1980). The relationship of maternal attitude to pregnancy outcomes and obstetrical complications. A cohort study of unwanted pregnancy. *Am. J. Obstet. Gynecol.,* **136,** 374–9

Lauritzen, Chr. (1985). Medikamente in der Schwangerschaft: Auch im 2. und 3. Trimenon sowie in der Stillzeit ist große Umsicht geboten. *Gyne,* Sept., 292–6

Leboyer, F. (1975). *Birth Without Violence.* (London: Wildwood House Ltd.)

Lecron, L. (1963). The uncovering of early memories by ideomotor responses to questioning. *Int. J. Clin. Exp. Hypnosis.,* **11**(3), 137–42

Lederman, R. P., Lederman, E., Work, B. A. and McCann, D. S. (1978). The relationship of maternal anxiety, plasma catecholamines, and plasma cortisol to progress in labor. *Am. J. Obstet. Gynecol.,* **132,** 495–500

Leiderman, P. H. and Seashore, M. J. (1975). Mother–infant neonatal separation: some delayed consequences. In *Parent–infant interaction* (Ciba Foundation Symposium 33-new Series). (New York: Elsevier)

Leifer, M. (1980). *Psychological Effects of Motherhood: a Study of First Pregnancy.* (New York: Praeger Science)
Leiter, R. G. (1966). *Instructions for Giving and Scoring the Individual Tests.* (Chicago: Stoelting Co.)
Leroy, W. (1986). Ethical issues in intrauterine diagnosis and therapy. *Fetal Therapy,* **1,** 32–7
Levi-Strauss (1969). *The Raw and the Cooked.* (UK: Penguin)
Liebenberg, B. (1973). Expectant fathers. In Shereshefsky, P. M. and Yarrow, L. J. *Psychological Aspects of a First Pregnancy and Early Postnatal Adaptation.* pp. 103–14. (New York: Raven Press)
Lieberman, M. (1963). Early developmental stress and later behavior. *Science,* **141,** 824
Lieberman, M. (1973). In Schwartz, L. (ed.) *The World of the Unborn: Nurturing your Child before Birth.* p. 71. (New York: R. Marek Publishers)
Liedloff, J. (1976). *The Continuum Concept.* (London: Futura Publications Ltd.)
Liharzik, F. (1858). *Das Gesetz des menschlichen Wachstumes.* (Wien: Gerold)
Liley, A. W. (1963). Intrauterine transfusion of the fetus in haemolitic disease. *Br. Med. J.,* **2,** 1107
Liley, A. W. (1972). The foetus as a personality. *Aust. N.Z. J. Psychiatr.,* **6,** 99–105
Lind, J. (1981). Personal communication, Stockholm
Lind, J. and Hardgrove, C. B. (1978). Lullaby bonding keeping abreast. *J. Human Nurturing,* **3,** 3, 184–90
Linderkamp, O. (1982). Placental transfusion: determinants and effects. *Clin. Perinatol.,* **9**(3), 559–92
Lipsitt, L. P. (1969). Learning capacities of the human infant. In Robinson, R. J. (ed.) *Brain and Early Behavior Development in the Fetus and Infant.* pp. 227–49. (London: Academic Press)
Lipsitt, L. P. (1977). The study of sensory and learning processes of the newborn. In Volpe, J. (ed.) *Clin. Perinatol.,* **4**(1), 163–86
Lipsitt, L. P. (1979). The pleasures and annoyances of infants: approach and avoidance behavior. In Thoman, E. B. (ed.) *Origins of the Infant's Social Responsiveness.* pp. 125–54. (Hillsdale, New Jersey: Erlbaum)
Lipsitt, L. P. and Werner, J. S. (1981). The infancy of human learning processes. In Gollin, E. S. (ed.) *Developmental Plasticity.* pp. 101–33. (New York: Academic Press)
Low, J., Galbraith, R. and Muir, D. *et al.* (1968). Intrauterine growth retardation: a preliminary report of long-term morbidity. *Am. J. Obstet. Gynecol. Br. Cwtlth.,* **75,** 903

Lowen, L. (1982). Breastfeeding when your baby is premature. *Mothering*, **22,** 68–70

Lozoff et al. (1977). The mother–newborn relationship: limits of adaptability. *J. Pediatr.*, **91,** 1: 1–12

Ludington, S. (1985). *How to Have a Smarter Baby*. (New York: Rawson Associates)

Lukesch, H. and Rottmann, G. (1976). Die Bedeutung sozio-familiärer Faktoren für die Einstellung von Müttern zur Schwangerschaft. *Psychologie und Praxis*, **XX,** 4–18

Lumley, J. (1980). The image of the fetus in the first trimester. *Birth and the Family J.*, **7**(1)

Luna, L. E. (1986). *Vegetalismo: Shamanism among the Mestizo Population of the Peruvian Amazon*. (Stockholm: Almquist and Wiksell International)

Lüpke, H. von (1984). Prophylaxe und Therapie bei frühen Formen auffälligen Verhaltens: Risiko und Regulation in Entwicklungsprozessen. In *Wege zum Menschen*. 36. Jhg., 8: 436–53. (Göttingen: Vandenhoeck & Ruprecht)

Luria, A. R. (1973). *The Working Brain: an Introduction to Neuropsychology*. (New York: Basic Books)

Luteyn, F., Hamel, L. F., Bouman, T. K. and Kok, A. R. (1984). *HSCL Hopkins Symptom Checklist*. (Lisse: Swets & Zeitlinger)

Macfarlane, A. (1977). *The Psychology of Childbirth*. (Cambridge, Massachusetts: Harvard University Press)

Macy, C., and Falkner, F. (1979). *Pregnancy and Birth: Pleasures and Problems*. (London: Harper and Row)

Magoun, H. I. Snr. (1971). A pertinent approach to pituitary pathology. *The D.O.*, **11,** 133–41

Magoun, H (1976). *Osteopathy in the Cranial Field*. 3rd edn. (Kirksville, Missouri: Journal Printing Co.)

Mahler, M. et al. (1975). *The Psychological Birth of the Human Infant: Symbiosis and Individuation*. (London: Hutchinson)

Marschak, M. (1960a). Imitation and participation in normal and disturbed young boys in interaction with their parents. *J. Clin. Psychol.*, **97,** 1960

Marschak, M. (1960b). A method of evaluating child–parent interaction under controlled conditions. *J. Genet. Psychol.*

Marschak, M. (1967). Child-parent tie in present day Japan. *Child and Family*, **6,** 1967

Marschak, M. (1980). *Parent–Child Interaction and Youth Rebellion*. (New York: Gardner Press)

Marshall, R. E. and Kasman, C. (1980). Burnout in the neonatal intensive care unit. *Pediatrics*, **65,** 6, 1161–5

Marshall, R. E. et al. (1982). *Coping with Caring for Sick Newborns*. (Philadelphia: W. B. Saunders Co)

Marton, P. et al. (1979). The interaction of ward personnel with infants in the premature nursery. *J. Infant Behav. Dev.*

Marty, P. (1958). La relation objectale allergique. *La Revue Française de Psychoanalyse*, **22**, 5–35

Maslow, A. (1968). *Toward a Psychology of Being*. (New York: D. Van Norstrand Co.)

Maslow, A. (1972). *The Farther Reaches of Human Nature*. pp. 168–79. (New York: Viking Press)

Mathiessen, P. C., Trolle, D. and Zachau-Christiansen, B. (1967). Infant and perinatal mortality in Denmark. *Vital Health Statistics*, **3**, no. 9

May, K. A. (1982). Three phases of father involvement in pregnancy. *Nursing Res.*, **31**(6), 337–42

Mayer, N. K. and Tronick, E. Z. (1985). Mother's turn-giving signals and infant turn-taking in mother–infant interaction. In Field, T. and Fox, N. (eds.) *Social Perception in Infants*. (Norwood, NJ: Ablex)

McCall, Kennedy, Bellows and Dodds (1977).

McDaniel, C. (1983). Fetal surgery results not as dramatic as reported. *The Medical Post*, 1 November, p. 60

McDonald, R., Gynther, M. and Christakes, A. (1963). Relations between maternal anxiety and obstetric complications. *Psychosom. Med.*, **25**, 74–7

McDonald, R. L. (1965). Personality characteristics in patients with three obstetric complications. *Psychosom. Med.*, **27**, 383–90

McDonald, R. L. (1968). The role of emotional factors in obstetric complications: a review. *Psychosom. Med.*, **30**, 222–37

McRae, J. (1981). Psychophysiological aspects of birth. Doctoral Dissertation, California School of Professional Psychology, Berkeley.

Mead, M. (1949). *Male and Female: a Study of the Sexes in a Changing World*. (London: Victor Gollancz)

Medical World News (1979). Amniocentesis kills 1.5% of fetuses in British study. Feb. 19th, pp. 25, 29

Medical World News (1984a). Call for improved fetal monitoring refuels debate among physicians. Feb. 27th, pp. 46–7

Medical World News (1984b). Consensus panel opposes routine use of ultrasound in pregnancy. March 12th, pp. 19–20

Mednick, S. A. and Baert, A. E. (1981). *Prospective Longitudinal Research*. (Oxford: University Press)

Mehl, L. and Peterson, G. (1979). Berkeley Family Health Center: an existential-phenomenological approach to health care. In Stewart, L. and Stewart, D. *Freedom of Choice in Childbirth*. (Marble Hill, MO.: NAPSAC Press)

Mehl, L. E. and Peterson, G. H. (1981). Existential prenatal risk screening. In Ahmed, P. (ed.) *Pregnancy, Birth and Parenting: Coping With Medical Issues*. (New York: Elsevier-North Holland)

Mehl, L. and Peterson, G. (1985). *Pregnancy as Healing*. (Berkeley: Mind Body Press)

Mehl, L. E. and Peterson, G. H. (1986). *Casarean Birth: Risk and Culture*. (Palo Alto, C.A.: Mindbody Press)

Mellin, G. W. (1964). Drugs in the first trimester of pregnancy. *Am. J. Obstet. Gynecol.*, **90,** 11–69–1180

Meltzoff, A. and Borton, W. (1979). Intermodal matching by human neonates. *Nature*, **282,** 403–4

Meltzoff, A. and Moore, M. K. (1983). The origins of imitation in infancy: paradigm, phenomena, and theories. In Lipsitt, L. P. and Rovee-Collier, C. (eds.) *Advances in Infancy Research*. Vol. 2, pp. 265–301. (Norwood, NJ: Ablex)

Merrick, J., Teasdale, T. W. and Merrick, Y. (1983). School health screening of a birth cohort. *Int. J. Rehab. Res.*, **6,** 461–8

Merz, F. et al. (1986). Stilldauer, Geschlecht und Persönlichkeitsentwicklung. Institutsbericht Universität Marburg, FB Psychologie, Nr. 88

Meyer, A. W. (1931). *Essays on the History of Embryology*. (California: University Press Stanford)

Meyer, A. W. (1938). The discovery and earliest representations of spermatozoa. *Bull. Inst. Hist. Med.*, **6,** 89

Meyer-Bahlburg, H. F. L. and Ehrhardt, A. A. (1983). Sexual orientations after prenatal exposure to exogenous sex hormones. *Neuroendocrinology Lett.*, **5,** 133

Michejda, M. and Pringle, K. (1986). In *Fetal Therapy*, **1,** 3–7

Milakovic, I. (1967). The hypothesis of a deglutitive (prenatal) stage in libidinal development. *Int. J. Psycho-Anal.*, **48,** 1, 76–82

Milani Comparetti, A. (1981). The neurophysiological and clinical implications of studies on fetal motor behavior. *Sem. Perinatol.*, **5,** 2

Milani Comparetti, A. (1985). Ontogenesi dell'identità personale e della appartenenza relazionale. *Giorn. Neuropsich. Età Evol.*, **5,** 47–52

Milani Comparetti, A. (1986). Fetal and neonatal origins of being a person and belonging to the world. *Maturation and Learning*, Suppl. 5, April

Milani Comparetti, A. and Gidoni, E. A. (1967a). Pattern analysis of motor development and its disorders. *Dev. Med. and Child Neurol.*, **9,** 5

Milani Comparetti, A. and Gidoni. E. A. (1967b). Routine developmental examination in normal and retarded children. *Dev. Med. and Child Neurol.*, **9,** 5

Milani Comparetti, A. and Gidoni, E. A. (1976). Dalla parte del neonato: proposte per una competenza prognostica. *Neuropsichiatria Infantile*, **175**

Minde, K. et al. (1975). Interactions of mothers and nurses with premature infants. *CMA J.*, **113**, 741–5

Minot, C. S. (1908). *The Problem of Age, Growth and Death.* (London: Murray)

Mistretta, C. M. and Bradley, R. M. (1977). Taste *in utero:* theoretical considerations. In Weiffenbach, J. M. (ed.) *Taste and Development: The Genesis of Sweet Preference.* pp. 51–69. (Washington DC: US Government Printing Office)

Mitchell, J. (1982). In Mitchell, J. (ed.) *Man in Society.* (London: Mitchell Beazley encyclopaedias)

Molinski, H. (1972). Die unbewußte Angst vor dem Kind (als Ursache von Schwangerschaftsbeschwerden und Depressionen nach der Geburt — mit zwölf anschließenden Falldarstellungen), München

Money, J., Ehrhardt, A. A. and Masica, D. N. (1968). Fetal feminization induced by androgen insensitivity in the testicular feminizing syndrome: effect on marriage and maternalism. *Johns Hopkins Med. J.*, **123**, 105–14

Money, J. and Schwartz, M. (1977). Dating, romantic and nonromantic friendships, and sexuality in 17 early-treated adrenogenital females, aged 16–21. In Lee, P. A., Plotnick, L. P., Kowarski, A. A. and Migeon, C. J. (eds.) *Congenital Adrenal Hyperplasia.* pp. 419–51. (Baltimore, Maryland: University Park Press)

Moniz, H. and Tyano, S. (1973). Le Syndrome de Cotard chez un transplant du rein. *Liberte Medical*, **4**, 6

Montagu, A. (1961). The origin and significance of neonatal and infant immaturity. *J. Am. Med. Assoc.*, **178**, 156–7

Montagu, A. (1962). *Prenatal Influences.* (Springfield: Charles Thomas)

Montagu, A. (1978). *Touching: The Human Significance of Skin.* (New York: Harper & Row)

Mosidze, V. M. (1976). On the lateralization of musical function in man (In Russian). In Kaznacheyev, V. P., Semyonov, S. F. and Chuprikov, A. P. (eds.) *Functional Asymmetry and Adaptation in Man.* Moscow

Motyka, M. and Golańska, Z. (1981). Psychologic characteristics of women with impaired fertility. *Gin. Pol.*, **52**, 51

Muasher, S. F., Garcia, J. E. and Rosenwaks, Z. (1985). The combination of follicle-stimulating hormone and human menopausal gonadotropin for the induction of multiple follicular maturation for *in vitro* fertilization. *Fertil. Steril.*, **44**, 62

Murchison, L. and Langer, S. (1927). Tiedemann's observation on the development of the mental faculties of children. *J. Genet. Psychol.*, **34**, 205–30

Murdock, G. P. and White, D. R. (1969). Standard cross-cultural sample. *Ethology*, **8**, 329–69

Murken, J. (1987). *Pränatale Diagnostik und Therapie*. (Stuttgart: Enke)
Murray, M. A. (1930). *The Bundle of Life. Ancient Egypt*. p. 65
Mussen. P. H., Conger, J. J. and Kagan, J. (1956/1974). *Child Development and Personality*. (New York: Harper & Row)
National Institute of Child Health and Development Project (1976). The safety and accuracy of mid-trimester amniocentesis. DHEW Publication No. (NIH) 78–190
Neal, M. (1968). Vestibular stimulation and developmental behavior of the small premature infant. *Nursing Res. Rep.*, **3**, 1, 2–4
Needham, J. (1954). Science and Civilization in China. 10 Vols. Cambridge
Neel, J. V. and Schull, W. J. (1956). The effect of exposure to the atomic bombs on pregnancy termination in Hiroshima and Nagasaki. (Washington: Nat. Acad. Sciences)
Neligan, G. A., Prudham, D. and Steiner, H. (1975). *The Formative Years*. (London: Oxford University Press)
Neue Osnabrücker Zeitung (1986). Schweden: zu hohe Dioxinwerte in der Muttermilch. May 17th
Neumann, E. (1955). Narzißmus, Automorphismus und Urbeziehung. In *Stud. z. analyt. Psychol. C. G. Jungs*. Vol. 1. (Zürich: Rascher)
Neumann, E. (1963). *The Great Mother (1955)*. (New Jersey: Princeton University Press)
Neumann, K. (1983). Der Beginn der Kommunikation zwischen Mutter und Kind. Strukturanalyse der Mutter–Kind- Interaktion. Bad Heilbrunn
Newton, R. (1985). The influence of psychosocial stress in low birth weight and preterm labour. In Beard, R. W. and Sharp, F. (eds.) *Preterm Labour and its Consequences*. pp. 225–41. XIIIth Studygroup on preterm labour, London
Nickel, H. and Kocher, E. M. T. (1985). Ökopsychologische Analysen von Eltern–Kind-Spielgruppen. In Montada, L. (ed.) *Bericht über die 7. Tagung Entwicklungspsychologie*. Universität Trier
Nickel, H. and Kocher, E. M. T. (1986a). The father's role – in West Germany and the German speaking countries. In Lamb, M. E. (ed.) *The Father's Role: Cross-cultural Perspectives*. (Hillsdale, NJ: Lawrence Erlbaum Associates) (in press)
Nickel, H. and Kocher, E. M. T. (1986b). Väter von Säuglingen und Kleinkindern – Zum Rollenwandel in der Bundesrepublik Deutschland. *Psychologie in Erziehung und Unterricht,* **33**, 174–87
Nickel, H., Arora, I., Thilmann, A. and Vetter, J. (1981). Zusammenhänge zwischen Mütterverhalten und Verhaltensmerkmalen von Kleinkindern. Ergebnisse einer Längs-schnittstudie zur Mutter–Kind-Interaktion im ersten und vierten Lebensjahr. *Psychologie in Erziehung und Unterricht,* **28**, 193–203

Nickel, H., Bartoszyk, J. and Wenzel, H. (1986). Eltern–Kind-Beziehung im ersten Lebensjahr: Der Einfluß von Vorbereitungskursen auf das Verhalten des Vaters und seine Bedeutung für die Entwicklung des Kindes. Forschungsbericht Universität Düsseldorf 2. revidierte un ergänzte Auflage

Nicolaides, K. and Rodeck, C. H. (1984). Fetoscopy. *Br. J. Hosp. Med.*, **6**, 396–405

Nijhuis, J. G., Prechtl, H. F. R., Martin, C. B. Jr and Bots, R. S. G. M. (1982). Are there behavioural states in the human fetus? *Early Hum. Dev.*, **5**, 87–94

Nissen, G. (ed.) (1982). *Psychiatrie des Säuglings – und des frühen Kleinkind alters.* (Bern, Stuttgart, Wien) (darin insbes, Beitrag von Bürgin, pp. 23–55)

Noble, E. (1983). *Childbirth with Insight.* (Boston: Houghton Mifflin)

Nolan, G. H. et al. (1981). The effect of ultrasonography on mid-trimester genetic amniocentesis complications. *Am. J. Obstet. Gynecol.*, **140**, 531

Nuckolls, K. B., Cassel, J. and Kaplan, B. H. (1972). Psychological assets, life crises, and prognosis of pregnancy. *Am. J. Epidemiol.*, **95**, 431–41

Oakley, A. (1980). *Women Confined: Towards a Sociology of Childbirth.* (Oxford: Robertson)

Oakley, A. (1981). *From Here to Maternity: Becoming a Mother.* (UK: Penguin Books)

Odent, M. (1984). *Birth Reborn.* (New York: Pantheon Books) (Orig. French ed. 1976)

O'Driscoll, K. and Meagher, D. (1980). *Active Management of Labor.* (Philadelphia: W. B. Saunders)

Ogden, T. H. (1979). On projective identification. *Int. J. Psycho-Anal.*, **60**, 357–73

Ogle, W. (1982). *Aristotle on the Parts of Animals,* (London: Kegan Paul)

Ohkawa, T., Arai, K., Okinaga, S., Götz, F., Stahl, F. and Dörner, G. (1986). Tyrosine administration combined with stress exposure in prenatal life prevents the diminished male copulatory behaviour in adult rats. In Dörner, G., McCann, S. M. and Martini, L. (eds.) *Systemic Hormones, Neurotransmitters and Brain Development.* pp. 167–71. (Basel: Karger)

Oliver, C. M. and Oliver, G. M. (1978). Gentle birth: its safety and its effect on neonatal behavior. *JOGN Nurs.*, **7**(5), 35–40

Olkin, S. K. (1981). *Positive Pregnancy through Yoga.* (Englewood Cliffs, NJ: Prentice Hall)

Olson, G. A., Olson, R. D. and Kastin, A. J. (1985). Endogenous opiates in 1984. *Peptides*, **6**, 769–91

Oribasius of Pergamos: French tr. by Bussemaker and Daremberg. 6 Vols. Paris 1851–1876

Ornston, D. (1985). The invention of 'cathexis' and Strachey's strategy. *Int. Rev. Psycho-Anal.,* **12,** 4, 391–9

Ortner, S. (1974). Is female to male as Nature is to Culture? In Rosaldo and Lamphere (eds.) *Woman, Culture and Society.* pp. 65–87. (Stanford: Stanford University Press)

Pancheri, P. et al. (1985). ACTH, – endorphin and met-enkephalin: peripheral modifications during the stress of human labour. *Psycho-Neuro-Endocrinology,* **10,** 289–301

Papiernik, E. (1969). Coéfficient de risque d'accouchement prématuré. *Presse Med.,* **77,** 793–4

Papousek, H. (1967). Experimental studies of appetitional behavior in human newborns and infants. In Stevenson, H. W., Hess, E. H. and Rheingold, H. L. (eds.) *Early Behavior: Comparative and Developmental Approaches.* pp. 249–77. (New York: John Wiley)

Papousek, H. and Papousek, M. (1977a). Mothering and the cognitive head-start: psychobiological considerations. In Schaffer, H. R. (ed.) *Studies in Mother–Infant Interaction.* Chap. 4. (London: Academic Press)

Papousek, H. and Papousek, M. (1977b). Die ersten sozialen Beziehungen: Entwicklungschance oder pathogene Situation? *Praxis der Psychotherapie,* **23**(3), 97–108

Papousek, H. and Papousek, M. (1978). Interdisciplinary parallels in studies of early human behavior: from physical to cognitive needs, from attachment to dyadic education. *Int. J. Behav. Dev.,* **1,** 37–49

Papousek, H. and Papousek, M. (1982). Integration into the social world: survey of research. In Stratton, P. (ed.) *Psychobiology of the Human Newborn.* pp. 367–90. (New York: Wiley)

Papousek, H. and Papousek, M. (1987). Intuitive parenting: a dialectic counterpart to the infant's precocity in integrative capacities. In Osofsky, J. D. (ed.) *Handbook of Infant Development.* 2nd Edn., pp. 669–720. (New York: Wiley)

Parasara (1968). *Parāśarasmrti,* Edited by Daivajnavacaspati Sri Vasudeva. (Benares: Chowkhamba Sanskrit Series Office)

Parke, R. D. (1978). Parent–infant interaction: progress, paradigms and problems. In Sackett, G. P. (ed.) *Observing Behavior.* Vol. 1.: Theory and applications in mental retardation. (Baltimore: University Park Press)

Parke, R. D. and O'Leary, S. E. (1976). Father–mother–infant interaction in the newborn period: some findings, some observations and some unresolved issues. In Riegel, K. and Meacham, J. (eds.) *The Developing Individual in a Changing World.* Vol. II: Social and environmental issues. (The Hague: Mouton).

Parke, R. D., O'Leary, S. E. and West, S. (1972). Mother–father–newborn interaction: effects of maternal medication, labor and sex of infant. *Proceedings of the American Psychological Association*, 85–6

Parke, R. D., Hymel, S., Power, T. G. and Tinsley, B. R. (1980). Fathers and risks: a hospital-based model of intervention. In Sawin, D. B., Hawkins, R. C., Walker, L. O. and Penticuff, J. H. (eds.) *Experimental Infant: Psychological Risks in Infant-Environment Transactions.* Vol. 4. (New York: Brunner/Mazel)

Parke, R. D., Grossmann, K. and Tinsley, B. R. (1981). Father–mother–infant interaction in the newborn period: a German–American comparison. In Field, T. M., Sostek, A, M., Vietzke, P. and Leidermann, P. H. (eds.) *Culture and Early Interactions.* (Hillsdale, NJ: Lawrence Erlbaum Associates)

Parkinson, C. E., Wallis, S. et al. (1981). School achievements and behaviour of children who were small for dates at birth. *Dev. Med. Child. Neurol.*, **23,** 41

Paruthos, C. (1984). *Transformation through Birth.* (South Hadley, Mass.: Bergin & Garvey)

Payer, L. (1983). Use of ultrasound on fetus showing no bad effects. *Medical Post*

Pearce, J. C. (1980). *Magical Child.* (New York: Bantam)

Pearn, J. H. (1973). Patient's subjective interpretation of risks offered in genetic counselling. *J. Med. Genet.*, **10,** 129–33

Pelletier, K. R. (1977). *Mind as Healer, Mind as Slayer.* (New York: Dell Publishing Co.)

Perrez, M. (1984). Analyse sozialer Kontingenzen bei Säuglingen. In *Bericht 34. Kongreß der DGfPs*, p. 137

Pert, C. (1986). Neuropeptides link brain, immunity. *Brain/Mind Bull.*, **11**(4), Jan 20

Peterson, G. (1984). *Birthing Normally: A Personal Growth Approach to Childbirth.* (Palo Alto, C.A., California: Mindbody Press)

Petersen, P. (1986). Empfängnis und Zeugung: Phänomene der Kindesankunft. *Z. Klin. Psych., Psychopathol., Psychother.*, **34,** 19–31

Peterson, G. and Mehl, L. (1978). Some determinants of maternal attachment. *Am. J. Psychiatr.*, **135,**

Peterson, G. and Mehl, L. (1985). *Pregnancy as Healing.* (Palo Alto, C.A., Mindbody Press)

Peterson, G., Mehl, L. and Leidermann, H. (1979). The role of some birth-related variables in father attachment. *Am. J. Orthopsychiatr.*, **49,**(2), 330–8

Petitti, D. B. (1984). Effects of *in utero* ultrasound exposure in humans. *Birth*, **11,** 159

Pfeiffer, C. A. (1936). Sexual differences of the hypophyses and their determination by the gonads. *Am. J. Anat.*, **58,** 195–225

Phillips, J. M. (1975). Fetoscopy: an overview. *J. Reprod. Med.,* **15,** 69–72

Phoenix, C. H., Goy, R. W., Gerall, A. A. and Young, W. C. (1959). Organizing action of prenatally administered testosterone propionate on the tissues mediating behavior in the female guinea pig. *Endocrinology,* **65,** 369–82

Piontelli, A. (1986). *Backwards in Time.* Clunie Press for the Roland Harris Trust Library, Monograph No. 1.

Pincus, L. and Dare, C. (1978). *Secrets in the Family.* (London: Faber & Faber)

Plato (1970). *The Laws,* Book VII, §12, Education: The Importance of Movement. pp. 273–4. (London: Penguin Classics) Transl. T. J. Saunders

Plutarch of Chaeronea (1603). Moralis. tr. by Philemon Holland, Hatfield, London

Pollack, M. (1981). New answer for amniocentesis: Who's the father? *Med. World News,* Dec. 7th, 68

Polybus: See Hippocrates

Portmann, A. (1944). *Biologische Fragmente.* (Basel: Benno Schwalbe & Co.)

Powledge, T. M. and Fletcher, J. (1979). Guidelines for the ethical, social, and legal issues in prenatal diagnosis. *N. Engl. J. Med.,* **300,** 168–72

Prechtl, H. F. R. (1977). The neurological examination of the full-term newborn infant. Second revised and enlarged edition. *Clinics in Developmental Medicine,* 63. (London: William Heineman Books)

Prechtl, H. F. R and O'Brien, M. J. (1982). Behavioural states of the full-term newborn. The emergence of a concept. In Stratton, P. (ed.) *Psychobiology of the Newborn.* pp. 52–73. (New York, NY: John Wiley & Sons)

Pribram, K. H. (1968). The cognitive revolution and mind/brain issues. *Am. Psychol.,* **41**(5), 507–20

Provence, S. and Lipton, R. C. (1962). Infants in institutions. (New York: Int. Univ. Press)

Prugh, D. G. (ed.) (1960). *The Healthy Child.* (Cambridge, Mass.)

Pudenz, R. E., Russell, F. E. and Hurd, A. H. (1967). Venticulo-auriculostomy. A technique for shunting cerebrospinal fluid into the right auricle. *J. Neurosurg.,* **27,** 525–9

Purpura, D. (1974). Neuronal migration and dendritic differentiation: normal and aberrant development of human cerebral cortex. In *Biologic and Clinic Aspects of Brain Development, Mead-Johnson Symposium on Perinatal and Developmental Medicine,* No. 6

Purpura, D. (1975a). Dendrite differentiation in human cerebral cortex; normal and aberrent developmental patterns. *Adv. Neurol.,* **12,** 91–116

Purpura, D. (1975b) Consciousness. *Behavior Today,* June 2, p. 494

Quasthoff-Hartmann, U. (1982). Frageaktivitäten von Patienten in Visitengesprächen. In Köhle, K. and Raspe, H. H. (eds.) *Das Gespräch während der arztlichen Visite.* pp. 70–102. (München: Urban & Schwarzenberg)

Raikov, V. L. (1980). Age regression to infancy by adult subjects in deep hypnosis. *Am. J. Clin. Hypnosis,* **22**(3), 156–63

Rajhvajn, B. and Kurjak, A. (1981). Ultrasound measurements of umbilical blood flow in normal and complicated pregnancies. In Kurjak, A. and Kratochwil, A. (eds.) *Recent Advances in Ultrasound Diagnosis.* Vol. 3: *Proceedings of the 4th European Congress on Ultrasonics in Medicine,* Dubrovik, May 17–24. (Amsterdam, Excerpta Medica). International Congress Series, 553, 240–2

Rank, O. (1923). Zum Verständnis der Libidoentwicklung im Heilungsvorgang. *Int. Zeitschr. Psychoanalyse,* **IX,** 434–71

Rank, O. (1924). Das Trauma der Geburt und seine Bedeutung für die Psychoanalyse. (Wien: Int. Psychoanal. Verlag)

Rank, O. (1926). Die analytische Situation. Technik der Psychoanalyse. Vol. I. (Wien, Leipzig: Deuticke)

Ranke-Graves von, R. and Patai, R. (1963). *Hebrew Myths: The Book of Genesis.* (New York: Doubleday & Co.)

Raphael-Leff, J. (1980). Psychotherapy with pregnant women. In Blum (ed.) *Psychological Aspects of Pregnancy, Birthing and Bonding.* pp. 174–205. (New York: Human Sciences Press)

Raphael-Leff, J. (1984). Myths and modes of motherhood. *Br. J. Psychother.,* **1,** 6–30

Raphael-Leff, J. (1986). Facilitators and regulators: conscious and unconscious processes in pregnancy and early motherhood. *Br. J. Med. Psychol.,* **59,** 43–55

Rau, H. (1982). Frühe Kindheit. In Oerter, R. and Montada, L. (eds.) *Entwicklungspsychologie.* (München, Wien, Baltimore: Urban & Schwarzenberg)

Rau, H. (1983). Frühkindliche Entwicklung. In Silbereisen, R. K. and Montada, L. (eds.) *Entwinklungspsychologie.* (München, Wien, Baltimore: Urban & Schwarzenberg)

Reading, A. (1980). Psychological effects on a mother of real-time ultrasound. Paper presented at the *Conference of the Division of Clinical Psychology,* British Psychological Society, London

Reinisch, J. M. (1977). Prenatal exposure of human foetuses to synthetic progestin and oestrogen affects personality. *Nature,* **266,** 561–2

Retzlaff, E., Mitchell, F. L. Jr., Upledger, Vridevoogd, J. and Walsh, J. (1980). Neurovascular mechanisms in cranial sutures. *J. Osteopathic Assoc.,* **80,** 218–19

Rice, R. (1977). Neurophysiological development in premature infants following stimulation. *Dev. Psychol.,* **13,** 69–76

Rice, R. D. (1979). The effects of the rice infant sensorimotor stimulation treatment on the development of high-risk infants. The National Foundation. *Birth Defects: Original Article Series,* **XV,** 7, 7–26

Rich, A. (1977). *Of Woman Born*. (London: Virago)
Richard, R. *Osteopathic Lesions of the Sacrum*. (Thorsons)
Richards, M. (1978). *New Scientist,* 847–9
Ringler, M. and Krizmanits, A. (1983). Zur Psychosomatik der Emesis Gravidarum: Wahrnehmungs und Einstellungsmuster von Frauen in der Frühschwanger schaft. *Z. Geburtsh. u. Perinat.,* **187,** 246–9. (Abstract also in *Bericht 34. Kongreß der DGfPs,* 1984, p. 144)
Robertson, J. (1970). *Young Children in Hospital*. (London: Tavistock Publications Ltd.)
Robillard, A. B. *et al.* (1983). Between doctor and patient: informed consent in conversational interaction. In Fisher, S. and Todd, A. D. (eds.) *The Social Organization of Doctor–Patient Communication*. pp. 107–33. (Washington DC: Center for Applied Linguistics)
Robinson, A. *et al.* (1973). Intrauterine diagnosis: potential complications. *Am. J. Obstet. Gynecol.,* **116,** 937–41
Robinson, H. P. (1973). Sonar measurements of fetal crown-rump length as a means of assessing maturity in the first trimester of pregnancy. *Br. Med. J.,* **4,** 48
Robinson, H. P. and Fleming, J. E. E. (1975). A critical evaluation of sonar crown-rump length measurements. *Br. J. Obstet. Gynaecol.,* **82,** 702
Robson, K. M. and Kumar, R. (1980). Delayed onset of maternal affection after childbirth. *Br. J. Psychiatr.,* **136,** 347–53
Rodgers, B. (1978). Feeding in infancy and later ability and attainment: a longitudinal study. *Dev. Med. Child Neurol.,* **20,** 421–6
Roffwarg, H. P., Muzio, J. N. and Dement, W. C. (1966). Ontogenetic development of the human sleep-dream cycle. *Science,* **152,** 604–19
Rosso, P. and Winick (1974). Intrauterine growth retardation. A new systematic approach on the clinical and biochemical characteristics of this condition. *J. Perinat. Med.,* **2,** 147
Rothman, B. K. (1986). *The Tentative Pregnancy*. (New York: Viking)
Rottmann, G. (1974). Untersuchungen über Einstellungen zur Schwanger schaft und zür fötalen Entwicklung. In Graber, G. H. (ed.) *Pränatale Psychologie*. (München: Kindler Verlag)
Rovee-Collier, C. (1985). Baby's memory. *Am. Psychol. Assoc. Monitor,* Oct. 1985, 25
Rowbotham, S. (1973). *Woman's Consciousness, Man's World*. (London: Pelican)
Rush, D., Stein, Z. and Susser, M. (1978). A randomized control trial of prenatal nutritional supplementation in New York City. *Pediatrics,* **33,** 32
Ryan, V. S. (1977). Effect of prenatal and postnatal nutrition on development, behaviour and physiology of the rat. PhD Thesis, Wayne State University. (Abstract in *Diss. Abstr. Int. B. Sci. Engl.,* **37,** 5875)

Rycroft, C. (1986). *A Critical Dictionary of Psychoanalysis*, p. 16. (London: Nelson)
Sacks, H. (1972). Spring Lectures 1–5. (University of California: Irvine)
Sacks, H., Schegloff, E. A. and Jefferson, G. (1978). A simpler systematics for the organization of turn taking for conversation. In Schenkein, J. (ed.) *Studies in the Organization of Conversational Interaction*. pp. 7–57. (New York: Academic)
Sadger, J. (1974). Preliminary study of the psychic life of the fetus and the primary gene. *Psycho-Anal. Rev.,* **28,** 327–58
Sagi, A. and Hoffman, M. L. (1976). Empathic distress in the newborn. *Dev. Psychol.,* **12,** 175–6
Salk, L. (1962). Mother's heartbeat as an imprinting stimulus. *Trans. N. Y. Acad. Sci.,* **24,** 753–63
Salk, L. (1966). Thoughts on the concept of imprinting and its place in early human development. *Can. Psychiatr. Assoc. J.,* **11,** S295–S305
Salk, L. (1973). The role of the heartbeat in the relations between mother and infant. *Sci. Am.,* **220,** 24–9
Salk, L. et al. (1985). Relationship of maternal and perinatal conditions to eventual adolescent suicide. *Lancet,* **1** (8429), 624–7
Sameroff, A. See Spezzano, Ch. (1981), p. 27
Sanabria, E. R. and Gomez, H. M. Rational handling of the premature child. Prepublication report by UNICEF, Geneva
Sander, L. (1980). New knowledge about the infant from current research: implications for psychoanalysis. *J. Am. Psychoanal. Assoc.,* **28,** 181–98
Scammon, R. E. (1927). The first seriatim study of human growth. *Am. J. Physiol. Anthropol.,* **10,** 329–36
Schaefer, E. S. and Manheimer, H. (1960). Dimensions of perinatal adjustments. Paper presented at *The Eastern Psychological Association Convention,* New York
Schaffer, R. (1978). *Mütterliche Fürsorge in den ersten Lebensjahren.* (Stuttgart)
Schaffer, H. R. (1979). Acquiring the concept of the dialogue. In Borenstein, M. H. and Kessen, W. (eds.) *Psychological Development from Infancy: Image to Intention.* pp. 279–305. (Hillsdale, NJ: Erlbaum)
Schindler, S. (1982). *Geburt: Eintritt in eine neue Welt.* Verlag für Psychologie, C. J. Hogrefe, Göttingen
Schindler, S. and Zimprich, H. (1983). *Ökologie der Perinatalzeit.* (Stuttgart: Hippokrates Verlag)
Schmidt, E. (1979). Vorzüge der Muttermilchernährung des Säuglings. *Monatsschr. Kinderheilkd.,* **127,** 525–8. (Vortrag gehalten in May, 1978)
Schmidt-Denter, U. (1984). *Die soziale Umwelt des Kindes.* (Berlin: Springer)
Schmidt-Kolmer, E. (1984). *Frühe Kindheit,* Berlin

Scholz, C. (1984). Das genetische Beratungsgespräch am Beispiel der Arzneimittelberatung. Unveröffentl. Diplomarbeit. Ludwig-Maximilian-Universität, München

Schröder-Kurth, T. M. (1985). Indikation zur pränatalen Diagnostik, Grundsätze und Konflikte. *Zeit. für evangelische Ethik*, **29,** 30–50

Schulman-Galambos, C. and Galambos, R. (1979). Assessment of hearing. In Field, T. M. (ed.) *Infants Born at Risk: Behavior and Development*. 117f. (New York: S. P. Medical & Scientific Books)

Schwartz, L. (1980). *The World of the Unborn: Nurturing your Child before Birth.* (New York: Richard Marek)

Schwerdtfeger, J. (1981). Das Erleben der frühen Schwangerschaft: eine kasuistische Studie bei zehn erstgebärenden Frauen und ihren Partnern. *Diss. Med. Hochschule,* Hannover

Scott, E. M. and Thompson, A. M. (1956). A psychological investigation of primigravidas. IV. Psychological factors and the clinical phenomena of labor. *J. Obstet. Gynecol. Br. Empire,* **63,** 502–8

Shaw, E. and Darling, J. (1985). *Strategies of Being Female: Animal Patterns, Human Choices.* (Brighton, UK: Harvester Press)

Sheldrake, R. (1981). *A New Science of Life: The Hypothesis of Formative Causation.* (Los Angeles: J. P. Tarcher)

Shereshefsky, P. M. and Yarrow, L. J. (eds.) (1973). *Psychological Aspects of a First Pregnancy and Early Postnatal Adaptation.* (New York: Raven Press)

Shnider, S. M. et al. (1979). Uterine blood flow and plasma norepinephrine changes during maternal stress in the pregnant ewe. *Anesthesiology,* **50,** 524–7

Siegrist, J. (1976). Asymmetrische Kommunikation bei klinischen Visiten. *Medizinische Klinik.,* **71,** 1962–6

Silberer, S. (1914). *Probleme der Mystik und ihre Symbolik.* (Darmstadt: Wiss Buchgem)

Simner, M. (1971). Newborns' responses to the cry of another infant. *Dev. Psychol.,* **5,** 136–50

Simoni, G., Gimelli, G., Cuoco, C., Romitti, L., Terzoli, G., Guerneri, S., Rossella, F., Pescetto, L., Pezzolo, A., Porta, S., Brambati, B., Porro, E. and Fraccaro, M. (1986). First trimester feta karyotyping: one thousand diagnoses. *Hum. Genet.,* **72,** 203–9

Singer, C. (ed.) (1917). *Studies in the History and Method of Science.* Vol. 1. Oxford

Sinosich, M. J., Ferrier, A. and Saunders, D. M. (1985). Monitoring of postimplantation embryo viability following successful *in vitro* fertilization and embryo transfer by measurement of placental proteins. *Fertil. Steril.,* **44,** 70

Skynner, A. C. R. (1976). *One Flesh: Separate Persons*. (London. Constable & Co.)
Slater, A., Morison, V. and Rose, D. (1982). Visual imagery at birth. *Br. J. Psychol.*, **73,** 519–25
Smilkstein, G., Helsper-Lucas, A., Ashworth, C., Montano, D. and Pagel, M. (1984). Predicting pregnancy complications: an application of the biopsychosocial model. *Soc. Sci. Med.*, **18,** 315–21
Smith, R. E. (1975). Standardization of the Leiter International Performance Scale. Thesis. (Los Angeles: Univ. Southern California)
Sontag, L. W. (1941). The significance of fetal environmental differences. *Am. J. Obstet. Gynecol.*, **42,** 996–1003
Sontag, L. (1944). Differences in modifiability of fetal behavior and physiology. *Psychosom. Med.*, **6,** 151–4
Sontag, L. W., Steele, W. G. and Lewis, M. (1969). The fetal and maternal cardiac response to environmental stress. *Hum. Dev.*, **12,** 1–19
Soranus of Ephesus (1894). *Die Gynäkologie d. Soranus von Ephesus*. German tr. by H. Lüneberg, Münich
Sosa, R., Kennell, J., Klaus, M. et al. (1980). The effect of a supportive companion on perinatal problems, length of labor, and mother–infant interaction. *N. Engl. J. Med.*, **303,** 597–600
Spender, D. (1980). *Man Made Language*. (London: Routledge & Kegan Paul)
Spezzano, C. (1981). Streß in Mutterleib. In *Psychologie Heute,* 8 Jg., No. 11, pp. 22–9
Spielberger, C. D., Gorsuch, R. L. and Lushene, R. E. (1970). *STAI Manual for the State-Trait Anxiety Inventory.* (Palo Alto: Consulting Psychologists Press)
Spielberger, C. and Jacobs, G. (1979). Emotional reactions to the stress of pregnancy and obstetrics complications. In Carenza, L. and Zichella, L. (eds.) *Emotion and Reproduction*. 20-A, p. 13. (London: Academic Press)
Spielrein, S. (1912). Destruktion als Ursache des Werdens. *Jahrbuch für psychopathologische und psychoanalytische Forschung,* Vol. IV
Spitz, R. A. (1945a). Diacritic and coenesthetic organizations. *Psychoanal. Rev.*, **32**(2), 146–62
Spitz, R. A. (1945b). Hospitalism: an inquiry into the genesis of psychiatric conditions in early childhood. *Psychoanalytic Study of the Child.* Vol. I, pp. 53–74. (London: Imago Publishing)
Spitz, R. A. (1946). Hospitalism: a follow-up report. *Psychoanalytic Study of the child.* Vol. II, pp. 113–17. (New York: Int. Univ. Press)
Spitz, R. A. (1950). Relevancy of direct infant observation. *Psychoanalytic Study of the Child.* Vol. V, pp. 66–73. (p. 70). (New York: Int. Univ. Press)
Stahl, F., Götz, F., Poppe, I., Amendt, P. and Dörner, G. (1978). Pre- and early postnatal testosterone levels in rat and human. In Dörner, G. and

Kawakami, M. (eds.) *Hormones and Brain Development. Developments in Endocrinology*, Vol. 3. pp. 99–109. (Amsterdam, New York, Oxford: Elsevier/North-Holland Biomedical Press)

Star, R. B. (1986). *The Healing Power of Birth*. (Austin, Texas: Star Publishing)

Starkman, M. N. and Youngs, D. D. (1980). Reactions to electronic fetal monitoring. In Youngs, D. D. and Ehrhardt, A. A. (eds.) *Psychosomatic Obstetrics and Gynecology*. pp. 145–7. (New York: Appleton-Century-Crofts)

Staudt, J., Stüber, P. and Dörner, G. (1978a). Morphologische Untersuchungen des Corpus amygdaloideum der Ratte nach der neonatalen Applikation von Reserpin und anderen Substanzen. *Folia anatomica jugoslavica*, **7**, 89–93

Staudt, J., Stüber, P. and Dörner, G. (1978b). Permanent changes of sexual dimorphism in the rat brain following neonatal treatment with psychotrophic drugs. In Dörner, G. and Kawakami, M. (eds.) *Hormones and Brain Development. Developments in Endocrinology*, Vol. 3, pp. 35–41. (Amsterdam, New York, Oxford: Elsevier/North-Holland Biomedical Press)

Steiner, J. E. (1979). Human facial expressions in response to taste and smell stimulation. In Reese, H. W. and Lipsitt, L. P. (eds.) *Advances in Child Development and Behaviour*. Vol. 13, 257–95

Steingruber, H.-J. and Plugmacher, C. (1982). Geburt in der Klinik: Frühe Mutter–Kind-Interaktion. In Beckman, Davies-Osterkamp, Scheer (eds.) *Medizinische Psychologie*. pp. 449–92. (Berlin, Heidelberg, New York)

Stern, D. (1980). Panel report by L. W. Sander: new knowledge about the infant from current research: implications for psychoanalysis. *J. Am. Psychoanal. Assoc.*, **28**, 181–98

Stern, D. (1985). *The interpersonal world of the infant: a view from psychoanalysis and developmental psychology*. (New York: Basic Books)

Stillman, R. J. (1982). In utero exposure to diethylstilbestrol: adverse effects on the reproductive tract and reproductive performance in male and female offspring. *Am. J. Obstet. Gynecol.*, **142**, 905–21

Stockman, J. A. (1979). *1979 Year Book of Pediatrics*. (Chicago: Year Book Medical)

Stone, L. J., Smith, H. T. and Murphy, L. B. (1974). *The Competent Infant*. (London: Tavistock) (New York: Basic Books 1973)

Stott, D. H. (1966). A general test of motor impairment for children. *Dev. Med. Child Neurol.* **8**, 523–31

Stott, D. H. (1973). Follow-up study from birth of the effects of prenatal stresses. *Dev. Med. Child Neurol.*, **15**, 770–87

Stratmeyer, M. E. (1980). Research in ultrasound bioeffects: a public health view. *Birth Family J.*, **7**(2), 92–100

Strato of Lampsacus: See Allbutt
Strauss, S. (1984). Microwaves may cause gene damage. *The Globe & Mail*, 29 March, p. 612
Streek, J. (1983). Konversationsanalyse. Ein Reparaturversuch. *Zeitschrift für Sprachwissenschaft*, **2**, 72–104
Stuart, H. C., Reed, R. B., Pyle, S. I. et al. (1959). Longitudinal studies of child health and development. *Pediatrics*, **24**, 875–974
Suśruta, Suśrutasamhitā (Sārirasthānam and Cikitsāsthānam). (1954). Edited by Ambikadatta Sastri. (Benares: Chowkhamba Sanskrit Series Office)
Sutherland, J. D. (1980). The British object relations theorists: Balint, Winnicott, Fairbairn, Guntrip. *J. Am. Psychoanal. Assoc.*, **28**, 829–61
Sutherland, W. *Cranial Bowl*. (SCTF)
Sutherland, W. (1967). *Contributions of Thought*. (Sutherland Cranial Teaching Foundation)
Švejcar, J. (1983). Ernährung des Säuglings durch Stillen. In *Schrifterreihe des Instituts für Fortbildung von Ärzten und Pharmazeuten*. Prag. Nr. 22, H, 4, pp. 235–53
Swaab, D. F. and Fliers, E. (1985). A sexually dimorphic nucleus in the human brain. *Science*, **228**, 1112–15
Swenson, E. A. (1928). *Anat. Rec.*, **42**, 40
Tanner, J. M. (1962). *Growth at Adolescence*. (Oxford: Blackwell)
Taylor, S. H. (1980). The association between pregnancy anxiety and the self concept in married primigravidae. Unpublished Doctoral Dissertation, University of Northern Colorado
Teasdale, T. W. (1979). Social class correlations among adoptees and their biological and adoptive parents. *Behav. Genet.*, **9**, 103–4
Terman, L. M. and Oden, M. H. (1947). *The Gifted Child Grows Up*. (Stanford: Stanford University Press)
Ter Vrugt, D. and Pederson, D. R. (1973). The effects of vertical rocking frequencies on the arousal level in two-month-old infants. *Child Dev.*, **44**, 205–9
Teuscher, H. (1888). *Fortschritte d. Medizin*, **6**, 863
Thomas, F. A. et al. (1982). Influence of medication, pain and progress in labor on plasma beta-endorphin-like immunoreactivity. *Br. J. Anesth.*, **54**, 401–8
Thompson, M. (1979). Another view. *The People's Doctor Newsletter*, **3**(11)
Thurmann, L. and Langness, A. P. (1986). *Heartsongs: A Guide to Active Pre-Birth and Infant Parenting Through Language and Singing*. (Engelwood, Colorado: Music Study Services)
Timor-Tritsch, I. E. (1986). The effect of external stimuli on fetal behaviour. *Eur. J. Obstet. Reprod. Biol.*, **21**, 321–9
Tönjes, R., Kitzrow, W., Poppe, I. and Dörner, G. (1984). Possible role played

by monoamines in the control of puberty onset in female rats. *Exp. Clin. Endocrinol.,* **83,** 1–5

Trampuz, V. (1968). Partial refractoriness to cortisone therapy in the adrenogenital syndrome. In *Research on Steroids.* 3rd meeting International Study group for Steroid Hormones, Vol. 3. Cassano, C., Finkelstein, M., Klopper, A. and Conti, C. (eds.) pp. 347–8. (Amsterdam: North-Holland Publishing)

Trethowan, W. H. and Conlon, M. F. (1965). The Couvade syndrome. *Br. J. Psychiatr,* **111,** 57–66

Trevarthen, C. (1974). The psychobiology of speech development. *Neurosci. Res. Prog. Bull.,* **12**(4), 570–85

Trevarthen, C. (1979). Communication and co-operation in early infancy: a description of primary intersubjectivity. In Bullowa, M. (ed.) *Before Speech: The Beginnings of Interpersonal Communication.* pp. 321–47. (Cambridge)

Trevarthen, C. (1980). The foundations of intersubjectivity: development of interpersonal and co-operative understanding in infants. In Olson, D. R. (ed.) *The Social Foundations of Language and Thought: Essays in honor of Jerome S. Bruner.* pp. 316–42. (New York: W. W. Norton)

Troisfontaines-De-Marneffe, F. (1984). Dynamique des Neuro-Hormones Maternelles et Foetales lors de l'Accouchement. *Mémoire de Licence en Gyn. Obst.,* Université de Liège, Belgium

Tronick, E. and Adamson, L. (1980). *Babies as People: New Findings on our Social Beginnings.* (New York: Collier Books)

Tronick, E. Z., Als, H., Adamson, L., Brazelton, B. and Wise, S. (1978). The infants response to entrapment between contradictory messages in face-to-face interaction. *J. Am. Acad. Child Psychiatr.,* **17**(1), 1–13

Tronick, E. Z., Ricks, M. and Cohn, J. F. (1982). Maternal and infant affective exchange: patterns of adaptation. In Field, T. M. and Fogel, A. (eds.) *Emotion and Early Interaction.* (Hillsdale, NJ: Erlbaum)

Trout, M. (1986). The psychological dimensions of pregnancy, labor and delivery. In *The Awakening and Growth of the Human: Studies in Infant Mental Health.* Videotape produced and narrated by Michael Trout. (Alma, Michigan: The Center for the Study of Infants and their Families)

Truby, H. M. (1971). Prenatal and neonatal speech, 'pre-speech', and an infantile-speech lexicon. *Word,* **27,** 57–101

Truby, H. M. and Lind, J. (1965). Cry sounds of the newborn infant. In Lind, J. (ed.) *Newborn Infant Cry. Acta Paediatrica Scandinavica,* Supplement 163

Tulving, E. (1985). How many memory systems are there? *Am. Psychol.,* **40**(4), 385–98

Uddenberg, N., Fagerstrom, C. and Hakanson-Zaunders, M. (1976). Reproductive conflicts, mental symptoms during pregnancy and time in labor. *J. Psychosom. Res.,* **20,** 575–81

Uexkull, Th. V. (ed.) (1981). *Lehrbuch der Psychosomatischen Medizin.* (München, Wien, Baltimore)

Ungerer, J. A., Brody, L. R. and Zelazo, P. (1978). Long-term memory for speech in 2–4 week old infants. *Infant Behav. Dev.,* **1,** 177–86

Upledger and Vredevoogd (1983). *Craniosacral Therapy.* (Eastland Press)

Vāgbhata (1956). *Astanghrdayam.* Edited by Taradatta Panta. (Benares: Haridas Sanskrit Series 106)

Van den Bergh, B. (1983). De psychische toestand van de zwangere en de prenatale ontwikkeling. *T. Orthoped. Kinderpsych.,* **8,** 18–37

Van de Carr, F. R., Lehrer, M. and Van de Carr, K. (1984). Prenatal university. *New Horizons for Learning,* **4**(3), 9–10

Van der Ploeg, H. M., Defares, P. B. and Spielberger, C. D. (1980). *Handleiding bij de Zelfbeoordelingsuragenlijst ZBV. Een Nederlandse bewerking van de Spielberger State-Trait Anxiety Inventory, STAI-DY.* (Lisse: Swets & Zeitlinger)

Van Dongen, L. G. R. and Goudie, E. G. (1980). Fetal movements in the first trimester of pregnancy. *Br. J. Obstet. Gynecol.,* **87,** 191–3

Van Look, P. F. A., Hunter, W. M., Corker, C. S. and Baird, D. T. (1977). Failure of positive feedback in normal men and subjects with testicular feminization. *Clin. Endocrinol.,* **7,** 353–66

Vaṣistha (1930). *Vaṣistha Dharmasutra.* Edited by A. A. Führer, 3rd Edn. (Poona: Bhandarkar Oriental Research Institution)

Vaughn, H. G. Jr. (1975). Electrophysiological analysis of regional cortical maturation. *Biol. Psychiatr.,* **10,** 513–26

Veldman, F. (1982). Life welcomed and affirmed. *The St. Cloud Visitor,* Newspaper of the Catholic Diocese of St. Cloud, Minnesota, Vol. LXXI, Nov. 11th

Verny, T. and Kelly, J. (1981). *The Secret Life of the Unborn Child.* (New York: Summit Books) (1982 edn. Dell)

Vinci, Leonardo da (1911). *Quaderni d'Auatomia.* 6 Vols. Eds. Vaugenstein, Fohnahn and Hopstock, (Christiania: Dybwad)

Visser, G. H. A., Zeelenberg, H. J., de Vries, T. I. and Dawes, G. S. (1983). External physical stimulation during episodes of low heart rate variation. *Am. J. Obstet. Gynecol.,* **145,** 579–84

Vries de, J. I. P., Visser, G. H. A. and Prechtl, H. F. R. (1982). The emergence of fetal behaviour. I. Qualitative aspects. *Early Hum. Dev.,* **6,** 301–22

Wachtler, J. (1896). *De Alcmaeone Crotoniata.* (Leipzig)

Waelder, R. (1936). The principle of multiple function. *Psychoanal. Q.,* **5,** 45–62

Wald, N. J. et al. (1983). Congenital talipes and hip malformation in relation to amniocentesis: a case-controlled study. *Lancet,* **2,** 246–9

Walker, A. H. C. (1957). Liquor amnil studies in the prediction of haemolytic disease of the newborn. *Br. Med. J.,* **2,** 376

Walther, D. *Applied Kineseology.* Vol. 2. (Systems DC)

Watson, J. S. (1973). Smiling, cooing and 'the game'. *Merrill Palmer Q. Behav. Dev.,* **18,** 323–39

Welch, G. (1985). Variability of practice and knowledge of results as factors in learning to sing in tune. *Bull. Council Res. Music Education,* **85,** 238–47

Welch, G. (1986). A developmental view of children's singing. *Br. J. Music Education,* **3,** 295–303

Werner, J. S. and Siqueland, E. R. (1978). Visual recognition memory in the preterm infant. *Infant Behav. Dev.,* **1,** 79–94

Whitelaw, A. and Sleath, K. (1985). Myth of the marsupial mother: home care of very low birth weight babies in Bogota, Colombia. *Lancet,* May 25, 1206–8

Wiesbauer, E. (1982). *Das Kind als Objekt der Wissenschaft.* (Wien: Löcker)

Wimmer-Puchinger, B. (1985). Konsequenzen Familien-orientierter Geburtshilfe. *Zentralblatt für Gynäkologie,* B. 107, H. 13, pp. 785–92

Winick, M., Rosso, P. et al. (1970). Cellular growth of cerebrum, cerebellum and brainstem in normal and marasmic children. *Exp. Neurol.,* **26,** 393

Winnicott, D. W. (1947). Hate in the countertransference. In *Through Paediatrics to Psycho-Analysis.* Chap. XV. (London: Hogarth Press, 1982)

Winnicott, D. W. (1949). Birth memories, birth trauma and anxiety. In *Through Paediatrics to Psycho-Analysis.* Chap. XIV. (London: Hogarth Press, 1982)

Winnicott, D. W. (1951). Transitional objects and transitional phenomena. In *Through Paediatrics to Psycho-Analysis.* Chap. XVIII. (London: Hogarth Press, 1982)

Winnicott, D. W. (1952). Anxiety associated with insecurity. In *Through Paediatrics to Psycho-Analysis.* Chap. VIII. (London: Hogarth Press, 1982)

Winnicott, D. W. (1957). *Mother and Child: A Primer of First Relationships.* (New York: Basic Books)

Winnicott, D. W. (1958). *Through Paediatrics to Psycho-Analysis.* (London: Hogarth Press & Inst. of Psycho-Anal., 1982)

Winnicott, D. W. (1965). *The Maturational Processes and the Facilitating Environment: Studies of the Theory of Emotional Development.* (London: Hogarth Press & Inst. of Psycho-Anal., 1982)

Winnicott, D. W. (1978). Aggression in relation to emotional development. In *Through Paediatrics to Psycho-Analysis.* pp. 204–18. (London: Hogarth, 1978)

Wladimiroff, W. Y., Tonge, G. M. and Stuart, P. D. (1986). Doppler ultrasound assessment of cerebral blood flow in the fetus. *Br. J. Obstet. Gynecol.,* **93,** 471–5

Wolf, B. (1983). 1st jede entwicklungspsychologische Forschung auch ökopychologisch? In Grossmann, K. E. and Lütkenhaus, P. (eds.) *Bericht 6. Tagung Entwicklungspsychologie.* p. 129 f. (Regensburg)

Wolff, S. (1986). Das Gespräch als Handlungsinstrument. *Kölner Zeitschrift für Soziologie und Sozialpsychologie,* **38,** 55–84

Wolkind, S. (1981). Prenatal emotional stress-effects on the fetus. In Wolkind, S. and Zajiceck, E. (eds.) *Pregnancy: a Psychological and Social Study.* pp. 177–93. (London: Academic Press)

Wolkind, S. N. (1974). Psychological factors and the minor symptoms of pregnancy. *Psychosom. Res.,* **18,** 161–5

Woodman, M. (1985). *The Pregnant Virgin: A Process of Psychological Transformation.* (Toronto: Inner City Books)

World Health Organization (1984). *Health Promotion: a Discussional Document on the Concept and Principles.* (Copenhagen: WHO Regional Office for Europe)

Wucherer-Huldenfeld, A. K. (1973). Ursprung und Anfang des menschlichen Lebens. In Graber, G. H. and Kruse, F. (eds.) *Vorgeburtliches Seelenleben.* (München: Goldmann)

Yalom, I. D., Green, R. and Fish, N. (1973). Prenatal exposure to female hormones: effect on psychosexual development in boys. *Arch. Gen. Psychiat.,* **28,** 554–61

Zachau-Christiansen, B. (1981). Follow-up of infants with perinatal hazards. In Korobkin, R. and Guilleminault, C. (eds.) *Progress in Perinatal Neurology.* Vol. 1. (Baltimore: Williams & Wilkins)

Zachau-Christiansen, B. and Ross, E. M. (1975). *Babies.* (London: Wiley)

Zeno of Citium: See Allbutt

Zilboorg, G. (1974). Masculine and feminine, some biological and cultural aspects (1944). In Miller-Baker (ed.) *Psycho-analysis and Women.* pp. 96–131. (New York: Penguin)

Zimmer, E.Z., Divon, M. Y., Vilensky, A., Sarna, Z., Peretz, B. A. and Paldi, E. (1982). Maternal exposure to music and fetal activity. *Eur. J. Obstet. Gynecol. Reprod. Biol.,* **13,** 209–13

Zuspan, F. P., Cibels, L. A. and Pose, S. V. (1962). Myometrial and cardiovascular responses for alterations in plasma epinephrine and norepinephrine. *Am. J. Obstet. Gynecol.,* **84,** 841–51

Index

abortions, habitual 447
adoption studies 41
AIDS, ISPP research xxi, 613
anemia 58
anthropology, research 617
Aristotle 516 ff
  as father of modern embryology 516
  development of the embryo 517, 518, 522
  enzyme action 517
  on generation 517
Apgar scores, prenatal stimulation 494
asphyxia, perinatal hazards 56
attachment
  cathexis 165 ff
  concepts 217 ff, 384 ff
  early loss and adult personality 41
  father–child 160 ff, 123 ff
  mother–child postnatal 37, 40, 549
  mother–child prenatal 253 ff, 489
  parental 256 ff
  perinatal deprivation 41
  prenatal 51, 217 ff
attitudes
  maternal and preterm labor 87 ff
  maternal postnatal 490
  maternal prenatal 75 ff, 88
  paternal 123 ff

Balint 28
birth
  anxiety 180
  Caesarian 184
  communication 486
  complications 399 ff
  fantasies 177
  hypnotherapy 189 ff
  low birth weight and later schooling 53
  normal 284
  pain 486
  postpartum separation 284
  premature xxi
  preparation xviii
  resistance 486
  social support 469
  symbolism 178
  trauma 28, 177 ff
birth and labor
  parturition 596
  post-birth care 500
  psycho-prophylactic preparations 499
birth memories
  after fantasy journey 539
  birth regression therapy 292
  fetal scripts 537

693

imprinting 292
relationship to womb
environment 590
therapeutic model 293
unconscious guideline 292
bonding 590 ff
adoptive families 284 ff, 287
birth experiences 283
cathexis 165 ff
concepts 217 ff, 383
facilitator 554, 581, 590 ff
mother–child 253 ff
nursing 283, 285 ff
prebirth 267
prebirth bonding program 268 ff
prenatal 217
prognostic indicator 258
touching 285
brain
hormone-dependent
development 419
sexual differentiation 420, 423
Brazelton 255
breast feeding 39, 549
mother's milk 39
Breuer 179
Buddha, beginning of life 543, 548

Caesarian section
preparaton 487
psychiatric diagnosis 399 ff
stress 191
unfulfilled transitions 482 ff
Capra, F. xxv
Caraka 525 ff
embryo development 525
fertilization 525
fetal development 526
genetics 525
Cartesian philosophy
dualistic outlook xix
psychophysical parallelism xix
cathexis
definition 165
narcissistic 214
ultrasound 169
usefulness for prenatal
psychology 165 ff
childbirth education
concepts 483 ff
educators 601

infant stimulation 275
limitations 483 ff
parenting 274, 556
parenting and singing for prenatal
stimulation 274 ff, 278 ff
parenting education 602, 604
parents 599 ff
postnatal care 604
preventative aspects of 599 ff
childbirth preparation
bonding and attachment
promotion xviii
pedagogy xvii
preventative health xviii
programs xvii
technology 481
unfulfilled transitions 481 ff
childbirth techniques 499
current character of 566
Lamaze 600
warm bath (Grodeck) 596
competence
in communicating 9
of the child 27
of the mother xvii
conception
ancient Egyptian ideas 509
conscious 271, 316
conditioning
classical 14
in utero 153
congenital abnormalities 340
conscious parenting xvii
crying 9
cultural/ethnological aspects
abortion/birth control in China 357
archaic mother/matriarch 585
belief in birth memory 541
in myths 584 ff
lack of modern motherhood rituals 588
mother–son cultural perpetuation 586
phenomenological base 46 ff
sexual stereotypes 552 ff, 556
sociocultural expectations 599
woman's role 554, 555, 586

da Vinci, Leonardo 534
anatomical notebooks 533
exponential growth in utero 534
developmental psychology
competence of the infant 27

INDEX 695

development of language 27
hormone-dependent
   development 419
   prenatal period 23, 295
development of the embryo
   ancient ideas 515, 516
   Jewish wisdom literature 525 ff
doula, supportive laywoman during
   labor 469 ff
dreaming 10

ecology research xxii, 611
EEG measurement, prenatal 7
Ekins, P. 614
embryologists of Antiquity
   Allmaeon of Crotona 513
   Aristotelian 517 ff
   Greek 513
   Hippocrates 515
   Hippocratic School 514 ff
   Susruta 519 ff
embryology
   ancient 515
   Indian 519, 528
   theological 512
ethics
   and accelerated development
     controversy 275 ff
   centrist position 276
   endomorphine hormones 277
ethology research 613
experience of pregnancy
   competency of the mother xvii
   mother–child dialog xx
   primal togetherness xxiii
   psychological development xvi

father
   attachment 106
   attention on the fetus 259
   at the birth 112 ff
   birth preparation 103 ff
   bottle feeding 112
   encounter with the child 112
   expectant 124
   father–child interaction 106 ff
   interactive behavior 119
   socialization 119
femininity, fulfilment 212
Ferenczi, S. 27, 28

fertility
   donor insemination 463 ff
   ethics 462 ff
   infertility treatment 463 ff
   in vitro fertilization 448 ff, 461 ff
   psychological disorders 94
fetal
   activity 137 ff
   behavior 134 ff
   heartbeat 254
   mortal behavior 347 ff
   movements 347 ff
   psyche 178 ff
fourth trimester 546, 593
Freud 545
   conception as primal scene 548
   Ur-fantasien 548
Freud, A. 30, 166 ff
Freud, S. 6, 27, 166 ff

Galen 531 ff
   generative process 532
   on embryology 532
   work dedicated to midwife 531
genetic counseling 356, 366 ff, 375 ff
   and conversation analysis 366
   implications of 374 ff
   meaning of utterances 379
   notation system/import of 369
   techniques of 370
   turn-constructural components 369
   turn-taking system 366
Graber, G. H. 29 ff, 168, 178, 607
Grodeck, G. 541
   Freud's view on 595
   on prenatal psychology 595
   prenatal life 595
   prenatal development 596
growth retardation
   ultrasound 338
gynecologists
   Cleopatra and fetal development 534

habituation 11
health
   definitions xxiv ff
   primal 439 ff
hearing, development of 8
high-risk pregnancy 566
   medical technology 579
   premature birth, causes of 392, 393

holding therapy
  developmental impairment 297 ff
hormones
  brain organizers 419 ff
  in labor 434
  in stress 433
  primal health 439 ff
hyperemesis gravidarum 132
hypnotherapy
  facilitating normal birth 189 ff
  techniques 15
hypothalamo-pituitary system
  synthesis of peptides 432
hypothalamus 326 ff, 439 ff
hysteria
  symbolism 179 ff

imitation 11
intermodal fluency 11
International Society of Prenatal and
  Perinatal Psychology & Medicine (ISPP)
  congresses 608
  funding xiv, 607
  goals xiii ff, 607 ff
  philosophy xiii ff, 607 ff
  research 607 ff

Janov 535 ff
Jung, C. G. 181, 382

Kruse, F. 168, 182 ff

labor
  and birth 592
  in warm bath 431
lactation
  psychosis 210
learning
  adaptation xv
  conditioning 14
  experience xv
  habituation 14
  imitation 14
  imprinting 15
  infants 14
  joy in 15
  newborns 13
  prebirth memory xv
  prenatal memory imprint 306
  process xv, 4 ff, 156 ff
  reinforcement 14
  storage xv
life continuum 51

Marschak Interaction Method
  (MIM) 253 ff
Maslow, A.
  and fear experiences 279
maternal
  ambivalence 153
  attachment 267, 271, 283, 285, 489
  anxiety 132
  experience of birth 385 ff
  fantasies 79 ff
  morbidity 469
  psychological condition 254
  psychosociobiological barriers 447
  self-identity 200
  separation 490
  socialization 83
  stress 381
memory
  before birth 17 ff, 306
  birth 18 ff
  imprints 306
  learning process 34 ff
  organismic 221
  prebirth imprinting xv
  tissue 325
midwifery 391 ff, 499 ff
  birth preparation xviii
  educating mother 395
  illusion of incapacity 588
  research 617
  treatise on the Art of Midwifery 588
mind
  human life of newborn 6 ff

neonatal development
  'at-risk' babies 236
  intensive care 235
  psychological aspects 235
neonatal intensive care (NIC)
  psychological aspects 217 ff
nervous system, development of 6
neuropeptides
  modulation of neurotransmission 432
neurotransmitters
  brain organizers 419 ff, 432 ff
  information processing 419
  primal health 439 ff

INDEX

NIC units 217 ff
  medical/nursing staff 292
  naming 239
  noise 236
  psychological effects on preterm
    infant 238
  research 611
  stress 292 ff
  therapeutic task 247
non-Western perceptions of prenatal
  experience 542
  Anbarbra of Arnheim Land 542
  Buddhist 542 ff
  Hindu 542
  Tibetan 593 ff

Oedipal complex 138
osteopathy, cranial 321
ovulation
  induced 343
  spontaneous 343
  ultrasound monitored 343

perinatal development
  early skin contact 251 ff
perinatal hazards
  asphyxia 56
  CNS symptoms 55 ff
  diabetic mothers 56
  later schooling 53
  low birthweight 56
  smoking mothers 56
  social influence 55 ff
perinatal morbidity and mortality 611
pituitary 326 ff
postnatal bonding
  male and female 587
  mother–child interaction 550, 583, 595
  psychosexual identification 580
postpartum 47
  rooming-in 39, 549
prebirth memories
  and reactive patterning 309 ff
  determined by cultural
    perceptions 541
  import of 314
  of prenatal experiences 314
  theoretical model 311
  therapy workshop model 311
pregnancy, experience of 37, 209 ff, 582
  anxiety/stress reduction methods 396

  challenge xviii
  dynamic process xx, xxiii
  course of 37, 551
  hyperemesis 37 ff
  maturation crisis 210
  mother–child bonding 358
  mother–child dialog xxiii, 583
  opportunity for mother's creative
    growth 590
  psychosocial factors 546, 581, 586
  psychosocial stress 392, 394
  risk xviii ff, 357, 497
  unconditional omnipotence 583, 590
  undergoing changes 393
  unfavorable outcome 93 ff
  unwanted 42
pregnancy, current methods 356 ff, 577
  second trimester 355
premature birth
  infant morbidity and mortality xxi
  maternal attitudes 76 ff
  maternal fantasies 82
  premature babies 217 ff
  premature mothers 217 ff
  prevention xxi
prematurity
  and bonding 237
  'at-risk' parents 238
  pathology of circumstance 239
  psychological aspects 235, 243 ff
prenatal and antenatal diagnosis
  and bonding 360 ff, 363
  and chromosomal diseases 355, 356
  and first trimester 355
  as confirmation of health 363, 576,
    577
  current methods 356 ff
  diseases of the fetus 355
  from client's point of view 358 ff,
    360, 362 ff
  psychological effects 355
  selective abortion 577
pre- and perinatal methodology 43, 45 ff
  diachronic studies 40
  disparate design 41, 43
  selective 37
pre- and perinatal philosophy/ethics
  584, 595
  'biology is destiny' 588, 589
  devaluation of women 583 ff
  in China 357

mother mystique 581 ff
parenting 560
women's silence on self-identity/
 culture 588 ff
pre- and perinatal psychology and
 medicine
 continuum of life xxiii
 developmental impairment 295
 developmental psychology 23
 discontinuity xxiv
 hormone-dependent brain
  development 419
 interdisciplinary field xxiii
 philosophy xiii ff
 preventive interdisciplinary science of
  life xxiv
 quality of life xiii ff
pre- and perinatal research 56, 501 ff
pre- and perinatal risk factors 42, 50
 psychosocial assistance 498
 treatment 498
pre- and perinatal studies 501
 coherency 43
 interdisciplinary 46 ff
 long-term 45
 project design 44 ff
 research plan 44 ff
prenatal
 bioengineering 561
 optimized potential 562
 precocious imprinting 561
 stimulation/enhancement 559, 561
prenatal bonding
 and ethology 587
 antenatal diagnosis effect on 360 ff,
  363
 mother–child interaction 51, 277,
  498, 502, 546, 555, 556, 583, 584
prenatal experience
 biological and psychological functions
  of 548
 navel as center of 597
prenatal health
 ecological/environmental hazards 36
 economic costs 502
 vulnerability 38
prenatal preventative health care 552,
 556
 and maternal attitudes 556
 economic costs 396, 502
 maternal ambivalence 595 ff

primary health care practitioners 582
prenatal psychology 42
 and psychosocial future of child 274
 memory 'imprints' 275, 278
prenatal stimulation
 and singing 274, 278 ff
 newborn preference for human
  voice 277
 practical application 280 ff
psychoanalysis
 prenatal psychology 165 ff
 theoretical concepts 178
psychoneuroendocrinology
 continuum xiv
 methodology 419 ff
 neuroendocrine immune system 419
 primal health 439 ff
 prophylaxis 420
 psychobiological basis 32
 research xiii ff, 7, 607
psychotechnology of pregnancy 563 ff
 fetal heart monitor 572 ff
 fetoscopy 575
 fiberoptics 575
 high-tech obstetrics 566
 home vs. hospital 564
 hospitalization of birth 569 ff
 interventionist bent 565
 physical effects on mother 564 ff
 psychological effects on mother 564 ff
psychotherapies
 birth memory 291 ff
 birth regression therapy 292
 fantasy-journey/directed dream 538
 pre- and perinatal therapeutic
  model 293, 310
 reactive patterning 310
 tree-therapy 537

Rank, O. 28, 172, 177, 544
Rascovski 178
rebirth symbolism 178, 187
regression
 creative 17
 crisis in use 185
 primary 178
 traumatic 178
Reich, W. 547
reinforcement learning 14
REM sleep
 fetal movement 137

INDEX 699

in infant 12
In newborn 10
premature babies 10
rhythmicity
   continuum 145
   parental stimulation of infants 143 ff
risk pregnancy xviii ff

separation of mother and infant 490
sexuality
   animal experiments 425
   behavior 425 ff
   'congenital' homosexuality 153
   deviations 425
   differentiation of the brain 423
   homosexuality 424 ff
   identification 155
   Kinsey Institute report 424
   orientation 155
   perinatal alterations 425
   psychotropic drugs 525
smell, development of 7
smiles, development of 10
socioeconomic considerations 614
sociopedagogic research 612
stress
   birth complications 399 ff
   emotion in pregnancy 96
   geopathic 322
   in labor 433
   maternal 381
   prenatal 134
Sudden Infant Death Syndrome (SIDS)
   ISPP research 613
   prevention 313
Susruta 519 ff
   conception of soul 519 ff
   embryonic growth 522 ff
   fertilization 519
   genetics 521
   nourishment of fetus 524
   planned parenthood 521
symbols
   as polyvalent 538
   connected with pre- and perinatal experience 536
   tree as placenta 536 ff

taste, development of 7
technology
   childbirth preparation 481

   course of pregnancy 356
   embryo transfer 344
   ethical issues 569
   fetal therapy 576
   fetoscopy 334
   impact on society 461 ff
   in vitro fertilization 344, 461 ff
   mother–child dialog, effect on 362 577, 579
   reproductive 461 ff
   selective abortion 577 ff
   ultrasound 333 ff, 356 ff, 566 ff, 570 ff
thermodynamics
   low 449 ff
   maternal 447 ff
   medical 459
   psychosocial barriers 458

ultrasound 566, 569 ff
   and fetoscopy 575
   behaviour of the fetus 134
   cathexis 169
   congenital abnormalities 366
   diagnostic 333
   early diagnosis 256
   early monitoring 343
   intrauterine growth retardation 338
   prevention 333 ff
   psychological benefits of 571
   treatment of infertility 343
ultrasound technology 356, 566
   amniocentesis 356, 566 ff
   chorion villi biopsy 356, 357
   psychological effect on prenate 568, 577
unborn
   gender and social/class expectations 555, 556
   gender preference 549, 551, 556

vision, development of 8

Western perceptions of prenatal
   experience 544
   as suffering/illness 544
   as trauma 544
   Xtian 544
Winnicott 253
World Health Organization (WHO) 550, 614, 615